P9-ARK-345

Advanced Microprocessors

OTHER IEEE PRESS BOOKS

Biological Effects of Electromagnetic Radiation, *Edited by John M. Osepchuk*
Engineering Contributions to Biophysical Electrocardiography, *Edited by Theo C. Pilkington and Robert Plonsey*
The World of Large Scale Systems, *Edited by James D. Palmer and Richard Saeks*
Electronic Switching: Digital Central Systems of the World, *Edited by Amos E. Joel, Jr.*
A Guide for Writing Better Technical Papers, *Edited by C. Harkins and D. L. Plung*
Low-Noise Microwave Transistors and Amplifiers, *Edited by H. Fukui*
Digital MOS Integrated Circuits, *Edited by M. I. Elmasry*
Geometric Theory of Diffraction, *Edited by R. C. Hansen*
Modern Active Filter Design, *Edited by R. Schaumann, M. A. Soderstrand, and K. R. Laker*
Adjustable Speed AC Drive Systems, *Edited by B. K. Bose*
Optical Fiber Technology, II, *Edited by C. K. Kao*
Protective Relaying for Power Systems, *Edited by S. H. Horowitz*
Analog MOS Integrated Circuits, *Edited by P. R. Gray, D. A. Hodges, and R. W. Brodersen*
Interference Analysis of Communication Systems, *Edited by P. Stavroulakis*
Integrated Injection Logic, *Edited by J. E. Smith*
Sensory Aids for the Hearing Impaired, *Edited by H. Levitt, J. M. Pickett, and R. A. Houde*
Data Conversion Integrated Circuits, *Edited by Daniel J. Dooley*
Semiconductor Injection Lasers, *Edited by J. K. Butler*
Satellite Communications, *Edited by H. L. Van Trees*
Frequency-Reponse Methods in Control Systems, *Edited by A.G.J. MacFarlane*
Programs for Digital Signal Processing, *Edited by the Digital Signal Processing Committee, IEEE*
Automatic Speech & Speaker Recognition, *Edited by N. R. Dixon and T. B. Martin*
Speech Analysis, *Edited by R. W. Schafer and J. D. Markel*
The Engineer in Transition to Management, *I. Gray*
Multidimensional Systems: Theory & Applications, *Edited by N. K. Bose*
Analog Integrated Circuits, *Edited by A. B. Grebene*
Integrated-Circuit Operational Amplifiers, *Edited by R. G. Meyer*
Modern Spectrum Analysis, *Edited by D. G. Childers*
Digital Image Processing for Remote Sensing, *Edited by R. Bernstein*
Reflector Antennas, *Edited by A. W. Love*
Phase-Locked Loops & Their Application, *Edited by W. C. Lindsey and M. K. Simon*
Digital Signal Computers and Processors, *Edited by A. C. Salazar*
Systems Engineering: Methodology and Applications, *Edited by A. P. Sage*
Modern Crystal and Mechanical Filters, *Edited by D. F. Sheahan and R. A. Johnson*
Electrical Noise: Fundamentals and Sources, *Edited by M. S. Gupta*
Computer Methods in Image Analysis, *Edited by J. K. Aggarwal, R. O. Duda, and A. Rosenfeld*
Microprocessors: Fundamentals and Applications, *Edited by W. C. Lin*
Machine Recognition of Patterns, *Edited by A. K. Agrawala*
Turning Points in American Electrical History, *Edited by J. E. Brittain*
Charge-Coupled Devices: Technology and Applications, *Edited by R. Melen and D. Buss*
Spread Spectrum Techniques, *Edited by R. C. Dixon*
Electronic Switching: Central Office Systems of the World, *Edited by A. E. Joel, Jr.*
Electromagnetic Horn Antennas, *Edited by A. W. Love*
Waveform Quantization and Coding, *Edited by N. S. Jayant*
Communication Satellite Systems: An Overview of the Technology, *Edited by R. G. Gould and Y. F. Lum*
Literature Survey of Communication Satellite Systems and Technology, *Edited by J.H.W. Unger*
Solar Cells, *Edited by C. E. Backus*
Computer Networking, *Edited by R. P. Blanc and I. W. Cotton*
Communications Channels: Characterization and Behavior, *Edited by B. Goldberg*
Large-Scale Networks: Theory and Design, *Edited by F. T. Boesch*
Optical Fiber Technology, *Edited by D. Gloge*
Selected Papers in Digital Signal Processing, II, *Edited by the Digital Signal Processing Committee, IEEE*
A Guide for Better Technical Presentations, *Edited by R. M. Woelfle*
Career Management: A Guide to Combating Obsolescence, *Edited by H. G. Kaufman*
Energy and Man: Technical and Social Aspects of Energy, *Edited by M. G. Morgan*

Advanced Microprocessors

Edited by
Amar Gupta
Hoo-min D. Toong

Sloan School of Management
Massachusetts Institute of Technology

A volume in the IEEE PRESS Selected Reprint Series,
prepared under the sponsorship of the
IEEE Computer Society.

The Institute of Electrical and Electronics Engineers, Inc., New York

PRINTED IN THE UNITED STATES OF AMERICA

Sole Worldwide Distributor (Exclusive of the IEEE)

JOHN WILEY & SONS, INC.
605 Third Ave.
New York, NY 10158

Wiley Order Number: 471-88176-7

IEEE Order Number: PC01602

Library of Congress Cataloging in Publication Data
Main entry under title:

Advanced microprocessors.

(IEEE Press selected reprint series)
"Prepared under the sponsorship of the IEEE Computer Society."
Includes bibliographies and indexes.
1. Microprocessors—Addresses, essays, lectures.
I. Gupta, Amar. II. Toong, Hoo-min D. III. IEEE Computer Society.
QA76.24.A34 1983 001.64 83-6092
ISBN 0-87942-167-3

Contents

Dedicated to Our Parents

Acknowledgment

This book has been made possible by the encouragement provided by the IEEE Press Editorial Board. We are also grateful to the staff of the IEEE Press for bringing out this book in minimum time. Last, but not least, we thank Nona Jenkins for her valuable assistance in putting this book together.

AMAR GUPTA
HOO-MIN D. TOONG

Part I
Overview

THE TERM "microprocessor" was first used in 1972. However, the era of microprocessors commenced in 1971 with the Intel 4004, a "microprogrammable computer on a chip" composed of an "integrated CPU complete with a four-bit parallel adder, 16 four-bit registers, an accumulator and a push-down stack on a chip" [1]. The 4-bit 4004 CPU contained 2300 transistors, and could execute 45 different instructions. Subsequently, 8-bit, 16-bit, and 32-bit microprocessors were introduced in 1972, 1974, and 1981, respectively. Today, the Hewlett-Packard 32-bit microprocessor contains 450 000 transistors and offers a repertoire of 230 instructions. In less than twelve years, we have seen four generations of microprocessors. For a long time, the computer revolution was considered unparalleled in history in terms of its pace. The progress in the domain of microprocessors is even more significant, and the pace two to three times faster than in the case of computers.

A microprocessor is the central arithmetic and logic unit of a computer, together with its associated circuitry, scaled down so that it fits on a single silicon chip (sometimes several chips), holding tens of thousands of transistors, resistors, and similar circuit elements [2]. Microprocessors are characterized along several dimensions as follows:

Chip Technology

In view of the large number of transistors, most manufacturers have opted to fabricate mircroprocessors using MOS (metal oxide semiconductor) technology in preference to bipolar transistor technology. Currently, the most popular MOS technology is n-channel MOS (NMOS), by virtue of its high packing density and fast switching speeds. CMOS (complementary MOS) circuits provide faster speed and lower power consumption than circuits implemented with traditional PMOS and NMOS technology; the disadvantage of CMOS lies in its lower packing density. In coming years, CMOS may become the most popular technology for fabricating microprocessors [3].

Word Size

Word size reflects the basic unit of work for the microprocessor. A larger word size implies more processing power and addressing capabilities. In the early years of microprocessors, size of registers, size of internal instruction paths and data paths, and size of external instruction and data paths were all identical. This is rarely true now. Large external data paths require the chip package to have a high number of pins, which implies high packaging and production costs. Thus, chips nowadays tend to have larger internal paths than external paths. For example, the Motorola 68000 and the National NS16032 have 32-bit internal paths and 16-bit external paths. A true 32-bit microprocessor has all external paths and all internal units designed to communicate or process at least 32 bits in parallel.

Type of Microprocessor

Some microprocessors process all bits of one word in parallel. Others work with "slices" of data and/or instruction words. In the latter case, called "bit-slice architecture," several identical chips can be used to process different slices in parallel. In the past, the lack of ability to fabricate a large number of transistors on the same chip made it essential to use multiple bit-slice chips to obtain large word widths. Today bit-slice architecture offers potential for creating a customized CPU with a word length that is an integral multiple of the bit-slice width. However, for most applications, word sizes of 16 bits or 32 bits are more than adequate, permitting use of standard (nonbit-slice) 16-bit and 32-bit microprocessors.

Microprogramming

Early microprocessors used "hard-wired architectures" with functions determined by fixed circuit paths. A microprogrammed CPU, although inherently slower than a hard-wired CPU, offers greater flexibility in terms of easier incorporation of changes or additions to the instruction set. The trend is towards microprogrammed microprocessors. Only a few of these chips can be microprogrammed by the user.

Clock Frequency (Hertz)

This is the number of clock cycles per second of the fundamental driving clock circuit. Two clocks of the same frequency, but phase shifted with respect to each other, can be used to generate a clock of higher frequency. An increase in the clock frequency results in a proportionate decrease in the execution of an instruction.

Number of Instructions

The enhanced ability to fabricate large numbers of transistors on a chip facilitates implementation of a larger instruction set. These instructions are frequently of varying sizes, depending on instruction type, size of data, and addressing mode used. As the instruction size has increased, the complexity of the chip has increased, and so has the design effort, from under a man-year to over 100 man-years of engineering time [1]. To reduce this massive effort, reduced instruction set architectures have been implemented [4], [5]. In coming years, commercial microprocessors will not offer much larger instruction sets—individual instructions will, however, become more powerful.

Addressing Capability

Early microprocessors could reference only limited memory space. Larger word sizes enable direct addressing of larger memory space. In addition, a number of auxiliary addressing modes (such as indirect, indexing, autodecrementing) have become popular on microprocessors. Specialized memory management chips provide even more enhanced capabilities for efficient memory management. Finally, virtual memory facilities are becoming a standard feature on the newer microprocessors.

Number of Registers

Registers are required for arithmetic operations, for stack operations, for storing base and index values, and for a variety of other operations, depending on the architecture. General-purpose registers can be used for multiple uses. Some microprocessors offer general-purpose registers only, others dedicated only, but most offer some combination of the two.

Data Types

All microprocessors support data in the form of bytes and words. However, only some support data in the form of bits, binary coded decimal words, floating-point numbers, words longer than 4 bytes, and character strings. Floating-point capabilities are useful for scientific work. Character string manipulation capability is required for text editing applications. Auxiliary chips, co-processors, or slave processors are sometimes used to perform these functions. As technology improves, it will be feasible to incorporate more functions on the main chip itself.

Direct Memory Access (DMA) Capability

DMA capability enables a processor to offer a higher overall performance by allowing input and/or output to proceed concurrently with processing. In most cases, an auxiliary chip is used to take over the task of controlling input and output operations, leaving the microprocessor free to process instructions.

Software

Two decades back, the Burroughs 5000 series introduced a trend of architectures designed to support high-level languages alone. Today there is the Intel iAPX 432, designed to be programmed entirely in a high-level language; its system architecture is consciously oriented toward supporting ADA. This trend will become widespread in the industry as it enables reduced user programming costs. Some new microprocessors provide high-level language-oriented instruction sets and enhanced support for switching from one process to another.

Multiprocessing Capabilities

In order to increase computational bandwidth and/or system resilience, it becomes necessary to integrate several microprocessors in a single system. The overall throughput and efficiency of such systems is directly dependent on the hardware and software interconnection mechanisms supported by the basic microprocessor chips. Although all chips offer some facilities for multiprocessing, it is essential to examine exact features to determine overall maximum efficiency of multiprocessor configurations and to estimate software overheads.

Number of Chips

The Intel iAPX 432 comes as a three-chip set. Other 32-bit microprocessors require auxiliary chips to perform meaningful functions. Thus, high performance configurations are comprised of multiple chips. Single-chip microcomputers, on the other hand, contain processor, memory, and input/output logic on the same chip. Because of the chip area needed for functions other than processing, these single-chip microcomputers are less powerful than microprocessors fabricated using the same technology. Two conflicting trends will continue; that is, single-chip microcomputers will become increasingly complex and powerful, and multichip microprocessor-based configurations will be used in increasing numbers to undertake more complex tasks (database, transaction processing) that have traditionally been done on larger mainframes.

In addition to the above, cost, availability of support chips, second-sourcing considerations, reliability of product, upward software compatibility with an earlier chip, and the nature of applications will influence the choice of a microprocessor.

A comprehensive analysis of all the diverse issues indicated above is a massive task because of the incredible pace of the microprocessor revolution. Handbooks published by chip manufacturers highlight the merits of their products, but present meager information on the design problems and the faults of their products. Also, designers find it virtually impossible to meaningfully compare and contrast products of different manufacturers.

This reprint book is intended to fill this void. It is organized into six parts as follows.

Part I: Overview

An introduction to the realm of microprocessors, including a history of the development of microprocessors.

Part II: 16-bit Microprocessors

A comprehensive collection of articles on contemporary 16-bit microprocessors and auxiliary support chips. Almost all of these papers are written by the persons who designed the chips.

Part III: 32-bit Microprocessors

A description of several high performance 32-bit microprocessors, including chips designed exclusively for internal use within sponsoring organizations. These internal chips, harbingers of similar capability public domain products, present an interesting overview of emerging trends in microprocessors.

Part IV: Performance Comparisons

Comparison of performance of 16-bit and 32-bit microprocessors for several different application scenarios, using theoretical methods and benchmark programs.

Part V: Related Technologies

A state-of-the-art overview of two related technologies—bit-slice architecture and single-chip microcomputers.

Part VI: System Issues

Summary of standards for interconnection mechanisms and for languages.

Read in sequence, these parts provide a tutorial to the rapidly growing microprocessor field. Persons with previous background will find it convenient to refer directly to the part that they are interested in. In proportion to the greater interest and higher usage of the newer chips, this book concentrates on 16-bit and 32-bit microprocessors and contains papers written during the 1980's only. The Bibliography refers to papers published in the 1980's, and provides sources of additional information on related topics.

This part (Part I) includes three general papers that look at the field of microprocessors from three different perspectives. In the first article, Dennis Moralee provides a history of important landmarks during the first decade of microprocessors and an analysis of how the architectural evolution of microprocessors is linked to that of mainframe computers and minicomputers. The second article, by Ian H. Witten, examines the economics of information processing, coming to a significant conclusion—as hardware costs plummet, it becomes increasingly relevant to decrease software costs by offering high-level languages; this article also shows the advantages of 16-bit processors over 8-bit processors in terms of extended addressing range, memory segmentation and protection, regularity of instruction set, string manipulation capabilities, and support of more data types. The third article, by Paul M. Russo, emphasizes the intimate relationship between trends in very-large-scale-integration (VLSI) and the evolution, usage, and system design of microprocessors. The paper shows that the advent of early microprocessors caused the LSI development to be reoriented towards design of chips with potential for use in industrial, commercial, and consumer applications.

Before the turn of this century, the population of microprocessors in use will exceed the population of people living on this planet. Hopefully, even in light of being outstripped in terms of numbers, this book will help the human race to remain in control!

References

[1] R. N. Noyce and M. E. Hoff, Jr., "A history of microprocessor development at Intel," *IEEE Micro*, vol. 1, pp. 8–21, Feb. 1981.

[2] H. D. Toong, "Mircroprocessors," *Sci. Amer.*, pp. 146–161, Sept. 1977.

[3] D. L. Wollesen, "CMOS LSI—The computer component process of the 80's," *Computer*, pp. 59–67, Feb. 1980.

[4] D. A. Patterson and C. H. Sequin, "A VLSI RISC," *Computer*, vol. 15, pp. 8–21, Sept. 1982.

[5] G. Radin, "The 801 minicomputer," in *Proc. Symp. Architectural Support for Programming Languages and Operating Syst.*, Mar. 1-3, 1982, pp. 39–47.

Bibliography

[1] "Microprocessors," *Elec. Eng.*, pp. 60–85, Sept. 1981.

[2] R. Bernhard, "More hardware means less software," *IEEE Spectrum*, pp. 30–37, Dec. 1981.

[3] R. M. Cushman, "CMOS microprocessor and microcomputer ICs," *EDN*, pp. 88–100, Sept. 29, 1982.

[4] H.M.J.M. Dortmans, "Application of microprocessors," *J. Phys. E. Sci. Instrum.*, vol. 14, pp. 777–782, 1982.

[5] D. A. Fairclough, "A unique microprocessor instruction set," *IEEE Micro*, vol. 2, pp. 8–17, May 1982.

[6] E. H. Frank and R. F. Sproull, "Testing and debugging custom integrated circuits," *ACM Comput. Surveys*, vol. 13, pp. 425–451, Dec. 1981.

[7] H. W. Lawson, Jr., "New directions for micro- and system architectures in the 1980s," in *Proc. Nat. Comput. Conf.*, 1981, pp. 57–62.

[8] C. M. Lee and C. G. Lin-Hendel, "Current status and future projection of CMOS technology," in *Proc. Compcon Fall*, Sept. 20–23, 1982, pp. 716–719.

[9] S.-M. S. Liu, C.-H. Fu, G. E. Atwood, H. Dun, J. Langston, E. Hazani, E. Y. So, S. Sachdev, and K. Fuchs, "HMOS III technology," *IEEE J. Solid-State Circuits*, vol. SC-17, pp. 810–815, Oct. 1982.

[10] D. J. McGreivy and K. A. Pickar, *VLSI Technologies Through the 80s and Beyond* (IEEE Computer Society Reprint Book). New York: IEEE Press, 1982.

[11] S. P. Morse *et al.*, "Intel microprocessors—8008 to 8086," *Computer*, pp. 42–60, Oct. 1980.

[12] D. A. Patterson and R. S. Piepho, "Assessing RISCs in high-level language support," *IEEE Micro*, pp. 9–19, Nov. 1982.

[13] R. Rice, *VLSI Support Technologies—A Tutorial* (IEEE Computer Society Reprint Book). New York: IEEE Press, 1982.

[14] P. C. Treleaven, "VLSI processor architectures," *Computer*, vol. 15, pp. 33–45, June 1982.

Microprocessor architectures: ten years of development

Ten years ago the first true microprocessor became commercially available. What were the origins of the microprocessor, how has it evolved since then, and how has its architectural evolution been linked to that of mainframe computers and minicomputers?

by Dennis Moralee

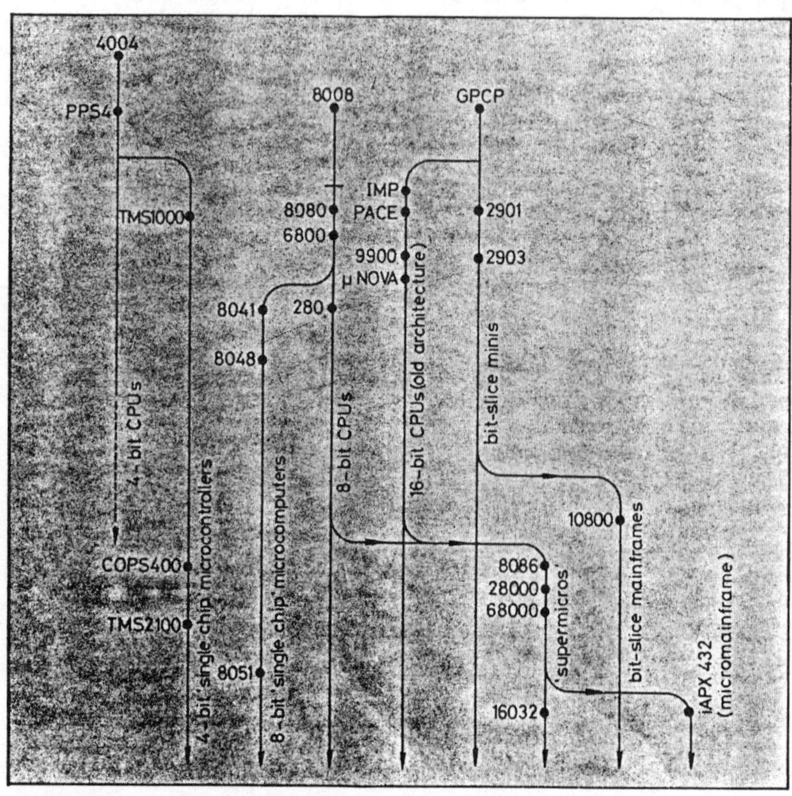

1 Genealogy of the microprocessor family

Just ten years ago, a small and at that time relatively little known semiconductor company called Intel launched an unusual new product, the MCS-4 'microprogrammed minicomputer' system based on a single-chip central processing unit (CPU) designated the 4004. This small PMOS device, containing the now very modest total of 2250 transistors, was in fact the first microprocessor, the very first of a now long line of microelectronics devices that, in only 10 years, have come to dominate modern electronics design and become the focus not only of intense engineering interest but also of an increasingly widespread public debate. Although at the time of its introduction the 4004 may have seemed to many to be little more than a minor technological curiosity unlikely to have any real long-term significance, with hindsight its development can now be seen as signalling the start of one of the most remarkable periods of technological change to occur in modern times. As the 4004's designers correctly predicted, the introduction of the new device was merely the first step along a whole new line of technological development: 'The MCS-4', they wrote,[1] 'is really only a beginning'.

However, even the 4004's designers would have had difficulty in correctly

Reprinted with permission from *Electron. and Power*, vol. 27, pp. 214–221, Mar. 1981.

predicting just how rapidly the microprocessor would evolve during its first 10 years. Some idea of how dramatic this evolution has been can be obtained by comparing the 4004 with the microprocessor device Intel launched just a few weeks ago, the iAPX 432 'micro-mainframe', an undoubted — if not directly lineal — descendant of the original MCS-4 family. Perhaps the most obvious comparison is in terms of 'raw' processing power: the 4004 was very much less powerful than even the basic minicomputers of the day, whereas the iAPX 432 is in some configurations as powerful as a contemporary midrange mainframe, the type of conventional computer that will typically fulfil all the traditional computing needs of a medium-sized manufacturing company.

In many ways more significant, however, is the comparison in terms of architecture, the distinctive functional organisation of the devices' computational resources. While the 4004, viewed as a general-purpose computing device, had an architecture that was primitive even when compared to the minicomputers of the day, the architecture of the iAPX 432 is not just more sophisticated than those of today's commonly used mainframes, it is in many respects more sophisticated than practically any general-purpose computing device yet put on the market. After only a single decade, in fact, microprocessor design has evolved from a situation in which it lagged far behind conventional-computer design to a place where it is beginning to take the lead.

Dramatically as such comparisons illustrate the rapid evolution of microprocessor design, however, they falsely suggest that this evolution has followed a single line of development. In fact, several very different types of microprocessor have evolved over the last 10 years, of which the general-purpose CPUs such as the iAPX 432 are perhaps the best known, if not necessarily the most important.

Microcontrollers

Still the most commonly used type of microprocessor device is the 4-bit 'single chip' *microcontroller*, a type that has changed only in detail from the first-generation chip-set such as the MCS-4, most importantly by the integration of the originally separate CPU, memory and I/O units onto a single chip.

Alone of all the microprocessor devices in production today, these microcontrollers still use the original PMOS technology, largely because of its extremely low cost, which tends to be an important factor in the low-end 'logic replacement' applications in which they are mainly used[2] (see Collie pp.236-239, this issue). More recently, these devices have been joined by the more powerful 'single-chip' *microcomputers*, essentially a reworking of the same concept but with a second-generation 8-bit CPU on the chip instead of a first-generation 4-bit unit: these devices, available in both NMOS and CMOS implementations, are typically used in the more demanding of the logic-replacement applications.

Bit-slice devices

At the other end of the processing-power scale, are the *bit-slice* devices, LSI processor components that are traditionally classed as a type of microprocessor, even though they differ in very many ways from all the other types. In use, several of these devices are combined to form the nucleus of a specific form of CPU, a *microprogrammed* processor that acts as a sort of 'computer within a computer', performing the overall CPU function not by the operation of a mass of hard-wired circuitry but by the execution of specialised *microprograms*. Working with these devices involves the use in the detailed internal design of the CPU, an advantage in certain specialised applications (see Clements pp.230-235, this issue), but an unjustified extra complication in applications for which 'ready-made' CPUs of the right characteristics are available. Because of this, bit slices have tended to be used in conventional microprocessor applications only when their intrinsically higher processing power has been required: the fast bipolar logic normally used in their construction has allowed the construction of CPUs in the mainframe performance category for some time.

Although the bit slices are thus a rather specialised form of microprocessor device, their ancestry can be traced back to the early days of microprocessor design, if not to the Intel 4004 at least to the National Semiconductor GPCP, a pioneering device that was developed almost simultaneously with the 4004, appearing only about a year afterwards. Since then, the bit slices have evolved from 2-bit and 4-bit models of limited throughput, via the now industry-standard 4-bit Advanced Micro Devices' 2901 and 2903, to newer 8-bit and even 16-bit models, the last mentioned being a complete 'unsliced' microprogrammable CPU.

Between these two very different types of somewhat specialised microprocessor device are perhaps the best-known microprocessors, the general-purpose single-chip CPUs. Because of their general-purpose nature, these devices have been used in the widest variety of microprocessor applications, ranging from low-end 'logic replacement' applictions beyond the power of the microcontrollers and microcomputers, to high-end 'information system' applications once the province of conventional minicomputers. Originally descended from the 8-bit PMOS 8008, a specifically general-purpose device designed almost simultaneously with the 4004 and released only a few months later, this type of microprocessor has gone through three distinct generations, and with the introduction of the iAPX 432 seems currently about to enter a fourth.

After the introduction in 1974 of the first generation of these devices, typified by the 8008 itself, perhaps the greatest advance in their design was made with the adoption of the superior NMOS technology in 1974. The change

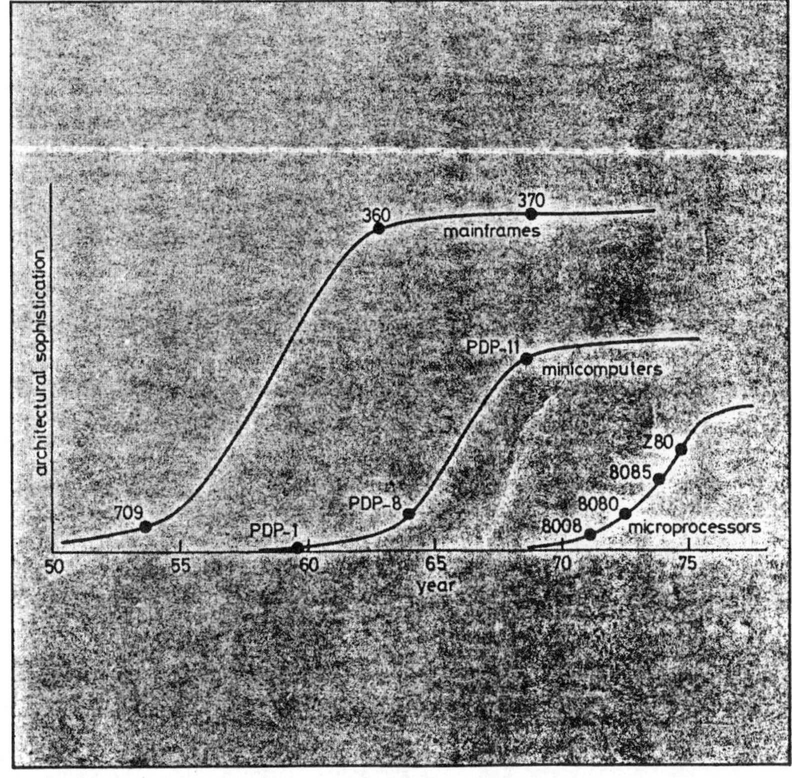

2 Architectural evolution of three types of computing device

to NMOS allowed more subsidiary functions to be incorporated on the chip, the architecture of the devices to be improved and their performance to be increased dramatically: the devices of this NMOS second generation, such as the 8080, 6800, 8085, Z80, 6502 etc., continue to be the best known microprocessors in use today. The fact that these influential mainstream devices all have an 8-bit architecture has led this wordlength to be associated almost exclusively with this generation of devices, but in fact a number of 16-bit devices date from this time: PACE, INS8900, 9900, microNOVA, CP1600 etc. The fact that these devices have a 16-bit wordlength does not, however, indicate *a priori* that they are more powerful or more sophisticated than their 8-bit contemporaries.

Third-generation CPUs

A range of more powerful and more sophisticated 16-bit devices did become available, however, with the introduction of the third generation CPUs in 1978. Based on the then newly developed high-density versions of NMOS, variously called HMOS, XMOS etc., this new generation of devices brought general-purpose microprocessors into the performance class of traditional minicomputers for the first time. Much more than 'souped up' versions of the second-generation devices, however, these new 'supermicros' are more importantly distinguished by their advanced architectures which, in some cases, outdo in general sophistication even those of the best-known mainframes.

The advanced architectures of these 'supermicros' — the Intel 8086 and its follow-up devices, the Zilog Z8000, the Motorola 68000 and the new National Semiconductor 16000 range — have not come about by accident, but by careful consideration by the microprocessor manufacturers of the characteristics that a high-end general-purpose microprocessor will have to possess in order to be a commercial success over the next decade or so.

After long development projects, which in some cases began in the early 1970s even before the second-generation NMOS devices were released, the manufacturers have all come out in favour of certain architectural concepts that are now reflected, with differing degrees of emphasis, in all the third generation designs. The current third-generation of general-purpose microprocessors could, in fact, be quite accurately called the 'advanced architecture' generation.

This shift in microprocessor design towards the implementation of more advanced architectural concepts is undoubtedly one of the most important developments in the short but already eventful history of the microprocessor. While the numerical dominance of the 4-bit and 8-bit logic-replacement devices will no doubt continue, and the second-generation 8-bit CPUs will certainly be around for many years to come, the new advanced-architecture 'supermicros' can be expected to exert a gradually increasing influence over the whole spectrum of microprocessor applications. This increasing influence will be the direct result of their advanced architectures, architectures based on concepts that, although often represented as being significant only in the high-end applications opened up by the greatly increased processing power of the 'supermicros', are likely to become recognised in the near future as just as significant for the less-demanding applications now in the province of the older second-generation devices.

This relevance of the third generation architectures to other than high-end applications has already been demonstrated to some extent by the introduction of the 'midi' microprocessors, devices such as the Intel 8088, Motorola 6809 and National Semiconductor 16008, which combine the implementation of advanced architectural concepts with the use of 8-bit interfaces that allow them to be used as replacements for the second-generation 8-bit devices with only a minimum of redesign. The scope for using these more advanced architectural concepts in the design of logic-replacement devices may be somewhat less, but important architectural developments can ultimately be expected in this area too.

Computer architecture

Before considering in detail the architectural advances embodied in the third-generation microprocessors, it may be best to specify more closely what characteristics of a computer-like device are included in the term 'architecture'. Essentially, by 'architecture' is meant the overall functional organisation of the device as seen from the applications viewpoint, i.e. the view of the device commonly taken by the user rather than the manufacturer.

Among the characteristics of a microprocessor that contribute to its overall architectural specification are: its instruction set; the data types on which its instructions operate; the

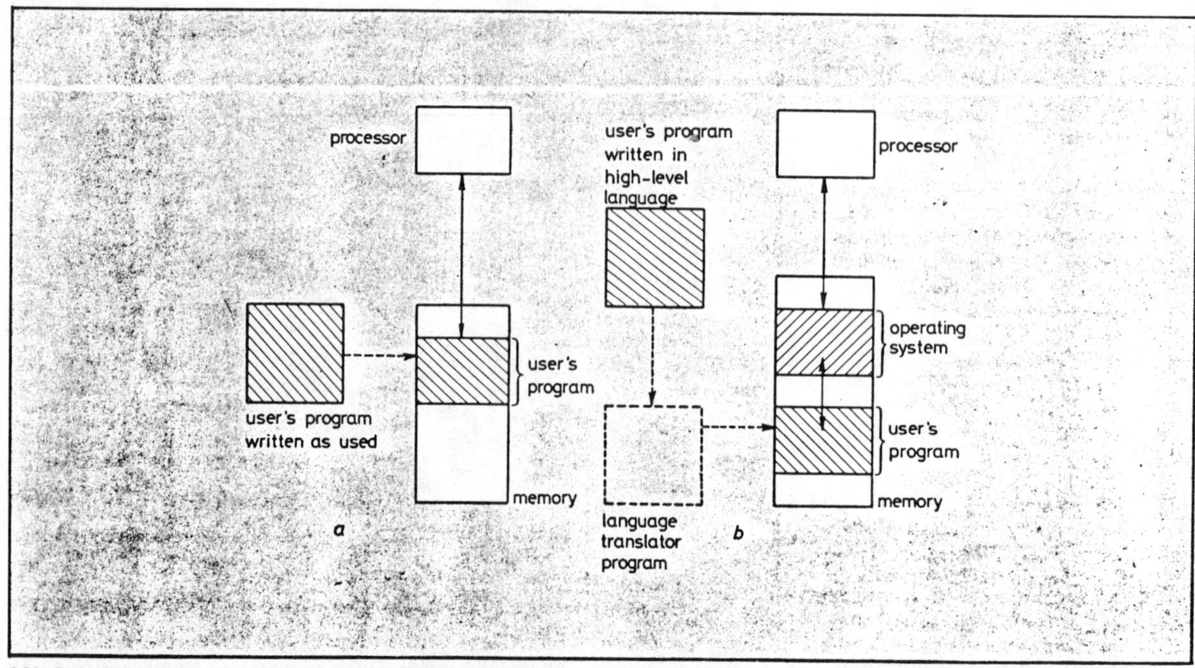

3 Modern approach to computer use. In the traditional approach (a), now rarely used in mainframe and minicomputer applications but still the norm for microprocessor use, the user programs directly in low-level hardware oriented code that runs unaided in the system. In the modern approach (b), the user programs in a high-level language and the translated low-level program drives the hardware via the operating system

number, bit-length and function of its registers; the addressing modes by which it can refer to specific locations in its memory; and the logical organisation of the input/output (I/O) units that it uses to exchange data with external equipment.

Concepts and features

Clearly, the concept of architecture is a highly multivariate one, and there is no simple measure of architectural sophistication, although several formal systems have been proposed. Clearly also, the desirability of certain architectural features will vary greatly with application, so that, for example, what is a good architectural arrangement for a logic-replacement device designed to control individual I/O lines will not be very suitable for a general-purpose CPU designed to interface with a system bus: for this reason there is little point in directly comparing the architectures of microcontrollers and general-purpose devices. In spite of these complications, however, it is possible to summarise concisely what a good architecture should do: it should allow all of the computing resources of the device to be utilised as effectively as possible.

Perhaps the best way of illustrating this concept of architectural 'goodness' is to consider the problems caused by architectural features that inhibit the effective use of a device's computing resources. Typically, this might be due to the lack of an instruction that performs a type of operation required by the application, or the lack of a data type required by the application, or, more subtly, the inability to use a particular instruction on an item of data solely because it happens to be located in one particular register. It is in the nature of computing devices that all these problems can be overcome — after all, any processor can eventually be programmed to do anything, but only at the cost of additional complexity in the software.

This additional complexity has two main consequences, one of which is that the additional operations required for the processor to 'work around' the architectural block can severely slow down the useful work of the application: improving the architecture of a processor can greatly increase its effective throughput even though the actual circuitry it employs continues at the same speed. Also, the additional complexity required in the software makes life much more difficult for the programmer, particularly if the architectural restrictions are themselves arbitrary and not easy to remember, and this leads to costlier and more error-prone software.

In case it should be thought that this effect is likely to be relatively minor, it should be remembered that programmers who have worked on both conventional minicomputers and second-generation microprocessors have often found that coping with the restricted architectures of the latter can almost double the time needed to complete a program.

By the time the design of the new 'supermicros' came to be finalised, the fact that the second-generation microprocessors had such architectural deficiencies was well known to their manufacturers. The manufacturers were also well aware that their business was founded on their ability to provide their customers with readily usable computing power: there was clearly no advantage in selling devices that were unnecessarily difficult to use, and every possible advantage in selling devices that were easy to use and would therefore tend to be in greater demand.

Consequently, the decision was taken to use the greater capability of the HMOS technologies to remove as many as possible of the second-generation devices' architectural limitations. For example, the limitations on data types would be removed: instead of the typical second-generation limitation to just 8-bit data words (with 16-bit address pointers), the new-generation devices would directly support all the data types commonly used in microprocessor applications: bits, BCD digits, 8-bit data (bytes), 16-bit data, 32-bit data and variable-length character strings of practically unlimited (64k bytes) length.

Limitations

Similarly, the limitations on addressing modes would be removed: instead of the typical second-generation limitation to modes such as pointer, register, immediate and indexed, the third-generation devices would also allow many others, such as indirect, indirect indexed, base indexed, autoincrement etc. Also, more and longer registers would be provided, and care would be taken to make the instruction set as *regular* (or *orthogonal*) as possible, so that *any* instruction should, in principle, be able to operate on *any* data type contained in *any* register or in *any* memory location specified by *any* addressing mode.

In choosing to generalise the architectures of their future third-generation devices in this way, the microprocessor manufacturers were reacting to limitations in the architectures of their second-generation devices that had been identified as a result of practical experience in their application. However, they also

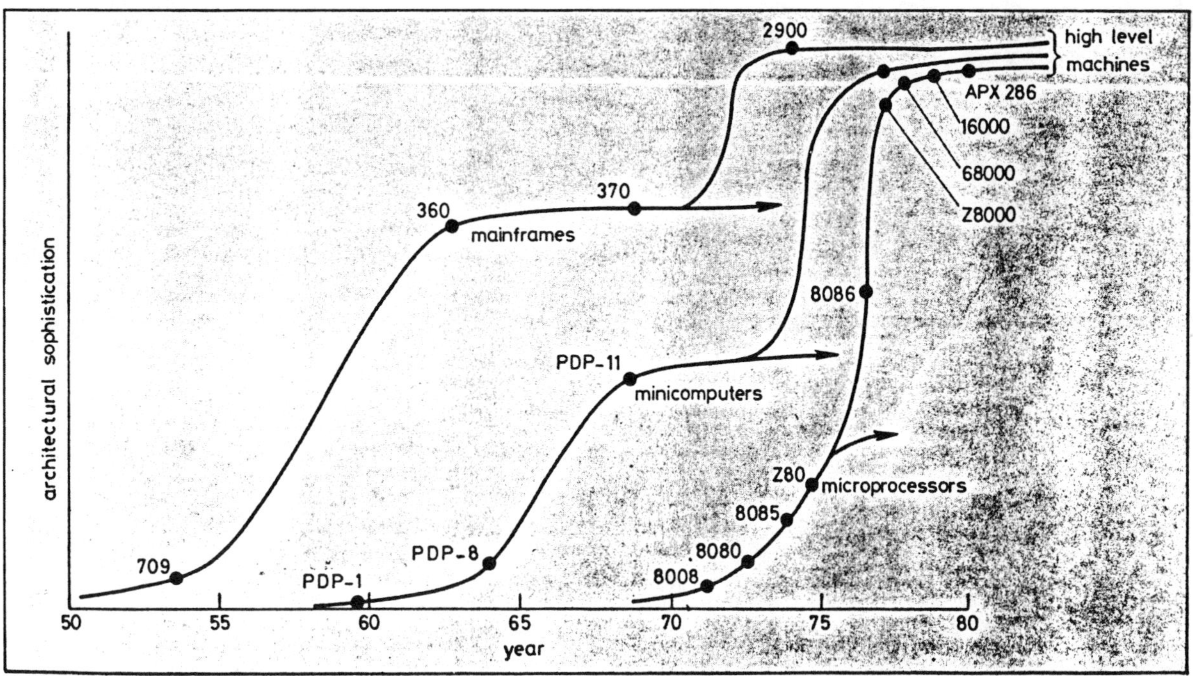

4 Enter the high-level architectures. The need to support high-level use of all types of computing device has led to the emergence of a new generation of high-level machines, developments of mainframes, minicomputers and microprocessors all based on very similar architectural concepts

had theoretical guidance in their choice as a result of a clear two-fold precedent for what they were doing, which had in fact been done before by the mainframe manufacturers at the beginning of the 1960s and by the minicomputer manufacturers at the end of the same decade.

The parallels between the evolution of these two older types of computer and that of the microprocessor are very noticeable (Fig.2) but this is not perhaps surprising: each of the three types of computing device has been brought into existence by the emergence of a particular form of electronics technology, and its evolution during at least the early years of its existence has been determined largely by the gradual maturing of that technology. Thus, mainframes were originally developed with discrete-component technology, and the early limitations on the components, first valves and then primitive transistors, meant that very unsophisticated architectures were originally adopted and that the rate of architectural advance was relatively slow. Only by the later 1950s had transistor technology matured to the point when hardware limitations were no longer a real restraint on architectural advance, and this then allowed the introduction of the first advanced-architecture main-frame, the IBM 360. Similarly, minicomputers based on SSI technology, started off with very basic architectures that continued until the maturing associated with the emergence of MSI devices, which then allowed the introduction of the first advanced-architecture mini, the DEC PDP-11.

Evolutionary pressures

In the case of the microprocessor, exactly the same evolutionary pressures were at work. First implemented in the relatively immature PMOS technology of the early 1970s, microprocessors were restricted by hardware constraints to very basic architectures, which in their broad characteristics were very similar to the mainframe architectures of the early 1950s and the minicomputer architecture of the early 1960s. Once the much more capable NMOS technology emerged, however, many of the hardware constraints were lifted, and microprocessors, like the mainframes and minicomputers before them, went through a stage of rapid architectural development, as typified by the transitions from the 8080 to the 8085 and then to the Z80.

Finally, with the then imminent commercial availability of the HMOS technologies, hardware limitations were no longer a real restraint to architectural advance, and the 'supermicros' were planned. It thus seemed likely that the evolution of the microprocessor was destined to go much the same way as the evolution of the earlier types of computer device, with the emergence of a definitive microprocessor architecture characterised by the provision of a substantial number of 16-bit or 32-bit registers, a useful range of data types and addressing modes, and a very regular instruction set.

Such a definitive architecture, or so it seemed at the time, would then 'fossilise' as a result of a number of stabilising factors, notably the large base of software that would quickly be built up for use with it, so forcing a virtual halt to major architectural development. After all, it was pointed out, very few new mainframe architectures have been developed since the introduction of the IBM360 and its 370 follow-up, and very few new minicomputer architectures had been developed since the emergence of the PDP-11.

Other factors were at work, however, to prevent this coming about. One of these was the effect that LSI technology was having on all forms of computing: by dramatically reducing the cost of all hardware resources, particularly memory, the new technology was highlighting the restrictions of existing architectures as evidenced in unnecessarily high programming and usage costs. In addition, the progressive

Origins of the microprocessor

Intel's launch of the MCS-4 system just a decade ago certainly deserves recognition as the first commercial introduction of a microprocessor range, but in fact the 4004 was just one of three pioneering microprocessor devices that were developed almost simultaneously and launched within just a year or so of each other. The remarkable thing is that each of these three devices was the first example of one of the three very different types of microprocessor that have developed down to this day: the Intel 4004 was the forerunner of the microcontrollers and microcomputers designed for logic-replacement applications; the Intel 8008 was the first general-purpose single-chip CPU; and the National Semiconductor GPCP was the first of the bit-slice microprocessors. Behind the development of each of these devices lies an interesting story.

Behind the development of the 4004 lies the steady increase in the scale of microelectronics integration that continued throughout the 1960s. By the end of that decade, it was clear that the new LSI technologies offered remarkable benefits in a wide range of application areas, but only if the volume of devices demanded by the application was large enough to justify the high costs of 'custom' LSI design. For lower-volume applications, the problem was the now classic one of the lack of any really practical way of 'customising' mass produced, and therefore inexpensive, LSI devices to meet the specific needs of the application. Until such a way was discovered, the majority of users were effectively disbarred from exploiting LSI technology.

Ironically, the impetus to the solution of this problem by means of the programmable-logic LSI device or microprocessor resulted from the actions of a company that believed its volume of production could fully justify the use of custom LSI devices. The company was Busicom, a Japanese manufacturer that had designed a set of 11 low-density LSI devices to form the basis of a new product, a compact new desktop calculator. In spite of the fact that these devices were destined for use in a calculator, they were in no sense programmable, but just a collection of hardwired logic capable of handling the very simple 'four-function' calculations then required. Having designed these custom-LSI devices, however, Busicom then found that there was no Japanese semiconductor company capable of making them, a difficulty that it solved by approaching Intel in the USA.

Then a relatively young company, Intel was glad of the opportunity to manufacture Busicom's devices, but in the end decided that high-volume production of 11 different chips would tie up more of its manufacturing resources than it then wanted to divert from the production of its own designs. The solution seemed to be to redesign Busicom's logic to make use of Intel's relatively high-density PMOS technology and so make them fit on fewer devices. A young engineer called M.E. Hoff was then assigned to the project, and began working on the more general problem of how to design a set of readily customisable logic chips. Being from a computer-engineering background, Dr. Hoff eventually realised the similarity between what he was trying to do and what was done in computer design when a standard hardwired CPU was implemented instead by *microprogramming*, i.e. by using a basic but relatively fast 'computer within a computer' to perform the same functions as the hardwired CPU but with a greatly reduced amount of logic.

Using this analogy with microprogramming, Dr. Hoff then realised that the same approach could be used in the design of the Busicom calculator, with the original hardwired calculator logic being replaced by an appropriately microprogrammed 'computer within a calculator' built from just a few LSI devices. Equally well, any other suitable array of hardwired logic could also be replaced by exactly the same LSI devices, only the microprograms requiring any change. Within a few months, Dr. Hoff's ideas had been taken up within Intel, and the detailed design of the world's first logic-replacement microprocessor, later to be designated the 4004, had begun.

The development of the other two pioneering

development of improved software techniques had made a re-orientation of hardware design overdue: existing architectures, whether mainframe, minicomputer or microprocessor, were all, to a greater or lesser extent, hardware-oriented designs geared to simple low-level programming techniques.

What was instead required were architectural designs geared to more modern techniques of programming and using computers, particularly the use of high-level programming languages and sophisticated operating systems, both of which act as 'bridges' between, on the one hand, the high-level approach to utilising computing resources that the user naturally wishes to adopt, and, on the other hand, the low-level approach actually allowed by conventional architectures. The use of such software 'bridges' to overcome the deficiencies of low-level hardware architectures can certainly be made to work, but usually only at the cost of providing very elaborate language-translation and operating-system software, and of accepting considerable inefficiency and general clumsiness in the overall operation of the system.

This need to develop new 'high-level' architectures, coupled with the availability of the new LSI technology from which new 'high-level' machines could be built, led to a rethinking of architectural concepts followed by development programmes dating from the beginning of 1970. In the mainframe world, these led most notably to the advanced architecture of the more recent Burroughs machines and of the ICL2900, and, although the mainframe industry is still dominated by the IBM 360/370 architecture there are signs of architectural change even in the IBM world. In the minicomputer world, perhaps the most notable development has been that of the DEC VAX-11, a 'high-level' extension of the PDP-11 that, among many other enhancements, takes the traditionally 16-bit minicomputer architecture up to 32 bits.

Supermicros

Finally, in the microprocessor world there have been the 'supermicros', devices that are based to a very large extent on the same 'high-level' architecture concepts as the new mainframe and minicomputer models. Indeed, reading the published design criteria for the new devices is rather like reading slightly adjusted versions of the design criteria published for machines such as the ICL2900[3] and DEC VAX-11[2]. This similarity is most notable with the later 'supermicros' the Z8000, 68000 and 16000, which at the time of their respective introduction each displayed progressively more similarity to the VAX-11 design in particular.

As an example of the high-level facilities provided by these new advanced-architecture microprocessors, consider National Semiconductor's remarkable new high-end device, the 16032. This powerful CPU, supported as desired by coprocessors for floating-point arithmetic and memory management, is essentially a 32-bit machine with eight 32-bit general-purpose registers, eight 32-bit floating-point registers, and six 24-bit pointer registers. With its 24-bit addresses, the device can address directly 16Mbytes of memory (larger memories based on 29-bit addresses will be supported in later releases), and it also includes facilities that will allow full virtual-memory operation[4]. Memory can be addressed by eight different addressing modes, including all those usually found on advanced-architecture devices, and the data types include bits, bit-fields, BCD digits, 16-bit words, 64-bit double words, single-precision and double-precision floating-point numbers, and variable-length strings. The instruction set includes over 100 basic types, and is highly orthogonal. In all these respects, the device shows an architectural sophistication up to traditional mainframe levels.

More than this, however, the device

---

devices was carried out for different reasons: the aim in both cases being not to find a way of replacing generalised hardwired logic with 'customised' LSI, but to adapt the newly emerged LSI technology to the needs of minicomputer manufacturers. Ideally, these manufacturers would have liked to have been provided with a single-chip LSI device having the same characteristics, including processing power, as their existing MSI CPUs, but everyone believed, rightly as it turned out, that this would not be possible until well into the 1970s. The alternative approach, as adopted by engineers at National Semiconductor, was to try to develop a set of LSI components that, while not being full CPUs in themselves, could be used in relatively small numbers to construct a CPU according to each individual manufacturer's specific requirements. What the National Semiconductor engineers were looking for, in fact, was a very versatile set of LSI devices that could be used to build a readily 'customisable' minicomputer CPU.

Again, the solution to this problem was found in the existing concept of microprogramming. By designing a set of LSI devices that could form a microprogrammed 'computer within a computer', National Semiconductor realised that it could provide users with all the benefits of LSI in a form that only required suitable microprogramming to allow full customisation. The limitations of the then PMOS technology, coupled with the need to optimise the devices for speed in order to attain the required minicomputer-like performance, meant, however, that several devices would be necessary to provide even the nucleus or 'microinstruction execution unit' of a CPU, a further problem that received an elegant solution in the form of the 'bit slice' concept.

Following this concept, an assembly consisting of only four GPCP 4-bit 'slices', 15 - 20 TTL support devices and a ROM to hold the microprograms, could form a complete minicomputer CPU, a point that National Semiconductor clearly demonstrated by launching a pre-assembled model called the IMP-16, the first single-board minicomputer. Although the bit slices could be used to build lower-performance 4-bit and 8-bit processors, they remained identified with 16-bit minicomputer-like systems, and this led National Semiconductor to go on to develop single-chip versions of the IMP-16 such as the late first-generation PMOS PACE, and the second-generation NMOS INS8900.

Even while the GPCP bit slices were still being developed, however, another project aimed at bringing LSI technology to computer design was under way. The aim of this other project was crucially different, however, for it was meant to result not in an LSI-based CPU of minicomputer-like performance, but in a specially low-powered CPU for a specific range of low-end applications, actually for relatively simple local processing in 'intelligent' terminals. The idea of using a low-power 8-bit LSI CPU for such applications was first promoted in 1968 by a small company called Viatron, which unfortunately went bankrupt before its development project was complete. The idea was revived, however, by Datapoint, a computer company then as now specialising in 'intelligent terminals' and what has more recently become known as 'distributed processing'. Datapoint approached Intel with its ideas, and a project was started with the aim of integrating as much as possible of a low-power 8-bit CPU onto a single chip.

In fact, it was only because a specifically low-power CPU was being built that this project had any hope of success: if minicomputer-like performance had been required, the Intel engineers could have had to resort to the sort of multichip solution that had been chosen by their National Semiconductor colleagues. As it was, the limitations of the then available PMOS technology meant that not all of even a low-power CPU could be squeezed onto a single chip, and the resulting device had to be supported by usually some 20 - 40 TTL devices to give a full-function CPU.

Nonetheless, the new device, designated the 8008, was much nearer to a single-chip CPU than many had at the time thought possible, and its capabilities were enough to establish it and its second-generation successor, the 8080, as almost the definitive general-purpose microprocessor.

DENNIS MORALEE

also provides specific hardware support for high-level operation. The use of operating-system software, for example, is aided by the provision of two levels of operation, the normal level used by the users' programs, and a supervisory level used by the operating software. User programs executing at the normal level are debarred from using many of the device's instructions, so that all operations that will crucially affect the state of the system have to be carried out by passing control to the operating software, which is thus able to supervise at all times the overall operation of the system.

Similarly, the efficient execution of code generated by translator software from programs written in high-level languages is promoted by an instruction set geared to this task. In particular, the distinctive 'block' structuring of programs written in modern high-level languages such as Pascal and Ada is directly supported by sophisticated ENTER and EXIT instructions, each of which is equivalent to a series of several instructions in conventional architectures. Also, a series of special instructions and other facilities directly support the use of independently constructed program modules, with the links between modules being handled by the processor's hardware without the need for complex and performance-limiting linking software.

Facilities such as these mean the removal of many of the limitations that in the past have made programming microprocessor systems unnecessarily difficult. The high speed of the HMOS third-generation devices, their more efficient architectures, and the availability of coprocessors and other multiprocessing facilities, all add up to a practical removal of all computing-power limitations for the great majority of applications. Similarly, the large addressing range of the third-generation devices, their use of memory-management techniques, and the possibility of virtual-memory operation, all add up to a practical removal of all memory-size limitations.

Finally, the ability of the devices to efficiently execute machine-translated code, their direct support of the most commonly used data types and structures, and their suitability for use with sophisticated operating software designed to take responsibility for detailed control of system resources away from the user, all add up to a removal of the practical limitations on high-level programming and operation. Since it has proved to be the limitations on computing power, memory size and level of programming imposed by the second-generation devices that have created most of the difficulties in using them, the removal of these limitations in the case of the third-generation devices can be expected to make them very much easier to use.

In the wider context of the evolution of computer architectures, what the introduction of the advanced-architecture third-generation devices means is that the microprocessor manufacturers have effectively made two significant jumps in architectural sophistication at the same time. The first jump is that from the restricted and irregular architectures of the second-generation devices to the more capable, more commodious and more regular architectures typical of such successful if now ageing computer designs as the IBM 360 and PDP-11. The second jump, made simultaneously with the first, is from these enhanced but still hardware-oriented architectures to the very advanced 'high-level' architectures of the third-generation devices.

By making this twofold jump in architectural sophistication in the last few years, what the microprocessor manufacturers have managed to do is to close the gap between themselves and the mainframe and minicomputer manufacturers. Now, although there are still major generic differences between the mainframe, minicomputer and microprocessor realisations of the high-level architectural concepts, no one can any longer say that the microprocessor devices are architecturally much less sophisticated than their mainframe and minicomputer counterparts.

Full potential

This greatly increased sophistication of the new-generation microprocessors is bound to be reflected in a corresponding increase in the sophistication of the new products that will be based upon them. At the moment, products based on the pioneering if relatively low-end 8086 are becoming fairly common, while products based on the newer Z8000 and 68000 devices are just beginning to make an appearance. It seems safe to say, however, that none of the products yet introduced manages to exploit anywhere near the full potential of the third-generation devices, which will only be fully realised in product form much later into the 1980s.

One restricting factor here is the very magnitude of the change from the second-generation to the third-generation devices, which means that users have a great deal to assimilate before they can be expected to use the new devices in the high-level way intended by their designer. High-level facilities may indeed be easier to use, but, to the unprepared user at least, they are not necessarily easier to understand.

The development of the 'supermicros' has thus provided a firm basis on which the user community can be expected to build well into the 1980s, gradually incorporating more and more of the devices' increased sophistication into their products. What will be the full effect of this increased sophistication on the end-user markets is hard to imagine — after all, it would be difficult to say that the full impact of even the second-generation microprocessors has yet been felt by the end-users of electronics-based equipment. Nevertheless, it now seems at least possible that, even before the advanced features of the third-generation devices have been fully assimilated by those who will eventually exploit them, the first example of a yet more advanced fourth-generation of microprocessors has been introduced.

This yet more advanced device is, of course, the new iAPX 432, which may prove to be, after the 8008, 8080 and 8086, yet another new-generation 'first' for Intel. What the 432 represents is not just another triumph for Intel's microelectronics technology — the three chips making up the 432 range contain some 225 000 transistors compared to the 2250 in the 4004, an increase of 100 times in just 10 years — but also another example of its willingness to incorporate into its products the most advanced concepts available from the user community. Although many, but not all, of the 432's features have been discussed in computer-science circles for some years, sometimes built into research-oriented machines, and occasionally implemented in a partial way in some of the most advanced computing systems, usually mainframes, to reach the market, there is no doubt that, for a mainstream product soon to be available in high volume, it represents probably the most sophisticated general-purpose computing device yet built.

As an example of this sophistication, the 432 implements a version of the 'capabilities' approach to memory management, an approach formerly limited to a few research-oriented machines. This approach effectively limits access to each item of data in memory on a 'need to know' basis, the hardware itself checking each attempted access to ensure that it is legal, an arrangement that can do much to detect, contain and even correct execution errors. Memory accesses are also made on a 'descriptor' basis, in which programs access data not by an address but by what is effectively a description of what the data are, the actual accessing then being carried out by the hardware according to its own 'knowledge' of where the data are stored in gigantic 2^{40} byte virtual-memory space. The hardware also monitors the 'type' of each data item, thus for the first time supporting one of the more powerful features of the most modern high-level languages.

It is interesting that all these features — data typing, descriptor addressing and 'capabilities' phased memory management — were actually considered by the VAX-1 project team in 1976, but were in fact rejected. The reason given for rejecting the 'capabilities' approach is particularly significant: 'the complexity of the capabilities design was inappropriate for a minicomputer system'.[2] Few would have disagreed with this at the time, but even fewer would have dreamt that only 5 years later the approach would be implemented on a microprocessor.

Just as remarkable is the 432's approach to supporting high-level operation, via both high-level programming languages and sophisticated operating software. While the third-generation devices take a significantly advanced approach to this kind of support by offering hardware facilities tuned to the needs of the relevant software, the 432 goes much further by actually incorporating a large proportion of the software's functions into the hardware. Thus, programming in the much-discussed new Ada language is supported by an instruction set that is very nearly identical to the statements used in Ada itself. Consequently, only relatively simple translator software is needed, and it is significant that the Intel translator will be probably the first to become available for the still very new language.

The 432 is also notable in that it incorporates most of the necessary operating-software functions into hardware, giving effectively a 'silicon operating system'. This approach should not be confused with the widely mooted but much less sophisticated idea of simply incorporating a conventional operating system in a ROM-based form: the 432's operating-system facilities are directly incorporated into the device's internal microcode, an arrangement that has been used before, but to a much more limited extent, in advanced mainframe implementations, such as more recent models of the IBM 370. The 432's built-in operating-system facilities are in fact very extensive and account for some 40% of its microcode, compared to the mere 6% needed to implement its basic instruction set. What this means is that the actual operating-system software, called iMAX, can be relatively small, manageable and efficient, unlike the great majority of operating systems now in use.

Perhaps the best way of looking at the effects of these high-level facilities is to regard the 432 devices as having substantial inherent 'intelligence'. Conventional microprocessors, and indeed conventional computers, are incorrigibly 'dumb', and cannot even manage to control their own internal computing resources without the help of detailed user-written or operating-system software. The 432 devices are capable of controlling a great deal of their operation by themselves, however, as can be seen by their way of handling multitasking and multiprocessing.[5] Instead of relying on software to control the allocation of processing time to individual tasks, the 432 processors perform all the necessary scheduling and dispatching themselves, co-operating with each other in multiprocessing configurations to optimise the overall throughput. All that is required to increase a 432 based system's computing power is to literally plug in a two-chip processing unit: conversely, removing a processing unit merely slows the system down, without even noticeably interrupting the processing task that the removed unit was executing just before it was unplugged.

This transparent form of multiprocessing may in fact prove to be one of the 432's most influential features. Ever since the introduction of the microprocessor, its potential for cost-effective multiprocessing has been recognised, even being mentioned in the original 4004 article,[1] but the necessary hardware facilities have been slow to emerge in general-purpose designs. Thus, the second-generation devices do not in general include even the most basic facilities to support multiprocessing, and building them into multiprocessor configurations has therefore involved considerable design effort on the part of users. The third-generation devices all have the basic hardware facilities to support multiprocessing, notably special interface arrangements and instruction types, but still require all the real work of co-ordinating the multiple processors to be performed by the operating-system software. The 432, however, has removed this final limitation on ease of use, and the device's capability for 'intelligent interconnection' via generalised inter-chip protocols may prove to be an important feature usable with considerable advantage in all other forms of VLSI-based-electronics systems.

5 The start of a fourth generation of microprocessor devices? One of the 3 VLSI chips that make up Intel's new 32-bit iAPX 432 'micromainframe', not only the most powerful microprocessor device yet produced but also one of the most sophisticated computing devices ever put on the market. Compared to the 4004's 2250 transistors, the VLSI 432 contains 225 000 — an increase of 100 times in just 10 years

To sum up, what the introduction of the 432 appears to represent is a considerable further extension of the already remarkable developments that have led up to the introduction of the third-generation devices. Taken together, these events can be regarded as a 'coming of age' of the microprocessor, its clear arrival at a stage where the limitations of its early days no longer hold back its future progress, and where it is no longer regarded as either just a more economical substitute for a custom-LSI device or a cut-down version of a conventional minicomputer. Instead, the microprocessor must now be accepted in its own right as a uniquely important technological development that has made the great power of software-based engineering applicable to almost every type of application. All this has come about in just 10 years: what will the next decade bring?

References

1 FAGGIN, F., and HOFF, M.E.: 'Standard parts and custom design merge in four-chip processor kit', *in* 'Microprocessors' (McGraw-Hill, Electronic book series, 1975)

2 BELL, C.G.: 'Computer engineering: a DEC view of hardware systems design' (Digital Press, 1978)

3 BUCKLE, J.K.: 'The origins of the 2900 series', *ICL Tech. J.,* Nov. 1978. (1), p.5

4 STEVENS, D.: 'An introduction to memory management', *Electron. & Pow.*, 1980, **26**, (4), pp.317-323

5 DUFF, M.J.B.: 'Array processing', (and panels by MORALEE, D.) *ibid.*, 1980, **26**, (11), pp.888-893

The new microprocessors

Ian H. Witten, M.A., M.Sc., Ph.D., C.Eng., M.I.E.E.

Indexing term: *Microprocessors*

Abstract: Many developments have taken place recently in the microprocessor market. New devices range from processor chips designed for use in analogue and digital communication systems to architectures which readily support high-level language run-time environments and compilers. Some of these architectures have a sophistication which was rare in large computers until recently. The paper is a tutorial survey of recent products in both low and the high ends of the microprocessor market. It explains the motivation behind the new 16-bit devices in terms of economical factors behind the market, and provides some technical background in the area of high-level language run-time software structures, necessary to understand the architectures.

1 Introduction

The microprocessor market is moving so fast it is impossible to 'keep up' with it; it is not just the pace of progress in any particular sector of the market, but the wide range over which new developments occur. For example, the progression from DEC's PDP-8, a computer programmed predominantly in machine code and assembly language, through the PDP-11 to VAX-11, very much a high-level language machine, took 15 years, whereas analogous improvements have been made in microprocessors in less than half that time. Such a progression portends change in the pattern of use of the computer: from tightly-coded 'bit-twiddling' programs to large, high-level language systems with emphasis on economising human, rather than machine, resources. Furthermore, the large market for microprocessor-based products has encouraged physical encapsulation of microcomputer components on to a single chip, intended for high-volume applications where human effort used on tight coding can be economical. Use of digital-processing techniques for analogue signals has led to microcomputers tailored for signal processing. Increased interest in small-scale digital communications for monitoring and control is responsible for further new chips. The range of developments is extremely wide.

This paper endeavours to give an idea of the wide range of activity involved, and describes recent trends in microprocessor design, rather than speculating about future products. However, much support effort is needed before new chips become usable; thus it considers the virtually new generation of microprocessors that will be seen by application engineers.

The next Section discusses examples of products recently available at the low end of the market. The rest of the paper concentrates on the new appearance, at the high end, of rather sophisticated processor chips – the 16-bit micros. It may be questioned if we really need such powerful and complex chips; their use as the processing unit of general-purpose computer systems is clear, but have they relevance to the larger market of microprocessor-based products? To understand this need, one must appreciate the economical factors influencing the market, as considered in Section 3. In later Sections, the requirements of high-level languages are developed in tutorial form, followed by consideration of key architectural features of 16-bit microprocessors. The broad discussion is intended not only to reveal what motivates the new generation of processors, but also to give a sound basis for perceiving and evaluating change in the future.

Paper 1500E, first received May 1980 and in revised form 10th February 1981

The author is with the Man-Machine Systems Laboratory, Department of Computer Science, University of Calgary, Canada T2N 1N4, and was formerly with Man-Machine Systems Laboratory, Department of Electrical Engineering Science, University of Essex, Colchester CO4 3SQ, England

2 Small microprocessors

2.1 Developments in 8-bit microprocessors

One important trend is enhanced versions of popular 8-bit micros, which started some time ago with the Zilog Z-80, an upwards-compatible version of the 8080. Recently, Motorola brought out the 6809 [1] which is a very considerable enhancement of the 6800. Unlike Zilog, whose major design goal was to produce a machine on which binary 8080 programs could run without modification, Motorola achieve their compatibility at the assembly-language level by providing a special assembler which takes a 6800 program and produces 6809 code. This has allowed them to design a very much more powerful machine than the 6800.

Motorola began by examining a large number of programs written for the 6800, provided by their customers. They added many more addressing modes, expanded the indexing facilities, incorporated arithmetic on 2-byte quantities, and took the opportunity to regularise and make consistent the rather muddled 6800 instruction set. The result is an attractive 8-bit processor which is as suitable for the implementation of high-level languages as some of the new 16-bit machines.

Another extremely interesting machine is Intel's 8088 [2]. This implements precisely the same architecture and instruction set as the 16-bit 8086, which is described later, but uses an 8-bit external bus. Thus, 16-bit data words are fetched in two bus cycles, which means that the 8088 can be twice as slow as the 8086. However, this is the worst case, and for certain applications, typically those with a predominance of multiplication and division, the speed difference will be very small. But it is compatibility, rather than speed, that is the 8088's major advantage. Any software (such as language compilers or operating systems) written for the 8086 can automatically be used on a cheaper system with an 8-bit bus, and this is a very real advantage because extensive software development is being undertaken for the 8086.

2.2 Single-chip microcomputers

Many manufacturers have brought out complete computers on a single chip, comprising a processor together with a small amount of store (both ROM and RAM) and some I/O lines. This is not a new development, for devices like the Texas TMS 1000 (the world's best-selling computer – about 10 million sold in 1978) have been used since late 1974. However, these older chips are extremely limited 4-bit machines, with peculiar and difficult-to-program architectures, and find application only in very large markets like those for electronic calculators.

Typical of the newer single-chip microcomputer is Intel's 8048. Driven from a single 5 V supply, this has an 8-bit CPU, 1 kbytes of ROM, 64 bytes of RAM, and 27 I/O lines, all on one chip. It has a fairly straightforward single-accumulator architecture, with immediate and direct addressing modes, and a proper 8-level subroutining facility. In volume production, the chip is mask-programmed at the factory (like the

Reprinted with permission from *Proc. Inst. Elec. Eng.*, vol. 128, part E, pp. 197–204, Sept. 1981.

TMS 1000), but Intel sell a pin-compatible EPROM version for prototypes and preproduction systems.

A similar device, the 3870, is marketed by Mostek. This is a complete Fairchild F8 processor, with onboard ROM (2–4 kbytes) and RAM (up to 128 bytes) timer, and 32 I/O lines. The device is mask-programmed at the factory (the minimum order is 250, and the masking charge is refunded when the 1000th part is shipped). However, a version exists which brings the ROM address and data bus out to a 24-pin socket piggy-backed on top of the chip, so that standard EPROMs can be employed for prototyping.

Particularly interesting is a cut-down version of the 8048, the 8022, which implements a subset of the 8048 instruction set and works at a slower rate, but has an onchip A/D convertor. It is intended as a controller for domestic devices which require analogue information, such as temperature, to be sensed.

2.3 Analogue communications

Announced very recently is a microcomputer which is designed for signal-processing applications [3, 4, 5]. The growing interest in artificial speech output for consumer electronics has undoubtedly spurred this development [6]. However, some say that the new analogue processor, the Intel 2920, is to the analogue design engineer what the first microprocessor was to the random logic engineer in the early 1970s.

The 2920 contains an onchip D/A convertor, which can be used in successive-approximation fashion for A/D conversion under program control. Although the precision of conversion is 9 bits, internal arithmetic is done with 25 bits to accomodate the accumulation of roundoff errors in arithmetic operations. An onchip PROM holds a 192-instruction program, which is executed in sequence with no program jumps allowed. This ensures that each execution of the program takes the same time, so that the analogue waveform is regularly sampled and processed. At the fastest operating speed of the device, an instruction takes 400 ns. The 192-instruction program therefore executes in 76.8 μs, corresponding to a sampling rate of almost 13 kHz. Thus the processor can handle signals with a bandwidth of 6.5 kHz – ample for high-quality speech (the telephone bandwidth is around 3.4 kHz).

However, a special EOP (end of program) instruction is provided which causes an immediate jump back to the beginning. Hence if the program occupies less than 192 instructions, faster sampling rates can be used. For example, a 2nd-order filter requires only 10 instructions and so can be executed at 250 kHz.

2.4 Digital communications

The importance of digital communications is at last being realised by chip manufacturers. Mostek's recently-announced SCU-1 serial control unit is designed to be used as a front-end communications controller operating under direction from a central processor, and up to 255 of them can be accomodated in one system [7].

The chip connects to an ordinary serial line, and interprets a byte-oriented protocol defined by Mostek. Five characters constitute a message; namely, device address, command, data, data address, and check bits (the last are handled automatically by the chip). The chip acknowledges the message to the central processor, so that line failures can be detected centrally.

When a message is received, it is acknowledged and processed by the chip whose device address is specified. Mostek has implemented 128 out of the 256 possible commands, leaving the rest free for user-specific tasks. These predefined commands allow the central processor access to the I/O ports of the chip, via single-bit input and output, and byte input and output. A local timer is also provided which can be set centrally.

2.5 Support chips

A number of specialised support chips for microprocessors are now available. For example, the AMD arithmetic processor does floating-point operations in around 50–100 μs – much faster than calculator chips. There are high-speed fixed-point add-and-accumulate devices. DMA controllers perform the rather complicated protocol needed to gain and release the bus for a direct memory access transfer. Memory management chips, which allow protected access to segments of a large store in a controlled way, will be discussed in Section 5. Floppy-disc controllers, VDU controllers, and data-encryption devices are all available as single supporting chips for microcomputer systems.

3 Economics of information processing

Information processing is a truly remarkable economic phenomenon. Before considering the new generation of 16-bit microprocessors, it is worth looking at the overall economic picture, for it is this that motivates new developments. There are two separate, strong forces that bring down the real cost of information processing. The first is simply mass-market economics. Microprocessors, together with their associated components, are general-purpose, and their development costs are therefore shared between many users. The raw material is insignificant – a chip of silicon, a plastic pack, some metal legs. You pay for organisation, for testing, for quality control, for distribution. Yet the development of a microprocessor, including design, chip development, generation of test procedures, setting up a production line, is very expensive. It is precisely because the final product is totally uncommitted as to how it is to be used, that it is cheap; sales are high and the development cost is shared among a multitude of users. Microprocessors are the perfect example of mass-market economics.

The second force which reduces the cost of information processing is improvement in the technology itself. We know of 64 kbit static RAM chips, 256 kbit dynamic RAMs, 2 Mbit ROMs – devices that were unimaginable a few years ago. The M68000 16-bit microprocessor has about 68,000 transistors on a single chip. It is difficult not to feel a sense of awe at today's technology, let alone tomorrow's. The late Chris Evans, in his book 'The mighty micro' [8] gives an example of how an analogous improvement would have affected motor-cars: you could buy a Rolls-Royce, doing 3 million miles to the gallon, with enough power to drive the Queen Elizabeth II, for about \$3! Although such a remark may seem trite and sensation seeking, it is important to appreciate the amazing rate of change that we are now experiencing.

In an article published in late 1977 [9], James Bell of the Research and Development Group at DEC, a large mini-computer manufacturer, stated that, for semiconductor store, we get 90% more bytes/\$ per year, and for disc we get 40% more bytes/\$ per year. The increase is lower for disc storage because of the significant mechanical component: processor costs will follow the trend for semiconductor store but are much more difficult to quantify. Table 1 shows what happens on extrapolation from 1977 prices. Although these figures may seem super-optimistic, for example, almost 8 Mbyte of semiconductor store for \$1000 in 1987, experience since 1977 has shown that they are, if anything, a little conservative. Current prices for 'bargain buys' in computer hobbies magazines are just over 100 byte/\$ for semiconductor store, and up to 10000 byte/\$ for disc (admittedly, with rather slow access).

Table 1: Price projections for storage (made in 1977)

Bytes for $1	Late 1977	Late 1979	1981	...	1987
Semiconductor store	11	40	140	...	7000
Disk store	1000	2000	2800	...	30000

The snag, however, is to be seen in the cost of software. Here, figures are notoriously difficult to obtain. Bell estimated a constant figure of 1 byte/$. Other sources mention from 600 to 10000 debugged instructions per man-year, depending on the type of program being created [10]. A US Department of Defence estimate is $45 per line of code. There seems to be general agreement on two points: that the cost depends upon the number of instructions regardless of whether they are high- or low-level ones, and that the real cost is not changing significantly with time.

There are three ways to combat this predominance of software over hardware costs. One is simply to sell products in greater volumes. Since software is (virtually) free to copy, the development cost should be shared between replicas. If one considers the hardware and software expense to be 'balanced' when each byte of main store costs the same as the software which occupies it, and takes Bell's figures, then 11 copies of the system would have to be sold in 1977 to balance it, whereas 7000 must be sold in 1987! As long as systems are unbalanced, the economic pressure to reduce cost will fall chiefly on the more expensive component. Currently for, say, calculators and watches, this is the hardware part, while for small business systems it is the software. Most of the chips mentioned above are aimed at reducing the cost of products where imbalance falls on the hardware side. However, the most important lesson is how the balance is changing with time.

The second way to cheapen software is to work with high-level languages. It is a fact that all current 8-bit microprocessors are extremely poorly suited to high-level language implementation. This means that

(*a*) compilers for them are hard to write

(*b*) compilers produce code which is markedly less efficient, both in time and space, than hand-written code.

The third way is to allow software to be easily modularised, with effective hardware-supported firewalls between different modules which prevent bugs from spreading. It has been shown empirically [10] that programming time = constant × (number of instructions)$^{1.5}$. Techniques of structured programming encourage the development of software as a number of weakly-interacting modules, but in live systems it is impossible to implement complete protection between modules by compiler-generated checks – there are always some parts of the program which run 'naked', either because they are especially time-critical, or because they involve closer interaction with the hardware than high-level languages allow. Hardware techniques of memory segmentation can permit effective firewalls to be erected, and we will return to these later.

4 Requirements of high-level languages

Code produced by high-level language compilers is rather different in character from that written by hand in assembly language. This is primarily for three reaons:

(*a*) Compilers allocate space for temporary variables (needed, for example, when evaluating arithmetic expressions) in a more regular fashion than assembly-language programmers.

(*b*) Modern high-level languages require a different structure for holding named variables than assembly language, because different procedures, and (worse) different invocations of the same procedure, can share the same name but not (necessarily) the same storage location.

(*c*) Compilers, lacking the intelligence of people, cannot easily take advantage of any irregularities in the design of the machine.

Both of the first two features are best handled by a structured stack which holds variables, data structures, and temporaries generated during expression evaluation.

Even older languages like Fortran and Basic need a stack for arithmetic expression evaluation, although the effect of a stack can be simulated by software when stack-manipulation primitives are not provided by the basic hardware. However, they can use normal assembly-language techniques for storage of variables. For example, in Basic all variables are global just as they are in a single assembly-language program. In Fortran, subroutines are compiled independently and each variable is global within its enclosing subroutine, thus the normal assembly-language technique of assembling modules separately and loading them together into distinct areas of store can be used for Fortran.

However, block-structured languages, like Pascal, allow procedures access to variables defined in outer, calling, procedures; with the restriction that, if the new procedure declares a variable with the same name as an existing one, the old value becomes temporarily inaccessible during execution of the procedure, and reappears (with its old value intact) when the procedure is left. This is a very significant departure from assembly-language techniques of variable storage. For one thing, the 'scope' of variables (what parts of the program they can legally be accessed from) depends on the nesting structure of procedures as they appear in the printed version of the program (the so-called 'static' structure) and the pattern of execution at run time (the 'dynamic' structure) depends on the sequence of calls to procedures, which can be quite different. The dynamic calling sequence cannot be predicted by the compiler, even in principle, because it may depend on the particular data values which are read in at run time. The situation is further complicated by the possibility of recursion, where a procedure can call itself: here the variables which are defined in the new invocation must be kept separate from the old ones, which will eventually be revealed again when the recursion 'unwinds'.

4.1 *Storage structure: an extended example*

To appreciate the techniques used to store variables in the implementation of a block-structured language, let us look in detail at a particular procedure. 'Printint' of Fig. 1 prints an integer in decimal. It is recursive, because to print an integer you isolate the last digit by

i = *n div* 10;   *div* is integer division, eg 123 *div* 10 is 12

last_digit = *n* − 10*i

print the earlier digits of the number by

printint (*i*)   only necessary if $i > 0$

and then print the last digit

write (last_digit)   or, equivalently, 'write ($n - 10*i$)'

Notice incidentally that 'printint' checks the sign of its argument, and if negative it prints a '–' and makes it positive. A *recursive* procedure is used here because it is the easiest way to get an interesting example without having to work through a more complex program.

Fig. 2 shows what happens when printint is called to print '123'. It calls itself recursively until *i* becomes 0, and then it unwinds. Each unwinding causes a new digit to appear.

It is clear that, during recursion, the old values of i and n need to be retained, because they are used in the unwinding for the calculation

$$n - 10*i$$

The best way to store printint's variables is in a stack, as in Fig. 3. At each recursion, a new frame with slots for i and n is created on the stack. A 'frame pointer' FP points to the current (top) frame on the stack and is used within printint to access the current values of i and n. For example, in the M6800 microprocessor, FP would be kept in the index register and the current n and i values retrieved by

```
lda a 0,X      ; load value of n into accumulator a
lda a 1,X      ; load value of i into accumulator a
```

This creates a requirement for *indexing*: variables in the current stack frame are accessed by indexing off the frame pointer. To create a new stack frame whenever a procedure

```
procedure printint (n    :    integer);
var i    :    integer
begin
    if n < 0 then begin
        n    : = -n;
        write ('—')
    end;
    i    : = n div 10;
    if i <> 0 then printint (i);
    write (n — 10*i)
end.
```

Fig. 1 *Recursive procedure (in Pascal) to print an integer*

```
printint (123)
 i = 12,   n = 123
              printint (12)
               i = 1,   n = 12
                              printint (1)
                               i = 0,   n = 1
                              writes 1–10*0
                                     = '1'
              writes 12–10*1
                     = '2'
writes 123–10*12
       = '3'
```

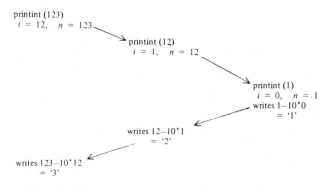

Fig. 2 *Sequence of events when printint is called to print '123'*

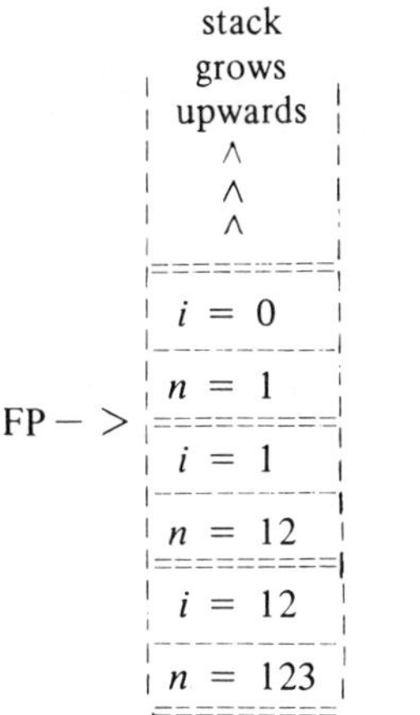

Fig. 3 *Variables being saved on stack during recursion of printint*

call occurs, we need to

```
        tsx    ; load old stack pointer (new FP) into
                 index register
sp <— sp + 2   ; increment stack pointer to leave space
                 for frame
```

Note that we have already encountered a deficiency in the 6800's architecture: you can't add to the stack pointer. Of course, the effect could be accomplished by performing two dummy pushes, like

```
psh a     ; increment sp by 1
psh a     ; increment sp by 1
```

but this would be cumbersome if there were, say, 37 variables in printint instead of just two. Since n is a parameter to printint, its value must be placed in the appropriate slot of the stack frame when printint is called, but we will ignore this in our slightly simplified discussion.

The storage structure of Fig. 3 has a serious shortcoming.

```
          | i = 0     |
          | n = 1     |
FP — >    |-----------|
            .....|......
          | i = 1     |      .
          | n = 12    |      .
          |-----------| < ...
            .....|......
          | i = 12    |      .
          | n = 123   |      .
          |-----------| < ...
```

Fig. 4 *Stack with pointers to previous stack frames*

```
program test_printint (output);
var radix, j    :    integer;

        procedure printint (n    :    integer);
        var i    :    integer;
        begin
            if n < 0 then begin
                n    : = -n;
                write ('—')
            end;
            i    : = n div radix;
            if i <> 0 then printint (i);
            write (n — radix* i    :    1)
        end;

    begin
        for j    : = 1 to 5 do begin
            for radix    : = 2 to 10 do begin
                printint (10*j);
                write (' ')
            end;
            write ln ();
        end
    end.
```

output:

1010	101	22	20	14	13	12	11	10
10100	202	110	40	32	26	24	22	20
11110	1010	132	110	50	42	36	33	30
101000	1111	220	130	104	55	50	44	40
110010	1212	302	200	122	101	62	55	50

Fig. 5 *Variable-radix version of printint, embedded in test program*

How is the previous FP value found when recursion unwinds? A double line has been drawn in the stack, but of course this will not be there in the computer store, when printint is executed. A pointer to the previous stack frame is needed at the beginning of each frame, as shown in Fig. 4. Then, to enter printint, the existing FP is pushed on to the stack before making the new frame.

```
psh X       ; save FP [NB cannot do this on the
                M6800]
tsx
sp <− sp + 2
```

To exit from printint, simply load the index register from the old, saved, FP

```
txs
pul X       ; [again, not implemented on M6800]
```

A further problem occurs if printint needs to access a variable declared in an outer procedure. Fig. 5 shows a new version of printint which can work with any radix (not greater than 10), embedded in a test program which prints 10, 20, 30, 40, and 50 in radices from 2 to 10. The output is also shown. During, say, the printing of 10 in base 10, the stack will be as shown in Fig. 6. Because access to 'radix' (which is defined at the outer level) is required from 'printint' (at the inner level), we must generalise the notion of frame pointer. What is needed is a *current environment vector* which points to all the 'accessible' stack frames. The top element of the environment vector is the frame pointer; lower elements correspond to outer (statically enclosing) levels of the program.

This example shows that the storage structure needed for variables in high-level languages is quite different to that used in handwritten assembly code. It would be a rare programmer who produced a structure like that in Fig. 6 to solve the problem of Fig. 5! A machine architecture which supports this kind of storage structure should be able to

(*a*) stack variables (it is clear that parameters should be stacked when a procedure is called, although this has not been discussed in the example)

(*b*) index off a hardware register (the frame pointer)

(*c*) increment the stack pointer by a constant (to reserve storage for variables)

(*d*) stack the index register (to preserve the old FP when entering a new procedure)

(*e*) manipulate the current environment vector, as well as the main stack.

None of the existing generation of 8-bit microprocessors can do many of these operations (with the exception of the new 6809 and 8088), although most of them have some hardware stacking facilities. This illustrates the mismatch between existing 8-bit microprocessors and high-level languages mentioned earlier.

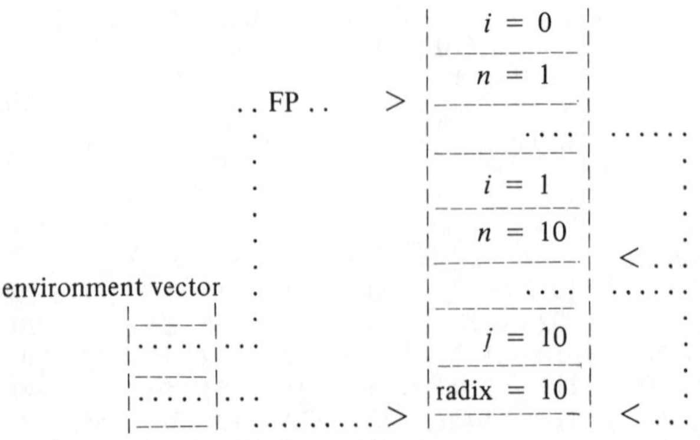

Fig. 6 *Stack with current environment vector*

5 16-bit microprocessors

Several 16-bit microprocessors are now on the market. The earliest was Texas's TMS9900, which was followed by the Intel 8086, and then, more recently, by the Zilog Z-8000 [11] and the Motorola M68000 [12, 13, 14]. National Semiconductor have announced the INS61000, but it is not yet available. For several years, DEC have marketed a microcircuit version of their PDP-11, the LSI-11; but this is not generally considered to be a microprocessor because the processor itself occupies several chips. This paper will concentrate here on the Intel, Zilog, and Motorola products: they are the 'big three' at present, and compete very strongly with each other.

There are several features which distinguish these microprocessors from all the 8-bit ones.

5.1 Extended addressing range

8-bit micros have an address space of 64 kbytes. This seemed quite sufficient when they were introduced in the early 1970s (the popular PDP-8 minicomputer was designed with a limit of 6 kbytes in 1963; and the PDP-11, designed in 1968, had a limit of 64 kbytes, although both have been extended over the years). However, 64 kbytes now seems a little restrictive, especially for large high-level language applications, and for multiprogrammed systems where several programs may be resident in store simultaneously. Nevertheless, this restriction will probably have little effect on the small domestic products which dominate the micro market.

The major disadvantage of an address space larger than 64 kbytes is that addresses can, in general, occupy more than two bytes (16 bits). The 16-bit microprocessor designers have tackled this problem in different ways; in fact, only the M68000 is fully and permanently committed to a large address space. The 8086 provides its programmer with a 64 kbyte 'window' on a much larger address space – up to 1 Mbyte. (In fact, four independently specified windows are operative at any one time.) To move the window, special instructions must be executed to load the hardware current-segment register, which points to the beginning of the window, with a new value. The Z-8000 is made in two versions. The cut-down 'unsegmented' version is restricted to a 64 kbyte address space (in fact, there are 6 such spaces, each dedicated to different kinds of code and data), while the 'segmented' version can work in conjunction with another memory management chip to provide address spaces of up to 8 Mbyte. The M68000 has a maximum address space of 16 Mbyte, but instructions generally need to specify only 16 address bits.

Note that address spaces of several megabytes really are enormous, by present standards. For example, only the largest models of IBM's top-range System 370 series have 16 Mbytes of store.

5.2 Memory segmentation and protection

Both the Z-8000 and M68000 offer memory management systems (on a chip separate from the processor) which allow one to set up protected areas of store. If a program disobeys the rules and attempts to access an area which is forbidden to it, the hardware detects this and a special exception routine is executed automatically. This allows firewalls to be erected between parts of a program, or between one program and another. The 8086 has much cruder segmentation facilities (but does not require a special memory management chip) which does not help to protect store but allows free access to all.

It is interesting that other manufacturers are already stepping in to provide alternative memory management systems for 16-bit micros. Central Data Corporation, for example, recently described a memory management board designed for the Z-8000 which is substantially more powerful than Zilog's own product [15].

5.3 *Protected modes of operation*

Allied to memory management facilities is the fact that the Z-8000 and M68000 both have dual modes of operation – *system mode* and *normal mode* (called 'supervisor' and 'user' mode on the M68000). These are provided for use when a system (supervisory) program, for example an operating system, wishes to exert control and protection over normal (user) programs. Only in system mode can the portion of the address space available to normal programs be reallocated. Furthermore, whenever an interrupt or other exceptional condition occurs, control reverts automatically to system mode, so that the user program can be unaware of such events. Full use of the dual-mode operation can only be made after considerable effort has been spent on writing an operating system for the processor which allows normal programs to run oblivious of the real complexities of the system.

5.4 *More data types*

The data-types supported by instructions on 8-bit micros are generally restricted to BCD (4-bit characters), bytes, and 16-bit addresses. 16-bit micros offer much more than this. For example, the Z-8000 has instructions which operate on bits, BCD characters, bytes, 16-bit words, 32-bit longwords, byte strings, and word strings. It provides multiply and divide instructions for both 16- and 32-bit integers. The M68000 has a similar repertoire of instructions, and may be extended in the future to deal with floating-point data as well.

With respect to hardware-supported data types, as in other ways, the 8086 is rather less sophisticated than the other two. It does not have any arithmetic operations on 32-bit quantities, although there are 16-bit multiply/divide instructions.

5.5 *Regularity of instruction set*

The 16-bit micros place increasing emphasis on the regularity of the instruction set, for this encourages high-level language use. Compilers cannot easily generate code which takes advantage of special tricks of the machine, so beloved of assembly-language programmers. In fact, compilers usually generate only a subset of the possible machine-language instructions, for they must confine themselves to a regular part of the machine and ignore its other features.

The 8086 has four 16-bit general registers, and the high and low byte of each can be referenced individually. In addition, there are two pointer registers (used as stack pointer and frame pointer), and two index registers. The memory management hardware has four segment registers, each providing a separate 64 kbyte window on the address space. Although the instruction set is much more regular than that of the 8080 and Z-80, it does present difficulties to compiler-writers. For example, one particular register is always implied as one of the operands of a multiply or divide instruction. This is not too awkward for assembly-language programmers, but places a severe restriction on compilers.

The Z-8000 has 16 16-bit registers, one of which is reserved as the stack pointer for procedure entry and exit. (There is a 17th register which is used for the stack in system mode, i.e. on occurrence of an interrupt.) The high and low bytes of the first eight registers can be accessed independently. Pairs of adjacent registers participate in 32-bit operations, and adjacent quadruples hold the 64-bit result of a 32-bit multiply operation. Although the stack pointer is reserved, any register can be used for push and pop instructions. The instruction set is regular in that any register can be used by any instruction as an accumulator, a source operand or operand address, or an index register. There are eight addressing modes (plus some extra ones used solely for string operations). However, the Z-8000 does not permit independent specification of addressing modes for both source and destination operands: it is primarily a memory-to-register architecture.

The M68000 has a highly regular instruction set. There are 16 32-bit registers, and from a logical point of view the architecture is a 32-bit one. Eight of these registers are used for data manipulation and index calculation, while the other eight are primarily used for addresses. The stack pointer is one of the address registers: like the Z-8000, there is a 17th register which is a system stack pointer. Several addressing modes, very similar to those of the Z-8000, are provided. Although addresses occupy 24 bits, 16-bit addresses can be specified instead in almost every situation, so that small systems do not pay a severe penalty by having to handle 24-bit addresses.

Behind this apparent similarity there are some subtle but important differences between the Z-8000 and M68000 instruction sets. Some of these are summarised in Table 2. While both are primarily register-to-memory architectures, the M68000 provides a flexible memory-to-memory move instruction where the source and destination address modes can be specified independently. It was noted above that the high and low bytes of the first eight Z-8000 registers can be accessed independently, but this is not so for the M68000. Its 32-bit registers can of course hold 16-bit or 8-bit quantities, but the higher-order part will be unused. Although the extra flexibility given by the Z-8000 may be used by assembly-language programmers, it will almost certainly not be taken advantage of by compilers, for which the simpler choice of the M68000 facilitates register allocation.

Table 2: Some architectural differences between the Z-8000 and M68000

Z-8000	*M68000*
memory-to-register architecture	memory-to-register architecture; but with memory-to-memory MOVE
16-bit registers; bytes can be packed	32-bit registers; bytes cannot be packed
several addressing modes, but	several addressing modes, but
(*a*) relative addressing for branches only	(*a*) relative addressing for any instruction
(*a*) push and pop instructions	(*a*) push and pop addressing modes

Relative addressing can be used in the M68000 for *any* instruction, and not just for branches and subroutine jumps as on the Z-8000. Furthermore, a push or pop (using any address register as stack pointer) can be specified as an addressing mode, rather than as a specific operation, and so can be performed on the fly in conjunction with arithmetic instructions. Autoincrement and autodecrement addressing modes (which are the same as push and pop) are implemented on the Z-8000 only in conjunction with string operations, although there are of course special push and pop instructions.

5.6 *High-level language support*

There are several features which a processor designer can add to enhance his machine for high-level languages. Earlier, we saw the need for a stack-frame-oriented approach to storing variables, and the three machines under consideration all support this. For example, a procedure call on the 8086 can be done by

```
                ; code to implement 'call proc (parm 1,
                  parm 2)'
push parm 1     ; push parameters on to stack
push parm 2
call proc.
```

The called procedure looks like

```
proc: push FP          ; save old frame pointer register
                         [called BP in 8086]
      mov FP,SP        ; make new frame pointer
                       ; [NB 8086 convention is 'mov
                         ⟨destination⟩ ⟨source⟩']
      sub SP,nlocals   ; reserve space for local variables
                         on stack
         .             ; [NB stack grows downwards]
         .
         .
      mov SP,FP        ; restore old SP
      pop FP           ; restore old FP
      ret 4            ; return, discarding 4 bytes of
                         parameters
```

The Z-8000's procedure call facilities are rather similar. In contrast, the M68000 provides a very sophisticated mechanism. The procedure-entry process

```
push FP
mov FP,SP
sub SP,nlocals
```

is accomplished by a single instruction,

```
link FP,nlocals
```

and an 'unlink' instruction does the return sequence. Furthermore, it is usually necessary to save some of the registers on entry to the procedure and restore them on exit, so that they can be used within it without altering their contents for the calling program. The M68000 provides a multiple-register move instruction, which moves a selected subset of the registers (indicated by a 16-bit mask within the instruction), typically stacking them. The registers can be restored by a similar instruction.

It is worth pointing out that the detailed decisions which have to be made when designing an instruction set can have a large effect on the high-level languages which are handled efficiently. For example, the 8086 code in 'proc' above discards the 4 bytes of parameters from the stack *within the procedure*, whereas the parameters are stacked outside the procedure as part of the calling sequence. This means that the caller and the procedure have to agree on the number of parameters. Although this convention is enforced by the Pascal language, other high-level languages allow procedures to have variable numbers of parameters. These cannot take full advantage of the 8086 'ret' instruction. The M68000 'unlink', however, does not attempt to remove parameters from the stack: this must be done by the calling code after the procedure has returned, by

```
add SP,nbytes
```

In this instance, the M68000's designers have made a sensible decision which will help to support a variety of high-level languages. However, the 'save-multiple-register' instruction has a flaw, if it is possible to have procedures with multiple entry points. The bit mask which determines the registers to be saved is embedded in the code, in both the 'save' and 'restore' instructions, and naturally these should agree. However, it is more useful for it to be placed on the stack by the 'save' instruction and retrieved automatically from the stack by 'restore'. This permits a procedure to be entered at different places, with different register subsets being saved at each. The exit code can be common because the stack records which registers have been saved. (This scheme is implemented by the VAX-11/780 processor [16].)

Another instruction which helps to support high-level languages is *push effective address*, which pushes a parameter address on to the stack instead of a parameter value. This facility is provided on all three microprocessors, although it requires two instructions on the 8086 and Z-8000.

The M68000 has further high-level instructions. An extremely useful one is the 'bounds check' instruction, which compares an array index, situated in any data register, against 0 and an upper limit situated in memory. This single instruction strongly encourages compiler-generated checks of array accesses, which are extremely helpful when debugging code.

5.7 String manipulation instructions

The 8086 and Z-8000 both provide instructions which deal with whole strings of data at once. For example, on the 8086 you can

move a string from one place in memory to another
compare two strings
scan a string for a specified byte
set each element of a string to a byte.

Although such instructions can speed up execution very considerably, they are rather awkward to generate by a compiler. They rely on using particular registers to hold particular operands, which causes considerable difficulty with register allocation. The Z-8000 avoids this by providing multioperand instructions which specify the operands in a more general way. However, special addressing modes are provided for strings which cannot be used in other instructions, and this detracts from the regularity of the addressing architecture. Motorola have promised that new versions of the M68000 will also provide string manipulation primitives.

6 Conclusion

This article has largely concentrated on some important aspects of the run-time representation of high-level language programs, and the steps which microprocessor designers have taken in order to assist with their implementation. This is certainly the high end of the market, at present. However, these are the crucial issues for the future, and will filter down to the lower levels of cheaper, single-chip, micros; indeed, they are doing so already, to a limited extent, with the 6809 and 8088. History has shown that software is much more conservative than hardware; e.g. the 22-year reign of Fortran (how many 22-year old computers are still being used?). Recent years have seen a slow shift of emphasis to block-structured languages like Pascal (and Ada), and they will probably be with us for years to come.

Hardware, on the other hand, will certainly not stay static. At present, about 70000 transistors can be squeezed onto a single chip, but it has recently been estimated that this will rise to 1,000,000 by 1985 [17]. Thus a single-chip microcomputer comprising a processor as powerful as the M68000 with around 64 kbytes of RAM or ROM should be possible by then. This will place increasing emphasis on the economic advantages obtained by writing software in high-level languages, even for mass-produced domestic products. Perhaps there will come a time when the devices of hand-crafted assembly-language programming will never be cost-effective.

7 Acknowledgments

It is a pleasure to acknowledge the help of Chris Corbett, John Foster, Paul Griffith, Phil McCrea, and Chris Rowden in gathering and assimilating material for this paper.

8 References

1 RITTER, T., and BONEY, J.: 'A microprocessor for the revolution: the 6809', *Byte*, 1979, 4, pp. 14–42

2 THOMAS, I.H.: '8-bit microprocessor harbors 16-bit performance', *Electronics*, 1980, **53**, pp. 163–167
3 TOWNSEND, M., HOFF, M.E., and HOLM, R.E.: 'An NMOS microprocessor for analog signal processing', *IEEE Trans.*, 1980, **C-29**, pp. 97–102
4 HOFF, M.E., and TOWNSEND, M.: 'Single-chip n-MOS microcomputer processes signals in real time', *Electronics*, 1979, **52**, pp. 105–110
5 'Anatomy and applications of the analogue microprocessor', *Electronic Product Design*, April 1980, pp. 40–45
6 HOFF, M.E., and LI, W.: 'Software makes a big talker out of the 2920 microcomputer', *Electronics*, 1980, **53**, pp. 102–107
7 BURCKLE, R.A.: 'Microcomputer brings flexibility and power to communications control', *ibid.*, 1980, **53**, pp. 127–131
8 EVANS, C.: *The mighty micro* (Gollancz, London, 1979)
9 BELL, J.R.: 'Trends in computing: predicting the areas of investment', *Europa Digital*, 1977, **3**, pp. 6–8
10 BROOKS, F.P.: 'The mythical man-month' (Addison-Wesley, Reading, MA, 1975)
11 PEUTO, B.L.: 'Architecture of a new microprocessor', *IEEE Computer*, Feb. 1979, pp. 10–21
12 STRITTER, E., and GUNTER, T.: 'A microprocessor architecture for a changing world: the Motorola 68000', *ibid.*, 1979, **C-28**, pp. 43–52
13 LeMAIR, I.: 'Complex systems are simple to design', *Electron. Des.*, 1978, **18**, pp. 100–107
14 HARTMAN, B.: '16-bit 68000 microprocessor camps on 32-bit frontier', *Electronics*, 1979, **52**, pp. 118–125
15 ROLOFF, J.J.: 'Managing memory to unloose the full power of microprocessors', *ibid.*, 1980, **53**, pp. 130–134
16 STRECKER, W.D.: 'VAX-11/780 – A virtual address extension to the DEC PDP-11 family'. National computer conference, 1978, pp. 967–980
17 PATTERSON, D.A., and SEQUIN, C.H.: 'Design considerations for single-chip computers of the future', *IEEE Trans.*, 1980, **C-29**, pp. 108–116

VLSI Impact on Microprocessor Evolution, Usage, and System Design

PAUL M. RUSSO, SENIOR MEMBER, IEEE

Abstract—**The rapidly expanding capability of Large-Scale and Very-Large-Scale Integration (LSI and VLSI) and their interaction with computer technology gave birth to the now ubiquitous microprocessor. Recent trends in digital integrated-circuit technology and their impact on microprocessor technology will be reviewed. Additionally, we will categorize microprocessors, discuss the microprocessor industry, and overview their impact on industrial, commercial, and consumer applications. Finally, we will discuss the impact VLSI will have on both chip and system design.**

INTRODUCTION

THE ONGOING REVOLUTION in digital Large-Scale Integration (LSI) spawned in the late 1960's, is leaving a permanent imprint on all aspects of our lives. The first computer revolution began with Von Neumann's work in 1945 [1], and has rapidly evolved to today's highly computerized and data-oriented society. The second computer revolution began with the commercialization of the microprocessor (μP) in 1971, when INTEL introduced the 4004, 4-bit single-chip Central Processing Unit (CPU) [2]. It took a few years for the business impact of microprocessors to be understood and a few more years before its potential impact on the consumer began to be visualized [3].

The rapid progress in computer and digital electronics technology is illustrated in Fig. 1. It took a decade from the 1945 invention of the stored program computer (instructions and data stored in same memory) to develop the first all-transistor machine. A decade later, standard digital logic families such as Texas Instruments' TTL and RCA's COS/MOS families began to emerge. This is the era when LSI capability, which allowed one to interconnect large numbers of transistors on a single piece of silicon substrate, began to evolve.

It is interesting to note that the INTEL 4004 concept arose from attempting to satisfy several custom calculator chip designs with a single family of LSI parts. INTEL quickly realized that this same part could be used in many other applications, and thus the microprocessor was born. More recently, we have entered the age of Very-Large-Scale Integration (VLSI) which is characterized by increasingly complex technologies, very complex integrated circuits, and a host of problems that relate to design of both the devices themselves and the systems that use them.

In this paper we will overview the trends in LSI and VLSI and the impact of the evolution of μP's and microcomputers (μC's) on that technology. We will categorize μP's and μC's, discuss the microprocessor industry, and identify the ingredients associated with successful participants in that business. Additionally, we will overview the impacts μP's and μC's are having on industrial, commercial, and consumer applications. Finally, we will discuss IC and systems design implications of VLSI, dwell a little on the impending software crisis, and present a comprehensive list of references for those seeking to delve deeper into any of the above areas.

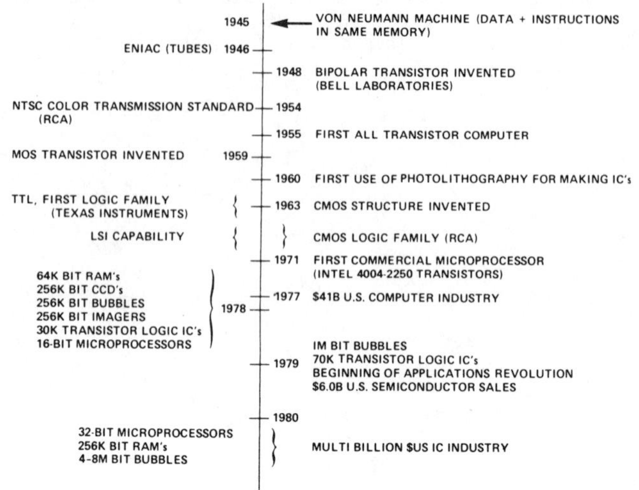

Fig. 1. Evolution in technology.

MICROPROCESSORS AND MICROCOMPUTERS

Any computer system, from the simplest microwave-oven controller to a sophisticated VLSI tester, consists of a combination of three classes of subsystems—CPU's, direct-memory subsystems, which can be READ/WRITE (RAM) and/or READ-ONLY (ROM), and input/output (I/O) interfaces for peripheral control, Fig. 2. The CPU subsystems perform all the classical arithmetic, logic, and control functions. The direct-memory subsystems contain both the programs (instructions to be executed by the individual CPU's) and the currently active data on which the CPU's are operating. The I/O interfaces represent the critical communication links between the internal computer operations and the external world of I/O devices such as mass memory, keyboards, displays, etc.

μP's are single-chip realizations of the CPU functions. μC's, in the context of this paper, are single-chip realizations of a major portion of the computer system function, i.e., CPU, RAM and ROM, and I/O. Many μC's sport an option of having either mask-programmed ROM (low-cost for high-volume ap-

Manuscript received February 4, 1980; revised April 24, 1980.
The author is with RCA Laboratories, Princeton, NJ 08540.

Reprinted from *IEEE Trans. Electron Devices*, vol. ED-27, pp. 1332–1341, Aug. 1980.

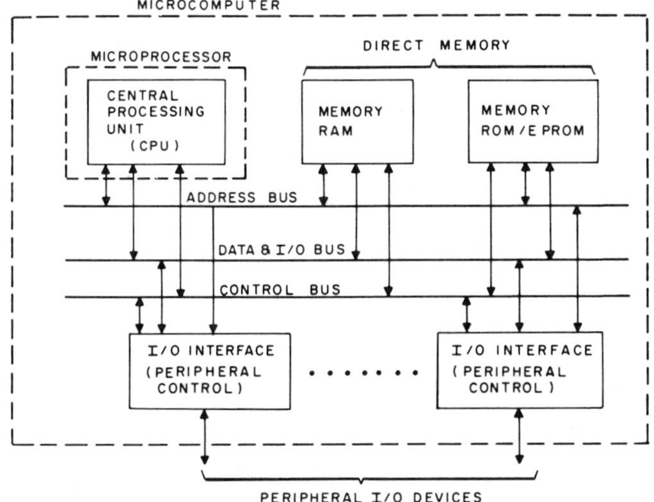

Fig. 2. The fundamental subsystems of any computer system.

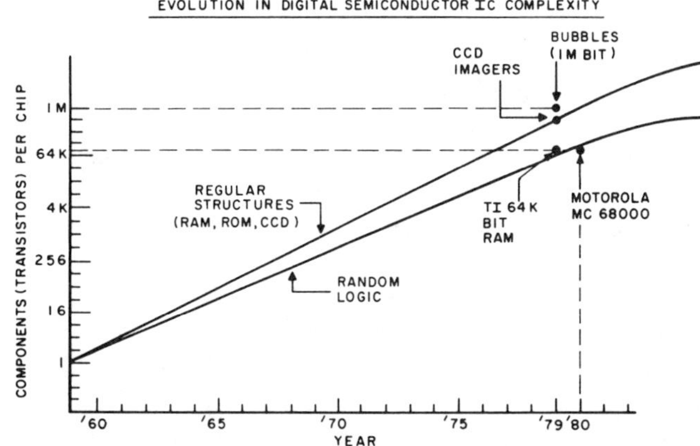

Fig. 3. Evolution in digital semiconductor IC complexity.

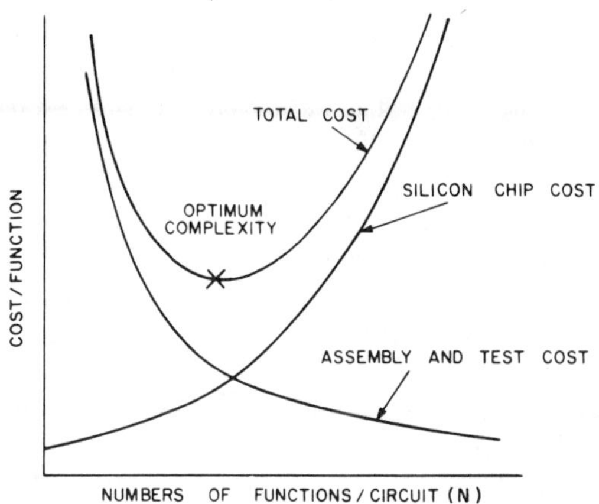

Fig. 4. LSI IC cost contributing factors showing optimum complexity for lowest cost per function.

plications) or EPROM (UV light erasable and reprogrammable for low-volume applications). The design of μP-based system architectures will not be discussed below, since considerable literature exists on the subject [4]-[6].

Trends in LSI/VLSI Technology

The history of LSI and VLSI is brief but explosive. Fig. 3 illustrates the rapid evolution in IC capacity, with the upper boundary representing regular structures such as RAM's and ROM's, while the lower boundary represents random logic. Since the development of the metal-oxide-semiconductor (MOS) transistor in the late 1950's, through the late 1970's, device complexity has doubled every year. The primary contributing elements to this growth rate were larger die size, higher density (finer microstructure), and advances in device design. Beyond 1979, the growth rate in IC complexity has slowed to doubling every 1.5 to 2 years. The reasons for this slowing are due to technological limits being approached, which is especially true for regular structures, and to the fact that it is not yet clear how designers can effectively make use of random-logic IC's containing hundreds of thousands of transistors [7], [8].

The growth in complexity has a direct effect on the cost of integrated circuits. The cost of LSI integrated circuits consists of two major components: silicon chip cost and assembly/test cost. Based on the available design techniques and process technology, silicon chip cost is roughly an exponential function of complexity. On the other hand, the assembly/test cost, as a first approximation, can be treated as independent of complexity. This leads to an inverse relationship between assembly/test cost per function and complexity. By combining these two components, the cost per function will have a minimum corresponding to the optimum complexity for the current state-of-the-art design technique and process technology, Fig. 4. As time goes on, the silicon chip cost will decrease due to improving density, processing technology, and material. Assembly and test costs, however, will stay approximately constant. Thus the optimum cost per function will decrease with time (in uninflated dollars). This will allow more and more of the system to economically fit on a single IC, and the cost per computation function will decrease exponentially. This will make possible distributed intelligence in the broadest sense, where every subsystem will have local processing capability and the ability, where needed, to interact with other intelligent subsystems or systems.

Microprocessor Impact on LSI/VLSI Technology

The rapid growing use of LSI and VLSI in non-memory applications would not have occurred if the μP had not been invented. Prior to the introduction of μP's and related peripheral circuits, ever more complex IC's were developed to perform ever more specialized functions. Hence, except for a few large volume market segments (e.g., data communications), IC volume decreased rapidly with complexity.

With the invention of the μP, it became economically viable to develop large complex random-logic IC's and then specialize their application in software. In fact, it is the invention of the stored-program computer itself (of which μP's and μC's are embodiments) that has spurred the use of RAM and ROM and has generated the volumes needed to attain the exponentially decreasing per bit costs. For example, in excess of 50 million 16K NMOS dynamic RAM's were produced in 1979. The 64K bit RAM represents the current technological limit, and 256K bit RAM's will be a reality by the mid 1980's.

Categorizing Microprocessors and Microcomputers

In categorizing μP's and μC's, we will restrict our discussion to MOS devices. Bipolar devices, to date, have been extensively used only in specialized applications requiring high thruput. Also, we *will not* discuss 4-bit μP's (we *will* discuss 4-bit μC's), since they are obsolete and their days are numbered.

μC's range from relatively simple 4-bit devices (Texas Instruments TMS 1000 series, National COPS 400 series, etc.) with volume costs in the 1-3 dollar range, to more powerful 8-bit devices (MOSTEK 3870 series, INTEL 8048 series, etc.) with volume costs in the 3-10 dollar range.

μP's, on the other hand, vary from mid-range machines (INTEL 8085, RCA 1802, ZILOG Z80, etc.) with volume CPU costs in the 2-10 dollar range, through higher performance 16-bit CPU's (MOTOROLA 68000, ZILOG Z8000, INTEL 8086, TI 9900, etc.) whose capability approaches that of mid-1970's minicomputers, and whose chip costs may range from tens to hundreds of dollars. These latter devices are relatively new to the market (8086 sampled in 1978, Z8000 and MC68000 sampled in late 1979), and hence their costs will tumble as we move down the learning curve.

Fig. 5 presents a rough view of processor performance ranges versus computer category. Note that the dollar figures shown represent mature product, i.e., those in volume production. Note also that even though many 8-bit microprocessors cost less than 8-bit μC's, the latter have on-board RAM, ROM, and I/O, which usually results in far lower system cost.

μP's and μC's exist in a wide variety of technologies. p-channel MOS (PMOS) is fading as a viable technology. n-channel MOS is the dominant technology and is the standard for all existing 16-bit machines. In the 4- and 8-bit categories, CMOS parts are available for low-power applications at nominal cost premiums (RCA 1802, CMOS TMS 1000, etc.), along with bipolar devices (FAIRCHILD 9440, etc.) for higher performance. Silicon-on-sapphire (SOS) parts are just becoming commercially available.

The unquestionable technological leader in the microprocessor industry has been INTEL Corporation. Fig. 6 illustrates the evolution of its μP and μC families. Note the rapid improvements in technology (average transistor area) which went from 8.6 mil^2/transistor for the 8008 in 1972 to 1.8 mil^2/transistor for the 8086 in 1978. The RCA 1802 CMOS microprocessor is included for comparison. Photomicrographs of the INTEL 8080 and 8086 are presented in Figs. 7 and 8.

A closer look at Figs. 6-8 reveals that the apparent large gains in "average transistor area" are at least partially due to architectual changes in the CPU giving rise to more regular structures. More will be said about this trend below. For similar reasons, the INTEL 8048, which contains significant amounts of on chip RAM and ROM, also shows a low "average transistor area." It should be noted that IC manufacturers are constantly shrinking the die size of their high-volume products to maximize yield and hence margin, so the chip areas shown in Fig. 6 represent moving targets and are apt to change.

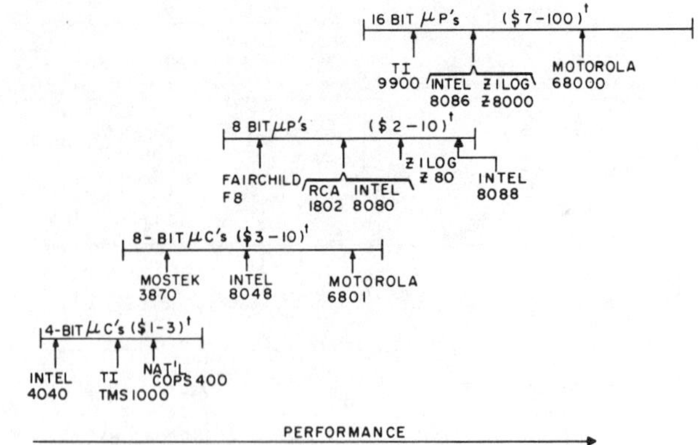

† ALL COSTS ASSUME MATURE PRODUCT AND 1980 DOLLARS

Fig. 5. Categorizing μP's and μC's.

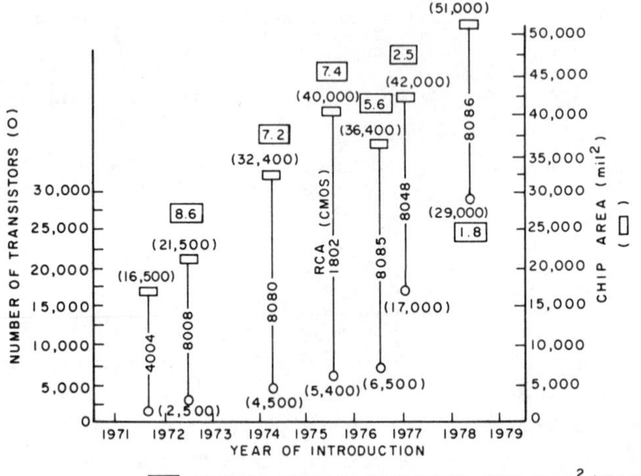

Fig. 6. INTEL microprocessor products showing chip area and complexity evolution.

The Microprocessor Industry

The microprocessor has changed the early trends of LSI development and has reoriented those efforts to the design of CPU's, memories, and ever more complex peripheral IC's which permit the rapid development of low chip count dedicated computer systems. As the industry matures, it is rapidly moving towards having full system capability. INTEL, the leader in IC technology, is also a leader in the development of support circuits, single-board computer systems, and development systems. More recently, INTEL has begun to market preprogrammed devices which satisfy desired system level functions. The manufacturing cost of these devices is the same as that of unprogrammed devices, but, since there is added value in the eyes of the customer, margins can be improved.

Below, we will attempt to summarize business trends and to project them a few years into the future. Before doing so, it is noteworthy to point out that most published sales figures and forecasts relate to noncaptive markets. Captive markets (such as TI, IBM, DEC, and ATT production for internal use) account for a significant fraction (close to 50 percent) of world production.

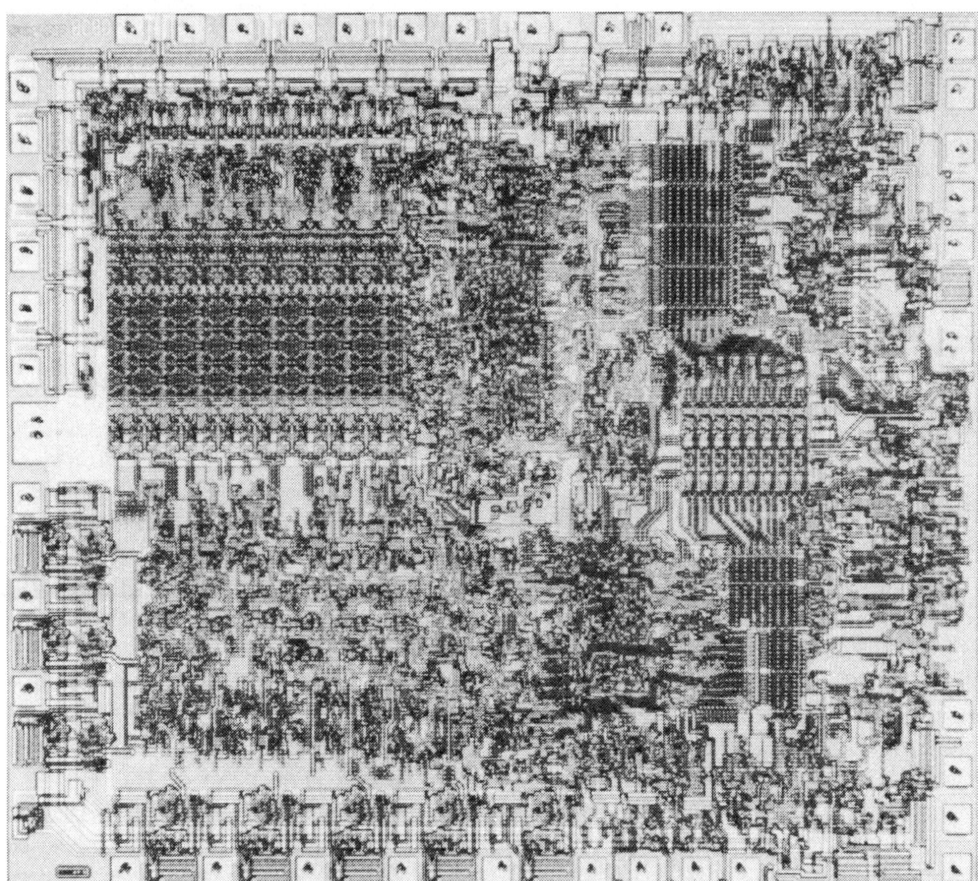

Fig. 7. INTEL 8080 die (4500 transistors, 32400-mil^2 area, NMOS) (Courtesy of INTEL Corporation).

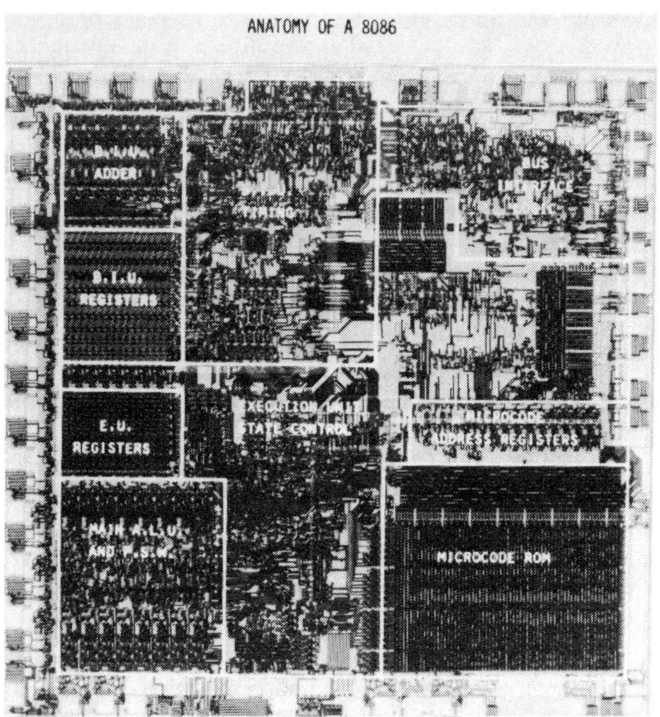

Fig. 8. INTEL 8086 die (29 000 transistors, 51 000-mil^2 area, HMOS) (Courtesy of INTEL Corporation).

The market for μP's will have a compound growth rate of about 25 percent through the early 1980's, approaching an annual volume of 200 million units by 1983, with a market value approaching 500 million dollars. When one adds sales of supporting IC's such as peripherals, RAM's, ROM's, and EPROM's, the market swells to about 1.5 billion dollars per year. Fig. 9 projects how noncaptive unit sales for 4-bit μC's, 8-bit μP's and μC's, and 16-bit μP's are expected to grow. Additional information is available in [9]-[12].

The numbers for 8- and 16-bit devices are similar to the ones generated in a recent Creative Strategies report [11]. Fig. 9, however, projects significantly larger unit sales for 4-bit devices than the 19.5 million units indicated by Creative Strategies for 1983. It should be noted, however, that the Creative Strategies numbers are not consistent with current industry production trends. Texas Instruments, in their sales presentations, claims that it has a capacity to produce "several million" TMS 1000 machines per month. Additionally, as we will discuss below, the real volume applications for 4-bit devices are in the consumer area, and this area is just beginning to explode. The trend in this area will be to pull more system capability onto the 4-bit chip to lower system cost rather than to go for unneeded computing power represented by 8-bit architectures.

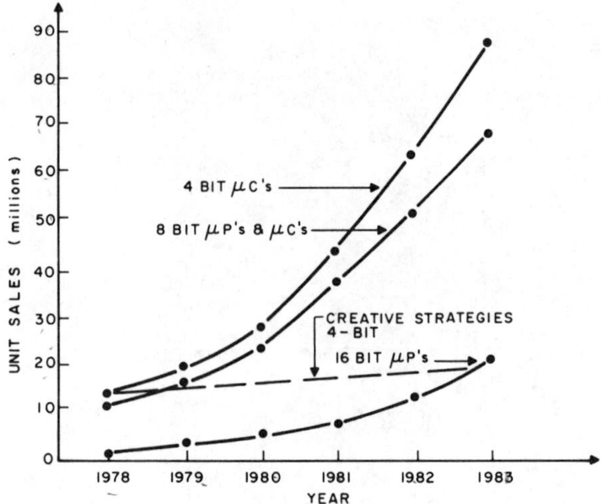

Fig. 9. Forecast of annual unit μP and μC sales through 1983.

Key ingredients in the success of a microprocessor manufacturer, in addition to price and delivery, are system development support and the availability of support chips and of single-board computer families. The μP itself usually represents a small fraction of the system LSI cost, usually less than 1 percent for industrial and commercial applications and perhaps 5-25 percent for consumer products (note that for μC's, the CPU portion usually takes up much less than half the IC area). Because of the above, μP applications are *rarely* designed to maximize CPU utilization but rather to minimize system cost (development and production). Thus the ease with which one can develop a system (development support) and the availability of peripheral IC's (low system chip count) usually dominate the CPU selection process [13], [14].

Microprocessor/Microcomputer Applications Overview

The μP revolution is truly an applications revolution. By the year 2000, 5 to 10 *billion* μP's and μC's will be in service—about one for each living person on earth. In the majority of cases, the person interacting with the μP or μC will not know that a computer is involved. One will simply have improved service or functionality for the task at hand.

The applications of μP's and μC's break down into three broad categories—industrial, commercial, and consumer. Industrial applications include those that employ microprocessors in the design or manufacturing processes of the industry under consideration. Commercial applications include those used in providing new or improved services and/or ways of doing business such as communications and word processing. Consumer applications include those that add features or improve the cost/performance of existing consumer products or give rise to entirely new classes of consumer products. These three categories of μP and μC applications are briefly reviewed below. In each area, references are listed to permit the interested reader to pursue the subjects in depth.

Industrial Applications

μP's are having a major impact on industrial applications, including the areas of testing, control, instrumentation, data acquisition, numerical machine control, and even robotics. In all these areas, equipment offering expanded functions, better human interfaces, improved reliability, and lower cost are emerging.

Testing: Microprocessor-based test systems, which can be used to automatically identify component, subsystem, and system faults, are increasingly used to improve product quality and reduce manufacturing costs. Quality is improved since marginal components and subsystems are replaced prior to equipment shipment, resulting in a lower probability of field failure. Manufacturing costs are reduced since system-level tests can identify the probable subsystem failures, and hence yield more efficient repair. We should note that product reliability is more a function of design than testing and there is no assurance that increased testing will, in fact, improve reliability. The advent of μP's has opened many avenues for low-cost dedicated testers, which means that industries can now economically justify automated and more complete testing of low-cost/low-complexity subsystems right on down to the component level. Marcantonio [15] describes a very successful application of RCA's COSMAC microprocessor to 100-percent testing of populated TV convergence boards. Other RCA examples are presented in [16] and [17].

Process Control and Data Acquisition: The process-control and data-acquisition areas differ from testing in that they must operate in real time. This implies that the μP must have time responses rapid enough to accommodate the process control or data-acquisition system under consideration. The advent of low cost μP's means that dedicated, intelligent subsystems are now viable. For example, a μP system can be dedicated to data acquisition alone. A dedicated μP can perform statistical analysis on the fly, format data for more efficient off-line processing, and perform periodic self-checking and autocalibration. However, its main advantage may, in fact, be the flexibility resulting from distributed software control. Simple software changes can alter the sampling rate, specify new data formats, or alter the self-checking algorithms. This results in better human engineered outputs, modularity in hardware (improved maintenance), and slower system obsolescence.

Through the use of low-cost μP's it became possible to decentralize the control function and use intelligent controllers dedicated to specific tasks. Many advantages result from local-loop and distributed control, including lower cabling costs, reduced noise pickup, improved overall reliability (if one small system fails, the remainder keep operating), simpler maintenance, and more flexibility.

An example of a μP-based process control system is a prototype wafer slicing machine developed at RCA Laboratories. Keeping the cutting force constant, via μP control, resulted in fewer wafers being damaged [18].

Instrumentation and Manufacturing: The impact μP's are having on instrumentation is just beginning to be felt [19]-[21]. From simply adding new features to instruments (digital readouts, averaging, etc.) to autocalibration, instruments are evolving into self-contained systems with a substantial amount of computing capability.

A major factor in the increasing sophistication and flexibility of instruments has been the development of the IEEE Standard 488 Instrumentation Bus pioneered by Hewlett-Packard. The

IEEE 488 Interface Bus provides a versatile effective communication link for exchanging digital information in an unambiguous manner [22], [23]. It can accommodate a wide range of devices with similar protocols and is being proposed as an international standard. The number of instruments supporting the bus grows almost daily, and currently exceeds 300. The availability of standards such as IEEE 488 encourages distributed intelligence which implies extensive and increasing use of μP's in instruments.

Other more specialized industrial applications of μP's abound. Energy-subsystem control, motor-speed control, numerical-machine control, and robotics, all are increasingly applying μP's to obtain new levels of performance at economically viable cost levels. Additional information on these subjects may be found in [24]-[26].

Commercial Applications

Commercial applications of μP's include their uses in communications (telephony and data), in medical applications, and in business applications (from word processing to localized data processing).

The most significant emerging trend in communications is the switch from prediminantly analog (voice) traffic to a more balanced mix between voice and data. By 1985, communications traffic will be evenly divided between voice and data. This will most certainly spur the development of all-digital communication channels. This, in turn, will greatly accelerate the use of distributed intelligence within the network. Intelligent multiplexers, concentrators, PABX's, modems, etc., incorporating the ubiquitous μP, will emerge. More and more, computers will take over the traditional role of operators. As all-digital networks emerge, there will be an increasing need for efficient techniques for transmitting voice in digital form. A variety of μP applications to communications is discussed in [27]-[30].

μP's are being increasingly used in medical applications. Because of the technical and legal complexities of using new technologies in diagnosing, monitoring, or treating humans, μP's today are being widely used on an experimental basis. Their routine use is only at the embryonic stage of development. Klig [31] overviews the entire subject and cites a bibliography of 129 papers.

Word processing and intelligent terminals are emerging as major users of μP technology. For example, approximately 13 million Americans have a hearing or speech defect. This represents a major potential market for a portable telephone terminal. Except for the lowest end "dumb" terminal, most terminals sport some μP control. Many typewriters and other word-processing machines employ μP control—not only to add capability but also for internal use to reduce cost.

Other commercial applications of μP's include their use in security systems, environmental control systems, and intelligent weighing devices. In the latter, for example, the store clerk need only type in "price per pound" or "price per quarter-pound," and the price will be computed automatically and displayed. A prototype multi-microcomputer energy management system is described in [32]. Other examples include taxi meters, automated gasoline dispensing pumps, and traffic controllers.

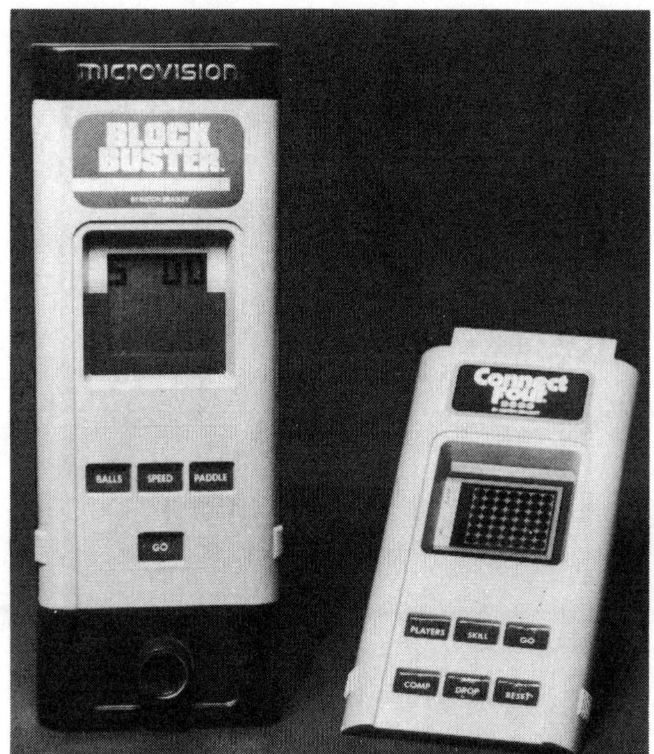

Fig. 10. "Microvision," a hand-held game system based on a 16 × 16 pixel LCD.

Consumer Applications

μP's and associated LSI technology are having a revolutionary impact on consumer products. New features are being added to standard products and entirely new product categories are becoming possible. Low-cost μC's are already changing a host of products. From exercise and coffee machines to electric ranges, from sewing machines to microwave ovens, from white goods to home security systems, a whole new generation of intelligent consumer products is emerging. Most home appliances typically need only relatively simple controls. For that reason 4-bit devices, with their low costs, are being shipped by the millions. In fact, it can be said that the 1979-1980 timeframe represents the transition period during which it is becoming cheaper to implement timing functions with a 4-bit μC than with traditional methods. This will result in the across-the-board use of these devices in appliance control rather than only in the higher feature-oriented models. The products discussed above were predominantly examples where electronics has replaced mechanical controls in consumer applications. More interesting, however, are the host of new consumer products spawned by the ongoing revolution in LSI.

Nonvideo μC-based games have just recently appeared, but already most of the major toy manufacturers are getting heavily involved [33]-[36]. Judging from the success of action games such as Parker Brothers "Stop Thief" and Milton Bradley's "Microvision," Fig. 10, a 16 × 16 pixel LCD-based game system that supports a variety of plug-ins—a revolution in toys is underway. An interesting twist to "Microvision" is that each plug-in contains its own μC, probably because the LCD display is the most expensive subsystem in the product. The Texas Instruments "Speak and Spell," Fig. 11, which

Spell

Fig. 11. "Speak and Spell," a talking education game from Texas Instruments.

contains voice synthesis circuitry [37], is being shipped at a rate in excess of 60K per month.

The videogame revolution began in the early 1970's on two fronts. Atari pioneered the development of video arcade games with the 1972 introduction of "Pong." That same year, Magnavox introduced "Odyssey," a consumer ball-and-paddle game based on circuitry patented by Sanders Associates. More recently, the consumer market has begun to evolve away from dedicated games and towards μP-based programmable games. The most successful example is, of course, the Atari VCS.

Automotive applications of μP's will have a major impact on the car of the future. From "Under-the-Hood" functions such as engine control (spark timing, fuel metering, etc.) and braking to "dashboard" functions (e.g., digital display of MPG), new levels of performance, economy, and information display will be achieved [38].

Another area of major current interest is that of the home computer. Early products in this area were aimed either at the "hobby" market, or at the "programmer" market (e.g., Radio Shack TRS-80). More recently, we are seeing a host of product introductions aimed more directly at the consumer. The TI 99/4 and Atari 400 and 800 models are in this category. The consumer computer area is of major interest to both computer and consumer oriented corporations. Related developments in home data services such as Viewdata and Teletext offer intriguing potential. References [39]-[41] discuss the ongoing revolution in personal computing and television-related data information systems. An entire issue of the IEEE TRANSACTIONS ON CONSUMER ELECTRONICS is dedicated to consumer text-display systems [42].

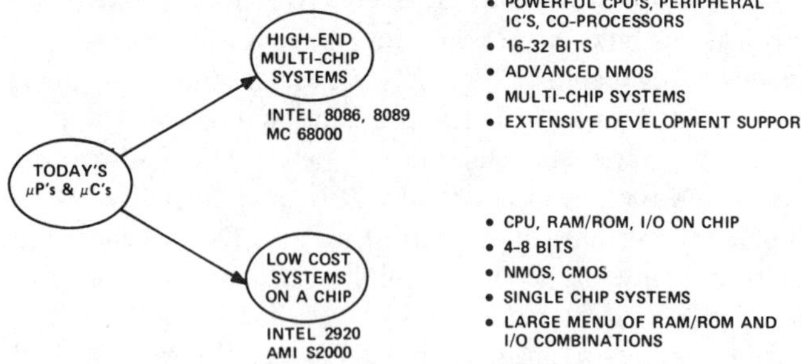
TODAY'S
µP's & µC's
HIGH-END
MULTI-CHIP
SYSTEMS
INTEL 8086, 8089
MC 68000
• POWERFUL CPU'S, PERIPHERAL IC'S, CO-PROCESSORS
• 16-32 BITS
• ADVANCED NMOS
• MULTI-CHIP SYSTEMS
• EXTENSIVE DEVELOPMENT SUPPORT
LOW COST
SYSTEMS
ON A CHIP
INTEL 2920
AMI S2000
• CPU, RAM/ROM, I/O ON CHIP
• 4-8 BITS
• NMOS, CMOS
• SINGLE CHIP SYSTEMS
• LARGE MENU OF RAM/ROM AND I/O COMBINATIONS

Fig. 12. Evolution of μP's and μC's.

The intelligent (programmable) thermostat is also emerging as a major consumer product. Selling in the 100-200-dollar range to a market of 70 million U.S. homes, annual volumes of 3-5 million units will be reached in a few years. This is but one of many examples of products that were not economically feasible prior to the invention of the μP.

Other consumer applications of μP's are under development (e.g., simple home control systems, electronic calendar/reminders, and wireless security systems), although it is not yet clear which of these developments will evolve into viable volume markets. Russo *et al.* [43] present an overview of the impact microprocessors are having on the consumer market.

VLSI Impact on Microprocessor and Microcomputer IC Design

It is becoming increasingly clear that the traditional "standard-cell" design and "hand-packing" layout techniques will not apply to IC's containing hundreds of thousands of devices. Instead, complex IC's will be designed by interconnecting and integrating a variety of standard subsystems to achieve the desired architecture and performance level. These subsystems, however, will likely have been designed via traditional techniques to ensure minimum area and hence, minimum cost.

Before addressing IC design techniques for μP's and μC's, let us project their future evolution. As shown in Fig. 12, the continuum that currently exists between very low-end 4-bit devices and high-end 16-bit devices will give way to two clearly separate classes of devices. On the one hand, high-end μP, memory, and peripheral building blocks, probably based on advanced NMOS technologies, will give rise to powerful multichip systems. On the other hand, single-chip μC's, probably based on standard NMOS or CMOS technologies, will emerge and will give rise to devices having lowest cost at the "system" level for volume products. Based on the above, we see that at the low-end, the "standard-cells" will be low-end CPU's, RAM and ROM blocks, analog interfaces (A/D, D/A, etc.), timers, and other I/O subsystems. Thus the IC designer will have to consider not only the interconnection of these subsystems at the IC level, but also the pin limits imposed by the various packaging options, which must be standard to ensure minimum cost.

At the high-end, on the other hand, multichip systems will be forgone conclusions. Hence complex IC's capable of being used as general-systems building blocks will emerge. These IC's themselves will be designed with "standard-cells" which now will consist of very fast RAM or ROM blocks (for microcoding), register arrays, ALU's, etc. A comparison of Figs. 7 and 8 confirms this evolution. The INTEL 8086 clearly consists of integrated subsystems whereas the 8080 looks more like a conventional random-logic design. Patterson and Sequin [44] provide additional detail, from a somewhat different perspective, on the evolution of future single-chip computers.

Systems Design Implications and the Software Issue

In the previous section we discussed the impacts VLSI technology will have on μP and μC design at the IC level. Here we will explore the impacts of VLSI parts at the system design level.

For cost-sensitive volume products (e.g., the consumer market), single-chip systems will dominate. Hence a successful vendor will have to satisfy such varied requirements within a product family as multiple technologies (NMOS and CMOS), multiple sourcing, a large selection of ROM, RAM, and I/O options, and, of course, low cost. Typically, a manufacturer will have a product concept in mind, for example a hand-held game or a TV tuning system, where broad system level requirements such as power consumption and the I/O would be specified. A wide variety of IC's will, in general, satisfy the requirements. Final selection will be made on the basis of cost, availability, and multiple sourcing.

For higher end μP applications, the systems architect will be concerned with throughput, system development, and software-related issues. Since technology limits place bounds on the processing power of any one subsystem, multi-CPU architectures will dominate in applications where performance is a primary goal. The emergence of powerful coprocessors such as the INTEL 8089 attest to this trend. More such devices are underway.

With the ability to generate powerful systems with a handfull of IC's, system development aids become essential and their availability will often dictate the choice of CPU. This need, along with the requirement of a large selection of peripheral IC's, imply very heavy investments on the part of the IC family vendors. Fig. 13 illustrates the point. Major corporate commitments are essential to the success of a high-end microprocessor product line.

Finally, we come to an issue that will be central in the evolution of powerful multichip architectures. This is the software issue, often labeled the software crisis. The tremendous strides witnessed by hardware over the past decade have not been matched in the software area.

This crisis is not as severe for low-end single-chip systems since the software is typically less complex and the software development costs are ammortized over large volumes (sometimes in the millions).

For high-end systems, however, the problem is severe. The cost per line of debugged code is in the 10-dollar range and rising while a severe shortage of manpower skilled in the various software disciplines looms ahead. No simple solutions are in sight though a mixture of several emerging trends may somewhat ease the problem. High-level languages are becoming the norm for both the systems portion of the software (operating systems, I/O drivers, etc.) and, even more strongly, for the applications programs. This results in some inefficiency in memory use and some sacrifice in throughput. Still, real cost advantages are gained (except, perhaps, in extremely high-volume applications). This is especially true when the costs of documenting and "maintaining" software (i.e., fixing bugs after product introduction) are included.

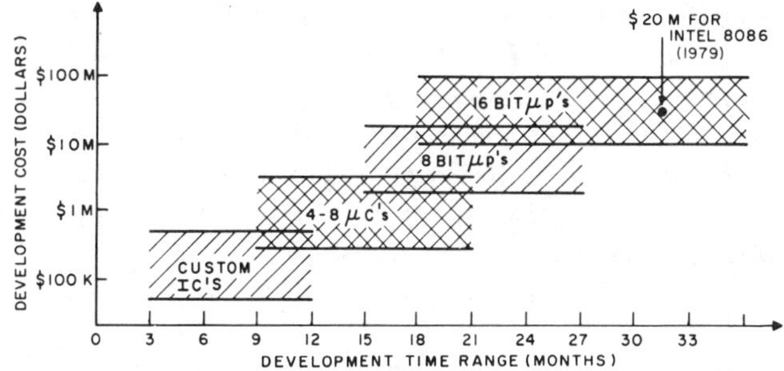

Fig. 13. Investment required and development time as a function of IC type and complexity.

Another viable approach is to use distributed or loosely coupled multi-computer architectures where, by definition, very complex systems functions are partitioned into somewhat independent subsystems whose software requirements are manageable. Yet a third, and perhaps more revolutionary, approach is the one recently put forth by INTEL where "software" modules are cast in silicon and can be used as system building blocks along with the conventional hardware IC subsystems [45], [46]. This will give rise to transportable high-level languages, data-base management systems, operating systems, run-time packages, etc. However, the software communication interface may be a major problem area and the success of this approach, though it appears promising, is in no way guaranteed.

Concluding Remarks

The computer and LSI/VLSI revolutions are moving ahead hand in hand, and are becoming an integral part of our society. The computer industry, born only 35 years ago has passed 50B dollars/year in sales and is streaking towards the 100B dollars/year mark. IBM received orders for over 32 000 system/38's, small business systems which range in price from 100 000 to 600 000 dollars, during the first year following product announcement. By 1983, the minicomputer business will grow to an annual volume of over 500 000 units per year. Marketing Development, Concord, MA, predicts that the market for under 2000-dollar computers will grow from 442 million dollars in 1979 to 1.5 billion dollars in 1984. All of the above attest to the fact that computer technology has become inextricably entwined both in our lives and in the world economy.

The semiconductor business which is growing 15-20 percent annually, has exceeded 6 billion dollars in sales in 1979 and will grow to 90 billion dollars by 1990. Explosive developments in digital LSI and VLSI are the fuel of the computer revolution. These developments led to the μP and the beginning of the second computer revolution where distributed intelligence systems will be used by the millions. Each year, the complexity of IC's doubles and the cost per function falls by about 25 percent. This is resulting in powerful computing elements costing but a few dollars. These costs are coming into the area required to impact volume consumer products—and the existing consumer applications are but the tip of the applications iceberg.

An LSI/VLSI technology continue to evolve, μP's and μC's will evolve in two directions. At the low-end, IC's will be designed with standard cells representing entire subsystems (e.g., RAM, ROM, CPU, A/D, D/A, etc.). Entire systems, including analog interfaces, will be put on the same chip to reduce system cost. At the high-end, ever more powerful CPU's, peripheral IC's, and coprocessors along with ever larger and faster memories will yield exponentially increasing computing power with but a handfull of chips. Software will emerge as a dominant problem in the 1980's. Few solutions are on the horizon but a mixture of high-level languages, multi-μP architectures, and software modules in IC form may render the problem tractable.

Increasingly, especially in μC-based consumer applications, low power dissipation and product portability will become realistic design goals. The potent mix of liquid-crystal displays (LCD's) with CMOS circuitry will yield an array of portable games, computers, and other intelligent products. Though CMOS technology trails NMOS in density by about three years, the price differential for equivalent parts will decrease to small levels as we move down the learning curve. For this reason, the current exploding usage of 4-bit NMOS μC's will be duplicated by CMOS devices in the next few years. Furthermore, since the bulk of true volume applications do not require 8-bit CPU throughput, the trend will evolve toward pulling more subsystems onto the chip resulting in lower system cost.

Finally, the question whether we will run out of technology to satisfy increasingly complex applications or whether we will run out of applications that need increasingly complex IC's, has not yet been answered. Nor has the question as to which VLSI technology will be dominant in the 1980's. NMOS is currently the leading contender but CMOS is not too far behind.

References

[1] J. von Neumann, "First draft of a report on the EDVAC," University of Pennsylvania, Philadelphia, Tech. Rep., June 1946.

[2] "Here comes the second computer revolution," *Fortune*, Nov. 1975.

[3] "The computer society," *Time*, Feb. 20, 1978.

[4] J. L. Hilburn and P. M. Julich, *Microcomputers/Microprocessors: Hardware, Software, and Applications.* Englewood Cliffs, NJ: Prentice-Hall, 1976.

[5] J. B. Peatman, *Microcomputer-Based Design.* New York: McGraw-Hill, 1977.

[6] P. M. Russo, "Interprocessor communication for multi-microcomputer systems," *IEEE Computer*, pp. 67–75, Apr. 1977.

[7] R. D. Noyce, "From relays to MPU's," *IEEE Computer*, pp. 22–29, Dec. 1976.

[8] G. Moore, "VLSI: Some fundamental challenges," *IEEE Spectrum*, Apr. 1979.

[9] *Electronics*, May 10, p. 90, 1979.

[10] G. Chao, "Future microcomputers promise greater diversity, higher performance," *High Technology*, Mar. 1980.

[11] Creative Strategies International, "The microprocessor industry," May, 1979.

[12] "U.S. markets forecast 1979," *Electronics*, p. 144, Jan. 4, 1979.

[13] "Peripheral chips shift microprocessor systems into high gear," *Electronics*, pp. 93–106, Aug. 16, 1979.

[14] J. M. Kelley, "Cut hardware, software development costs–Take advantage of in-circuit emulators," *Electron. Des.*, pp. 66–71, Aug. 16, 1979.

[15] A. R. Marcantonio, "Microprocessor-based printed circuit board tester," in *Proc. IECI '78* (Philadelphia, PA, Mar. 20–22, 1978).

[16] N. O. Ny, "An alignment and test system for TV remotes," in *Proc. IECI '80* (Philadephia, PA, Mar. 17–20, 1980).

[17] N. Fedele, "Dedicated microprocessor-based keyboard tester," in *Proc. IECI '80* (Philadelphia, PA, Mar. 17–20, 1980).

[18] D. Van Le, R. Demers, K. R. Etzold, and A. H. Firester, "Wafer slicing with microprocessor-based controller," in *Proc. IECI '79* (Philadelphia, PA, Mar. 19–21, 1979). pp. 231–233.

[19] W. C. Randle and N. Kerth, "Microprocessors in instrumentation," *Proc. IEEE* (Special Issue on Microprocessor Applications), vol. 66, pp. 172–181, Feb. 1978.

[20] B. M. Oliver, "The role of microelectronics in instrumentation and control," *Scientif. Amer.*, Sept. 1977.

[21] "Instruments '79," Special Report, in *Electron. Des.*, Nov. 22, 1978.

[22] D. C. Loughry and M. S. Allen, "IEEE Standard 488 and microprocessor synergism," *Proc. IEEE* (Special Issue on Microprocessor Applications), vol. 66, pp. 162–172, Feb. 1978.

[23] IEEE, "IEEE standard digital interface for programmable instrumentation," IEEE Std. 488–1975.

[24] N. Sohrabji, "Microprocessors extend scope of automated manufacturing," *EDN*, Mar. 5, 1978.

[25] Y. Doi, "Robots get smarter and more versatile," *IEEE Spectrum*, Sept. 1977.

[26] K. Goksel and E. A. Parrish, Jr., "The role of microcomputers in robotics," *Comput. Des.*, Oct. 1975.

[27] D. C. Stanzione, "Microprocessors in telecommunications systems," *Proc. IEEE* (Special Issue on Microprocessor Applications), vol. 66, pp. 192–199, Feb. 1978.

[28] R. Gundlach, "Large-scale integration is ready to answer the call of telecommunications," *Electronics*, Apr. 28, 1977.

[29] D. K. Melvin, "Microcomputer applications in telephony," *Proc. IEEE* (Special Issue on Microprocessor Applications), vol. 66, pp. 182–191, Feb. 1978.

[30] J. S. Mayo, "The role of microelectronics in communication," *Scientif. Amer.*, Sept. 1977.

[31] V. Klig, "Biomedical applications of microprocessors," *Proc. IEEE* (Special Issue on Microprocessor Applications), vol. 66, pp. 151–161, Feb. 1978.

[32] A. Abramovich, "A microcomputer system for remote process control," in *Proc. IECI '80* (Philadelphia, PA, Mar. 17–20, 1980).

[33] D. Ahl and B. Stables, "Electronic games roundup," *Creative Comput.*, Nov. 1979.

[34] D. Ahl, B. Staples, and R. Heuer, "Electronic games roundup," *Creative Comput.*, Dec. 1979.

[35] "Those beeping, thinking toys," *Time*, Dec. 10, 1979.

[36] "Turned-on toys," *Newsweek*, Dec. 11, 1978.

[37] "Single silicon chip synthesizes speech in $50 learning aid," *Electronics*, June 22, 1978.

[38] J. Marley, "Evolving microprocessors which better meet needs of automotive electronics," *Proc. IEEE* (Special Issue on Microprocessor Applications), vol. 66, pp. 142–150, Feb. 1978.

[39] A. C. Key, "Microelectronics and the personal computer," *Scientif. Amer.*, Sept. 1977.

[40] J. Doerr, "Low-cost microcomputing: The personal computer and single-board computer revolutions," *Proc. IEEE* (Special Issue on Microprocessor Applications), vol. 66, pp. 117–130, Feb. 1978.

[41] S. J. Lipoff, "Mass market potential for home terminals," presented at the IEEE Chicago Fall Conf. on Consumer Electronics, Nov. 6–7, 1978.

[42] *IEEE Trans. Consumer Electron.* (Special Issue on Consumer Text Display Systems), July 1979.

[43] P. M. Russo, C. C. Wang, P, K. Baltzer, and J. A. Weisbecker,

"Microprocessors in consumer products," *Proc. IEEE* (Special Issue on Microprocessor Applications), vol. 66, pp. 131–141, Feb. 1978.

[44] D. A. Patterson and C. H. Sequin, "Design considerations for single-chip computers of the future," *IEEE J. Solid-State Circuits*, vol. SC-15, pp. 44–52, Feb. 1980.

[45] "Intel sees software modules, 32-bit μP in its future," *Electron. Des.*, pp. 44–52, Mar. 29, 1980.

[46] "The microprocessor champ gambles on another leap forward," *Business Week*, Apr. 14, 1980.

Part II
16-Bit Microprocessors

THE era of 16-bit microprocessors began in 1974 with the introduction of the PACE chip by National Semiconductor. The Texas Instruments TMS9900 was introduced in 1976. Subsequently, the Intel 8086 was introduced two years later in 1978, the Zilog Z8000 in 1979, and the Motorola MC68000 in 1980. Several higher performance versions of the original chips are now available. It is difficult to analyze in depth the characteristics of all 16-bit microprocessors that have been developed, or even the subset of chips that is currently available. As such, only the more popular and better documented chips are considered.

The first reprint article compares and contrasts the Intel 8086, the Zilog Z8000, and the Motorola MC68000 on the basis of their architecture, register organization, system structure, memory addressing, stack organization, input/output mechanisms software, and multiprocessing capabilities. It presents estimates of execution speeds for different operations on these microprocessors and a discussion of technical and nontechnical issues that influence the selection of a microprocessor for a given application. The issues discussed in this article constitute a general framework for analyzing any new 16-bit microprocessor, especially the higher performance versions of the original three considered in this paper.

Except for the first article, each of the other articles deals specifically with a chip or chips of a particular make. Since most of these articles are written by persons actually involved in the design of the chip, they represent a designer's perspective of his/her creation; these articles highlight all the merits of the chips.

The papers are organized in alphabetical order of manufacturers' names as follows.

1) *Intel*

a) *"The Intel iAPX 286 Microprocessor,"* by Peter Heller

An introduction to the Intel iAPX 286 microprocessor. By using faster clock speeds, additional instructions, and several design improvements, this chip (130 000 transistors) performs two to five times faster than the iAPX 86/10 (29 000 transistors).

b) *"Memory Protection Moves Onto 16-Bit Microprocessor Chip,"* by Peter Heller *et al.*

Unlike its predecessor, the 286 has multilevel memory management and protection features built into the CPU. This paper explains this feature.

c) *"A Task Driven Peripheral Interface,"* by Daniel Tjoa and Tom Rossi

This paper explains the need for placing increased intelligence in peripherals in order to get higher system throughput.

2) *Motorola*

a) *"MC68000—Break Away from the Past,"* by Jack W. Browne, Jr.

The MC68000 microprocessor is described in terms of its instructions, addressing modes, cycle times, and exception vectors.

b) *"The M68451 Memory Management Unit,"* by J. F. Stockton

A description of the memory management unit and the method used to translate addresses, to provide memory protection, and to enable fast context switching. Virtual memory is *not* supported.

c) *"16-Bit-μP Peripheral ICs Provide Datacomm Support,"* by Dennis R. Snyder

A description of the design and functions of three peripheral chips that enable an MC68000 microprocessor to communicate in a synchronous or asynchronous environment.

3) *National*

a) *"The NS16000 Family—Advances in Architecture and Hardware,"* by Subhash Bal *et al.*

The NS16000 family of microprocessors is introduced, and its design methodology explained.

b) *"Design Considerations of the NS16082 Memory Management Unit,"* by Gary Martin and Yoav Lavi

An explanation of the operation of the NS16082 memory management unit to do address translation, memory protection, and to provide support for virtual memory.

c) *"High-Performance Peripherals Complement NS16000 Family,"* by Gary R. Martin

A comprehensive description of features and support chips that aid interfacing of peripherals to NS16000 family chips.

4) *Texas Instruments*

a) *"An Overview of the 9900 Microprocessor Family,"* by Richard V. Orlando and Thomas L. Anderson

A description of the TI9900 microprocessor family and a detailed comparison of its features with those offered on other 16-bit microprocessors.

b) *"Intelligent Peripherals of VLSI Era,"* by Gerald R. Samsen

The article presents a comparison of microprocessor performance during the first decade and emphasizes the importance of application processors and peripheral processors to yield increased system throughput.

5) *Zilog*

a) *"Benefits of Z8000 Family Planning,"* by Richard Mateosian

The design philosophy and structure of the Z8000 family of chips is explained in detail.

b) *"Memory Management Made Easy with the Z8000,"* by Stephen Walters

The operations of the Z8010 and Z8015 memory management units are explained, and the differences between them summarized.

c) *"A Coherent Family of Peripherals for the Z8000 16-Bit Microprocessor,"* by Mike Pitcher

The operation of the Z-BUS is explained, and block diagrams and functions of several key Zilog support chips are explained.

6) *Others*

a) *"Chip Set Bestows Virtual Memory on 16-Bit Minis,"* by Jan Beekmans *et al.*

Philips Data Systems developed the SPC/10 microprocessor in 1979, followed by the SP 16C/20 instruction unit, and the SP 16C/23 memory management unit. The bus arbitration and interrupt chips are implemented in bipolar technology. These chips are described.

b) *"16-Bit C-MOS Processor Packs in Hardware for Business Computers,"* by Norio Inui *et al.*

The Fujitsu FSSP chip used 20 000 transistors and microprogrammed architecture. The chip is described, and its characteristics are compared to those of Intel 8086 and the Motorola 68000.

c) *"Low-Cost 16-Bit Microprocessor Has Performance of Midrange Minicomputer,"* by Raymond Ochester

The T-11 microprocessor, developed by Digital Equipment Corporation, uses the PDP-11 instruction set. Its performance compares with that of the PDP-11/34. This chip reflects the the trend of implementing popular instruction sets on microprocessors to enable low-cost direct emulation of the computational power of power series like the PDP-11.

In addition to the above, 16-bit chips are available from several other manufacturers. Rockwell [1], for example, has implemented the circuits not in the traditional N-MOS silicon, but in C-MOS silicon-on-sapphire. The Rockwell chip is the first 16-bit chip that is intended to be programmed exclusively in a high-level language.

The trend in 16-bit microprocessors can be summarized as follows.

1) *Chip technology:* Growing use of C-MOS technology.

2) *Chip density:* Increased number of transistors. The Intel 286 uses 130 000 transistors.

3) *Architecture:* Direct emulation of mainframes with popular instruction sets.

4) *Software:* Marked trend towards support of high-level languages.

Until 1984 it is expected that the use of 16-bit microprocessors will be higher than the use of 32-bit microprocessors.

References

[1] D. W. Best, C. E. Kress, N. M. Mykris, J. D. Russell, and W. J. Smith, "An advanced-architecture CMOS/SOS microprocessor," *IEEE Micro*, vol. 2, pp. 10–26, Aug. 1982.

Bibliography

[1] "General-purpose microprocessors: Performance and features," *Electron. Des.*, pp. 118–139, Oct. 14, 1982.

[2] D. Bursky, "16-bit families swell with greater integration," *Electron. Des.*, pp. 103–112, Oct. 14, 1982.

[3] D. G. Fairbairn, "VLSI technology," *Computer*, pp. 87–96, Jan. 1982.

[4] R. D. Grappel, "Design powerful systems with the newest 16-bit μP," *EDN*, pp. 127–140, Sept. 29, 1982.

[5] W. D. Hopkins, "Speed/cost tradeoffs of using the TMS 99110 microprocessor," in *Proc. Electro 1982*, Session 18, Paper 3, pp. 1–7.

[6] J. Klovstad, G. M. Catlin, and T. Zingale, "16-bit μP crams peripheral support on chip," *Electron. Des.*, pp. 191–196, June 10, 1982.

[7] R. Rubinstein *et al.*, "Compatibility about μeclipse and speed: Goals of a small machine," *Comput. Des.*, pp. 69–76, Aug. 1982.

[8] T. W. Starnes, "Cost-effective numeric processing," in *Proc. Electro 1982*, Session 18, Paper 2, pp. 1–6.

[9] D. Stevenson, "Floating-point processing with Zilog's Z-8000 CPU," in *Proc. Electro 1982*, Session 18, Paper 4, pp. 1–2.

[10] J. F. Stockton, "A virtual breakthrough for micros," *Comput. Des.*, pp. 153–162, Aug. 1982.

[11] W. Twaddell, "EDN's ninth annual μP/μC chip directory," *EDN*, pp. 98–204, Oct. 27, 1982.

[12] T. Zingale, "Broadening the scope of microcomputer numeric applications with the 8087 numeric processor extension," in *Proc. Electro 1982*, Session 18, Paper 1, pp. 1–7.

Today's microprocessors exhibit powerful computing capabilities. Their characteristic differences favor each machine for a distinct portion of the applications spectrum.

An Architectural Comparison of Contemporary 16-Bit Microprocessors

Hoo-min D. Toong and Amar Gupta
Massachusetts Institute of Technology

The evolution of microprocessor architecture during the past decade has progressed at an incredible pace. From the primitive 4004, introduced in 1971, to the present spectrum of sophisticated microprocessors, the growth has been swift, dramatic, and almost revolutionary. Today's products possess astonishing computational capabilities and support primary memories of up to 64M bytes. They incorporate high-level languages and technical innovations only recently introduced on larger mainframes. Microprocessor-based systems now offer facilities for direct support of multiuser/multitask environments and sophisticated operating system implementations.

The current single-chip, 16-bit microprocessor market has three major contenders:

- the 8086 (iAPX 86): designed by Intel; second-sourced by Mostek in the US and by Siemens in Europe;
- the Z8000: designed by Zilog; second-sourced by AMD in the US, by SGS/ATES in Europe, and by Sharp in Asia;
- the MC68000: designed by Motorola; second-sourced by AMD and Rockwell in the US, by EFCIS in Europe, and by Hitachi in Asia.

Several of these devices are also being produced by major systems houses for internal use. In addition, National Semiconductor has recently announced the NS16000 microprocessor chip family, scheduled to be introduced during 1981. In the following paragraphs, we examine and compare the architectures of the three processors. A section is devoted to the preliminary data on the National 16000 series.

General characteristics

The characteristics of the microprocessors being discussed here are summarized in Table 1.

The 8086. Of the three processors, the Intel 8086 is the oldest and simplest. Basically, it is an improved, 16-bit version of the 8080; an 8080-type multiplexed bus is expanded to a 16-bit external bus. As in the 8080, the instructions are byte-oriented. One of the major enhancements is a six-byte instruction prefetch queue. This buffer feeds instructions to the execution unit in eight-bit segments. The queue decreases address bus/data bus idle times by prefetching data, thus increasing processor speed. The 8086 register structure is very similar to the 8080's. Registers in both machines are special-purpose. Rooted in a basic design philosophy requiring storage efficiency, special-purpose registers allow implied register addressing in most instructions and permit shortened instructions. Most addressing modes are the same in both machines. An address space of one megabyte is implemented in the 8086 through a memory segmentation scheme using 64K segments. Memory segments of up to 64K bytes can be placed on an eight-bit boundary, allowing a maximum of one megabyte to be addressed. By basing the segmentation and addressing mechanisms on 16 bits, Intel has preserved close compatibility between the 8086 and the 8080.

The 8086 has 95 basic instructions, of which a substantial number are only eight bits long. In the few 16-bit instructions, only the first eight bits are used for operation codes; the additional byte specifies data displacement. Instructions longer than two bytes use the remaining bytes for specifying data. The 8086 instruction set is an expanded version of the 8080 instruction set. Hence 8080 code can be converted easily to 8086 code. Many enhanced programming features are available in the 8086 instruction set. Base segment registers have been added to provide software support for certain operating system functions and for extended addressing range. Changing these segment registers allows the programmer to do process swaps with relative ease. Internally, the 8086 retains an eight-bit instruction path similar to the 8080's. The ALU is 16 bits wide, like the 8080's ALU. Thus, the 8086

Reprinted from *IEEE Micro*, vol. 1, pp. 26–37, May 1981.

is a widened 8080 with enhanced addressing and instruction prefetch. In all, 24 addressing modes are supported. With a clock frequency of 5 MHz, the fastest instruction time is 0.4 microseconds.

The Z8000. A register-rich 16-bit processor, the Z8000 is not an enhancement of Zilog's Z80 family and has a different internal structure. The Z8000 is based on a regular register use and a symmetric instruction set. Its operating system support is far more sophisticated than that available on eight-bit machines. An entire set of registers controls systems calls and manages process swaps. Internal registers allow 32-bit double-word operations. Traps of illegal addresses and illegal instructions serve as debugging tools through the use of an expanded flag register, also permitting software expansion of the instruction set. The Z8000 is a true 16-bit machine, as data and instruction paths are 16 bits wide.

Table 1.
Specifications of 16-bit microprocessors.

	8086	Z8000	68000	16008/16016	16032
YEAR OF COMMERCIAL INTRODUCTION	1978	1979	1980	1981	1981
NO. OF BASIC INSTRUCTIONS	95	110	61	100	100
NO. OF GENERAL-PURPOSE REGISTERS	14	16	16	8	8
PIN COUNT	40	48/40	64	40	48
DIRECT ADDRESS RANGE (BYTES)	1M	48M*	16M/64M	64K/16M	16M
NUMBER OF ADDRESSING MODES	24	6	14	9	9
BASIC CLOCK FREQUENCY	5MHz (4-8MHz)	2.5-3.9MHz	5-8MHz	10MHz	10MHz
SYSTEM STRUCTURES					
UNIFORM ADDRESSABILITY			•	•	•
MODULE MAP AND MODULES				•	•
VIRTUAL					•
PRIMITIVE DATA TYPES					
BITS		•	•	•	•
INTEGER BYTE OR WORD	•	•	•	•	•
INTEGER DOUBLE-WORD		•	•		•
LOGICAL BYTE OR WORD	•	•	•	•	•
LOGICAL DOUBLE-WORD			•		•
CHARACTER STRINGS (BYTE, WORD)	•	•		•	•
CHARACTER STRINGS (DOUBLE-WORD)					•
BCD BYTE	•	•	•	•	•
BCD WORD				•	•
BCD DOUBLE-WORD					•
FLOATING-POINT				•	•
DATA STRUCTURES					
STACKS	•	•	•	•	•
ARRAYS				•	•
PACKED ARRAYS				•	•
RECORDS	•	•	•	•	•
PACKED RECORDS				•	•
STRINGS	•	•		•	•
PRIMITIVE CONTROL OPERATIONS					
CONDITION CODE PRIMITIVES		•	•	•	•
JUMP	•	•	•	•	•
CONDITIONAL BRANCH	•	•	•	•	•
SIMPLE ITERATIVE LOOP CONTROL	•	•	•	•	•
SUBROUTINE CALL	•	•	•	•	•
MULTIWAY BRANCH				•	•
CONTROL STRUCTURE					
EXTERNAL PROCEDURE CALL				•	•
SEMAPHORES	•	•	•	•	•
TRAPS	•	•	•	•	•
INTERRUPTS	•	•	•	•	•
SUPERVISOR CALL		•	•		•
OTHERS					
USER MICROCODE			•		
DEBUG MODE			•		

*6 SEGMENTS OF 8M EACH

The machine's 110 basic instructions are either 16 or 32 bits long, and the instruction set is word-oriented with vector operations strongly represented. These instructions are the basis of the performance of the Z8000, as is most evident in the block operations. A single 32-bit instruction is used for set and move operations, while in the 8086, six single-byte instructions must be used. For future expansion, the designers of the Z8000 have left one register unused and unassigned. With the present 4-MHz clock speed, the fastest and the slowest instruction times are 0.75 microseconds and 90 microseconds, respectively. A 6-MHz version is being made available.

The MC68000. The designers of this microprogrammed machine have chosen to implement a very wide engine. The external 16-bit bus is multiplexed from the 32 bits inside the engine. A wide, 32-bit ALU has been coded as the user machine. Unlike the general-purpose registers of the Z8000, the 16- by 32-bit registers of the 68000 are partitioned into eight address registers and eight data registers. Motorola has made a great effort to design the engine with a very regular instruction set, making available several general addressing modes for most instructions. This design permits easy implementation of stacks and queues without special instructions. Two 32-bit stack pointers are provided for aiding in systems calls. A special flag register can be set to move the machine into a debugging, single-step mode for program development. Traps for illegal instructions can be used for software extension of the basic instruction set and for floating-point operations. Besides reducing software development problems, the traps allow software compatibility with future hardware improvements.

The MC68000 supports 56 basic instructions and 14 addressing modes. The total number of instructions is misleading, however, because many instructions perform triple functions and are encoded differently. The number 56 is an artifact of the assembler. Instruction sizes vary from one to five words. The address bus uses 23 bits for word addressing, providing an addressing capability of 16M bytes.

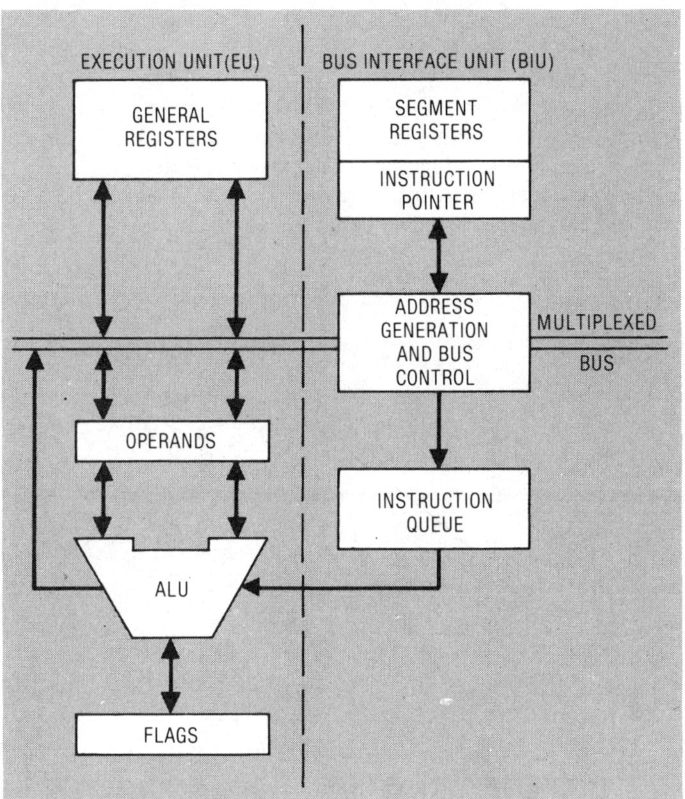

Figure 1. Basic structure of the Intel 8086.

Architectural details

Basic principles of operation. The basic structure of the Intel 8086 is shown in Figure 1. The 8086 (and the 8088) CPU consists of two separate processing units, the execution unit, or EU, and the bus interface unit, or BIU, connected by a 16-bit ALU data bus and an eight-bit Q bus. The EU obtains instructions from the instruction prefetch queue, IQ, maintained by the BIU, and executes instructions using the 16-bit ALU. Execution of instructions involves maintenance of CPU status and control logic, manipulation of general registers and instruction operands, and manipulation of segment offset addresses within 16-bit limits. The EU accesses memory and peripheral devices through requests to the BIU, which is the second processing unit, performing all bus operations for the EU on a demand basis. This involves generating physical addresses from segment register and offset values, reading operands, and writing results. The BIU is also responsible for prefetching instructions from the IQ whenever possible, to keep the EU busy with prefetched instructions under normal conditions, and for resetting the IQ when the EU transfers control to another location. The execution unit and the bus interface unit operate independently of each other, enabling the 8086 to overlap instruction fetch and execution.

The Z8000 is a random-logic-based CPU; its basic structure is shown in Figure 2. The internal 16-bit data bus is used for internal addressing and data communication. The instructions are fetched through the Z-bus interface and executed by the instruction execute control unit. Throughput is enhanced through "limited" pipelining, which allows prefetching of the next single-word instruction (or the first word of the next multiword instruction) from the memory into the instruction buffer. This occurs only during execution of the current instruction, provided the current instruction does not require the bus to complete the execution cycle. No instruction prefetching occurs when the bus is assigned to another bus master. The 16-bit ALU manipulates data and generates logical offset addresses in the general-purpose register block in accordance with the instruction executed. The CPU status and control flags are maintained in the program status registers, and the CPU, which can operate in a system mode or normal mode, can execute privileged instructions only in the system mode. Interrupts and traps are handled by the exception-handling control unit, and there is provision for multiple interrupt tables. A refresh

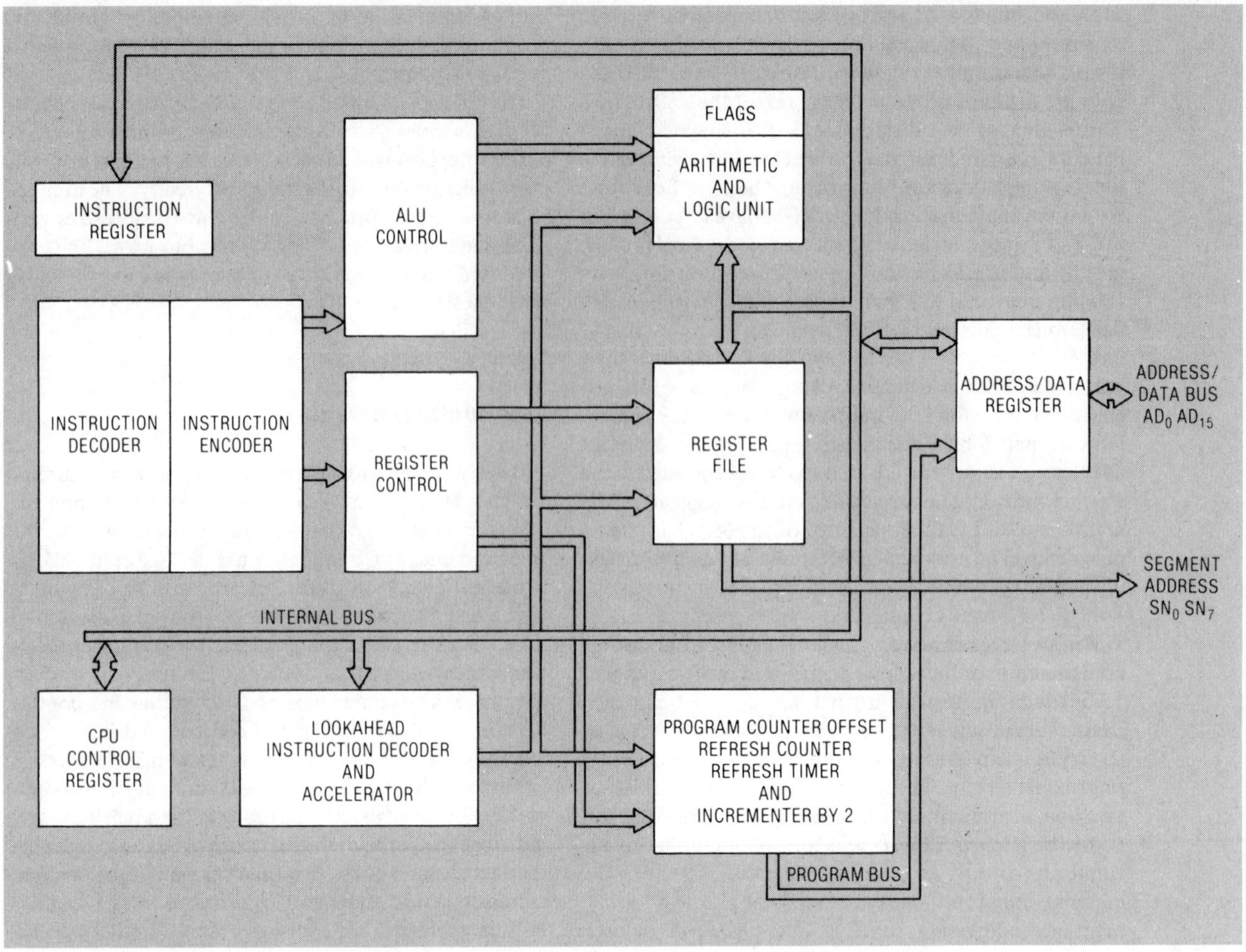

Figure 2. Basic structure of the Z8000.

counter provides the refresh control logic with timing information for CPU-driven memory refresh operation.

The MC68000 is architecturally quite distinct from the others. Its block structure is shown in Figure 3. The microcode-based CPU is centered around a microprogram-controlled execution unit. The control store area size is minimized through the use of a two-level control structure. At level one, the machine instructions are produced by sequences of micro-instructions in the micro-control store. These micro-instructions are actually pointers (addresses) to nano-instructions in the nano-store at level two. The nano-control store contains an arbitrarily ordered set of unduplicated machine-state control words, which control the execution unit. All information that is machine instruction static (timing-independent) bypasses the control store and is transmitted directly to the execution unit. In all, about 22.5K bits of control store is used, 50 percent less than the control store required for a single-level implementation. However, the two-level structure increases total access time. An attempt has been made to overcome this by means of a pipelined architecture, in which the instruction fetch, instruction decode, and instruction execute cycles are fully overlapped across every macro-instruction boundary. An attempt has also been made to minimize delays in looping (branching) by prefetching instructions associated with the most likely branch condition. The MC68000 execution unit is a dual bus structure that performs both address and data processing. The CPU may run in either a

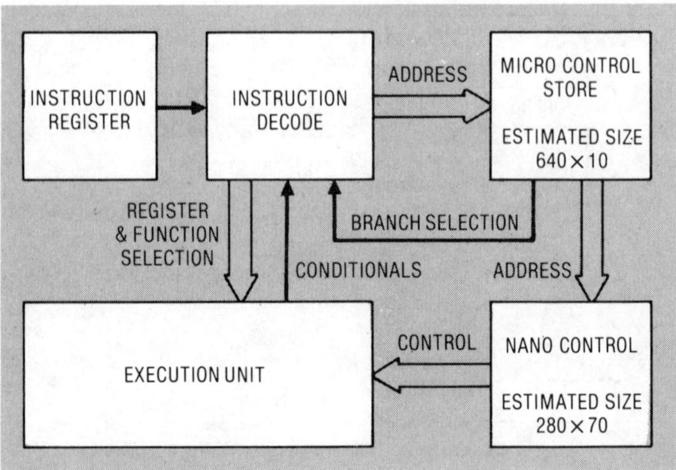

Figure 3. Basic structure of the MC68000.

supervisor mode with privileged instructions or in a user mode. Although internal data paths are all 32 bits wide, the packaging limitation on the number of pins constrains data paths to and from memory to be only 16 bits wide. The 64 pins are comprised of 23 pins for address bus, 16 for data bus, five for asynchronous bus control, three for bus arbitration control, three for interrupt control, three for system control, three for peripheral control, three for processor status, and the remaining five for power supply ground and for clock. The chip specifications provide for floating-point and string operations, but current versions do not have these features because of technological limitations on circuit density and size. At present, these unimplemented instructions cause traps for software emulation. Overall, the MC68000 CPU implements as large a subset of the complete 68000 system architecture as is feasible under current technology. It is expected that on-chip memory, faster clock speeds, custom microprogramming, and facilities for run-time changes in microprogram will be provided by Motorola during the lifetime of the 68000 architecture.

Register organization. The Intel 8086 execution unit contains four 16-bit pointer and index registers and four 16-bit data registers addressable on an individual byte basis. These eight registers are used implicitly by the instruction set, providing compact encoding at the cost of reduced flexibility. The BIU contains one 16-bit instruction pointer, which contains the offset of the next instruction to be fetched. This pointer is updated by the BIU but cannot be directly accessed by programs. The BIU also contains four 16-bit dedicated segment registers for segment base addressing, which enables programs to access up to four 64K-byte segments at a time. Finally, the EU contains six one-bit status flags and three one-bit control flags.

The Z8000 family is characterized by sixteen 16-bit general-purpose registers. All can be used as accumulators, and all but one can be used as index pointers or memory pointers. The one exception is an escape mechanism for address changes. The general register architecture avoids bottlenecks inherent in dedicated or implied registers. Register grouping and overlapping provide for byte, double-word, and 64-bit registers. Two registers are used as implied stack pointers for system mode and normal mode. All Z8000 family chips contain one 16-bit segment offset register, and the Z8001 also contains one 16-bit segment number register. The Z8001 also contains a 16-bit reserved register, two 16-bit program status area pointers, one 16-bit flag and control register, and one 16-bit refresh counter.

The MC68000 has eight 32-bit data registers, seven 32-bit address registers, and two implied 32-bit stack pointers. The data registers can be addressed as byte registers, word registers, or double-word registers. The address registers are used for 32-bit base addressing, 32-bit software stack operations, and word and long word address operations. The implied stack pointers are used for 32-bit base addressing and for word and long word address operations. The MC68000 also contains a 32-bit program counter and a 16-bit status register. The program counter addresses one large linear address space from a full 32-bit address, but only 24 bits are available in the present version. There is no segmentation at the CPU level. The status register contains one user byte and one system byte. The user byte contains five control bits, including the extend bit for extended operations. The system byte contains a trade mode bit, a supervisor state bit, and a three-bit interrupt mask.

System structure. The 8086 utilizes two types of multimaster buses, the local bus and the system bus. Microprocessors are always connected to a local bus, and memory and I/O usually reside on a system bus. The two buses are linked by interface components, the number of which depends on the size and complexity of the system. On the local bus, the address and data lines are multiplexed to reduce the number of processor pins. Signals coordinate up to three processors with an implied priority structure. On-chip arbitration logic enables both independent processors and coprocessors to share the bus. The system bus is functionally and electrically compatible with the Intel Multibus and provides for interconnection of multiple processing modules. This bus is composed of address lines, data lines, control lines, interrupt lines, and arbitration lines. Because it is modular in design, only a subset may be implemented, according to the needs of the application. All memory and I/O modules on the system bus are accessible to all the processing modules.

The Z-bus interconnects Z8000 family components in a master/slave fashion. The CPUs obey the Z-bus protocol directly at the chip level, and no extra circuitry is needed to generate bus signals. Multiplexing of address and data minimizes pin count without significant performance loss in "read-oriented" applications. Demultiplexing is performed when necessary within the individual modules. The daisy chain serial priority philosophy resolves interrupts/traps, bus requests, and requests for shared resources. The Z-bus is always controlled by one of the devices, which, on request, grants control to legal bus masters for bus transactions. Multiple CPUs communicate on a bus-to-bus basis, using the FIFO input/output interface units, or FIOs. Multiple FIOs may be connected to one Z-bus.

The MC68000 family is supported by two different master/slave-based multimaster buses for interconnection of components—the local bus and the global bus. The local bus connects microprocessor, memory, and I/O devices to form individual microcomputer modules, and the global bus interfaces to various local buses through bus arbitration modules. In the minimum version, the local bus uses transmission and control lines as they appear directly at the CPU. The extended version of the local bus, the Versabus, designed to support all future versions of the 68000 family, utilizes additional control lines.

Memory. The one megabyte of real addressing space in the 8086 is treated as a group of segments, each segment 64K bytes in size. Four segments are addressable at one time, providing up to 64K bytes of code, 64K bytes for stack, and 128K bytes for data. The starting address is obtained through segment registers. Segmentation permits writing of position-independent programs. Two portions of the memory are dedicated and reserved. Physical addresses are generated by shifting the segment base value four bits to the left and adding the offset. In the case of programming code, the offset is obtained from the instruction pointer, and, in the case of operands, it is the result of calculation based on the addressing mode. This organization of memory does not provide easy management and protection.

On the Z8000 chips, addresses are always expressed in bytes. Single bytes can be read and written using the byte/word output line. The eight megabytes of directly addressable memory is split up as 128 segments, each of 64K bytes. The 23 address lines (on the Z8001) provide a seven-bit segment number and a 16-bit segment offset pointer. The two address parts can be manipulated separately or together by all the available word and long word operations. The CPU generates processor status information, which enables the address range to be increased beyond its nominal limits by physically separating code, data, and stack spaces in system and normal modes (6 × 8M bytes = 48M bytes). External logic is needed for this memory extension. The Z8010 memory management unit, or MMU, can be used with the Z8001 microprocessor to improve and expand memory addressing capabilities, randomly relocating all 128 segments in the six address spaces with translation tables for each space.

The MC68000 has 23 address lines, providing a 16M-byte addressing capability. The address space is linear with no internal segmentation. Although words are normally addressed, single bytes can be read or written using upper and lower data strobes. Instructions and multibyte data are always aligned on even byte boundaries. Similar to that of the Z8000, the processor status information separates address space into four areas: the supervisor program, the supervisor data, the user program, and the user data. The proposed memory management unit, MC68451, would support sophisticated management and protection of 32 variable-sized segments, ranging from 256 bytes to 16M bytes in increments of 256 bytes, and would allow trapping of unauthorized accesses. Without the MMU, it is possible to equip the MC68000 with a simple memory protection mechanism by separating user and supervisor space into high and low memory.

Stack organization. While Intel 8086 systems can have many stacks, each less than or equal to 64K bytes, only the current stack is directly addressable. Other stack pointers are located in memory and are implemented through the stack segment register, SS. Thus, multiple concurrent stacks are not feasible on Intel systems.

In contrast, the Z8000 can have multiple concurrent stacks; stacks can be located anywhere in memory and are addressed via stack pointer registers. Any register except RO can serve as a stack pointer by means of PUSH and POP. Call return, interrupts, and traps use implied stack. The system stack can be accessed only in system mode, whereas the normal stack can be accessed in both modes.

The MC68000 has two implied stack pointers for use in user mode and supervisor mode. Multiple concurrent user stacks and queues can be created and maintained by employing the address register indirectly with post-increment and predecrement addressing modes.

I/O mechanisms. The Intel 8086 has a 64K-byte (32K words) separate I/O space. A memory-mapped I/O capability that can respond like a memory device is available for linking I/O devices, but Intel does not recommend its use for the Multibus. Any memory reference instruction can be used to access an I/O device, providing additional programming flexibility. Word-based devices should use even addresses for maximum throughput. Intel has reserved eight locations for future products. High-speed I/O operations can be carried out with traditional DMA controllers. Intel also offers the 8089 IOP, an independent processor with two DMA channels and an instruction set tailored for I/O operations.

The Z8000 family CPUs support two different I/O address spaces of 64K bytes through special I/O instructions, which can be executed only in the system mode. Standard I/O instructions transfer data between the CPU and peripherals, and special I/O instructions transfer data to and from external CPU support chips. Processor status information enables separation of address spaces. The I/O addressing scheme is identical to the basic memory addressing scheme. For DMA operations, two signals, bus request and bus acknowledge, are available, Inhibited from controlling the bus during DMA operations, the CPU must wait for the bus to be given up by the DMA controller.

The MC68000 possesses no separate I/O space. All I/O is memory-mapped and all I/O protection must occur at the memory protection level. Three signals, bus request, bus grant, and bus grant acknowledge, allow master devices to get control of the bus for DMA operations. The three signals are used by potential bus masters to decide who will be the next bus master. The actual arbitration protocol handles overlapped arbitration and data transfer and resolves multiple simultaneous bus requests. The CPU has been designed to operate in conjunction with the MC68450, a direct memory access controller scheduled to be available during 1981, which will allow block transfer rates of up to four megabytes per second.

Software. As mentioned previously, the 8086 is an improved and expanded version of the 8080. The 8080's basic eight-bit instructions have been retained, and expanded with extended instruction lengths when necessary. For efficient code, the instructions most often executed are only a single byte long. Implied register addressing also reduces code size. To allow for expansion of the instruction set, an "escape" facility is available for transferring control to a coprocessor. The 8086 instruction set provides automatic repetition of many non-decision-making instructions, large I/O space with register indirect addressing, decimal operations, error traps, and software traps. The addressing highlights of the 8086 include the ability to finely segment memory, and the facilities for indexing with displacement and without displacement.

The Z8000 achieves high speeds through random logic encoding. Code is space-efficient because the instructions most often executed are shortest in length, and because it distinguishes between long branches and short branches. The Z8000 also has an expandable instruction set. Unlike the 8086, it does not use implied registers. Zilog provides

16 completely general registers and consciously avoids specialized ones. The instruction set facilitates multiprogramming through a context switching facility. Other instruction highlights include signed 32-bit multiply and divide, decimal operations, multiple load, vector-based instructions, and the test and set instruction, which is especially valuable in multiprocessor applications. Addressing schemes include indexing, with and without displacement, and multiple increment indexing. Multiple stacks, segmented memory, and the very large address space (48M bytes) ease programming effort. Finally, the user/supervisor stacks are all hardwired.

The MC68000 has a regular instruction set and provides multiuser support. It emphasizes space-efficient code through "quick" instructions and short jumps on loops. The MC68000 offers the advantage of excellent debug tools like single-step execution, traps on illegal instructions, and debug mode. The instruction set can be expanded by remasking the microcode or by traps. Context switching facilitates multiprogramming, and the test and set instruction aids in multiprocessor and data-base applications. Other advantages include complex push and pop capabilities, the 32-bit internal structure, and instructions for multiple load and signed multiply and divide. It is possible to address 16M bytes directly and 64M bytes through functional segmentation. Post/pre increment/decrement facilities are available for most instructions. Real-time control applications are aided by multilevel interrupt and seven auto-vector interrupt capabilities.

National 16000. National Semiconductor has announced a family of 16-bit microprocessors, and sample production is expected to begin in 1981. The 16000 series consists of the NS16008, NS16016, and NS16032 processors. Of these, the NS16008 and the NS16016 are very similar, each offering an internal data ALU bus 16 bits wide and a direct addressing range of 64K bytes. Further, either of these two chips can operate in two distinct modes:

(1) native mode, in which the two processors have 100 basic instructions and are directly compatible with the NS16032;
(2) 8080 compatibility mode, which permits direct emulation of the 8080, with a speed four times that of the 8080.

Transfer from one mode to another within a program is implemented with an ESCAPE instruction. No separate translator and assembly programs are needed.

The NS16008 and NS16016 processors are designed to bridge the gap between the 8080 and the high-end members of the NS16000 family. The NS16008 and 16016 have 16-bit address pointers that are upwardly compatible through software to the 16032 address space. The primary difference between them is that the NS16016 has a 16-bit data bus, whereas the NS16008 has only an eight-bit data bus and is primarily suitable for use in systems with eight-bit-wide memory and peripherals.

The NS16032 achieves an address range of 32M bytes by means of a memory management unit, or MMU. However, it does not have an 8080 compatibility mode. The NS16032 has an internal data ALU bus that is 32-bits wide and a direct address range of 16M bytes using 24-bit address pointers. Unlike the 16032, the 16008 cannot be supplemented with an MMU to increase the address space.

All the National microprocessors have eight general-purpose registers that can be used (without any restrictions) as base registers and index registers. Instructions are not register-specific and can make use of every relevant addressing mode, including scale index (powerful when using high-level languages), external address (used to construct modular software), and memory relative. Furthermore, the symmetry between registers and memory means that each memory location can serve as an accumulator or base register as needed. The NS16081 floating-point unit, or FPU, has an additional set of eight general-purpose registers, supplementing the GPRs on the master processor. The MMU, NS16082, can serve as a second slave processor.

The main CPU has eight dedicated registers: program counter register, processor status register, user stack pointer, interrupt stack pointer, frame pointer, static base register, mod register (for module map), and interrupt base register. The MMU provides eight dedicated registers, and the FPU provides one floating-point status register. The NS16000 family offers several symmetric addressing modes, including top of stack addressing, memory relative addressing, external addressing, and scaled indexing. National is unique in providing modular software capabilities for the new microprocessors, permitting a user to develop a software package independent of all other packages and without regard to individual addressing. This provides flexibility in system design and lower programming costs. The ROM code is totally relocatable and easy to access. Within the system, a module consists of three components: a code component (contains the code that the processor executes in a given module), a static data component (contains local variables and data for the particular module), and a linkage component (contains all information required to link references from one module to another).

National has attempted to provide as much compatibility as feasible. The floating-point unit, the NS16081, is compatible with the proposed IEEE floating-point formats by means of its hardware and software features. It can be driven not only by National microprocessors but also by any Microbus-compatible CPU.

Microcomputers

Several microcomputers configured around 16-bit microprocessors are now available. Intel Corporation offers the SDK-86 based on the 8086, Zilog offers the Z8000 Development Module based on the Z8002, and Motorola offers the MEX-68-KDM based on the MC68000. Several independent system houses offer equivalent systems. The broad features of various systems are summarized in Table 2.

Multiprocessor capabilities

To increase computational bandwidth and/or system resilience, integration of several microprocessors in a single system frequently becomes necessary. The overall throughput and efficiency of such systems is directly dependent on the hardware and software interconnection mechanisms supported by the basic microprocessor chips. Many different interconnection systems have evolved over the years, but the single timeshared bus offers distinct advantages as an interconnection mechanism for multimicroprocessor systems. Under such a scheme, different modules can share the bus resource equally on a time-multiplexed or demand-multiplexed basis. However, the internal design of the present 16-bit microprocessors does not facilitate efficient concurrent operation of a large number of processors on such a bus.

Intel 8086. The Multibus is the structure for interfacing Intel's 8080/85/86 products. It supports a one-megabyte address space. The 8289 bus arbiter controls Multibus accesses by multiple masters. The control lines are designed according to a master-slave concept: a master (processor) in the system takes control of the Multibus; then the slave device (I/O or memory), upon recognizing its address, acts upon the command provided by the master. An asynchronous handshaking protocol allows modules of different speeds to use the bus. Although the basic definition in the bus standard specifies only two types of units—bus masters and bus slaves—the system also can include "intelligent" slaves, which cannot control the bus, but put more processing power into the bus slave. Multiple masters can be connected in either a daisy chain priority scheme or in a parallel priority scheme.

Coordination features of the 8086 multiprocessor include

- the 8289 bus arbiter, which decides which master may use the bus during the next cycle;
- the bus lock signal, activated on execution of lock prefix instructions, blocking interrupts and requests by other processors until the lock sequence is completed;
- semaphore using the lock prefix in conjunction with the XCHG instruction;
- synchronization to an external event using a WAIT instruction and the test input signal;
- escape instruction allowing other processors to obtain an instruction and/or a memory operand from the host;
- two bidirectional request/grant lines, used to share the local bus between one host and two other pro-

Table 2.
Microcomputer characteristics.

	ADVANCED MICRO COMPUTERS 96/4016	ADVANCED MICRO COMPUTERS 96/4116	INTEL ISBC 86/12A	INTEL SDK-86	MICRODA-SYS MD-68K	MOTOROLA MEX-68-KDM	ZILOG 05-6101-01
GENERAL							
PROCESSOR USED	AMZ8002	Z8000	8086	8086	68000	68000	Z8002
WORD SIZE (BITS)	16	16	16	16	16	16	16
ADDRESSING							
ADDRESS SIZE (BITS)	16	16	20	20	24	24	16
TOTAL MEMORY ADDRESSABLE (BYTES)	64K	160K	1M	1M	4M	16M	64K
AMT. OF RAM ON CARD (BYTES)	8K	32K	32-64K	2-4K	128K	32K	32-48K
AMT. OF ROM ON CARD (BYTES)	0-12K	0-8K	0-32K	8K	0-16K	8-64K	4-16K
DMA CAPABILITY	NO	YES	YES	YES	YES	NO	YES
FREQUENCY, ETC.							
CLOCK FREQUENCY (MHz)	4	4	5	2.5 or 5.0	?	8	2.5 or 3.9
SUPPLY VOLTAGES	+5, +12	+5, +12	+5, +12	+5	+5, +12	+5, +12	+5, +12
BOARD SIZE (IN)	6.75×12	6.75×12	6.75×12	12×13.5	12×15	9.75×14	11×14
I/O CAPABILITY							
BUS TYPE	SPECIAL	MULTIBUS	MULTIBUS	SPECIAL	SPECIAL	EXORCISER	SPECIAL
PARALLEL I/O LINES	24+	24+	24	48+	32+	32+	32+
NUMBER OF I/O PORTS	2	2	1	1	4	2	2
MAX I/O RATE (K BAUD)	38.4	19.2	38.4	4.8	300	9.6	19.2
ADDTL. H'WARE DETAILS							
INTERRUPT PROVISIONS	YES	YES	YES	YES	YES	YES	YES
MULTIPROCESSING CAPABILITY	NO	YES	YES	NO	YES	YES	NO
NO. OF TIMERS	3	5	2	?	4	3	5
BITS PER TIMER	16	16	16	?	16	16	8
SOFTWARE							
OPERATING SYSTEM	YES	YES	YES	YES	NO	YES	YES
HIGH-LEVEL LANGUAGE(S)	YES	YES	YES	YES	NO	YES	YES
ASSEMBLER	YES	YES	YES	YES	YES	YES	YES
DEBUGGING AIDS	YES	YES	YES	YES	YES	YES	YES
APPLICATION PACKAGES	NO	NO	YES	NO	NO	NO	YES

cessors via a handshake sequence—request, grant, release;

- the 8288 bus controller that outputs system bus signals compatible with Multibus.

Z8000. Two different multimicroprocessor mechanisms are possible on the Z8000. Zilog has designed a FIFO buffer communication module, which can run each processor as a separate system and pass messages back and forth through buffers to achieve total system communication. The processors are very loosely coupled, and any high-speed resource sharing is virtually impossible.

The second multiprocessor mechanism employs two signal pins called micro-in and micro-out (MI and MO) for implementation of a daisy-chained, software-controlled, global priority scheme. A processor examines the chain for busy condition (global resource allocation locked). If the bus is not busy, the processor places a request into the chain and then re-examines it after a settling delay (to prevent races). The result of the operation is reported with a flag handled in software. Thus, with an appropriate software driver, a single global locking scheme can be implemented. However, the time required to operate this locking mechanism rules out any high-speed communication.

Multimicroprocessor operation with the Z8000 is facilitated by the following features:

- four special, privileged "multimicro" instructions—MBIT, MREQ, MRES, and MSET;
- pins for bus request, bus acknowledge, multimicro in, multimicro out, and segment trap;
- test and set instructions, TSET and TSEB;
- special output instructions;
- bus arbitration mechanisms;
- normal and system modes;
- provision for asynchronous Z-bus to Z-bus communication using the Z8038 FIO;
- simple external SSI logic to establish actual daisy-chain;
- semaphore using TSET (test and set) to synchronize software processes that require exclusive access to certain data or instructions at one time;
- sharing of large memory by various processors under the memory management scheme.

On the Z8000, six op-codes have been reserved for extended instructions to be used in conjunction with extended processing units (coprocessors).

MC68000. In a Motorola environment, each processor has a local bus with local memory and peripherals. A global bus connects all local buses together through bus arbitration modules (BAMs). A processor is free to execute at full speed in its own bus space until it needs something from another processor's area, or until another device needs something from the former's domain. This is not a true multiprocessing system, but rather a connected group of individual microcomputer systems. Resources are not equally available to each processor. Any access involving the global bus takes longer than a simple local access. Access from the global bus back to a local bus is obtained through a DMA operation. There are no strictly global, shared resources, and the mechanism is suitable only for low, nonlocal access rates. Also, there is nothing to prevent several processors from making continuous accesses into one processor, effectively stopping that processor entirely. With the priority on the global bus fixed, a processor with the lowest priority may never get a global transaction started or completed.

MC68000 multimicroprocessor operation is facilitated by

- bus arbitration modules (BAMs), which provide support in global bus multiprocessor design;
- the TAS (test and set) instruction;
- signals for bus request, bus grant, and bus grant acknowledge, which provide necessary input signals for arbitration purposes. Such arbitration requires some external hardware.

Interlocked multiprocessor communication is achieved through an indivisible read-modify-write cycle. For this purpose, the TAS instruction is used, and the address strobe is asserted throughout the cycle to inhibit other bus members from accessing the bus. The bus arbitration handles overlapped bus arbitration and transmission; however, it is not very powerful for multiple CPUs. The extended bus arbitration provided by Versabus is more powerful, but the inherent master/slave nature of its protocol presents a major bottleneck as the number of processors increases.

NS16000. The NS16000 series uses local buses and system buses. The local bus can connect the NS16032 CPU to the NS16081 floating-point unit, the NS16082 memory management unit, and the NS16203 DMA controller. The system bus is used for communications to other processors and global memory, and also to the bus arbiter and the interrupt control unit. The two buses communicate through "drivers" and "address latch" circuitry. It is too early to comment on specific system capabilities and potential bottlenecks of the National bus protocols.

Multiprocessing overview. In all the 16-bit chips, support for multiprocessing is rather primitive, and one must consciously avoid the various pitfalls mentioned above. National Semiconductor still has to make known the details of its more sophisticated mechanisms. Among the other multiprocessors, the amount of resource sharing in the 8086 Multibus design is more restricted than that in the MC68000 local/global bus structure. Although all resources on the system bus can be accessed by any master, local bus resources are directly accessible only by the resident 8086. A further constraint imposed by Multibus is the fixed master-slave relationship of devices on the system bus, limiting interprocessor communication to the level of mailbox messages via global memory. Multibus, like the MC68000 local/global structure, is subject to saturation by high-priority devices. Individual transactions on Multibus are much faster than those on the MC68000 bus for two reasons: fetches from MC68000 local memory involve contention with the local processor, while Multibus global memory fetches do not; MC68000 inter-BAM communication adds two additional steps to the global memory access procedure. The Z8000 offers special signal pins, MI and MO, and four special instructions to support multiprocessing.

Selection strategy

In selecting a microprocessor for a particular application, one must analyze a spectrum of issues, both technical and nontechnical. Let us consider the relevant technical issues first.

Technical issues. The operational speeds of all the 16-bit microprocessors have improved over the previous generation 8080, Z80, and MC6800 processors. The shortest execution (assuming sufficiently fast memory) is 400 ns for the 8086, 750 ns for the Z8000, and 500 ns for the MC68000. In all three microprocessors, extended address ranges allow large memory sizes to be directly accessed. The upper limit on directly addressable memory is one megabyte on the 8086, 48M bytes on the Z8000, and 64M bytes on the MC68000. Such large memory space requires some form of management. The internal segment registers of the 8086 provide internally controlled memory management via relocation. Both the Z8000 and the MC68000 are designed to be used with an external memory management chip, which allows increased function by increasing silicon area. These management units can relocate, check bounds, and check functions of all references to support very sophisticated memory mapping and protection facilities.

The 8086 and Z8000 have separate I/O addressing facilities, while the MC68000 uses memory-mapped I/O. Separate I/O space makes system memory design and management easier. Memory-mapped I/O allows all memory referencing instructions to also be I/O-referenced. This saves instructions, but the I/O cannot be protected at the instruction level; it can be protected only at the memory level.

A valuable feature of the Z8000 and MC68000 processors is the implementation of supervisor/user mode separations, allowing the protection of certain instructions and separate system/user stack pointers. The 8086 does not offer such facilities. Also, the Z8000 and the MC68000 can handle 32-bit operands.

The basic speed of instruction execution is an important selection criterion. Available independent benchmark studies do not cover the NS16000 series, which is not yet commercially available. Hence, we must use the figures published by National Semiconductor. The speed data, listed in Table 3 for the four microprocessors, must be interpreted with caution. Actual throughput is a function of the exact instruction sequence, displacements, data lengths, clock frequency, and other factors. Also, the numbers may represent a slight positive bias in favor of National. Overall, the MC68000 is the best on the various branch operations. For simple data transfer operations, the NS16032 and the MC68000 are superior to the 8086 and the Z8000.

The direct address sizes supported by the various microprocessors are considerably different, making the machines suitable for different application areas. Simple text editing, for example, generally requires less memory than data-base management, and memory requirements increase in direct proportion to the number of users simultaneously on-line. Thus, each processor has its own application niche (see Figure 4). The sophisticated addressing modes and segmentation schemes used in both the MC68000 and the Z8000 families simplify the implementation of large programs. Conversely, the small address space of the NS16008 and the NS16016 prevents their use for any large-scale programs.

Software is another factor determining application suitability of the various microprocessors. The Z8000 is

Table 3.
Execution speeds (in microseconds) of 16-bit microprocessors.

OPERATION	DATA TYPE	8086	Z8000	MC68000	NS16032
REGISTER-TO-REGISTER MOVE	BYTE/WORD	0.40	0.75	0.50	0.30
	DOUBLE-WORD	0.80	1.25	0.50	0.30
MEMORY-TO-REGISTER MOVE	BYTE/WORD	3.40	3.50	1.50	1.00
	DOUBLE-WORD	6.80	4.25	2.00	1.40
MEMORY-TO-MEMORY MOVE	BYTE/WORD	7.00	7.00	2.50	1.60
	DOUBLE-WORD	14.00	8.50	3.75	2.40
ADD MEMORY TO REGISTER	BYTE/WORD	3.60	3.75	1.50	1.10
	DOUBLE-WORD	7.20	5.25	2.25	1.50
COMPARE MEMORY TO MEMORY	BYTE/WORD	7.00	7.25	3.00	1.80
	DOUBLE-WORD	14.00	9.50	4.00	2.60
MULTIPLY MEMORY TO MEMORY	BYTE	13.00	20.25	N/A	2.80
	WORD	23.00	16.00	8.75	4.60
	DOUBLE-WORD	115.20	85.75	43.00	7.60
CONDITIONAL BRANCH	BRANCH TAKEN	1.60	1.50	1.25	1.40
	BRANCH NOT TAKEN	0.80	1.50	1.00	0.70
MODIFY INDEX BRANCH IF ZERO	BRANCH TAKEN	2.20	2.75	1.25	1.30
BRANCH TO SUBROUTINE		3.80	3.75	2.25	2.50

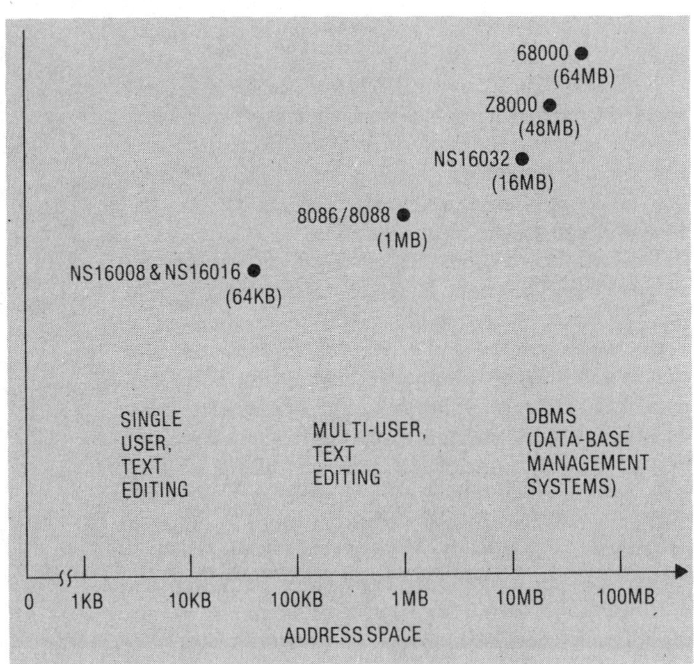

Figure 4. Application niches for 16-bit microprocessors.

best suited for word processing and text editing applications because of its sophisticated string instruction repertoire. On the other hand, the MC68000 lacks this capability but offers excellent support for handling interrupts and thus is suitable for real-time and control systems and also for multitasking. The perceived market for Intel 8086 systems is largely to upgrade earlier Intel products and to serve as a steppingstone to 16-bit applications. The National products, according to current specifications, are attractive across the range because of their direct upward compatibility with the Intel 8080, as well as their string-processing and interrupt-handling capabilities.

Another major evaluation dimension is the availability and type of support chips. Such chips greatly facilitate particular functions—e.g., memory management, bus arbitration, floating-point operations, array processing, and a whole spectrum of I/O operations. Although all chip vendors are involved in the development of "coprocessor," "slave," or support chips, only a few such chips are commercially available. Since the 8086 has been in existence much longer than the other processors, it possesses a distinct advantage in this realm. Table 4 presents a listing of the various support chips. In most cases, the new 16-bit microprocessors will interface with support chips designed earlier for eight-bit microprocessors. This may result, however, in a substantial performance loss, as the earlier chips use relatively obsolete technology, operate at lower speeds, and use fewer data lines. The new chips cost more than the earlier ones—thus the price-performance trade-offs of the two options must be considered in the design of any new system.

The software conversion costs of upgrading to a 16-bit microprocessor are not insignificant. A system presently using an Intel 8080 must convert either to an Intel 8086 or a National Semiconductor 16008/16016. These alternatives will yield a speed increase of a factor of 4-6. It is possible to obtain higher speeds with an NS16032 or a Motorola 68000, but the costs of rewriting software plus the associated costs of debugging can more than offset the gain. Likewise, the only appropriate upward path from an MC6800 is to an MC68000. The Z8000 has a basic structure different from the previous Z80; hence, one must fully analyze present programs before making a final choice.

The major features discussed in this section are listed and evaluated in Table 5 (A is excellent; B is good; C is fair; D is poor).

Commercial issues. The availability of vendor support and second sourcing is critical, especially for high-volume systems. (Second sources for the 16-bit microprocessor-based systems were listed in the second paragraph of this article.) It is unwise to depend on a single source for the supply of all chips. So far, no second source has been identified for the National microprocessors, and this constraint must be kept in mind.

We come finally to the pertinent issue of new product versus old product. The Intel 8086 has been available since 1978, the Zilog 8000 since 1979, and the Motorola

Table 4.
Support chips for 16-bit microprocessors.

TYPE OF CHIP	INTEL 8086	Z8000	MC68000	NS16000
MEMORY MANAGEMENT		Z8010	68451	NS16082 (NOT USEABLE W/NS16008)
BUS ARBITER	8289	Z8001/8002 MAY BE USED		NS16024
FLOATING-POINT	8087		68000X	NS16081
DMA CONTROLLER	8089/8237	Z8016	68450	NS16023
INTERRUPT CONTROL UNIT	8259A			NS16202
I/O PROCESSOR/INTERFACE	8089	Z8038		
PERIPHERAL CONTROLLER	8041A/8741A	Z8034	68120	
FLOPPY DISK CONTROLLER	8271/8271-6/8271-8			
CRT CONTROLLER	8275	Z8052		
ARRAY PROCESSOR				
BUBBLE MEMORY CONTROLLER			68453	

68000 since January 1980. The number of Intel users is the largest. Hence, the company's spectrum of support chips is also the largest, and there is a much lower probability of a bug in the software. The MC68000 can use the large number of support chips designed earlier for the MC6800 family. However, very few support chips designed exclusively for the MC68000 are presently available. National Semiconductor support products will be available this year. But by that time, Intel will also have new iAPX series products, which will offer higher speeds, wider data paths, and superior addressing facilities. Microprocessing is a dynamic world, and we can always expect newer and more powerful chips. ■

Table 5.
Ranking of 16-bit microprocessors.

	INTEL 8086	Z8000	MC68000	NS16000
SPEED	C	B	A	A
NUMBER OF REGISTERS	B	A	A	C
ADDRESS RANGE	D	A	A	B
COMPATIBILITY W/EARLIER MICROPROCESSORS	A	B	B	B
SUPPORT CHIPS	A	B	C	D
MULTIPROCESSING CAPABILITY	B	B	B	C
SECOND SOURCE	A	A	A	D

Acknowledgment

The authors sincerely thank John-Francis Mergen and Svein Ove Strommen for their valuable assistance in the preparation of this article.

Bibliography

Brooks, F. P., "An Overview of Microcomputer Architecture and Software," *Micro Architecture,* EUROMICRO 1976 Proceedings, pp. 1-3a.

Childs, R. E., "Multiple Microprocessor Systems: Goals, Limitations and Alternatives," *Digest of Papers COMPCON Spring 79,* pp. 94-97.

Enslow, P. H., Jr., ed., *Multiprocessors and Parallel Processing,* John Wiley, New York, 1974.

Franklin, M. A., S. A. Kahn, and M. J. Stucki, "Design Issues in the Development of a Modular Multiprocessor Communications Network," *Sixth Ann. Symp. Computer Architecture,* Apr. 23-25, 1979, pp. 182-187.

Fung, K. T., and H. C. Torng, "On the Analysis of Memory Conflicts and Bus Contentions in a Multiple-Microprocessor System," *IEEE Trans. Computers,* Vol. C-27, No. 1, Jan. 1979, pp. 28-37.

Harris, J. A., and D. R. Smith, "Hierarchical Multiprocessor Organizations," *Fourth Ann. Symp. Computer Architecture,* Mar. 23-25, 1977, pp. 41-48.

Intel Corp., "8086 User's Guide," and other 8086 technical publications, 3065 Bowers Ave., Santa Clara, CA 95051.

Lipovski, G. J., "On Virtual Memories and Micronetworks," *Proc. Fourth Ann. Symp. Computer Architecture,* Mar. 23-25, 1977, pp. 125-134.

Motorola Semiconductor, "MC68000 Microprocessor User's Manual," and other MC68000 technical publications, Motorola IC Division, 3501 Ed Bluestein Blvd., Austin, TX 78721.

Myers, G., *Advances in Computer Architecture,* John Wiley, New York, 1978.

National Semiconductor Corp., "The NS16000 Family of 16-Bit Microprocessors," and other NS16000 technical publications, 2900 Semiconductor Dr., Santa Clara, CA 95051.

Patel, J. H., "Processor-Memory Interconnections for Multiprocessors," *Proc. Sixth Ann. Symp. Computer Architecture,* Apr. 23-25, 1979, pp. 168-177.

Thurber, K. J., and G. M. Masson, *Distributed Processor Communication Architecture,* Lexington Books, Lexington, MA, 1979.

Toong, H. D., J. F. Mergen, and C. J. Smith, "Issues of Advanced Microprocessor Architecture," Technical Report #4, M.I.T. internal monograph, July 1979.

Toong, H. D., S. O. Strommen, and E. R. Goodrich II, "A General Multimicroprocessor Interconnection Mechanism for Non-Numeric Processing," *Proc. Fifth Workshop on Computer Architecture for Non-Numeric Processing,* 1980, pp. 115-123.

Zilog Corp., "Z8000 User's Guide," and other Z8000 technical publications, 10460 Bubb Rd., Cupertino, CA 95014.

THE INTEL iAPX 286 MICROPROCESSOR

Pete Heller
Product Marketing Manager
Intel Corporation
2625 Walsh Ave.
Santa Clara, CA 95051

INTRODUCTION

The iAPX 286 is a new 16-bit microprocessor. The iAPX 286 has three key attributes which differentiate it from other 16-bit microprocessors. These attributes are:

1. The 286 is a very high speed processor. System throughput (the total amount of work accomplished) of a 286 system will be two to five times greater than that of systems based on other 16-bit microprocessors. This is due to two major advances in the 286 over other microprocessors. First, the 286's technologically leading internal architecture processes applications code up to 10 times faster than existing microprocessors. Second, totally new "operating system accelerator" instructions have been added specifically to increase system software performance.

2. The 286 CPU offers new functions never before supplied in a 16-bit microprocessor. The 286 has memory management and protection functions built into the CPU. These functions complement the processor's high performance architecture. The 286, therefore, addresses the need for isolation of users or tasks in memory yet still provides very high system throughput.

3. The 286 is easy to use. The 286's new functions and high performance simplify the task of writing operating systems and system software. For example, the 286 can respond to an interrupt and start a completely new task to process the interrupt with only one iAPX 286 instructions.

APPLICATIONS

The 286 is an excellent choice for:

1. Performance Critical Applications: Such systems must be able to process a given event or a given number of transactions within a specified time. These applications generally have an imbedded processor. Examples would include communications processors for mainframe computers and central office switches for a telephone company. Such applications could take advantage of the 286's performance leadership.

2. Multi-User Reprogrammable Applications: Such systems generally have multiple users and/or tasks which execute independently from the same memory space. These applications generally require memory management and protection. For example, medium size multi-user business systems could use the 286's memory protection mechanisms to completely isolate users. And, because the 286's memory protection degrades performance by less than 10%, upgraded business systems could increase the number of users supported.

3. Upgrades of iAPX 86 based systems: Code written for the iAPX 86 processor family is directly transportable to the 286. A straightforward CPU board upgrade would increase performance by a factor of two to five times with no software modifications.

KEY FEATURES

Extremely High Performance

The iAPX 286/10 CPU performance ranges from two to five times faster than the iAPX 86/10 (8086) or other competitive 16-bit microprocessors. Many instructions, particularly those for arithmetic, execute ten times faster than on a 5 MHz iAPX 86/10 (see Table 1). The iAPX 286/10 provides an excellent performance upgrade path for iAPX 86 based systems.

High Performance for Numerics

The iAPX 286 family includes a Numeric Data Processor (NDP) configuration just as the iAPX 86 family does. The NDP, called the iAPX 286/20, performs the same functions as the iAPX 86/20 (8086 + 8087) and is software compatible with the 86/20. The 286/20 will offer twice the performance of the 86/20 for numerics oriented applications, however. That makes the 286/20 an excellent performance upgrade path for systems now using the 86/20 numerics processor.

Reprinted with permission from *Wescon Conf. Rec.*, 1981, pp. 1.3.1-1.3.4.

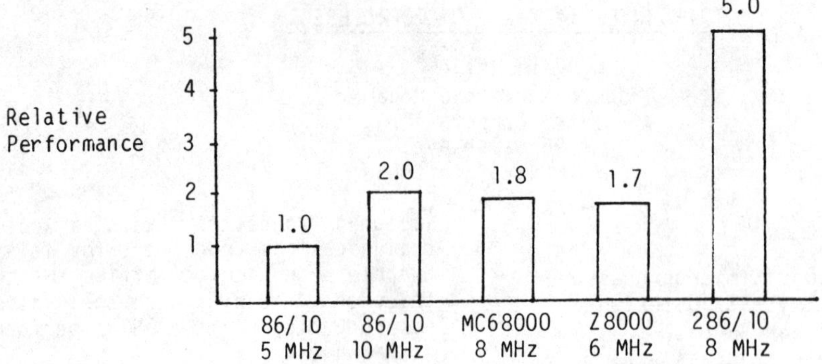

Fig. 1 Relative Throughput Benchmark
(Based on Intel Standard
Application Benchmarks)

Instruction	Execution Speed (Microseconds) 286	86	iAPX 86/286 Ratio
Move Register to Memory	.38	3.4	8.9
16-bit Register Multiply	2.62	25.0	9.5
32-bit Register Divide	2.88	30.0	10.4
Shift/Rotate Memory	.88	5.0	5.7
Conditional Jump	1.00	3.2	3.2

Table 1. 286 vs. 86 Instruction Speed Comparison

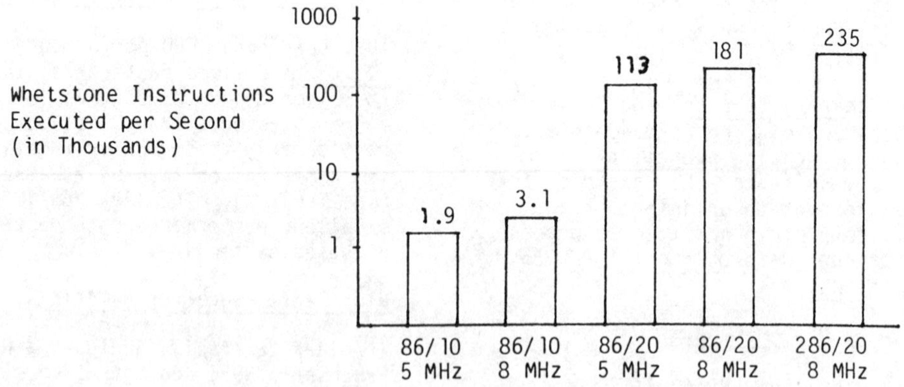

Fig. 2 Floating Point Throughput Benchmark

New Microprocessor Functions

In addition to the 286's high performance it offers new levels of function in a 16-bit microprocessor. The capability to efficiently support memory management, memory protection, and virtual memory is built into the silicon of the 286/10 CPU.

The concepts of memory management, protections, and virtual memory, are not entirely new to microprocessors. In fact, silicon devices external to the processor have been built to "add" these capabilities to a CPU. The 286 attacks memory protection and virtual memory differently. These capabilities are an integral part of the 286 CPU itself.

There are three main reasons for building memory management and protection into the CPU. First, and foremost, performance of a protected 286 system is much higher than that of a 2-chip solution. Second, virtual memory can be implemented much more cleanly. Third, hardware design is much simpler with the 286 and significantly slower memory devices can be used.

Memory Management and Protection

It is generally desirable (and often required) to have memory management and memory protection in reprogrammable systems with multiple users or multiple tasks in memory. In a multi-user or multi-tasking system it can be difficult and time consuming to effectively manage the memory space. It is even more difficult to protect each task or user from being interfered with by another since they all share the same memory space.

The 286 addresses these problems directly. The 286 can protect and manage nearly 8000 tasks simultaneously with little software intervention or performance reduction. This includes verifying every memory access for address range and access rights violations. Tasks attempting to make unauthorized memory accesses are flagged and trapped to the operating system. The advantage to the end user is much increased system integrity with little performance degradation over an unprotected system.

Tasks can be managed in either real (physical) or virtual (secondary) storage. The iAPX 286 directly addresses up to 16 megabytes of real memory. In addition, the 286 supports up to 2^{30} bytes of logical memory per user.

Virtual Memory

The 286 CPU has capability to support virtual memory built in. All instructions which can cause a segment fault are fully restartable. This allows a not-present segment to be retrieved from secondary storage and the task restarted at the point the fault occurred.

Virtual memory can be beneficial in systems requiring large programs or large amounts of data. In general, not all of the data or all the program is needed for processing in memory at any one time. By reducing the size of main memory and putting programs and data on a secondary storage device, system cost can be dramatically reduced with only a small performance decrease. As sections of the program are required for processing they are brought into main memory from the secondary storage device.

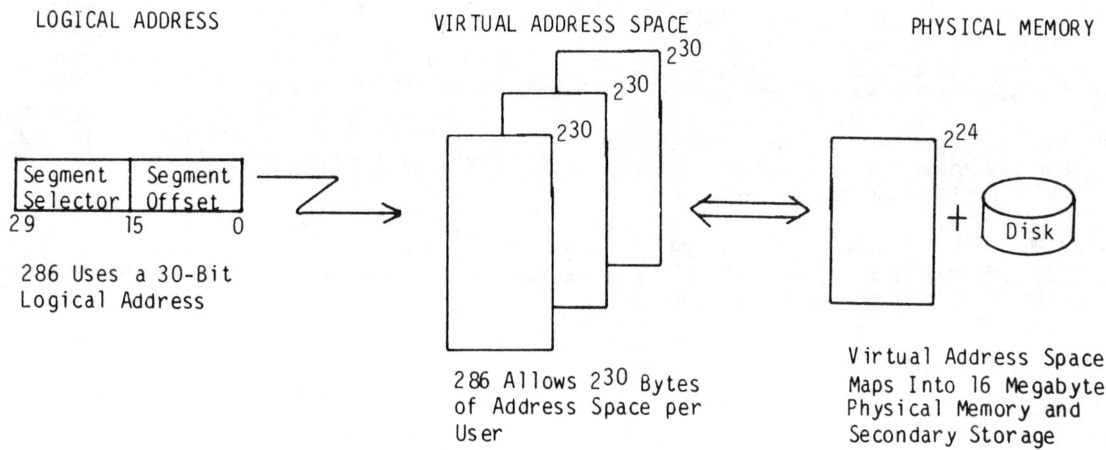

Fig. 3 iAPX 286 Supports Real and Virtual Memory

Simple to Use

The assembly language programmer will find the iAPX 286 processor easy to use. The 286 has a straightforward set of eight 16-bit general purpose registors, a large set of addressing modes, and an excellent set of instructions to make use of these resources.

The iAPX 286 is advantageous for those who plan to write their own operating system. The 286 allows the system designer to do functions never before possible on a microprocessor. The 286 also greatly simplifies writing an operating system. This is especially true for a multi-user or multi-tasking operating system.

The needed functions for memory management and memory protection exist as capabilities of the 286 itself. Three key examples of this fact are:

- o Only a single 22 microsecond instruction is needed to make a task switch (i.e. save old task parameters and start a new task).
- o All memory access instructions are checked by the CPU for violations of segment boundaries, illegal accesses, or improper use of data.
- o Operating system service calls are fast and only require one instruction.

These features allow the system programmer to concentrate on writing the best operating system. The 286 handles much of the "dirty" work. And the 286 does this work more efficiently than the programmer could. The benefits of this approach are:

- o More powerful operating systems can be constructed. For example, memory protection can be implemented with performance only slightly below that of the same system without protection.
- o System programmers are more productive because they code at a higher level. This shortens the development cycle.
- o High system throughput is assured. More processing power available per user or more users per system can be supported.

From an applications programmer's standpoint the 286 is also simple to use. It is supported by high level languages including PL/M, Pascal, and FORTRAN as well as 286 assembler. Programmers familiar with the iAPX 86 family will need minimal training to master the 286. Other assembly language programmers will quickly learn the 286.

The 286 efficiently supports applications programming, especially in high level languages such as Pascal or Ada. The 286's register set and instructions are well suited for compiler generated code. Code generated for the 286 generally requires less memory than other 16-bit processors and executes faster as well.

It should be noted that the 286 virtually eliminates the need to program application software (vs. system software) in assembler language. The 286's performance level is high enough that a high-level language such as Pascal generally can be used in place of assembler code. Programmers write code in high-level languages much more efficiently than assembler language. Using high-level languages reduces software development and maintenance costs.

CONCLUSION

The iAPX 286 is an extremely high performance VLSI processor. It provides a comprehensive and powerful memory management and protection mechanism. A large logical address space is directly supported. The protection mechanism is highly efficient thus allowing high performance protected systems to be built.

The 286 is perfectly suited for performance critical embedded applications, multi-user reprogrammable applications, and iAPX 86 based product upgrades. For all applications, the 286 will be fully supported with software development tools and high level languages.

Memory protection moves onto 16-bit microprocessor chip

Hardware implementations of virtual-memory management and protection adapt this device to sophisticated multiuser, multitasking applications

by Peter Heller, Robert Childs, and Jim Slagev, *Intel Corp., Santa Clara, Calif.*

□ The 16-bit microprocessor has won rapid promotion from its comfortable early jobs running simple terminals and instrumentation controllers to the more strenuous responsibilities of organizing multiterminal word processors and small business systems. But its success in a multi-tasking and -user role has brought with it pressures for memory-management and -protection hardware to increase system performance and to simplify system implementation.

In order to run a reprogrammable, multiuser, multitasking system, a 16-bit microprocessor needs higher throughput than it does for a single-task, single-user setup. It also needs to protect its operating-system software against its users and its users against each other. And it could support more users or more tasks if it had virtual memory. Moreover, both memory protection and virtual-memory management should be implemented in hardware, rather than software, so as not to compromise throughput.

Intel's iAPX-286 has been engineered with these requirements in mind. And it achieves its goal on a single chip without the need for cumbersome external memory-management units. Applications like financial transaction systems, in banks or for stock transfers, can benefit from the 286's ability to protect confidential data. Real-time process control systems can profit from its fast interrupt response time, automatic task switching, and ample address space. The 286 supports the needs of multiuser business systems and can serve as the host of a distributed-processing network by managing a number of work stations and local communications lines. It is also closely matched to the needs of telecommunications and data-communications systems like private branch exchanges.

In sum, the 80286 processor, together with its family of support circuits, offers performance and features previously available only from minicomputers. On-chip circuitry provides powerful yet flexible memory protection, completely controlling access to operating-system resources and isolating individual application programs and programmers from each other. A physical address space of 16 megabytes maps into a full gigabyte of virtual memory per task.

Also, the 80286 processor has six times the throughput of its predecessor, the 8086. Compared with the 29,000 or so transistors of the 8086, the 80286 has 130,000.

Lastly, to minimize software development costs, which can become very steep for complex applications, the 286 system is equipped to run high-level languages and has a complete set of software development tools. Its instructions are a superset of the 8086's, maintaining complete compatibility with software for the 8086 and 8088.

No forgetting

Large computer systems normally allocate portions of a sizable virtual-address space to multiple tasks or multiple users. To enforce the memory boundaries and also prevent unauthorized access to or modification of information stored, these systems use hardware support. The 80286 is the only microprocessor that has such a protection mechanism built into its own silicon.

The system designer may exploit the 286 protection mechanism in different ways to accommodate systems of varying complexity. One possibility is to split all memory between user and supervisor functions. But this traditional two-level system is seldom reliable enough for

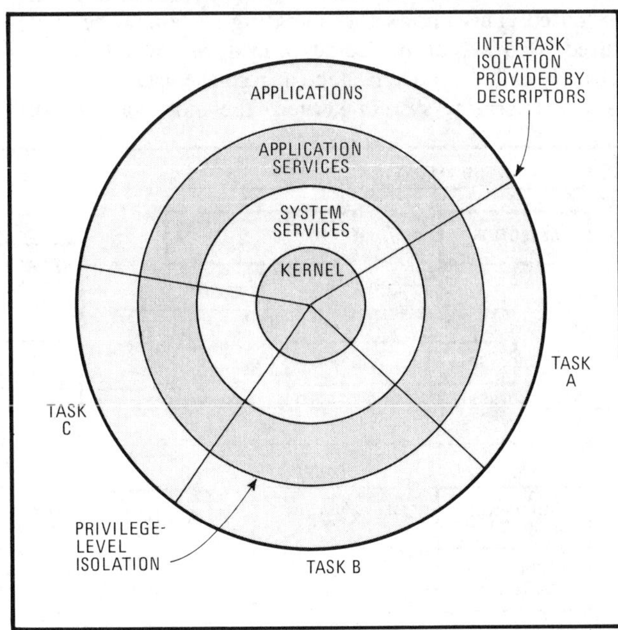

1. Lines of defense. Each task running in a 286 system can operate on any of four privilege levels. This form memory of protection is augmented by isolation between tasks. Hardware implements all forms of protection for higher performance and throughput.

Reprinted with permission from *Electronics*, vol. 55, pp. 133–137, Feb. 24, 1982.

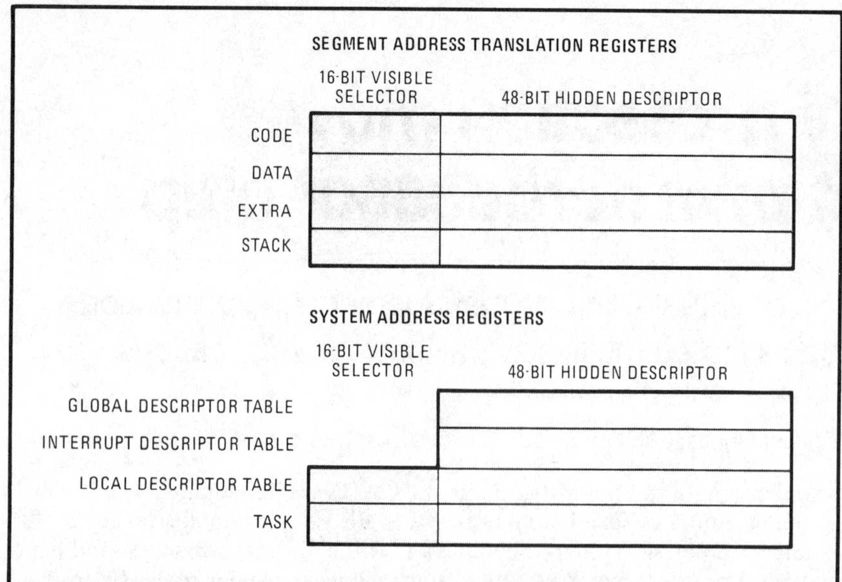

2. Extended registers. The four segment registers of the 8086 are expanded with 48-bit descriptors on the 286. The 16-bit segment register selectors are virtual addresses that are mapped into physical memory via the descriptors containing access rights.

complex systems or flexible enough for customization.

The 286 instead has four hierarchical protection levels, creating a structured environment that promotes reliable system design. For instance, the programs written for each level can be smaller and easier to develop and maintain. Being in hardware rather than software, the protection mechanism also speeds operation and means there is no software overhead for these functions.

In terms of a processor's operation, memory protection levels may be more meaningfully described as software privilege levels. Whenever the 286 is executing a procedure, it is doing so at the privilege level assigned to that task. The task's position in the hierarchical organization of the system software determines its privilege level.

Therefore a task in the system may be executing at any of the levels depending on the procedure being executed. This allows the operating system to be structured as a set of protected procedures, which can be directly called yet are protected from the user.

The operating-system kernel—the most trusted software—operates at the highest of the four privilege levels. The kernel is typically assigned the critical responsibilities of managing memory space, scheduling tasks, and handling intertask communications. A small, fast operating-system kernel takes the best advantage of the high-speed capabilities of the 286 and indeed may be treated as an extension of the actual processor.

Below the kernel comes the supervisor level. The supervisor manages input/output resources, allocates data buffers, and does more global job scheduling. Whereas the kernel serves as an extension to the processor, the makeup of supervisor programs depends more on the intended applications. Because they perform more complex tasks, supervisor programs are usually larger than those at the kernel level.

On the third level of privilege are application services. Programs located at this level are dedicated to the support of the application programs. File-control systems, job-control language processing, and application support utilities are all to be found here.

Least trusted software, such as unproven user programs, operates at the fourth or lowest privilege level to prevent interference with more trusted software.

The multilevel protection mechanism of the 286 is extremely flexible. System designers have the option of using two, three, or four protection levels for system software to provide the level of protection required in any system. By reserving a privilege level for operating-system extensions, they may customize systems without compromising the original software.

Controlled memory access is fundamental to the 286 protection mechanism (Fig. 1). Control of memory references must be strict and continuous to isolate operating-system software from destruction by user programs, as well as to isolate user tasks from each other. To this end, each task has controlled access to two areas of virtual memory, one public and one private as defined by the contents of two kinds of descriptor tables.

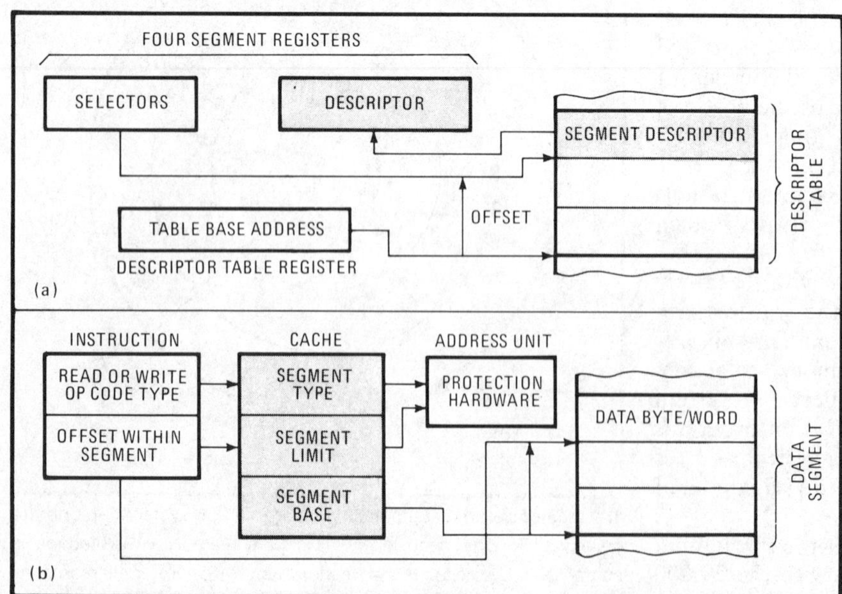

3. Mapping mechanism. Descriptors are stored in main memory (a) until selected, whereupon they are loaded transparently into a segment register. Thereafter all access rights and protection modes are checked (b) in parallel with virtual-address translation.

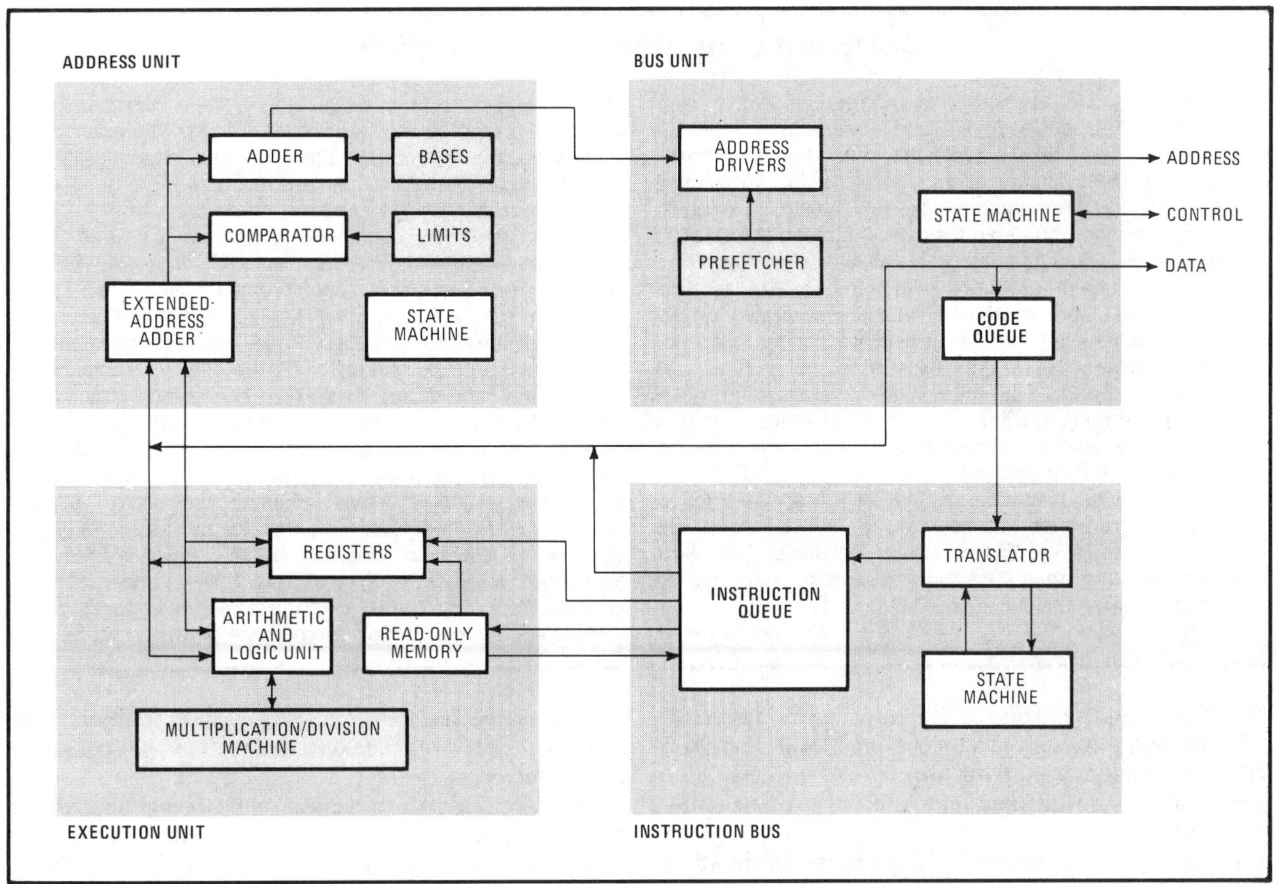

4. Pipelined operation. The four separate subunits of the 286 operate in parallel to address, fetch, decode, and execute instructions. Throughput is further increased over the 8086 by demultiplexing the address and data bus and by the use of improved microcode.

The global descriptor table lists those segments that all system tasks may access, subject only to privilege-level restrictions. A local descriptor table lists those segments available to only one task; as each task includes such a table as part of the description of its state, a typical 286 system will have many local descriptor tables. A register pointing to this table is automatically loaded, along with the other registers, during a task-switching operation.

The descriptor for each segment contains the base address and size of the segment and an access rights field. This field defines how the information in the segment may and may not be used. For example, code segments are always write-protected and may be read-protected as well, whereas data segments can always be read but may be write-protected if desired.

Other bits in the access rights field include the present bit and the descriptor privilege level. The present bit indicates whether the segment is present in real memory or whether it is located in secondary storage for virtual memory systems.

The descriptor privilege level is compared with the processor's current privilege level and, if higher, does not allow the program to gain access to the segment. Any attempted access to such a segment results in a protection fault.

The 286's flag register is similar to the 8086 in containing six arithmetic and three system status flags. Where it differs is in adding further system status flags—the nested flag and the 2-bit I/O privilege level flag. These new flags control protected I/O operations.

Altogether, the 286 has 17 registers. It has the same eight programmer-visible registers as the 8086 for general-purpose arithmetic and offset address computation to ensure compatibility with the 8086 and 8088 software base (Fig. 2).

Protective register structure

Four segment registers define the four segments of the virtual address space currently visible to the executing task. They are the code, data, extra, and stack segment registers. Wider versions of the 8086's 16-bit segment registers, the 286's 64-bit segment registers each contain a 16-bit selector and a 48-bit descriptor. Though a task utilizes only four hardware segment registers, up to 16-K segments are accessible to a single task. The hardware registers are reloaded each time a new segment is requested in a manner that is completely transparent to the programmer.

A selector is an index to a table of descriptors kept in external main memory. As before, the descriptor includes the base address of a segment, the segment length, and the specific access rights for that segment. The processor copies this descriptor information from main memory into the segment register where it is used for high-speed address translation and protection-checking operations.

Three descriptor-table registers are provided in the

Software simplifies 286 evaluation

When a new microprocessor was introduced in the past, customers had to wait until silicon devices were available to evaluate the chip. To avoid this delay, Intel has developed the iAPX-286 evaluation package for an Intellec series III microcomputer development system. It enables system designers to begin their development of 286 software before an actual processor is available.

Four evaluation programs with support libraries help programmers become familiar with the operation of the 286 instruction set and memory-protection mechanism. The demonstration program illustrates the architectural features of the 286 with an evaluation version of a multitasking operating system and a series of utility programs and can be used as a model for customers to develop their own operating systems.

The evaluation version of the 286 macroinstruction assembler translates 286 source code into an object file and a source listing. The evaluation builder accepts that object file and creates an executable task that may be debugged using the evaluation simulator.

The evaluation simulator contains a loader and a monitor/debugger. It provides built-in system functions for input and output as well. After loading a task into memory, it initializes the descriptor tables, the task-state segment, and the code- and data-segment registers. The symbolic debugger is also controlled by the loader program.

The simulator itself is an 8086 program that runs on the Intellec development system. It runs 286 programs, either normally or a step at a time, enforcing all of the 286 protection rules and executing all supported instructions.

Though the 286 evaluation package can familiarize designers with the operation of the 286, it does not provide the total support required to develop large systems. Intel's planned releases of development software include a full-scale macroinstruction assembler, a system builder program, a linker-binder program, a librarian program, and several high-level–language translators. PL/M will be the first high-level language to be offered for the 286, with Pascal to follow in 1982. Future high-level languages will include Fortran and other standard languages from the 8086 family. Hardware support will include in-circuit emulation and a single-board computer.

---

286. These registers point to the three active descriptor tables in main memory. The global and local descriptor tables contain descriptors for the segments accessible to a task. The interrupt descriptor table is used to vector interrupts.

A task register is the seventeenth and last of the set of 286 registers. It indicates the segment reserved to describe the state of the currently executing task and is used to save and restore the machine state automatically when one task is being swapped for another.

A gigabyte of virtual memory

Because all the 286's instructions refer to virtual rather than physical addresses, the operating system can relocate a program to any available segment of physical memory. This addressing scheme potentially gives every user access to a gigabyte of virtual memory.

A segment of the 286 is a portion of the virtual address space that may vary in length from 1 byte to 64-K bytes. This approach makes more efficient use of available memory space than would a page, which has a fixed length. The variable-length feature enables a segment to match the length of a procedure or data area exactly for more efficient swapping operations.

A virtual address on the 286 is composed of a selector and an offset. The selector is an index from the base address of a descriptor table to the desired location of the descriptor within the table. The offset is the byte location of the data within the segment (Fig. 3).

The process of addressing memory begins when a selector is placed in one of the segment registers. When the processor receives the new selector, it compares the access rights of the current task with the access rights indicated in the selector's associated descriptor while the latter is still in main memory.

When access is granted, the descriptor is automatically copied from main memory into the segment register and thus installed alongside the selector. Only the selector is visible to the program. The descriptor being used by the processor makes the absolute physical reference to memory.

At this point, the processor may access the code or data within the new segment. Subsequent accesses to that segment need specify only the desired offset, thereby minimizing the software overhead of managing and using the virtual-address space.

On-the-fly virtual-memory management is implemented through a present bit in each descriptor. If the operating system has marked a segment as nonpresent, a nonpresent fault initiates procedures to bring the segment into main memory. Once that segment is brought into main memory, the present bit is modified and the instructions loading the segment may be restarted.

Software compatibility

Software developed for either the iAPX-86 or -88 processors—the 8086 or 8088—can be run directly on the 286. The 286 even offers a mode of operation that will execute unmodified 8086 and 8088 object code. Called the real address mode, it greatly increases throughput but does not support protection or virtual-addressing features. The other operating mode, called the protected virtual-address mode, invokes the 286's memory-protection and memory-management hardware and is upwardly compatible with both 8086 and 8088 source code.

A system designed around 286 hardware can be used immediately with 8086 software, since the instruction set of the 8086 is a subset of the 286 instructions. Later, as operating systems are developed to use the full power of the 286, this system may be upgraded to operate in the protected mode without hardware modifications of any kind being necessary.

Virtual-address translation and protection checking operations are transparent to the 8086 application programs, which normally require only recompilation or reassembly to make them fully compatible with the 286 protected mode.

Most microprocessors must fetch, decode, and execute each instruction in serial fashion before starting the next instruction. Computing effective address values typically adds more steps and more time to this sequence. However, the 286 carries out these operations in parallel. Pipelining makes maximum use of the system bus by enabling one part of the processor to fetch instructions while other parts are decoding and executing previous instructions. In addition, the 286 can utilize available bus cycles to get as many as three instructions ahead of the processor's arithmetic and logic unit. As a result, the 286 provides much greater throughput than previous microprocessors, without requiring faster memory.

A pipelining plus

Instruction pipelining also makes it possible to detect invalid instructions before they can be executed and to check the protection attributes of a memory segment before granting access to that segment.

The 8086 provides two levels of pipelining. However, the 286 contains four separate logical units: the bus, address, instruction, and execution units (Fig. 4). These four units operate simultaneously so that memory accesses, address calculation and protection checks, instruction decoding, and execute cycles can overlap, partially accounting for the sixfold increase in throughput the 286 offers over the 8086.

The bus unit transfers information from its code queue to the instruction unit at a rate of 1 byte per clock cycle. The instruction unit then decodes and formats complete instructions and places them in an instruction queue to await execution.

The execution unit contains the working registers, the ALU, and the microcode read-only memory. The ROM defines the internal microinstruction sequencing, which executes instructions. As the microinstruction sequence for an instruction nears completion, the ROM generates a signal that causes the execution unit to take the next ROM address from the instruction queue. This technique keeps the execution unit continually busy.

The address unit translates addresses at the same time as it checks access rights. This unit maintains a cache that contains the base address, the boundary limit, and the access rights for all virtual-memory segments currently selected for use by the executing task. By minimizing the need to read this information from memory, the explicit cache enables the address unit to perform its function in a single clock cycle.

The parallel operation of these four internal units enables the 286 to support virtual-memory management and to provide total memory protection without degrading its high-speed operation.

Another reason for its high speed is that the 286 microprocessor is equipped with separate data and address lines, as opposed to the multiplexed scheme of the 8086, thus doubling bus bandwidth and requiring a 68-lead package. This interface is highly optimized—pipelined bus cycles let successive bus operations take place at a rate of one bus cycle every two processor cycles—200 nanoseconds with a 10-megahertz clock.

Hardware supports of multitasking

In anticipation of multitasking environments, dedicated task-switching hardware has been included in the 286, which is the only microprocessor with this capability. This hardware automatically handles transitions between tasks to support task dispatch operations and to handle interrupts. The hardware-supported switching operation requires less than 18 microseconds at 10 MHz.

Most contemporary microprocessors require numerous instructions to save the state of one task and then recall the state of another. The task-switching hardware of the 286 lets programmers make transitions much faster and more easily using just a call or jump instruction or by an external interrupt.

All of the dynamically variable registers for an inactive task reside in a part of memory called the task-state segment. When a task switch is invoked, the processor automatically verifies all protection requirements before the switch takes place. After these requirements are satisfied, the hardware saves the state of the current task in that task's task-state segment and then loads the processor registers with new information from another task-state segment.

Nested interrupts are supported by a linkage word within a task-state segment. When these occur, the linkage word points to the previous task-state segment. The linkage then provides a return path to the task that was originally interrupted and eliminates all software overhead for these operations.

The 286 instruction set facilitates the implementation of sophisticated systems developed in modern high-level languages (see table). To the 8086 instructions, the 286 adds others that improve high-level language execution. These new instructions simplify handling stack operations, calculating and checking dynamic-array indexes, and executing procedure entry and exit commands in structured high-level languages. With privileged instructions that are accessible only to the highest-level priority, the kernel can set up or reconfigure the memory-protection parameters for the system. □

NEW iAPX 286 INSTRUCTIONS

Instruction	Function	Comments
BOUND	Verifies that a variable's value is within a user-specified upper and lower bound. If the variable value is outside of the specified range, a bounds-exceeded exception is caused.	This is extremely useful for array index checking.
ENTER	Creates the stack frame required by most block-structured high-level languages for procedure calls (this includes allocating space for dynamic variables and maintaining stack frame pointers to previous stack frames).	——
LEAVE	The converse of ENTER deletes stack frames and de-allocates the stack space.	——
PUSHA, POPA	Pushes or pops all eight general registers.	These instructions simplify and speed up interrupt handling and high-level language procedure calls.
BLOCK I/O	Inputs or outputs a block or string of data using a single instruction.	——

A TASK DRIVEN PERIPHERAL INTERFACE

Daniel Tjoa, Tom Rossi
Intel Corporation, Santa Clara

Summary:

The limitations of the traditional CPU-Peripheral Component interface, both I/O type and direct memory access is explored. A better means of communication, especially suitable for high speed peripheral devices, is introduced. An example of this type of interface, which the authors named Task Driven Interface, in a CRT controller is presented.

I. Introduction

To complement the new 16 bit microprocessors, such as the Intel 8086, new peripheral components have been made available or are being announced. As larger systems are being designed to take full advantage of the capabilities these new microprocessors offer, users realize that the traditional methods of CPU-Peripheral Component communications is limiting the system's performance. An improved communication method is being designed into the newer high performance periphperal components.

In a microcomputer system communication between the CPU and its peripheral components consists of exchanges of commands, status and data. Command and status are usually exchanged sporadically between the CPU and the peripheral component, depending on the changes in states occuring at the peripheral device under control. On the other hand, data in many cases is not processed by the peripheral component and is exchanged over a broad spectrum of size (number of bytes) and speed, depending on the particular peripheral device. Most human interface peripherals are slow in nature, while devices like mass storage require large blocks of data at high speed. Keyboard and switch sensing are performed at rates of no more than 100 bytes/sec while high speed local area network controllers demand data transfer rates of up to 1 Mbyte/sec or more.

The simplest and most widely used means of CPU-peripheral component communication is through the CPU's various data move instructions; input, output or memory data moves. As a result, this type of communications (let's call it I/O type) is slow. The CPU always needs to be involved. A diagram depicting this type of communication is shown in Fig. 1.

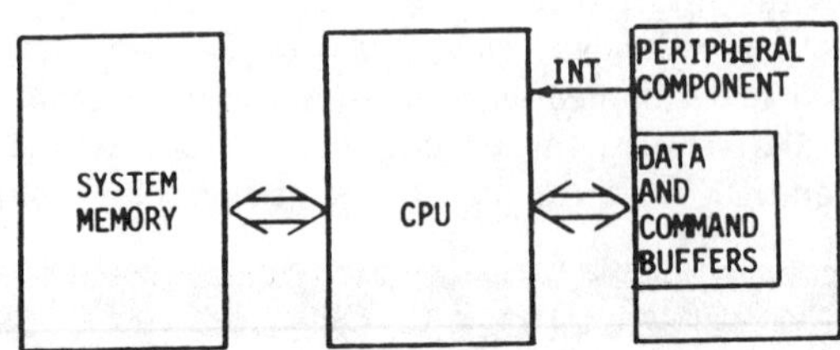

Fig. 1. I/O Type Interface

In systems with high speed peripherals, communication improvements are achieved by direct memory access through the use of a DMA controller such as the 8257 or 8237 in systems with Intel CPUs. With these DMA controllers whole blocks of data can be transferred from memory to peripheral component, and the other way around, at high speed without CPU intervention. Command and status processing still require CPU interaction, as shown diagrammatically in Fig. 2A.

Reprinted with permission from *Wescon Conf. Rec.*, 1981, pp. 5.4.1-5.4.6.

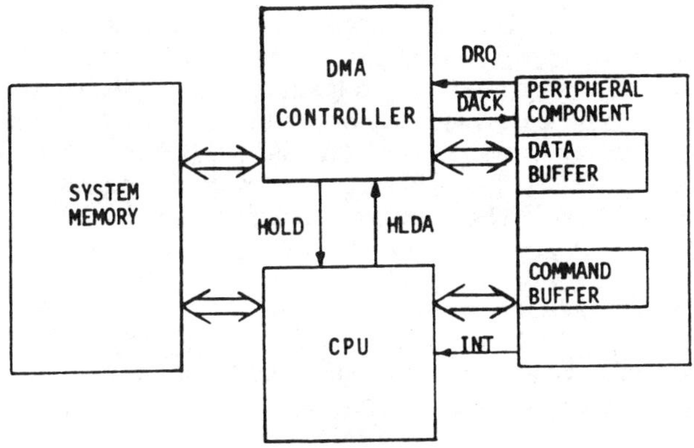

Fig. 2A DMA Type Interface

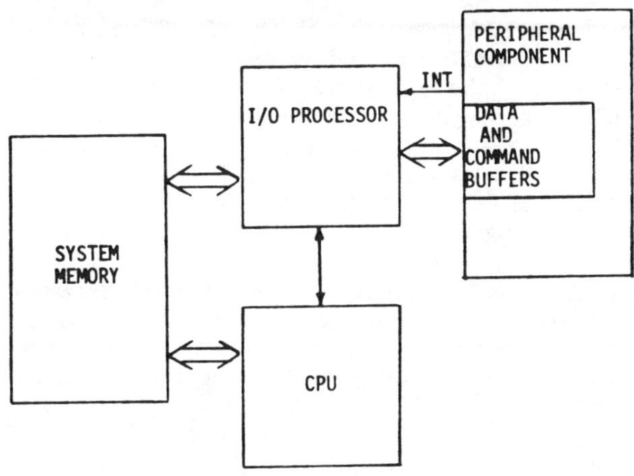

Fig. 2B. IOP Type Interface

With high speed peripherals, the frequent intervention by the CPU to service command and status can be so severe to reduce the CPU's usefullness beyond servicing this peripheral component. To reduce this problem, I/O Processors such as the 8089 were developed for 8088 and 8086 based systems. The inherent intelligence of the I/O Processor allowed the removal of one more level of control from the CPU. The I/O Processor assumes all peripheral component control overhead, does DMA transfers and can recover from some I/O errors; all these are done while the CPU is attending to other tasks. To service a wide range of applications, the I/O Processor's intelligence is of a general purpose nature. See Fig. 2B.

With a DMA controller, data transfer is a one cycle process, moved directly from memory to the peripheral component and from peripheral component to memory. To be able to utilize the I/O Processor's intelligence, for example to implement pattern matching, data has to pass through the I/O Processor during transfer between memory and peripheral component. This process understandably reduces the maximum data transfer rate to less than the maximum the system bus is capable of handling. As peripheral device speed increases and as larger systems are being built, this 2 cycle data transfer process could limit total performance.

One solution to the above problems is to place the task of intelligent data transfer into the peripheral component itself. This way, not only is the transfer rate improved, but specialized dedicated intelligence tailored to the specific tasks of the peripheral device under control can also be added. For example, in a CRT controller, this specialized intelligence might be the ability to follow linked lists and quickly recognize and execute special commands to ease the handling of text editing data structures. Such a system is shown in Fig. 3.

All communications take place via "Message Areas" shared in the common memory. The CPU performs an I/O operation by building a message in memory that describes the function to be performed. The peripheral component reads the message, carries out the command and notifies the CPU when it is finished. All peripheral components appear to the CPU as transmitting and receiving whole blocks of data. This type of CPU-Peripheral Component interface is what we call "task driven".

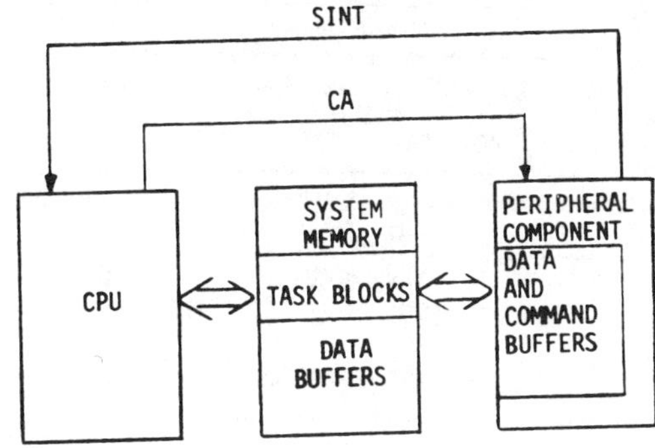

Fig. 3. Task Oriented Interface

II. The Communication Channel

In a peripheral component with a task driven interface, communication between the CPU and the peripheral component is performed through messages placed in communication blocks in shared memory. Commands from the CPU to the peripheral component are passed by preparing message blocks and directing the peripheral component's attention by asserting the Channel Attention (CA) input pin on the peripheral component. The CA signal is an interrupt signal from the CPU to the peripheral component. Communication from the peripheral component to the CPU is performed in a similar manner via the System Interrupt (SINT) output pin on the peripheral component. By providing a hierarchical data structure, this communication mechanism can be enhanced. The data structure is built in several levels, each level has direct connection only with levels immediately above or below it. This results in flexible and efficient memory use. It also makes the special processing function of the peripheral component easy to use. This communication hierarchy, which consists of blocks of linked messages, is diagrammed in Fig. 4.

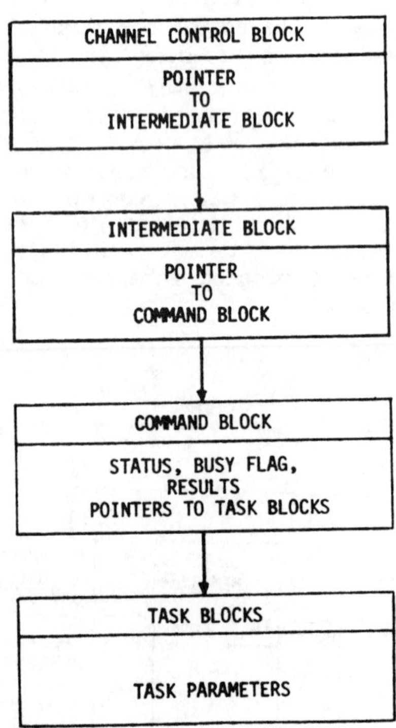

Fig. 4. Communication Hierarchy

Two distinct modes of communications are required: Initialization and Command. The initialization sequence is performed after system power up or system reset. Upon receipt of the first CA after power up or reset, the peripheral component reads a message from the Channel Control Block, which has a fixed location in memory and is shared with all peripheral components with task driven interfaces and the 8089. This Channel Control Block contains information about the systems data bus configuration and a pointer to an Intermediate Block.

The Intermediate Block contains a pointer to specific Command Blocks for each peripheral component in the system. The command Block is where all communications are centered after initialization. It also contains a Busy Flag that indicates whether the channel is in the midst of an operation or is available for a new command. Messages placed in the Command Block are status, results of operations and pointers to various Task Blocks. A typical Command Block organization is shown in Fig. 5. Some of the commands in a CRT controller are commands to set its operating mode (MODESET), starting and stopping the display process (START DISPLAY, STOP DISPLAY), reading the status (READ STATUS), loading the cursor coordinates (LOAD CURSOR), etc. Depending on the command, the peripheral component then accesses one of the Task Blocks which contain parameters associated with the command.

COMMAND	BUSY
⋮	
LIST BASE	
COMMAND BLOCK POINTER	
STATUS	
CURSOR COORDINATE	
MODE BLOCK POINTER	
⋮	

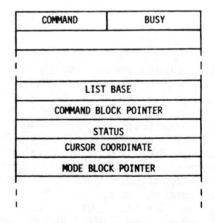

Fig. 5. Command Block Organization

HORIZONTAL MODES
VERTICAL MODES
DMA MODE
CURSOR MODE

Fig. 6. Mode Block Organization

To clarify this concept further, the sequence of events in the MODESET command is as follows. After receipt of the MODESET, the CRT controller addresses the associated Task Block, the Mode Block. This Mode Block contains parameters describing the screen format and other operational characteristics of the display. The mode parameters read by the peripheral component is loaded into registers inside the peripheral component. They set the number of characters to be displayed in a row, the number of rows on a screen, the type of cursor to be displayed, etc. The organization of the mode block is shown in Fig. 6.

III. The I/O Control Process

A peripheral component is designed to provide a peripheral device interface solution. Through its built-in function, it offloads the CPU from performance sensitive real time operations. While the CPU is capable of processing only one task at a time, the peripheral component may be busy running two or more processes simultaneously. An SDLC controller in full duplex could be receiving and transmitting serial data at the same time for example.

To perform this I/O control task without CPU intervention, the peripheral component should be capable of executing certain preprogrammed tasks repeatedly once it is activated. In a CRT controller, this task might be the display process, which consists of fetching linked strings of data from memory which are interpreted as either character data to be displayed or of a Data Stream Command. Character data is to be used to refresh the screen and Data Stream Commands are commands that are immediately interpreted as they are encountered. These Data Stream Commands may be interspersed with display data. Examples of Data Stream Commands are: NEXTSTRING (end of Datastring), END OF SCREEN (last character of the page), END OF ROW (last character of a row).

The hierachy of the data structure associated with the display process is as follows. Character data to be displayed are organized in blocks called Datastrings. Each Datastring is terminated by a NEXT STRING Data Stream Command. These Datastrings are indexed by data in another block called the Stringlist, which in turn is indexed by the Listbase located in the Command Block.

The display process is shown in Fig. 7. It is activated by the START DISPLAY Channel Command. Internally, the CRT controller has two register, the Listpointer and the Stringpointer, which are used as address registers to access data from memory. The first action of the CRT controller after the START DISPLAY command is

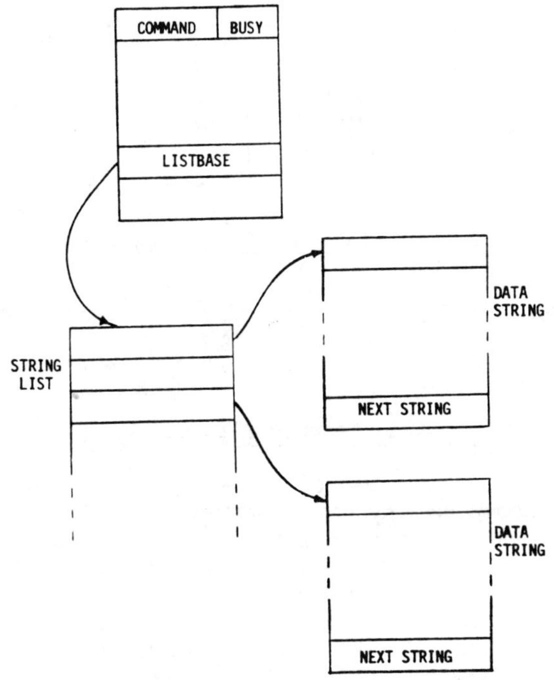

Fig. 7. Display Process

to read the Listbase and Load it into the Listpointer. Next, the data indexed by the Listpointer (data in the stringlist) is fetched and used as the initial value for the Stringpointer. The Listpointer then is incremented, ready to address the next data on the Stringlist. Finally, data indexed by the Stringpointer (data in the Datastring) is fetched and displayed on the screen. After each data fetch, the Stringpointer is incremented in anticipation of fetching the next data on the Datastring. The Datastream Command NEXTSTRING causes the Stringpointer to be reloaded with memory data indexed by the Listpointer. This linked string memory access will continue until the end of the display screen has been reached.

By including this specialized intelligence in the peripheral component, the I/O control process can be very efficient and is easy to use by the user. A disk controller or data communication peripheral component will have a different I/O control process tailored to its particular tasks.

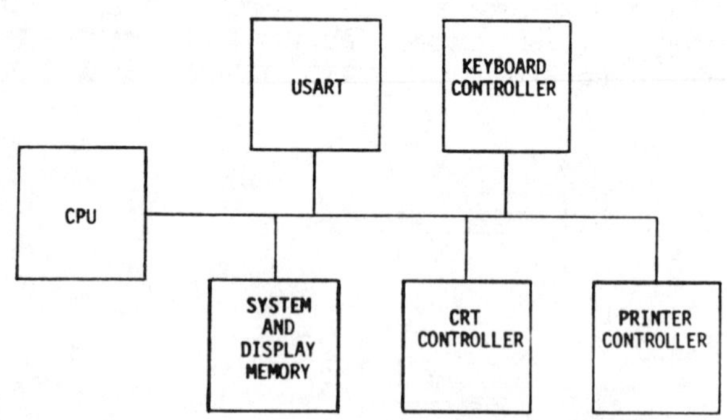

Fig. 8. Stand Alone Display System

IV. System Architecture Flexibility

Since users' needs, and thus microcomputer systems, vary widely depending on the application from small to large and complex, it is important that the design of a peripheral component takes this into consideration. From a system architectural standpoint, the task driven interface is the most flexible yet. Several examples of how different systems can be configured follow. In these examples a task driven peripheral interface such as might be used in a high performance CRT controller is shown.

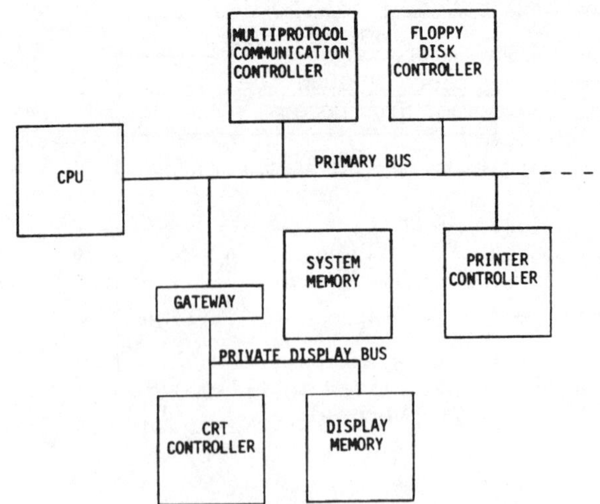

Fig. 9. Stand Alone Display with Private Display Memory

Fig. 8 shows a simple microcomputer system, for example a typical CRT terminal. The system consists of a CPU, memory, the CRT controller and a few more peripheral components such as keyboard and USART. This type of system has one bus through which all communications flow and so has a limited throughput.

To make more efficient use of the system bus, the high speed task driven peripheral component can be isolated from the main bus as shown in Fig. 9. The CRT controller has a private display memory shared only between it and the CPU. Unless an update of the display memory is needed, or a command is sent from the CPU, the CRT controller has total possession of the display memory while all other communication in the system flows through the main bus.

An even larger system, consisting of several CPUs, is shown in Fig. 10. In systems like this one, the high performance I/Os are isolated in subsystems, each controlled by a dedicated private CPU. A typical system like this would be a very high performance terminal where the full use of a CPU for the processing of graphics data is required.

V. Conclusions

In microcomputer systems with high speed peripherals such as high density CRT displays and high speed datacommunications, traditional CPU-Peripheral Component communication may no longer be sufficient. A Task Driven Interface, characterized by a high speed data transfer capability and dedicated intelligence, overcomes these limitations. Advantages of the Task Driven Interface can be summarized as follows:

- Efficient use of system bus
- Configuration flexibility
- Specialized intelligence, reducing CPU overhead.

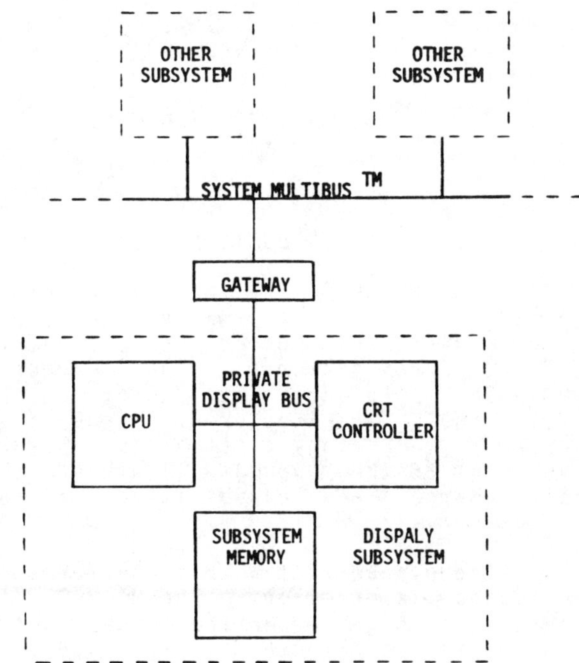

Fig. 10. Multiple Subsystems

MC68000 - Break Away From The Past

Jack W. Browne, Jr.
Manager, Applications Engineering
Motorola, Inc.
3501 Ed Bluestein Boulevard
Austin, Texas 78721

INTRODUCTION

The MC68000 is the first of a family of high performance processors whose design is based on a complete 32-bit architecture. The present MC68000 implements the subset of the full 68000 architecture allowed by current technology constraints. Future versions of the MC68000 will extend the performance and cabablities of the processor.

Acceptance of this high performance processor is excellent. The MC68000 is getting a high percentage of design-ins as shown in Figure 1. In addition Motorola has signed five other manufacturers--Hitachi, Rockwell, Thompson EFCIS, Signetics/Phillips and Mostek--to produce and design the MC68000 and its family of peripherals. Customers are the main beneficiaries as the licensing agreements are for "true second sources". In addition to a full set of production the masks, Motorola transfers all the technology, including the vital HMOS process, necessary for the second source to manufacture the family of microcomputer products. In return, the second source commits to design new additional products to extend the capabilities of the 68000 family.

MC68000 IS THE BEST 16-BIT MPU TODAY

The MC68000 is world acknowledged as the best 16-bit MPU available today. Its performance is 25 times better than that of the MC6800. The general purpose architecture satisfies market requirements for diverse applications. The MC68000 provides the user with seventeen 32-bit registers, 56 basic instructions, an efficient hardware implementation and extensive exception processing.

FIGURE 1 -: MC68000 DESIGN INS

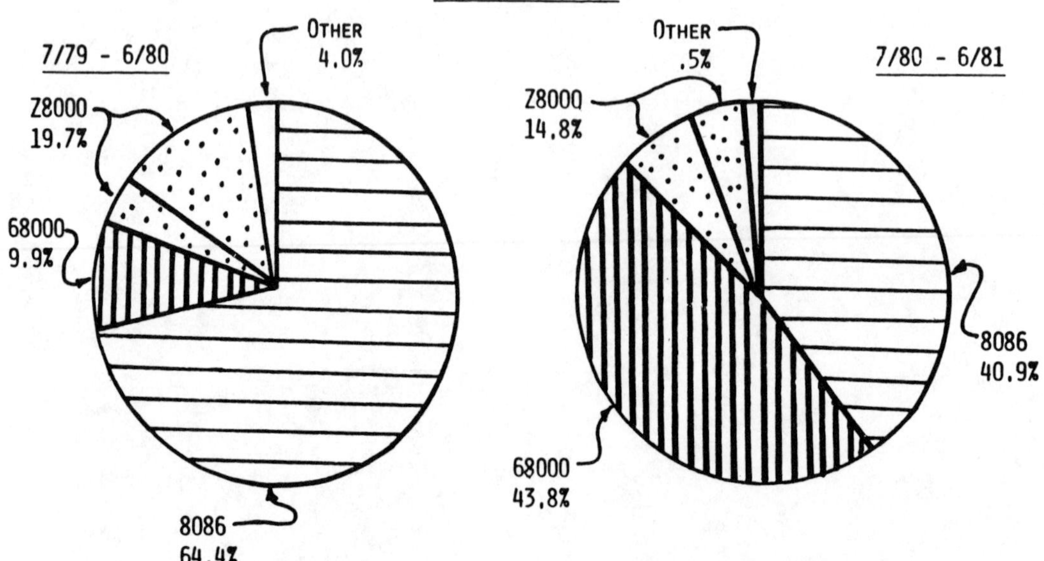

Reprinted with permission from *Wescon Conf. Rec.*, 1981, pp. 1.4.1-1.4.8.

Register Structure

Figure 2 shows the seventeen 32-bit registers, the 32-bit program counter and the 16-bit status register. The first eight registers (D0-D7) are used as data registers for byte (8-bit), word (16-bit) and long word (32-bit) operations. The second set of seven registers (A0-A6) and the system stack pointer (A7) may be used as software stack pointers and base address registers. In addition, the registers may be used for word and long word operations. All of the seventeen registers may be used as index registers.

The system stack is used by many instructions. The addressing modes allow the creation of user stack and queues. The system stack pointer is either the supervisor stack pointer (SSP) or the user stack pointer (USP), depending on the state of the S-bit in the status register. If the S-bit is set, indicating that the MPU is in the supervisor state, then the SSP is the active system stack pointer and the USP cannot be used or accessed. If the S-bit is low, indicating that the MPU is in the user state, then the USP is the active system stack pointer and the SSP cannot be referenced.

The 23-bit address bus provides the MPU with a memory addressing range of 16 Megabytes (16,777,216 bytes). This large address space coupled with the MC68451 Memory Management Unit, allows large modular programs to be developed and executed efficiently. The MC68000 allows program segment sizes to be determined by the application rather than forcing the designer to adopt an arbitrary segment size without regard to his individual requirements.

The status register, shown in Figure 3, may be considered as two bytes--the user byte and the system byte. The user byte contains five bits defining the overflow (V), zero (Z), negative (N), carry (C) and extend (X) condition codes. The system byte contains five bits. Three bits are used to define the current interrupt priority; any interrupt level higher than the current mask level will be recognized. (Note that level 7 interrupts are non-maskable--that is level 7 interrupts are always processed. Two additional bits indicate if the processor is in a trace (T) mode and/or in a supervisor (S) state. Ample space remains in the status register for future extensions of the M68000 Family.

FIGURE 2 : PROGRAMMING MODEL

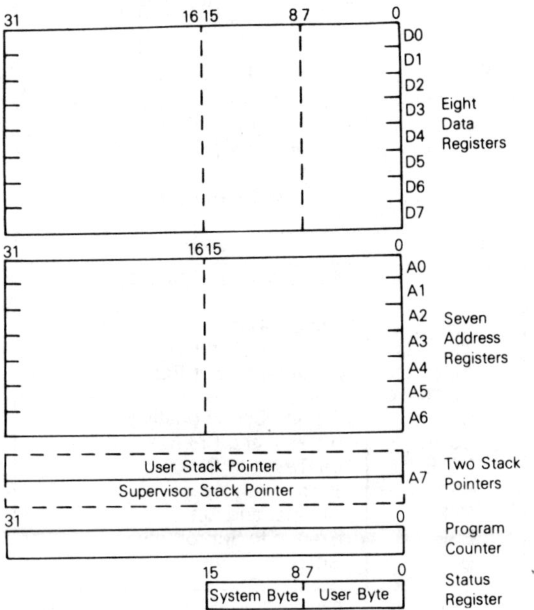

FIGURE 3 : STATUS REGISTER

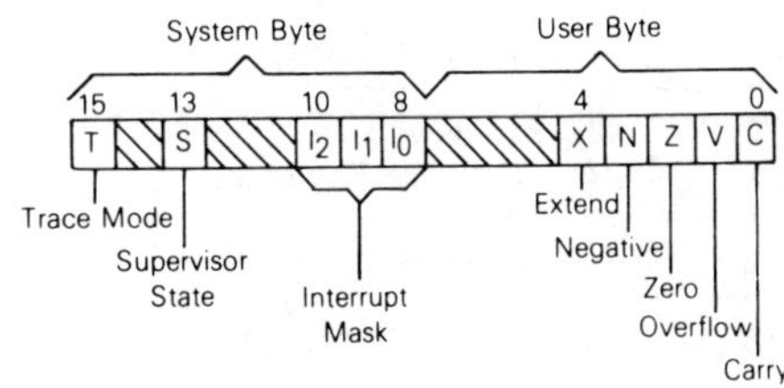

Instruction Set

The MC68000 instruction set was designed to minimize the number of mnemonics remembered by the programmer. To further reduce the programmer's burden, the addressing modes are orthogonal. During development of the processor, instruction useage studies reveiwed dynamic instructions in several major systems (IBM 360/370, DEC-10, PDP-11, Interdata 3200, etc.).

The resultant MC68000 instruction set, shown in Table 1, forms a set of programming tools that include all processor functions to perform data movement, integer arithmetic, logical operations, shift and rotate operations, bit manipulation, BCD operations and both program and system control. Some additional instructions are variations or subsets of these and appear in Table 2.

Each instruction, with few exceptions, operates on bytes, words and long words. The instruction vary from one to five words in length. The length of the instruction and the operation to be performed are specified by the first word of the instruction. This first word is called the operation word. The remaining words specify the operands. These words are either immediate operands of extensions to the effective address mode specified in the operation word.

Most instructions can use any of the 14 addressing modes listed in Table 3. These addressing modes consist of six basic types--register direct, register indirect, absolute, immediate, program counter relative and implied.

TABLE 1 : INSTRUCTION SET

Mnemonic	Description
ABCD	Add Decimal with Extend
ADD	Add
AND	Logical And
ASL	Arithmetic Shift Left
ASR	Arithmetic Shift Right
Bcc	Branch Conditionally
BCHG	Bit Test and Change
BCLR	Bit Test and Clear
BRA	Branch Always
BSET	Bit Test and Set
BSR	Branch to Subroutine
BTST	Bit Test
CHK	Check Register Against Bounds
CLR	Clear Operand
CMP	Compare
DBcc	Test Cond., Decrement and Branch
DIVS	Signed Divide
DIVU	Unsigned Divide
EOR	Exclusive Or
EXG	Exchange Registers
EXT	Sign Extend
JMP	Jump
JSR	Jump to Subroutine
LEA	Load Effective Address
LINK	Link Stack
LSL	Logical Shift Left
LSR	Logical Shift Right
MOVE	Move
MOVEM	Move Multiple Registers
MOVEP	Move Peripheral Data
MULS	Signed Multiply
MULU	Unsigned Multiply
NBCD	Negate Decimal with Extend
NEG	Negate
NOP	No Operation
NOT	One's Complement
OR	Logical Or
PEA	Push Effective Address
RESET	Reset External Devices
ROL	Rotate Left without Extend
ROR	Rotate Right without Extend
ROXL	Rotate Left with Extend
ROXR	Rotate Right with Extend
RTE	Return from Exception
RTR	Return and Restore
RTS	Return from Subroutine

TABLE 1 : INSTRUCTION SET (continued)

Mnemonic	Description
SBCD	Subtract Decimal with Extend
Scc	Set Conditional
STOP	Stop
SUB	Subtract
SWAP	Swap Data Register Halves
TAS	Test and Set Operand
TRAP	Trap
TRAPV	Trap on Overflow
TST	Test
UNLK	Unlink

TABLE 2 : ADDITIONAL INSTRUCTIONS

Instruction Type	Variation	Description
ADD	**ADD**	Add
	ADDA	Add Address
	ADDQ	Add Quick
	ADDI	Add Immediate
	ADDX	Add with Extend
AND	**AND**	Logical And
	ANDI	And Immediate
CMP	**CMP**	Compare
	CMPA	Compare Address
	CMPM	Compare Memory
	CMPI	Compare Immediate
EOR	**EOR**	Exclusive Or
	EORI	Exclusive Or Immediate
MOVE	**MOVE**	Move
	MOVEA	Move Address
	MOVEQ	Move Quick
	MOVE from SR	Move from Status Register
	MOVE to SR	Move to Status Register
	MOVE to CCR	Move to Condition Codes
	MOVE to USP	Move to User Stack Pointer
NEG	**NEG**	Negate
	NEGX	Negate with Extend
OR	**OR**	Logical Or
	ORI	Or Immediate
SUB	**SUB**	Subtract
	SUBA	Subtract Address
	SUBI	Subtract Immediate
	SUBQ	Subtract Quick
	SUBX	Subtract with Extend

The register indirect adddressing modes also have the capability to perform postincrementing, predecrementing, offsetting and indexing. The program counter relative mode may used in combination with indexing and offsetting.

Combining instruction types, data types and addressing modes, over 1000 useful instructions are provided. These instructions include signed and unsigned multiply and divide, "quick" arithmetic operations, BCD arithmetic and expanded operations (through traps).

Hardware Implementation

The MC68000 is an embodiment of several innovative concepts. Communication with memory (Note that I/O is memory mapped), occurs via a high performance non-multiplexed asynchronous address and data bus. The proprietary microcode of the MC68000 simplified the design and provides expandability of the MPU. Exception processing is used to guarantee the state of the machine at all times.

Figure 4 shows the MC68000 signal lines. Note the functional grouping:

address bus
data bus
asynchronous bus control
MC6800 peripheral control
processor status
bus arbitration
interrupt control
system control

The asynchronous bus structure gives the customer the flexibility to choose the access time required for the application thus optimizing both performance and cost. A non-multiplexed bus was chosen for the 30% throughput increase as opposed to a multiplexed address and data bus.

Figure 5 shows the read and write cycle timing for the MC68000. A basic MC68000 cycle is initiated by the rising edge of S2 which causes AS to fall. If DTACK is asserted prior to the falling edge of S4 no wait states are inserted. For a read cycle the falling edge of S6 strobes data into the MPU and terminates the bus cycle. During a write cycle the falling edge of S6 terminates the bus cycle.

The MC6800 peripheral control signals are used to interface

TABLE 3 : ADDRESSING MODES

Mode	Generation
Register Direct Addressing	
Data Register Direct	EA = Dn
Address Register Direct	EA = An
Absolute Data Addressing	
Absolute Short	EA = (Next Word)
Absolute Long	EA = (Next Two Words)
Program Counter Relative Addressing	
Relative with Offset	EA = (PC) + d_{16}
Relative with Index and Offset	EA = (PC) + (Xn) + d_8
Register Indirect Addressing	
Register Indirect	EA = (An)
Postincrement Register Indirect	EA = (An), An ← An + N
Predecrement Register Indirect	An ← An - N, EA = (An)
Register Indirect With Offset	EA = (An) + d_{16}
Indexed Register Indirect With Offset	EA = (An) + (Xn) + d_8
Immediate Data Addressing	
Immediate	DATA = Next Word(s)
Quick Immediate	Inherent Data
Implied Addressing	
Implied Register	EA = SR, USP, SP, PC

NOTES:
EA = Effective Address
An = Address Register
Dn = Data Register
Xn = Address or Data Register used as Index Register
SR = Status Register
PC = Program Counter
d_8 = Eight-bit Offset (displacement)
d_{16} = Sixteen-bit Offset (displacement)
N = 1 for Byte, 2 for Words and 4 for Long Words
( ) = Contents of
← = Replaces

FIGURE 4 : SIGNAL LINES

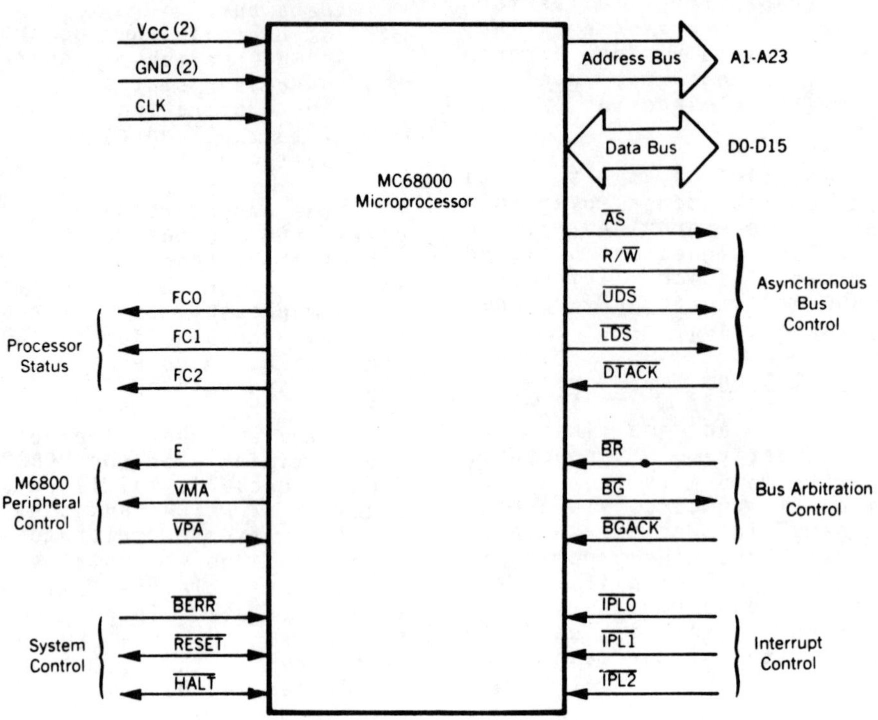

FIGURE 5 : CYCLE TIMING

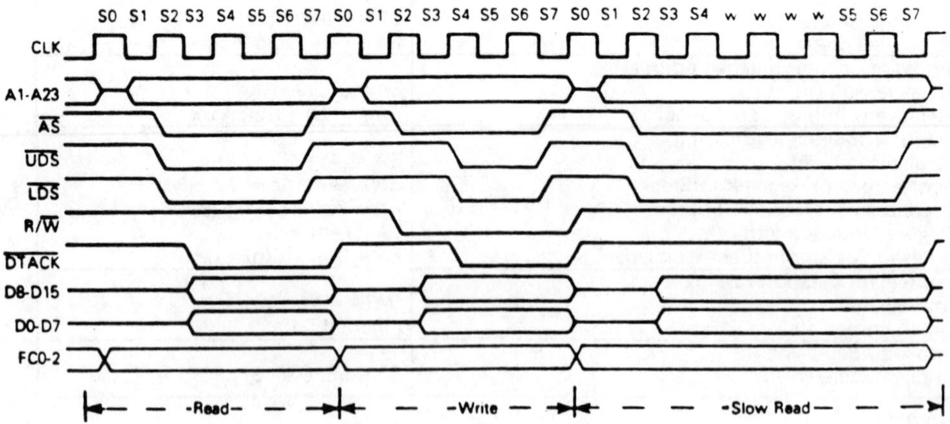

synchronous M6800 family peripherals to the asynchronous MC68000. Enable is gnerated by the MC68000 with a period of ten MC68000 clock periods (six clocks low; four clocks high). VPA is an input to the MC68000 which is generated by the decoder which generates the chip selects for the M6800 peripherals. After VPA is asserted, the MC68000 sychronizes its bus cycle to Enable and asserts VMA. VMA should be used to qualify the M6800 peripheral chip select to meet the required chip select setup requirements.

The processor status outputs indicate the state(user or supervisor) and the access currently underway (program or data). The MPU also uses the status outputs to indicate execution of an Interrupt Acknowledge (IACK) cycle.

Bus arbitration control is accomplished via a three line interface formed by Bus Request (BR), Bus Grant (BG) and Bus Grant Acknowledge (BGACK). In a system with multiple bus masters--processors or DMA devices--these signals determine which device will be the bus master device.

The three interrupt control input indicate the encoded priority level of the device requesting the interrupt. Level seven is the highest level interrupt and may not be masked while level zero indicates that no interrupts are present.

The three system control lines, RESET, HALT and BERR, are used to reset the processor and/or the system, halt the processor or indicate that a bus error has occurred. A bus cycle may be rerun if the original error was corrected.

The microcoded architecture simplifies design changes. These design changes are accomplished by changing the microcode ROM patterns. In a conventional MPU, the control logic is composed of random logic. A "simple" change may require many man-months for layout and checking before processing.

The exception processing allows the MC68000 to handle interrupts, address errors, unimplemented instructions and other commonly encountered glitches while mantaining absolute system integrity. Table 4 shows the exceptions and the memory location for the corresponding vector to the service routine.

The exception processing state is associated with interrupts, trap instuctions, tracing and other exceptional conditions detailed in Table 4. The exception may be generated internally by an instruction of by an unusual condition occuring during program execution. Exception processing provides an efficient context switch to enable the processor to handle unusual conditions without degrading system integrity.

PERFORMANCE

Performance is the key issue with the MC68000. Emphasis on performance has resulted in the introduction of a 10MHz version of the processor(in addition to the already existing 4MHz, 6MHz and 8MHz versions).

TABLE 4 : EXCEPTION VECTORS

Vector Number(s)	Address Dec	Address Hex	Address Space	Assignment
0	0	000	SP	Reset: Initial SSP
–	4	004	SP	Reset: Initial PC
2	8	008	SD	Bus Error
3	12	00C	SD	Address Error
4	16	010	SD	Illegal Instruction
5	20	014	SD	Zero Divide
6	24	018	SD	CHK Instruction
7	28	01C	SD	TRAPV Instruction
8	32	020	SD	Privilege Violation
9	36	024	SD	Trace
10	40	028	SD	Line 1010 Emulator
11	44	02C	SD	Line 1111 Emulator
12*	48	030	SD	(Unassigned, reserved)
13*	52	034	SD	(Unassigned, reserved)
14*	56	038	SD	(Unassigned, reserved)
15	60	03C	SD	Unitialized Interrupt Vector
16-23*	64	04C	SD	(Unassigned, reserved)
	95	05F		–
24	96	060	SD	Spurious Interrupt
25	100	064	SD	Level 1 Interrupt Autovector
26	104	068	SD	Level 2 Interrupt Autovector
27	108	06C	SD	Level 3 Interrupt Autovector
28	112	070	SD	Level 4 Interrupt Autovector
29	116	074	SD	Level 5 Interrupt Autovector
30	120	078	SD	Level 6 Interrupt Autovector
31	124	07C	SD	Level 7 Interrupt Autovector
32-47	128	080	SD	TRAP Instruction Vectors
	191	0BF		–
48-63*	192	0C0	SD	(Unassigned, reserved)
	255	0FF		–
64-255	256	100	SD	User Interrupt Vectors
	1023	3FF		–

*Vector numbers 12, 13, 14, 16 through 23 and 48 through 63 are reserved for future enhancements by Motorola. No user peripheral devices should be assigned these numbers.

Benchmark programs are used by many customers to evaluate the performance of the MC68000 in different applications. References 6 through 9 detail several benchmarks done by Motorola, Motorola's competitors and independent sources. Table 5 shows one set of benchmark results for typical system operations.

Future product definitions are best illustrated in Figure 6. These peripherals are intended to augment the standard M6800 peripheral functions. The MC68000 was designed to support the M6800 peripherals thus providing a unified system solution. Many other peripherals are emerging to fufill additional system requirements (hard disk controllers, operating system firmware, math coprocessor, etc.).

SUMMARY

The MC68000 is the basis of a high performance processor family intended for use through the 80's. This family of products will provide designers with the most advanced tools for their applications. Emphasis on the M68000 family is directed towards providing the highest performance possible.

References

1. M68000 Family Brochure, document M68KFM-1, (Austin, TX: Motorola Semiconductor Products, Inc., 1981).

2. MC68000 Article Reprints, (Austin, TX: Motorola Semiconductor Products, Inc., 1981).

3. MC68000 Advanced Information Data Sheet, (Austin, Tx: Motorola Semiconductor Products, Inc.,1981)

4. MC68000 User's Manual, Second Edition, document MC68000UM(AD2),(Austin, Tx: Motorola Semiconductor Products, Inc., 1980).

5. Stan Groves, The Inter-Relationship Between Access Time and Clock Rate in an MC68000 System, document EB-83, (Austin, Tx: Motorola Semiconductor Products, Inc., 1980).

6. The MC68000 Competitive Benchmarks, (Austin, Tx: Motorola Semiconductor Products, Inc., 1981).

7. Christopher Titus, Phd. ed., 16-bit Microprocessor Handbook, (Howard W. Sams and Company, 1980).

8. V. P. Nelson and H. T. Nagle, Jr., "Digital Filtering Performance Comparison of 16-bit Microcomputer", (IEEE Micro, Feb 1981).

9. Robert Grappel and Jack Hemenway, " A tale of four uPs: Benchmarks quantify performance", (Boston, MA: Cahner Publishing, EDN, April 1, 1981).

TABLE 5 : BENCHMARK RESULTS

Code		Ratio Z/M	Z8001 (6 MHz)	MC68000 (10 MHz)	8086-1 (10 MHz)	Ratio I/M
64-Bit Binary Addition	Time	1.58	14.50	9.20	19.70	2.14
	Lines	1.50	6	4	9	2.25
	Bytes	1.50	18	12	25	2.08
64-Bit Binary Negate	Time	2.99	14.33	4.80	18.20	3.79
	Lines	5.00	10	2	11	5.50
	Bytes	4.00	24	6	30	5.00
16-Bit BCD Addition	Time	2.88	75.00	26.00	63.50	2.44
	Lines	2.00	12	6	10	1.67
	Bytes	1.40	28	20	22	1.10
32-Bit Array Scan	Time	2.20	246.16	112.00	264.60	2.36
	Lines	1.75	7	4	9	2.25
	Bytes	1.29	18	14	18	1.29
String Translation	Time	1.91	7338	3850	5606	1.46
	Lines	0.80	8	10	13	1.30
	Bytes	0.81	26	32	27	0.84

Z8001 — 6 MHz, MC68000 — 10 MHz, 8086-1 — 10 MHz

FIGURE 6 : MC68000 FAMILY

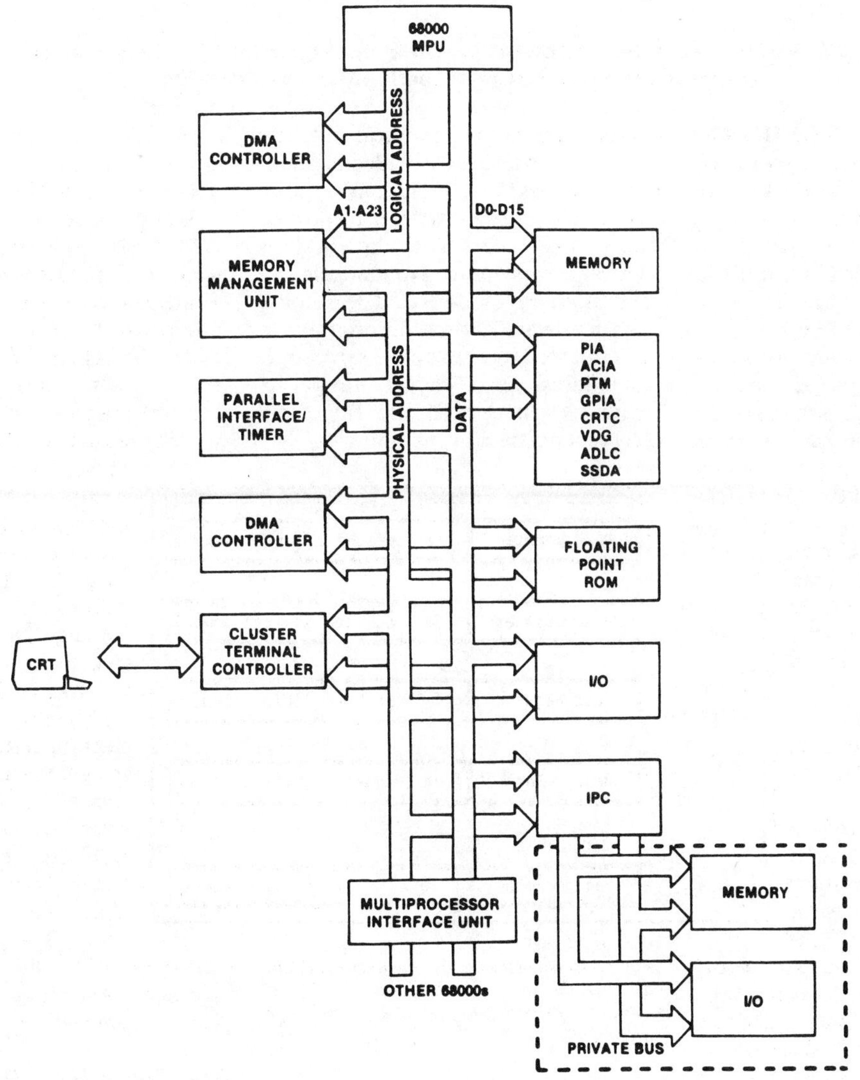

The M68451 memory management unit

J. F. Stockton **describes the M68451 memory management unit, discussing its concepts, features, functions, performance and benefits**

The microprocessors of the MC68000 generation will be used in applications that microprocessors typically have not been in previously.

This new generation of microprocessors will be used in multi-user and multi-tasking systems that place heavy demands on memory management support that has not necessarily been included in previous microprocessor families. Some specific requirements of the hardware to support memory management are the ability to translate addresses for dynamic memory allocation, to support dynamic address relocation, and to provide memory protection. To provide these features, the MC68451 memory management unit is being introduced as the latest member of the MC68000 family.

When a task is started, it is not always known exactly how much memory that the task will require, so while the task is running, the operating system will have to allocate memory for the task. Since the allocation does not take place until the task is running, the allocation is dynamic since the memory that the operating system gives the task might not be located in contiguous memory. The processor must support address translation, so that the physical memory may be mapped to appear to be contiguous in logical memory.

When a task is suspended for long periods of time, and a request is made for more space in primary storage — frequently to make room for the new program — the task that has been suspended the longest will be swapped out to disk until it is again ready to run. Later, when ready to run again, it will be reloaded into primary memory, and then be restarted since the probability of being able to reload the task at exactly the same physical address that it was previously loaded is small, the task will probably have to be reloaded at some different address. Since this occurs fairly often, it is desirable to support dynamic address allocation in hardware. The relocation hardware allows the program to be relocated at exactly the same logical address as it was at previously, while not necessarily at the same physical address in memory.

The author is with Motorola Semiconductor, Texas, USA.

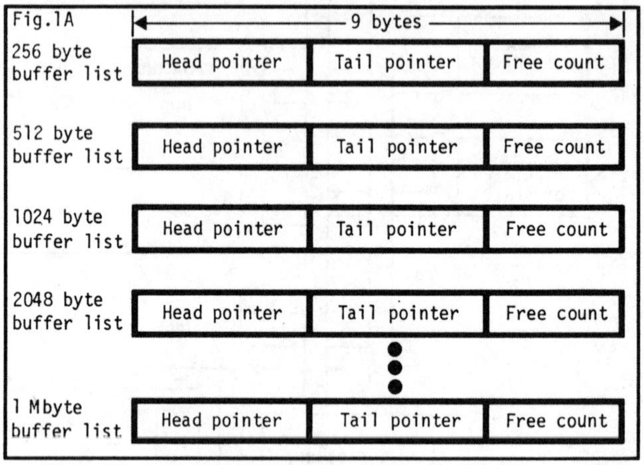

Fig.1A

	← 9 bytes →		
256 byte buffer list	Head pointer	Tail pointer	Free count
512 byte buffer list	Head pointer	Tail pointer	Free count
1024 byte buffer list	Head pointer	Tail pointer	Free count
2048 byte buffer list	Head pointer	Tail pointer	Free count
⋮		⋮	
1 Mbyte buffer list	Head pointer	Tail pointer	Free count

Fig. 1a. Arrangement of memory available lists for the binary buddy system. (Fig. 1b shows the information contained in the buffer descriptors.)

One of the most important requirements of a multiprocessing system is the need of system security. It is important that one task does not inadvertently wipe out another task or interfere with its operation. Illegal memory operations by both the processor, and peripherals such as DMA devices should be aborted before the contents of memory are changed. This sort of protection is particularly important in real time process control applications where there is more at stake than just cpu time.

It is also important that one task is not able to access another task's data. Some mechanism has to be available to let some processes have access to privileged data, while keeping other tasks out. This is particularly important when dealing in applications involving "sensitive" information such as bank account balances and credit information.

While it is necessary to ensure privacy of data, sometimes there is the need to share data with other tasks. Sometimes it is desirable to allow the other task to only read the contents of the buffer, and thus the need for read-only protection. Read only protection is necessary for applications where user tasks might want to access a system resource, like a real time clock, but should not be able to change them. The read-only provision allows for this level of protection in hardware, thus saving a call to the operating system.

One other important aspect about resource protection is that it is necessary to guarantee proper operation of the operating system itself. If some other task can alter the operating systems tables, then there is no way to guarantee its operation. The protection features of the MC68451 memory management unit allow for all of these kinds of protection.

The Binary Buddy System

The Buddy System is an algorithm for dynamically allocating and deallocating storage that is both fast and efficient. The first application of the Buddy System was described in a paper by Knowlton (4). Where Bell Laboratories used this storage algorithm in their "L-Sixth" computer. Since then, there have been numerous other articles in the trade journals about this topic (other refs.). The basic concept of the Buddy System is that when memory is requested, a search is made of the memory buffer available tables to see if an appropriately sized buffer is available. If one is not, then a search is made for the next larger sized buffer. If a larger buffer is found, then it is split into two pieces, one being allocated to the requesting

Reprinted with permission from *Electron. Eng.*, vol. 54, pp. 59, 63, 64, 66, 69, 73, May 1982.

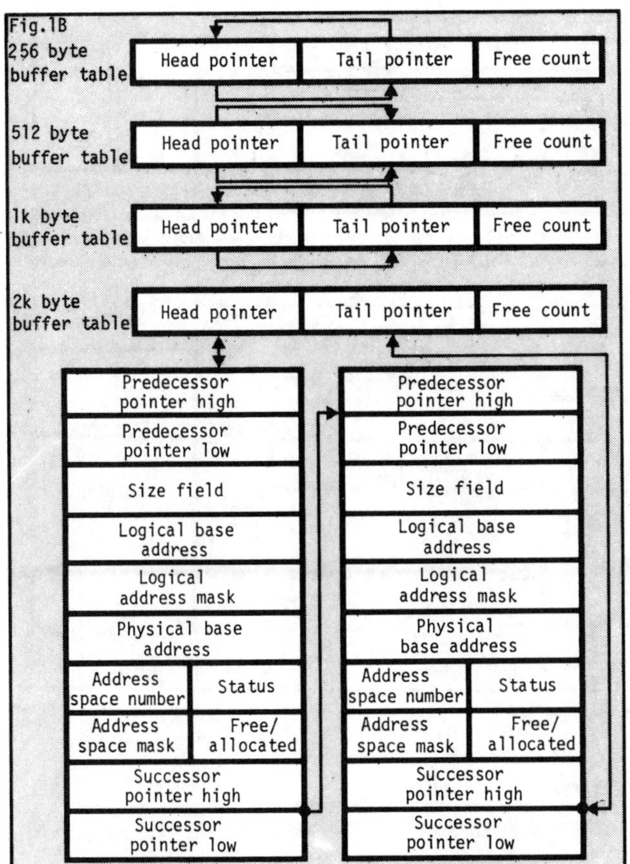

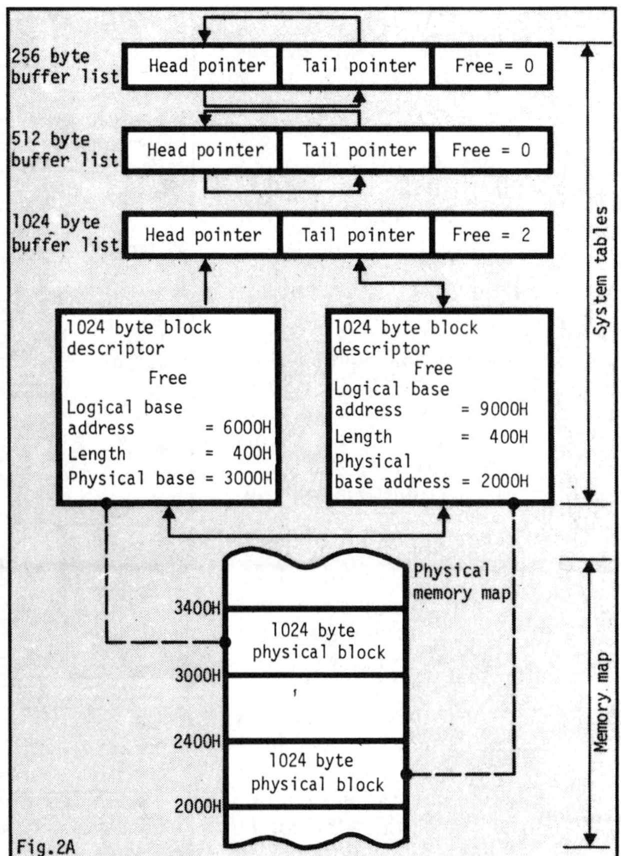

Fig. 1b. Structure of buffer descriptors. In this example there are no free 256, 512 or 1024 byte buffers, but there are two 2K buffers that have been defined. These buffers might or might not be free.

Fig. 2a. "before" — there are no 256 byte buffers that are free to satisfy a 256 byte request.

task, and the other being placed on the memory-available list. If a larger buffer is not found, the process continues until either the largest sized buffer is split into multiple pieces and the request is honoured, or the request is put onto a queue to wait until sufficient memory is released to honor the request.

When a task is done with a memory block, it returns the block back, and if the Buddy that corresponds to that block is available, they are joined back together to make the next larger sized block.

The conceptual layout of the memory available tables is shown in Fig. 1. In this application, a separate table is maintained for each possible size buffer that might be requested. Possible buffer sizes are typically limited to a reasonable range to simplify operation of the storage algorithm. A typical range that is well supported by the MC68451 MMU is 256-bytes to 256 k-bytes. The MC68451 MMU will support buffers up to the entire address space of the MC68000, but as discussed by Knuth (1), empirical data suggests that the buffer size should be limited to about one-tenth of the total memory space available, (16 megabytes in the case of the MC68000).

Each entry in these memory available tables consists of two links (successor and predecessor pointers), and sometimes a free buffer count (to lower the search time when no buffers are available).

In Fig. 2a, there are currently no 256-byte or 512-byte buffers currently available. The respective predecessor and successor pointers point to themselves to indicate a full list, and the free buffer count is set to zero. Fig. 2b shows what happens after a 256-byte buffer request. The first thing that happens is that the memory available table for 256-byte buffers is scanned and found to be empty. Then the 512-byte buffer table is also scanned, and also found to be empty. The routine continues to scan the next higher binary sized buffer table until an entry is found. In this example, a 1024-byte buffer is available. When the buffer is found, it is removed from the 1024-byte buffer available list, and is then split into halves. The 512-byte halve is added onto the 512-byte buffer available list, and the remaining 512-byte buffer is again split to honor the request for a 256-byte buffer. One half of the 512-byte buffer is allocated for the request. And the other 256-byte piece is added to the 256-byte buffer availability list. The resulting structure is shown in Fig. 2b. Note that to add a buffer onto a list, it is simply a matter of rewriting four pointers a free/allocated bit, and a size field.

Since the buffer sizes are powers of two, the Binary Buddy System naturally operates most efficiently when buffer requests are in powers of two. When they are not, requests must be treated as if they were larger than they actually are, so more memory will be allocated to a task than was requested. The results of all requests between 257 and 512 bytes being treated as a request for 512 bytes is that on the average somewhere between 1.3 and 1.5 times as much memory will be requested as is actually being used (1).

The inefficiency caused by the binary restrictions of buffer size is measured as the fraction of memory allocated over and beyond what was actually requested. Since this waste occurs inside a buffer, it is called internal fractioning, and is the prime cause of inefficiency in the Buddy System. Studies performed (2), show that a modification of the Binary Buddy System. (The Fibonacci System) can reduce this internal fractioning from an average of 38 per cent excess memory to 25 percent excess, at the expense of a slighty more complicated allocation algorithm. Fig. 3 illustrates this inefficiency.

There is another kind of inefficiency caused by the way that Buddies are defined, which means that although two buffers of a given size exist and could be combined to create a buffer that was large enough to satisfy a request, they might not be Buddies and cannot be combined. Figure 4 shows an example of a memory map illustrating external fractioning. Since this fractioning occurs external to the buffers, it is caused external fractioning. This typically is not as much of a problem as internal fractioning, since sooner or later enough memory will be freed up to honor the request. Figure 5 shows a typical memory map that would result from usage of the Buddy system. Note that the entire map is considered to be one buffer, and that it is broken into two equal sized pieces that are each Buddies. These pieces are in turn broken into even smaller pieces and so. Note also that two available buffers might exist on the same level (being of equal size), and yet cannot be combined since they come from different parents.

Algorithms

The algorithm for allocating a block of memory is relatively straightforward. The routine starts by checking to see if a segment size is available within a power of two of the request.

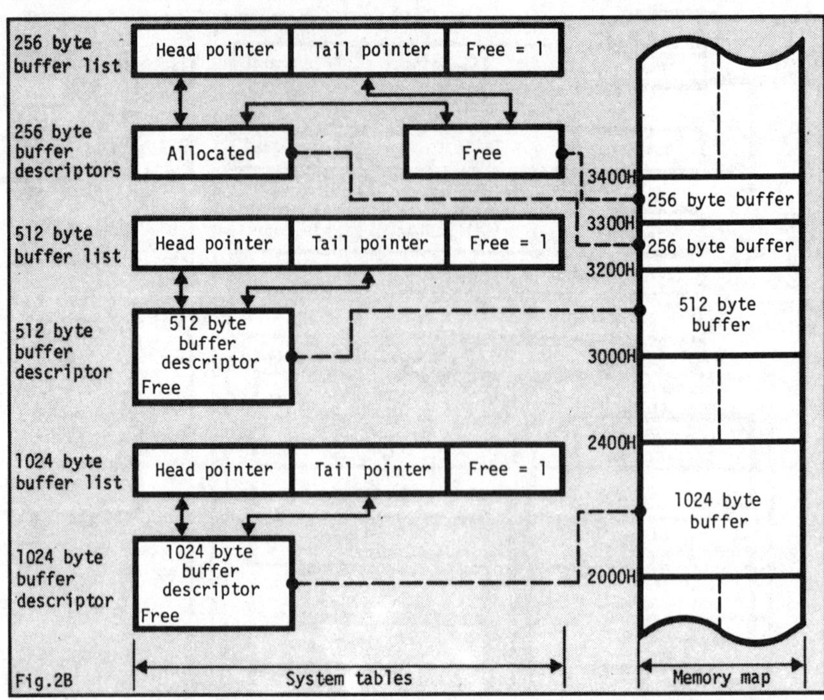

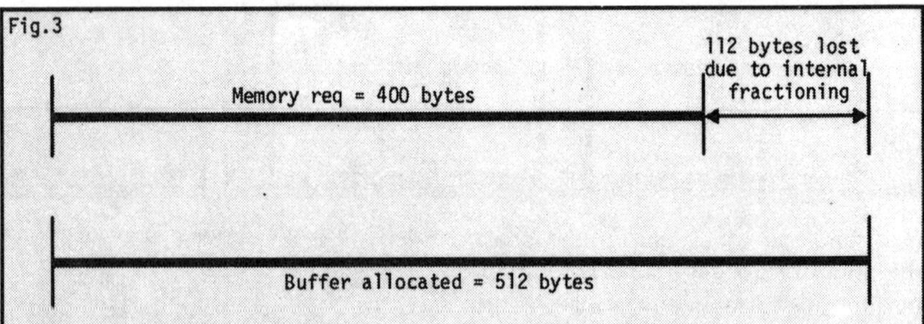

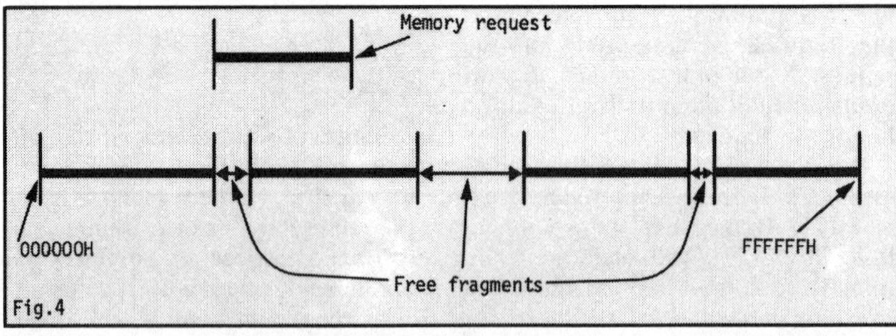

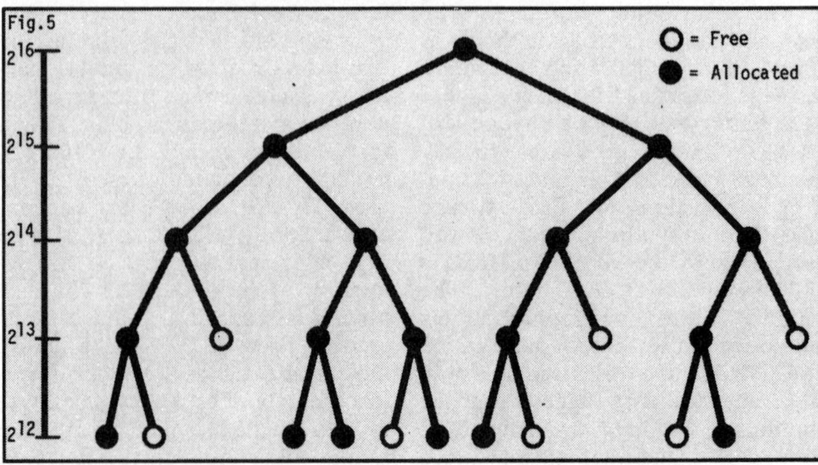

Fig. 2b. "after" — a 1024 byte buffer was split into a 512 byte and 2 256 byte buffers to satisfy the request for a 256 byte buffer.

Fig. 3. Internal fractioning.

Fig. 4. External fractioning.

Fig. 5. Buddy system memory mapping showing external fragmentation.

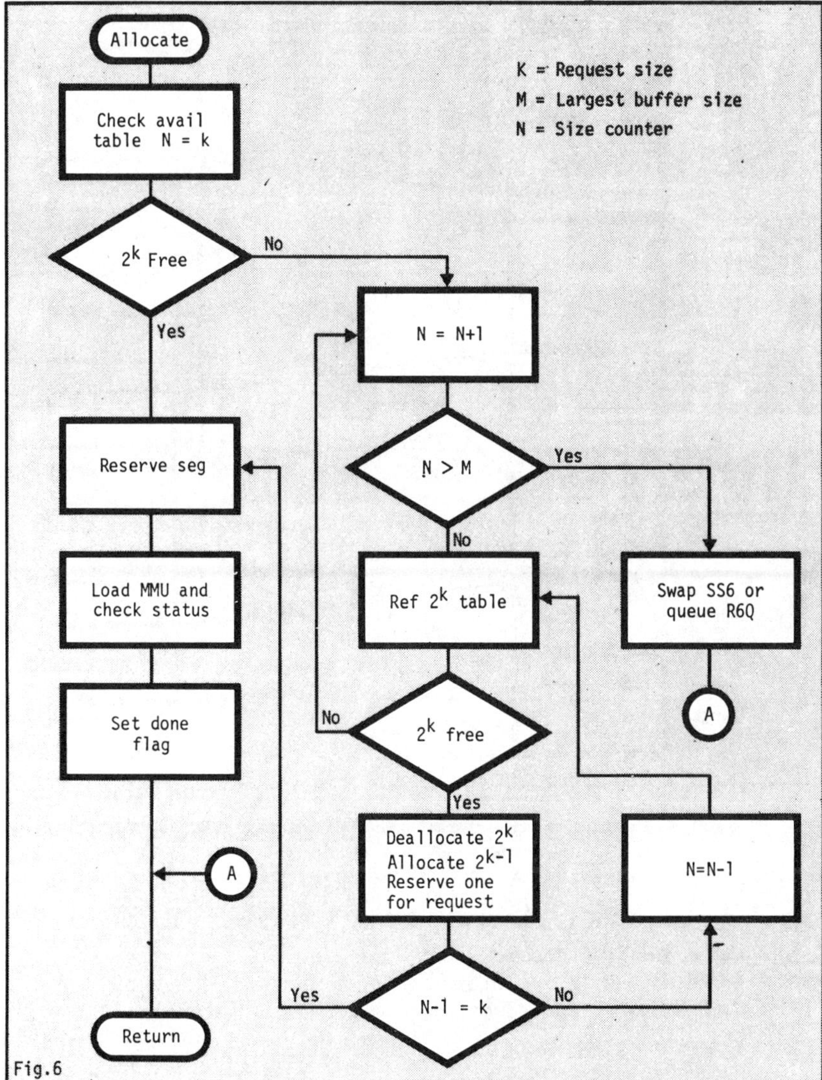

Fig. 6. Buffer request.

Fig. 7. Recombination flow chart.

If so, the segment is removed from the available list, and tagged as being in use at this time. A descriptor is loaded into the memory management unit to describe the segment if a segment is not available, then the tables of the next larger size segments are scanned to check for an available segment. If the process continues and no segment is available to fill the request, then the operation of checking the available list for the next higher size segment continues. If the maximum segment size is reached, which typically is one-tenth the total memory size. Then the requesting task must be suspended until memory becomes available, or other descriptors must be swapped out to make room for the new request.

If a larger segment is available, then it is broken into two pieces, a left half and a right half. One half is used to honor the request, so it is tagged and entered into the MMU, and the other segment is entered into the available list of the smaller size segment. Figure 6 is a flow chart for this operation. Note that if the first power of two segment size was not available, then the next one up, if available, would be broken into three pieces, one quarter for the request, one quarter sized segment, and a half sized segment would then be available for other requests.

The algorithm for deallocation is also relatively simple, and is illustrated in Fig. 7. When a buffer is returned to the pool, the segment descriptor in the MMU is immediately freed up, and the segment is added to the available table. Also, its buddy is checked for availability. If both buddies are available, then they are both removed from the available list, and recombined to become a larger segment. This recombination prevents the accumulation of a large number of small segments that tend to choke the system, so system performance is maintained.

Systems concepts

The concepts of unique address spaces, fast context switching, a simple address translation mechanism, and virtual memory support were important to the design of the memory management unit. These concepts are discussed here in more detail.

Address space concept

The MC68000 provides four lines indicating what the type of bus cycle is that is currently executing. These

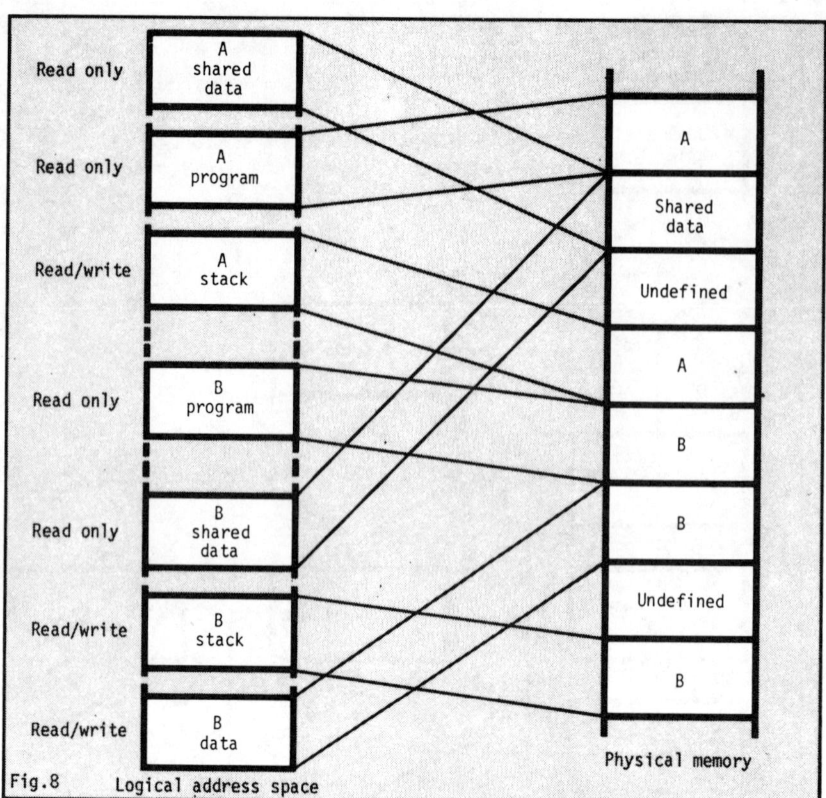

Fig. 8. Logical to physical address mapping.

lines are the three function code lines (FC0-FC2) and the bus grant acknowledge line (BGACK). They specify if the processor is in the user or supervisor mode — if it is making an instruction fetch or a data fetch, and if the processor has control of the bus, or if a slave device such as a DMA controller currently has control of the bus. Each of these conditions specifies a unique address space and thus the function codes and BGACK are looked at as being address space modifiers. The memory management unit uses these to provide a fast context switch, and to allow user data areas to be shared without necessarily forcing the program areas to be shared also.

Table 1 shows the address space correspondence table within the memory management unit. The table is basically a 16 byte long table. The function codes associated with each memory cycle are used as an address in the table where they effectively point to a tag that will be used for that address reference. The table supports 8 processor fetch types and 8 DMA or other bus master fetch types. The primary use for the address space correspondence table is to speed up context switches by using the tags in an associative look-up scheme.

Fast context switching

The MMU allows for a fast context switch by changing a program and a data descriptor tag in the address space correspondence table of the MMU. These bytes are used on a cycle basis to determine which segment descriptors should be considered for an address and privilege match. This is possible since each segment descriptor has a tag associated with it that is considered for a match only when the tags match. By changing two bytes in the address space correspondence table, it is possible to have a completely different set of segment descriptors used for address translations. This makes for a very fast context switch, at the expense of having all of the segment descriptors resident at the same time. (The memory management unit context switch time = 2 write cycles at 625 nanoseconds each = 1.25 microseconds.) This turns out to not be a limitation since each MMU has 32 segment descriptors, and up to 8 MMUs can be configured in a system. The obvious advantage of lowering the time taken for context switching is that the processor can spend less time taking care of overhead and have more time left over to run user tasks.

Translation mechanism

The concept of address translation allows the programmer to think in terms of logical memory allocations rather than just physical memory terms. The memory management unit translates logical addresses into physical addresses. So that a program that was assembled to run at 2000 HEX could actually be located at 2A00 Hex, and still run. The advantage of this is that programs can be swapped out to disk, and not have to be restored to exactly the same physical address that they were at before. In smaller systems, a programmer can assemble his programs to run at any convenient location, and if he reconfigures his system he can relate them without reassembling them. Fig. 8 shows an example of the mapping of logical segments to physical memory.

The memory management unit can map both program and data segments so that they can be either shared or private segments. Since the function codes are used in the mapping function, the segments can be execute only segments by making them available to the processor only during instruction fetches. Segments

Address correspondence table

BGACK	FC2	FC1	FC0	
0	0	0	0	Reserved
0	0	0	1	User Data
0	0	1	0	User program
0	0	1	1	Reserved
0	1	0	0	Reserved
0	1	0	1	Supervisor data
0	1	1	0	Supervisor program
0	1	1	1	Interrupt acknowledge
1	0	0	0	DMA/other bus masters
1	0	0	1	DMA/other bus masters
1	0	1	0	DMA/other bus masters
1	0	1	1	DMA/other bus masters
1	1	0	0	DMA/other bus masters
1	1	0	1	DMA/other bus masters
1	1	1	0	DMA/other bus masters
1	1	1	1	DMA/other bus masters

can also be defined so that an interrupt will be generated upon access to the segment, thus allowing for dynamic stack allocation.

Address translation takes place in two stages, consisting of an address range and privilege comparison, and then the actual driving out of the physical address onto the address bus. The first stage actually consists of three parts, the first being the matching of tags between the address space correspondence table and the tag associated with each segment descriptor.

Virtual memory support

Future versions of the MC68000 will support virtual memory, and in designing the peripherals, it makes sense to include the things that will be required in the future now. Things such as the ability to indicate that a page fault has taken place, through the fault line, and to indicate that a segment has been written into, or that it has not been used in some period of time, are all important to virtual memory systems. □

References

1 Knuth, Donald E. The Art of Computer Programming, Vol. 1. Second printing, Addison-Wesley, Reading, Mass. 1968. pp. 435-455.

2. Hirschberg, Daniel S. A Class of Dynamic Memory Allocation Algorithms, Communications of the ACM, October 1973, Volume 16, Number 10, pp.615-618.

3. Peterson, James L and Norman, Theodore A. Buddy Systems, Communications of the ACM, June 1977, Volume 20, Number 6. pp.421-431.

4. Knowlton, Kenneth C. A Fast Storage Allocator, Communications of the ACM, October 1965, Volume 8, Number 10, pp.623-625.

5. Taylor, Mitchell B. Efficient Memory Allocation with the Buddy Algorithm, Motorola, November 1981.

6. Purdom, Paul W. and Stigler, Stephen M. Statistical properties of the Buddy System, Journal of The Association for Computing Machinery, Volume 17, Number 4, October 1970, pp.683-697.

16-bit-μP peripheral ICs provide datacomm support

A programmable communications interface, a multiprotocol communications controller and a polynomial generator/checker ease data transfers between and within μP-based systems.

Dennis R Snyder, Motorola Inc

Individually or in combination, three 68000-μP peripheral chips support virtually all standard data-communications protocols. Additionally, they integrate many functions not previously available in hardware (thus reducing software overhead), and they allow you to efficiently use pc-board area.

Specifically, the chips include

- The MC68661/MC2661 enhanced programmable communications interface (EPCI), which furnishes either asynchronous or synchronous operation
- The MC68652/MC2652 multiprotocol communications controller (MPCC), which furnishes only synchronous operation
- The MC68653/MC2653 polynomial generator/checker (PGC), which provides full error checking with such chips as the EPCI or the MPCC.

Modernizing the USART

The MC68661/MC2661 furnishes all the functions of first-generation USARTs but requires less μP intervention and software overhead. It provides asynchronous and synchronous byte-control-protocol (BCP) support and furnishes on-chip features such as baud-rate generation and modem control.

In operation, the system μP initializes the EPCI to either Asynchronous or BCP mode and then sets the parameters for EPCI data-link communications. For Asynchronous-mode operation, these parameters tailor the device to the UART at the other end of the link—the EPCI's Mode and Command registers permit programming of variable character lengths (five to eight bits); optional odd, even or no parity bit; and one, 1½ or two stop bits.

Moreover, you can independently select data-clock sources for transmit and receive operations. For example, although the transmitter always operates at the clock rate of the internal baud-rate generator (BRG), Isochronous-mode operation (see **box,** "Observing the protocol") maintains an asynchronous character format while allowing a clock applied to the chip's TxC input to transfer data.

You have additional options with receive clocking. In asynchronous operation, the receive clock operates at 16 times the programmed BRG-set data rate. In isochronous operation, an external clock on the RxC input brings in the data. You can program the EPCI to accept this clock at one, 16, or 64 times the data rate.

Operating in Synchronous mode, the EPCI achieves improvements in Bisync (or IBM BCP) capability by automatically providing in hardware such features as DLE (Data Link Escape) searching, stuffing or stripping. (DLEs serve to preface control characters, differentiating them from other text.) In its Transparent mode, it compares all serial data characters with the DLE-register contents and strips and does not transmit to the μP any received DLE or DLE-SYN1 characters. (However, only the first DLE character of a DLE-DLE pair gets stripped.) In its Nontransparent mode, the chip strips only SYN1 or SYN1-SYN2 characters from the incoming data.

Additionally, the EPCI can handle transmitter underruns, which plague most synchronous protocols. Aided by double buffering, the chip's transmitter provides automatic line fill of SYN or DLE-SYN characters to prevent this problem. Furthermore, the double buffering helps prevent overruns on the received data stream. And if they should occur, the chip detects and reports them.

Additional EPCI Synchronous-mode features include internal or external clock generation, external jam synchronization, selectable character lengths (five to eight bits) and odd-, even- or no-parity options.

Making the connection

In a typical interface circuit (**Fig 1a**), the EPCI's data bus connects to the 68000's lower eight bits. The EPCI's A_0 and A_1 lines connect to the 68000's A_1 and A_2 lines to accommodate word-boundary addressing.

Normal address decoding generates the EPCI's Chip Enable (CE) signal with a half-clock-cycle delay

Reprinted with permission from *EDN*, vol. 55, pp. 181–187, 189, 190, Feb. 17, 1982.

Double buffering in the MC68661 minimizes underrun problems

inserted to allow for data-setup time. The 74LS161 adds an Inhibit, preventing CE reassertion until the end of the chip-enable period (t_{CE}), and prevents certain μP instructions (such as MOVEP) from accessing consecutive addresses on consecutive bus cycles.

The chip-enable period equals 600 msec; thus, the 74LS161 must generate a 5-cycle (625-nsec) or 8-cycle (640-nsec) delay for 8- and 12.5-MHz 68000s, respectively. The first rising clock edge after CE assertion generates the 68000's Data Transfer Acknowledge (DTACK) signal, causing the μP to insert one Wait state in the bus cycle. Inhibit assertion delays both DTACK and CE, and the μP then inserts more Wait states in the bus cycle. **Fig 1b** shows these timing relationships in detail.

MPCC suits synchronous operation

The MC68652/MC2652 multiprotocol communications controller serves systems requiring only synchronous communication. Available in two versions that accommodate data rates to 1M or 2M bps, it supports both

Observing the protocol

In the Asynchronous/Isochronous format **(figure),** a frame is one character long. (A frame is defined as one message unit that includes the data and required overhead support.) The start bit is a MARK-to-SPACE transition that must be at least half a bit period long. The parity bit (odd or even) is optional, and the stop bit(s) can span one, 1½ or two bit periods.

Byte-control-protocol (BCP) message frames are usually termed blocks. An elementary block might consist of only one or two sync characters and data, formatted as 5- to 8-bit characters. BCP error-checking schemes generally employ some form of cyclic redundancy check (CRC), although a longitudinal redundancy check (LRC) can also serve.

The frame can include several special control characters and data-field subdivisions between the sync characters and the error-checking field (BCC). The **figure** illustrates a typical Bisync frame. Control information might be sent independently without text/control-character transmission.

Unique flag characters define frame limits in bit-oriented protocols (BOPs). Essentially, a BOP uses three unique control characters—Flag, Abort and Go Ahead. All have at least six consecutive ONEs—no other bit configuration in a frame can have more than five.

The Address field (consisting of one or more 8-bit characters) follows the opening flag and determines the secondary-station address as either sender or receiver. The control field (also based on an 8-bit character) comes next and defines whether the frame contains information transfers, commands or responses. An optional information field follows; it can be any length.

The frame-check sequence (FCS)—16 bits long and based on a cyclic redundancy check (CRC) of all frame data—is the final field. In a BOP, error checking involves division of frame data by the CRC-CCITT polynomial; the remainder gets used as the FCS.

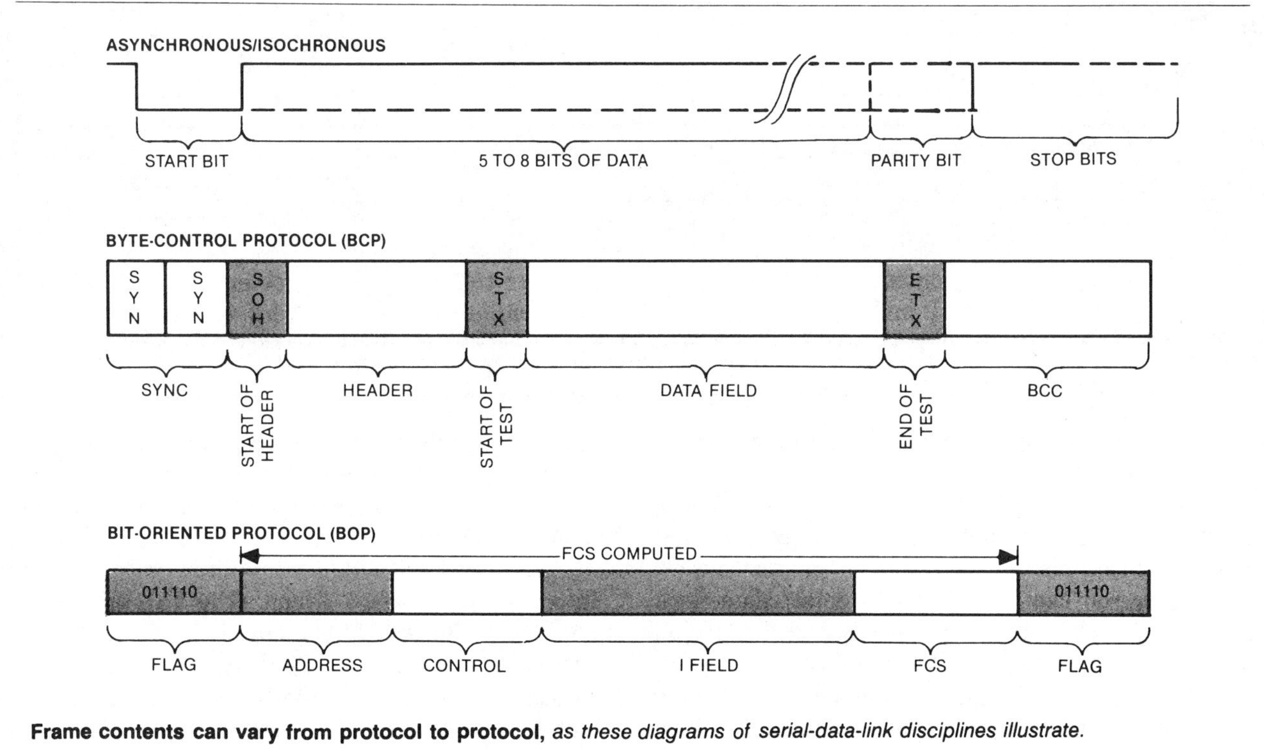

Frame contents can vary from protocol to protocol, *as these diagrams of serial-data-link disciplines illustrate.*

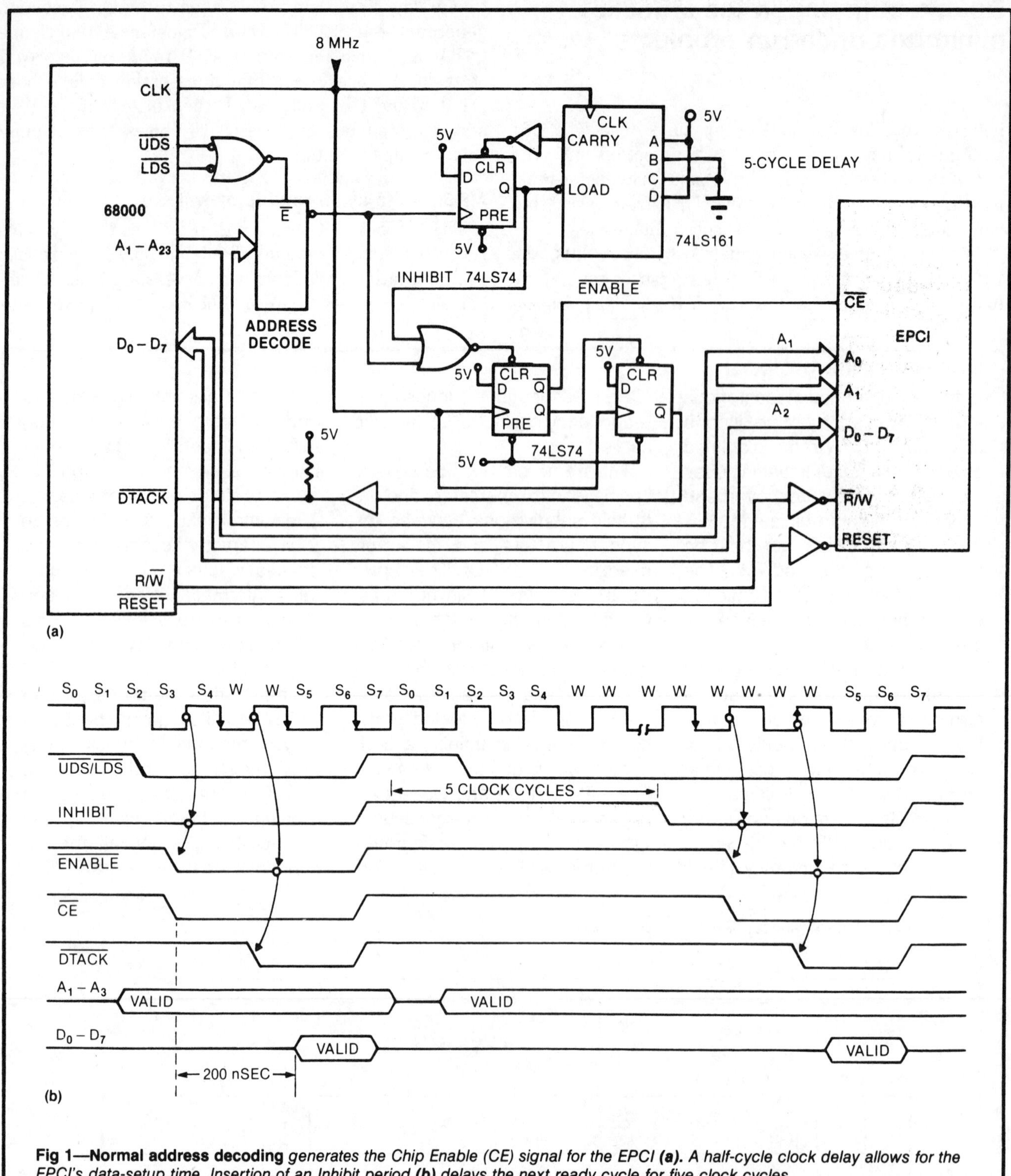

Fig 1—Normal address decoding *generates the Chip Enable (CE) signal for the EPCI* ***(a)****. A half-cycle clock delay allows for the EPCI's data-setup time. Insertion of an Inhibit period* ***(b)*** *delays the next ready cycle for five clock cycles.*

BOP (bit-oriented protocol) and BCP disciplines on an 8- or 16-bit bus.

The MPCC supports BCP in a manner similar to the EPCI. To start, you initialize it with the desired data-link parameters. It then searches for two successive sync characters that match the 5- to 8-bit characters stored in its Sync/Address register. If you specify sync stripping, the MPCC presents the next nonsync character to the μP; in Nonstripping mode, it presents the first character following the second sync character to the μP. The MPCC continues inputting, deserializing and presenting received data until the μP determines the end of input and resets the receiver.

The final two message bytes contain the CRC field. The MPCC can utilize CRC-16 or CRC-CCITT polynomials, although CRC-16 is most often associated with BCP. It also transparently handles odd or even Vertical Redundancy Checks (VRC=parity).

In a CRC or VRC error-checking mode, the MPCC's Receiver Status register reflects the μP error status at the end of a message. (Note that because all received data characters accumulate in the CRC checker, use of

Bit-oriented protocols mandate bit-by-bit data handling

IBM's Bisync protocol requires external CRC generation and checking.)

BCP operation starts with serialization and transmission, on the TxSO pin, of the two 5- to 8-bit sync characters stored in the Sync/Address register. The µP must then supply data to the MPCC each time the Transmitter Buffer register empties. Otherwise, a transmitter underrun results, asserting TxU (transmitter underrun) and TERR (transmitter error) and sending either Mark or Sync idle-line-fill characters. This character string is incompatible with the Bisync protocol; thus, you must ensure that the transmitter doesn't underrun when supporting Bisync.

An in-depth look at the EPCI

Major MC68661/MC2661 sections include the transmitter, receiver, timing, modem control, operation control and SYN/DLE control **(figure).** µP-to-EPCI interface occurs via an 8-bit data bus (and associated control lines), with all data exchanges passing through the data-bus buffer. Transmit and Receive registers provide double buffering between the µP and serial lines, freeing the µP for tasks other than EPCI servicing.

The EPCI provides various modem-interface control lines to establish a data link. Data Set Ready (DSR) and Data Carrier Detect (DCD) line information (including any state changes) gets stored in the Status register. The modem control also inputs Clear to Set (CTS) signals for use in controlling the TxD output. Request to Send (RTS) and Data Terminal Ready (DTR) are also available at the modem control.

If a system develops problems, the EPCI can provide diagnostic self help using two hardware capabilities—local loopback and remote loopback. Local loopback checks the µP and EPCI by connecting the transmitter and receiver serial-data and clock lines together and passing data through the EPCI. In remote loopback, the data line and part of the EPCI are tested by inputting and assembling data in the receiver and transferring the data to the transmitter holding register for retransmission.

The three MC68661/MC2661 versions each provide 16 selectable baud rates. A and B units require 4.9152-MHz TTL clock inputs and accommodate 50- to 19.2k-bps and 45.5- to 38.4k-bps baud rates, respectively. C versions operate with a 5.0688-MHz clock and have the same baud-rate range as A models (the baud rates aren't identical, however).

For more information on MC68661/MC2661 chips, **Circle No 722**

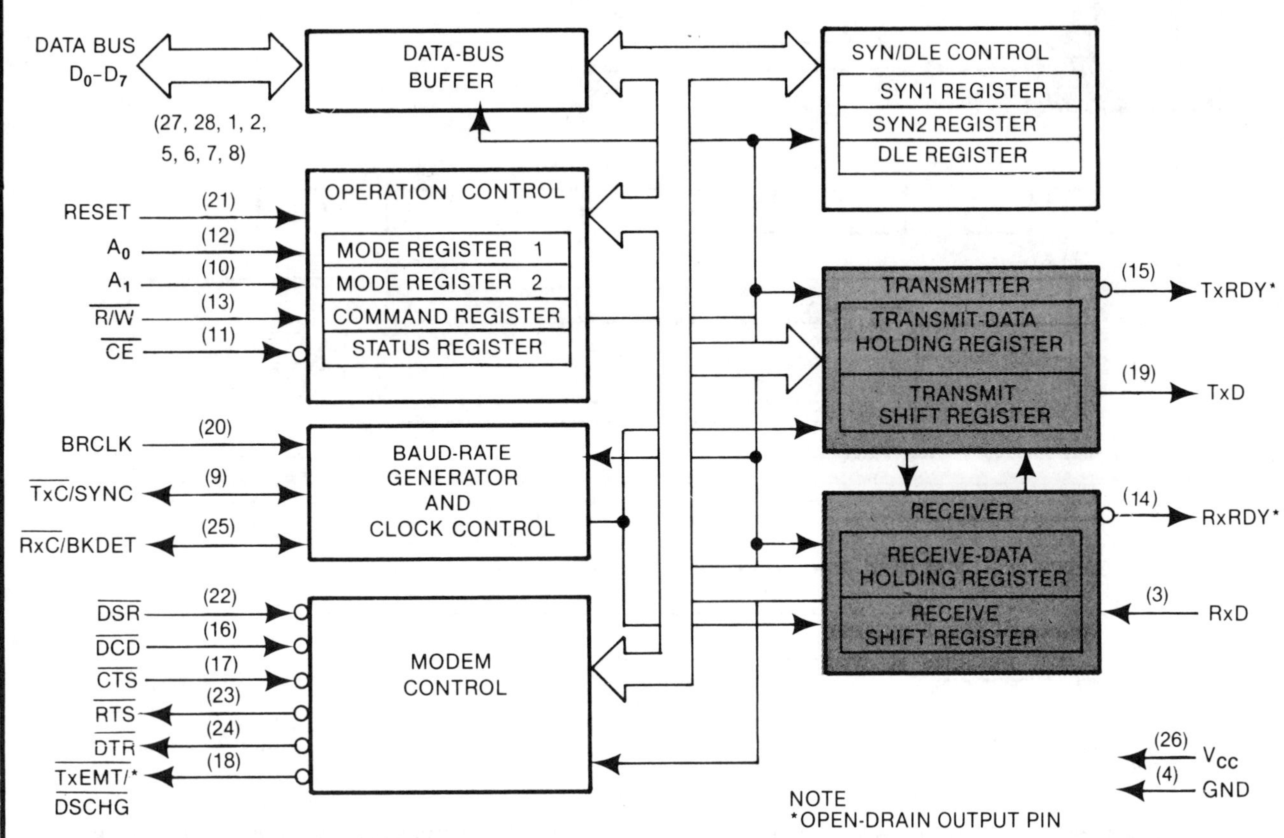

To free the µP for tasks other than EPCI servicing, *the MC68661/MC2661's Transmit and Receive registers feature double buffering between the µP and serial lines.*

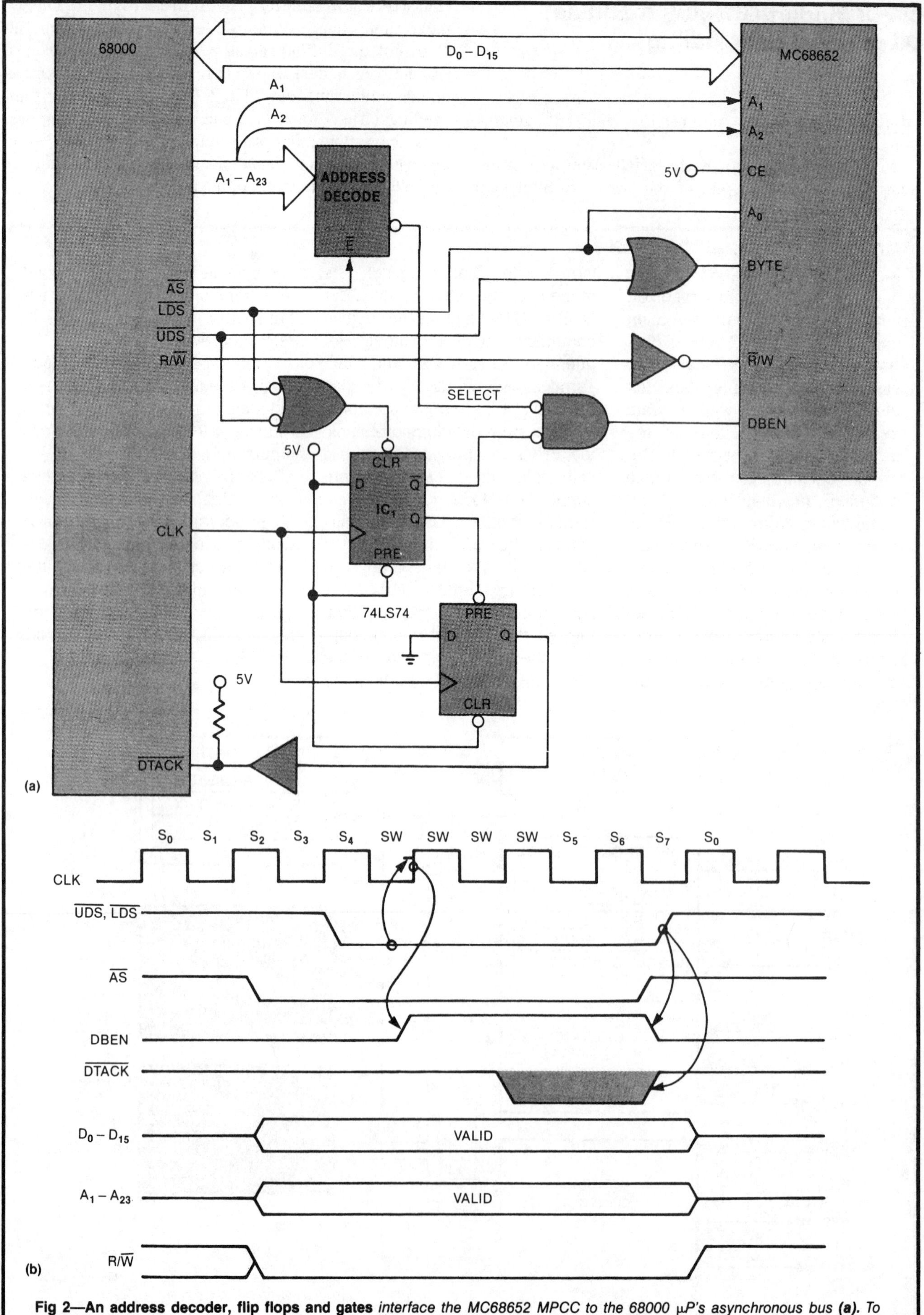

Fig 2—An address decoder, flip flops and gates *interface the MC68652 MPCC to the 68000 μP's asynchronous bus* ***(a).*** *To guarantee the MPCC access time, the μP inserts four Wait states by asserting DTAC on the first rising clock edge after assertion of DBEN* ***(b).***

EPCI modem-interface lines ease serial-data-link setup

As its name implies, a bit-oriented protocol (BOP) requires that you handle the serial data stream one bit at a time. During Receive operation, the MPCC continuously monitors the incoming data for the special Flag, Abort or GA (go ahead) 8-bit BOP characters. Between frame-delimiting flags, it inserts the required ZERO after five ONEs when receiving.

The first byte following the flag contains the secondary-station address. In the secondary mode, the MPCC compares this byte with the address-register contents, and if a match occurs, it passes the address byte and the remainder of the frame on to the μP. If no match occurs, the MPCC discards the byte, ignores the rest of the frame and doesn't interrupt the μP.

Some BOPs allow address- and control-field extensions of more than one byte. In these cases, software handles address comparisons beyond the first byte.

The Information (I) field follows the Control field, and the MPCC can dynamically change the received character length from one to eight bits to match the incoming data stream. If the final I-field character is shorter than eight bits, the MPCC transfers it to the μP along with status bits that reflect its actual length.

The final two frame bytes following the I field contain the frame-check sequence (FCS). After recognizing the final frame flag, the MPCC examines this FCS. All frame data passes through the CRC-CCITT polynomial

Inside the MPCC

The MC68652/MC2652 are each organized into three main functional blocks: μP interface, transmitter and receiver. All share a 16-bit internal bus **(figure)** that you can convert to eight bits by asserting the Byte input. Because this bus is buffered, the μP needn't service the MPCC immediately after the transmission or reception of a data character, freeing the μP to perform other tasks.

If problems develop, you can easily test the μP-to-MPCC link by asserting the Maintenance Mode (MM) input, which connects the MPCC's Transmitter output to its Receiver input. The μP can thus compare data sent to the MPCC with data coming back from the MPCC and verify both interconnections and MPCC synchronous functions.

Built-in CRC-16 or CRC-CCITT polynomical generators facilitate error checking. All data following the two sync characters passes through the CRC generator. When the μP signals the MPCC to send the last data character, the MPCC transmits the 2-byte CRC field.

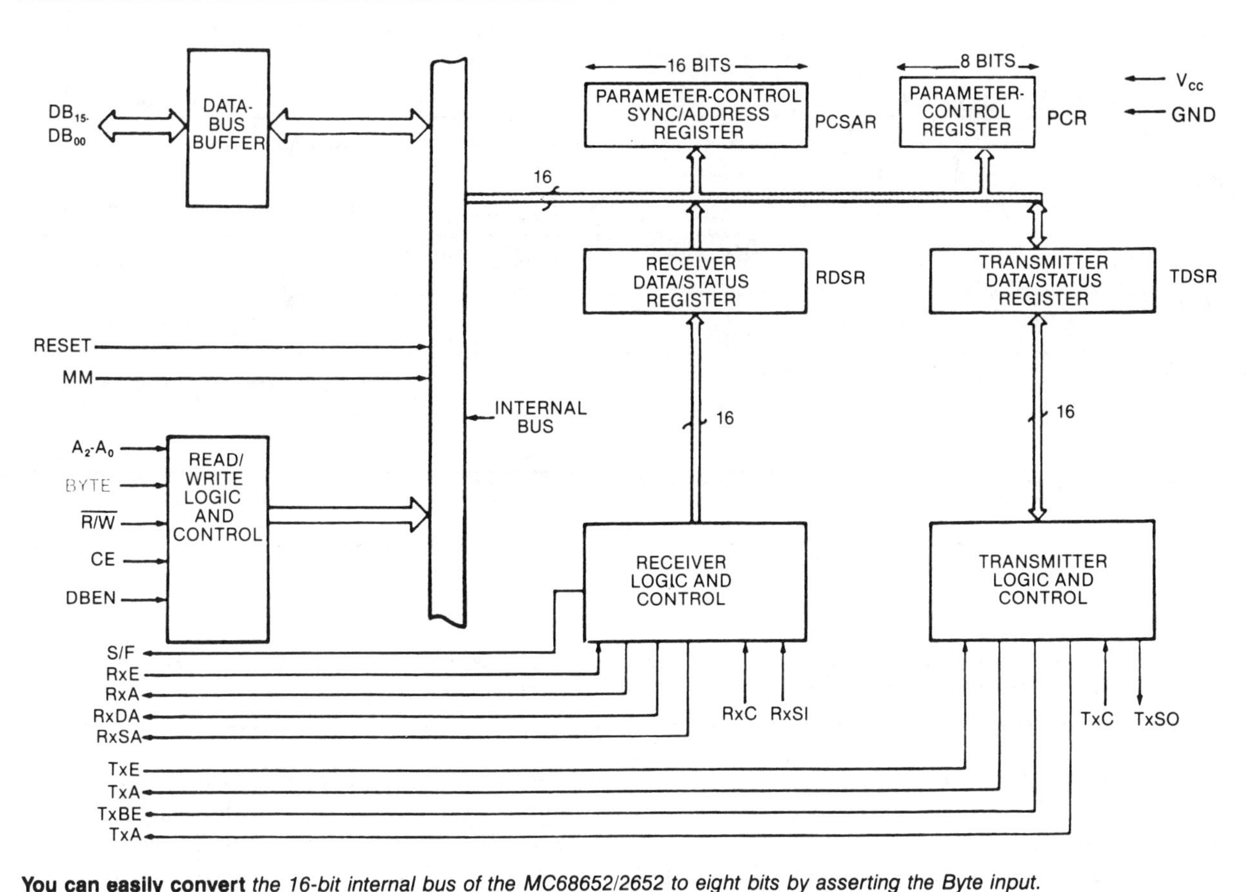

You can easily convert *the 16-bit internal bus of the MC68652/2652 to eight bits by asserting the Byte input.*

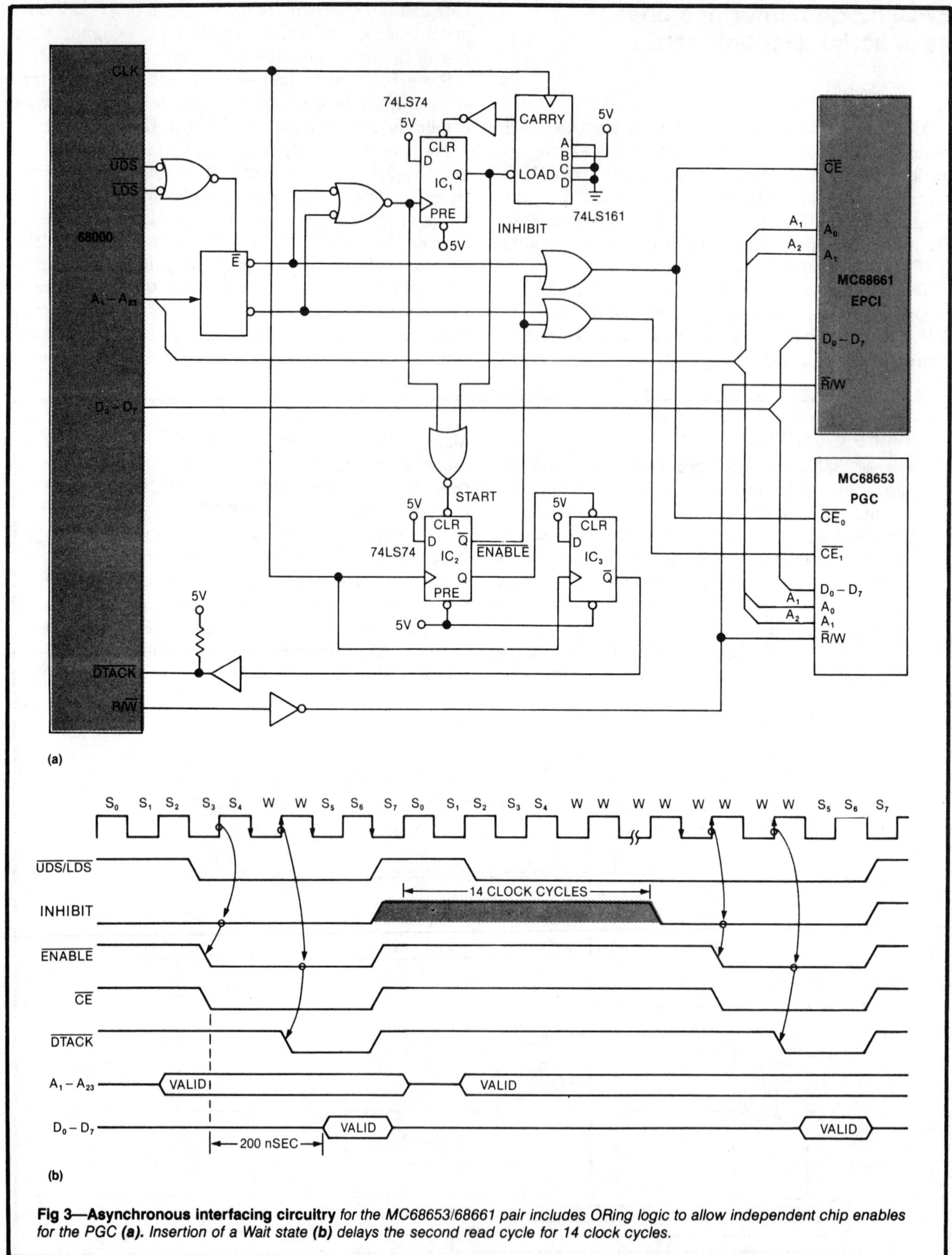

Fig 3—Asynchronous interfacing circuitry *for the MC68653/68661 pair includes ORing logic to allow independent chip enables for the PGC* ***(a)****. Insertion of a Wait state* ***(b)*** *delays the second read cycle for 14 clock cycles.*

checker. If the received frame contains an error, the accumulated CRC-CCITT code is incorrect, and the appropriate error status gets set.

When programming the MPCC, you have the options of presetting the CRC-CCITT bits to ONEs or ZEROs, or choosing CRC-16 preset ZEROs. If at any time during the frame reception the MPCC inputs a series of seven ONEs, the remainder of the frame gets ignored and the Received Abort/Go-Ahead bit is set. The MPCC also provides support for a Loop mode by

The MC68652 MPCC suits synchronous-only system needs

providing GA-character detection.

BOP transmission follows the same format as BOP reception. When the μP sets the Transmit Start of Message bit, the MPCC sends a Flag character. Contiguous flags get sent until the μP loads the first message character into the MPCC. It serializes this character, checks for five consecutive ONEs and inserts a ZERO into the data stream to ensure that no data character matches the Flag, Abort or GA control characters. FCS gets updated after each character transmission.

If underrun occurs, the MPCC automatically starts sending Abort or Flag characters (depending on which one signifies an Idle character). At the end of the I field, the residual character length of one to eight bits

A detailed look at the PGC

Major MC68653/MC2653 functions include the data-bus buffer, BCC and parity generators, operation control, a 3-byte DLE ROM, character register and 128×2 character-class array **(figure).** A 68000 μP interfaces with the PGC's internal 8-bit data bus via the data-bus buffer.

Before system operation, the μP configures the PGC to the desired operating mode, error-checking/generating scheme and character properties. It accomplishes this initialization by programming the Mode register to define the block-check-character (BCC) polynomial; odd, even or no parity; Receive or Transmit mode; and type of accumulation mode.

After master reset, the character-class array must always be programmed to define the class associated with each of the possible 128 7-bit characters. The Command register selects the four character classes to control BCC accumulation in Bisync mode, detect control characters and set the control-character-detect bits in the Status register.

The Command register also controls the control-character-detect interrupt enables, plus VRC (Vertical Redundancy Check) and BCC error-interrupt enables. Several 1-time commands serve to start accumulation, clear the BCC register and provide master reset.

The error polynomial uses three DLE characters stored in ROM for DLE-character detection. DLE comparison, character-class array and BCC/VRC generation share the Character register for input and isolation from the internal bus.

The BCC/VRC function computes the three polynomials used to generate and update BCC accumulation on a character-by-character basis. CRC generation involves the division of a character's binary value by the selected CRC-16 or CRC-12 polynomial. The remainder's two 6-bit (CRC-12) or 8-bit (CRC-16) characters serve as the BCC and are stored in the upper and lower BCC registers.

Any BCC or VRC errors detected in a received message set a corresponding bit in the Status register. During transmission, BCC-register contents serve as the end-of-message BCC.

For more information on MC68653/MC2653 chips, **Circle No 724.**

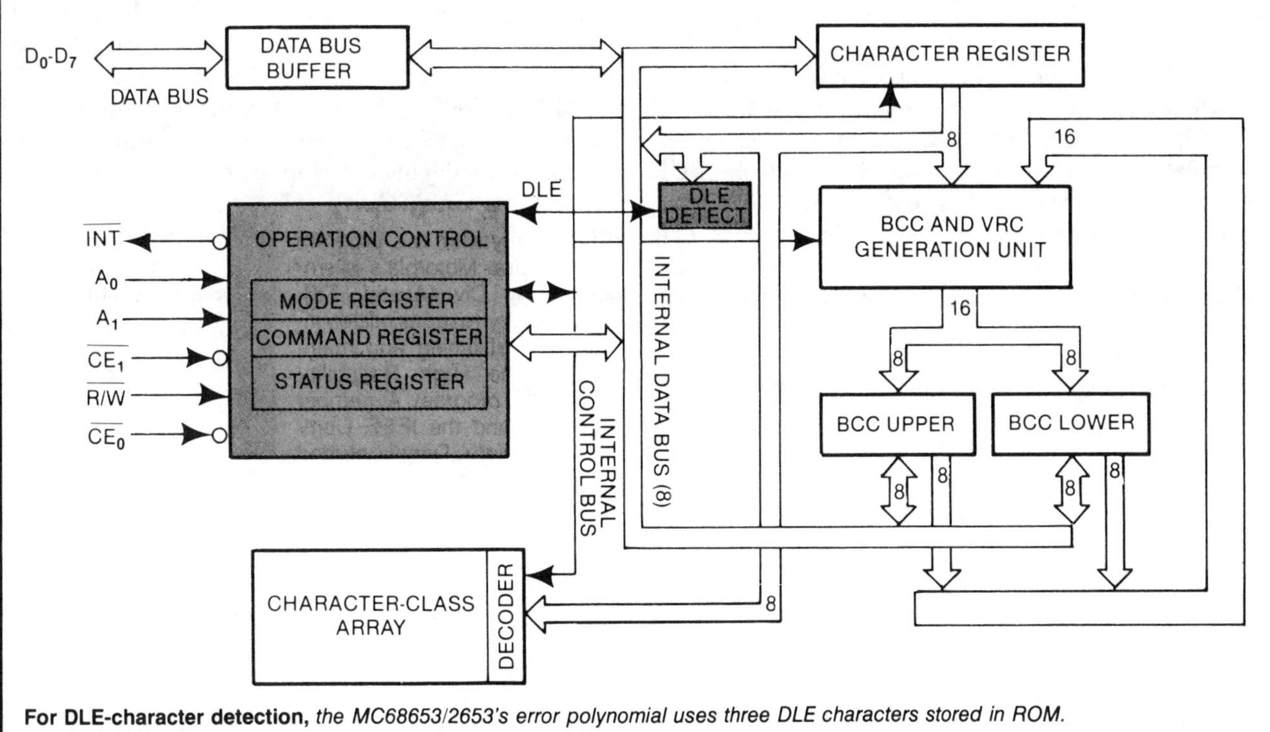

For DLE-character detection, *the MC68653/2653's error polynomial uses three DLE characters stored in ROM.*

can be written along with the final character to be transmitted. The MPCC then transmits the final character's remaining data bits, the FCS and the frame's final flag.

Configuring a datacomm system

Fig 2a illustrates the interfacing of the MPCC to the 68000's asynchronous bus, including connection of the 16-bit data bus and R/W, address and decode lines. UDS, LDS and Byte connections determine byte or word transfers. If both UDS and LDS are LOW, the Byte input is also LOW, allowing the 68000 to make word transfers. But if either UDS or LDS is HIGH, Byte is also HIGH, and byte transfers occur. LDS ties to the MPCC's A_0 input to select either its upper or lower byte.

Examining the MPCC/68000 timing **(Fig 2b)**, you can see that the cycle starts with the μP asserting AS (Address Strobe), indicating the presence of a valid address on the address bus. Flip flop IC_1 asserts DBEN (Data Bus Enable) on the first rising clock edge after assertion of UDS or LDS, satisfying MPCC setup-time requirements by ensuring a 1-clock-cycle delay between the generation of the addresses and DBEN. Asserting DTACK on the first rising clock edge after DBEN assertion forces the μP to insert four Wait states to guarantee the MPCC access time.

Add full error-checking support

The MC68653/MC2653 polynomical generator/checker serves applications requiring the error-checking capability of BCPs (such as Bisync) with special control characters. It can support one or more BCP serial or parallel data-link controllers. Monitoring the parallel data-character transfer between the μP and the BCP data-link controller, the PGC performs block-check accumulation or checking of the three major BCP error-checking codes—LRC-8, CRC-16 and CRC-12.

The PGC supports both Bisync Transparent and Normal modes with either automatic or single-character-accumulation operation. It accommodates 1- or 2-character sequence detection to support the transparent Bisync mode.

After initialization and selection of Receive or Transmit mode, the PGC is ready for character accumulation. Operation is similar in both modes until the end of the message. Here, the PGC makes an error check in Receive mode and outputs a block-check-character (BCC) string in Transmit mode. During the message transfer, characters load into the Character register. Whether or not they accumulate depends on the current accumulation mode.

Four BCC accumulation modes exist; two support Bisync. In Bisync Normal mode, the register accumulates all characters except those in the SYN/Bisync class. In Transparent Bisync mode, you can embed in the message data that resembles control characters.

You accomplish this operation by designating a special Data Link Escape (DLE) character. The PGC excludes accumulation of the first DLE of a DLE-nonsync sequence (the nonsync character can be in any format, even another DLE). It also excludes all DLE-SYN pairs not preceded by an odd number of DLE characters.

Receipt of a BTC/SC (Block Terminate Character/ Search Character) lets the character register accumulate the following one or two characters (depending on whether the BCC mode is LRC-8 or CRC-12/16) and causes the PGC to automatically stop accumulation until given a Restart command.

The PGC also supports Automatic and Single Accumulate modes. In the first, it accumulates all characters loaded into the character register. BTC/SC and SSC (Second Search Character) detection are enabled, but the Bisync mode's automatic accumulation termination doesn't occur. In Single Accumulate mode, the μP can selectively accumulate characters or accumulate additional characters that other modes exclude.

Final system integration

Fig 3a shows the 68000 asynchronously interfacing with an MC68653/MC68661 pair (**Fig 3b** shows the timing for two consecutive read cycles). The MC68653/ MC68661 support circuits are similar to those serving the MC68661/MC2661 EPCI; the primary difference is the additional address decoding and ORing circuitry that permit independent chip enables to the PGC.

Asserting the PGC's CEO input accesses the Character register to allow BCC accumulation. The PGC's CEO input ties to the EPCI's CE input to permit simultaneous data transfers between both chips. CE_1, the other PGC enable, accesses the Status, Command, Mode and BCC registers and has an address code different from that of the EPCI's data-transfer address. **EDN**

With the aid of features such as 32-bit architecture and slave processors, this group of microprocessors addresses a wide range of system applications.

The NS16000 Family—Advances in Architecture and Hardware

Subhash Bal, Asher Kaminker, Yoav Lavi, Abraham Menachem, Zvi Soha

National Semiconductor

When LSI/MOS chips were first developed, it was possible for designers to place approximately 1000 active elements on a single chip. Now, ten years later, the number of active elements per chip has risen to over 100,000. As we enter the second decade of LSI/MOS technology, applications for its use are continually expanding as the computational power of newly developed 16- and 32-bit microprocessors approaches that of mainframe computers. In short, microprocessor designers have their work cut out for them.

Currently, software development efforts are becoming responsible for ever larger shares of product development costs. To offset these costs, microcomputer designers are shifting toward high-level language programming. Increasingly, users expect microprocessors to provide a cost-effective solution for HLL support with minimal degradation in overall system performance; this sets tougher requirements for microprocessor designers.

Sophisticated future systems will require a combination of capabilities. Anticipating these needs, National Semiconductor has developed the NS16000 microprocessor family to incorporate various architectural features into a new generation of devices. Utilizing National Semiconductor's XMOS technology, the design of the NS16000 family is implemented with 3.5-micron gate technology. This allows for a smaller die size, leading to a reduction in chip cost.

The design challenges in creating this new family were met only after thoroughly considering market requirements and LSI technology limitations. This article describes some of the capabilities provided by the NS16000 architecture.

Supporting system software

Operating system design can be simplified with built-in hardware features. The powerful NS16000 control instructions aid the implementation of efficient operating systems and of systems oriented to high-level languages. These NS16000 facilities include semaphores, traps, interrupts, supervisor calls, easy context switching, and procedure calls.

One feature of the NS16000 architecture is virtual memory support, which includes the instructions-abort facility. This facility allows an instruction to be reexecuted after it as been aborted due to an address fault (that is, virtual memory page fault).

With the increasing level of multiprocessor system complexity, we expect to see a concurrent increase in the number of users demanding some level of system protection. In the multitasking/multiuser system environment, absolute protection is desired. To achieve a high level of protection, we must assure total isolation of one user's environment from another and from system resources. Any attempt to violate this protection, either accidentally or maliciously, should result in a trap which will transfer control to a system supervisor.

The NS16032 MPU (microprocessing unit) and the NS16082 MMU (memory management unit) together provide a high level of system protection with a set of 11 privileged instructions supported by the NS16032 user and supervisor modes and stack pointers:

- Set and clear bit in the processor status register,
- Load and store processor register,
- Return from interrupts and traps,
- Four MMU instructions, and
- Set system configuration.

To reduce system development cost, the NS16032 was designed to utilize the debugging facilities implemented on the MMU (16082). The MMU has built-in debugging tools to support both high-level and assembly-level programming in a virtual machine environment and hardware debugging in an in-system emulation environment.

Reprinted from *IEEE Computer*, vol. 15, pp. 58–67, June 1982.

Several MMU instructions are available to activate breakpoints and the memory access trace. Among other features used by the debugging software are memory protection and user/supervisor modes.

Managing large address space

The decreasing price of mass storage serial access devices now allows their use in microprocessor applications. Extended addressability is required for the ever-growing number of users expanding their system memory to sizes greater than 65K bytes. To manage large address space, microprocessor designers have adopted segmentation techniques previously used by minicomputers. To avoid the disadvantage associated with the minicomputer approach to segmentation, the NS16032 architecture has incorporated an important feature in its addressability: a large, uniform, unsegmented address space. This provides for a flexible memory management scheme without additional expense and simplifies the operating system and compilers. For example, if a user wants data handling in large address space but does not need sophisticated memory management, then there is no need to pay for it.

For more sophisticated memory management support, generally in multitasking environments, the NS16032 can be linked with the MMU to provide additional system capabilities: dynamic virtual-to-physical address translation, dynamic page table handling, and memory protection. The MMU can treat both main memory and a secondary mass storage as one large, uniform space completely transparent to the programmer, and special control instructions have been included in the architecture to support the MMU operations.

An on-chip cache memory enables the MMU to perform most mappings without actually referring to the translation tables in memory. The cache memory contains direct virtual-to-physical mapping of the presently used pages. With a hit-ratio of better than 95 percent, the overhead caused by translation is minimal.

When page swapping is required, the MMU aborts the execution on the MPU. A dedicated hardware mechanism, integrated within the CPU chip, guarantees graceful recovery from the abort function. This is an essential feature for virtual memory support. Unlike classic interrupt schemes, the abort cannot be suspended until the end of instruction execution. Also, the execution cannot be terminated since some of the operands are not in physical memory. While some processors supply an abort mechanism, they do not guarantee that an aborted instruction will yield correct results when retried.

The NS16032 CPU execution algorithms assure that whenever a processor register or a memory location is referenced, the access will not prevent reexecution. The CPU verifies either that the specific access allows graceful recovery or that no abort can possibly occur at this phase of the instruction execution (that is, there are no more memory accesses in the current instruction). If these conditions are not present, the CPU saves the old contents of the register in an on-chip back-up register, so that they can be recovered in case of abort.

NS16000 architecture

Register set. The architecture supports 16 registers forming two register files: eight dedicated registers and eight general-purpose registers (see Figure 1). The eight dedicated registers on the CPU are

• Program counter. The PC points to the first byte of the currently executing instruction.

• Static base register. The SB register points to a RAM data storage area for the currently running module. All references to the module's data are relative to this register, making them easily relocatable.

• Frame pointer. The FP points to the stack frame of the currently executing procedure. This is also referred to as the "activation record," containing the parameters for the currently executing subroutine and also the volatile (as opposed to static) local variables.

• User stack and interrupt stack pointers. Two stack pointers controlled by the U bit in the PSR: US is used as the stack pointer when U = 0, IS when U = 1. The U bit may be altered only in supervisor mode or by an interrupt.

• Interrupt base register. The INTBASE register points to an interrupt table for traps and interrupts.

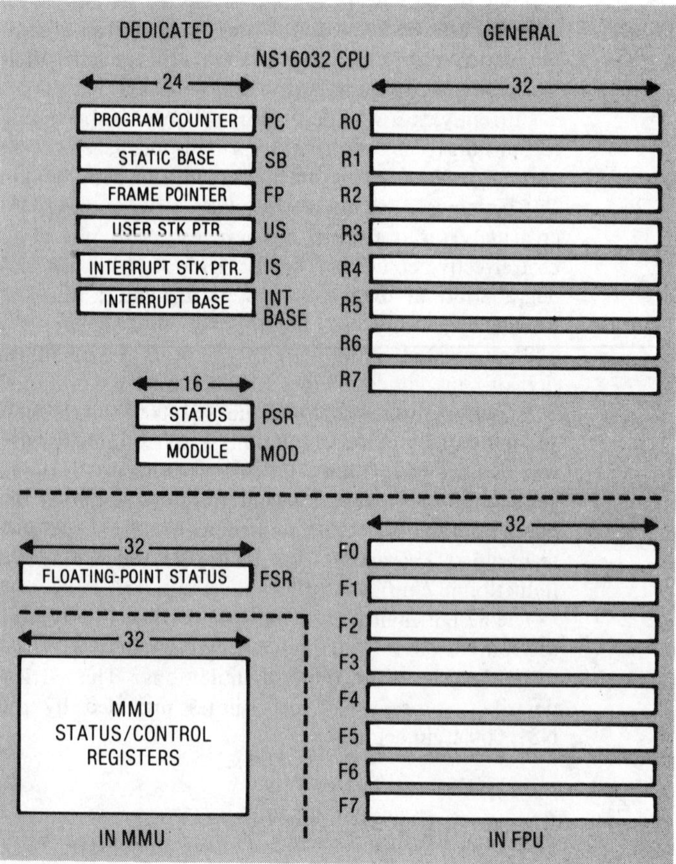

Figure 1. NS16000 register set.

• Processor status register. The PSR contains status information such as the arithmetic flags. It also contains supervisor state information for the operating system. This information is automatically saved on interrupt.

• Module register. The MOD register points to the appropriate area of the module map that indicates the module under current execution. The module map is a directory containing all the necessary address pointers for each module, which is applicable even to ROM-based codes.

The above are 24-bit registers, except for the 16-bit PSR and MOD registers. The eight general-purpose registers (R0-R7) are 32-bit registers.

Addressing modes

The NS16000 addressing modes, combined with the instruction set, contribute to efficient high-level language support. The basic instructions reference two operands, each of which is addressable by nine general addressing modes. The standard addressing modes, common to other processors, are:

- *Register addressing*—direct reference to a general purpose register,
- *Immediate addressing*—operand is provided as part of the instruction,
- *Absolute addressing*—absolute operand's address is specified, and
- *Register-relative addressing*—the operand's address is derived by adding a displacement to the contents of a specified general-purpose or dedicated register.

In addition to these four modes, the NS16000 architecture introduces five addressing modes oriented to high-level-languages and not usually found in other machines:

• *Memory-space addressing.* This allows relocatable reference to memory areas commonly used in high-level languages—specifically, the problem, static (or global), frame, and stack areas.

• *Top-of-stack addressing.* Any operand or operands of an instruction may be referred to by the TOS addressing mode. The operand is pushed into the current stack, popped from it, or referenced without modifying the stack pointer—all according to the role of the operand within the instruction. For example, the instruction SUBD TOS, TOS performs standard stack subtraction of two 32-bit operands in a single instruction. (Operands 1 and 2 are popped from the stack, and the result is pushed into the stack). Thus, efficient stack machine operation is achieved.

• *The memory-relative addressing mode.* This is a powerful addressing mode that is useful for handling address pointers and manipulating fields in a record. This mode uses two displacements. The first is added to one of the dedicated registers (static base register, stack pointer, or frame pointer), which is specified by the mode. The resulting double-word intermediate address is added to the second displacement for the final address of the operand.

• *The scaled-index addressing mode.* This mode, one of the most powerful features of the machine, computes the effective address by adding the contents of any of the general-purpose registers, multiplied by 1, 2, 4, or 8, to the basic address, as defined by the basic addressing mode. The scaled index mode is quite useful for indexing into an array while the basic addressing mode points to the head of the array. The elements of the array can be bytes, words, double words, quad words, floating-point numbers, or long floating-point numbers. Any memory addressing mode has the option of being indexed.

• *The external addressing mode.* Unique to the 16000, this supports the modular software (described below) and allows modules to be relocated without linkage editing. This mode is used to reference operands external to the current executing module. Associated with each module is a linkage table containing the absolute addresses of external variables and relative addresses of operands to be accessed by other modules. The external addressing mode specifies two displacements: the ordinal number of the external variable (the linkage-table entry to be used) and an offset to a subfield of the referenced variable (a subfield of a Pascal record, say). Since code need not be edited for external reference or for relocation, it is completely relocatable even in ROM form. This addressing mode has the capability of going through the tables and accessing the external operands. (See the listing in the box starting at right for more details.)

Supporting high-level languages

The NS16000 architecture is designed to support high-level languages, such as Pascal, Ada, and Fortran. Its architectural features increase the efficiency of HLL compilers to generate compact code, and special emphasis has been put on modular programming. Its address pointers are large enough to address directly the entire addressing space. In the NS16032, address pointers are 24-bits wide and address 16M bytes of memory. Future CPUs can use a larger addressing space with complete software compatibility. This uniform, unsegmented addressing provides a flexible memory management scheme and allows upward compatibility with future CPUs. It also eliminates artificial limitation to segment size.

Instruction set. The NS16000 instruction set includes over 100 basic instruction types coded in variable-length machine codes. The basic instruction code is one byte to three bytes long. There are genuine two-operand instructions, supporting a variety of addressing modes for both operands. However, some instructions use up to five operands, with one to three displacements (of one to four bytes each).

The instruction codes were carefully assigned, so that frequently used instructions have very short codes while rarely used, yet extremely powerful instructions utilize longer opcodes.

Instruction set summary

The instruction column gives the instruction as coded in assembly language and the description column provides a short description of the function provided by that instruction.

NOTATIONS:

i = Integer length suffix: B = Byte
W = Word
D = Double word

f = Floating-point length suffix: F = Standard floating
L = Long floating

gen = General operand. Any addressing mode can be specified.

short = A 4-bit value encoded within the basic instruction.

imm = Immediate operand. An 8-bit value appended after any addressing extensions.

disp = Displacement (addressing constant): 8, 16, or 32 bits. All three lengths legal.

reg = Any general-purpose register: R0-R7.

areg = Any dedicated/address register: SP, SB, FP, MOD, INTBASE, PSR, US (bottom 8 PSR bits).

mreg = Any memory management status/control register.

creg = A custom slave processor register (implementation dependent).

cond = Any condition code, encoded as a 4-bit field within the basic instruction.

MOVES

INSTRUCTION		DESCRIPTION
MOVi	gen,gen	Move a value
MOVQi	short,gen	Extend and move a 4-bit constant
MOVMi	gen,gen,disp	Move multiple:disp bytes
MOVZBW	gen,gen	Move with zero extension
MOVZiD	gen,gen	Move with zero extension
MOVXBW	gen,gen	Move with sign extension
MOVXiD	gen,gen	Move with sign extension
ADDR	gen,gen	Move effective address

INTEGER ARITHMETIC

INSTRUCTION		DESCRIPTION
ADDi	gen,gen	Add
ADDQi	short,gen	Add 4-bit constant
ADDCi	gen,gen	Add with carry
SUBi	gen,gen	Subtract
SUBCi	gen,gen	Subtract with carry (borrow)
NEGi	gen,gen	Negate (2's complement)
ABSi	gen,gen	Take absolute value
MULi	gen,gen	Multiply
QUOi	gen,gen	Divide, rounding toward zero
REMi	gen,gen	Remainder from QUO
DIVi	gen,gen	Divide, rounding down
MODi	gen,gen	Remainder from DIV (Modulus)
MEIi	gen,gen	Multiply to extended integer
DEIi	gen,gen	Divide extended integer

PACKED DECIMAL (BCD)

INSTRUCTION		DESCRIPTION
ADDPi	gen,gen	Add packed
SUBPi	gen,gen	Subtract packed

INTEGER COMPARISON

INSTRUCTION		DESCRIPTION
CMPi	gen,gen	Compare
CMPQi	short,gen	Compare to 4-bit constant
CMPMi	gen,gen,disp	Compare multiple:disp bytes

LOGICAL AND BOOLEAN

INSTRUCTION		DESCRIPTION
ANDi	gen,gen	Logical AND
ORi	gen,gen	Logical OR
BICi	gen,gen	Clear selected bits
XORi	gen,gen	Logical exclusive OR
COMi	gen,gen	Complement all bits
NOTi	gen,gen	Boolean complement:LSB only
Scondi	gen	Save condition code (cond) as a boolean variable of size i.

SHIFTS

INSTRUCTION		DESCRIPTION
LSHi	gen,gen	Logical shift, left or right
ASHi	gen,gen	Arithmetic shift, left or right
ROTi	gen,gen	Rotate, left or right

BITS

INSTRUCTION		DESCRIPTION
TBITi	gen,gen	Test bit
SBITi	gen,gen	Test and set bit
SBITIi	gen,gen	Test and set bit, interlocked
CBITi	gen,gen	Test and clear bit
CBITIi	gen,gen	Test and clear bit, interlocked
IBITi	gen,gen	Test and invert bit
FFSi	gen,gen	Find first set bit

BIT FIELDS

Bit fields are values in memory which are not aligned to byte boundaries. Examples are PACKED arrays and records used in Pascal. ''Extract'' instructions read and align a bit field. ''Insert'' instructions write a bit field from an aligned source.

INSTRUCTION		DESCRIPTION
EXTi	reg,gen,gen,disp	Extract bit field (array oriented)
INSi	reg,gen,gen,disp	Insert bit field (array oriented)
EXTSi	gen,gen,imm	Extract bit field (short form)
INSSi	gen,gen,imm	Insert bit field (short form)
CVTP	reg,gen,gen	Convert to bit field pointer

ARRAYS

INSTRUCTION		DESCRIPTION
CHECKi	reg,gen,gen	Index bounds check
INDEXi	reg,gen,gen	Recursive indexing step for multiple-dimensional arrays

STRINGS

String instructions assign specific functions to the general-purpose registers:

R4—Comparison value
R3—Translation table pointer
R2—String 2 pointer
R1—String 1 pointer
R0—Limit count

Options on all string instructions are

B(Backward): Decrement string pointers after each step rather than incrementing
U(Until match): End instruction if String 1 entry matches R4
W(While match): End instruction if String 1 entry does not match R4

All string instructions end when R0 decrements to zero.

INSTRUCTION		DESCRIPTION
MOVSi	options	Move String 1 to String 2
MOVST	options	Move string, translating bytes
CMPSi	options	Compare String 1 to String 2
CMPST	options	Compare, translating String 1 bytes
SKPSi	options	Skip over String 1 entries
SKPST	options	Skip, translating bytes for Until/While

JUMPS AND LINKAGE

INSTRUCTION		DESCRIPTION
JUMP	gen	Jump
BR	disp	Branch (PC relative)

The data types in the instruction set include bytes, words, double words, and BCD operands as well as floating-point numbers (single and double precision), strings, bits, and bit-fields. These can be arranged in a variety of data structures.

In addition to conventional CPU instructions such as data movement, arithmetic/logic operations, and shifting (all with inherent memory-to-memory capability), the architecture includes advanced instructions that are very useful in an HLL environment. The CHECK instruction determines whether an array index is within bounds and adjusts it to a zero-based value. The INDEX instruction implements the recursive indexing step for multiple-dimensioned arrays. The STRING instructions manipulate data strings with optional translation, escape-characters test, and limit counting. The CXP instruction allows automatic calls of external routines by a simple "call external procedure" type of statement. ENTER and EXIT instructions minimize the overhead in procedure calls by managing the resources (registers and stack frame) allocated at the beginning of a procedure and reclaimed at the end. The INTERLOCKED instructions (test and set/clear) provide interlocked semaphore primitives for multitasking and multiprocessing coordination. And the FLOATING POINT instructions handle single precision (32-bit) and double precision (64-bit) arithmetic, move, and conversion operations.

Supporting modular programming

As we stated at the beginning of this article, modern high-level languages implement modular software techniques as a means of reducing development cost and increasing design flexibility. The NS16000 allows the creation of a library of independently developed software

Bcond	disp	Conditional branch
CASEi	gen	Multiway branch
ACBi	short,gen,disp	Add 4-bit constant and branch if non-zero
JSR	gen	Jump to subroutine
BSR	disp	Branch to subroutine
CXP	disp	Call external procedure
CXPD	gen	Call external procedure using descriptor
SVC		Supervisor call
FLAG		Flag trap
BPT		Breakpoint trap
ENTER	[reg list],disp	Save registers and allocate stack frame (enter procedure)
EXIT	[reg list]	Restore registers and reclaim stack frame (exit procedure)
RET	disp	Return from subroutine
RXP	disp	Return from external procedure call
RETT	disp	Return from trap (privileged)
RETI		Return from interrupt (privileged)

CPU REGISTER MANIPULATION

INSTRUCTION		DESCRIPTION
SAVE	[reg list]	Save general-purpose registers
RESTORE	[reg list]	Restore general-purpose registers
LPRi	areg,gen	Load dedicated register (privileged if PSR or INTBASE)
SPRi	areg,gen	Store dedicated register (privileged if PSR or INTBASE)
ADJSPi	gen	Adjust stack pointer
BISPSRi	gen	Set selected bits in PSR (privileged if not byte length)
BICPSRi	gen	Clear selected bits in PSR (privileged if not byte length)
SETCFG	[option list]	Set configuration register (privileged)

FLOATING POINT

INSTRUCTION		DESCRIPTION
MOVf	gen,gen	Move a floating-point value
MOVLF	gen,gen	Move and shorten a long value to standard
MOVFL	gen,gen	Move and lengthen a standard value to long
MOVif	gen,gen	Convert any integer to standard or long floating
ROUNDfi	gen,gen	Convert to integer by rounding
TRUNCfi	gen,gen	Convert to integer by truncating, toward zero
FLOORfi	gen,gen	Convert to largest integer less than or equal to value
ADDf	gen,gen	Add
SUBf	gen,gen	Subtract
MULf	gen,gen	Multiply
DIVf	gen,gen	Divide
CMPf	gen,gen	Compare
NEGf	gen,gen	Negate
ABSf	gen,gen	Take absolute value
LFSR	gen	Load FSR
SFSR	gen	Store FSR

MEMORY MANAGEMENT

INSTRUCTION		DESCRIPTION
LMR	mreg,gen	Load memory management register (privileged)
SMR	mreg,gen	Store memory management register (privileged)
RDVAL	gen	Validate address for reading (privileged)
WRVAL	gen	Validate address for writing (privileged)
MOVSUi	gen,gen	Move a value from supervisor space to user space (privileged)
MOVUSi	gen,gen	Move a value from user space to supervisor space (privileged)

MISCELLANEOUS

INSTRUCTION	DESCRIPTION
NOP	No operation
WAIT	Wait for interrupt
DIA	Diagnose. Single-byte "branch to self" for hardware breakpointing. Not for use in programming

CUSTOM SLAVE

INSTRUCTION		DESCRIPTION
CCAL0c	gen,gen	Custom calculate
CCAL1c	gen,gen	
CCAL2c	gen,gen	
CCAL3c	gen,gen	

modules to be linked at runtime. This feature provides totally relocatable code that can be stored in ROMs to suit various applications.

Each module consists of three components:

- a code component, which contains the code to be executed in a given module,
- a static data component, which contains the module's local variables and data, and
- a linkage component, which contains the information required to make link reference from one module to another.

In a typical system, the static data and linkage components would be in RAM and the code component would be in either RAM or ROM.

The MOD register contains the number of the currently executing module and points to the appropriate area of the module table, which in turn specifies the relevant component addresses of the module. The module table pointers are only used for external procedure calls. When referencing static data, the MPU uses the static base register, shown in Figure 2.

The external procedure call sequence is

CALL (external descriptor) =

push	MOD
push	PC of next instruction
MOD	= mod from the external-procedure descriptor in the link table
SB	= ((MOD))
PC	= ((MOD) + 8) + offset from descriptor

The procedure return sequence is

CMOV0c	gen,gen	Custom move
CMOV1c	gen,gen	
CMOV2c	gen,gen	
CCMPc	gen,gen	Custom compare
CCV0ci	gen,gen	Custom convert
CCV1ci	gen,gen	
CCV2ci	gen,gen	
CCV3ci	gen,gen	
CCV4DQ	gen,gen	
CCV5QD	gen,gen	
LCSR	gen	Load custom status register
SCSR	gen	Store custom status register
CATST0	gen	Custom address test (privileged)
CATST1	gen	(privileged)
LCR	creg,gen	Load custom register (privileged)
SCR	creg,gen	Store custom register (privileged)

NS16032 addressing modes

ENCODING	MODE	ASSEMBLER SYNTAX	EFFECTIVE ADDRESS
REGISTER			
00000	Register 0	R0 or F0	None. Operand is in the register
00001	Register 1	R1 or F1	
00010	Register 2	R2 or F2	
00011	Register 3	R3 or F3	
00100	Register 4	R4 or F4	
00101	Register 5	R5 or F5	
00110	Register 6	R6 or F6	
00111	Register 7	R7 or F7	
REGISTER RELATIVE			
01000	Register 0 relative	disp(R0)	Disp + register
01001	Register 1 relative	disp(R1)	
01010	Register 2 relative	disp(R2)	
01011	Register 3 relative	disp(R3)	
01100	Register 4 relative	disp(R4)	
01101	Register 5 relative	disp(R5)	
01110	Register 6 relative	disp(R6)	
01111	Register 7 relative	disp(R7)	
MEMORY SPACE			
11000	Frame memory	disp(FP)	Disp + register; "SP" is either SP0 or SP1, as selected in PSR
11001	Stack memory	disp(SP)	
11010	Static memory	disp(SB)	
11011	Program memory	disp(PC)	
MEMORY RELATIVE			
10000	Frame memory relative	disp2 (disp1(FP))	Disp2 + Pointer; Pointer found at address Disp1 + register. "SP" is either SP0 or SP1, as selected in PSR
10001	Stack memory relative	disp2 (disp1(SP))	
10010	Static memory relative	disp2 (disp1(SB))	
IMMEDIATE			
10100	Immediate	value	None. Operand is input from instruction queue
ABSOLUTE			
10101	Absolute	@disp	Disp
EXTERNAL			
10110	External	EXTERNAL (disp1)+ disp2	Disp2 + pointer; pointer is found at link table entry number disp1
TOP OF STACK			
10111	Top of stack	TOS	Top of current stack using either user or interrupt stack pointer as selected in PSR. Automatic push/pop included
SCALED INDEX			
11100	Index, bytes	mode[Rn:B]	Mode + Rn
11101	Index, words	mode[Rn:W]	Mode + 2 × Rn
11110	Index, double words	mode[Rn:D]	Mode + 4 × Rn
11111	Index, quad words	mode[Rn:Q]	Mode + 8 × Rn "Mode" and "n" are contained within the index byte
10011	(Reserved for future use)		

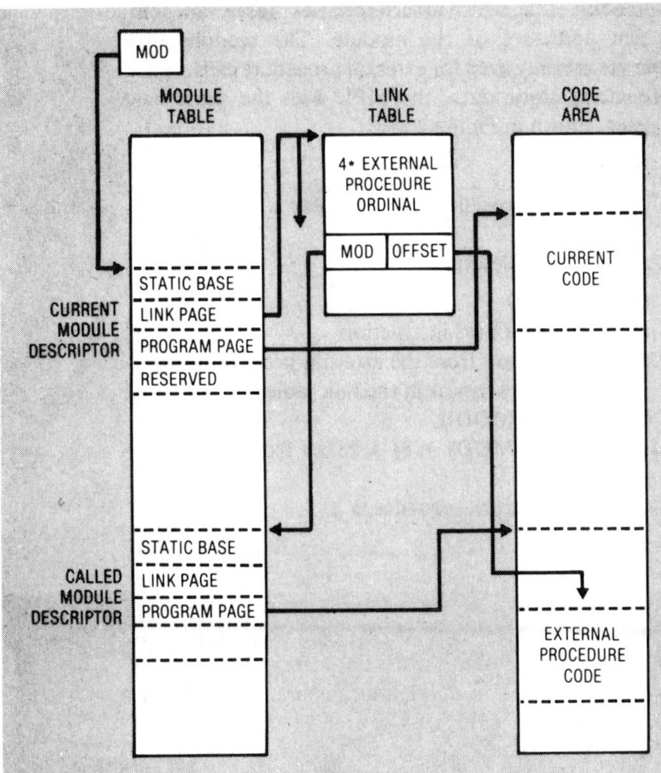

Figure 2. Module table and external procedure referencing.

```
RETURN =
  pop    PC
  pop    MOD
  SB     = ((MOD))
```

As mentioned above, reference to external variables is done via the external addressing mode. In this case, no CPU registers are affected. The CPU indirectly references the external variable through the linkage table of the current module.

In short, NS16000 programs can consist solely of a library of ROM modules. As modules are loaded, the linking loader need only update the module table and fill the linkage table entries with the appropriate values.

Expandable architecture

As each "new generation" of microprocessors makes its predecessors obsolete, users are forced to reinvest in software development as they adopt these advanced microprocessor systems. National Semiconductor has attacked the future expansion problem by introducing the slave processor concept. Slave processor chips are defined as hardware extensions of the basic CPU chip. The slave processor "instructions" are an integral part of the instruction set. Presently, they are implemented by dedicated chips.

The communication protocol between the master CPU and the slave processors is transparent to the software. As technology advances, slave-processor hardware will be incorporated within the CPU chip. This means that no software modifications will be required and that the same programs will execute much faster. Moreover, if the present system requirements do not justify the inclusion of slave processors, the user can set up a "nonslave system" configuration. If a slave is not connected to the system and a slave instruction is encountered, the program traps to a software routine, emulating the nonexisting slave. In the future, slave processors or future "super CPUs" may be used without software modifications.

The NS16000 microprocessor family presently has two slave processors—the NS16081 floating-point unit and the NS16082 memory management unit. The slave instructions are executed by the slaves with complete software transparency. A fast, self-contained protocol is used for communicating between the master CPU and the slave processors. The fact that there are two or three different chips is transparent to the system designer.

Since the slave processor is designed as a subset of a "super CPU," it takes advantage of CPU functions already implemented on the master CPU chip such as effective address calculation, memory bus interface, etc. This results in low cost, high performance, and software symmetry. The user can treat floating-point numbers (both single and double precision) like any other NS16000 data types and may use any of the NS16000 addressing modes to reference them.

The slave processors and the CPU are tightly coupled by a well-defined, simple and yet effective, protocol. To the programmer, the CPU and the slaves present an integrated monolithic architecture, as shown in Figure 3. The slave processor instructions have a three-byte basic instruction field, consisting of an ID byte followed by a operation word. The ID byte has three functions:

- it identifies the instruction as being a slave processor instruction,
- it specifies which slave processor will execute it, and
- it determines the format of the following operation word of the instruction.

Upon receiving a slave processor instruction, the CPU initiates the sequence outlined below:

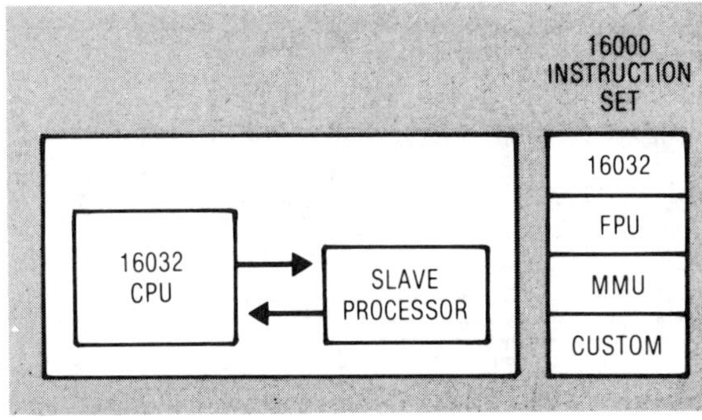

Figure 3. NS16000 CPU-slave architecture.

Step	Action
1	CPU sends ID byte
2	CPU sends operation word
3	CPU sends required operand
4	Slave starts execution. CPU ---
5	Slave sends termination indication at the end of operation
6	CPU reads status word (flags, etc.)
7	CPU reads results

The instruction set and the slave-processors' protocol provide support for additional future slave processors. Future technology will allow integration of the slave processor functions as part of the master CPU chip.

Internal description

The NS16032 chip design, shown in Figure 4, is tailored to support all of these features while achieving high performance. (For more details, see pages 61-63.) This requires the introduction of novel elements, not previously required in microprocessor implementations, as well as the use of current VLSI/MOS technology.

Pipelining. The powerful instruction set includes a variety of instructions with execution times ranging from 300 nanoseconds to tens of microseconds. The compact code yields instructions coded in one or two bytes versus instructions consuming up to 25 bytes of code (including associated displacements). An instruction look-ahead mechanism prefetches the instruction stream into an 8-byte on-chip queue. The NS16032 pipelined architecture ensures high throughput in this environment.

The instruction code is extracted from the queue by the loader where it is manipulated, separated into appropriate fields, and loaded into the instruction register. The code is transferred to the execution machine only when the previous instruction execution is terminated. Thus, three successive instructions can be processed simultaneously by the NS16032. While one instruction is being executed, the following one is loaded into the instruction register, and the next instruction is shifted through the queue.

Two-level microcode. The architecture represents a two-operand machine, with each operand being addressable by all the addressing modes. A two-level microcode technique was implemented, to allow the sharing of common, effective address calculation routines by all the instructions and to avoid time-consuming subroutine calls or space-consuming repeated microcode flows. The outer level is a preprocessor, which controls the effective address calculation and execution sequences while the inner level details the execution steps.

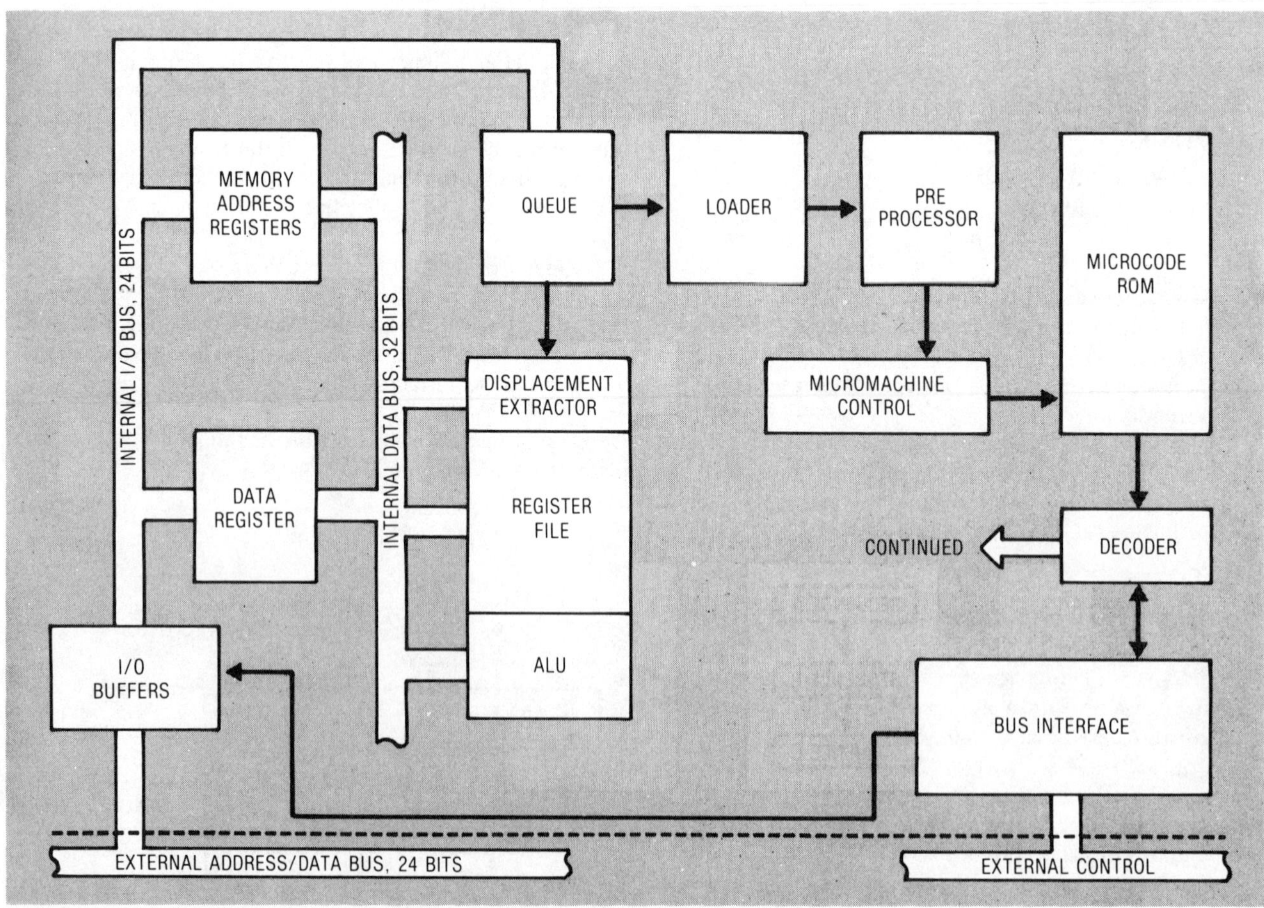

Figure 4. NS16032 block diagram.

The micromachine control unit controls the microcode execution and provides a flow control mechanism for microsubroutine calls, looping, and conditional branching. The microprogram counter is loaded with the sequence start address determined by the instruction opcode and the preprocessor. The microinstruction decoder decodes the microcode ROM outputs and controls the execution steps. A handshake protocol synchronizes the microcode execution to the bus interface unit whenever memory reference is required. The instruction execution flow is depicted in Figure 5.

Internal buses. Internally, the NS16032 is a parallel 32-bit machine and includes a 32-bit data bus, 32-bit registers, and a 32-bit arithmetic logic unit. The internal data bus allows the transfer of 32-bit data between bus elements—the NS16000 register set members, temporary registers, memory registers, the data register, and the ALU. The displacement extractor transfers displacements from the instruction stream via the queue, to any on-chip register.

Additionally, the internal I/O bus is used for external memory access. It communicates with the internal bus, the memory address registers (for address transfers), and the data registers (for memory data transfers).

32-bit ALU. The arithmetic and logic operations are carried out by a 32-bit ALU. The ALU is configured by the ALU control unit into one of 12 operating modes. Each ALU operation handles the accumulator and any register as operands, and can transfer the result to any NS16032 register. The ALU source and destination are specified by microcode. Certain ALU operations modify the NS16032 condition-code flags.

In addition to the standard arithmetic and logic operations (add, subtract, and, exclusive or, etc.), the ALU is capable of performing complex operations. Dedicated ALU operations support binary coded decimal addition and subtraction (8 digits at a time) and multiply/divide algorithms. As a result, the NS16032 performs multiplication and division of two 32-bit operands in 9.4 microseconds. Addition and subtraction of two 32-bit (8-BCD-digit) numbers is carried out in two microseconds.

Bus interface. The bus interface unit, or BIU, controls the communication between the CPU and the external

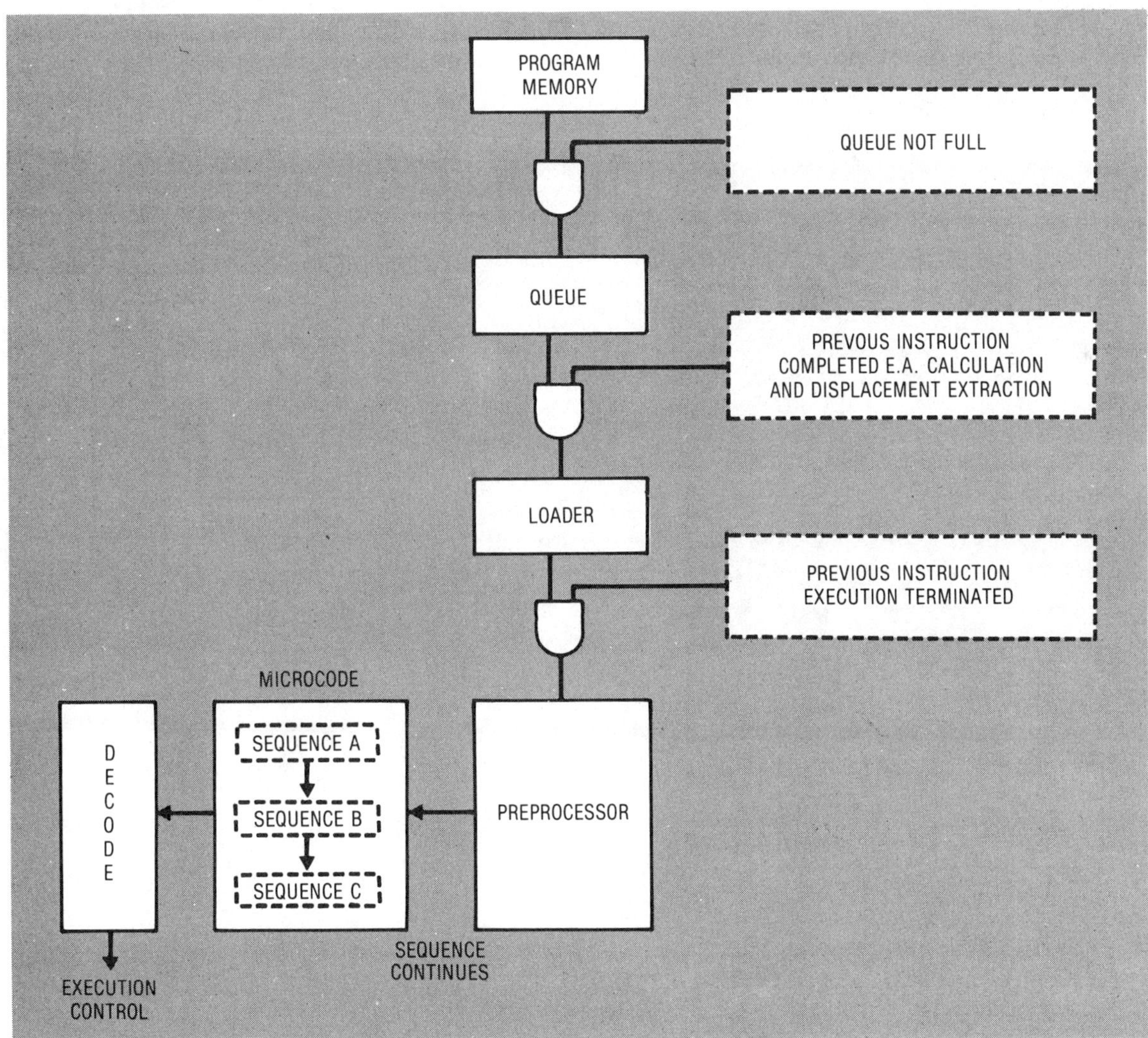

Figure 5. Processing of an instruction by the NS16032.

bus. It generates the various memory cycles and drives the status flags and external control signals. The bus interface unit controls memory data transfers through the internal I/O bus and initiates memory cycles upon requests from the execution machine's microcode. When no request is pending, instruction prefetch cycles are generated. The operand types with lengths of one to eight bytes (non-aligned to any memory location boundaries) are supported by the BIU, which determines the exact number of memory cycles required for each operand.

Summary

In summary, the NS16000 family addresses a wide range of system applications, including the development of modular software and the support of high-level language and operating systems through the use of its 32-bit architecture, powerful instruction set, uniform and unsegmented address space, and slave processors. ■

June 1982

DESIGN CONSIDERATIONS OF THE NS16082 MEMORY MANAGEMENT UNIT

Gary Martin and Yoav Lavi
Product Marketing Engineer
Design Manager
NATIONAL SEMICONDUCTOR CORPORATION
2900 Semiconductor Drive
Santa Clara, CA 95051

INTRODUCTION

The NS16082 Memory Management Unit is a versatile product designed to support the NS16000 family microprocessors in memory management tasks. Its main features are:

* automatic translation of virtual to physical addresses

* memory protection

* virtual memory support

* software/hardware debugging facility

The NS16082 is fabricated on a 270 square mil die using 3.5 micron NMOS technology. It is housed in a 48-pin DIP. This paper describes some features of the device and why these particular features and implementation are chosen.

VIRTUAL MEMORY

When the NS16000 family architecture was outlined, there were two ways to support the mainframe characteristics we had in mind. We could:

a. preserve the 16 bit architecture and expand address space beyond 64K bytes through memory management tricks such as segments. This seemed to be the easiest approach considering the silicon area requirements and had already been chosen by some semiconductor and minicomputer vendors. The problem with this approach is the extra software overhead needed to manage segments and the resulting performance degradation.

b. adopt a completely 32-bit architecture in which all instructions operate on up to 32-bit integers. This approach supports a complete 32-bit uniform address space. The only disadvantage is the extra silicon required.

   The uniform address space approach yields a much more powerful and clean architecture. Addresses as well as data can be manipulated with the entire instruction set. Moreover, any program can generate a practically unlimited virtual address space.

In the NS16000 family a subset of (b) above is chosen. This is a result of the following compromises:

a. the external data bus is 16 bits wide, so that a 32-bit data transfer takes two memory cycles (although the MPU has 32-bit wide data paths internally).

b. 24 bits of address are implemented, (i.e. - a 16 MB memory rather than a 4 GB one).

In environments such as multi-user or virtual memory, this large, uniform address space has to be managed by a hardware/software combination.

Managing A Large Uniform Address Space

The management of a non-segmented address space is traditionally done with fixed size pages. Page size is usually between ½K and 4K bytes. Fixed page size yields simple memory management schemes in which:

a. Virtual memory can be implemented on a demand-paged basis (a secondary storage page replaces an identically sized, least-recently-used page in main memory and the translation tables are updated accordingly.) Virtual memory management for variable size segments tends to be very cumbersome.

b. When a new task is activated or when a task requests storage allocation dynamically, the translation tables can be easily updated. This scheme also avoids fragmentation problems. Supporting segments (fixed or variable sizes) is not ruled out, but segments must be an integral number of pages.

Speeding Up Address Translation

As mentioned above, the translation of a virtual address to a physical one requires

Reprinted with permission from *Midcon Conf. Rec.*, 1981, pp. 10.5.1–10.5.6.

access to memory tables. This may badly impact performance if the implementation is simple-minded. There are three ways to solve this problem:

a. in segmented systems the translation for each segment might be stored in registers. This approach is very fast if all active segment translations can be stored in registers and if the set of active pages is not changed very frequently. However, it is not applicable for the NS16000 which avoids variable-sized segments because of the extra software overhead.

b. store the translation for useful pages in registers using special instructions. This approach is rejected since it tends to limit the number of segments available to the user (to the number which can be stored in the MMU or else it might decrease performance too drastically.

c. use a translation cache for frequently-used pages. Several studies were done which suggest the performance of dynamic address translation is directly related to the number of cache entries included. A price/performance compromise of 32 entries seems a practical solution and this approach is adopted.

The important advantage of a translation cache over fixed registers is that it is transparent to the user, needs little operating systems support and is changed dynamically as the program wanders around various parts of memory.

The Translation and Protection Algorithm

A two-stage translation algorithm is used by the NS16082 MMU as illustrated in figure 1. The Page Table Base (PTB) register is in the MMU and is used as a base address to the first table of page table entries (PTE). The high-order nine bits of the virtual address is used to read the next PTE. This PTE contains an address offset to the second translation table, protection information and a bit which indicates if the physical page is valid (i.e., present) in memory. If the page is valid and the access is allowed under the protection level, then the address offset is concatenated to bits 15-24 of the virtual address getting an entry address into the second level page table. In this table, each entry contains the physical page address, a Modified bit (M), and a referenced bit (R) which indicate the status of the current page. These bits may be used by the operating system to implement more efficient page swapping algorithms. After the M and R bits are updated (as necessary), the MMU outputs the physical address and the memory cycle continues.

Note that the table-access is used in one of two cases:

a. the translation for the current page is not in the MMU cache

b. it is necessary to update the M bit of the second page table entry.

In either case, directly following the page tables access, the second level PTE will be stored in the cache.

VIRTUAL MACHINE SUPPORT

A Virtual Machine is a technique used to emulate an arbitrary configuration of hardware under control of some particular program. For instance I/D, physical memory and Operating System support can all be set up to support a certain application. The programmer using these resources thinks that they define a complete machine -- and in a sense this is true, since these resources are all that are available. These resources are really under direct control of a larger, more universal operating system. This operating system emulates the function of the virtual resources.

The Dual Space feature enables the virtual machine to access the full extent (or some subset) of memory using its own translation tables. Appropriate software routines simulate the virtual machine I/O and system calls.

Virtual machines are very easy to implement with this dynamic address translation scheme. All we need do is separate references to supervisor and user spaces. This is trivially implemented by using the U/S status pin in the MPU to distinguish between the two translation tables. Figure 2 demonstrates.

DEBUGGING YOUR SOFTWARE/HARDWARE

A very important feature in computers in general and microprocessors in particular is tools for rapid debugging of software and hardware. In typical mainframe computers this is done by a combination of extra hardware and special software routines. In a typical microprocessor application it is necessary to provide real time debugging aids. This means that some mechanism is needed to debug the MPU during full speed operation while asynchronous devices are attached. For example, if we wish to debug an automobile engine control routine while the engine is running at a moderate speed (rev = 20 msec), we need hardware which can monitor the program flow in actual operation. The software debugging becomes meaningless if we have to slow the engine to allow for the software monitor overhead.

The traditional solution for microprocessor debugging is an emulator which plugs into the MMU socket and executes a program at full speed. This technique additionally provides monitoring and breakpointing aids. A typical debugger/emulator provides users with one or two real-time breakpoints pluce a trace memory for the last several hundred memory cycles. The user can stop at a specified breakpoint and check the preceeding memory cycles. Appropriate software can support symbolic debugging - i.e., breakpoint on symbolic operands or instructions and trace assembler or high-level language lines.

This may be very difficult to implement in an advanced, pipe-lined microarchitecture MPU like the 16032. Several activities take place concurrently and, as a result, the mere monitoring of bus cycles does not reflect program flow. The most difficult part to filter out is the instruction prefetch feature. For example, suppose the MPU fetches the single byte instruction N, then 4 bytes of the 5 byte instruction N+1, writes an operand for instruction N-1 and then jumps to location N-100 as result of instruction N, N+1 or N-1. How can one easily trace the program flow of such activity? Obviously extra hardware and software tools are required. In the NS16000, the MPU has two special features to enable the tracing of program flow:

a. A Program Flow Status (PFS) pulse is generated in the execution phase of each instruction.

b. The MPU outputs different bus cycle status when it fetches sequential and non-sequential instructions.

These two features enable an external debugging emulator to keep trace of the program flow since all it must do is store the non-sequential fetch addresses along with the number of PFS pulses (the number of instructions executed between them).

In order to both decrease the cost of an emulator circuit and provide a stand alone debugging aid, the NS16082 MMU includes two software debugging features: (a) it traces the program flow, storing the most recent two non-sequential fetch locations and two PFS counts; (b) it has two breakpoints to stop the MPU when they match.

Program Flow Tracing

When a breakpoint is reached, the debugger software reads the MMU registers which contain the two last non-sequential fetch addresses and the two last PFS counts. It then disassembles the instruction stream defined by these location counters. The user is presented with a symbolic program flow from the last two branches to the breakpoint. Figure 3 illustrates a possible debugger output.

Breakpoints

The NS16082 has the capability for up to two breakpoints. The breakpoints have the following features:

a. Each can be enabled on an operand read, write, or instruction execution address.

b. A counter can be attached to breakpoint 1 allowing not just one occurrance of the event but N occurrances. The expression N*BP1+BP2 can occur before the program is stopped.

c. Breakpoints can detect both virtual and physical addresses.

Breakpoints can also be initiated in systems devoid of an NS16082 by placing a Breakpoint instruction (BPT) in the instruction address to be breakpointed, but this is not as flexible as the above method.

OTHER NS16082 FEATURES

In order to support a wider variety of applications, more programmable features are built into the NS16082:

a. Non-translate mode for both user and supervisor. This is necessary when response time is critical and the overhead of dynamic address translation is unacceptable. This feature is also necessary at power-up time because no tables are initialized. The NS16082 is reset to this mode.

b. Trace user only. In this mode, the program flow tracing registers are only active when the MPU is in user mode. This is useful when a program is debugged in a multitasking environment. When an interrupt occurs, the NS16082 will not monitor the interrupt routine. This makes it possible for the user to debug his/her routine alone, ignoring system activities.

c. Trace all branches. In this mode, a software routine can build a table of the last N branches (jump history table). This is useful when more than the last two branches are required.

SUMMARY

It is clear that the NS16082 is a very useful device for both virtual memory management, memory protection and software debugging. The quick dynamic address translation facility provides an automatic mechanism for both virtual memory and additionally for virtual machine support. The built in automatic registers for debugging save a great deal of time and expense in the emulation effort and provide a stand alone debugging tool.

```
NS16082 DEBUGGER

PROGRAM: ENGINE-CONTROL
MODE   : REAL TIME TRACE

BKPT1  : OFF
BKPT2  : OFF

MODULE : FEUL-VALVE-CONTROL

PROCEDURE CALCULATE
          100: MULW X,Y
          102: ADDW X,Z

          105: BEQ  POSITIVE

POSITIVE:
          500: ADDW A,B
          502: MOVW A,C
          504: MOVB 1,VALVE

** STOPPED BY NMI**
```

Figure 3: Sample 16000 Debugger Output.

Figure 1

VIRTUAL ADDRESS TRANSLATION

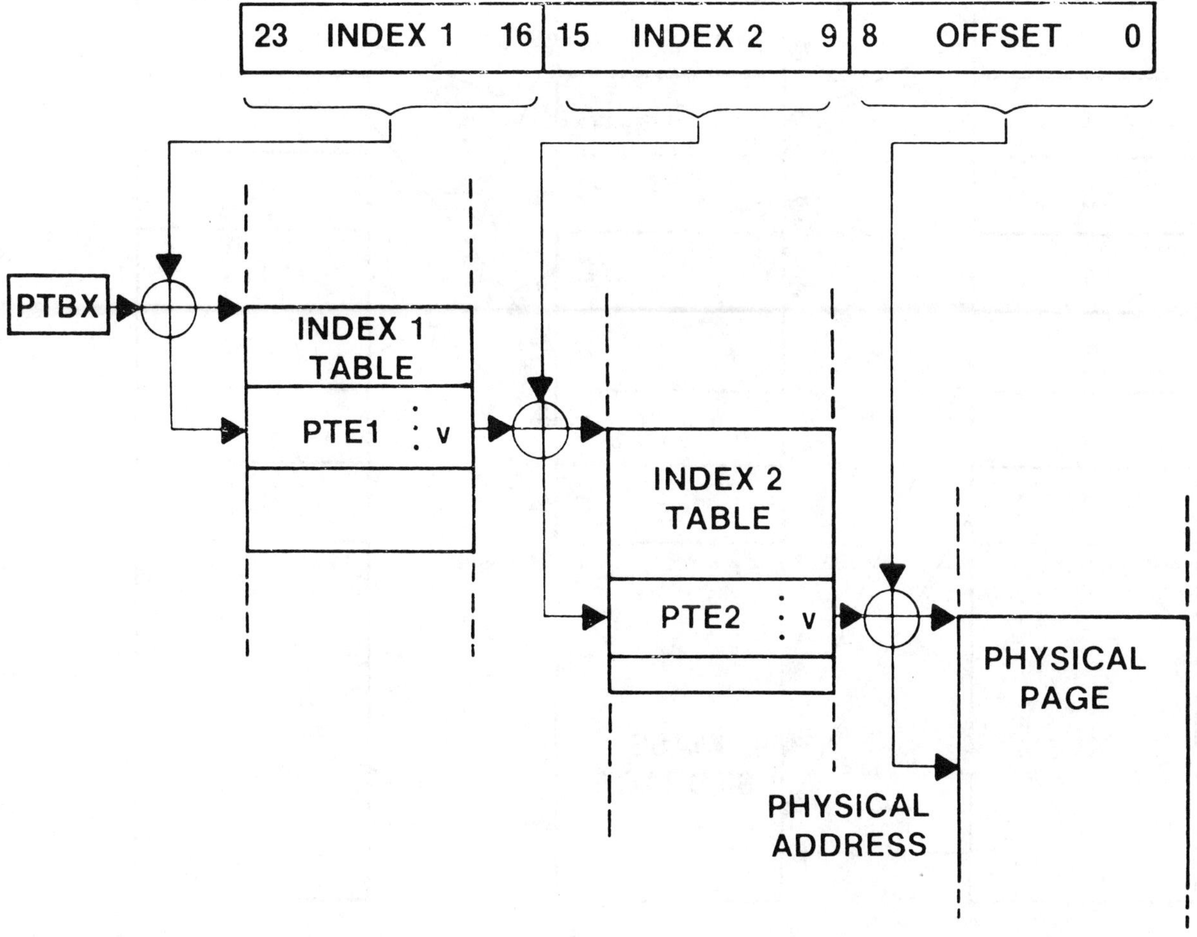

Figure 2

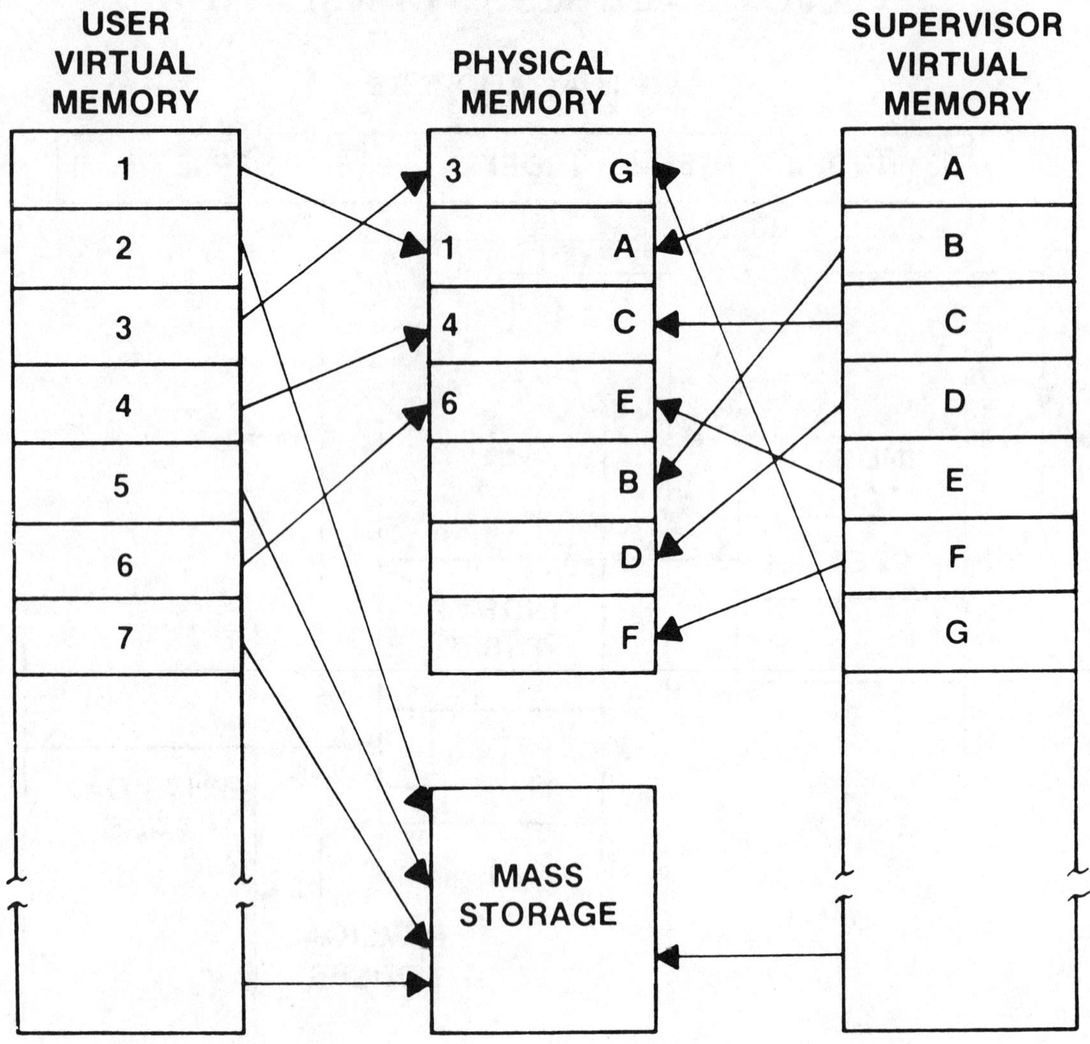
DUAL SPACE MODE
USER
VIRTUAL
MEMORY
PHYSICAL
MEMORY
SUPERVISOR
VIRTUAL
MEMORY
1
2
3
4
5
6
7
3 G
1 A
4 C
6 E
B
D
F
A
B
C
D
E
F
G
MASS
STORAGE

HIGH-PERFORMANCE PERIPHERALS COMPLEMENT NS16000 FAMILY

Gary R. Martin
Product Marketing Engineer
National Semiconductor Corp.
Santa Clara, California

INTRODUCTION

The NS16000 high-performance microprocessor family is being introduced by National Semiconductor this year. Led by the NS16032 microprocessor, the family promises to be an exciting new addition to the VLSI era. This paper surveys the capabilities of several of these components: the NS16082 Memory Management Unit, the NS16202 Interrupt Controller and the NS16203 Direct Memory Access Controller.

THE NS16082 MEMORY MANAGEMENT UNIT

Although the primary function of the MMU is, of course, virtual memory management (this is the subject of another paper here at WESCON), there is also a very useful secondary function: program debugging support. As the complexity and word width of microprocessors increases, it becomes more difficult and certainly more expensive to design and produce in-system emulators (ISE). To aid in ISE development and give the user an added edge during the program debugging phase of software development, the MMU has some "logic analyzer" functions built directly into the silicon.

PROGRAM DEBUGGING SUPPORT

Addresses issued from the processor reflect the behavior of the program it is executing. As such, they are a valuable diagnostic tool for program debugging. This is supported by the breakpointing and flow tracing facilities.

BREAKPOINTING

The breakpointing facility is an aid to program debugging provided by the Memory Management Unit. It is a separate feature from the BPT instruction provided by the processor. The memory management unit issues an ABT trap on receiving addresses matching the contents of one of the four breakpoint or BPR registers. The memory management unit can distinguish between virtual and physical addresses from either only user programs or both supervisor and user programs. It can also distinguish between addresses for instructions and addresses for operands and between addresses for modified operands and addresses for unmodified operands.

FLOW TRACING

The flow tracing facility is another aid to program debugging provided by the memory management unit. The addresses of the most recent nonsequential instructions are recorded in the four program flow or PF registers. A nonsequential instruction is an instruction executed as the result of a transfer of program control, such as a jump or branch. The number of sequential instructions between these nonsequential instructions are recorded in the four SC registers. Together, these facilities provided a profile of program execution up to the point at which the registers are sampled.

MEMORY MANAGEMENT UNIT REGISTERS

The NS16082 Memory Management Unit extends the basic processor architecture with the addition of eleven dedicated registers.

PTB The two, double word length PAGE TABLE BASE registers hold the addresses of level 1 page tables. The PTB0 register may be used to translate all virtual addresses, or the PBT0 register may be used to translate supervisor addresses and the PTB1 register may be used to translate user addresses (dual space mode.) (See figure 1).

The high bit of a PTB register corresponds to the MS bit of the physical address of the corresponding page table.

EIA The double word length ERROR/INVALIDATE ADDRESS register is used to invalidate addresses in the translation buffer. The translation buffer is a transparent cache of the most recently used page table entries, which typically eliminates the need for better than 97% of the accesses to the page tables. When an entry in a page table is modified, its copy in the translation buffer should be deleted by writing its address into the register. An entry is automatically cleared from the translation buffer when any modification is made to its corresponding PTB register.

The EIA register is also used to provide the address which caused the last page fault. When a page fault occurs, the address is obtained by reading the register. (See figure 2).

Reprinted with permission from *Wescon Conf. Rec.*, 1981, pp. 5.2.1–5.2.14.

On writing, the most significant bit of the register is used as the MS bit of the invalidated entry.

On reading, the most significant bit of the register specifies the untranslatable address was accessed with the PTB0 register when it is clear or the PTB1 register when it is set.

PF The two, double word length PROGRAM FLOW registers are used to hold the addresses of the most recent nonsequential instructions. The addresses of the most recent nonsequential instruction is held in the PF0 register. (See figure 3).

SC The two, word length SEQUENTIAL COUNT registers are used to hold the number of sequential instructions executed between the most recent nonsequential instructions. The register is accessed as a pair, with an even register in the lower word and an odd register in the high word of a double word. If the count is zero, it is not saved when the next nonsequential instruction is executed. If a sequential instruction is executed which would increment the SC0 register into overflow, counting stops. All of the SC and PF registers are cleared by any attempt to write into any of them, to provide quick initialization. (See Figure 4).

BPR The two, double word length BREAKPOINT registers hold addresses upon which to issue breakpoints. (See Figure 5).

AS the ADDRESS SPACE field indicates the PTB register used to translate the breakpoint address.

VP The VIRTUAL/PHYSICAL field indicates the address is untranslated.

BE The BREAKPOINT EXECUTION field causes a breakpoint to be issued when an instruction at the address is executed.

BR The BREAKPOINT READ field causes a breakpoint to be issued when an operand at the address is read.

BW The BREAKPOINT WRITE field causes a breakpoint to be issued when the operand at the address is written or is read during the read phase of a read/modify/write operation.

CE The COUNTER ENABLE field causes the breakpoint counter or BCNT register to be decremented on breakpoints issued by BPR register 0. The execution of the breakpoint is postponed until the counter reaches zero.

BC The double word length BREAKPOINT COUNT register holds the number of breakpoints on the BPR0 register to pass over before issuing the breakpoint.

MSR The double word length MEMORY STATUS REGISTER holds fields to control and examine the memory management unit. A reset initialization clears the NT, FT, BEN, TS, TU, and ERC fields An interrupt or trap resulting from breakpointing or flow tracing clears the NT, FT, and BEN fields. After writing into the MSR register, breakpointing and flow tracing are suppressed until after the next nonsequential instruction to allow entry into a program being debugged without an immediate interrupt or trap. (See Figure 6).

ERC The ERROR CLASS is a three bit field which holds the reason for the last interrupt or trap issued by the memory management unit. Its low bit is set on an address translation error (protection conflict, invalid page, etc.). Its middle bit is set on an external abort. Its high bit is set on breakpointing and cleared on flow tracing. Multiple errors can result in the accumulation of more than one set bit. The field is automatically cleared after being read.

TET The TRANSLATION ERROR TYPE is a three bit field which holds the kind of address translation error which occurred, if the last interrupt was caused by an address translation error. Its low bit is set on a protection level conflict. Its middle bit is set on an invalid entry in a level 1 page table. Its high bit is set on an invalid entry in a level 2 page table.

BN The BREAKPOINT NUMBER is a two bit field which specifies the BPR register which triggered the last breakpoint, if the last interrupt was caused by a breakpoint.

ED The ERROR DIRECTION field indicates a read operation or read phase of a read/modify/write operation caused the last address translation error or external abort.

BD The BREAKPOINT DIRECTION field indicates a read operation or read phase of a read/modify/write operation caused the last breakpointing or flow tracing interrupt or trap.

EST The ERROR STATUS field retains the value of the low three bits of the status lines from the processor bus control unit at the last address translation error or external abort.

BST The BREAKPOINT STATUS field retains the value of the three low bits of the status lines from the processor bus control unit at the last breakpointing or flow tracing interrupt or trap.

TU The TRANSLATE USER field causes addresses from user programs to be treated as virtual addresses.

TS The TRANSLATE SUPERVISOR field causes addresses from supervisor programs to be treated as virtual addresses.

DS The DUAL SPACE field causes translated addresses from supervisor programs to use the PTBO register and translated addresses from user programs to use the PTB1 register. Otherwise, all translated addresses are translated with the PTBO register.

AD The ACCESS OVERRIDE field gives user programs access to protected addresses. It is typically used when addresses from supervisor mode are either untranslated or translated with the DS field set.

BEN The BREAKPOINT ENABLE field causes the BPR registers to issue breakpoints.

UB The USER BREAK field prevents breakpoints from being issued for supervisor mode.

AI The ABORT/INTERRUPT causes the memory management unit to issue ABT traps on breakpoints. Otherwise, it will issue NMI interrupts.

FT The FLOW TRACE field causes the PF and SC registers to t rack program execution.

UT The USER TRACE field prevents the flow tracing of supervisor mode.

NT The NONSEQUENTIAL TRACE field causes the execution of the current instruction to be cancelled and an ABT trap to be executed on every nonsequential instruction.

THE NS1602 INTERRUPT CONTROL UNIT

The NS16202 Interrupt Control Unit is designed to minimize the software and hardware overhead in handling multiple interrupts. It has a wide variety of operating modes.

Some highlights are:

* Each 16202 handles up to 16 hardware or software, programmable, prioritized interrupts. Multiple 16202s can be cascaded providing up to 256 interrupts.
* When only 8 interrupts are required of a single 16202, the extra 8 interrupt sense lines can be programmed to function as independent parallel I/O lines.
* Two, 16-bit counters, each capable of generating interrupts or cascading to one 32-bit counter.
* Software interrupts can be set pending by the MPU.
* Independently programmable polarity, edge/level detection and masking for each interrupt line.
* Optional automatic rotation of priorities within each 16202.

THE NS16000 INTERRUPT SCHEME

In the NS16000 architecture, interrupts result in a transfer of control to a new program location. There are two operating modes for interrupts -- vectored and non-vectored. In the non-vectored mode, all interrupts are serviced with the same interrupt module. In the more flexible vectored mode, each of the possible 256 interrupts may be serviced with a different module. When the MPU acknowledges an interrupt, the ICU provides an index into the "Dispatch Table" within memory. The service vector pointed to by the sum of the dedicated MPU "Intbase" register and the index describes the module with which to service the interrupt.

CASCADING

When more than 16 interrupts are required, multiple 16202s can be cascaded to provide any number of interrupts between 16 and 256.

In this case, the index received from the ICU upon acknowledging the interrupt is negative and signals that the interrupt index should be fetched from a cascaded 16202. An additional memory cycle finds the Dispatch Table index in the vector register of the cascaded 16202. The address of the cascaded ICU is maintained in the "Cascade Table" in memory (indexed from Int-base register).

Each of the 16202s has a memory mapped register set. The master 16202 is assumed to reside at address Top-of-memory minus 511 (relocateable by means of the cascade table, which provides the address of the 0th register for each 16202 in the system.

EIGHT OR SIXTEEN BITS

If high-speed interrupt servicing is the ultimate goal, a 16-bit bus mode is provided. This allows the memory-mapped register pairs to be accessed in one bus cycle. If interrupt reaction time can be traded for flexibility, the 8-bit bus mode should be used. In 8-bit mode, the unused 8 data bus lines can be independently programmed for any of the following functions: a) an input line; b) an output line; or c) another hardware interrupt sense input. Note that in 16-bit mode only 8 hardware interrupts are useable, but in 8-bit bus mode, 16 are achievable.

REGISTER SET

Each 16202 has 32, 8-bit registers arranged in pairs. Each of these registers can be addressed by the MPU using byte reference instructions. In 16-bit bus mode, by word reference.

The registers are:

Vector Indicator a positive number is an index into Dispatch Table, a negative number is an index into Cascade Table.

Trigger Select each interrupt sense line can be independently programmed for edge/level and positive/negative polarity.

Interrupt Pending each bit in this register indicates a pending interrupt for the associated interrupt sense line. The MPU can write this location to indicate "Software" interrupts. Software interrupts are useful when we want to defer service on an incoming hardware interrupt.

In Service for each interrupt source a corresponding bit is set if the service routine for that source is executing.

Mask each source may be independently enabled and disabled by corresponding bit locations here.

Cascade Indicator each source which is actually a cascaded 16202 should be initialized to indicate so here.

First Priority the source with the highest priority is noted by a set bit. In AUTO-ROTATE mode, after each interrupt acknowledge from this 16202, the priority 2 interrupt is made priority 1 and so on.

Control the various control modes are programmed here (i.e. auto-rotate, 8/16-bit mode and others).

Clock Output Assignment in 8-bit mode, the unused lower four sense lines may be connected to the internal counter.

Counter Interrupt Pointer each counter may be assigned an interrupt to trigger when it counts down to 0. If the assignment is enabled, then the corresponding interrupt source is automatically masked out.

I/O Port Latch in 8-bit mode, if the unused sense lines are programmed as I/D, this register functions as a latch. It reflects the values of the pins, both input and output.

Interrupt/Port Select this register determines the independent function of the sense lines in 8-bit mode.

Port Direction independently programmed directions for the I/O port.

Counter Control programming for the various counter attributes is done by bits here.

Counter Starting Value holds the preset value for the 2 counters. When the counters count down to 0 they fire interrupts, reload the respective preset value and continue counting. The counters interrupts are maskable.

Counter Value the current value of each counter.

THE NS16202 DIRECT MEMORY ACCESS CONTROLLER

The NS203 DMA controller is a high-speed peripheral designed to reduce the I/O handling time of the MPU and improve system performance.

Like the Interrupt Controller, it also has a wide variety of operating modes. These are outlined below. Some highlights are:

* 2 modes of bus interface -- local and remote
* 4 independently controlled channels
* can use dedicated bus to minimize local bus traffic
* supports command chaining
* 3 different channel commands
* can be programmed to terminate on until match or while match conditions
* handles 8 and 16 bit devices and memories
* performs optional assembly/disassembly of byte and word values
* data rates to 5 megabytes/second
* cascadable.

REMOTE VS LOCAL CONFIGURATIONS

In local mode the 16203 resides on the microprocessors multiplexed bus. The controlled devices may reside either on the multiplexed or non-multiplexed busses. In this configuration, the 16203 shares the bus control signals from the 16201 Timing Control Unit.

In remote mode the 16203 controls its own dedicated bus to minimize local bus useage. All controlled devices reside on this dedicated bus. Each 16203 in this mode uses the bus control signals from an associated 16201 TCU.

Each mode supports up to 4, independent channels with 8 and 16 bit widths. In both modes the user can specify a transfer to occur in direct or indirect mode.

DIRECT AND INDIRECT MODE

In the direct mode the data is transferred between the device and local memory. No assembly or searching is allowed.

In the indirect mode, the data is first transferred into the 16203 where the controller has the capability of performing logical operations on it. Data may be assembled into words or disassembled into bytes. The controller may be programmed to stop when a certain bit pattern is found in the data stream.

REGISTERS

The 16203 has a memory mapped address space of 128, 8-bit registers organized as pairs. A large number of registers at this time are unimplemented and are reserved for future expansion. Each channel has 13 associated registers. In addition, there are one device control register and four device status registers.

A brief description of the register set follows:

Control sets the global operating characteristics of the device (i.e. local/remote and chaining)

Vector when used like a 16202 ICU this register provides the interrupt service vector index into the Dispatch Table.

Command bit patterns here indicate what kind of transfer to make, where the source and destinations are, whether they are devices or memory, the transfer width of each. Also indicated are the direct/indirect mode, assembly/disassembly, autorotate and burst type.

Source/Destination Address the absolute, physical address of each.

Search/Mask when search is specified, the bits not indicated by the mask register value are compared to the incoming byte. If the proper match/nomatch exists, the transfer terminates as programmed.

Other Features

Chaining When chaining is used, the termination of one channel command causes its complementary channel to begin operation. This allows non-stop channel operation.

Burst Two types of burst mode are supported. In semi-burst mode the DMA releases the local bus only when a request from the device is released. In full-burst the DMA maintains control of the bus until the transfer terminates.

Auto-Transfer Some devices do not issue a DMA request, instead they have the data ready right after the previous datum is read. With this capability the DMA controller issues a transfer whenever the priority is correct, regardless of the DMA request.

Assembly It is usually necessary to interface 8-bit peripherals to 16-bit wide memory. In this case two device accesses are made for every memory access.

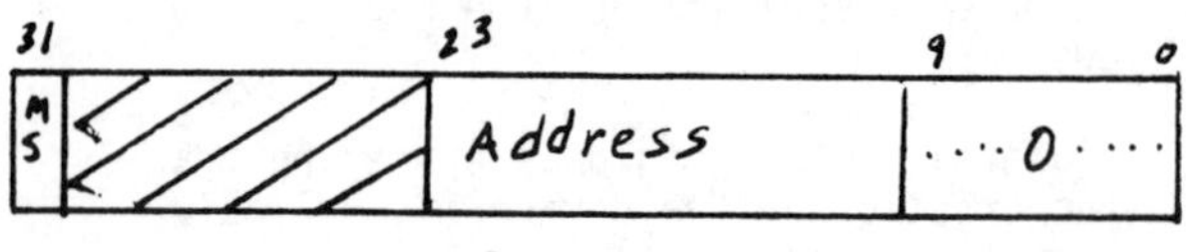

Fig. 1. A PTB REGISTER

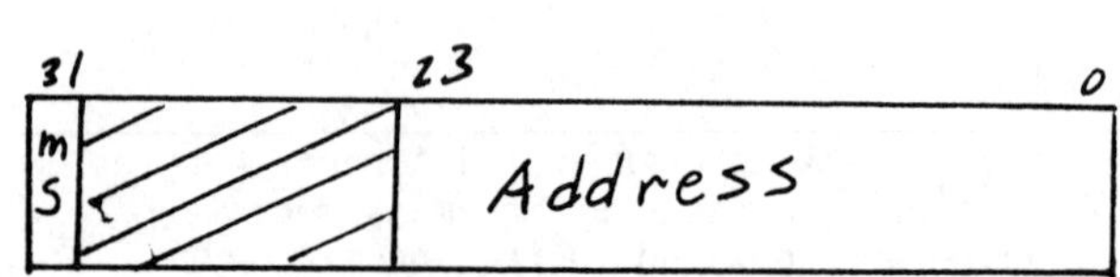

Fig. 2. THE EIA REGISTER

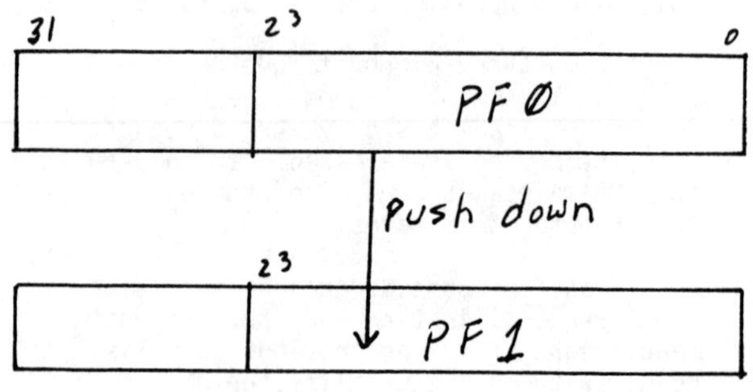

Fig. 3. THE PROGRAM FLOW REGISTER

<u>Termination Action</u> The device may be programmed for different actions at end-of-transfer. It may simply halt, or it may interrupt like a 16202. It may terminate on a search condition or it may not. Various other conditions may be programmed also.

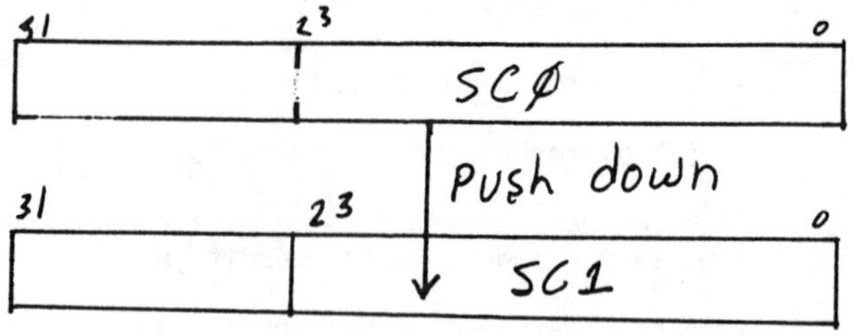

Fig. 4. THE SEQUENTIAL COUNT REGISTERS

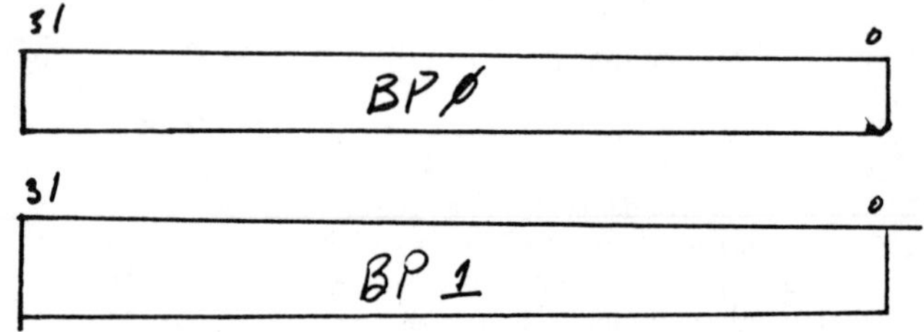

Fig. 5. THE BREAKPOINT REGISTERS

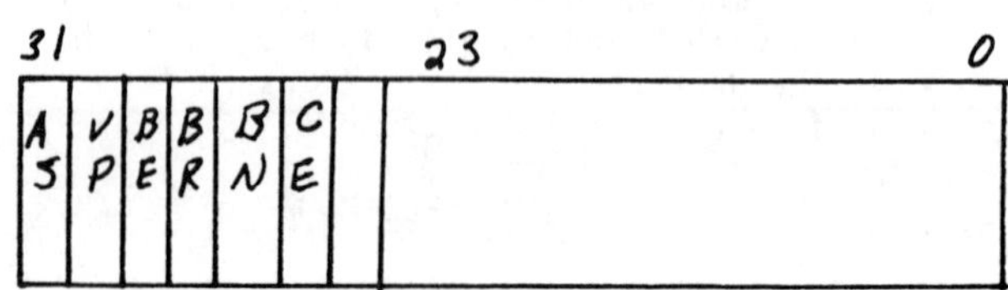

Fig. 6. THE MSR REGISTER

NS16202 INTERRUPT CONTROLLER/TIMER

- 16 Interrupt Sources
- Programmable Conditions
- Cascadable
- Two 16-Bit Counters

CPU/INTERRUPT CONTROLLER INTERFACE 8-BIT BUS MODE

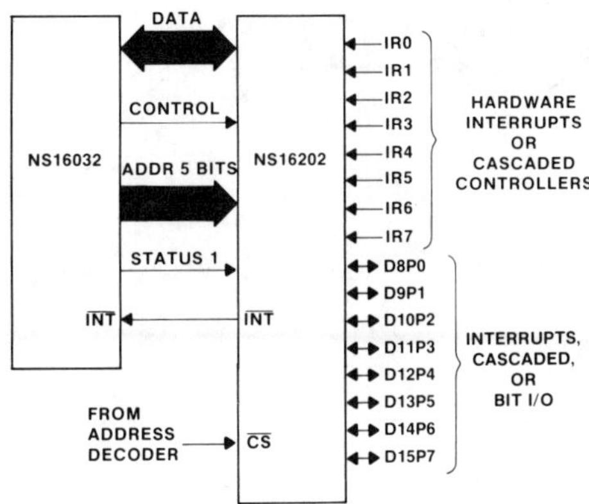

MEMORY ORGANIZATION FOR CASCADED NS16202's

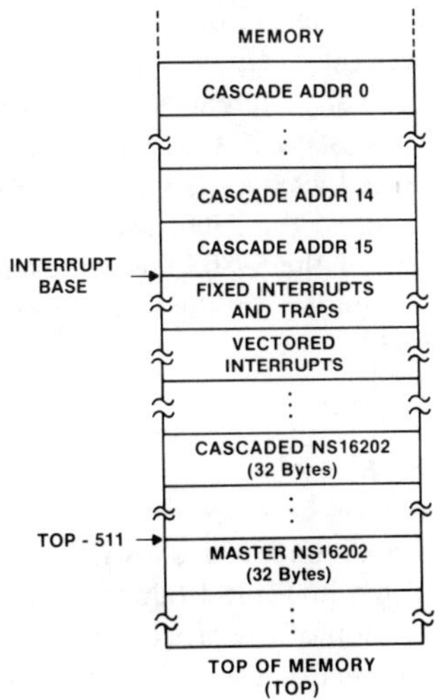

CASCADED INTERRUPT SEQUENCE

- Master ICU Interrupts CPU
- CPU Reads Master Vector
  — Sees Negative Value
- CPU Finds Cascaded ICU
  — Identifier from Master Vector
  — Backward from INT Table
- CPU Reads Cascaded Vector
- CPU Performs Interrupt Service Per Cascaded Vector

NS16202 INTERRUPT CONTROLLER ADDRESSABLE REGISTERS

SOFTWARE VECTOR	HARDWARE VECTOR	0
EDGE/LEVEL		2
TRIGGER POLARITY		4
INTERRUPT PENDING		6
IN SERVICE		8
INTERRUPT MASK		A
CASCADED SOURCE		C
FIRST PRIORITY		E
CLOCK OUTPUT ASSIGNMENT	COUNTER/MODE POINTER	10
PORT LATCH	COUNTER INT. POINTER	12
PORT DIRECTION	PORT/INTERRUPT	14
COUNTER INT. CONTROL	COUNTER CONTROL	16
COUNTER START VALUE (L)		18
COUNTER START VALUE (H)		1A
COUNTER VALUE (L)		1C
COUNTER VALUE (H)		1E

NS16203 DMA CONTROLLER

- Local/Remote Configurations
- Channels
  - Four in Local Mode
  - Two in Remote Mode
  - Cascadable
- Supports 8-Bit and 16-Bit Peripherals
  - Byte Packing Feature
- Direct or Indirect Cycles
- Powerful Commands
  - Chaining
  - Masked Search Options
- 48-Pin Dual-in-Line Package

NS16203 DMA CONTROLLER

- Channel Registers: n = 0, 1, 2, 3

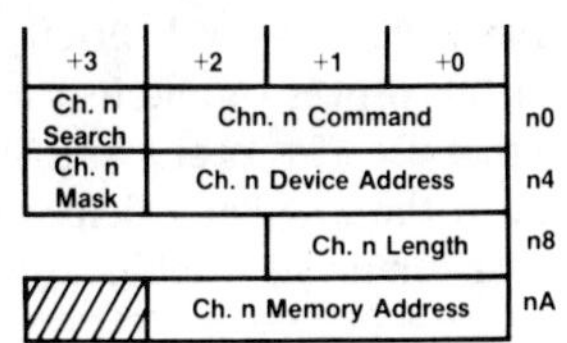

- General Control Registers:

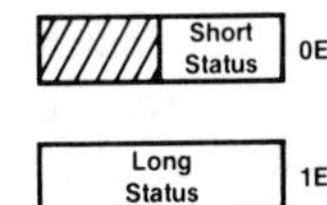

An established microprocessor family—especially its newest member—offers speed, compatibility with a large body of existing software, and multiprocessing capability.

An Overview of the 9900 Microprocessor Family

Richard V. Orlando
Thomas L. Anderson
American Microsystems, Inc.

A recent article in *IEEE Micro* (Toong and Gupta, May 1981[1]) discussed at some length the main features of several currently available 16-bit microprocessors. Although the authors made no pretense about covering all such processors, we feel they erred in omitting at least one machine, the 9900. As we will show, the 9900 microprocessor and its successor, the 9995, are powerful machines with architectural and performance characteristics rivalling those of the 8086, Z8000, and 68000. We will also discuss the recently disclosed 99000 family, a highly sophisticated, upward-compatible extension to the 9900 family.

Besides its power, the 9900 is notable for being the first commercially available 16-bit microprocessor—Texas Instruments first offered the TMS9900 in 1976 and it is still on the market. In addition, the 9900 is second-sourced by AMI as the S9900. We will briefly outline the salient features of this processor and its successors in a manner similar to that used by Toong and Gupta—by following the format of the original article, we hope to present a valid comparison to the machines discussed there.

General characteristics

Since the 9900 was the pioneering 16-bit microprocessor, it does not contain all the features found on later machines. However, it does provide 16-bit internal and external data buses, byte and word instructions, and most of the common addressing modes. The machine architecture provides 16 general-purpose registers, although these actually reside in main memory. This strategy achieves one of the benefits of register addressing: the coding efficiency gained by not having to specify full memory addresses. However, no increase in speed is attained by using register instead of memory instructions. The address space is 64K, with no internal provision for extension. The 9900 emphasizes the "family" approach to microprocessors, with several different software-compatible models available. The 9940 is a single-chip microcomputer with an enhanced 9900 as its CPU; the 9980 is an 8-bit data bus version of the 9900; the 9995 is a high-performance version of the 9980. We will examine the 9900 and the 9995, pointing out the differences between them where appropriate.

Architectural details

The basic structure of the 9900 is shown in Figure 1; its specifications are listed in Table 1 (along with those for the 9995). The operation of the processor is straightforward. There is no instruction prefetch or pipelining. The I/O interface is handled by a communications register unit, or CRU, which uses specific instructions to address external devices via the CRU lines and address bus. Most important, I/O bits can be addressed individually or in fields of 1 to 16 bits. The structure of the 9995 (Figure 2) is similar to that of the 9900, although it adds a single instruction prefetch, 256 bytes of internal RAM, and internal clock generation. To save pins and to allow the use of byte-wide memories, the 9995 provides only an eight-bit external data bus. However, the 16-bit-wide on-chip RAM prevents this from becoming a bottleneck.

Register organization. 9900 processors contain three primary internal registers: the program counter (PC), the status register, and the workspace pointer (WP). The

Reprinted from *IEEE Micro*, vol. 1, pp. 38–44, Aug. 1981.

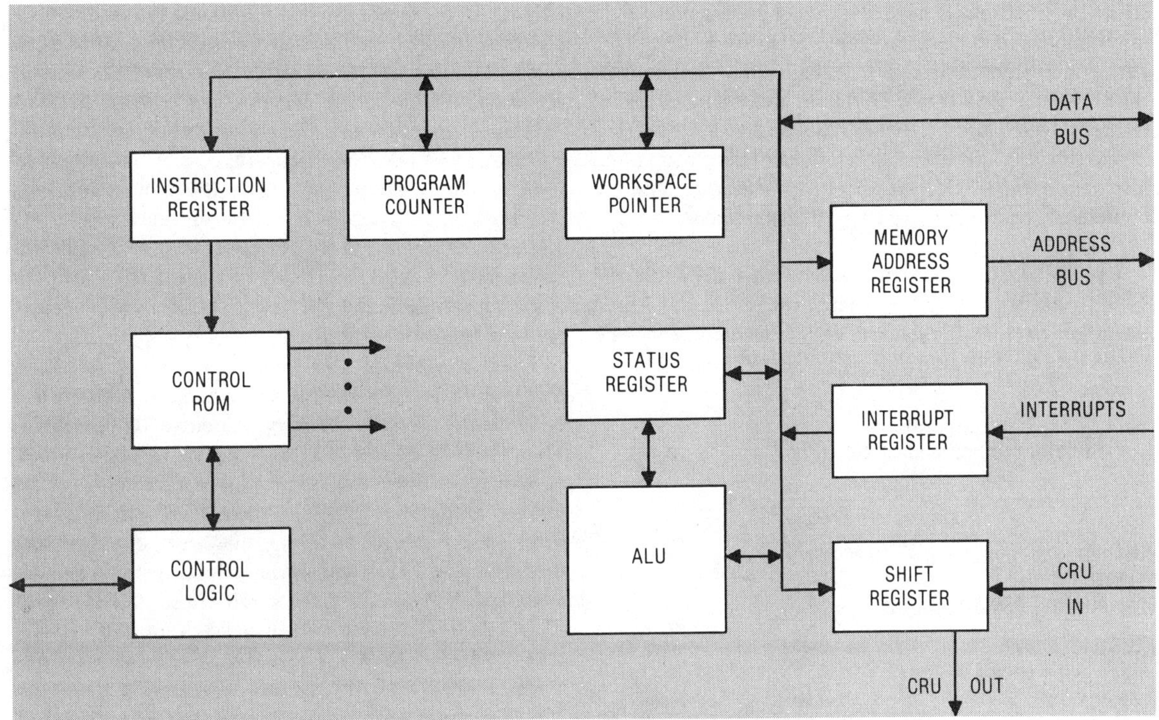

Figure 1. Basic structure of the 9900.

status register contains a four-bit interrupt mask and processor status bits (seven for the 9900 and eight for the 9995). The WP points to the starting location in memory of the 16 general-purpose "workspace" registers, which must be held in contiguous words. A "context switch" mechanism loads the WP with a new value, thus defining a new set of work-space registers in main memory. This multiple-register-set scheme allows the 9900 family to efficiently handle interrupt and subroutine calls without saving or stacking the contents of the workspace registers. In essence, the 9900 family uses a linked-list approach to program control linkage rather than the more traditional hardware stack. Since certain workspace locations are used to store processor status during subroutine calls, the "general-purpose" registers are not completely general. The 9995's 256 bytes of internal RAM are commonly used to store workspaces—this greatly improves the performance of register operations.

System structure. The microprocessor, memory, and I/O devices are interconnected by a local bus as defined by the processor pin-out. The data portion of this bus is used only for memory operations; I/O is handled by a separate serial interface (described in a later section). A microprocessor, memory, and I/O devices form a module which may be connected through bus control and arbiter modules to a global bus (see Hirschman, Ali, and Swan[5]).

Memory. The 9900 and 9995 use a straightforward 64K address space, which can be expanded only by external memory management. The 9900 always accesses an entire 16-bit word of memory at one time, although it has byte instructions to perform operations on either of the two bytes.

Stack organization. The 9900 and 9995 are not stack-oriented machines and provide no direct hardware support for stacks. For example, for a subroutine call or interrupt response, several of the work-space registers—rather than a stack—are used to save the processor state. However, it is a relatively straightforward matter to set up a stack of workspaces to permit recursive and multiple subroutine calls.

I/O mechanisms. Up to 4K bits each of input and output may be individually addressed by the CRU mechanism in the 9900, and up to 32K bits in the 9995. These bits may be addressed in fields of 1 to 16 bits, which allows single-operation flag testing or setting. Data transfer to and from I/O devices is handled serially through the CRUIN and CRUOUT lines. External decoding of the low-order address lines determines the actual number of I/O devices being addressed.

Software. Unlike other 16-bit microprocessors, the 9900 was designed to be software-compatible with a minicomputer family—the Texas Instruments 990 series—rather than with a microprocessor. Texas Instruments' philosophy of microprocessor design dictates that advances in minicomputer systems development be incorporated into new microprocessors as soon as improvements in VLSI technology permit it. The result is a parallel development of both a microprocessor and a minicomputer family, with software compatibility between families and among individual members of each family.

The 9900 family supports a full memory-to-memory architecture, although workspace registers are provided to reduce program size through encoding efficiency. The instruction set supports most addressing modes, some byte instructions, and bit-addressable I/O space. The 9995 contains arithmetic overflow traps to help handle run-time errors. The 9900 and 9995 both contain software interrupts, which allow a user to emulate a new instruction in macrocode. The 9995 also provides an unimplemented instruction trap (MID interrupt) to allow users to simulate complex instructions or to trap on illegal opcodes.

The 99000. Texas Instruments recently disclosed the 99000 family of 16-bit microprocessors.[6,7] Three members of this family are under development—the 99105 is a faster version of the 9900; the 99110 and 99120

Table 1.
Specifications for the 9900 family.

	9900	9995
YEAR OF COMMERCIAL INTRODUCTION	1976	1981
NO. OF BASIC INSTRUCTIONS	69	73
NO. OF GENERAL-PURPOSE REGISTERS	16	16
PIN COUNT	64	40
DIRECT ADDRESS RANGE (BYTES)	64K	64K
NUMBER OF ADDRESSING MODES	8	8
BASIC CLOCK FREQUENCY	3 MHz*	3 MHz
SYSTEM STRUCTURES		
UNIFORM ADDRESSABILITY		
MODULE MAP AND MODULES		
VIRTUAL		
PRIMITIVE DATA TYPES		
BITS	•	•
INTEGER BYTE OR WORD	•	•
INTEGER DOUBLE-WORD		
LOGICAL BYTE OR WORD	•	•
LOGICAL DOUBLE-WORD		
CHARACTER STRINGS (BYTE, WORD)	•	•
CHARACTER STRINGS (DOUBLE-WORD)		
BCD BYTE		
BCD WORD		
BCD DOUBLE-WORD		
FLOATING-POINT		
DATA STRUCTURES		
STACKS	•	•
ARRAYS	•	•
PACKED ARRAYS	•	•
RECORDS	•	•
PACKED RECORDS		
STRINGS		
PRIMITIVE CONTROL OPERATIONS		
CONDITION CODE PRIMITIVES	•	•
JUMP	•	•
CONDITIONAL BRANCH	•	•
SIMPLE ITERATIVE LOOP CONTROL	•	•
SUBROUTINE CALL	•	•
MULTIWAY BRANCH		
CONTROL STRUCTURE		
EXTERNAL PROCEDURE CALL		
SEMAPHORES		
TRAPS	•	•
INTERRUPTS	•	•
SUPERVISOR CALL	•	•
OTHERS		
USER MICROCODE		
DEBUG MODE		

*The 9900 clock frequency is 3.0 MHz, but since two clock cycles are required for each machine state, the effective clock frequency is actually only 1.5 MHz.

(Figure 3), however, provide numerous enhancements to the 9900 family which greatly increase their range of application. Each has single instruction prefetch, an internal oscillator and clock generator, arithmetic overflow and illegal opcode traps, and status output pins for multiprocessor and DMA configurations. The instruction set includes many extensions to the 9900, including long-word arithmetic, support for user-defined stacks, and test-and-set primitives for semaphores. The 64K address space may be extended to 16M by using the TIM99610 memory manager; the 99110 and 99120 include instructions to support this chip.

These processors also include a feature called the macrostore, an internal high-speed memory addressed independently of main memory and currently comprising 1K bytes of ROM and 32 bytes of RAM. This fast memory allows the software emulation of new instructions or frequently executed routines to operate considerably faster than if the instructions or routines were stored in main memory. The 99110 will contain floating-point routines as part of its macrostore; the 99120 will contain the kernel of TI's Real-Time Executive, which will support a Pascal-based operating system. These new architectural features, when coupled with the increase in operating frequency, will yield significant improvements over 9900 family execution times. In addition, the 99110 and 99120 can operate in either user or supervisor (privileged) mode.

Microcomputers

There are several single-card microcomputers based on members of the 9900 family. Table 2 summarizes the characteristics of the Texas Instruments TM990/101 single-card microcomputer, which contains a 9900 as its CPU.

Multiprocessor capabilities

As already mentioned, the designer can configure 9900 family processors in a multiprocessor system by interconnecting them on a global bus. Although no *specific* multiprocessing features were incorporated into the design of the 9900 and 9995, the 99110 and 99120 provide several features designed specifically for multiprocessing environments. They send out bus status codes so that other modules in the system know exactly what phase of instruction execution they are in. Such status information is critical to efficient arbitration of system bus contention. They provide primitives for testing and setting semaphores, with external signals to lock out other processors during atomic operations.

Selection strategy

Technical issues. The machines of the 9900 family have both advantages and disadvantages when compared to the 8086, Z8000, 68000, and NS16000. Their direct address space, 64K, is the smallest of the group, although this address space is externally extensible. Their I/O facilities are addressed separately from memory, allowing implementation of useful features such as individual bit access.

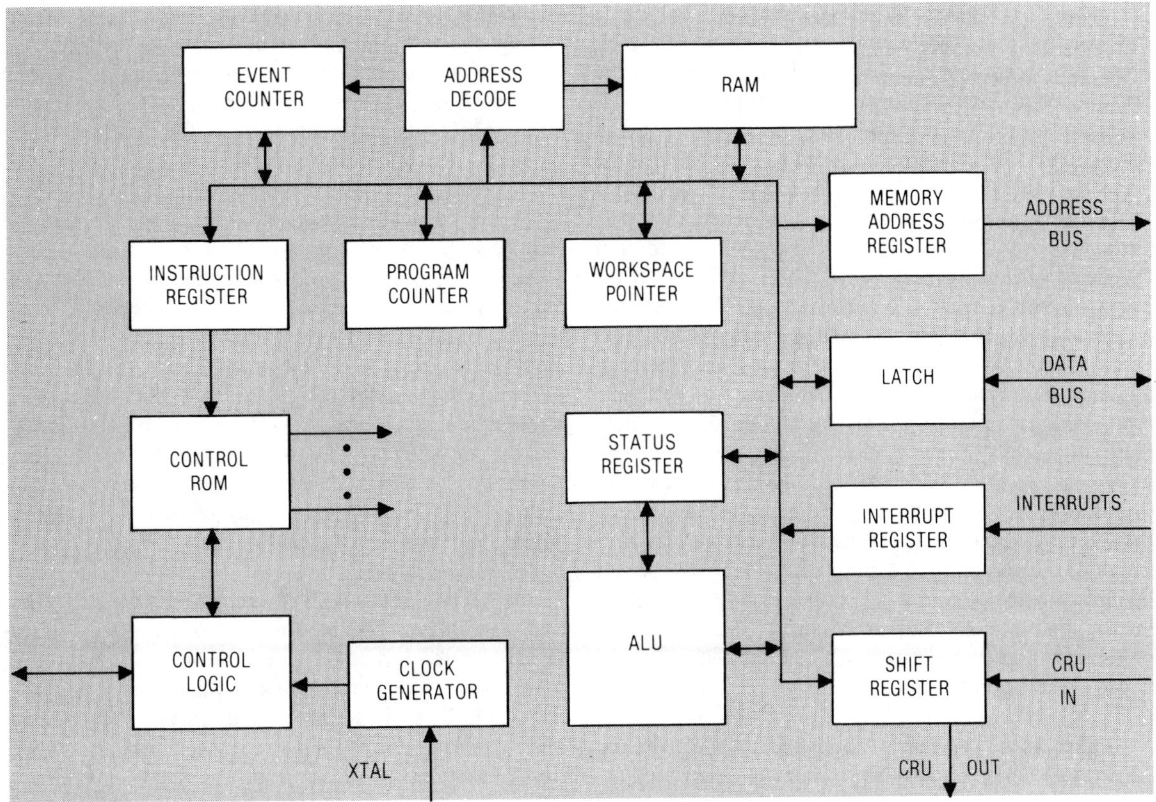

Figure 2. Basic structure of the 9995.

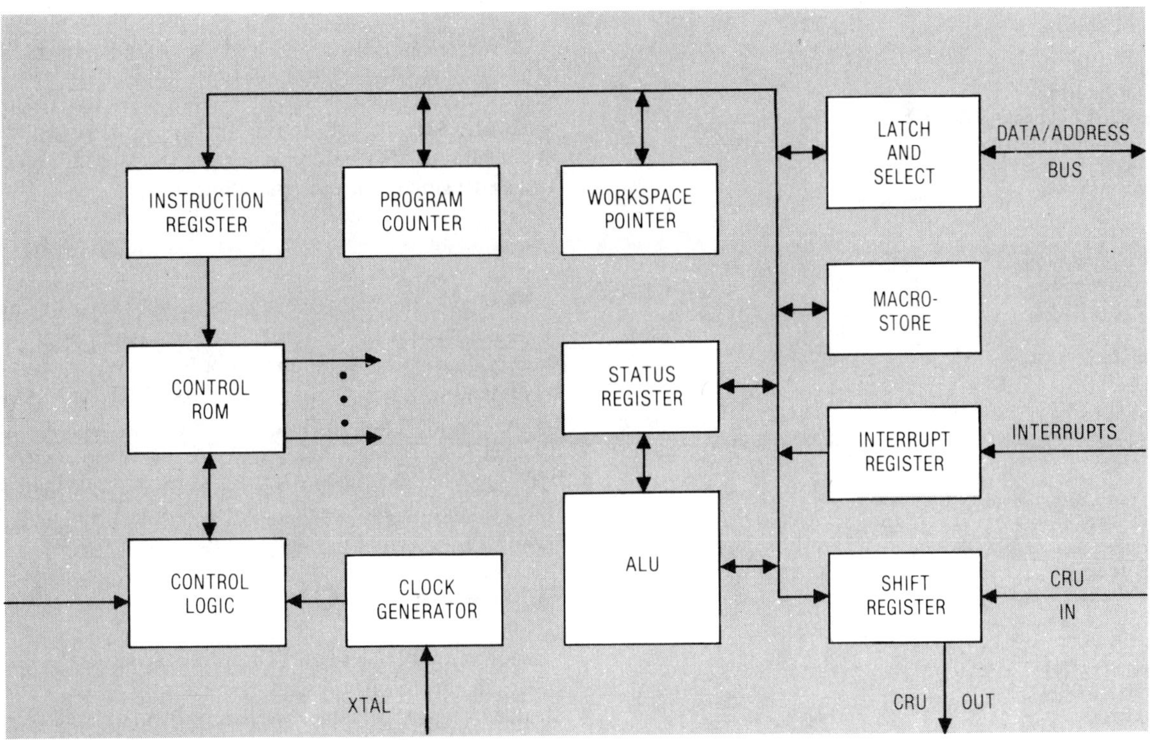

Figure 3. Basic structure of the 99110 and 99120.

Unlike the Z8000 and 68000, currently available members of the 9900 family do not support 32-bit operands, except in multiplies and divides. However, the family's memory-to-memory architecture provides an advantage not found in the other 16-bit micros by reducing the number of instructions required to access operands. The 99110 and 99120 support both long-word operations and a memory-to-memory architecture; hence, their performance benefits greatly. Table 3 lists the execution speeds of various instructions for the 3-MHz (1.5-MHz effective) 9900, the 3-MHz 9995, and the 6-MHz 99110.

The 9900 is obviously the slowest currently available 16-bit microprocessor, although it is the least expensive and most mature. Advances in VLSI technology and microprocessor architecture are responsible for the dramatic increases in the execution speeds provided by the newer processors. The 9900 and the 9995 exemplify this—they show great differences in performance even though they both operate at the same cycle time and with the same general internal architecture. This increase can be directly attributed to architectural techniques such as instruction prefetch. The performance of the 99110 is impressive, consistent with its high clock frequency and advanced architectural features.

Applications. The ideal "application niche" for the 9900 and 9995 is probably a control environment. Because such applications do not require large amounts of memory, the limited direct address space of the 9900 and 9995 is not a major factor. The 9900 family's fast interrupt response time (as can be seen from the figures in Table 3 for context switching and restoring) is a useful feature in such environments. Its ability to individually address I/O bits and fields without the need for masks makes it particularly useful in bit-map applications such as terminals and printers. On the other hand, the serial I/O is not particularly well-suited for applications which require large amounts of data transfer.

An important feature of the 9900 family is its provision for single-chip, 16-bit micro*computers*. The 9940, for example, contains 2K of ROM, 128 bytes of RAM, internal clock generation, and 32 bits of general-purpose I/O ports in a single, 40-pin package. The 9995 includes internal clock generation and 256 bytes of on-chip RAM, making it somewhat of a hybrid between a microcomputer and a microprocessor. The availability of microcomputers is important in many control applications, where space and speed constraints do not permit use of board-level systems.

The 99110 and 99120 have enough enhancements that their usefulness will extend well beyond control applications. The two devices provide multiprocessor and multiuser support of the same caliber as that found in the Z8000 and 68000. They do not provide support for demand paging, which may limit their use in certain large applications. However, they do support functional paging—e.g., of separate data and program memories—and this can be useful in numerous applications.

There are many support chips for the 9900 family (Table 4). Although the 9900 does not have a set of peripheral chips from an eight-bit predecessor to fall back on, it has been around longer than the other 16-bit microprocessors discussed. Thus, there has been sufficient time to develop support chips for typical applications.

Table 2.
TM990/101 microcomputer characteristics.

GENERAL	
PROCESSOR USED	TMS9900
WORD SIZE (BITS)	16
ADDRESSING	
ADDRESS SIZE (BITS)	15
TOTAL MEMORY ADDRESSABLE (BYTES)	64K
AMT. OF RAM ON CARD (BYTES)	4K
AMT. OF ROM ON CARD (BYTES)	0-8K
DMA CAPABILITY	YES
FREQUENCY, ETC.	
CLOCK FREQUENCY (MHz)	3
SUPPLY VOLTAGES	+5, +12, −12
BOARD SIZE (INCHES)	7.5 × 11
I/O CAPABILITY	
BUS TYPE	SPECIAL
PARALLEL I/O LINES	16+
NUMBER OF I/O PORTS	2
MAX. I/O RATE (K BAUD)	38.4
ADDITIONAL HARDWARE DETAILS	
INTERRUPT PROVISIONS	YES
MULTIPROCESSING CAPABILITY	YES
NO. OF TIMERS	3
BITS PER TIMER	8-14
SOFTWARE	
OPERATING SYSTEM	YES
HIGH-LEVEL LANGUAGE(S)	YES
ASSEMBLER	YES
DEBUGGING AIDS	YES
APPLICATION PACKAGES	YES

Commercial issues. The 9900 is second-sourced by AMI and, internationally, by ITT Intermettel. It is a mature product with the largest established software and hardware base in the 16-bit world. Both Texas Instruments and AMI will continue to support the family, as well as develop its future generations.

We have attempted to evaluate the 9900 family using the same metrics as those used by Toong and Gupta in their evaluation of 16-bit microprocessors. We conclude by presenting our own rating of the 9900, 9995, and 99000 family (Table 5) and include for comparison the ratings assigned by Toong and Gupta to the 8086, Z8000, MC68000, and NS16000. Our results show performance impressive enough to demand the 9900's inclusion in any treatment of currently available 16-bit machines. ■

Acknowledgments

The assistance of Dave Laffitte, John Schabowski, and others in the 16-bit microprocessor group at Texas Instruments was invaluable. Their proofreading and assistance in obtaining 99000 information contributed greatly to this article.

Table 3.
Execution speeds (in microseconds) of 9900 family microprocessors.

OPERATION	DATA TYPE	9900	9995	99110
REGISTER-TO-REGISTER MOVE	BYTE/WORD	4.60	(1.30)*	0.50
	DOUBLE-WORD	9.80	(2.60)	1.00
MEMORY-TO-REGISTER MOVE	BYTE	7.30	(1.99)	0.83
	WORD	7.30	(2.33)	0.67
	DOUBLE-WORD	14.60	(4.66)	1.33
MEMORY-TO-MEMORY MOVE	BYTE	9.90	(1.30),2.60	1.00
	WORD	9.90	(1.90),3.30	0.83
	DOUBLE-WORD	19.80	(3.90),6.60	1.67
ADD MEMORY TO REGISTER	BYTE/WORD	7.32	(2.60)	0.83
	DOUBLE-WORD	21.30	(5.30)	2.00
COMPARE MEMORY TO MEMORY	BYTE/WORD	9.90	1.99	1.00
	DOUBLE-WORD	19.80	3.98	2.00
MULTIPLY MEMORY-TO-MEMORY	BYTE	21.90	(7.90),8.60	4.17
	WORD	21.90	(7.90),8.60	4.17
	DOUBLE-WORD	180.64	59.95	26.38
CONDITIONAL BRANCH	BRANCH TAKEN	3.60	1.30	0.50
	BRANCH NOT TAKEN	2.90	1.30	0.50
MODIFY INDEX BRANCH IF ZERO	BRANCH TAKEN	7.60	2.60	1.00
BRANCH TO SUBROUTINE		7.90	3.90	1.00
CONTEXT SWITCH		13.60	5.60	2.00
RETURN CONTEXT		5.90	2.30	1.00

*Times in parentheses are for references to internal RAM.

Table 4.
9900 family support chips.

MEMORY MANAGEMENT	TIM99610
BUS ARBITER	
FLOATING-POINT	
DMA CONTROLLER	TMS9911
INTERRUPT CONTROL UNIT	TMS9901
I/O PROCESSOR/INTERFACE	TMS9901
PERIPHERAL CONTROLLER	TMS9901
FLOPPY DISK CONTROLLER	TMS9909
CRT CONTROLLER	TMS9927
ARRAY PROCESSOR	
BUBBLE MEMORY CONTROLLER	

Table 5.
Ranking of 16-bit microprocessors.

	8086	Z8000	MC68000	NS16000	9900	9995	99000
SPEED	C	B	A	A	D	B	A
NUMBER OF REGISTERS	B	A	A	C	A	A	A
ADDRESS RANGE	D	A	A	B	D	D	D
COMPATIBILITY WITH EARLIER MICROPROCESSORS	A	B	B	B	NA	A	A
SUPPORT CHIPS	A	B	C	D	A	A	A
MULTIPROCESSING CAPABILITY	B	B	B	C	C	C	A
SECOND SOURCE	A	A	A	D	B	D	D

References

1. Hoo-min D. Toong and Amar Gupta, "An Architectural Comparison of Contemporary 16-Bit Microprocessors," *IEEE Micro*, Vol. 1, No. 2, May 1981, pp. 26-37.*

2. Henry A. Davis, "Comparing Architectures of Three 16-Bit Microprocessors," *Computer Design*, Vol. 18, No. 7, July 1979, pp. 91-100.

3. *9900 Family Systems Design and Data Book*, Texas Instruments, Inc., Houston, 1978.

*Included in this book, pp. 33–34.

4. *TMS 9995 Microcomputer Preliminary Data Manual*, Texas Instruments, Inc., Houston, 1981.

5. Alan D. Hirschman, Gamil Ali, and Richard Swan, "Standard Modules Offer Flexible Multiprocessor System Design," *Computer Design*, Vol. 18, No. 5, May 1979, pp. 181-189.

6. David S. Laffitte and Karl M. Guttag, "Fast On-Chip Memory Extends 16-Bit Family's Reach," *Electronics*, Vol. 54, No. 4, Feb. 24, 1981, pp. 157-161.

7. David Laffitte, "New-Generation 16-Bit Microprocessors—Fast and Function-Oriented," *Electronic Design*, Vol. 29, No. 4, Feb. 19, 1981, pp. 111-117.

INTELLIGENT PERIPHERALS OF THE VLSI ERA

Gerald R. Samsen
Strategic Marketing Manager
Texas Instruments Incorporated
8600 Commerce Park Drive
Houston, Texas

ABSTRACT

If present trends in microprocessor performance continue, system performance may be adversely restricted by limitations in the hardware buses which interconnect the various system elements. This paper highlights this problem and proposes a direction for overcoming the limitations of past and present system architectures. The evolution in peripheral subsystems for the TMS 99000 microprocessor family is shown to address these limitations.

INTRODUCTION

The subject of advanced 16-bit microprocessor families has seen much discussion on processor architecture in recent years. However the advent of VLSI technology has provided the capability for peripheral subsystems to attain a much higher level of intelligence and a much higher degree of autonomy than previously realized in past generations of microprocessor peripherals. For this reason, peripheral functions are becoming more of a factor in overall system performance and cost. Thus the architecture of the peripheral subsystem becomes a key factor in systems design.

TRADITION – A LIMITING FACTOR?

Computer system architectures, especially microprocessor system architectures, have traditionally been based upon the computer architecture first proposed by Von Neumann in 1948. This architecture, shown in Figure 1, consists of a CPU, a memory system, and an input/output system connected locally through a common bus.

The factors, which influence system performance, include the throughput of the CPU and the bandwidth, or information rate, of the bus, which interconnects the various elements. Past microprocessors were limited in performance by the state-of-the-art technology in which they were manufactured. Thus system bus bandwidth requirements were low and were overshadowed by the CPU as a source of performance limitation. However, the evolution of technology has greatly increased the performance of microprocessors and has likewise placed an ever-increasing burden of performance degradation on the system bus. Thus microprocessor systems suffer from the "Von Neumann Bottleneck", or, in other words, are bound by the rate at which functions may be performed on the system bus.

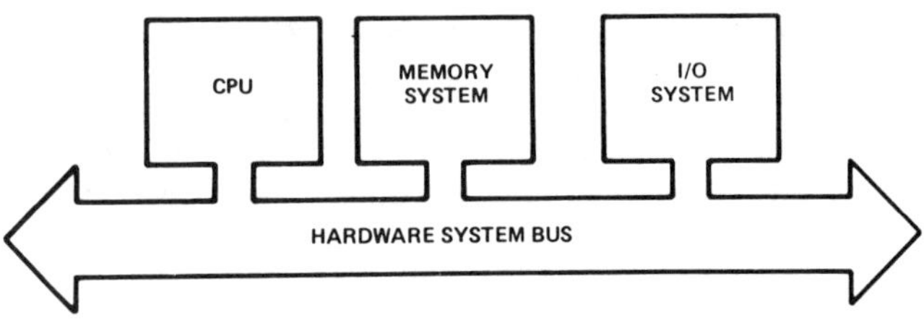

FIGURE 1 – VON NEUMANN COMPUTER ARCHITECTURE

Figure 2 illustrates the evolution of microprocessor performance from the 8008 in 1972 to the advanced TMS 99000 in 1981. As future processors further advance in performance, system buses must be capable of bandwidths in excess of 10 megahertz to avoid detrimental effects to system performance. It is conceivable that if trends continue bandwidth requirements will someday approach 100 megahertz and above.

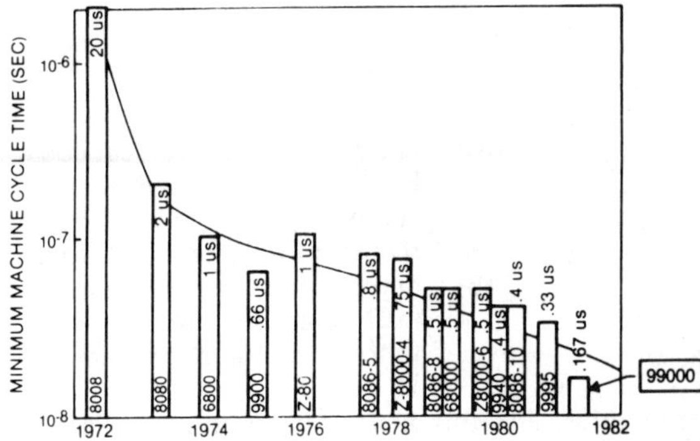

FIGURE 2 – MICROPROCESSOR PERFORMANCE EVOLUTION

As system designers are aware, the problems associated with the physical design of very high bandwidth buses can be a severe handicap to meeting the criteria of the system design goals. Thus it appears that an alternative approach must be explored to maintain consistency between CPU performance and system bus performance.

ELEVATING THE BUS IQ

An alternative to increasing the bus bandwidth to maintain system performance is to increase the functionality of bus level information transfers. Traditional microprocessor buses carry data objects and native instruction objects during information transfers. To raise the functionality of the system bus, additional intelligence must be integrated into the peripheral subsystems. The result of this is a single system bus transfer invoking a particular function at the peripheral subsystem level. Thus, a single bus transfer, or a small number of transfers, results in execution of a high-level function by the peripheral subsystem.

Utilization of peripheral computing elements, or peripheral processors, can increase the performance of the system bus to the point where the bus no longer proves to have a detrimental performance impact on CPU performance. An interesting analogy may be made with peripheral computing elements. This analogy is a logic signal line, which is typically limited by the amount of source and sink current, which it can provide to logic inputs. To increase the output power of the logic line, simple n-p-n transistors can be tied to the signal bus to increase fanout. In a similar manner, computing elements, or peripheral processor elements, can be tied to a bus of limited bandwidth, and effect a net functional gain at

Reprinted with permission from *Wescon Conf. Rec.*, 1981, pp. 5.5.1–5.5.3.

the system bus level much as the n-p-n transistor drivers netted the signal line much more signal gain. This analogy may be extended even further by comparing the beta ratio, or dc current gain, of the n-p-n transistor to the functional gain of the computing element. Whereas the beta ratio of the n-p-n ratio may be expressed as:

$$\beta = \frac{i(c)}{i(b)}$$

where;

i(c) = dc collector current
i(b) = dc base current

the functional gain of a computing element may be expressed as:

$$A = \frac{I(C)}{I(B)}$$

where;

I(C) = average number of object code level peripheral subsystem or computing element instructions required to perform function.
I(B) = number of system bus level instructions required to invoke function of computing element.

Figure 3 illustrates this analogy between n-p-n signal drivers and bus resident computing elements.

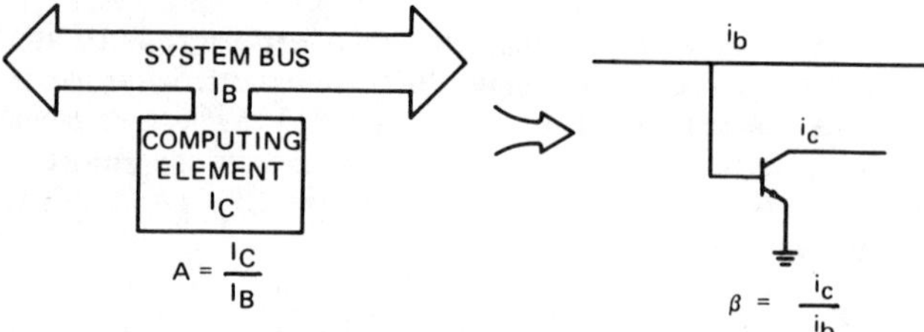

FIGURE 3 – BETA GAIN VS. FUNCTIONAL GAIN ANALOGY

Thus a computing element effectively increases the power and throughput of a system bus by accommodating a higher level of information transfer. In past Von Neumann architectures bus transfers consisted primarily of machine-level and data objects. To overcome future limitations of bus bandwidths and to capitalize upon state-of-the-art microprocessors, bus transfers must carry information at a much elevated level.

COMPUTING ELEMENTS

The term computing element may be defined as any subsystem resident on the bus, which has the facilities to execute a function autonomously either under the direction of a host-computing element or in an independent fashion. Under this definition two generic families of computing elements may be defined:

- Application processors
- Peripheral processors

Application Processors

An application processor is a microprocessor whose native functionality is application specific. Examples of application processors include:

- Control processors
- Data manipulation processors
  - Commercial
  - Scientific
  - Industrial

The advantage of application processors or "application specific" processors is that a much superior solution to specific systems may be realized. This direction in next generation microprocessors has taken a first step with the advent of the TMS 99000 microprocessor family.

The TMS 99000 family of microprocessors initially includes a floating point processor for instrumentation type applications (TMS 99110) and an operating system kernal processor which facilitates implementation of TI's software bus, the real-time executive (TMS 99120). Future variations of the TMS 99000 family of microprocessors can, for example, support linked-list, signal processing, and data communications type applications.

Peripheral Processors

Peripheral processors may be classified by the method of coupling to the system bus. The classifications chosen for this discussion are as follows:

- Attached processors/computers
- Direct I/O interface
- Message-oriented

Attached processors and attached computers employ a direct instruction coupling to the system bus. The instruction flow on the system bus to the host microprocessor is monitored on a real-time basis for instructions or function codes, for which the attached processor or attached computer is responsible. Once an instruction present on the bus is recognized, a context switch to the attached processor/computer is initiated by the host CPU. An attached processor halts the host CPU until completion of the instruction or function and then initiates a context switch back to the host. An attached computer has the resources of a private memory and thus may release the host CPU to access the system bus. Operation of the attached computer effectively increases the power of the system bus to invoke concurrent functions through a bus-level transfer. Likewise, attached processors increase the power of the bus by providing specialized hardware to perform system functions, reducing the number of bus cycles to perform a function.

The TMS 99000 family of microprocessors employ an attached processor/computer interface as shown in Figure 4. The TMS 99000 family can, for example, include attached processors and computers to support such functions as floating point, scientific, business, and high level language applications.

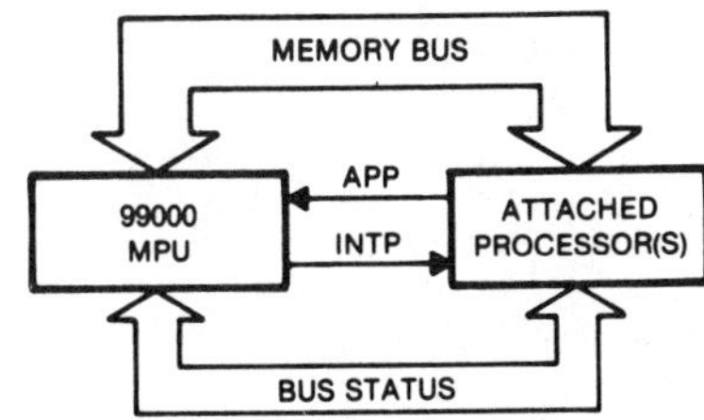

FIGURE 4 – TMS 99000 FAMILY ATTACHED PROCESSOR/ COMPUTER INTERFACE

Direct I/O Interface

Direct I/O interface peripherals are directly coupled to the memory or I/O space of the microprocessor. Past and current generation peripherals have typically fallen into this classification. Examples include floppy disk controllers, video display controllers, and communications controllers. The disadvantages of direct I/O coupling of peripherals are that very specific conventions must be learned for proper operation; each peripheral requires a unique software driver; and the architecture is typically not technologically portable as integration levels increase over time. Direct I/O coupling is very vendor/architecture specific in that usually specific interrupt or DMA conventions and interface are assumed.

Message Oriented Interface

The most promising peripheral processor interface employs a message oriented coupling to the system bus. By means of a "message bucket", or memory buffer area, a single set of conventions may be defined for a generic family of functions such that the "register" type assignments of the direct coupled I/O disappear into the message frame. Because the message bucket is non-specific, the peripheral function becomes very vendor independent, thus not tied to a particular microprocessor architecture.

The memory intensive orientation of the TMS 99000 family facilitates implementation of message-oriented peripheral function interfaces. Direct fusion and integration of processors with media interface functions and memory will provide for a bus architecture as shown in Figure 5. Initially implemented as chip sets, technological improvements will provide for a chip count collapse.

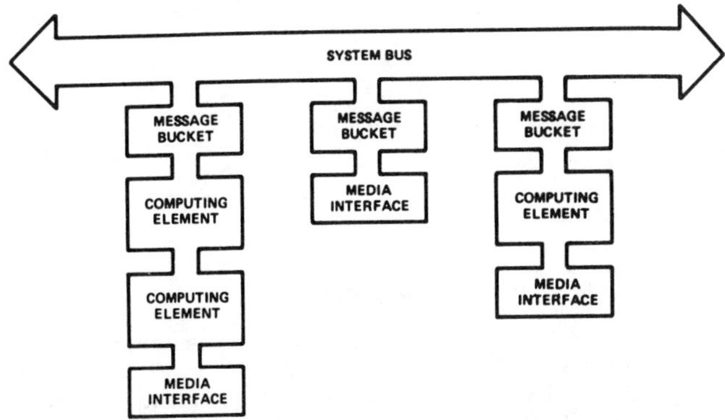

FIGURE 5 – MESSAGE ORIENTED PERIPHERAL FUNCTION INTERFACE

Software functions now implemented with TI's component software will provide direct support of message-oriented peripheral functions. Again as technological advances are realized, component software will be migrated to the silicon of the peripheral subsystem.

SUMMARY

Because of the physical limitations of hardware system buses, advanced generation microprocessors must elevate the "bus IQ" of the system bus to maintain throughput compatibility with the capabilities of the processor. The TMS 99000 family is presently pursuing this goal through attached processors and computers and message-oriented peripheral processors, which perform autonomous functions. This migration of functions from the host CPU software to alternative bus resident hardware will mark the beginning of what may be termed "function-to-function" system architectures of the '80s. This distributed processing at the local bus level provides the ability of VLSI to continue to capitalize upon the ability to integrate memory based functions to silicon.

Benefits of Z8000™ Family Planning

Richard Mateosian

Zilog Component Applications Group
10460 Bubb Road
Cupertino, CA 95014
(408) 446-4666

INTRODUCTION

The Z8000 CPUs were conceived as part of an integrated family of components designed to work well together. This concept recognized the fact that a CPU and its component family must be developed and introduced in stages--a process that might span several years and that thus requires careful planning.

The Z8000 Family plan centers around the Z-BUS™ protocol that defines the interfaces to all present and future Z8000 Family members. The Z8000 CPUs, the first family members to be developed, contain within them all the features necessary to support this planned family expansion.

THE EXTENDED PROCESSOR ARCHITECTURE

An important goal of the Z8000 Family design was to accommodate additional processing capabilities (such as what would be provided by a floating point chip) with no redesign of the overall system or software. This goal was achieved with a scheme that allows certain CPU instructions either to cause traps (allowing simulation of an absent chip's function) or to be executed cooperatively by the CPU and an extended processing unit (EPU). With this cooperative approach, the CPU's addressing capabilities are used to fetch or store the arguments, and the EPU performs the operations. EPU operation can proceed in parallel with the execution of subsequent instructions by the CPU; synchronization is achieved by the EPU's assertion of the CPU's $\overline{\text{STOP}}$ line if the CPU fetches another EPU instruction before the EPU is ready to execute it. Figure 1 illustrates the cooperation of the EPU and the CPU.

The Extended Processor Architecture gives designers a great deal of flexibility. For example, an EPU doing floating point operations could be used interchangeably with floating point software controlled by the same instruction stream; only a single bit in the CPU's Flag/Control Word (FCW) control register would need to change. Thus, a high-performance floating point chip could be an optional feature of a product that used floating point operations. The "slow" version would use software execution of the floating point instructions, and the "fast" version would use the chip to execute instructions. Both versions would have identical applications program code and circuitry.

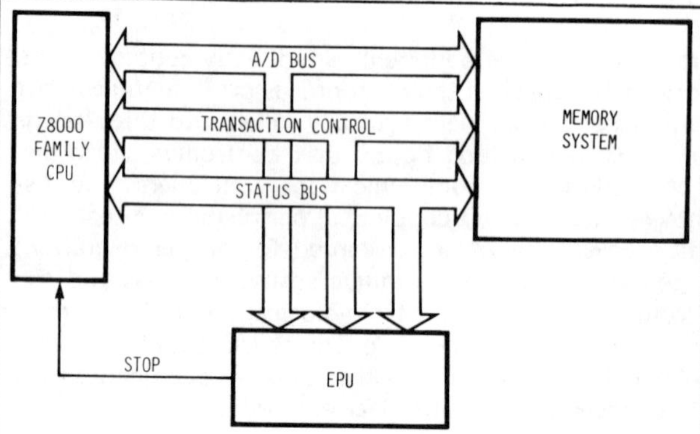

The EPU monitors the status lines, looking for "Instruction Fetch, First Word" status. When this occurs, it examines the instruction presented on the A/D bus. If the instruction is for that EPU, it either asserts $\overline{\text{STOP}}$ (if it is still busy executing a previous instruction), or initiates execution of the indicated instruction.

The EPU instruction can be entirely internal to the EPU, or it can include one or more transfers of data between the EPU and CPU, or EPU and memory. For each of these cases, the CPU generates the appropriate status signal (ST_3-ST_0) and transaction control (R/$\overline{\text{W}}$, B/$\overline{\text{W}}$, $\overline{\text{AS}}$, $\overline{\text{MREQ}}$, $\overline{\text{DS}}$) lines, and the EPU takes or supplies data as appropriate.

Figure 1. CPU and EPU Cooperate to Execute Instructions

DIRECT ADDRESSABILITY OF PERIPHERAL COMPONENT REGISTERS

An important feature of the Z8000 Family plan is the ability to address peripheral component registers directly. The design of the Z8000 I/O bus produces this feature at very small cost. The time-multiplexing of I/O addresses and data allows at least eight bits of address information to be provided to a peripheral component during the addressing phase of an I/O bus read or write transaction (see Figure 2). Since the data lines, which are obviously already required, are used for this address information, and since the demultiplexing occurs within the peripheral component, the cost of this feature is very small. Its benefits, on the other hand, are substantial.

Reprinted with permission from *Wescon Conf. Rec.*, 1981, pp. 1.5.1–1.5.7.

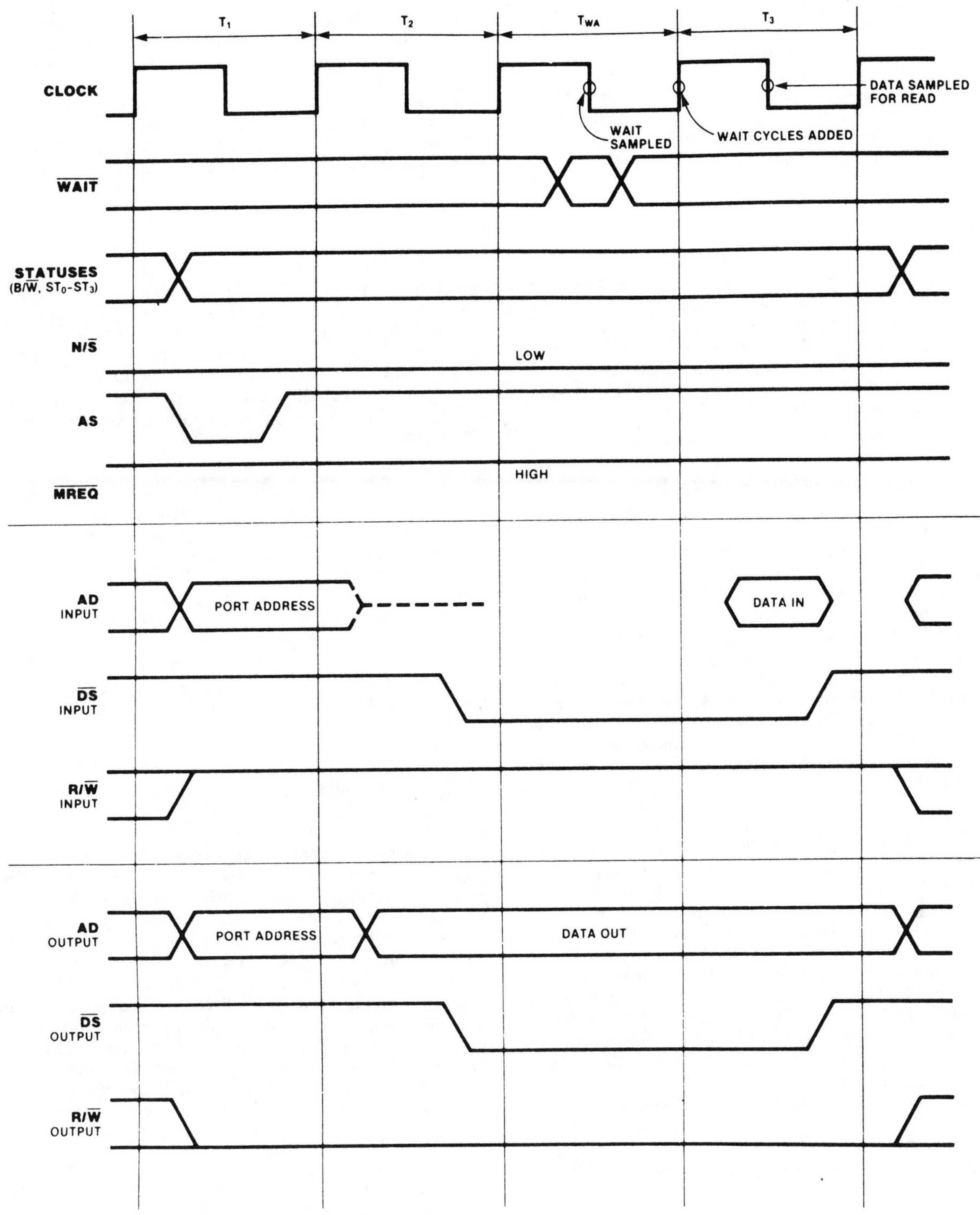

Figure 2. Multiplexed Bus Allows Direct Addressing of Peripheral Registers

The ability to address the internal registers directly provides a natural model for dealing with the complexity of VLSI components. Modern peripheral components are capable of operations defined by the contents of internal registers. The Z8010 MMU, for example, contains sixty-four 32-bit segment descriptor registers, three 8-bit control registers and six 8-bit status registers--a total of 265 bytes of internal register information that must be set or read by the CPU. This is achieved by allowing the MMU to recognize 22 separate addresses as internal register addresses or commands. The fact that 265 bytes of register storage can be accessed through 22 addresses depends on the use of an "autoincrementing" pointer register in the MMU in conjunction with the block I/O capability of the Z8000 CPUs.

Addressing internal registers directly makes transfers of blocks of data between the CPU and peripheral components easy to implement; no advance agreement or communication is required. The address information output by the CPU signals initiation or termination of the transfer. The block I/O instruction further simplifies and speeds this function.

COHESIVE MEMORY MANAGEMENT

A large logical address space is an essential feature of any modern CPU's memory addressing capability. Unfortunately, large address spaces can lead to difficult management problems for the system designer, so every modern CPU requires some sort of memory management scheme to provide access protection, relocation, sharing, and virtual memory. Memory management can have implications for the CPU design and for those of the peripheral components, so even if it is implemented as a separate component, its design cannot be left until after the CPU is designed.

Memory addressing in the Z8000 CPUs uses a segmentation scheme. For purposes of this paper, the Z8000 CPU can be thought of as having logical address spaces composed of 64K byte banks. Each CPU has four such address spaces, corresponding to the four combinations of system/normal and instruction/data. One version of the CPU is the Z8002 CPU, which uses 16-bit addresses and can address one such bank in each of the four address spaces; another version is the Z8001 CPU, which can address 128 banks simultanously, using 23-bit addresses. A special Z8001 mode allows Z8002 programs, with their shorter addresses, to be executed; these programs reside in and refer to a single bank of the Z8001 CPU's 128-bank memory address space.

This paper will not discuss the details of Z8000 memory management, since that has been done adequately elsewhere [1, 3, 5]. There are, however, several points to be made about how the Z8000 family approach to memory management affects system designers, for which it is necessary to understand three "practical" goals of the Z8000 Family plan:

- To encompass a broad range of processing capabilities with a single architecture, so that Z8000-based applications can grow without substantial redesign.
- To provide an easy transition to the Z8000 architecture for applications based on 8-bit multiprocessors, especially the Z80.
- To achieve high performance with an economy of means, so that Z8000-based designs are cost-effective.

The Z8002 CPU, which comes in a 40-pin package and has four 64K byte address spaces (and hence can represent any address in two bytes), provides an inexpensive first step for an application that has outgrown an 8-bit microprocessor. (Incidentally, the Z8000's memory-to-register architecture and its instruction set make adaptation of Z80 programs to the Z8000 relatively easy.)

The step from a Z8002-based system to a Z8001-based system is made easy by the Z8000's memory addressing scheme. Furthermore, the modular design encouraged by the Z8001 CPU's segmented addressing makes it easy to adapt Z8001-based applications to a Z8002. This interchangeability, within the limits imposed by the Z8002 CPU's smaller address space, is important to system designers, since it provides the same kind of flexibility discussed earlier in connection with the Extended Processing Architecture.

Finally, the Z8001 CPU and the MMU provide high-performance memory management at low cost. As with other aspects of the Z8000 Family plan, a wide range of capabilities is available with no change to the basic architecture. For example, context switching can be accompanied either by a block transfer of mapping information to an MMU or by the automatic selection of a new MMU. The first approach involves a greater overhead during context switches; the second achieves faster context switching at a greater cost and higher component count. The important point is that a change from one of these approaches to the other can be made with small, precisely localized changes to the context switching software and with no change to the application programs.

The high performance and flexibility of the multi-component approach is made possible by segmentation. The bank-like nature of the Z8001 logical address segments makes possible the early availability of the segment number during memory read and write bus transactions, so that the MMU is able to perform a flexible mapping and access-checking algorithm largely in parallel with CPU address computations (see Figure 3).

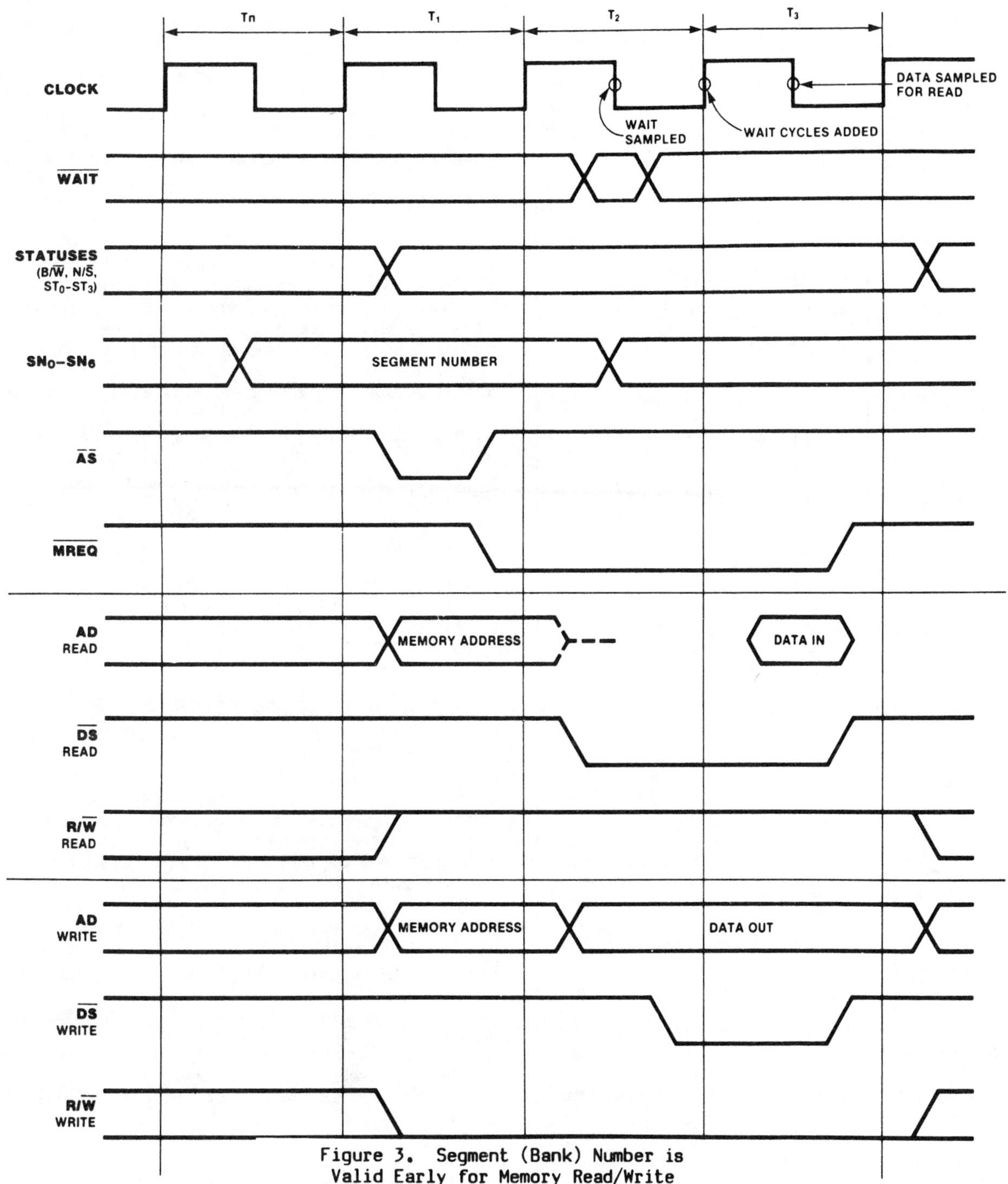

Figure 3. Segment (Bank) Number is Valid Early for Memory Read/Write

INTERPROCESS SYNCHRONIZATION

The Z8000 Family plan provides two interlock mechanisms to help synchronize the operations of concurrently running processes. The first of these, the Test and Set instruction, is widely used and understood and will not be discussed here. (Note that a special CPU status output warns other CPUs on the same bus that a Test and Set instruction is in progress.) The second interlocking mechanism is used by processes that do not share a common memory. Figure 4 shows a prosaic example: three CPUs sharing a line printer. When a CPU wishes to use the line printer, it merely executes the MREQ instruction, which conducts a transaction on the 4-line resource bus; condition code settings indicate to the program whether or not the CPU acquired control of the line printer through this transaction. If not, the MREQ instruction is executed again to retry; if so, the line printer is used, then released through execution of the MRES instruction. If another CPU executes an MREQ instruction while the line printer is being held, the resource bus transaction results in a "not available" indication.

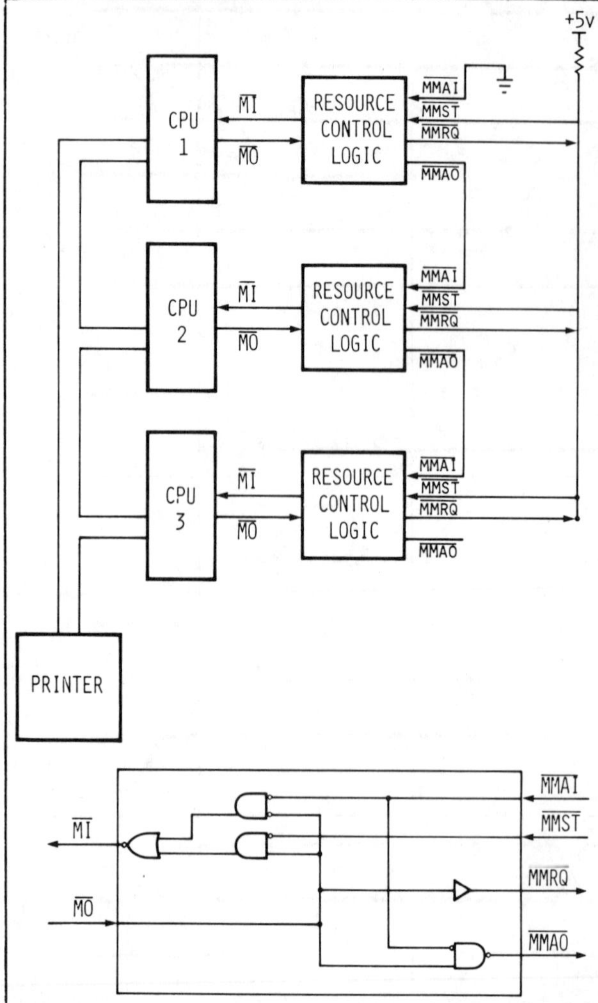

The printer is shared by the three CPUs. There is no default "owner" of the printer. A CPU that is not attempting to use the printer does not assert the MO output, i.e., MO is High. The resource acquisition protocol conducted by a CPU when the MREQ instruction is executed proceeds as follows:

> If MI is asserted (Low), acquisition fails. Otherwise, MO is asserted (Low) and MI is sampled repeatedly over a specified delay period. If it remains asserted (Low), acquisition has succeeded. Otherwise acquisition fails. If acquisition fails, MO is left unasserted (High).

Figure 4. Resource Bus Provides Non-Memory Synchronization

INTERPROCESS COMMUNICATION SUPPORT

The Z8000 Family plan provides good support for operating system functions. A principal operating system function is the support of interprocess communication, and one of the most flexible approaches to interprocess communication is through message passing. Support for message passing occurs throughout the Z8000 Family architecture.

A message is simply a string of characters emitted by one process to be received asynchronously by another process. This approach is quite general; it does not require that the communicating processes be assigned to the same CPU or that they both be active simultaneously. This generality makes message passing thoroughly compatible with the Z8000 Family design goal of allowing a wide range of processing capabilities with no change to the basic architecture.

The most important provisions for a message-passing philosophy in the Z8000 architecture are the following:

- Z8000 instructions and addressing modes that support efficient implementation of ring (FIFO) buffers in memory.
- Z8000 CPU block I/O instructions and the Z8038 Z-FIO FIFO I/O Interface Unit.
- Message-passing communication protocol established for fail-safe control of the Z8090 Z-UPC Universal Peripheral Controller by the Z8000 CPUs.

Support for the efficient implementation of ring buffers in memory is important to a message-passing approach, because ring buffers provide a natural means of implementing the asynchronous transmission of characters from one process to another. Discussion of the Z8000 CPU instruction set and addressing modes and samples of ring buffer routines can all be found elsewhere [2] and are not presented here.

The Z8038 Z-FIO is a ring buffer implemented externally to the CPU and its memory. It provides exactly the support needed to pass messages between processes assigned to different CPUs. Figure 5 shows a block diagram of a Z8038 Z-FIO serving as a buffer between two Z8000 CPUs.

The Z8090 Z-UPC Universal Peripheral Controller is intended to provide, through programming, the kind of control functions for a peripheral device (for example, a disk) that have traditionally been provided through hard-wired logic. As a result, programming errors can have serious physical consequences (for example, loss of stored material or even damage to the peripheral). To insulate the Z-UPC from errors in the principal (or master) CPU, a fail-safe message-passing protocol for control of the

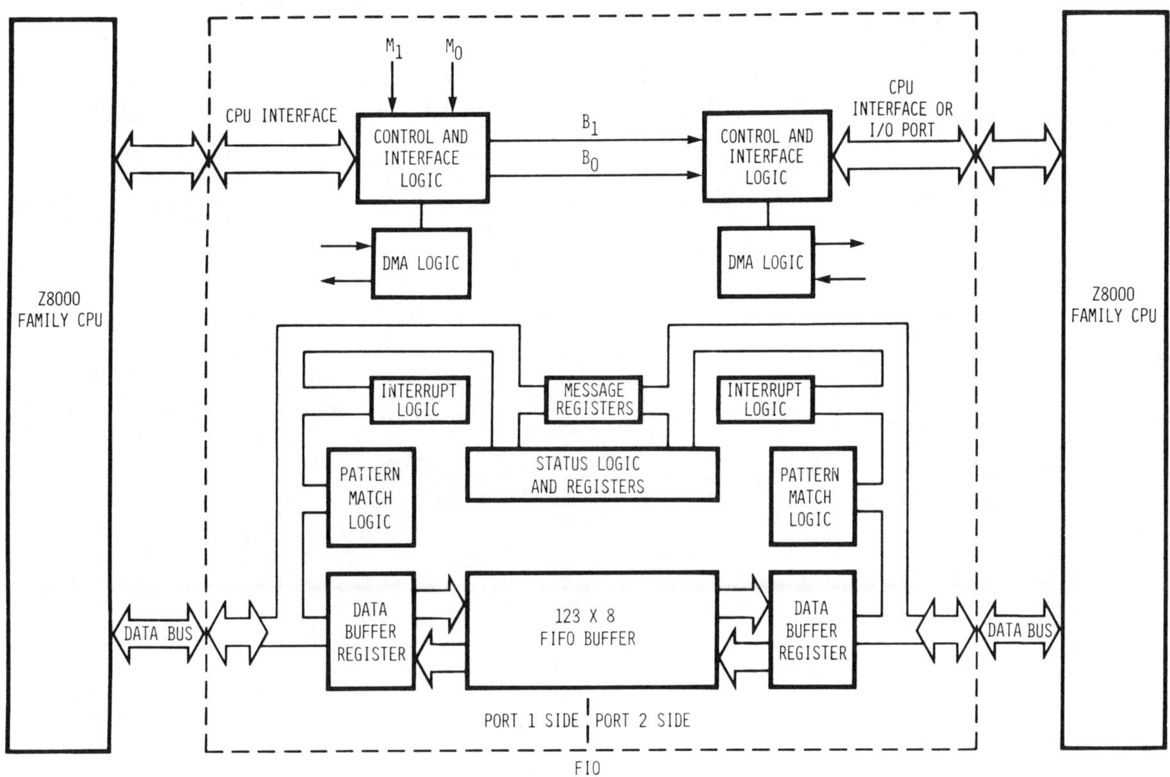

Figure 5. FIO Provides Asynchronous Inter-CPU Communication

Z-UPC by the CPU has been devised. In essence, the CPU initializes all transfers of data between the Z-UPC and the CPU, but the Z-UPC can prevent CPU accesses and has complete control over the location and the number of register accesses made by the CPU during a transfer. As with the MMU, the Z-UPC has been designed with an internal autoincrementing mode, which allows it to work well with the Z8000 CPUs' block I/O instructions.

SUMMARY

The Z8000 Family of components has been designed as a unit, resulting in an integrated set of parts that provide a broad range of capabilities within a single architecture. Family planning assures high-performance solutions with an economy of means, since functions can be allocated efficiently and without undue overlapping to family members.

The framework for the Z8000 Family design is provided by the Z-BUS protocol, which defines the interfaces among Z8000 Family members. The Z-BUS definition, in combination with the integrated Z8000 Family plan, led to the presence in Z8000 Family CPUs of many features whose purpose is to accommodate future developments.

The Extended Processor Architecture and the segmented memory addressing scheme are two examples of features designed with the needs and capabilities of future family members in mind.

The ability to address peripheral device registers directly, which arises out of the Z-BUS definition of a multiplexed address/data bus, gives rise to a natural model for interdevice communication. All of the Z-BUS peripherals are designed to take advantage of this feature.

Finally, the intended application of the Z8000 Family components to the implementation of integrated systems gives rise to the provisions in the Z8000 CPUs for interprocess synchronization and to the provisions made throughout the Z8000 Family architecture for interprocess communication support through message passing.

REFERENCES

1. Hu, Jackson, Hiroshi Yonezawa, and Bernard Peuto. "Memory Management Units Help 16-bit Microprocessors to Handle Large Memory Systems," Electronic Design, April 26, 1980, pp. 128-35.
2. Mateosian, Richard. "Programming the Z8000," Sybex, 1980.
3. Stevenson, David. "An Introduction to Memory Management," Electronics & Power, April 1980, pp. 317-23.
4. Zilog, Inc. Z8000 CPU Technical Manual, March 1981.
5. Zilog, Inc. Z8010 MMU Technical Manual, March 1981.

Memory Management Made Easy with the Z8000

Stephen Walters
Manager, Component Applications Engineering
Zilog, Inc.
10460 Bubb Road
Cupertino, CA 95014

INTRODUCTION

The basic issues of memory management have been considered at one time or another by the designers of all but the simplest microprocessor-based systems. For years these concepts have been described in literature for use in "big computing machines," but recognition of their relevance by microprocessor designers has been slow. Only since these memory management concepts have been provided for in leading-edge microprocessors, and deliberately applied in high-end microprocessor-based products, have microprocessor users become cognizant of their significance.

Some semiconductor companies have provided for memory management within their new 16-bit microprocessors, whereas other semiconductor companies have not designed in provisions for memory management and the facilities that are provided appear as external add-ons to the CPU. Zilog designed the Z8000 Family of microprocessors with features that anticipate implementation of an efficient memory management scheme in microprocesor-based systems.

This paper describes the features designed into the Z8000 Family of 16-bit microprocessors to ease implementation of memory management. Virtual memory environments for the Z8000 Family are also discussed.

A REVIEW OF MEMORY MANAGEMENT CONCEPTS

The two primary functions of memory management are the allocation and the protection of memory. The system design issues that suggest memory management as a solution include a scarcity of memory resources, system integrity, and the sharing of programs or data in a multi task environment (a task is the execution of a program on its data).

These functions and the issues that require some form of memory management consideration seem only remotely related to small microprocessor based-designs. But in fact, they are dealt with in one way or another in most microprocessor designs, and in a very significant way in large microprocessor-based systems. For example, when a small microprocessor-based product can be built with the entire program resident in 16K bytes of memory, the designer makes a conscious decision to use at least 16K bytes of semiconductor memory and to store the program in it. This is a trivial example of the designer making a memory resource management decision while designing a system. On the other end of the complexity spectrum, where a system provides for multiple tasks and not all the tasks can reside in main memory at the same time, memory resource allocation decisions must be made dynamically.

The latter example relates to a system where main memory is a scarce resource and its use must be managed. This type of system requires a secondary storage media such as disc storage. The various tasks are moved from secondary storage to main memory as they are needed and sent back again when they are no longer needed. The ability to store the tasks in different locations in the main memory on different occasions adds flexibility when implementing the resource management mechanism. Tasks that can reside at any location in main memory are referred to as "relocatable."

System integrity is another issue that requires memory management consideration. It is primarily an issue of protection. Protecting a task from itself, protecting one user task from another user task, protecting system tasks from user tasks, and protecting (or restricting) system functions (such as I/O) from user tasks are a few kinds of protection functions.

In the most elementary case, a program stored in read-only memory (ROM) is protected from being written over. But, programs stored in ROM are not usually relocated in the ROM space, so larger microprocessor systems use RAM with sophisticated protection techniques. One such technique is to create an "object" environment where programs and data are organized as collections of well-defined objects. Objects have a number of attributes assigned to them such as "read only," "execute only," and "system only". When a transaction occurs and an attribute associated with a given object is violated, the microprocessor is altered so appropriate action can be taken. In some cases, the attribute violation may cause the transaction to be suppressed at the memory itself. Any microprocessor architectural feature that enforces object organization will inherently simplify the task of maintaining system integrity.

Reprinted with permission from *Wescon Conf. Rec.*, 1981, pp. 9.3.1-9.3.9.

The issue of sharing programs or data comes into play in multi tasking environments in which the same program may need to be made available to more than one process, or more than one process may require access to the same data. An example of the first type of environment is a multi-user software development system in which language translators (such as a FORTRAN compiler) can be shared by several users rather than requiring each user to have a copy of the translator in main memory. Shared data can be exemplified by programs that use the same results of a questionnaire for different analyses. Figure 1 illustrates the latter example.

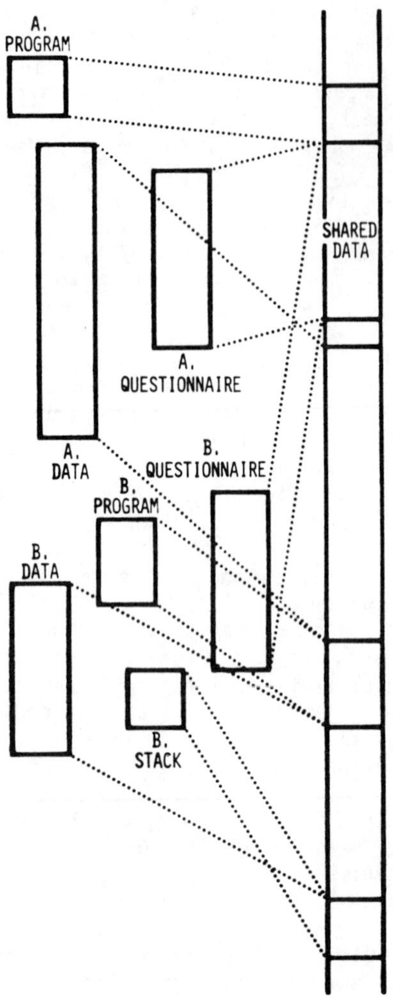

Figure 1. Two Users Sharing Common Data

In Figure 1, the boxes on the left show the system logical address space; the long box on the right shows the actual (physical) memory space. User A has program, data, and questionnaire space. User B has program, data, stack, and questionnaire space. The questionnaire data exists in physical memory as a single copy and is shared by programs A and B.

Modern programming techniques advocate a structured and modular approach to program generation. Large programs are more easily generated and managed if prepared as small independent tasks that are eventually tied together through a well-defined interface protocol. Each task communicates with a small number of other tasks, and the interface is tightly controlled. An object orientation is a natural model for implementing a modular programming environment. Objects can be defined as "segments" or "pages." Segments are distinct, unordered objects that may vary in size and are referred to with a segment number and a segment offset address. Pages are of fixed sizes and appear to the user and to operating systems as homogeneous collections of objects referred to by a single linear address.

There are advantages and disadvantages to both segmented and paged organizations. Segmentation provides an inherent protection mechanism, because attributes can be assigned to segment objects and movement from one segment to another can be strictly controlled. Segmentation also minimizes "internal fragmentation" of memory (in the logical address space), because its length can be adjusted to fit the task size. Paging minimizes "external fragmentation" (in the physical address space), because memory is treated as fixed-size blocks. The fixed-size blocks also simplify memory allocation and decisions of where to place the logical objects in the physical memory. A segmented memory scheme needs to be incorporated into the microprocessor itself, whereas a paging scheme can be added on to the microprocessor in the address translation hardware.

A microprocessor chip with segmentation designed into the architecture provides a basis for a highly effective protection mechanism. A microprocessor system that employs paging techniques provides a basis for an effective physical memory management scheme. Segmentation and paging can be combined to achieve the advantages of both techniques.

The elements of implementing a memory management scheme include address generation, address translation, object attribute assignment, and the attribute violation handling mechanism.

Address generation refers to the method by which logical addresses are generated. Two techniques are common. One technique has the entire address contained in the instruction; the second technique employs special registers to contain some of the address information, and the instruction carries only part of the address information. In the former technique, the instruction carries a segment number (address) and a segment offset address. The latter technique employs special registers to contain the segment number, and the instructions carry the segment offset address.

The technique using special registers reduces the size of the address field required in the instructions, potentially reducing program size and execution time. However, if the number of segments is much larger than the number of special registers, this technique may require a high overhead to manage the special registers. The special registers also require additional instructions to manipulate them and this manipulation adds to program size and execution time.

Address translation refers to the mapping of logical addresses to physical addresses. This translation is required when the logical address space is larger than the physical address space and the physical address space must be reallocated by the system. In a segmented environment, the segment offset is added to the starting physical address of the segment. The segment number is a logical identifier, which is mapped into a physical segment starting address by the address translation mechanism. The translation mechanism may be associative, which means the segment number is presented to a table of segment numbers, and if the table contains that segment number, it returns the starting physical address of the segment.

A second scheme for address translation is a table of physical addresses, each of which can be selected by using the segment number (logical address) to index into the table. This scheme has one physical address for every possible segment number.

The address translation device also contains the access attributes for each segment, such as segment length, read only, execute only, and system only. These access attributes implement the protection of objects (segments). If access to a segment is attempted and it violates the access attributes associated with the segment, the system is alerted and appropriate action can be taken. Object independence plays a crucial role in implementing a protection mechanism. A task operating within a segment cannot execute instructions across segment boundaries. That is, the Program Counter of the microprocessor will not increment the segment number when the segment offset address reaches its maximum count. Crossing segment boundaries must be a deliberate action and is easily controlled.

Handling access attribute violations can be accomplished in a variety of ways, including segment traps and suppressed memory transactions. A segment trap is a type of interrupt, which invokes a segment trap service routine that determines the cause of the trap and takes the appropriate action. Depending on the nature of the access violation, it may be desirable to suppress the memory transaction that caused the violation, either by preventing a write operation, returning special data during a read operation, or aborting the instruction all together.

THE Z8000 CPU FAMILY WITH DESIGNED-IN FEATURES FOR MEMORY MANAGEMENT:

The Z8000 CPU Family offers features that support the primary memory management functions of protection and allocation. These features are especially helpful to microprocessor users faced with the design issues of scarce main memory, systems integrity, and sharing of code and data. The Z8001 CPU provides an object orientation based on the concept of segmentation. Segmentation is designed into the architecture of the Z8001 CPU, with the segment number and the segment offset address carried throughout the architecture. Hardware enforces the independence of segment objects by preventing carries that result from address calculations on the segment offset address. The segment number field in the Z8001 is seven bits wide, allowing for 128 segments. The segment offset address field is 16 bits wide, so each segment can be up to 64K bytes long.

A "segment trap" input pin on the Z8001 handles violations of the access attributes associated with a segment. The segment trap has an assigned address in the Program Status Area, which contains the Flag and Control Word (FCW) register and the Program Counter (PC) values for the trap service routine. The PC is a two-word address including a segment number.

Another feature of the Z8000 Family provides additional support for improved system integrity: system and normal modes of operation. While in system mode, the CPU can execute all instructions and access any register. In normal mode, some instructions can not be executed (e.g., I/O operations) and the control registers can not be accessed. Z8000 Family architecture reinforces the system/normal modes of operation by automatically switching to system mode just before interrupts are acknowledged and through the use of a "system call" instruction. Also, if an attempt is made to execute a privileged instruction while the CPU is in the normal mode (S/N bit in the FCW is cleared), a "privileged instruction" trap occurs. The available, system/normal pin simplifies system hardware design by providing an external indication of which mode (system or normal) the CPU is operating in. Table 1 reviews the Z8000 Family features provided that support a memory management environment.

Table 1. Memory Management Features of the Z8000 Family of CPUs

Feature	Implementation	Benefit
Segmentation	o Separate segment number and segment offset address. o Segment number and segment offset address carried throughout the architecture.	o Object orientation designed into architecture. o Eliminates management of special segment number registers. o Supports protection and allocation mechanisms.
Segment Trap	o External Segment Trap pin (SEGT) and separate location in program status Area.	o Provides for interface to external memory management hardware. o Supports protection and allocation mechanisms.
System/Normal	o System/normal bit in Flag and Control Word register. o Normal/system pin.	o Provides for privileged mode of operation. o Supports protection mechanism.
Privileged Instruction Trap	o Automatic occurrence when attempted execution of privileged instructions in normal mode. Separate location in Program Status Area.	o Supports protection mechanism.

THE Z8010 MEMORY MANAGEMENT UNIT

Zilog planned for the need to provide sophisticated memory management features when it designed the Z8000 Family of CPUs. Part of that plan included companion chips that would fulfill the remaining requirements for the implementation of a complex memory management environment. Address generation and object access attribute violation handling are provided for in the Z8001 CPU. The other two implementation requirements, address translation and access attribute checking, are accomplished with the Z8010 Memory Management Unit (MMU).

A block diagram of the Z8010 MMU is shown in Figure 2. The translation and attribute checking is done using 64 segment descriptor registers that define 64 segments. The segment descriptor registers contain a 16-bit base address field, an 8-bit segment limit field, and an 8-bit attribute field (see Figure 3).

The base address in each segment descriptor register is used to generate the physical address. The upper eight bits of the logical segment offset address from the Z8001 are added to the lower eight bits of the 16-bit base address. The sum is then used as the upper 16 bits of the physical address. The lower eight bits of the physical address are the lower eight bits of the logical segment offset address, and they come directly from the Z8001. The address translation function is shown in Figures 4 and 5. There are several characteristics of MMU address translation that resulted from Z8000 Microprocessor Family planning. These characteristics simplify system implementation and improve translation efficiency:

- The MMU interfaces directly with the Z8000 Family of CPUs.
- The segment number from the Z8001, which is made available early in the transaction cycle, reduces the impact of translation time on transaction cycle time.
- The status lines from the Z8001, which are input to the MMU to control the type of transaction for which a translation is performed (e.g., no translation for I/O operations).

Attribute checking is accomplished with the remaining 16 bits of the segment descriptor registers. The limit field (see Figure 3) indicates the length of each segment. Since segments can be up to 64K bytes long and the limit field is eight bits wide, the limit field represents a number of 256-byte blocks. The limit field specifies a number "n" which indicates n+1 blocks for normal segments, which grow with ascending addresses, and 256-n blocks for segments defined as stacks, which grow with descending addresses. When the upper byte of the logical segment offset address from the Z8001 falls outside of the boundary established by the limit field, a segment length violation occurs.

The attribute field contains eight flags (see Figure 3). The attributes are briefly described as follows:

RD (Read Only) - The segment can only be read.
SYS (System Only) - The segment can be accessed only when the Z8001 is in system mode (the normal/system mode pin is input to the MMU).
CPUI (CPU Inhibit) - The segment is not accessable to the currently executing process. This attribute is useful when a segment is not residing in main memory.
EXC (Execute Only) - The segment can only be accessed during instruction fetch transactions or load relative data accesses.
DMAI (DMA Inhibit) - The segment cannot be accessed by a DMA device. This attribute prevents a DMA device from modifying a segment being used by an executing task.
DIRW (Direction and Warning) - The segment is organized as a stack and grows with descending addresses from the logical address 64K down to the limit.
CHG (changed) - The segment has been modified by the CPU or by a DMA device.
REF (Referenced) - The segment has been referenced by the CPU or by a DMA device.

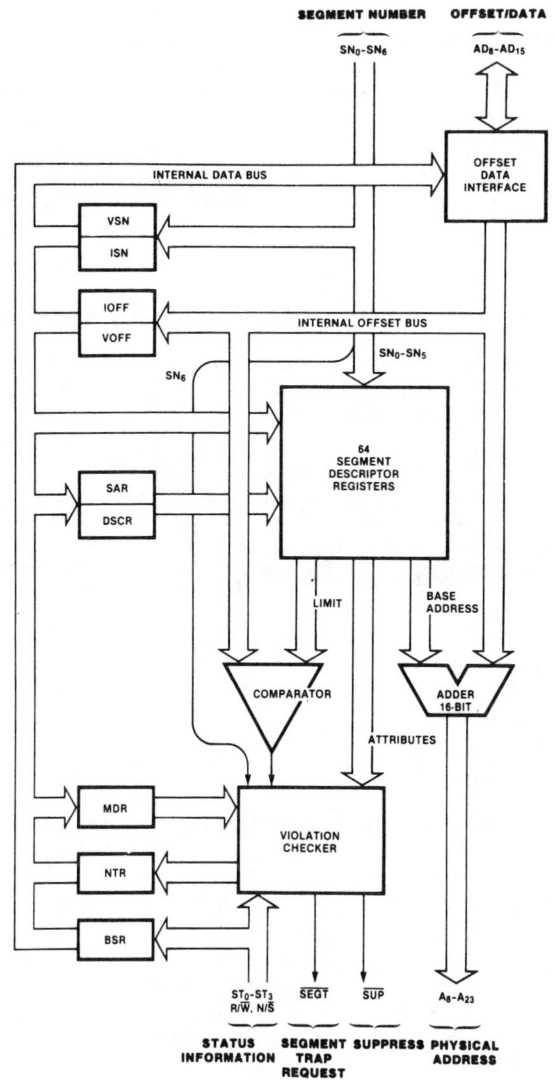

Figure 2. Z8010 MMU Block Diagram

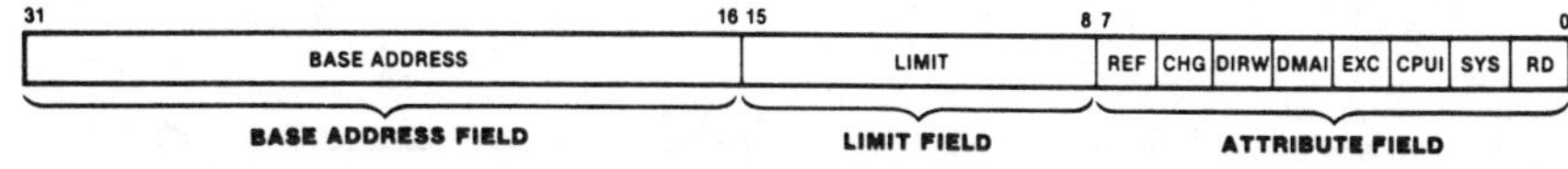

Figure 3. Segment Descriptor Register

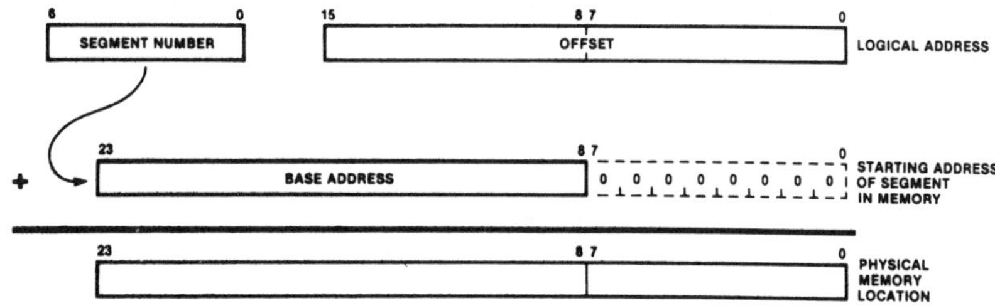

Figure 4. Address Translation in MMU

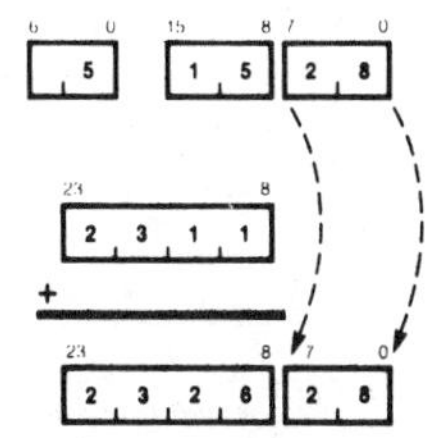

Figure 5. An Example of Address Translation Arithmetic in MMU

The last two attributes are automatically set by the MMU and are useful in the management of segments. If a segment has not changed (CHG is not set), for example, it need not be copied back onto secondary storage when no longer needed in main memory. If a segment has not been referenced (REF is not set), it is probably a task or data that is not being used and can be swapped out of main memory to make room for another task.

When an error condition occurs, violation status must be saved and the event must be signaled to the system. The following information is saved internally by the Z8010 MMU upon occurrence of an error condition:

- o Violation segment number
- o Violation offset (upper byte)
- o Bus cycle status
- o Instruction segment number
- o Instruction offset (upper byte)
- o Violation type

The Violation Type Register includes flags for the segment attribute violations and three violation type flags: Primary Write Warning, Secondary Write Warning, and Fatal Condition (see Figure 6). The Primary Write Warning occurs when the CPU writes into the last 256 byte block assigned to a stack segment. The Secondary Write Warning occurs when EXC, CPUI, RD, or SYS attribute violations occur or if the Primary Write Warning flag is set as a result of the execution of the previous instruction, and then a system stack reference causes a write warning. This situation occurs when the CPU is placed in system mode by a segment trap activated to service a segment violation, and then a stack reference places the system stack in jeopardy of overflowing. Once this flag is set, subsequent write warnings for accessing the system stack do not cause a segment trap request. This prevents the system from being continually interrupted for the same warning while it is attempting to remove the cause of the warning. The Fatal Condition occurs when an access attribute violation flag is set and either a violation is detected or a write warning condition occurs in normal mode or a write warning condition occurs in system mode during a non-stack write operation.

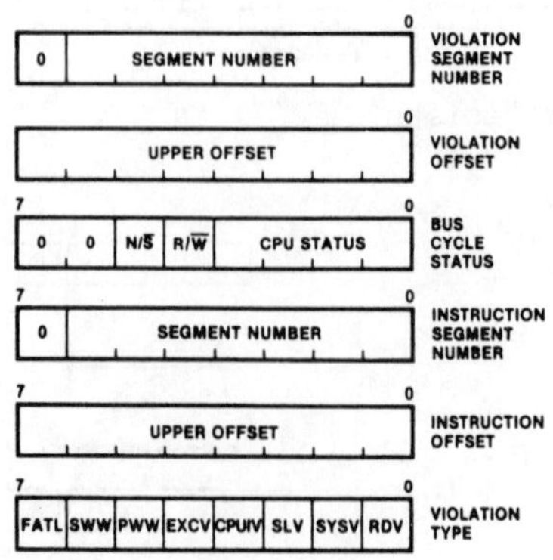

Figure 6. Violation Status

The error conditions are signalled to the system with the Segment Trap Request (SEGT) line and the Suppress (SUP) line. The MMU activates these signals differently, depending on whether the error was caused by a CPU access or a DMA access and whether the error was an attribute violation or a write warning. The memory can use the Suppress line to suppress a write transaction and to initiate the saving of error condition status. The Segment Trap line is similar to an interrupt to the CPU. Table 2 shows when these signals are activated.

Table 2. Segment Trap Request and Suppress Activation Summary

	CPU	DMA
Attribute Violation	Trap and Suppress	Suppress only
Write Warning	Trap	None

During write warnings, the transaction will be completed, but additional stack space may be needed. During DMA transactions, the segment trap request has no effect because the Segment Trap request is connected to the CPU.

Figure 7 shows a block diagram of an MMU in a Z8001-based system.

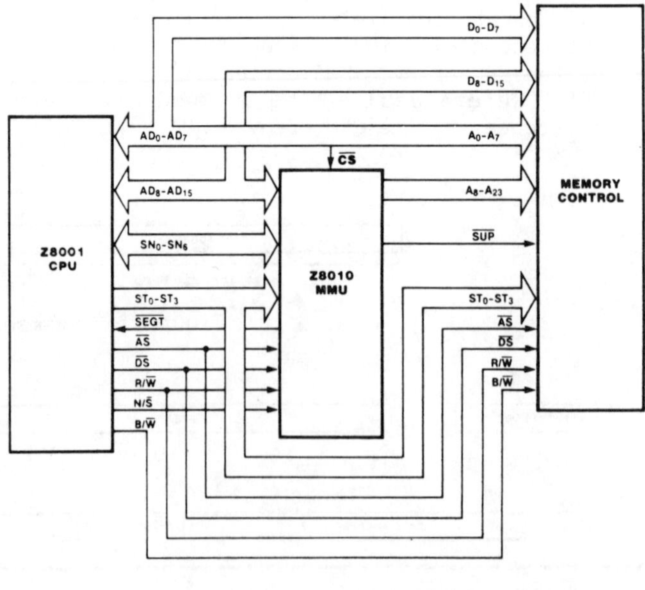

Figure 7. The MMU in a Z8001-Based System

A complete description of the status and control registers, transaction timing, interfacing, and programming techniques for the Z8010 MMU is available in the following Zilog documents:

- o An Introduction to the Z8010 MMU Memory Management Unit (document #00-2049-A).
- o Z8010 MMU Technical Manual (document #00-2015-A).

The Z8003 VMPU and the Z8015 PMMU

The Z8003 Virtual Memory Processor Unit (VMPU) offers all the features of the Z8001 CPU with the addition of two capabilities:

- o On-chip provisions for operating in a virtual memory environment.
- o External status line indication of the execution of a Test and Set instruction.

Physically, the Z8003 differs from the Z8001 only in the addition of an abort input (a reserved pin on the Z8001). The abort input and additional on-chip logic allow any memory transaction to be aborted. After the cause of the aborted instruction has been determined and remedied, the instruction can be restarted. The Test and Set instruction is a memory-based, mutual exclusion mechanism used by the Z8001 and Z8003 to control access to shared resources. The status lines on the Z8003 indicate when the Test and Set instruction is being executed. The Z8003 status line indication simplifies the hardware design of collision logic at the entry point to the memory where the shared resource status information is stored. This feature aids in making the Test and Set function atomic (non-interruptable), which minimizes the probability of simultaneous accesses to a shared resource.

Unlike the Z8001, the Z8003 can respond to separate trap and instruction abort requests. Traps in the Z8003 are handled the same way as in the Z8001, and they are sampled by both CPUs at the end of each instruction execution cycle. The on-chip provisions for aborted instructions is unique to the Z8003, and the abort input is sampled at the end of each machine cycle. The significance of this distinction is that aborted instructions must be terminated before any machine status or data is changed. Instructions that only cause a trap, such as stack write warnings, can be dealt with after the instruction causing the trap is executed.

The Z8015 Paged Memory Management Unit (PMMU) is similar to the Z8010 MMU in concept and organization. The Z8015, like the Z8010, provides for address translation and access attribute checking. The distinguishing characteristics of the Z8015 PMMU include:

- o The objects managed are 2048-byte pages instead of segments.
- o The page descriptor information is accessed through an associative memory using the logical page address as input.
- o The descriptor registers can be flagged as valid or not valid with a single bit.
- o Variable sized pages for a given application can be implemented with external hardware.
- o All status information necessary to implement a virtual memory environment is saved by the PMMU.

Figure 8 shows a block diagram of the Z8015 PMMU. The 64 descriptor registers are page descriptor registers instead of segment descriptor registers. The logical page address from the CPU does not address the page descriptor registers linearly. Instead, a content-addressable memory is used to determine if the logical page is defined in the page descriptor registers. A valid bit in the attribute field of each descriptor register indicates that the descriptor register contains valid page information for the currently executing process. Since pages are fixed-size objects, there is no need for a limit field in the page descriptor registers. If required,

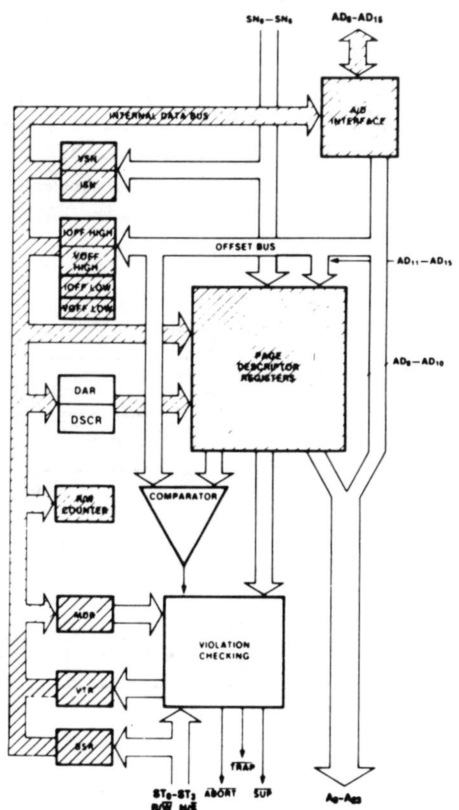

Figure 8. Z8015 PMMU Block Diagram

external logic can be used to implement larger or smaller page sizes. As shown in Figure 8, the upper and lower logical instruction offset address ($\overline{\text{IOff}}$ High, IOff Low), the upper and lower logical violation offset address ($\overline{\text{VOff}}$ High, VOff Low), and the read/write (R/$\overline{\text{W}}$) counter are saved by the PMMU. This information is used to restart an aborted instruction. The remaining information used during the trap and abort service operations is similar to what is saved during traps by the Z8001, such as bus cycle status and violation type.

Address translation is accomplished in the Z8015 PMMU by using the 12 most-significant logical address bits of the Z8003 (4096 pages of 2048 bytes each) to make an associative look-up into the page descriptor registers (see Figure 9). Logical address bits 8 through 10 are used untranslated in the physical address, and logical address bits 0 through 7 are connected directly from the CPU logical address bus to the physical address bus.

Each page descriptor register contains a logical address field (segment number and offset), a physical address field (translated page address), and an attribute field (see Figure 10).

The attribute field is detailed in Figure 11.

The Z8015 has a valid page bit, but the Z8010 does not have a valid segment bit. The Z8010 has DMA inhibit and CPU inhibit bits, and the Z8015 has combined these two functions into a single valid page bit. The five other attribute bits are common to both memory management units: read only, system only, execute only, direction and write warning (on a page basis in the last 128 bytes of a stack), changed page, and referenced page.

The concepts of Primary Write Warning, Secondary Write Warning, and Fatal Condition are carried over from the Z8010 to the Z8015 PMMU.

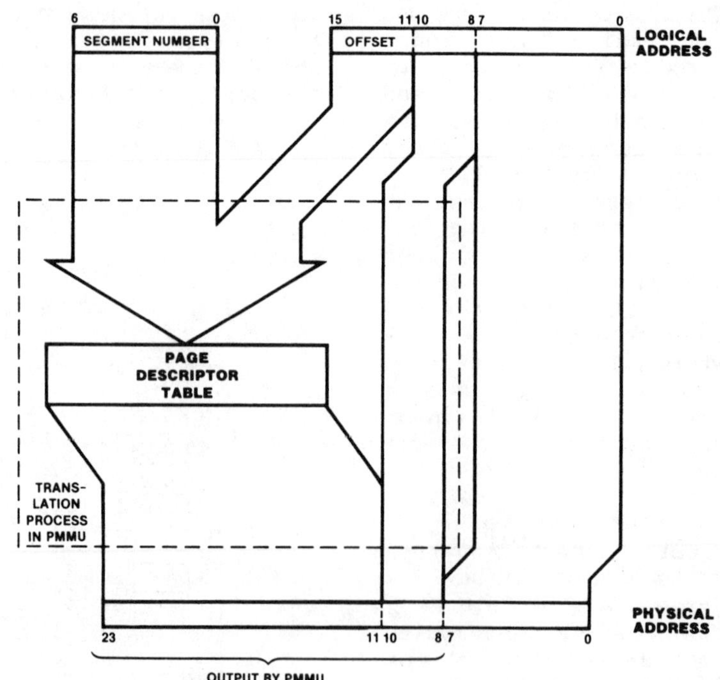

Figure 9. Address Translation in a Z8015 PMMU

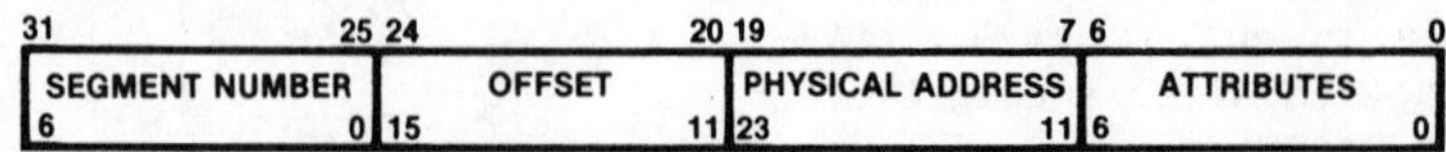

Figure 10. Page Descriptor Register Format

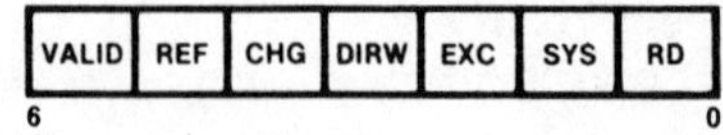

Figure 11. Attribute Field of Page Descriptor Register

The Z8015 PMMU has provisions for 64 page descriptor registers, but the Z8003 logical addresses can define 4096 pages in each of six address spaces (system, normal; and code, data, and stack). A page fault condition is generated when the upper 12 bits of a logical address applied to a selected PMMU do not match any of the logical addresses contained in the valid descriptor registers. The occurrence of a page fault causes a trap request to the CPU.

The PMMU directly supports pages of 2048 bytes. With the addition of external circuitry, the PMMU can support systems that require larger or smaller pages.

Detailed descriptions of the Z8003 VMPU and the Z8015 PMMU are available in the following Zilog documents:

- o Z8015 Paged Memory Management Unit Product Specification (Advance Copy) (Document #00-2081-01)
- o Z8003 VMPU Virtual Memory Processing Unit Product Specification (Advance Copy) (Document #00-2084-01)

VIRTUAL MEMORY WITH THE Z8000 MICROPROCESSOR FAMILY

Virtual memory is a technique that gives the programmer the illusion that memory is larger than it actually is. To accomplish this effect, the programmer uses a set of addresses that are different from the addresses actually driving the memory. Implicit in this scheme is an address translation mechanism. Addresses used by the programmer are referred to symbolically (the virtual address) and are said to be logical addresses. The logical addresses are translated or mapped into the address space that physically drives the memory and are called physical addresses. The requirements for implementing a virtual memory environment include address generation, address translation, and the ability to suspend the execution of instructions that cause accesses to programs or data not residing in physical memory. The requirements are a subset of the implementation requirements for memory management and have been effectively provided for by Z8000 Microprocessor Family products.

The Z8000 Microprocessor Family offers several approaches to designing systems with a logical address space larger than the physical address space. The Z8001 CPU and the Z8010 MMU can be used together without additional interface circuitry to implement a "demand swapping" environment. This scheme allows the logical address space to be greater than the physical address space, but assumes that when a task is active, it resides entirely in physical memory. The segmented address space of the Z8001 allows addresses to be named symbolically by segment numbers and segment offset addresses, and the Z8010 MMU provides a powerful and efficient method of translating addresses into a 24-bit physical address space.

The Z8003 VMPU and the Z8015 PMMU add two advancements to the architectural features of the Z8001 CPU and Z8010 MMU combination: virtual memory and paging.

Virtual memory is provided through address generation in the form of a segmented logical address space, address translation with page descriptor registers, the ability to suspend instructions at the machine cycle level, and the saving of all of the status information necessary to restart an instruction if aborted. This virtual memory capability is provided without the need for additional external logic and is transparent to the applications programmer. The paging scheme implemented with the Z8015 PMMU offers designers using Z8000 Family CPUs with a PMMU the protection advantages of segmentation and the physical memory allocation advantages of paging.

SUMMARY

The designers of the Zilog Z8000 Microprocessor Family have made every effort to utilize the advances in semiconductor technology in providing for the needs of microprocessor users faced with a broad range of application requirements. Application requirements that may range in complexity from process controllers implemented with the Z8002 in a conventional microprocessor design, to the most sophisticated 16-bit microprocessor application imaginable using the Z8003 VMPU and the Z8015 PMMU. Provisions for memory management were designed into the Z8000 Family, not added on. Zilog has taken advantage of the fact that today's semiconductor technology allows for the implementation of the most advanced processor architectural features. Features that have been proven over many years of large computing machine development.

Virtual memory was a natural evolution for the Z8000 Family, and it was an easy addition because it was planned for.

A COHERENT FAMILY OF PERIPHERALS FOR THE Z8000 16-BIT MICROPROCESSOR

Mike Pitcher
Applications Engineer
Zilog, Inc.
10460 Bubb Road
Cupertino, CA 95014

SUMMARY

Over a period of just a few years, microcomputer system requirements have changed dramatically. CPU memory space has typically increased by a factor of 128 or more, and prices of some semiconductor memory devices have dropped from a few cents to around $.0001 per bit. At the same time, integrated circuit technology has made possible the design of faster chips with more capabilities. These changes have led to systems with large memories, with performance approaching that of mainframe computers.

To keep pace with this rapid increase in central processing power, new peripheral products have been developed. The new peripheral devices enhance system performance by distributing processing power among the hardware components. At first glance, this seems like an expensive and overly complex approach. To fully appreciate the cost effectiveness of these hardware components, it is essential to examine the complete interaction of the system. This paper discusses two important aspects of the system: the Z-BUS interface and the individual peripheral components.

Z-BUS

A key feature of this distributed processing approach is a unified and coherent bus structure that allows easy expansion and flexible operation of all system elements. The Zilog Z-BUS architecture was developed to maximize system performance while minimizing hardware device count. Two notable characteristics of the Z-BUS are the multiplexed address/data bus, and a clean, standard interrupt structure.

The multiplexed address/data bus has several advantages over the nonmultiplexed bus. First, the hardware component count is kept to a minimum by integrating the address and data buses. Instead of using 16 data and 16 or 32 address lines, there are only 16. The savings in buffers and backplane connections are important, since costs per interconnect are steadily increasing. Second, more efficient use is made of device pins, which means lower component costs and lower device power-dissipation. Third, the bus can be expanded easily. All existing peripheral components can be used with a bus width of eight bits or more. Accomodating a 32-bit processor requires a minimum change in the existing system or no change at all. Finally, the registers within the peripheral are directly addressable. Two-step operations of writing a register pointer and transferring data are no longer required. Since 16 bits are used for addressing, the lower eight bits can be used for register selection, resulting in 256 addressable internal registers. The upper eight bits are the only address lines that need to be decoded for device selection. Again, this reduces component count and therefore cost.

A standard interrupt structure that can be adapted to a wide variety of user needs is a critical requirement. The Z-BUS interrupt structure offers a clean, efficient, and cost-effective method of dealing with interrupts. All Zilog peripherals have hardware and software provisions for using a daisy-chain interrupt priority scheme. This feature eliminates multiple interrupt request lines and the resulting extra priority-resolution circuitry found in many systems. If one wanted to use a parallel-priority resolution scheme, however, the Z8000 family peripherals would easily accomodate the configuration. The daisy chain has two basic functions: to determine which device is being acknowledged during the CPU interrupt acknowledge cycle, and to determine the priority in which devices can initiate interrupts.

Five pins are used to control interrupt actions within the peripheral device. $\overline{\text{INT}}$ is an open-drain output from the peripheral connected to the $\overline{\text{INT}}$ input of the CPU, which signals an interrupting condition within the peripheral. $\overline{\text{INT}}$ goes Low when the peripheral device has its internal IP (Interrupt Pending) bit set and IEI is High. Two pins, Interrupt Enable Input (IEI) and Interrupt Enable Output (IEO), enable interrupt action within the device and control interrupt priority within the chain. If IEI is Low, the device and all subsequent devices in the chain are prevented from requesting or acknowledging an interrupt. When IEI is High the device allows $\overline{\text{INT}}$ and IEO to go Low (if IP is set) or IEO to go Low and $\overline{\text{INT}}$ to go High (if IP is set and the CPU is acknowledging an interrupt request). It is during the latter condition that the IUS (Interrupt Under Service)latch for the corresponding IP bit is set. As long as IUS is set, IEO is Low and devices lower in the daisy chain are inhibited

Reprinted with permission from *Wescon Conf. Rec.*, 1981, pp. 5.1.1-5.1.6.

from responding to interrupts.

The last two pins, $\overline{INTACK}$ (Interrupt Acknowledge) and $\overline{DS}$ (Data Strobe), are used during the CPU interrupt acknowledge cycle. $\overline{INTACK}$ is derived from the CPU status lines and activates interrupt logic within the peripheral. When $\overline{DS}$ goes Low along with $\overline{INTACK}$, the peripheral presents an 8-bit interrupt vector to the data bus, if programmed to do so. The CPU processes the vector and branches to the appropriate service routine.

All Z8000 family peripherals are capable of operating in a wide variety of interrupt modes. First, vectored interrupt mode allows complete flexibility in software because the peripheral vector response is controlled by the programmer. The Z8000 family peripherals have the capability of altering the interrupt vector to reflect the specific cause of the interrupt. For example, if the user writes 10H into the IV (Interrupt Vector) register in the CIO and if the status affects vector (SAV) bit is set, the CIO can generate vectors 10H, 12H, 14H, and 16H depending on what the interrupt condition is. This greatly simplifies the programming task by minimizing the amount of processing effort used to determine the cause of the interrupt. Second, if one does not require the features of vectored interrupts, "standard" interrupts can be used. The peripherals can inhibit presentation of the vector in response to the CPU interrupt acknowledge cycle. This allows the user to implement a different interrupt scheme with additional hardware, if needed. Finally, interrupts can be inhibited altogether so that the peripherals can be polled. Generally, the peripheral registers are organized in such a way that the most important status information is contained in the most readily accessible register. As a result, the flexible interrupt operation of the Z8000 family peripheral products can support a wide range of system configurations.

Because of the way the Z8000 family peripherals interface to the CPU, the peripheral can function totally asynchronously from the CPU clock. This means that the PCLK (Peripheral Clock) input to the peripheral does not have to be related to the system or CPU clock. In fact, the peripheral clock can come from a source unrelated to the system clock.

BUS OPERATION

There are two basic operations that can occur on the Z-BUS: transactions and requests. Transactions include actions initiated by the bus master device and responded to by another device on the bus. The four types of transactions that can occur are memory, I/O, interrupt acknowledge, and null. A memory transaction transfers 8 or 16 bits of data to or from memory. An I/O transaction transfers 8 or 16 bits of data to or from a peripheral device. An interrupt acknowledge transaction transfers a vector from a peripheral to the bus master and acknowledges an interrupt request. A null transaction transfers no data. It is typically used for memory refresh.

A request action is initiated by a peripheral device or by some device other than the bus master. Request types include interrupt, bus, or resource requests. Interrupt requests signal the bus master to attend to the requesting peripheral device. A bus request transfers control of the bus from one master device to another, as in a DMA operation. A resource request requests a resource that is shared between two or more users, such as a two-port memory. In all of the requests, contention may be resolved through the daisy-chain priority mechanism.

PERIPHERAL DEVICES

Several devices are scheduled to be available during 1981 and early 1982. These include the following:

- Z8036 Counter/Timer Input/Output (Z-CIO) (available now)
- Z8038 FIFO Input/Output (Z-FIO) (available Q3, 1981)
- Z8030 Serial Communication Controller (Z-SCC) (available now)
- Z8090 Universal Peripheral Controller (Z-UPC) (available now)
- Z8016 DMA Transfer Controller (DTC)
- Z8065 Burst Error Processor (Z-BEP)
- Z8068 Data Ciphering Processor (Z-DCP)

Z8036 Counter/Timer Input/Output

The Z8036 Z-CIO is a counter/timer I/O device that can be used by any system. It contains three 16-bit counter/timers, two 8-bit individually programmed I/O ports, and a special 4-bit I/O port. The Z8036 Z-CIO is analogous to a combination of a Z80 CTC and Z80 PIO.

Z8038 FIFO Input/Output

The Z8038 Z-FIO is a 128-by-8-bit FIFO buffer that can be used in a variety of data transfer environments. It is particularly useful for high-speed block transfers, such as between processors, and can be programmed to operate in several ways. A FIFO device can be used between the CPU and a peripheral device to reduce interrupt servicing by as much as two orders of magnitude. Two or more FIFOs can be paralleled to provide data widths greater than eight bits.

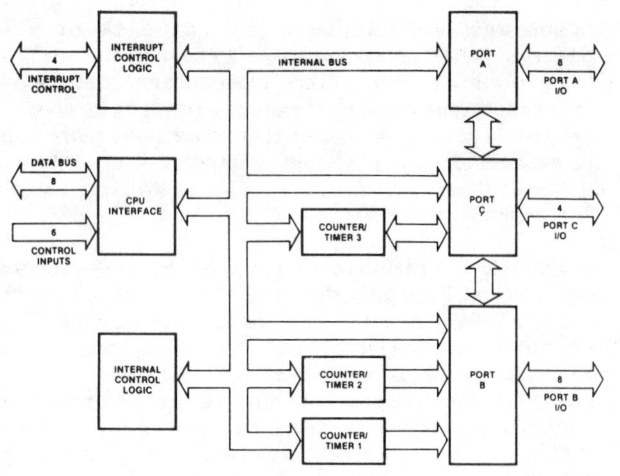

Figure 1. Z8036 Z-CIO Block Diagram

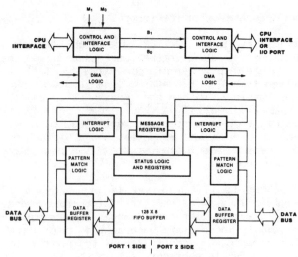

Figure 2. Z8038 Z-FIO Block Diagram

Z8030 Serial Communications Controller

The Z8030 Z-SCC is a dual-channel, full-duplex serial controller device in a 40-pin package. Similar to the Z80 SIO, the Z8030 Z-SCC contains many enhancements. Each channel has a separate oscillator and baud rate generator. The receiver for each channel also has a digital phase-lock loop for clock recovery during reception. The transmitter and receiver can encode data using standard NRZ format or using NRZI or FM encoding.

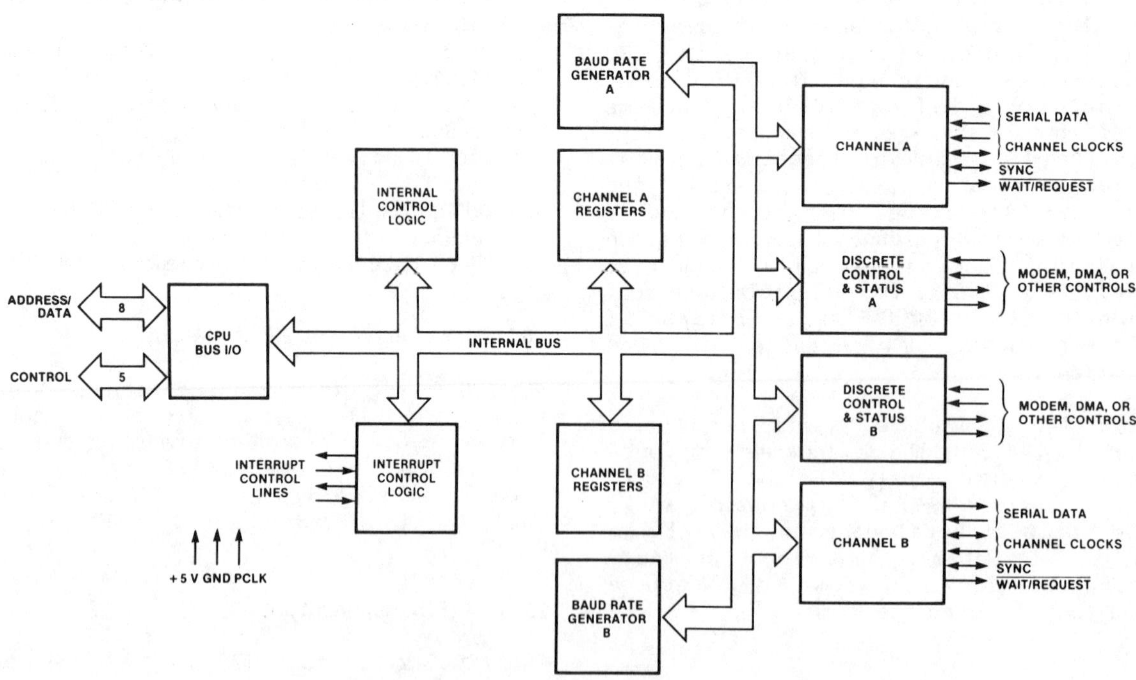

Figure 3. Z8030 Z-SCC Block Diagram

Z8090 Universal Peripheral Controller

The Z8090 Z-UPC is a slave microcomputer in a 40-pin package. It interfaces to the Z-BUS and is treated by the master CPU as a passive peripheral device. However, the Z-UPC contains 2048 bytes of program ROM and a 256-byte register file plus two counter/timers, three programmable I/O ports, and six levels of interrupt so that it can reformat data and control peripheral devices efficiently. The Z-UPC can request service from the master CPU but cannot initiate bus transactions.

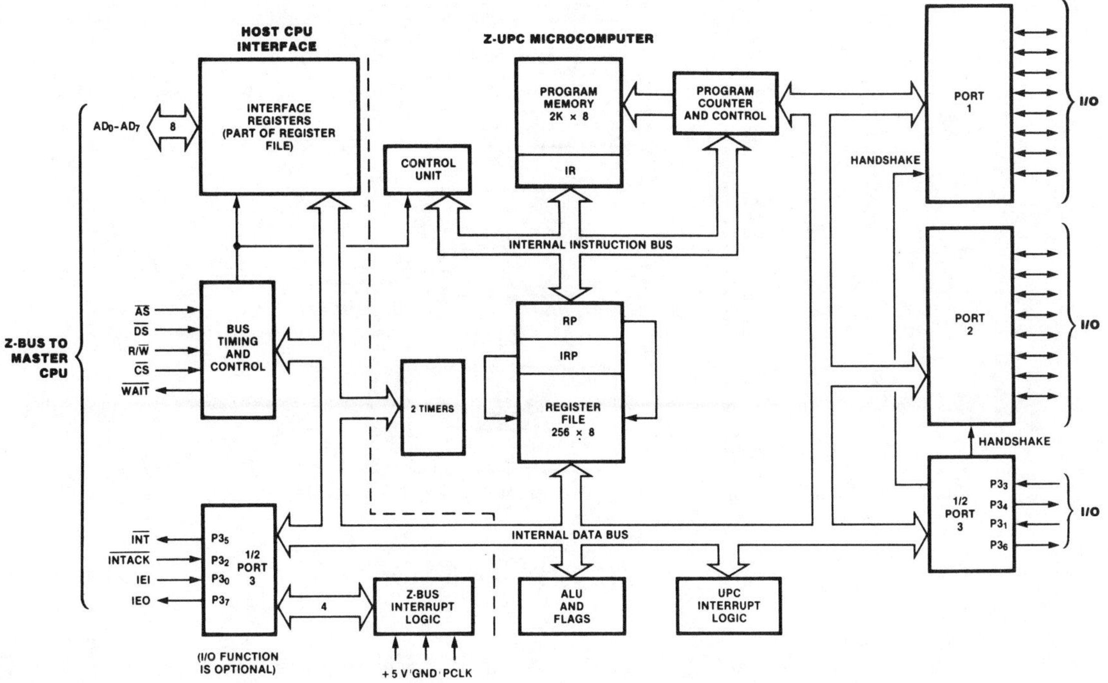

Figure 4. Z8090 Z-UPC Block Diagram

Z8016 DMA Transfer Controller

The Z8016 DTC is a dual-channel DMA controller that operates in a variety of modes. Data can be transferred between memory and peripheral, peripheral and peripheral, or memory and memory in groups of 8 or 16 bits.

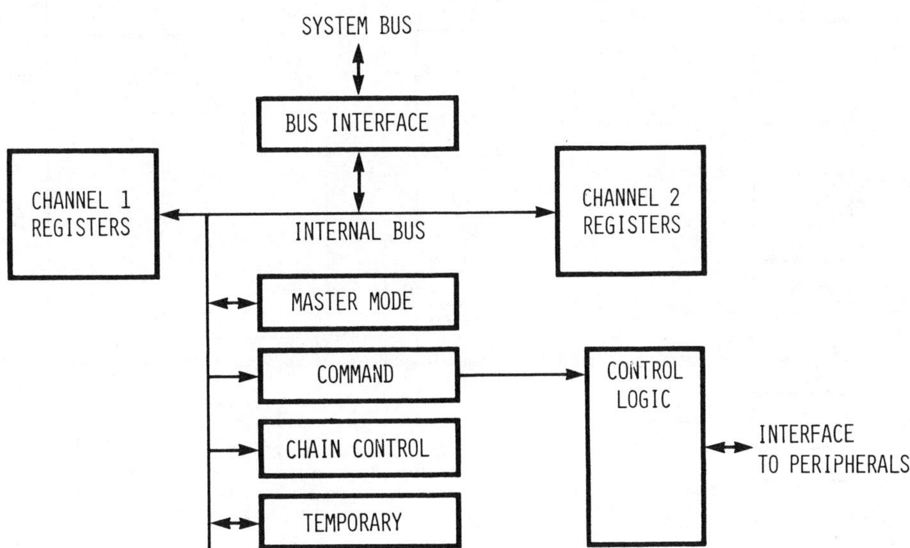

Figure 5. Z8016 DTC Block Diagram

Z8065 Burst Error Processor

The Z8065 Z-BEP is useful in systems that transfer large blocks of data rapidly. The Z8065 provides error detection and correction on a byte basis at speeds up to 20M bits per second. Using one of four industry-standard polynomials, errors of up to 12 bits can be corrected.

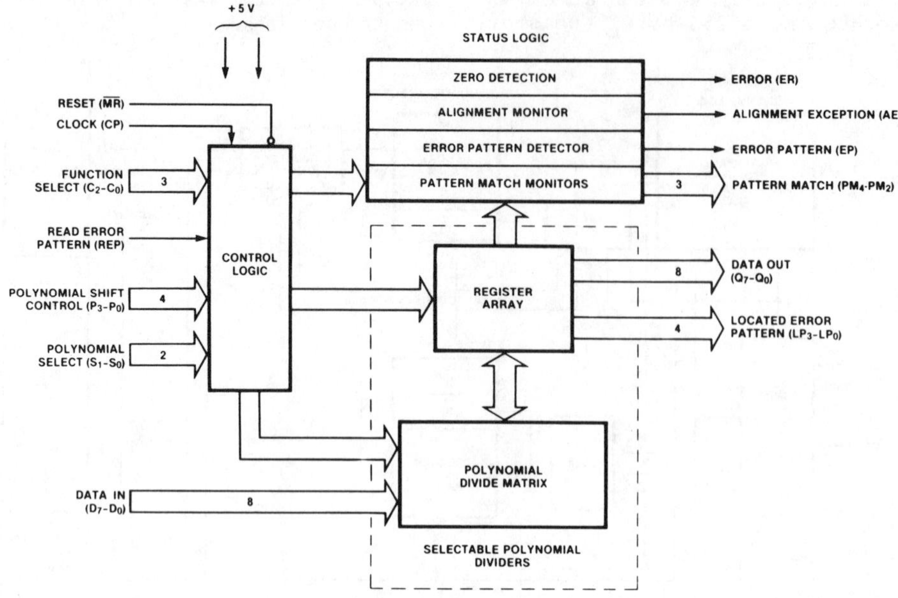

Figure 6. Z8065 Z-BEP Block Diagram

Z8068 Data Ciphering Processor

The Z8068 Z-DCP encrypts and decrypts data to maintain data security and integrity. The Z8068 can be used at rates of up to 1M bytes per second. Input, output, and ciphering operations occur simultaneously, so data can be transferred using DMA without processor interaction. The encryption algorithm used conforms to the National Bureau of Standards' algorithm for data encryption.

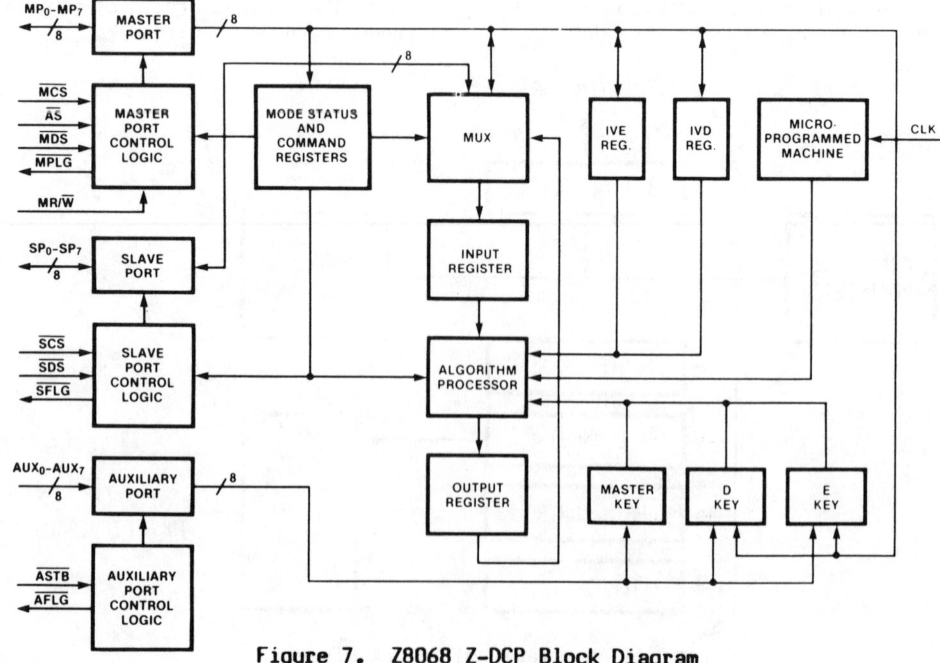

Figure 7. Z8068 Z-DCP Block Diagram

APPLICATIONS

The Z8000 family peripheral components are designed to fulfill a broad range of user needs. The appeal of the Z8000 family peripherals is increased by the unified and coherent features of the Z-BUS interface. Components are designed to support a building block approach to system design while maintaining a powerful subset of processor functions.

For example, the Z8038 Z-FIO could be used with the Z8030 Z-SCC in lieu of a DMA controller or interrupt data transfer via the CPU. To send a block of data would require the CPU to fill the FIO only once, eliminating further CPU interaction until transmission is completed or an error occurs.

The Z8000 family peripherals can be easily adapted to serve a minimum hardware configuration system or a complex, multiprocessor configuration. In a system with two or more separate buses, the Z8038 Z-FIO can be used as a data path between the two buses. If one of the buses happens to be a Z80-type bus, then the Z8000 family peripherals are available for the Z80 bus. These parts, called the Z8500 series, are similar to the Z-BUS parts, except they are nonmultiplexed and support a simple control-line protocol that matches the Z80 and most other 8-bit processors, like the 8080, 6800, and 6502. The Z8030 Z-SCC, for example, is available in a universal version called the Z8530 SCC. Other universal components include the following:

- Z8536 CIO
- Z8530 SCC
- Z8590 UPC

The Z8038 Z-FIO is configurable for either type of bus and does not require two part numbers.

CONCLUSION

How well the components work together, the chip count, and the design cycle time are among the most critical issues in any system. In this case, the adage that says "the whole is greater than the sum of the parts" is especially true where computer systems are concerned. The Z8000 family peripherals provide a powerful, flexible, and efficient system design when coupled with the Z8000 family processors.

Chip set bestows virtual memory on 16-bit minis

Second-generation chips add support for coprocessors and multiprocessors as well

by Jan Beekmans,* Gerard Duynisveld,* Claude Fernandes, Leo de Groot,* Louis Quéré,* Frans Schiereck,* and Arjaen Vermeulen
Philips Data Systems, Apeldoorn, the Netherlands, and Fontenay-aux-Roses, France

☐ The application of state-of-the-art MOS and bipolar custom circuitry to computer systems is boosting performance and the number of functions at a phenomenal rate. To protect its edge in system and software know-how over semiconductor houses, Philips Data Systems began a custom large-scale integrated-circuit design effort several years ago. It had the first building blocks by 1979: a 16-bit microprocessor (the SP 16C/10) and two bipolar circuits—one for bus arbitration (the SP16C/12) and one to support the interrupt system (the SP 16C/11).

But though this first generation was powerful, programs have become larger, requiring more addressable memory. Multiprocessing for multiusers demands virtual memory management, as well as strong memory protection. All this has led to a second-generation 16-bit processor—the SP 16C/20 instruction execution unit—and the SP 16C/23 memory management unit. This set supports virtual memory, dynamic code changes, and multiprocessor protocols, plus coprocessors for decimal and floating-point operations.

In addition, the new generation's instruction capabilities allow swapping of virtual memory into available physical space but do not restrict the swapping to fixed-size segments. By allowing segments to be of varying lengths, an entire task can be kept together.

Implementation

The SP 16C/10 was designed to execute a basic, 120-instruction set (called the primary, or P, set) using real, or physical, addressing. It was realized in static, depletion-load enhancement-driver n-channel MOS technology, initially with 6-micrometer minimum features, but now with 4 μm. The design is housed in a 40-pin package; the clock frequency of the 4-μm device is 4 megahertz. In that version, the shortest instructions take less than 2 microseconds. The processor works with both synchronous and asynchronous input/output interfaces, supports direct-memory-access requests, and has a nonmaskable interrupt input, along with four maskable ones. Its 16-bit data bus is multiplexed with the address bus. In its present version, the chip measures about 200 mils (5.1 millimeters) a side.

The addition of the virtual addressing scheme called for supporting an additional instruction class and led to a two-chip set for the new members of the computer family. Because the address translation is done in parallel with all instructions, it adds no appreciable delays to instruction execution. The block diagrams of the two new chips are shown in Figs. 1 and 2.

Complete compatibility

To preserve the vast investments of the last decade in system and application software, complete compatibility right down to the machine-code level is dictated. The best way to maintain compatibility and also add functions to an established computer line is to provide new instruction categories while incorporating more sophisticated address schemes, like support of virtual memory, into all instructions. Table 1 shows the four different instruction classes, including the two address schemes, along with the computer designed to execute them. All four classes are based on 16-bit-wide code and data.

Most of the 120 instructions in the P set have five different addressing modes: immediate, register, indirect, indexed, and indexed with indirection. Several data formats, including bits, bytes, words, and double words, are also supported. The set includes instructions like multiply and divide, 16 different shifts, and test and set or reset a bit, as well as 10 string-handling instructions that can move strings up to 64-K bytes long or search for a match with a specified character.

The D set acts on decimals up to 33 digits long and converts between the different formats currently in use for data processing. It comprises 22 instructions.

The F set covers floating-point instructions. Of the two addressing schemes—real and virtual—the real system is most widely used; here addresses directly indicate physical locations in main memory. Because the addresses are 16 bits wide in the real scheme and the smallest addressable unit is a byte, a 64-K-byte main memory can be addressed.

Virtual memory

In the virtual memory scheme, 32-bit addresses are handled in the program, whereas 24-bit physical addresses are computed. In this case, an extra instruction category, the V set, is added to support the wider addresses and the built-in protection mechanisms. Also, there are added instructions to support block-structured languages by implementing both a system stack, used for system parameters, and a user stack, for variables.

When instruction categories F and D are not being executed by hardware coprocessors, traps are generated to allow emulation of such instructions in software. There also are two privilege modes for instructions: system and user. Those instructions available only at the system privilege level control I/O operations, virtual memory management, and the system stack.

The segmented virtual memory management scheme

* Temporarily at Signetics Corp., Sunnyvale, Calif.

Reprinted with permission from *Electronics*, vol. 54, pp. 134–138, June 2, 1981.

of Fig. 3 meets the requirement of upward compatibility with the existing computer line while serving the need for a well-protected memory space much larger than 64-K bytes. Simply enlarging the address space without any protection—making a linear address space of several megabytes—is inadequate for multiuser applications.

The address space

A virtual memory scheme with 32-bit addresses yields an address space of 4 gigabytes. The address space is divided into 65,536 segments, each ranging from a minimal 256 bytes to a maximal of 64-K bytes, allowing for convenient execution of older programs at the machine-code level by placing them in a single segment. Segments with flexible lengths are chosen over the simpler page-based systems—where every page has a fixed length—because variable-length segments can each hold a complete software task.

Upward compatibility with the real addressing mode is preserved by dividing the 32-bit address into two parts—a 16-bit segment number and a 16-bit displacement. These are treated separately so that there is no overflow into an adjacent segment, which could destroy another user's program. When a user reaches beyond the end of his current segment a flag is set that is checked by the microprogram very early in each instruction's execution cycle, preventing illegal accesses.

A segment number signifies an entry in both the system context table and the segment index table. The system context table indicates the locations of the vari-

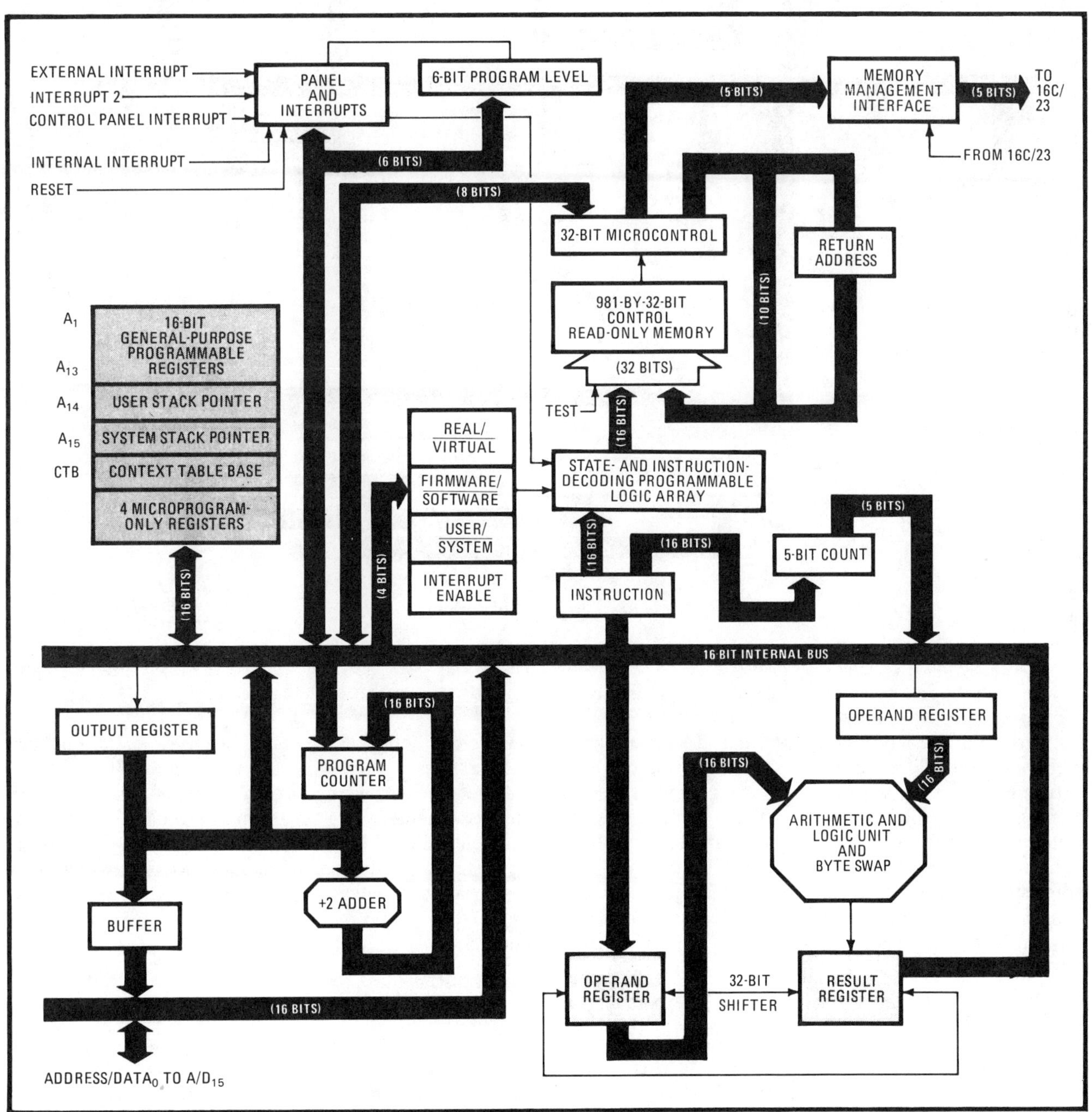

1. Inside the processor. The SP 16C/20 contains all the standard modules of a central processing unit, plus an interface to the SP 16C/23 memory management unit. It is fully microprogrammed and makes use of a programmable logic array to decode instructions.

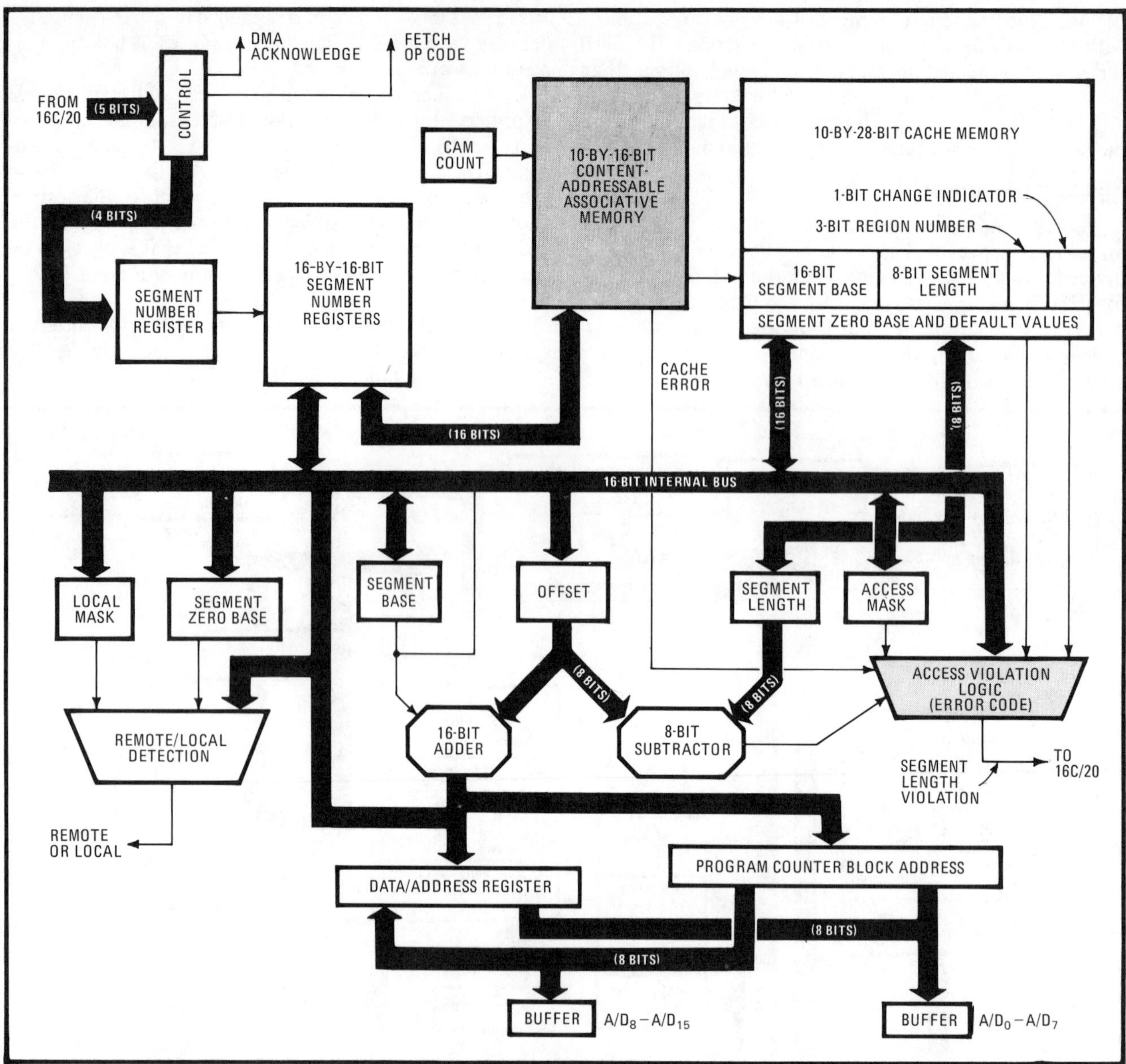

2. Virtual memory. A separate chip manages the virtual memory in parallel with the CPU's data calculations. The content-addressable memory and high-speed cache for descriptors keep protected address calculations from slowing down the processor.

ous parts of a user's program context. The segment index table holds the address of the segment descriptor, which in turn holds the address of the user's segment, as well as its length and protection status. These tables let users who by definition have different program contexts share the same segment without the need to copy it into different memory locations. The displacement and the first 16 bits of the segment descriptor (the segment base) form a 24-bit real address for the 16-megabyte on-line memory. The existence of segments is checked during the conversion through the tables, and the displacement is checked against the segment length. An abort trap is activated whenever one of those checks fails.

The protection scheme controls access to users' tasks being executed in the same virtual address space. Each task can be given different access rights to each individual segment (no access or read-only or read/write access). In addition, priority levels for tasks can either utilize 8 hierarchically organized task categories or 256 nonhierarchical ones.

A portion number is added on top of the segmented address scheme so as to group specific task segments. This scheme greatly eases the construction of the operating system's memory management function, which handles swapping between the 16-megabyte real address space (the on-line memory) and the 4-gigabyte virtual memory.

Not at home

Constructing a virtual memory space leads to requests for instructions or data that is not present in the on-line memory, causing a residence error. This type of error will occur frequently; depending on the execution speed of the instructions, the size of the on-line memory, and the regularity and size of the tasks, it will occur several times per second. Hence, a system must be able to

PHILIPS MINICOMPUTERS USING LARGE-SCALE INTEGRATED PROCESSORS								
Instruction classes supported	Using 16C/10 chip (real addressing only)				Using 16C/20 and 23 chips (real and virtual addressing)			
	P-853	P-858	P-400	*	*	*	*	*
Primary	√	√	√	√	√	√	√	√
Floating-point		√		√		√		√
Decimal			√	√			√	√
Virtual					√	√	√	√

*Proposed only

recover from it without intervention by the operator. Early in an instruction's microprogram decoding sequence, a check is run for this error to make an elegant restart possible in case it occurs. The procedure slightly complicates the microprogram but is preferable by far to checking at the moment a segment descriptor is loaded, because of the inherent software overhead and the possibility that between the loading of the descriptor and the execution of an instruction in that segment, interrupts might change the residency of segments. The checking also eliminates the need for redundant backup registers to save the previous state of the machine.

Both chips in the second-generation family have 40 pins and are implemented in a dense n-MOS process with 3.5-μm minimum features. Layout and initial fabrication were done at Signetics, and second sourcing is now being set up at Philips in Europe. The processor, like its predecessor, is about 200 mils (5.1 mm) on a side, and the memory management unit (MMU) about 160 mils (4.1 mm). Clock frequency ranges from 6 to 9 MHz for selected parts, giving instruction execution times of less than 700 nanoseconds for the shortest, most frequently used instructions at 6 MHz.

Similar interfaces

The microprogram size for the enhanced instruction set increased from 360 words of 32 bits in the case of the SP 16C/10 to nearly 1,000 words of 32 bits for the SP 16C/20, owing mainly to its virtual memory capability and the requirement that instructions be restartable in case of a residence error. Because processors are members of the same 16-bit computer family, the interfaces with the interrupt system and their buses remain functionally the same.

Translating the logical into the real addresses in the virtual scheme and their inherent checks would normally slow down the processor significantly. Implementing a cache memory on the SP 16C/23 for 11 segment descriptors has fully solved this performance disadvantage. The associate memory checks for valid addresses and loads new descriptors into the cache under microprogram control in order to preserve speed. One of the 11 segment descriptors is always the one used to execute the programs written in the real addressing scheme of the SP 16C/10.

The checks on access rights and segment length are done on the SP 16C/23 in parallel with instruction execution by the SP 16C/20. Thus the virtual memory scheme does not slow down the processor.

The more complex of the two, the SP 16C/20, has about 60,000 transistors, over half of which are used in the read-only memory and the programmable logic array structures. The microprocessor has an instruction prefetcher that also supports dynamic changes in the operation code. Although the capability to change the code slightly decreases the efficiency of the instruction prefetch, it can potentially allow the construction of very dense codes.

Coprocessors, too

Since the SP 16C/20 and 23 execute only the P and V instruction sets, the D and F sets have to be emulated in software. So that these sets may eventually be executed by separate processors, two interfaces have been microprogrammed into the SP 16C/20—one to pass a program context to a coprocessor, in case a decimal instruction is fetched, and one if a floating-point instruction occurs. The context is passed in less than 20 clock cycles, after which the coprocessor takes over the task, transmitting results and context back to the SP 16C/20 at its completion. The SP 16C/20 detects a coprocessor's presence on the fly, and either a context is passed or, in the absence of the dedicated processor, the emulation routine is started. Because the computer line is mainly for business applications, priority is given to the decimal coprocessor, which is now being microprogrammed.

The P instruction set enables the construction of semaphores for a multiprocessor system. In addition, the basic interrupt protocol of the SP 16C/11 can support such systems.

Multiple processors

With this foundation, a multiprocessor system built of identical processors is envisaged. Each processor is placed on a separate printed-circuit board of the Eurocard size, with a part of the general-purpose memory on board. All these distributed memory chunks make up the total on-line memory. Whereas the local memory is addressed synchronously, the second category employs an asynchronous handshake to allow time for other processors to get off the bus and to support the use of memories having a wide variety of access times. To make this memory organization transparent to the system software, the SP 16C/20 and 23 have extra logic to take the

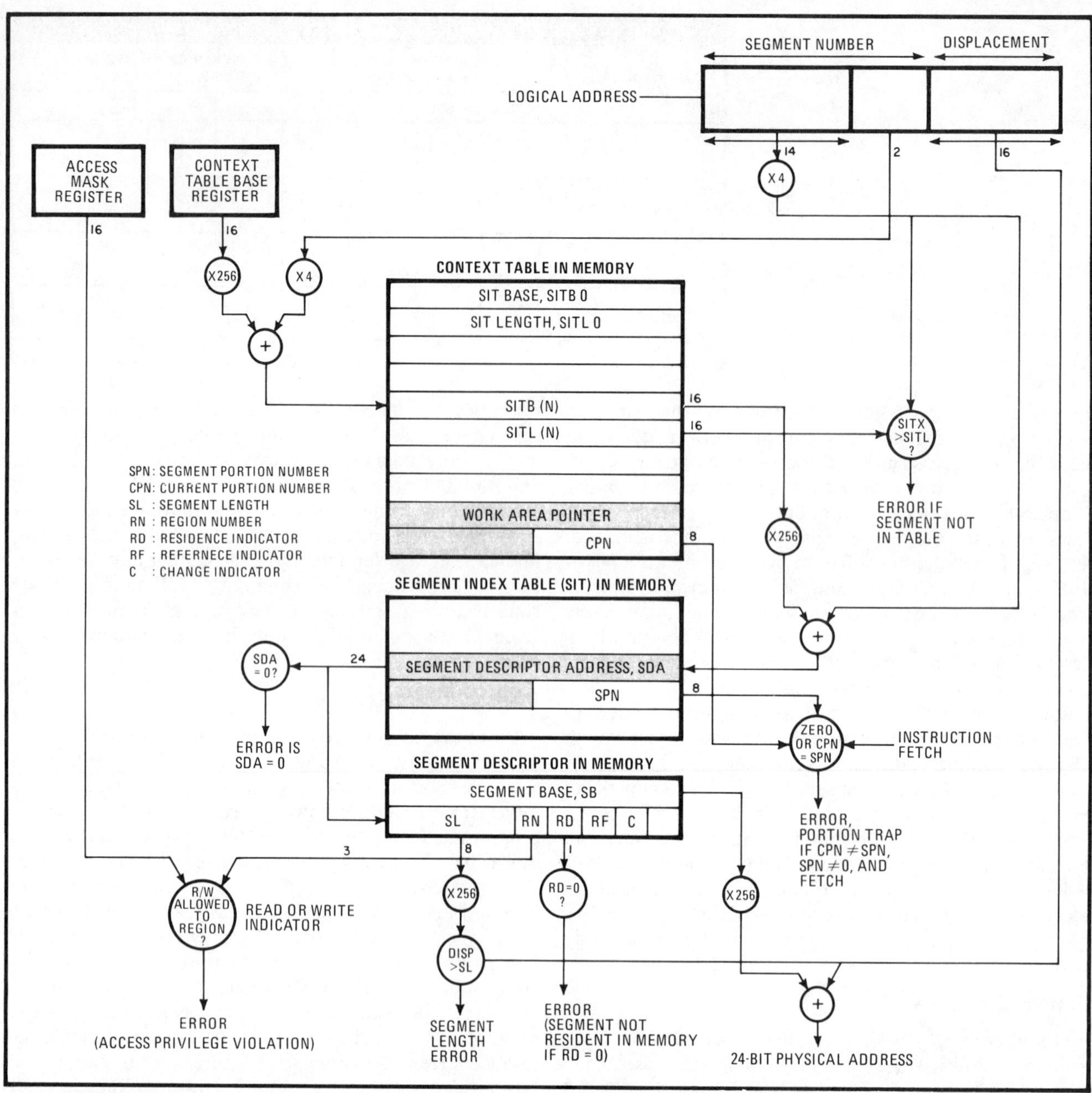

3. Logical to physical. The conversion of 32-bit virtual addresses into 24-bit real addresses is done in two steps. The logical address is used to locate the segment index table entry from the context table, and that entry in turn indicates the location of the segment descriptor.

memory partitioning into account. The idea is to have the processors accessing as much as possible their local (on-board) memory at full speed by a synchronous interface and to minimize the references to remote memory over the slower asynchronous system bus.

At the system level, the processor (or processors, in the case of a multiprocessor system), the on-line memory, and the I/O control units are connected by a system bus, which has as a physical form factor a 96-pin Euroconnector. A 28-pin bipolar device, the SP 16C/12, is designed to permit a bus master device—such as a central processing unit or direct-memory-access control unit—to request and gain control of the common system bus. The SP 16C/12 lets a bus master in a multimaster system communicate with other masters, as well as transfer data to common memory and I/O devices. The chip is about 160 mils (4.1 mm) on a side and allows modular expansion to any number of bus masters. To maximize throughput, the bus allocation runs in parallel with the other functions on the chip.

To support an interrupt system with as many as 63 different interrupt levels, the SP 16C/11 was designed. It is realized in bipolar technology, measures about 170 mils (4.3 mm) on a side, and is housed in a 22-pin package.

The bus interface of the SP 16C/11 comprises only two lines: a clock for the interrupt system and one for the encoded interrupt information. This concept has many features in common with the interrupt structure of the proposed P-896 bus interface standard that the Institute of Electrical and Electronics Engineers is working on for modern 16- and 32-bit multiprocessor systems. □

16-bit C-MOS processor packs in hardware for business computers

On-chip error detection, virtual memory support, and four operating levels equip 10,000-gate circuit for multiuser applications

by Norio Inui, Hideo Kikuchi, and Toshihiro Sakai, *Fujitsu Ltd., Kawasaki, Japan*

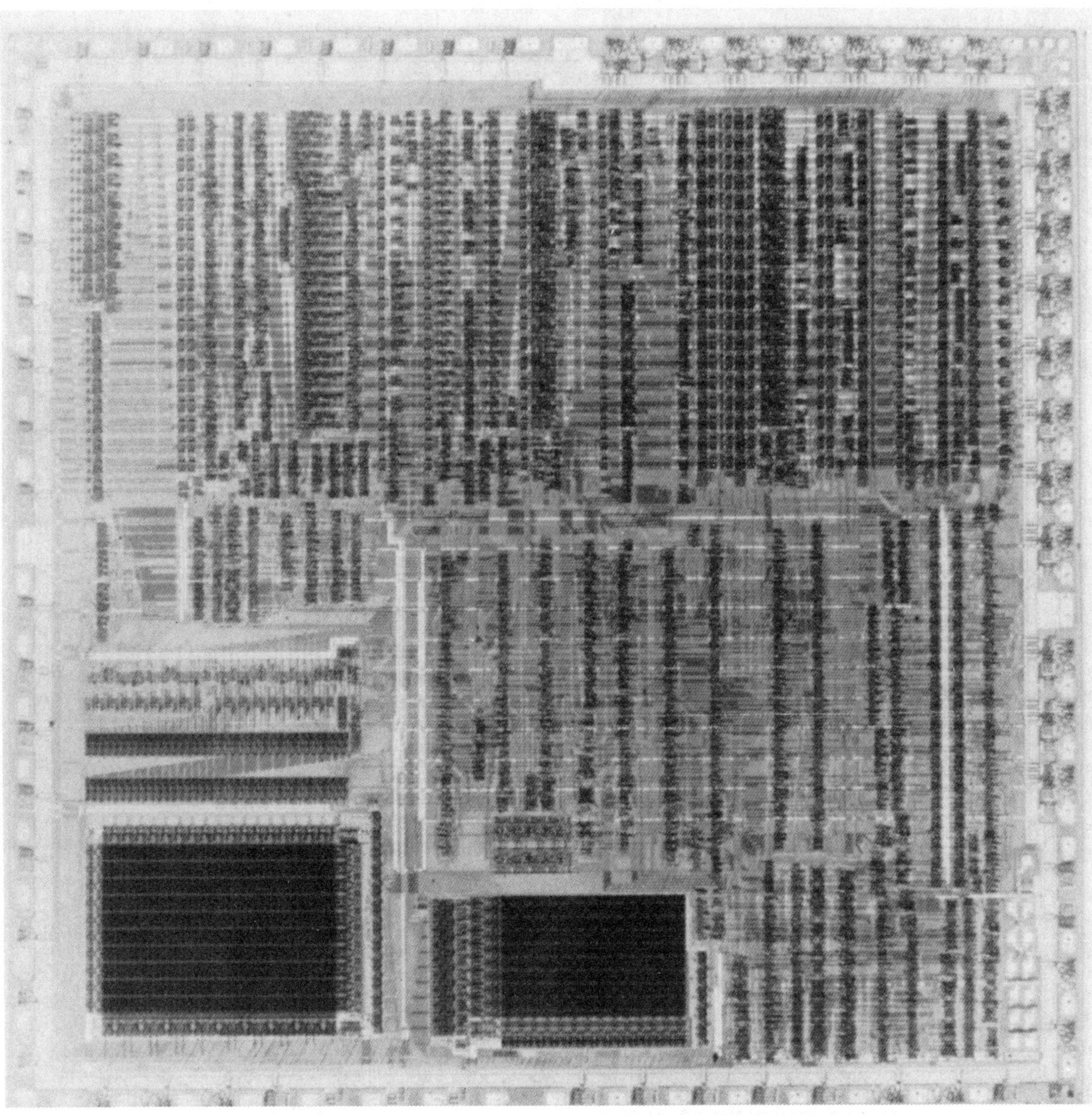

1. A real CAD. The FSSP 16-bit complementary-MOS microprocessor makes extensive use of computer-aided design, which acccounts for the regularity of its layout. Its multiple register sets occupy a large area on the die, but they speed along context switches.

Reprinted with permission from *Electronics*, vol. 54, pp. 182–186, June 16, 1981.

☐ Sixteen-bit microprocessors have attained the speed and sophistication that enable them to serve as the central data-processing unit for multiuser applications like small-business computer systems or as a cluster-control device for intelligent terminals. The small-system processor, dubbed the FSSP, from Fujitsu is one such device that carries an added advantage—it can be microprogrammed to emulate an existing processor, though in the Facom V series of small-business computers it emulates the Unios architecture developed in 1974.

Today's small-business computer systems perform on-site processing with a typical configuration consisting of a work station centered around a display unit at each work site. The improvement in processor capabilities and storage capacity, along with the decline in the price of terminal equipment, has made it possible to place work stations wherever needed and given rise to multiple work-station processing.

The FSSP (Fig. 1) aims at processing universality in this emerging market through its ability to emulate the Unios architecture of the Facom series, as well as the high-level architectures of other machines. It uses microcode to support virtual memory management in the Facom V series, though in the Facom system 80 it handles only real physical addresses. In both, the FSSP executes such multiuser channel functions as input/output control in microcode, in addition to its normal data-processing function, and high system reliability has been achieved by virtue of full error detection on all internal and external buses.

Designed with a silicon-gate complementary-MOS process the FSSP uses a double layer of metal for connecting over 40,000 transistors that make up 10,000 gates, each of which has a propagation delay between 4 to 10 nanoseconds. The chip is housed in a 64-pin package, requires only a 5-volt supply, and dissipates about 130 milliwatts at a 2.5-megahertz clock rate. It can address 16 megabytes of main memory, has decimal arithmetic, and uses four hierarchical levels of operation to efficiently handle multiprocessing.

The FSSP's architecture permits emulation of the architectures of other machines at the lowest level possible. That means that if the operating system is viewed as the highest level, then the machine language can be considered the next level, and the native microprogram-controlled architecture of the FSSP will be at the lowest.

To efficiently emulate the Unios architecture of the Facom V and Facom system 80 computers, the FSSP has special microinstructions, registers, and other hardware.

The microprogram is pulled up to the machine-language level of other computer architectures by an interpreter. Most of the other 16-bit microprocessors on the market have a preprogrammed machine language (see table). Under those circumstances, emulating the machine language of another computer through an interpreter can seriously degrade performance.

In order to efficiently emulate different architectures, it is necessary to have access to the microarchitecture of a machine, since it is the microinstructions that are executed at the highest speed. Although emulating machine language through the interpreter inevitably affects a processor's performance, this degradation can

COMPARING 16-BIT MICROPROCESSORS

	Fujitsu FSSP	Intel 8086	Motorola 68000
Addressable memory	16 megabytes (possible to support virtual storage)	1 megabyte (64-K bytes segment mapping)	16 megabytes (possible to support virtual storage)
Architecture	variable (oriented by microprogram on control storage)	fixed	fixed
Operating levels	4 levels	1 level	2 levels
Interrupt levels	3 levels	3 levels	7 levels
Addressing modes	3	6	12
Features of instructions	bit manipulation decimal addition and subtraction (packed/unpacked data) — — branch for codes	— decimal adjustment (packed/unpacked data) multiply and divide string manipulation —	bit manipulation decimal addition and subtraction (packed data) multiply and divide — —
Registers	⟨central processing unit level⟩ general registers, 16 bits by 16 words address registers, 16 bits by 8 words working registers, 16 bits by 8 words ⟨machine-check level⟩ working registers, 16 bits by 8 words ⟨input/output 1 level⟩ working registers, 16 bits by 8 words ⟨I/O 2 level⟩ working registers, 16 bits by 8 words	general registers, 16 bits by 4 words pointer registers, 16 bits by 2 words index registers, 16 bits by 2 words segment registers, 16 bits by 4 words	data registers, 32 bits by 8 words address registers, 32 bits by 7 words stack pointers, 32 bits by 2 words

2. Separate stores. A separate control store allows the FSSP chip to emulate the instruction set of other machines. A microcoded interpreter converts each instruction of the emulated machine into a series of microinstructions for the FSSP.

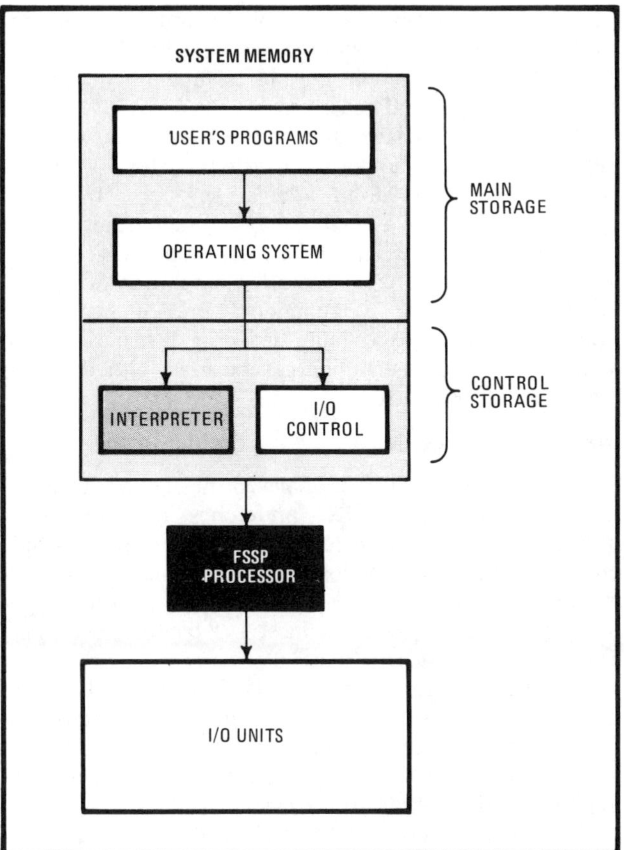

be reduced by supporting the most frequently used functions of the operating system through microprogramming and firmware.

The FSSP facilitates these functions by dividing storage into a control storage area and a main storage area. Figure 2 shows a typical example of how this storage scheme works. The control storage area contains an interpreter that emulates the architecture of the target machine, as well as microprogrammed routines for I/O control; the main storage area contains the target machine's operating system and user programs.

Microprogrammed architecture

The logical structure of the FSSP is designed for multiprocessing, especially in business environments. There are 117 microinstructions for binary arithmetic, logic operations, and shifting—all based on 16-bit data—and the shift instructions can shift from 1 to 16 bits in a single clock cycle. For accelerating the processing of business data of varying word lengths, there are also decimal arithmetic instructions, as well as decimal data-checking and -modification instructions.

The unit also has an ample set of data-transfer, I/O control, branch, and other instructions for fast and effi-

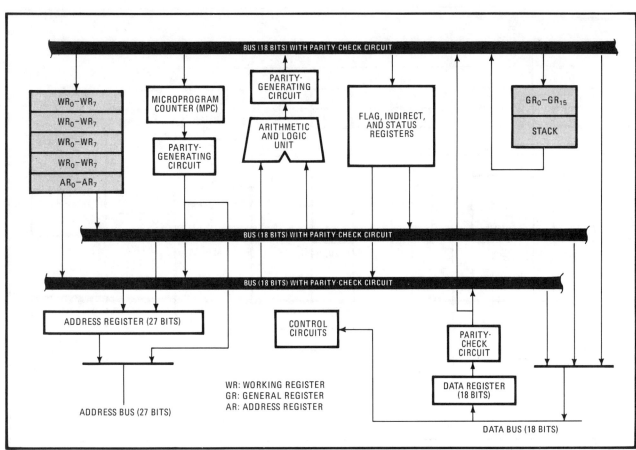

3. On-chip error detection. Each byte of data has a parity bit appended to it, making most of the data paths 18 bits wide. The FSSP also appends parity bits to its results, and whenever a parity error is detected, its source is logged and the offending operation retried.

cient microprogramming control. In addition, both the main and the control storage are accessed by a set of instructions that include an address-update function to streamline sequential accesses.

At the hardware level, four sets of 8-by-16-bit working registers furnish fast operating-system context switching. There are also 8 16-bit address registers, 16 16-bit general registers, a dedicated indirect register for address calculations, and other, more specialized registers—all arranged to facilitate the emulation of higher-level architectures. A functional branch instruction speeds emulation by quickly decoding instructions and commands. This instruction can be used with Unios or any other architecture.

Anticipatory control

High-speed operation is achieved through anticipatory control. Because the FSSP prefetches and predecodes microinstructions, most can be executed in a single machine cycle (400 nanoseconds). This extremely fast speed, coupled with the unit's interrupt-driven multiprocessing capability, enables most I/O control to be performed by microinstructions.

These instructions generate I/O control signals for up to 256 I/O ports, making it easy to add remote interfaces. Each signal transfers either 1 or 2 bytes of data, and a direct-memory-access circuit can be added when even higher transfer speeds are necessary.

The FSSP is designed to produce systems with high reliability and accordingly has a full range of error-detection functions not found elsewhere. On all the internal FSSP registers and buses, for example, 1 parity bit is attached to each byte of data, making most data paths 18 bits wide (Fig. 3).

Achieving parity

The arithmetic and logic circuits use the parity method to check for errors without interrupting the data flow. The input-section circuits also check the parity of data coming on chip, making it possible to separate internal from external errors—an operation that is extremely difficult to effectively accomplish on conventional microprocessors.

Backup registers behind all control registers give the machine-check level its own set of working registers. When an error occurs, the FSSP is designed to detect the source of the error, which is logged for later inspection, and then recovers by retrying the offending operation.

The FSSP has powerful multiprocessing functions that enable numerous I/O units to be processed simultaneously and in parallel with the execution of programs. A key factor in this capability is the chip's use of four operating levels, each of which has its own set of 8 16-bit working registers, a microprogram counter, and a area for saving condition codes (Fig. 4). No other microprocessor has such an extensive set of registers.

This duplication of register sets for each of the four levels of operation does consume die area, but the disad-

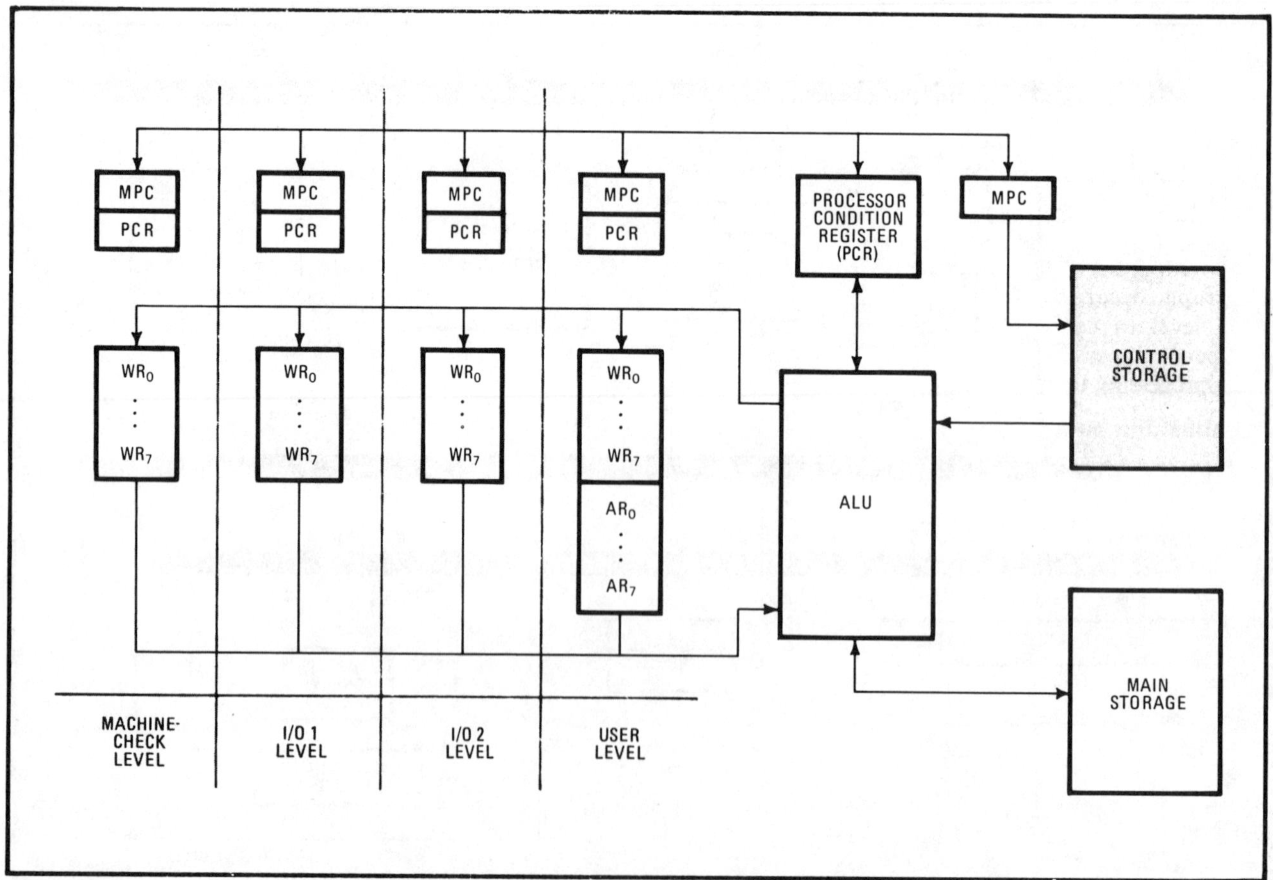

4. Multiple register sets. Four separate register sets and program counters on the FSSP eliminate the necessity for swapping values in and out of the FSSP when switching between the four operating levels. Switching is interrupt driven and is optimized for multiprocessing.

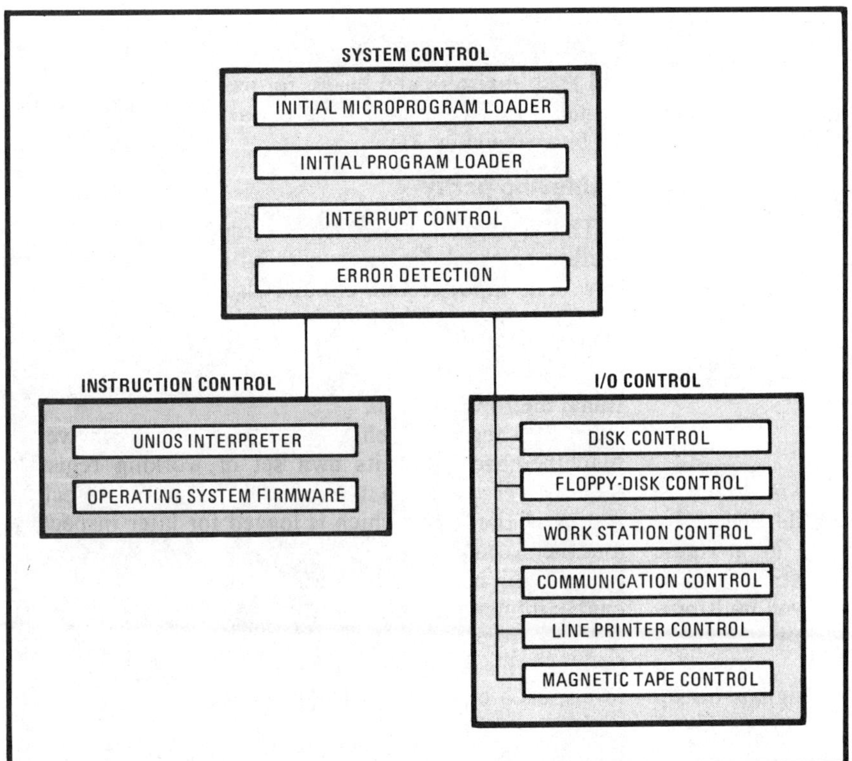

5. Firmware support. The Facom V-830 has extensive firmware support for system, instruction, and input/output control. The interpreter recognizes the Unios instruction set; other often-used functions such as disk control are also handled in firmware.

vantage is more than offset by the time saved during context switches. Specifically, in moving from one level of operation to another, an extremely frequent operation in multiuser environments, no time is wasted swapping register sets—an operation that can significantly slow down conventional processors.

Many computers have only two operating modes: a supervisory mode and a program mode. In contrast, the four mode levels of the FSSP are the machine check level (level 0), the I/O levels (1 and 2) and the normal user mode (level 3).

Switching between levels is done automatically when interrupts occur. These functions permit programs at each level to use the microprocessor as if they had independent possession of it, thereby achieving a high multiprocessing throughput not otherwise attainable.

Establishing an order

An order of processing priority is established among these levels, with level 0 as the highest and level 3 the lowest. Thus, tasks are automatically executed according to their degree of urgency, resulting in efficient multiprocessing. Since each level has its own working registers, program counter, and condition-code save area, there is no need to save either the registers or the condition codes when switching between levels.

The machine level answers two types of interrupts: those caused by hardware errors and those caused by program exceptions. I/O level 1 and I/O level 2 are reserved for interrupts from I/O devices, which are divided into two groups according to the time-critical nature of the peripheral. Slow devices like terminals and printers are assigned to the lower priority level, whereas higher-priority peripherals, such as disk and tape controllers, are assigned to level 1.

The FSSP has compiled a good service record in the Facom V series and Facom system 80. A representative example can be found in its use in the Facom V-830.

The functional components of the V-830 are a main memory capacity of 768-K bytes for storing the operating system and user's programs, all of which are written in the machine language of the emulated computer. A 192-K-byte control storage holds programs made up of FSSP microinstructions and their data.

The central processing card is the heart of the Facom V-830 and consists of the FSSP, plus storage and DMA control circuits. It uses microprograms held in the control store to execute Unios instructions, control I/O, convert virtual addresses, and execute DMA transfers over the high-speed bus. In addition, the V-830 has a disk file capacity of up to 464 megabytes and can support up to 16 work stations and 4 communication lines.

The central controller of this fairly large system is the FSSP along with the firmware residing in control storage to perform system, instruction, and I/O functions (Fig. 5). Under system control are two bootstrap programs for loading microprograms and user's programs, both initially from magnetic disk.

Another system firmware routine handles interrupt control. Yet another manages error detection whereby hardware status can be displayed and causes of machine checks are analyzed and reported to software.

The Unios interpreter, which emulates the Unios instruction set, is part of the instruction-control firmware, as shown. In addition, the operating-system firmware uses microprograms to carry out certain supervisory functions of the Unios control program. I/O control is also handled in firmware in order to efficiently execute the channel functions that control the I/O units. □

Low-cost 16-bit microprocessor has performance of midrange minicomputer

Designing to pare silicon real estate cuts cost and increases speed of the latest PDP-11 IC implementation

by Raymond Ochester

Digital Equipment Corp., Hudson, Mass.

1. Tiny 11. The 5-by-5-mm die of the T-11 contains three somewhat independent data-processing machines—a control machine, a data machine, and a bus machine. The data machine is roughly the upper three quarters of the left side; the control machine is mostly on the right, with the bus machine above and below it.

☐ Extending the cost-performance benefits of the PDP-11 family into a new realm, the T-11 16-bit microprocessor realizes lower cost than other single-chip processing solutions, yet delivers performance equal to a conventional minicomputer. The new integrated circuit offers the same PDP-11 instruction subset and functionality as lower-end members of the series, yet has a higher execution speed than any of them—about the same as the PDP-11/34 midrange minicomputer.

The architecture and design concepts in the T-11 were influenced primarily by DEC's emphasis on low cost, both for the chip itself and for microcomputer systems and other applications to be built around it. The number of transistors was minimized—there are only 13,000—so that the silicon die size could be small for low unit cost. To accomplish what amounted to a complete redesign, a number of space-saving techniques sparing in their use of transistors were adopted.

The execution speed of the T-11 is 1.6 microseconds for a register-to-register ADD instruction, which is roughly equivalent to that of the PDP-11/34 and twice the speed of the PDP-11/05. The chip operates at a 7.5-megahertz clock frequency with a maximum power consumption of less than 0.8 watt at 25°C. This figure is substantially lower than some other 16-bit n-channel MOS microprocessor designs (1.2 W is given as typical for one; 1.8 W as maximum for another).

The T-11 (Fig. 1) consists of three semiautonomous machines based on programmable logic arrays—the control, data, and bus subunits. The control machine interprets PDP-11 macroinstructions and triggers the next control state. The data machine, which consists mainly of a static register file based on random-access memory and of an arithmetic and logic unit on main and secondary internal buses, computes data-based results. The bus machine handles all input/output flow, including data, address, interrupt, and control signals.

Fabricated in a 5-micrometer process in place of the 6-μm process used for the LSI-11/23 two-chip implementation, the T-11 is faster, yet consumes 20% less power. The smaller-scale circuit geometry improves the speed-power product, as well as saving real estate. The higher transconductance and lower capacitance of the smaller transistors tend to increase speed and, potentially at least, reduce power.

Production ease

Production of the new chip uses existing DEC manufacturing equipment and does not require special processing that tends to reduce overall yield or requires further special processing to achieve acceptable yield. Moreover, the 5-μm process is more easily transferred to potential second sources than a finer process would be. Other microprocessor manufacturers have established processes with minimum features as small as 2 μm, but typical device cost is many times higher than what was considered acceptable for the T-11.

In moving to 5-μm geometry, it was necessary to rework layout rules in order to avoid possible merging of elements of the chip structure. If a linear shrink had been used to reduce all elements the same proportion, circuit density could have been increased only about 15% at a given production yield in going from 6 to 5 μm. In

Reprinted with permission from *Electronics*, vol. 54, pp. 129–133, Nov. 3, 1981.

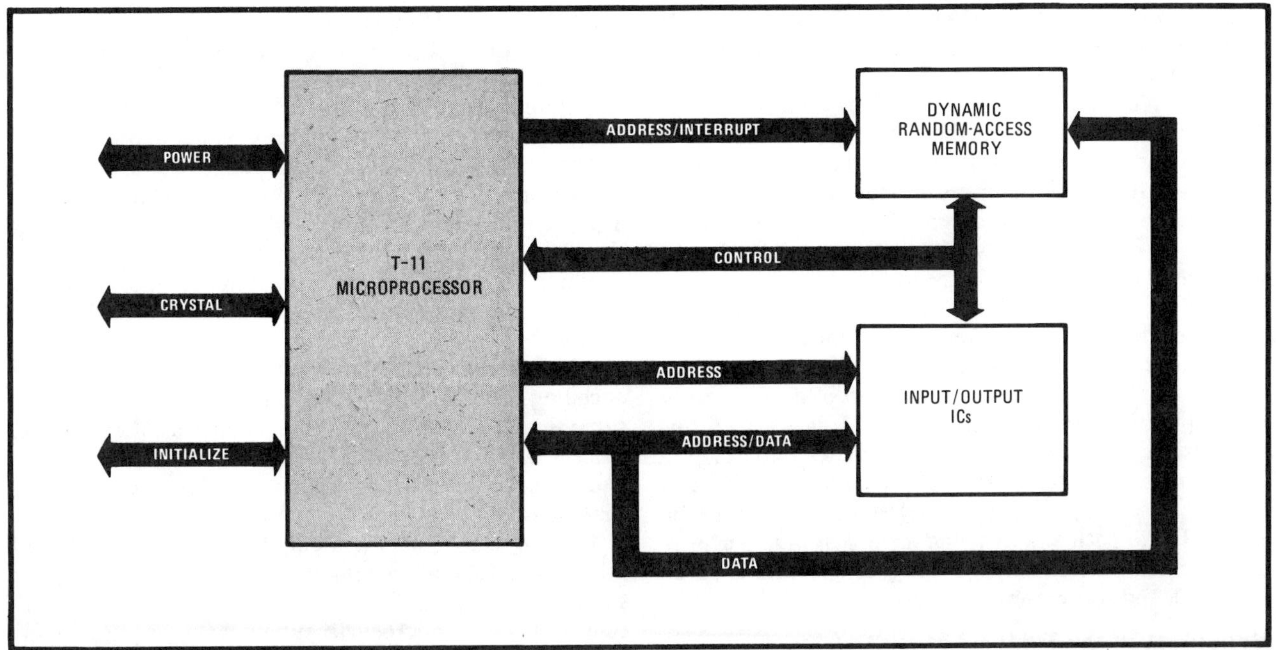

2. Double identity. The T-11 microprocessor in its 40-pin dual in-line package can interface with either an 8- or 16-bit bus. The 8-bit version is shown; in the 16-bit configuration, all the lines at right, except the control lines, become multiplexed address and data lines.

contrast, the density of the T-11 was increased about 30% and achieved the same yield through selective shrinking, a longer and more difficult design process in which various circuit elements are shrunk to the maximum allowed for each element for a given yield.

The new microprocessor was designed to provide greater application flexibility than do single-chip microcomputers and more integrated support functions than bit-slice processors. The trend toward embedded processors places a premium on flexibility in configuring support functions. With such peripheral products as a video display terminal or floppy-disk drive, the processor and its support hardware can match that unit's needs. Use of a microcomputer would mean that the peripherals must be adapted to its characteristics.

Cost-reduction goals

Size and power constraints for the new IC were established initially to insure a product that would be internally cost-competitive. Since manufacturing costs in today's production technology are proportional to silicon area rather than to the number of chips, a die size of 5 by 5 millimeters was selected. The decision to use a plastic dual in-line package rather than the more expensive ceramic packaging set maximum allowable heat dissipation at 0.9 W.

N-MOS semiconductor technology was selected in preference to a complementary-MOS process because of its higher transistor density. The higher power requirements of n-MOS were considered manageable.

Early in the design process, a number of cost-related decisions were made regarding chip and support functions. For example, plans are to use the T-11 with off-the-shelf large-scale integrated I/O chips for such external hardware functions as memory, serial communications lines, and floppy-disk and video-terminal control. Therefore, the processor design included intelligence to ensure timing compatibility with these support chips.

A single-voltage power supply of +5 volts was chosen with TTL-compatible signal input and output. This selection minimizes the number of power pins in the package, avoids the need for a second external power supply, helps to cut heat generation, and reduces the number of support chips.

The IC has a built-in oscillator clock for use with an external crystal. An external clock would have added substantially to the cost of support hardware, whereas a crystal is comparatively inexpensive.

Program memory was omitted from the T-11; however, the chip includes all the addressing and control signals required by low-cost external dynamic RAMs. The rationale for the first decision was that, with the tendency of program memory to grow rapidly from year to year, the limited chip real estate would require the periodic addition of memory chips anyway. On the other hand, the address- and control-signal configurations would remain constant with foreseeable increases in program-memory size.

Somewhere in time

One approach to help speed up the operation of other microprocessors has been to provide separate external buses for communications with dynamic RAM and I/O devices. However, a single-bus configuration was selected for the T-11 to simplify application and internal system design.

The dynamic RAM and I/O chips each receive control signals from the same pins of the microprocessor by precise positioning of these signals in time. Without time-multiplexed control signals, there would have had to be more pins on the chip package and more support chips, which would increase system costs.

A 40-pin plastic DIP was deemed capable of handling the functions assigned to the chip. A 48-pin package would have cost more, and production testers for DIPs with more than 40 pins could not be implemented fast enough or cheaply enough.

In order to compete for applications against both 8- and 16-bit microprocessors, the T-11's internal data path is 16 bits wide, and the processor can be operated on an external data bus of either 16 bits for performance or 8 bits for lower cost. The schematic diagram of Fig. 2 shows the T-11 in an 8-bit external bus configuration, with a total of eight pins assigned to the service functions at left and eight for each of the four lines at right. In a 16-bit environment, the only difference is that all address lines become address and data lines.

The bus machine handles all I/O flow of data, address, interrupt, and control signals. The T-11 chip's operating mode is matched to application needs by initializing a unique mode register in the bus machine. For low-cost designs, for example, the mode register is set for an 8-bit external data path and dynamic RAM. For high performance, on the other hand, the designer specifies a 16-bit data path and static RAM.

Geneology of the T-11

In 1973, the PDP-11/05 minicomputer was implemented in TTL technology, and a good deal of microcode was built into the processor. For its control machine, more than 40,000 array sites were provided on 33 densely packed LSI chips. In addition, the gates and registers in the 11/05's data machine were implemented in medium-scale and small-scale integration, with 100 chips providing a total of 5,000 transistors.

In 1979, the LSI-11/23 was designed entirely in LSI technology on two chips in which cost-effective architecture demanded a significant reduction in microcode. By then, cost was evaluated in terms of total silicon area rather than of the number of chips.

Microcode in the 11/05 was converted to implicit functions of the ALU in the 11/23. The ALU in the 5,500-transistor 11/23 data machine can handle every PDP-11 macroinstruction of the two predominant types. The control machine contains 15,700 array sites, about 40% the number found in the 33 chips of the 11/05's control machine.

The T-11 contains 17,000 transistor sites (potential devices) and about 13,000 actual transistors distributed among the three machines: 6,550 in the control machine, 5,450 in the data machine, and 1,000 in the bus machine. The major reductions in transistor count and chip real estate are found in the control machine, where the number of transistor sites was reduced 40%—from 15,700 to 9,400—compared to the 11/23.

The control machine contains four submachines. The instruction submachine computes and retains a new value each time a PDP-11 macroinstruction is fetched. Each time instruction execution enters a new phase (fetch instruction, fetch operand, or execution), the instruction phase submachine computes a new value. The microcycle submachine updates each cycle of the data machine, and the microcycle phase submachine computes a new value for each phase of the microcycle within which the data machine is controlled by strobes (timed commands to registers).

Because one of the prime goals for this design was to minimize the size of the chip, a number of functions were shifted among the submachines. Shifting functions to different parts of a chip can reduce the number and length of interconnections, thereby reducing the area.

The number of sites in the control machine was reduced first in the LSI-11/23 and then further in the T-11 by redistributing data-handling assignments among the four submachines. First, the instruction phase submachine was made more important in the 11/23 by increasing the maximum possible number of instruction phases. While this modification added transistor sites in the instruction phase submachine, it saved far more decoding sites in the microcycle submachine. At the same time, the microcycle submachine was changed over from RAM to programmed logic arrays because Boolean equations could be represented with fewer gates in PLAs than in RAM.

The number of sites was cut even further in the T-11 microprocessor by moving tasks from the microcycle submachine to its phase submachine. Gates are uniformly wide in the microcycle submachine because many tasks require large I/O sections. However, certain tasks that did not need such large I/O sections were transferred to fewer sites in the microcycle phase submachine. Additionally, some tasks were shifted from the microcycle submachine to the data machine, also reducing the number of sites that are required.

Simpler decoding

The decoding space of the microcycle submachine in the 11/23 must decode all 16 bits of the PDP-11 macroinstruction: 4 bits of operations code and 6 bits each of source and destination address. Depending on the operations code and particular instruction phase, however, only 10 bits are actually needed for the gate output of the operations code and either source or destination address. In the T-11, therefore, the instruction phase machine instead determines the appropriate 10 bits in advance, so that the microcycle submachine need decode only 10 bits. The move eliminated the address space needed for the additional 6 bits.

A branch instruction task was shifted from the microcycle submachine into the data machine, saving both the microword space for representing different branch possibilities and the time needed to select the microword in the control machine. To do this, a branch PLA was put between the 16-bit temporary instruction register at the bottom of the scratchpad memory and the processor status register below it.

Four bits in the branch PLA are compared to the 4 bits of condition code in the processor status register: a match switches the ALU to ADD, and no match switches it to NOP (no-operation). The entire matching function is performed in the data machine, using what would otherwise be open space between registers.

This shift of data-handling tasks out of the microcycle submachine has significantly reduced the total real estate, as well as the number of devices in the microprocessor. The area of the microcycle submachine has been cut nearly in half with only small increases in the smaller areas occupied by other circuit sectors. Also, putting the

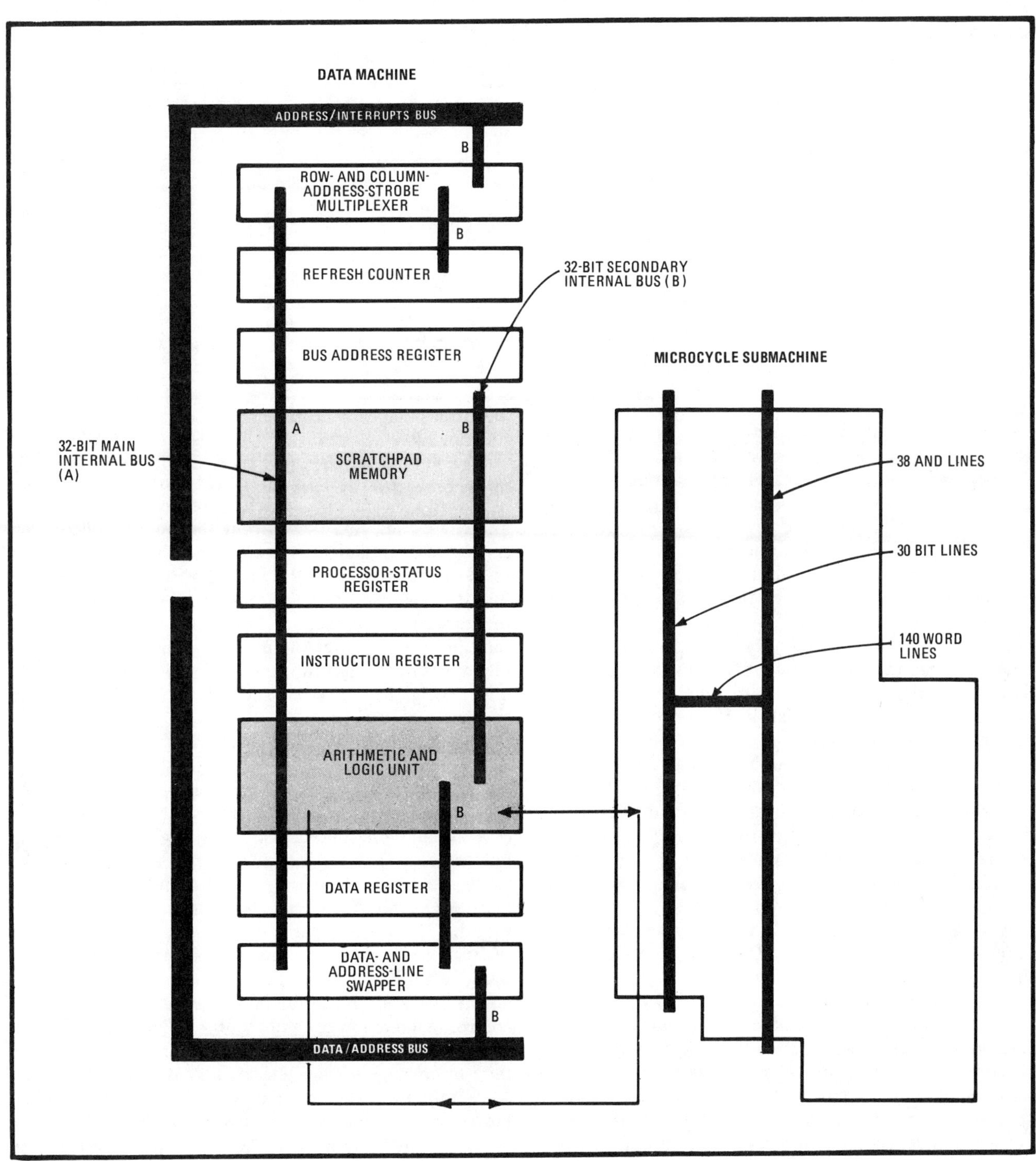

3. Machine parts. In the T-11 design, functions were shifted among the machines. For example, the branch-instruction task was moved to the data machine from the microcycle portion of the control machine in the form of a branch PLA. Control lines are shortened wherever possible, such as substituting the colored path for the solid black one for links between the microcycle submachine and the data machine.

control and data machines on the same IC eliminates about 1,000 transistors needed to interconnect circuits on separate control and data chips.

There are significant differences in the circuitry of the T-11's data machine that have increased its execution speed. Fast paths for the address from the bus address register and data from the scratchpad memory to pass around the ALU to the bus output latch are added without penalty in cost and real estate by timesharing the internal buses extensively. In the data machines of the earlier low-end PDP-11s, the bus address must be transmitted from the scratchpad through the ALU and back over the main bus to reach the bus address register.

The real estate occupied by the data machine was shrunk by adopting an internal architecture aimed at orderly geometry, which in turn minimizes the length and number of interconnections. In the data machine and microcycle submachine (Fig. 3), all the registers, including 12 in the scratchpad memory, are aligned for convenient multiplexing with the main and secondary

4. Relay race. The microcycle of the T-11 microprocessor has three phases that slightly overlap. The phases φ_1, φ_2, and φ_3 are shown in relation to a typical output sequence with a single-rank register. Because of circuit segment stability, each phase starts before the previous one ends.

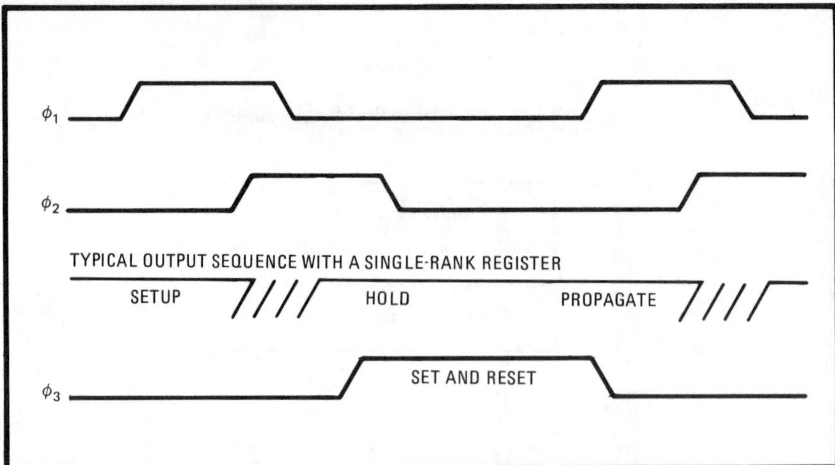

internal buses that are oriented vertically in the layer above. Similarly, parallel control lines in another layer and perpendicular to the internal buses (but not shown in the figure) cross over the registers and the ALU.

Buses A and B consist of seven lines for each of 16 bits. One of the seven, called the X line, is available for any assigned data transfer. The uniform spacing of the horizontal control lines is such that additional lines can be inserted wherever needed. As a result, the registers and logic for condition codes, branches, priorities, variables, and constants can communicate by means of short links to existing vertical and horizontal metal, thereby avoiding the jogs or angular lines that can handicap high-density circuit designs.

The characteristics of n-MOS technology have contributed to orderly geometry in several ways. Rather than requiring the positioning of transistors and then of the interconnections, n-MOS permits first laying out the mutually perpendicular bus and control lines. The gates are placed below the crossing of the lines, substantially reducing the number of interconnections.

In addition, bidirectional buses can be used in conjunction with multiplexers so that single transfer devices linking registers and buses can handle both reading to and writing from the bus. The B bus links at top and bottom to the time-split external bus are also connected through transfer devices for two-way transmission.

However, the concept of orderly geometry in the data machine was not applied blindly, regardless of other space-saving techniques. Two modifications to the geometry further reduced the number and length of interconnections in this unit.

In the first modification, the carry condition code requires linking the outputs of transistors at bit positions 15, 7, and 0 in the ALU. One way to accomplish this would be to add three long horizontal lines to bring the bit-position signals out to one side of the ALU.

Instead, the bit positions scattered in the lower part of the ALU are connected in step fashion by linking vertical X lines and short line segments inserted between existing control lines. Even though the ALU must be slightly wider to accommodate the 16 extra X lines, the area under these lines is used in other layers of the chip and so space is saved in the ALU's vertical dimension.

In the second modification of orderly geometry, there are a number of instances in which a position on a vertical bit line in the microcycle submachine must be connected to a horizontal control line in the data machine. Conventional practice would be to insert an interconnecting line down from the bit line out of the congested area and then back up to the control line in the data machine (the solid black line in Fig. 3).

Instead, wherever there are no transistors to the left of the particular bit line, the horizontal control line from the right is stopped at the bit line. Thus space is available to go directly left into the data machine (the colored line in Fig. 3)—a much shorter route than with the conventional method.

Overlapping clock phases

The simplest clocking scheme that operates effectively with the single-rank registers in the T-11 microprocessor is a three-phase microcycle with slightly overlapping phases (Fig. 4). A slightly overlapping arrangement like this is more process-tolerant and demands less total time and fewer circuit elements than a nonoverlapping clock would. The three-phase clock can overlap slightly because each circuit segment remains stable for two phases after its state changes.

With careful choice of the functions of the data and control machines in each phase, both machines can work together in a pipeline structure. All circuits have ample time to operate in each phase. Balancing data-handling tasks minimizes the number of devices and therefore power consumption in the control and data machines.

During the three microcycle phases, the data machine performs a complete operation by reading two registers and writing in one. Other logic on the chip modifies these operations by providing constants like vectors and addresses, indirect register addressing, and conditional data such as a branch or priority status based on data in particular registers. The control machine of the microprocessor computes new control signals during the last, or write, phase of the data machine.

The bus machine usually cycles in six phases. Its cycle begins one phase after the data machine reads and ends one phase after the data machine writes. During intervening phases, it generates external control strobes and waits for support chips to complete their portions of the data transfer. □

Part III
32-Bit Microprocessors

MICROPROCESSORS with 32-bit internal paths and 16-bit external paths have been in existence since 1980. However, the era of true 32-bit microprocessors began in 1981 with the commercial introduction of the iAPX 432 and Hewlett-Packard's use of its internally developed 32-bit microprocessor in an engineering workstation.

The first reprint article in this Part presents a very comprehensive report on the state of the art of 32-bit microprocessors. It discusses in detail the design, technology, architectural highlights, software, and overall performance of microprocessors that have been developed by four vendors—Bell Labs, Hewlett-Packard, Intel, and National. These chips offer a large instruction repertoire, an enormously large address space, and a marked trend to perform in hardware several operating system functions that have traditionally been done in software. The instructions on these chips are quite complex; thus, one higher level language statement frequently translates into one machine language statement instead of several simpler instructions on previous generation chips. If the potential of these instructions is not utilized efficiently, inherent overhead can cause the 32-bit microprocessor to result in overall throughput equivalent to, or even less than, 16-bit microprocessors [1]. The performance issue is examined in detail in Part IV of this book.

Valuable insight into the design objectives of different 32-bit microprocessor development teams is provided by the papers which follow.

1) *"An Architecture for the 80's—The Intel iAPX-432,"* by Howard I. Jacob

An introduction to the Intel iAPX-432, its architecture, its hardware and software, its multichip organization, its multiprocessing capabilities, its operating system implementation, and its emphasis on increasing programming productivity. Operating system *mechanisms*, such as "send message to a communications port," are distinguished from operating system *policies,* such as the scheduling algorithm. By implementing "mechanisms" in hardware, but allowing the "policies" to be specified in software, it is claimed that the operating system functional performance is significantly enhanced, while retaining sufficient flexibility for the systems programmer to tune the characteristics of the operating system.

2) *"The Execution Unit for the VLSI 432 General Data Processor,"* by David L. Budde *et al.*

The Intel iAPX-432 consists of three chips: the iAPX 43201 Instruction Decode Unit with 110 000 devices, the iAPX 43202 Execution Unit [2] with 49 000 devices, and the iAPX 43203 Interface Processor with 60 000 devices. This article describes the 43202 in detail. A functional overview is provided, and important design tradeoffs are described, including motivations for the particular partitioning of the functions on multiple chips. The circuit implementation details are discussed.

3) *"The Interface Processor for the Intel VLSI 432 32-Bit Computer,"* by John A. Bayliss *et al.*

The Intel 43203 interface processor (IP) chip is comprised of two functional units—the data acquisition unit (DAU) and the microexecution unit (MEU). The DAU is responsible for address mapping, data transfer, and access control; it provides up to five windows which access different objects in the 432 main memory. The MEU is a microprogrammed machine that executes 432 operations and handles interrupts. This paper describes the functions in detail, the design aspects, and the functional implementation.

4) *"A 32-Bit Microprocessor with Virtual Memory Support,"* by Asher Kaminker *et al.*

Unlike the strategy of distribution of a larger number of functions over three chips in the Intel case, National has implemented the processor on a single 290 mil^2 chip containing 60 000 transistors. The basic chip supports 82 instructions. If greater functionality is required, National offers a slave processor chip which implements 32- and 64-bit floating-point arithmetic. Another slave processor (Memory Management Unit) implements a demand-paged virtual memory system. In this paper, the software architecture is described, and the problems involved in supporting virtual memory discussed. The organization of the CPU is outlined, along with a system connection diagram.

5) *"The Operating System and Language Support Features of the BELLMAC-32 Microprocessor,"* by Alan D. Berenbaum *et al.*

Unlike the NS16032 which supports only a 16-bit external bus, the BELLMAC-32A microprocessor has a 32-bit bidirectional bus with status decoding, bus arbitration for external access, DMA control, interrupt handling, and test/debug access, all implemented on the same chip. It uses a higher performance, improved CMOS circuitry [3], and its implementation is outlined in [4]. This paper concentrates on the operating system and language support features of the BELLMAC-32A microprocessor.

6) *"A 32-Bit VLSI CPU Chip,"* by Joseph W. Beyers *et al.*

The Hewlett-Packard 32-bit VLSI CPU chip contains a very high number of transistors, 450 000 in all. A 32-bit binary integer add takes 55 ns, a 32-bit binary integer multiply 1.8 μs, and a 64-bit floating point multiply 10.4 μs. The complexity of the chip made careful design and testing essential to the success of the development. The chip is described in depth. Reference [5] provides details of the fabrication process.

7) *"Gate Array Embodies System/370 Processor,"* by C. Davis *et al.*

Reflecting the current trend of transplanting popular mainframe instruction sets and architectures as single-chip or multichip microprocessors, this paper describes the implementation of an IBM System/370 instruction set on a single chip. With the assistance of computer-aided design of gate arrays, the entire effort took only nine months. After reading this article, one eagerly awaits the day when such a System/370-on-a-chip will be released in the market.

Several new 32-bit microprocessors have been announced in the recent past. NCR Corporation offers a four-chip set [3] comprised of a CPU chip (32-000), an extended arithmetic chip (32-020), an address translator chip (32-010), and a system interface chip (32-100). The n-channel MOS CPU chip includes four internal 32-bit and two 16-bit data paths, and a 32-bit arithmetic and logic unit. A noteworthy feature is the external microprogramming capability achieved using a 128 kbyte store, accessible from the CPU through a 16-bit bus; this enables machine-language emulation of virtually any 32-bit minicomputer or mainframe. According to NCR [6], the Texas Instruments 9900 16-bit microprocessor operating system and instruction set can be emulated using 12 kbytes, whereas an optimized Cobol virtual-language machine would require 25 kbytes. Overall, the chip set is expected to offer performance four times that of the Motorola 68000.

As the microprocessor revolution continues, newer and superior 32-bit chips will become available. But if we recall that 4-bit, 8-bit, 16-bit, and 32-bit eras commenced one year, two years, and seven years after the start of the respective previous eras, the 32-bit era will probably last until the end of the 1980's.

References

[1] D. A. Patterson, "A performance evaluation of the Intel 80286," *Comput. Architecture News*, vol. 10, pp. 16–18, Sept. 1982.

[2] J. A. Bayliss *et al.*, "The instruction decoding unit for the VLSI 432 general data processor," *IEEE J. Solid-State Circuits*, vol. SC-16, pp. 531–537, Oct. 1981.

[3] R. H. Krambeck, C. M. Lee, and H.-F. S. Law, "High-speed compact circuit with CMOS," *IEEE J. Solid-State Circuits*, vol. SC-17, pp. 614–618, June 1982.

[4] H.-F. S. Law, "Layout technology for high performance VLSI," in *Proc. Compcon Fall*, Sept. 20–23, 1982, pp. 40–43.

[5] J. M. Mikkelson *et al.*, "An NMOS VLSI process for fabrication of a 32-bit chip," *IEEE J. Solid-State Circuits*, vol. SC-16, pp. 542–547, Oct. 1981.

[6] W. R. Iversen, "32-bit chip set will offer huge microprogram store," *Electronics*, pp. 47–48, Sept. 8, 1982.

Bibliography

[1] J. A. Bayliss *et al.*, "The interface processor for the 32 bit computer," in *Dig. Tech. Papers, 1981 IEEE Int. Solid-State Circuits Conf.*, pp. 116–117, 263.

[2] J. W. Beyers *et al.*, "A 32 bit VLSI CPU chip," in *Dig. Tech. Papers, 1981 IEEE Int. Solid-State Circuits Conf.*, pp. 104–105.

[3] D. L. Budde *et al.*, "The 32 bit computer execution unit," in *Dig. Tech. Papers, 1981 IEEE Int. Solid-State Circuits Conf.*, pp. 112–113, 261.

[4] J. Hennessey *et al.*, "The MIPS machine," in *Proc. Compcon Spring 1982*, pp. 2–7.

[5] W. W. Lattin *et al.*, "A 32 bit VLSI micromainframe computer system," in *Dig. Tech. Papers, 1981 IEEE Int. Solid-State Circuits Conf.*, pp. 110–111.

[6] W. S. Richardson *et al.*, "The 32 bit computer instruction decoding unit," in *Dig. Tech. Papers, 1981 IEEE Int. Solid-State Circuits Conf.*, pp. 114–115, 262.

[7] F. A. Ware *et al.*, "64-bit monolithic floating point processors," *IEEE J. Solid-State Circuits*, vol. SC-17, pp. 898–907, Oct. 1982.

[8] S. Zeigler *et al.*, "Ada for the Intel 432 microcomputer," *Computer*, pp. 47–56, June 1981.

The supermicros have arrived. Their 32-bit structure—and their performance—quite justifiably earn them the name "micromainframes."

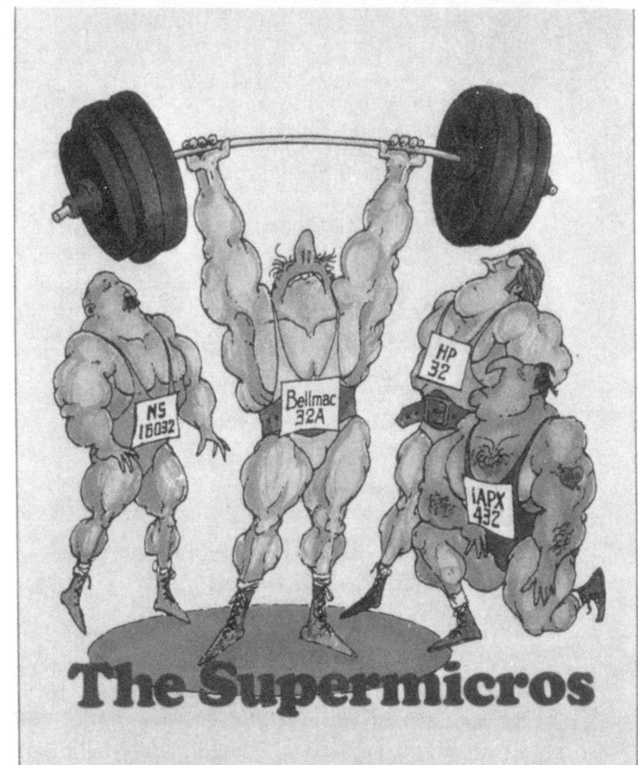

An Architectural Comparison of 32-bit Microprocessors

Amar Gupta and Hoo-min D. Toong
Massachusetts Institute of Technology

The pace of the current microelectronic revolution is unparalleled; it even outstrips the pace of development of the mainframe computer itself. In just a little over a decade, microprocessors have evolved from the Intel 4004, a four-bit machine, to 32-bit chips. In the case of mainframe computers, the "maturity" of a 32-bit word length came with the IBM 360 series, *two* decades after the first computers. The pace of microprocessor development is made even more impressive by the newest generation of microprocessors, which offers sophistications such as object-oriented architecture and easy network interfacing. Such features are considered innovative even in mainframe computers.

The semiconductor industry continues to invest heavily in the development of more complex and more powerful microprocessors. The characteristics and performance of single-chip 16-bit microprocessors have been summarized in earlier articles we have written.[1,2] Announcements of 32-bit chips have been made by several manufacturers in the US and abroad. Chips like the NS 16032 offer 32-bit internal data paths but only 16-bit external paths. One microprocessor, the Intel iAPX 432, uses three chips instead of one to implement a very sophisticated architecture. Other chips, designed by companies like IBM, Hewlett-Packard, Bell Labs, and Rockwell, are intended for internal use but are harbingers of similar public-domain products. A major contender from Japan is the 20,000-gate CMOS microprocessor fabricated by Nippon Telegraph and Telephone.

The MC68000, with 32-bit internal and 16-bit external data paths, was considered by us in an earlier article in *IEEE Micro*.[1] Its performance relative to other 32-bit microprocessors is considered later in this article. The MC68020, with 32-bit external data paths, and other unreleased 32-bit microprocessors of major commercial impact are not included here due to the preliminary nature of their specifications. A useful insight into the current direction of microprocessor innovation can be

Reprinted from *IEEE Micro*, vol. 3,pp. 9–22, Feb. 1983.

achieved by studying and comparing the following better-documented 32-bit products:

- the NS 16032 chip designed by National,[3,4]
- the Bellmac-32A chip designed by Bell Labs,[5,6]
- the "no name" 32-bit CPU chip designed by Hewlett-Packard,[7,8] and
- the iAPX 432 chip set designed by Intel.[9-14]

In the following sections, we examine and compare the architectures of these four processors.

General characteristics

The general characteristics of the four microprocessors are summarized in Table 1.

The NS 16032. This microprocessor represents the high end of the NS 16000 family. Internally, it uses 32-bit data paths and 32-bit address arithmetic to access memory without the overhead of segmentation registers. Externally, it uses a multiplexed address and data bus with 24 bits of external address and 16 bits of external data; this multiplexing has enabled the device to be packaged in a 48-pin package, at the cost of reduced external data rates.

The NS 16032 chip implements 82 basic instructions and has an address range of 16M bytes with 24-bit address pointers; this address range can be enhanced to 32M bytes with a memory management unit. The chip has a three-stage pipeline. Implementation of an eight-byte instruction fetch-ahead queue provides an overlapped instruction fetch and execute facility. Other highlights include modular software capabilities, a fully orthogonal instruction set, a virtual memory facility, and string processing capabilities. These features can be expanded through the use of auxiliary chips. The NS 16081, for example, provides 32-bit and 64-bit floating-point capabilities, while the NS 16082 memory management unit supports demand-paged virtual memory. Together, these three chips implement a software architecture comparable in sophistication to a VAX-11/780, with about half that machine's performance and a much lower price.[4] Communication between the NS 16032 CPU and an NS 16202 interrupt control unit may involve transfer of information on the local bus as well as on the system bus, and incur the overheads and delays inherent in such transfers.

The Bellmac-32A. Besides being a true 32-bit microprocessor, the Bellmac-32A is much more sophisticated technologically than the NS 16032. In general, CMOS circuits provide faster speed and lower power consumption than circuits implemented with traditional PMOS and NMOS technology. The Bellmac-32A single-chip CPU is fabricated in twin-tub CMOS and uses "domino circuits" that operate at twice the speed of previous CMOS circuits and enable a single clock pulse to activate many circuits simultaneously. The chip uses two non-overlapping clocks, each of 10 MHz and both generated from a 40-MHz external clock.[24]

The Bellmac-32A chip has been designed to provide support for the C programming language. Single instructions can move blocks of data from memory to memory, or push and pop a group of registers with respect to the stack. Sophisticated hardware facilities include a barrel-shift circuit that shifts 0 to 31 bits in a single cycle. The operating system, which can be included in the address space of every process, includes a hardware interface to assist process-oriented operating system control software. It also includes a set of exception handling mechanisms. The exception structure provides four levels of execution privilege and is intended for real-time control applications. Neither floating-point nor decimal arithmetic is supported, although an auxiliary processor to perform such operations is being investigated.[6] At present, "extension" instructions are provided for these functions. There is little compatibility with any existing microprocessor.

Table 1.
General characteristics of the four 32-bit microprocessors.

	NS 16032[15]	BELLMAC-32A[16,24]	HP 32-BIT CPU[17]	INTEL iAPX 432[18]
YEAR OF COMMERCIAL INTRODUCTION	1982	1982*	1982*	1981
TECHNOLOGY	3.5-μm NMOS	2.5-μm DOMINO CMOS	1.5/1.0-μm NMOS	HMOS
NO. OF TRANSISTORS	60,000	146,000	450,000	219,000 ON 3 CHIPS
SIZE OF CHIP	84,000 MIL^2	160,000 MIL^2	48,400 MIL^2	100,000 MIL^2 EACH
POWER DISSIPATION	1.25 WATTS	0.7 WATT AT 8 MHz	4 WATTS	2.5 WATTS/CHIP
PIN COUNT	48	63 ACTIVE 84 TOTAL	83	64 PER CHIP
BASIC CLOCK FREQUENCY	10 MHz	10 MHz	18 MHz	8 MHz
DIRECT ADDRESS RANGE (BYTES)	2^{24}; 2^{25} WITH MMU	2^{32}	2^{29} REAL; 2^{41} VIRTUAL	2^{24} REAL; 2^{40} VIRTUAL
NO. OF GENERAL-PURPOSE REGISTERS	8	16 USER-VISIBLE	28 (NOT ALL GENERAL-PURPOSE)	NO REGISTERS VISIBLE TO USER
NO. OF BASIC INSTRUCTIONS	82	169	230	221
NO. OF ADDRESSING MODES	9	18	10	5

*CURRENTLY FOR INTERNAL USE ONLY.

The Bellmac-32A chip was developed in a relatively short time through the extensive use of computer-aided design techniques. These techniques make the Bellmac-32A "technology updatable." They include a mask generation program that enables old mask sets to be easily updated to new rules, and a facility that provides automatic generation of new simulation files. With these techniques, an existing design can benefit from the advances in fabrication technology that permit thinner line widths. On the chip itself, special internal features provide access to most registers for test and debug purposes. Unlike the Hewlett-Packard chip, which will be discussed in the next section, the Bellmac has no facility for automatic self-test during power-up.

The HP 32-bit chip. This no-name, no-number device has the highest circuit density of any microprocessor—450,000 transistors on a single, 48,400 mil^2 chip. Implemented in double-layer-metal NMOS with a one-micrometer pitch, this microprocessor uses two nonoverlapping clocks, each of 18 MHz frequency and both generated from an external 36-MHz clock. The chip is microcoded with 9K (38-bit) words of ROM control store addressed via a set of 14-bit registers in the sequence stack. The microinstructions are decoded by a PLA. Most of the microinstructions execute in one clock cycle of 55 nanoseconds. Pipelining of memory operations permits initiation of a 32-bit memory read every two states (every 110 nanoseconds), even though the memory access time is longer. Like the other chips considered so far, the HP device has a three-level pipeline—this is implemented through a CIR (current instruction register), an NIR (next instruction register), and a PIR (prefetch instruction register). A self-test routine, executed by the CPU during power-up, automatically tests operations internal to the chip.

The HP chip offers several sophisticated hardware and software features. A hardware-implemented *n*-bit barrel shifter can shift a 32-bit quantity right or left 0 to 31 places in a single clock cycle. The load instruction includes automatic bounds checking and takes only 550 nanoseconds. The arithmetic and logical instructions can manipulate the 32- and 64-bit floating-point operands specified in the proposed IEEE floating-point standard. Text editing capabilities are inherent in the move and string instructions that manipulate byte arrays and string-type data. All communication to and from the chip uses the memory-processor bus. This 32-bit-wide multiplexed address/data bus permits pipelined data transfers at 36M bytes per second. Facilities to communicate with the memory and with peripheral devices are provided by a memory controller chip and an I/O processor chip, respectively.

The iAPX 432. In many respects, the Intel iAPX 432 is very different from the chips described above. The others are single-chip CPUs, but the iAPX 432 is a three-chip set. These three chips are tied together through a processor-memory interconnection bus that is different from the traditional Intel Multibus. In addition, the iAPX 432 was designed to support the Ada programming language. Just as the Burroughs 5000 initiated a trend, two decades ago, toward architectures specifically designed to support high-level languages, so the iAPX 432 may start a trend toward architectures specifically designed to be programmed in a particular high-level language.

The General Data Processor System, or GDP, is a subset of the iAPX 432. It consists of two chips—the iAPX 43201, with 110,000 transistors, which is responsible for instruction decoding; and the iAPX 43202, with 49,000 transistors, which performs actual instruction execution. The iAPX 43203 I/O interface processor, containing 60,000 transistors, performs I/O interface functions and possesses limited capabilities for execution of microcode. There is an additional chip—a multiprocessor memory interface—that provides the signals required for packet bus interconnection. The Intel iAPX 432 is architecturally very different from its predecessors, namely the 8080, 8085, and 8086. This difference, although providing hardware enhancements, newer functions, and higher overall throughput, greatly limits programming compatibility between the iAPX 432 and earlier Intel products.

The total physical address size is limited to 2^{24} bytes. The upper limit on the logical address space is 2^{40} bytes. However, at any instant the logical addressing environment of a program is restricted to 2^{32} bytes. The instructions are of variable length, ranging from six bits to 344 bits. Each instruction's operator can have zero, one, two, or three operands. The GDP chip set has built-in security mechanisms that restrict access to programs and data on a "need-to-know" basis. Other noteworthy features include hardware-implemented concurrent programming and self-dispatching processors with hardware-implemented process scheduling. In addition, the processor can perform specialized functions such as floating-point and string operations without needing to attach specialized auxiliary chips.

Architectural details

Technology. All the chips reflect a conscious attempt toward the integration of an enormously large number of transistors. Even with a significantly smaller chip size, Hewlett-Packard has packaged the largest number—450,000—on a single chip, almost twice what Intel has packaged on its three chips put together. In order to achieve this density, HP used an electron beam to generate masks that provide 1.5-micrometer wide lines and 1.0-micrometer-wide spaces, with ± 0.25-micrometer tolerances. The large number of devices and the narrowness of the lines contribute to the chip's relatively high power dissipation of four watts. To package the device, Hewlett-Packard uses a copper core, on which the CPU and auxiliary chips are directly mounted, and four layers of interconnect, which are separated by low-capacitance Teflon dielectrics. The HP chip, the NS 16032, and the iAPX 432 are all implemented in NMOS, although Intel prefers to call it N-channel, silicon-gate HMOS.

The NS 16032 and iAPX 432 have larger structures, and hence lower transistor densities, than the HP chip. National and Intel took this approach because their chips are intended to be openly sold in the world market. Needing large numbers of chips, the companies chose a structure size that would give them high yields.

Because of its CMOS implementation, the Bellmac-32A consumes the least power of the four microprocessors. The twin-tub CMOS process (Figure 1) provides high switching speeds in both N- and P-channel devices because each tub is separately implanted for optimum doping. Classical CMOS logic designs have an equal number of N- and P-channel devices. Newer CMOS designs use 80 percent N-channel devices and only 20 percent P-channel devices. This ratio of N-channel to P-channel devices makes it possible to have high circuit densities while retaining the CMOS advantages of fast speed and low power consumption.

Principles of operation. The basic structure of the NS 16032 is shown in Figure 2. The instructions are fetched via the 24-bit-wide multiplexed address/data bus. An instruction fetch-ahead queue provides overlap of instruction fetch and execution and aligns incoming instructions to 16-bit boundaries. The queue consists of a double-ended eight-byte FIFO with 16-bit input and output

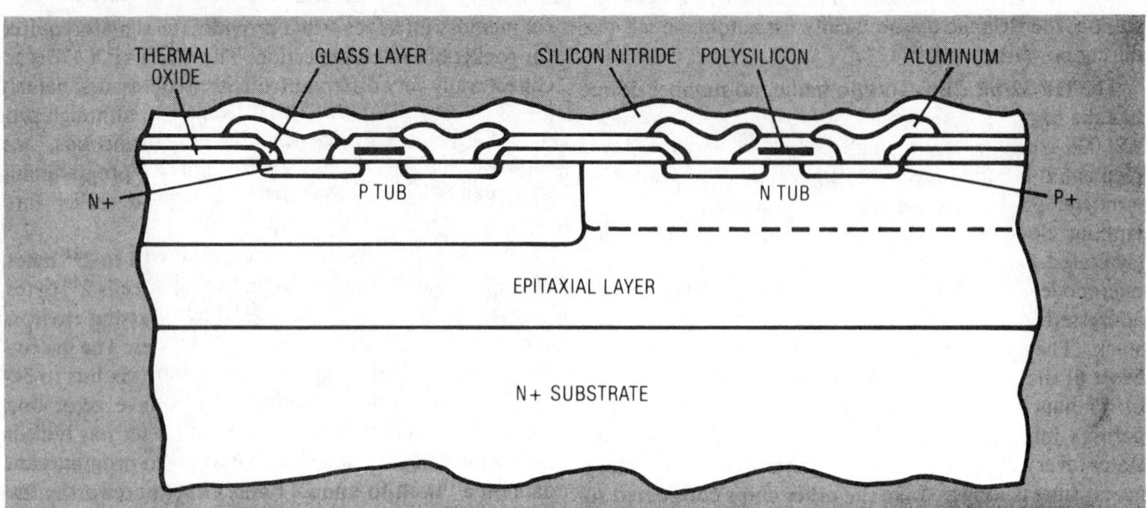

Figure 1. The Bellmac-32A is implemented in twin-tub domino CMOS. This process gives the microprocessor high switching speed in both N- and P-channel devices, because each tub is separately implanted for optimum doping. The process easily scales down for denser designs. The N+ substrate layer prevents the thyristor-like latch-up usually found in CMOS circuits. (Figure adapted from A. F. Shackil, "Microprocessors," *IEEE Spectrum*, Jan. 1982, page 33.)

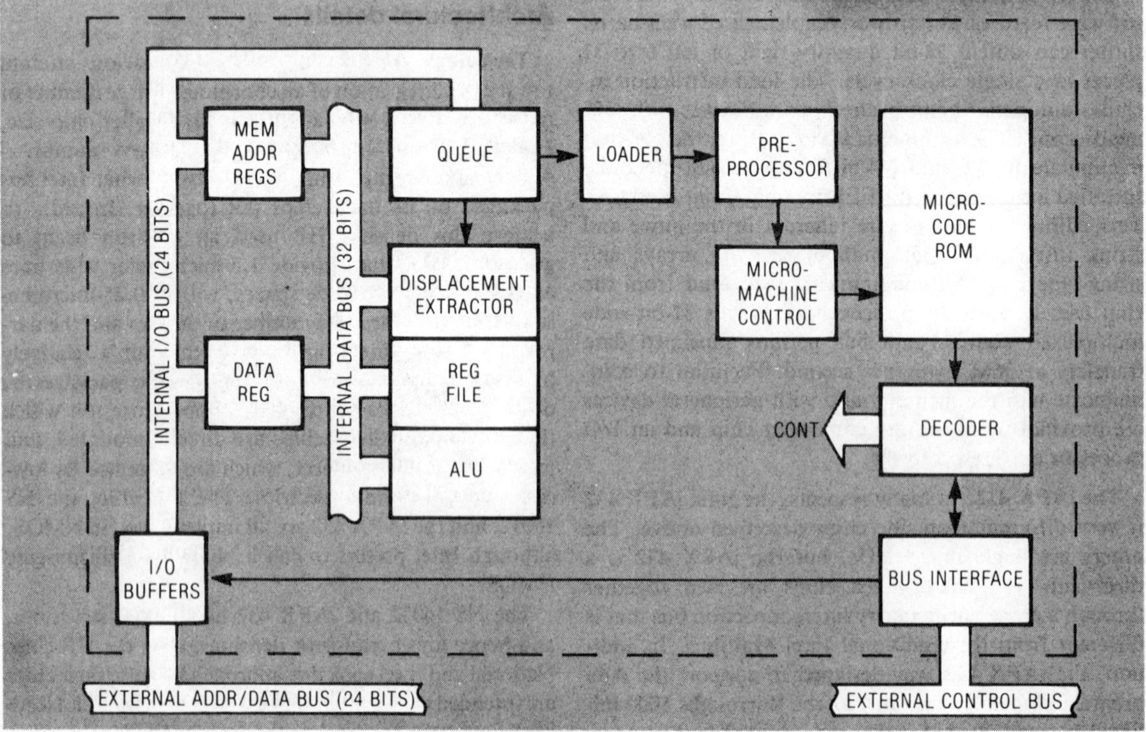

Figure 2. NS 16032 block diagram.

buses. The loader extracts the instruction from the queue and decodes it into a basic opcode, an operand length, address modes, and ALU control fields. The loader can decode two bytes every 100 nanoseconds. So that complex instructions can be efficiently executed without consuming excessive microcode ROM space, a two-level microcode (similar to that used in the Motorola 68000[1]) enables sharing of common effective address-calculation routines by all instructions and avoids both time-consuming subroutine calls and space-consuming repeated microcode flows. A preprocessor controls the sequence of instruction execution, while the micromachine controls the individual execution steps. As microinstruction n is executed, microinstruction $n+1$ is decoded, and microinstruction $n+2$ is selected by the microcode ROM address decoder. This procedure results in an effective 100-nanosecond microinstruction execution rate. A hardware backup mechanism saves contents of the processor status register, the stack pointer, and the program counter, and automatically restores them to their original values in the case of an instruction retry.

The structure of the Bellmac-32A is shown in Figure 3. Like the NS 16032, it consists of two distinct functional units—a fetch unit which controls interactions with the external memory and an execution unit which controls the manipulation and processing of data. Both units, as well as the bus, have full 32-bit capability. The instruction stream is byte-oriented. The first byte specifies the addressing mode and the register, and the subsequent bytes specify additional data. All byte and half-word operands are sign- or zero-extended to 32-bits when they are fetched. Instructions are monadic if there is one operator, dyadic if there are two operators, or triadic if there are three operators. Instructions fetched from the memory are stored in the instruction queue and translated into a series of microinstructions via a PLA. An arithmetic address unit performs all address calculations. An ALU in the execute block performs the actual execution of microinstructions. The emphasis on support of process-oriented operating systems generates a need to store instructions, data, and register values associated with a process whenever there is a switch from one process to another. The Bellmac-32A provides these storage functions in hardware.

The HP 32-bit chip, shown in Figure 4, is similar in operation to the previous two chips. It too uses a three-stage overlapping sequence for instruction prefetch and execution; it too uses a microcoded structure. The microcode control-store ROM is organized as 9216 words, each of 38 bits. Microinstructions accessed from the ROM are decoded by a PLA; they drive control lines which determine the operations of the 32-bit register stack and the ALU. The flow of instructions to the PLA is controlled by a sequencing machine, which contains a microprogram counter, a set of incrementers, three registers for microcode subroutine return addresses, and a machine instruction opcode decoder. The opcode decoder generates the starting address in the control store for the microcode routine that implements each machine instruction. The test condition multiplexer facilitates conditional jumps and skips in the microcode. The ALU contains an n-bit shifter, a 32-bit logical selector, and a 32-bit full look-ahead adder which also performs integer multiplication and division via special hardware.

The operation of the iAPX 432 involves communication among the iAPX 43201 instruction fetch and decode unit, the iAPX 43202 instruction execution unit, and the iAPX 43203 I/O interface unit. This communication is

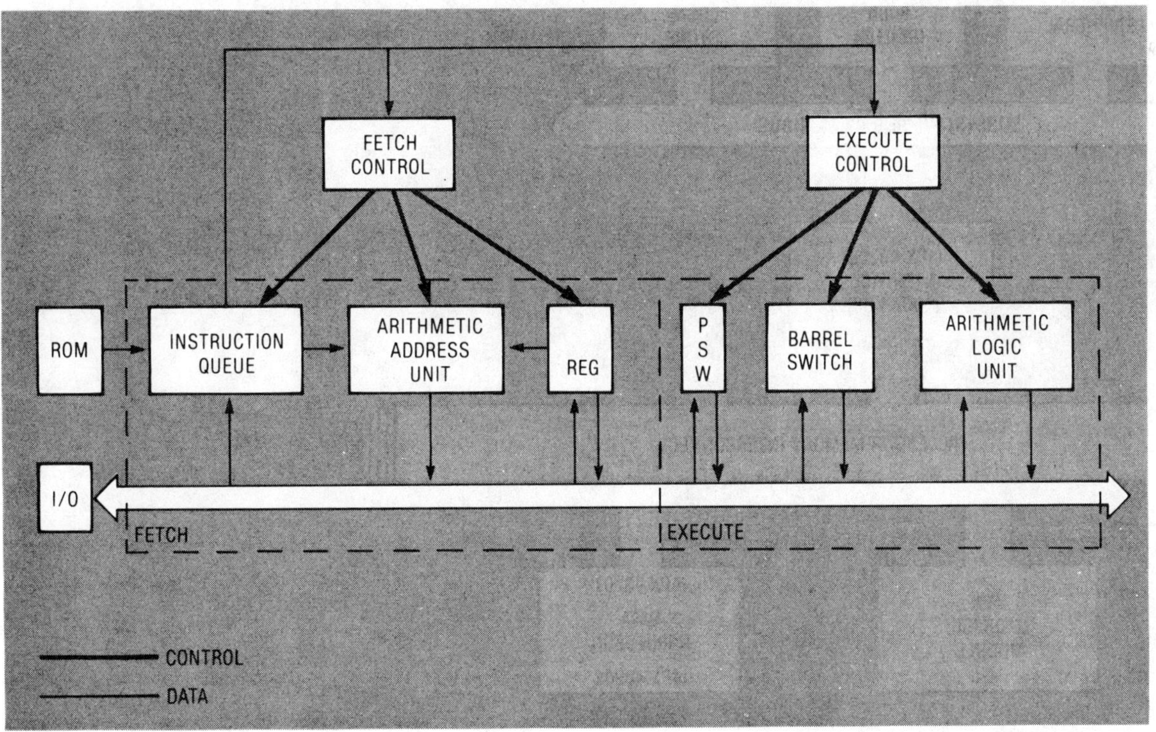

Figure 3. Bellmac-32A CPU architecture.

Figure 4. The HP 32-bit microprocessor.

handled over the processor-memory interconnect bus, as shown in Figure 5. The characteristics of the three iAPX 432 chips are summarized in Table 2. Data can be manipulated in the form of eight-bit characters, 16/32-bit ordinals, 16/32-bit integers, 32/64/80-bit floating-point variables, bit strings, arrays, records, or "objects," which are data structures containing information organized in some manner. Such objects can be referenced as a single entity; their internal organization is hidden and protected from all other procedures by hardware mechanisms. Each object has defined for it a set of operations (procedures or instructions) that are permitted to directly manipulate it. Examples of hardware-defined objects are

- processor objects, which represent the physical processors;
- process objects, which represent the individual computing tasks;
- context objects, which represent the activation of a program unit;
- dispatching-port objects, which provide a stream of work for a set of processors; and
- communications-port objects, which support interprocess communication and synchronization.

The iAPX 432 instruction set supports objects through messages (SEND, WAIT), context (CALL, RETURN), storage pools (ALLOCATE, TYPE), and processes (SCHEDULE, DISPATCH). At the macro level, the notion of objects permits each user to visualize a "virtual machine" that is exclusively his own. The concept of objects also makes multiprogramming and multiprocessing easier.

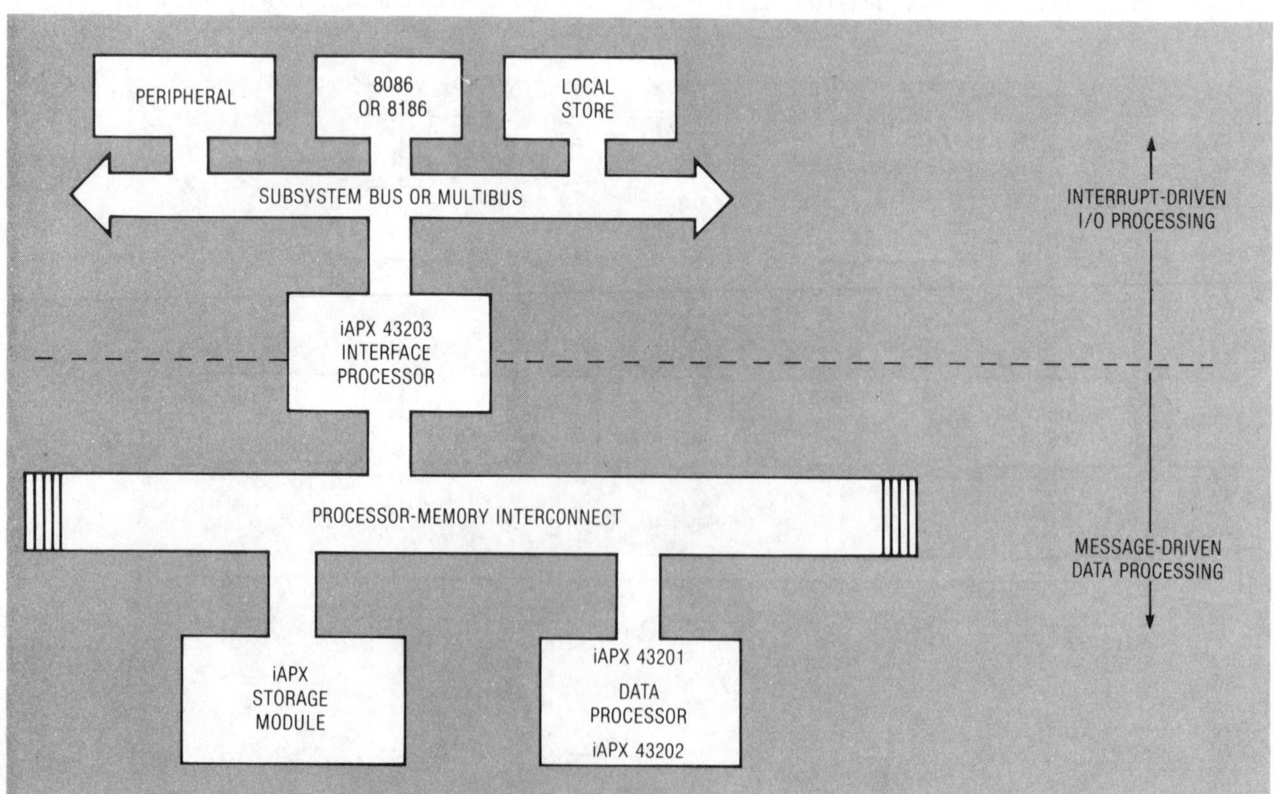

Figure 5. The Intel iAPX 432 three-chip 32-bit microprocessor.

Register organization. The NS 16032 contains sixteen registers—eight general-purpose ones (all 32 bits wide) and eight dedicated ones. The dedicated registers are as follows:

- The program counter register (24 bits) points to the current instruction being executed.
- The frame pointer register (24 bits) is used to access parameters and local variables on the stack.
- The static base register (24 bits) is used by software modules as a pointer to their respective global variables.
- The interrupt register (24 bits) points to the dispatch table for interrupts and traps.
- The two stack pointer registers (2 pointers each, 24 bits wide) point to the top of the stack used for interrupt routines and to the top of the stack used for other programs, respectively.
- The processor status register contains status codes.
- The module register points to the module description of the currently executing software module. The module register and the processor status register together use 32 bits.

To reduce register allocation problems, the instruction set has been designed to be symmetric with respect to memory and general register references.

The Bellmac-32A microprocessor contains a special program counter register and fifteen other registers, each 32 bits wide, that can be referenced in any addressing mode. Of these fifteen registers, three are used to support operating system functions (interrupt stack pointer, process control block pointer, processor status word) and can be written when the processor is in kernel execution level. Another three registers are used by certain instructions as a stack pointer, a frame pointer, and an argument pointer.

At the heart of the HP chip is a register stack, with 28 identical general-purpose registers, and an ALU, with four operand/result registers. Each of the general-purpose registers is 32 bits wide; not all are accessible by software. The register stack uses two databases and contains auxiliary logic such as top-of-stack and instruction registers. In any register, each of the 32 bit-cells can receive data from, or dump data to, either of the two data buses, as determined by the PLA outputs.

On account of the iAPX 432's multichip organization, its register structure cannot be equitably compared with that of the other chips. A microinstruction execution unit performs several functions traditionally associated with registers. Its functional subunit, the reference generation unit, or RGU, contains a 43-bit by 20-entry register array to support logical-to-physical address translation and access right verification. The other functional unit, the data manipulation unit, or DMU, contains its own set of operand registers, implemented as double-ended queues, to optimize arithmetic calculations on variable-length operands over a fixed-length (16-bit) bus. Intel claims that compiler complexity is reduced by keeping registers "behind the scenes" rather than as visible features of the architecture.[19]

Instruction set. Thirty-two-bit processors offer powerful instruction sets and support a wide spectrum of distinct data structures. These capabilities are summarized in Table 3.

The original specifications of the NS 16032 were too ambitious to be accommodated on a single chip with current technology. Several functions were offloaded from the main chip to auxiliary chips or slave processors. The total number of instructions was reduced from 100 to 82.

Floating-point instructions are trapped by the main processor and executed by the NS 16081 floating-point unit. The NS 16032 processor accepts data in bits, bytes,

Table 2.
Characteristics of the components of the iAPX 432.

CHARACTERISTIC	iAPX 43201		iAPX 43202		iAPX 43203	
DIE SIZE (IN μm)	318×323		366×313		358×326	
TOTAL DEVICE PLACEMENTS	110,000		49,000		60,000	
FUNCTION OF UNIT	INSTRUCTION FETCH AND DECODE		INSTRUCTION EXECUTION		I/O INTERFACE	
FUNCTIONAL SUB-UNITS	INSTRUCTION DECODER	MICROINSTRUCTION SEQUENCER (MIS)	DATA MANIPULATION UNIT (DMU)	REFERENCE GENERATION UNIT (RGU)	DATA ACQUISITION UNIT (DAU)	MICRO-EXECUTION UNIT (MEU)
FUNCTION OF SUBUNIT	DECODES VARIABLE-LENGTH, BIT-ALIGNED INSTRUCTIONS	SEQUENCES VERTICALLY ENCODED MICRO-INSTRUCTIONS AND INPUTS THEM TO THE MEU	CONTAINS OPERAND AND UNITS TO IMPLEMENT THE MACRO-INSTRUCTION SET EFFICIENTLY	CONTAINS REGISTERS AND FUNCTIONAL UNITS FOR LOGICAL-TO-PHYSICAL ADDRESS TRANSLATION AND ACCESS RIGHT VERIFICATION	PERFORMS PREFETCH AND POST-WRITE BUFFERING OF DATA AND GENERATES MAIN SYSTEM MEMORY ACCESSES	PERFORMS SYSTEM ACCESS, ENVIRONMENT MANIPULATION, INTER-PROCESSOR COMMUNICATION, AND ADDRESS MAP SET-UP

half-words, and words. Its ability to operate on variable-length character strings suits it to text processing applications. The NS 16032 offers instructions to operate on packed decimal quantities, on arrays, and on blocks. Instructions are of variable length. Common zero-operand instructions, such as the branch instruction, have a one-byte opcode. One-operand and two-operand instructions use a two-byte basic instruction. All instructions can use all applicable addressing modes. For code compactness, instructions are aligned on byte boundaries rather than on half-word or word boundaries.

The Bellmac-32A offers 169 instructions, 24 more than twice the number of the NS 16032. It too supports bytes, half-words, words, and bit fields. Strings are supported by special block instructions, and the string format conforms to the C language. C compatibility is manifest in the implementation of the instruction repertoire. The result of the unary operations NEGATE and COMPLEMENT (implemented as move instructions) can either replace the existing datum or be placed in a new location. The dyadic form stores the result in the second operand, and the triadic form places the result in the third operand, with the first two unaltered: these dyadic and triadic instructions are available for all operators. High-level procedure linkage operations assist in manipulating the stack frame, saving registers, and transferring control between procedures. Also, explicit instructions that permit the operating system to switch processes (CALL PROCESS and RETURN TO PROCESS) are provided. On the negative side, the Bellmac-32A does not support floating-point or decimal arithmetic.

Table 3.
Capabilities of the four microprocessors, not including functions provided by coprocessors or auxiliary chips.

	NS 16032	BELLMAC-32A	HP 32	iAPX 432
SYSTEM STRUCTURES				
UNIFORM ADDRESSABILITY	✓	✓	✓	✓
MODULE MAP AND MODULES	✓	X	X	✓
VIRTUAL	✓	✓	✓	✓
PRIMITIVE DATA TYPES				
BITS	✓	✓	✓	✓
INTEGER BYTE OR HALF-WORD	✓	✓	✓	✓
INTEGER WORD	✓	✓	✓	✓
LOGICAL BYTE OR HALF-WORD	✓	✓	✓	✓
LOGICAL WORD	✓	✓	✓	✓
CHARACTER STRINGS (VARIABLE)	✓	✓	✓	✓
BCD BYTE OR HALF-WORD	✓	X	X	X
BCD WORD	✓	X	✓	X
32-BIT FLOATING-POINT	X	X	✓	✓
64-BIT FLOATING-POINT	X	X	✓	✓
80-BIT FLOATING-POINT	X	X	X	✓
DATA STRUCTURES				
STACKS	✓	✓	✓	✓
ARRAYS	✓	✓	✓	✓
PACKED ARRAYS	✓	X	X	X
RECORDS	✓	X	X	✓
PACKED RECORDS	✓	X	X	X
STRINGS	✓	✓	✓	✓
PRIMITIVE CONTROL OPERATIONS				
CONDITION CODE PRIMITIVES	✓	✓	✓	✓
JUMP	✓	✓	✓	✓
CONDITIONAL BRANCH	✓	✓	✓	✓
ITERATIVE LOOP CONTROL	✓	X	✓	✓
SUBROUTINE CALL	✓	✓	✓	✓
MULTIWAY BRANCH	✓	✓	✓	✓
ORTHOGONAL INSTRUCTION SET		✓	✓	✓
CONTROL STRUCTURE				
EXTERNAL PROCEDURE CALL	✓	✓	✓	✓
SEMAPHORES	✓	✓	✓	✓
TRAPS	✓	✓	✓	✓
INTERRUPTS	✓	✓	✓	✓
SUPERVISOR CALL	✓	✓	✓	✓
OBJECTS	X	X	X	✓
HIERARCHICAL OPERATING SYSTEM	X	✓	X	✓
OTHER				
USER MICROCODE	X	X	X	X
DEBUG MODE	X	✓	✓	X
COMPATIBILITY WITH OTHER MICROPROCESSORS	X	X	X	X
SELF-TEST DURING POWER-UP	X	X	✓	X

✓ = FEATURE AVAILABLE
X = FEATURE NOT AVAILABLE

The HP 32-bit chip offers a still larger repertoire of 230 instructions as well as 32- and 64-bit floating-point arithmetic. The load and store instructions can transfer double-words in addition to bits, bytes, half-words, and words. MOVE and STRING manipulate both unstructured byte arrays and structured string data. Hardware support includes four top-of-stack registers to handle push and pop operations and to provide "data valid" indications. The large number of transistors enables hardware implementation of features that have traditionally been done by software. For example, run-time bounds checking of addresses, performed on all memory accesses, is supported in hardware.

The iAPX 432 supports integer data in hardware; this has traditionally been done by software. Like the HP processor, the iAPX 432 performs run-time bounds checking of addresses. The iAPX 432 supports integer data in the form of half-words and words, and floating-point data in the form of words, double-words, and as 80-bit quantities. The usual 80-bit-wide quantities, called temporary reals, are used to store intermediate results to improve the accuracy of final results. Instructions are bit-variable in length and are not constrained to coincide with byte or word boundaries. The total number of instructions is 230, and the longest is 344 bits long. By allowing both stack and memory-to-memory arithmetic, the iAPX 432 can provide denser code and faster speeds for evaluating expressions. An instruction contains four fields. The first two fields, the class field and the format field, specify how many operands are in the instruction and how they are to be accessed. The third field, the reference field, contains the logical addresses of up to three operands. The last field specifies the operator itself. The processor reads an instruction segment in units of 32 bits. The instructions are decoded by the 43201 decoding chip, and the resulting stream of microinstructions are executed by the 43202 execution chip.

Memory organization. The NS 16032 provides a 16M-byte uniform address space and nine types of address mode (register, memory, immediate, absolute, register relative, memory relative, top-of-stack, external, and scaled index). An autoindexing address mode is not supported, as National feels that compilers seldom produce such code.[15] Moreover, properly supporting both autoindexing and demand-paged virtual memory is difficult.

The lengths of address-mode offset constants are encoded in the upper two bits of the offset so that small offsets (-64 to 63) will require only one byte in the instruction stream and larger offsets will take two or four bytes. The integration of the memory management unit (see Figure 6) provides operating system and virtual memory support and enables addressing of up to 32M bytes. Virtual-address-to-real-address translation is accomplished through two levels of page tables and offset specifications. Each page, 512 bytes in size, is assigned a protection code, and this provides an access control mechanism. The memory management unit has eight registers and provides a flow tracing facility for both sequential and nonsequential instructions.

The Bellmac-32A chip offers several addressing modes: literal, byte/half-word/word immediate, register, register deferred, short offset (for frame and argument pointers), absolute, absolute deferred, byte/half-word/word displacement deferred, and expanded operand. The Bellmac-32A chip includes a set of exception handling mechanisms and a hardware interface for a process-oriented operating system; this operating system can be included in the address space of each process, enabling each to execute independently.

The HP 32-bit processor views the memory space for each program as an active code segment (one of 4096 code segments), a stack segment, a global data segment, and a set of 4096 external data segments. Segment pointers, maintained in 32-bit, on-chip registers, include ones to a base and limit register for the code, to stack and global data segments, to the current instruction address in the code segment, to the address of the most recent stack marker in the stack segment, and to the address of the top-of-stack in memory. External data segments are accessed via a set of memory-resident tables. A memory controller chip can control up to 20 RAM chips, each of 128K bits, or up to eight ROM chips, each of 640K bits, providing an effective memory space of up to 256K bytes of RAM or 512K bytes of ROM (Figure 7). The processor-memory bus has a transfer rate of 36M bytes per second, and the overlapped access method permits high throughput. The memory controller maps logical-to-physical addresses in 16K-byte blocks, and permits byte, half-word, word, and semaphore operations.

The iAPX 432 uses a segmented memory scheme having up to 2^{24} segments; each segment is 2^{16} bytes long, yielding a total virtual space of 2^{40} bytes. A two-step mapping process separates the relocation mechanism from the access control mechanism. Segments are of two types—access and data. The hardware recognizes them differently and rigorously enforces the distinction. The iAPX 432 provides four addressing modes: the base and index direct, used to access scalars; the base indirect, index direct, used to access records; the base direct, index

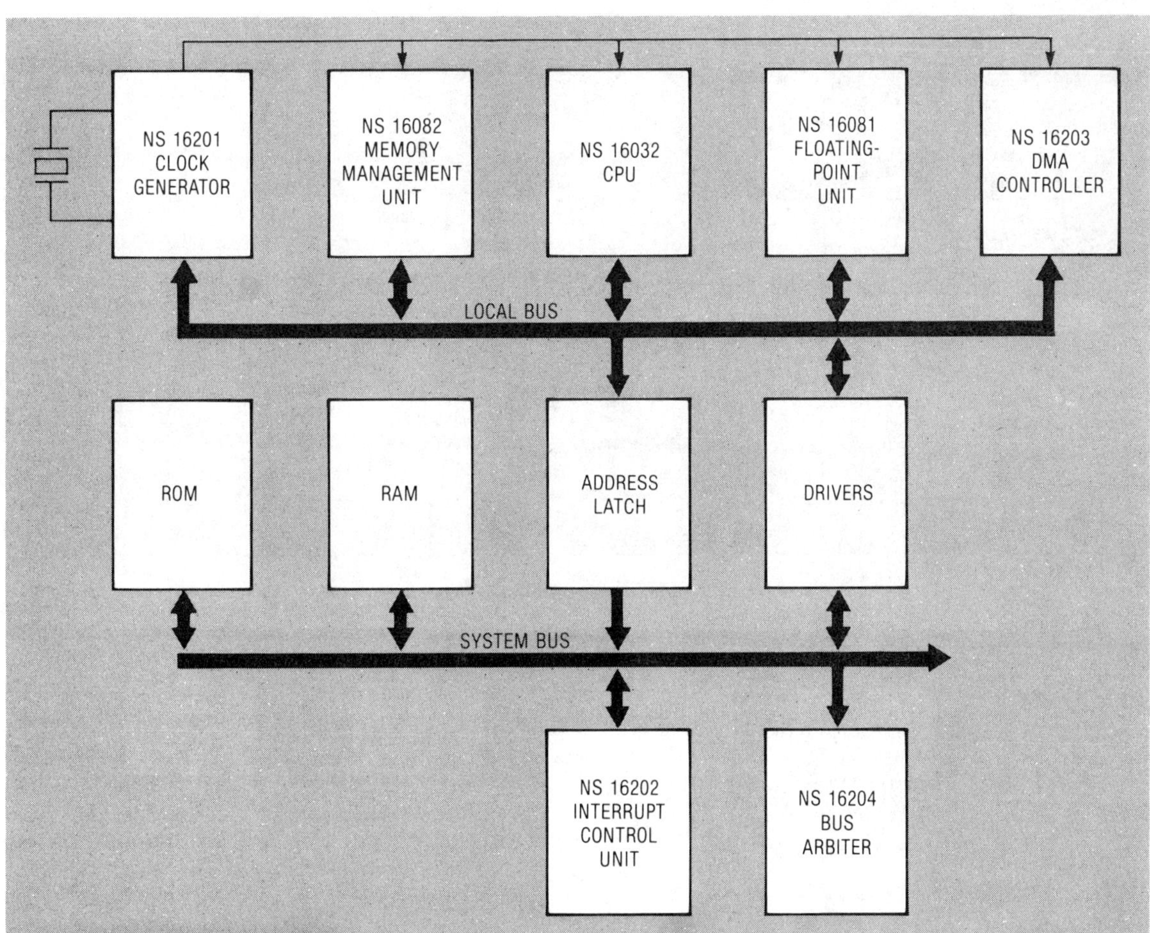

Figure 6. The National Semiconductor NS 16000 system.

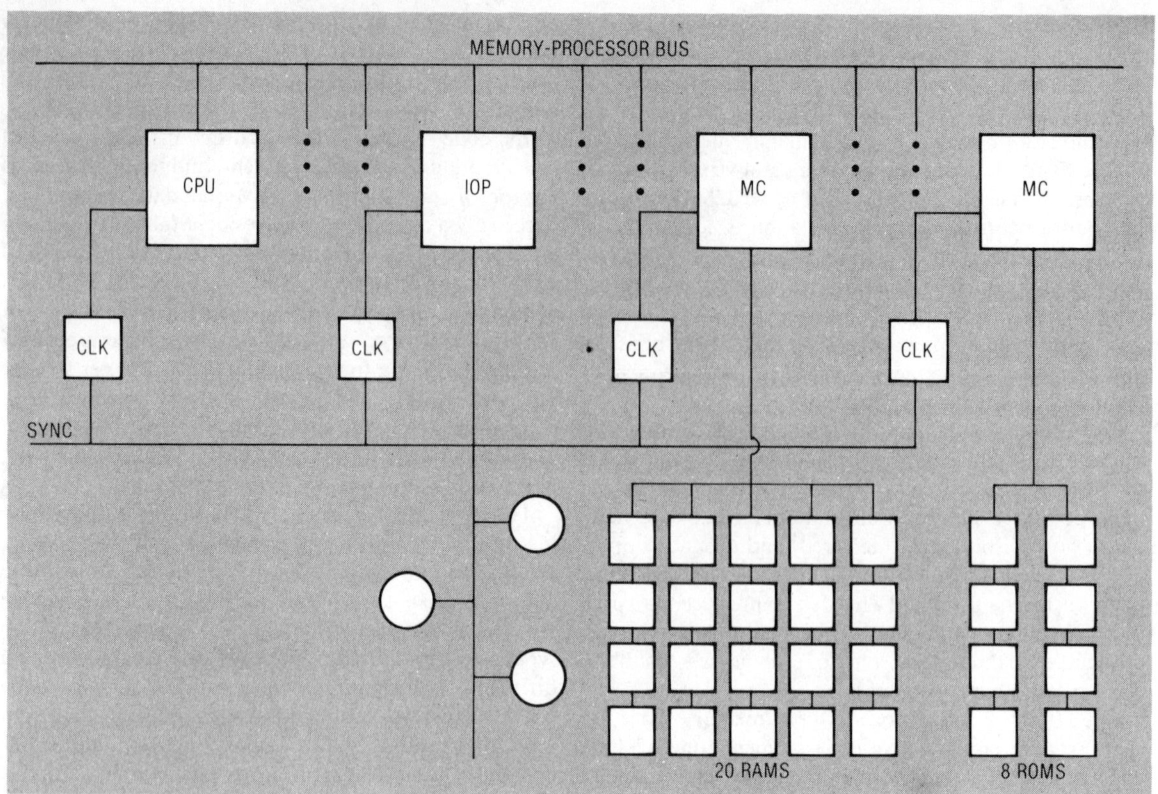

Figure 7. The HP 32-bit microcomputer system.

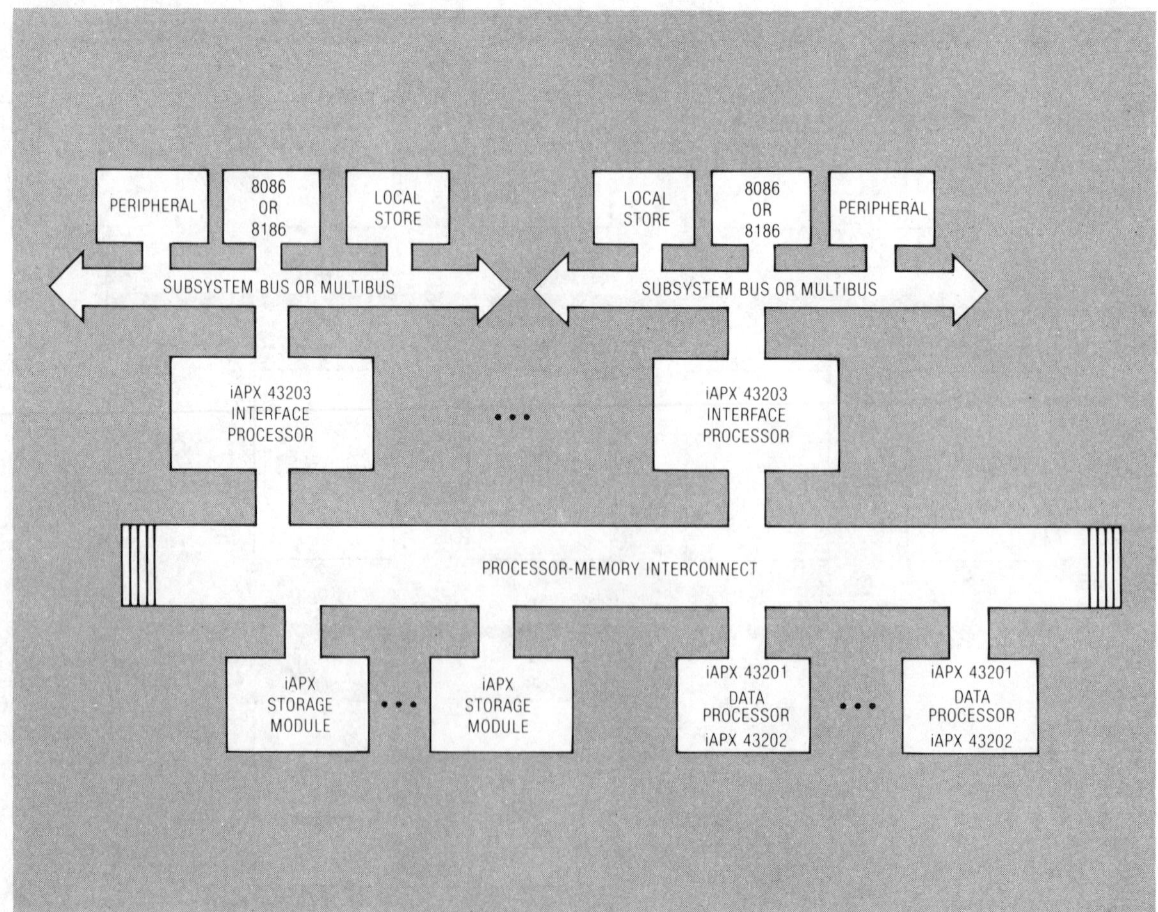

Figure 8. A typical multiple-iAPX-432 system.

indirect, used to access static arrays; and the base and index indirect, used to access dynamic arrays. The emphasis is on addressing objects through the use of access descriptors in the form of directory index and segment index. This object-oriented architecture facilitates implementation of high-level languages like Ada, Pascal, and PL/I.

Multiprocessing capabilities. To increase computational bandwidth and/or system resilience, the integration of several microprocessors frequently becomes necessary. The throughput and efficiency of integrated systems depend directly on the hardware and software interconnection mechanisms supported by the microprocessors. Many interconnection schemes have evolved over the years, but the single timeshared bus offers distinct advantages as an interconnection mechanism for multi-microprocessor systems. Under such a scheme, different modules can equally share the bus resource on a time-multiplexed or demand-multiplexed basis. National and HP indicate that their respective system-buses/processor-memory buses can provide the communications required for multiprocessing; the Bellmac also provides some multiprocessing support. Here, we will concentrate on the Intel product.

A typical iAPX-432-based multiprocessor configuration is shown in Figure 8. Different iAPX 432 processor pairs (each pair comprising the 43201 and the 43202) are connected to a single processor-memory interconnect bus. An existing 8086 processor cannot be connected directly to this bus; it must be connected through the Multibus and an interface processor, the iAPX 43203. Thus, if one 8086-based system is required to read information from a second 8086-based system in a configuration such as that shown in Figure 8, the request will involve the Multibus, an interface processor, the processor-memory interconnect bus, the second interface processor, and finally the second Multibus. The reply will involve the same interface/communication units, in the reverse order. In all, six distinct buses and four distinct interface processors will be used to complete a simple READ between the two 8086 systems. Such slave-to-slave operations are not efficiently supported by the suggested system organization.

Intel refers to the processor-memory interconnect bus as a Packetbus. This bus operates on a split-transaction basis. For example, a processor needing to access some data from memory will send a message to the appropriate storage module. The actual transfer of the message on the bus occurs when the arbitration mechanism grants the bus to the particular CPU. When the request for the data is received by the storage module, it accesses the data, but during this period of data access the bus is freed up for use by others. Finally, when the storage module is ready with the data, it requests the bus, gets it, and sends the "reply" to the CPU. The freeing up of the bus during the period of memory access—which is significantly longer than the bus service time—enables more processors to communicate on the same bus in a given span. In the iAPX 432, variable-length (1 to 10 bytes) data messages are used for request/reply; a 32-bit word can be transferred in 250 nanoseconds.

Hewlett-Packard also uses a demand-multiplexed bus,[17] with a single CPU using 30 percent of the total bus bandwidth for typical instruction mixes. In any multiprocessor environment, the number of bus users increases as the number of processors increases, resulting in greater bus contention. Also, additional overhead is incurred in controlling and coordinating multiple resources. The latter overhead is difficult to estimate, and most studies simply neglect to take it into account. Figure 9 reflects Intel's estimates of the effective number of processors versus the actual number of processors. Since a dual-processor configuration is shown as having twice the processing power of a single-processor one, the exclusion of software overhead is evident. Notice that the curve flattens off quickly. No matter the number of physical processors used, it is impossible to get an aggregate performance exceeding four times the power of a single processor on a single processor-memory bus. Hewlett-Packard[17] claims that with four processors overall multitasking performance ranges from 2.9 to 3.7 times the uniprocessor performance, depending on the instruction mix. Studies of other single-timeshared-bus systems[20] show that with proper interface circuitry and bus protocols, one can integrate up to 25 processors on a single bus, with positive incremental increases in overall system throughput.

Performance estimates

The timing estimates for several elementary operations, summarized in Table 4, must be interpreted with caution. Actual throughput is a function of the exact instruction sequence, displacements, data lengths, clock frequency, and other factors. Also, since the figures have been provided by the manufacturers, it is appropriate to assume that they reflect optimal estimates. Notice that the comparison is being made at dissimilar clock frequencies. In the case of Intel, several chips are involved and the timings include some operating overhead.

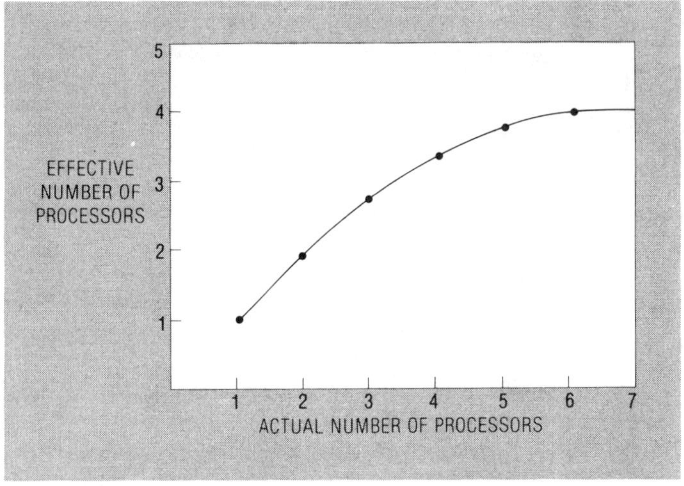

Figure 9. Intel's estimate of iAPX 432 bus efficiency for a single memory bus.

Table 4. Timing estimates for the four microprocessors (in microseconds unless otherwise specified).

OPERATION	NS 16032[15]	BELLMAC-32A[16,24]	HP 32[17]	iAPX 432
GENERAL: CLOCK SPEED	10 MHz	10 MHz	18 MHz	8 MHz
MOVE: MEMORY TO REGISTER	1.5	0.95	0.56	0.75
ADD: 32-BIT INTEGER	1.6	0.4	0.055 (HARDWARE TIME) 0.275 (INSTRUCTION TIME)	0.5
ADD: FLOATING-POINT	9.3 WITH NS 16081	NOT SUPPORTED IN HARDWARE	6.0 (FOR 64-BIT) 4.7 (FOR 32-BIT)	19.125 (FOR 80-BIT)
MULTIPLY: 32-BIT INTEGER	8.3	1.8-9.5, DEPENDING ON OPERANDS	1.8 (HARDWARE TIME) 2.9 (INSTRUCTION TIME)	6.375
MULTIPLY: FLOATING-POINT	7.1 (FOR 64-BIT) WITH NS 16081	NOT SUPPORTED IN HARDWARE	10.4 (FOR 64-BIT) 5.1 (FOR 32-BIT)	27.875 (FOR 80-BIT)
DIVIDE: 32-BIT INTEGER	9.2	DEPENDENT ON OPERANDS	9.4 (64-BIT/32-BIT) 5.2 (32-BIT/32-BIT)	10.625
DIVIDE: FLOATING-POINT	10.8 WITH NS 16081	NOT SUPPORTED IN HARDWARE	16.0 (FOR 64-BIT) 6.5 (FOR 32-BIT)	48.25 (FOR 80-BIT)

Table 5. Relative code sizes (from Hansen et al.[21]).

MACHINE	LANGUAGE	WORD SIZE	RATIO TO VMS PASCAL (<1 = > SMALLER)				
			SEARCH	SIEVE	PUZZLE	ACKER	AVG ± SD
VAX-11/780	C	32	0.60	0.38	0.77	0.45	0.5 ± 0.2
	PASCAL (UNIX)	32	0.95	1.24	1.49	0.72	1.1 ± 0.3
68000	C	32	0.79	0.55	1.01	0.50	0.7 ± 0.2
	PASCAL	16	0.72	0.29	0.60	0.36	0.5 ± 0.2
	PASCAL	32	0.74	0.31	0.64	0.38	0.5 ± 0.2
8086	PASCAL	16	0.94	0.85	0.79	0.91	0.9 ± 0.1
432 (REL. 3)	ADA	16	0.76	0.44	0.84	0.42	0.6 ± 0.2

(NUMBERS SMALLER THAN ONE INDICATE MORE COMPACT CODE THAN ON THE VAX.)

Table 6. Execution times (from Patterson[22]).

MACHINE	LANGUAGE	WORD SIZE	TIME (MILLISECONDS)			
			SEARCH	SIEVE	PUZZLE	ACKER
VAX-11/780	C	32	1.4	250	9400	4600
	PASCAL (UNIX)	32	1.6	220	11,900	7800
	PASCAL (VMS)	32	1.4	259	11,530	9850
68000 (8 MHz)	C	32	4.7	740	37,100	7800
	PASCAL	16	5.3	810	32,470	11,480
	PASCAL	32	5.8	960	32,520	12,320
68000 (16 MHz)	PASCAL	16	1.3	196	9180	2750
	PASCAL	32	1.5	246	9200	3080
8086 (5 MHz)	PASCAL	16	7.3	764	44,000	11,100
432/REL. 2 (4 MHz)	ADA	16	35.0	3200	350,000	260,000
432/REL. 3 (8 MHz)	ADA	16	4.4	978	45,700	47,800
80286 (8 MHz)	PASCAL	16	1.4	168	9138	2218
80286 (10 MHz)	PASCAL	16	1.1	135	7311	1774
HP 32-BIT CPU* (18 MHz)	PASCAL	32	NA	NA	7450	2590
NS 16032* (7 MHz)	PASCAL	32	NA	NA	24,000	9900

*VENDOR-PROVIDED INFORMATION

Hansen and his colleagues[21] used four programs (string search, sieve, puzzle, and Ackermann's function) to evaluate iAPX 432 performance in comparison to that of two 16-bit microprocessors and the VAX-11/780. Using a VAX-11/780 operating in a VMS Pascal environment as the base, they determined relative code sizes (Table 5). These figures indicate that in spite of bit-variable-length instructions, the code size was larger on the iAPX 432 as compared to the 68000, probably because of the inability of the former to refer to a local variable or constant with fewer than 16 bits of address. The execution timings are summarized in Tables 6 and 7.[22] In all these performance evaluation exercises, the iAPX 432 was tested as a high-level-language uniprocessor for integer and character programs; thus, any potential benefits arising from transparent multiprocessing, data security, or increased programmer productivity are not reflected.[21] Also, the timings for the Hewlett-Packard and National chips must be viewed with caution, as they have not been verified by any independent organization.

Overall, the performance of the newer microprocessors approaches that of mainframes. The Intel 432 takes 5.0 microseconds for a 32-bit integer multiply and 27.0 microseconds for an 80-bit floating-point multiply. The equivalent figures for an IBM 370/148 are 16.0 microseconds and 38.5 microseconds. In terms of basic computational power, the iAPX 432 is superior to an IBM 370/148. The Bellmac-32A chip and the HP 32-bit chip are expected to be superior to an IBM 370/158. However, the IBM 370 family is supported by many compilers and application programs; it will take some time for similar facilities to be available for 32-bit microprocessors. A typical end user will have to decide among several options: waiting for the desired application software to become commercially available, developing the desired software in house, or using an earlier-generation microprocessor that is already supported by necessary software.

Selection strategy

The 32-bit word size of the newer microprocessors permits higher throughput, greater precision, and larger addressing space than those supported by earlier chips. The power that traditionally characterized mainframes is now exhibited by the four 32-bit microprocessors we have considered here. Overall performance is determined by the hardware and by the efficiency of the several layers of software that determine how a user sees the chip. The trend in microprocessors is toward microcoding and performing traditionally software-based functions in hardware. For example, the operating system function of job dispatching is performed entirely by hardware in the iAPX 432. The hardware shift circuit is another example. No longer is it possible to base evaluations on register-to-register-level instructions alone. Today one must analyze the match between the user's application and the functions being implemented in hardware. The situation is analogous to the mainframe world, where evaluations once were based on clock frequencies and elementary instruction timings, but today are based on benchmarks and simulation studies. The trend in the "micromainframe" world is the same.

The Intel iAPX 432 is not the only multichip, 32-bit processor. The HP 32-bit machine requires a memory controller and I/O processor to do meaningful work. Similarly, the NS 16032, to demonstrate its virtual memory and floating-point capabilities, requires two auxiliary chips. The final decision of Bell Labs regarding the floating-point processor for the Bellmac is not known. However, to tap their full potentials, the NS 16032 and the HP 32-bit CPU both need at least two auxiliary chips.

The HP and Bell Lab micros are reserved for use with company products. The much simpler National chip is compatible with the firm's 16008. However, not one of these chips has established a market niche to date, nor does any offer compatibility with earlier chips. The iAPX 432 is the most complex of the four, and it will take some time before it will be fully accepted. Also, it offers no direct compatibility with Intel's 8080, 8086, or other chip. This noncompatibility tends to negate Intel's advantage of a large established user base and software library. The 432's increased hardware capabilities, however, favor its use in areas such as database and transaction processing.

We have evaluated the four chips (Table 8) on the basis of available technical information. A is excellent, B is good, C is fair, and D is poor. As vendors announce newer chips, designers will face even greater difficulty in the selection exercise. Motorola has announced the MC68020, its first true 32-bit microprocessor; it is upward-compatible with, and similar in architecture to, the MC68000. National plans to offer the NS32032, with 32-bit external data paths, in 1983.[15] NCR has announced the microprogrammable NCR/32 four-chip set.[23]

Table 7.
Performance at eight MHz (from Patterson[22]).

WAIT STATES	MACHINE	LANGUAGE	TIME (MILLISECONDS)			
			SEARCH	SIEVE	PUZZLE	ACKER
4	68000	PASCAL	5.3	810	32,470	11,480
	432 (REL. 2)	ADA	17.5	1600	175,000	130,000
	432 (REL. 3)	ADA	4.4	978	45,700	47,800
0	8086	PASCAL	4.6	448	27,500	6938
	68000	PASCAL	2.6	392	18,360	5500
	80286	PASCAL	1.4	168	9138	2218

Table 8.
Ranking of the four 32-bit microprocessors.

	NS 16032	BELLMAC-32A	HP 32-BIT CPU	iAPX 432
SPEED	B	B	B	C
ADDRESS RANGE	B	A	A	B
COMPATIBILITY WITH OTHER MICROPROCESSORS	C	C	C	C
SOFTWARE SUPPORT	B	B	B	A
LARGE-SCALE MULTIPROCESSING CAPABILITY	B	B	B	A

The microprocessor industry has been characterized by an incredibly fast pace of technical development. We have gone from four-bit chips to 32-bit chips in just over eleven years. However, we see one development that will parallel the mainframe world—just as most mainframes eventually settled on a 32-bit structure, so should microprocessors eventually settle on 32 bits as a lasting standard. ■

Acknowledgments

After this paper was accepted for publication, we asked the four vendors to correct any inaccuracies and to update facts and figures. We are grateful to the representatives of these vendors for their time and effort and their helpful comments and suggestions.

References

1. H. D. Toong and A. Gupta, "An Architectural Comparison of Contemporary 16-bit Microprocessors," *IEEE Micro,* Vol. 1, No. 2, May 1981, pp. 26-37.
2. H. D. Toong and A. Gupta, "Evaluation Kernels for Microprocessor Performance Analyses," *Performance Evaluation,* Vol. 2, No. 1, May 1982, pp. 1-8.
3. L. Kohn, "A 32b Microprocessor with Virtual Memory Support," *Proc. IEEE Int'l Solid-State Circuits Conf.,* Feb. 1981, pp. 232-233.
4. A. Kaminker et al., "A 32-bit Microprocessor with Virtual Memory Support," *IEEE J. Solid-State Circuits,* Oct. 1981, pp. 548-557.
5. B. T. Murphy et al., "A CMOS 32b Single Chip Microprocessor," *Proc. IEEE Int'l Solid-State Circuits Conf.,* Feb. 1981, pp. 230-231.
6. A. D. Berenbaum et al., "The Operating System and Language Support Features of the Bellmac-32 Microprocessor," *Proc. Symp. Architectural Support for Programming Languages and Operating Systems,* Mar. 1982, pp. 30-38.
7. J. W. Beyers et al., "A 32-bit VLSI CPU Chip," *IEEE J. Solid-State Circuits,* Oct. 1981, pp. 537-542.
8. J. M. Mikkelson et al., "An NMOS VLSI Process for Fabrication of a 32-bit CPU Chip," *IEEE J. Solid State Circuits,* Oct. 1981, pp. 542-547.
9. D.L. Budde et al., "The 32b Computer Execution Unit," *Proc. IEEE Int'l Solid-State Circuits Conf.,* Feb. 1981, pp. 112-113.
10. W. S. Richardson et al., "The 32b Computer Instruction Decoding Unit," *Proc. IEEE Int'l Solid-State Circuits Conf.,* Feb. 1981, pp. 114-115.
11. J. A. Bayliss et al., "The Interface Processor for the 32b Computer," *Proc. IEEE Int'l Solid-State Circuits Conf.,* Feb. 1981, pp. 116-117.
12. D. L. Budde et al., "The Execution Unit for the VLSI 432 General Data Processor," *IEEE J. Solid-State Circuits,* Oct. 1981, pp. 514-521.
13. J. A. Bayliss et al., "The Interface Processor for the Intel 432 32-bit Computer," *IEEE J. Solid-State Circuits,* Oct. 1981, pp. 522-530.
14. F. J. Pollack et al., "Supporting Ada Memory Management in the iAPX-432," *Proc. Symp. Architectural Support for Programming Languages and Operating Systems,* Mar. 1982, pp. 117-131.
15. S. Bal (National Semiconductor Corp.), personal communication, Nov. 19, 1982.
16. B. T. Murphy (Bell Laboratories), personal communication, Nov. 17, 1982.
17. D. Seccombe (Hewlett-Packard), personal communication, Nov. 8, 1982.
18. R. Martin (Intel Corp.), personal communication, Nov. 10, 1982.
19. *Intel 432 System Summary: Manager's Perspective,* Manual No. 171867-001, Intel Corp., Santa Clara, CA, 1981, p. 29.
20. H. D. Toong, S. O. Strommen, and E. R. Goodrich II, "A General Multi-Microprocessor Interconnection Mechanism for Non-Numeric Processing," *Proc. Fifth Workshop Computer Architecture for Non-Numeric Processing,* 1980, pp. 115-123.
21. P. M. Hansen et al., "A Performance Evaluation of the Intel iAPX 432," *Computer Architecture News* (ACM Sigarch newsletter), Vol. 10, No. 4, June 1982, pp. 17-26.
22. D. A. Patterson, "A Performance Evaluation of the Intel 80286," *Computer Architecture News* (ACM Sigarch newsletter), Vol. 10, No. 5, Sept. 1982, pp. 16-18.
23. W. R. Iversen, "32-bit Chip Set Will Offer Huge Microprogram Store," *Electronics,* Sept. 8, 1982, pp. 47-48.
24. J. Mao (Bell Laboratories), personal communication, Jan. 11, 1983.

AN ARCHITECTURE FOR THE 80's - THE INTEL iAPX 432

Howard I. Jacob
Senior Field Application Engineer
Intel Corporation
2550 Golf Road, Suite 815
Rolling Meadows, IL 60008

INTRODUCTION

The rate of proliferation of microprocessor technology over the past decade has been explosive. This has been driven by the tremendous strides that have been made in the development of integrated circuit technology; from the development of the Intel 4004, the world's first "computer on a chip", with 2000 integrated devices; to today's capability to produce, in volume, system building blocks with over 100,000 devices integrated on a single chip. The cost of computer hardware has consistently followed a steep downward trend, and since the initial applications of microprocessor technology were primarily to replace discrete hardware logic, the proliferation of microprocessor technology was driven by the cost effectiveness of the hardware. Today's applications transcend the scope of hardware logic replacement, to the point where software intensive applications, which could traditionally be solved only with the use of minicomputers and mainframes just five years ago, can now be cost effectively addressed by the computing power of today's microprocessors (Figure 1).

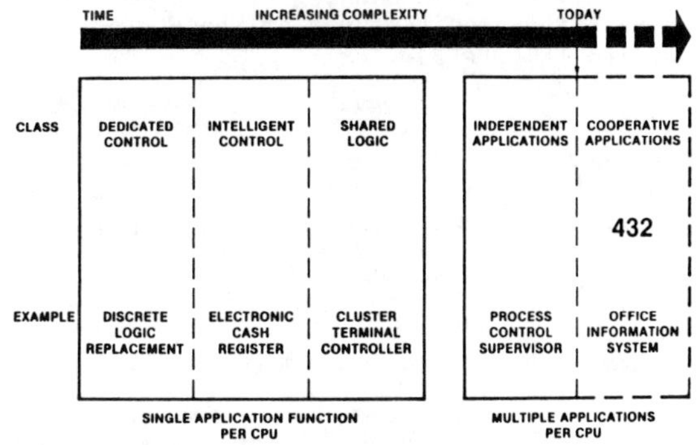

Figure 1
THE EVOLUTION OF MICROPROCESSOR APPLICATIONS

This transition, from the use of microprocessor technology to do general purpose logic replacement, to the use of microprocessor technology for the solution of complex, software intensive applications, brings with it a significant set of problems. First, the responsibility for the continued proliferation of microprocessor technology has moved from the mature discipline of hardware design, to the relatively new discipline of software engineering. Second, the scope of the problem has changed, from the design of a dedicated hardware system (such as a data entry terminal or a small PABX), to the design of a large, multi-function software system, with many independent but cooperating applications (such as a large PABX, which serves as the heart of the "office of the future"). Third, the cost of developing software currently represents eighty percent of the cost of developing a new microprocessor based product. The need to improve the productivity of the engineers who are responsible for this major portion of a product's development cost is therefore significant; as is the need to protect the investment made in the development of this software, by extending its useful life over the evolution of a product family. Finally, if we examine the scope of applications such as the "office and factory of the future", it becomes obvious that the impact of failures in these large systems is significant; therefore, the reliability of the system, as well as its component hardware and software, must be assured, and verifiable. If we are to see the continued proliferation of microprocessors in the next decade, these problems must be resolved.

MICROPROCESSOR APPLICATION ISSUES

We have seen the shift in emphasis from hardware design to software design as the major problem in successfully bringing a microprocessor based product to market. Let's now examine the evolution of software design methodologies, and the impact that this has had on the design of computer architectures.

Early machines, like the Intel 4004 microprocessor, were programmed by hardware design engineers, who were utilizing the processor to do dedicated logic replacement. These machines were programmed in non-relocatable assembly language, using essentially a "brute force" approach, with little or no structure. As the complexity of microprocessor applications, and the power of the available processors grew to the level of the Intel 8080/8085, the need for the more sophisticated software tools became apparent. While these machines were still not suitable for efficient high level language implementation, large multiprogrammer assembly language applications were being developed. This created the need for relocatable assemblers, to allow for the necessary modularization and indepedent development of programs. While the availability of these assemblers allowed several programmers to independently develop

Reprinted with permission from *Midcon Conf. Rec.*, 1981, pp. 19.2.1–19.2.6.

software for a given application, code quality and reliability were primarily the function of which programmer coded a particular module, and what kind of day the programmer was having. This was complicated by the wide gap between the "semantics" of the application (problem), and the semantics of the processor (solution). This so-called "semantic gap" required the programmer to translate the system function "sample input 1" into the low level machine instructions required to perform the high level function.

In an attempt to close the "semantic gap", it was necessary to allow the programmer to work in a high level language. This need was fulfilled by the next generation of microprocessors, as signified by the Intel 8086, a 16 bit microprocessor specifically designed to efficiently support structured high level languages, such as PLM, C, and PASCAL. While this reduced the gap between the application and the programmer, there was still a significant gap between the application and the capability of the machine to directly support the semantics of the application. To date, all microprocessors have supported the traditional Von Neumann model of computation, where instructions are fetched, executed, and the results stored, one at a time, in a sequential fashion. There have been attempts made in research laboratories to provide machine architectures which more closely match the semantics of their applications. Examples of these architectures would include the Data Flow and General Control Flow models of computation, each of which attempt to deal with the issues of concurrency and asynchrony in real life processes. Another architecture which has made an attempt at reducing the semantic gap is the object oriented architecture, which provides a very high level of hardware enforcement of structured programming methodologies. This includes finely grained, per data structure protection, with a high degree of programming flexibility, as well as a high level, easily understood interface for the programmer.

As architectures evolve, and as different implementations of specific architectures are introduced, system architects are faced with an ever-widening range of choices. All too often, it becomes necessary to re-evaluate the original design decisions of a system, when its evolution and enhancements begin to tax the limits of the underlying processor(s) implementation, long before the intended end of a system's life. Real time constraints, memory limitations, and cost constraints are some of the more common reasons that enhanced systems soon "run out of gas". Recalling that eighty percent of the cost of system development lies in the software, the impact of changing the architecture of the system, i.e., distributing some of the processing to more processors, changing the processor family, etc., in order to extend its capabilities and/or life, is significant. To date, the problem of developing a long-lived, extensible performance, system architecture has only been partially addressed.

THE INTEL iAPX 432 SYSTEM

The Intel iAPX 432 system was specifically designed to address the cost of developing large, software intensive applications. It provides a set of capabilities that allow for the efficient implementation of complex systems, achieving mid-range mainframe levels of performance, while insuring that these systems will be built upon reliable hardware and software. At the same time, the large investment represented by the development of these systems is protected through performance extensibility, which the iAPX 432 achieves through software transparent multiprocessing, and an attached processor I/O system architecture. We can achieve a better understanding of the iAPX 432 system by examining these four primary attributes of the system in more detail.

Large Scale Computing Power

The iAPX 432 system truly offers mainframe performance in a microcomputer form factor; performance in the range of two million IBM 370 normalized instructions per second, for the execution of parallel and/or concurrent processes, can be achieved. If we compare the attributes of the iAPX 432 with a mid-range IBM 370 machine, we can begin to compare and contrast the architectures of these two machines (Figure 2).

	IAPX 432 FUNCTIONALITY	TYPICAL MAINFRAME FUNCTIONALITY (IBM 370)
ADDRESS SPACE INSTANTANEOUS VIRTUAL	2^{32} 2^{40}	2^{16} 2^{24}
DATA TYPES	8, 16, 32, 64 and 80-BIT BOOLEAN, CHARACTER ORDINAL, INTEGER, REAL LONG ORDINAL, INTEGER, REAL	8, 16, 32, 64, 96, 128 BCD, CHARACTER, INTEGER, ORDINAL, REAL
INSTRUCTION SET	HIGH LEVEL (e.g., A B C) MULTI-OPERAND (0-3) VECTOR, RECORD	ASSEMBLY LEVEL TWO OPERAND REGISTER BASED
I/O	INDEPENDENT PARALLEL	DEPENDENT SLAVED
PROTECTION	FINELY GRAINED... PER DATA STRUCTURE	COARSE SUPERVISOR/USER

FIGURE 2
ARCHITECTURAL COMPARISON

Both machines support a large address space, with the iAPX 432 supporting a 2^{40} byte virtual address space on chip, with no external logic. Both machines support a rich repetoire of data types, the longest of which are the extended precision floating point types. In the iAPX 432, this is limited to the 80 bit temporary real data type that is defined in the IEEE floating point standard. At the instruction set level, we begin to see some of the unique attributes of the iAPX 432, in that the instructions are no longer of the assembly level, two operand, register based type. Instead, we find that the instructions are more like high level language statements, in that they can have from zero to three operands, with the operands being scalars, vectors or records. To achieve code density, the instructions are bit variable, ranging from 6 to >300 bits in length, and Huffman encoded by usage. As an example, the following PASCAL or Ada assignment statement translates to a single machine level instruction:

```
a(i) := b(j) * c(k)
   where the * operator could alternatively
      be /, +, -
   and a,b,c could be single or double
      precision integers or reals.
   For 32 bit integer operands, this
      instruction is 84 bits in length,
      including three, thirty-two bit
      address references.
```

The I/O in the iAPX 432 system is provided through intelligent, independent and decentralized attached processor subsystems, which not only are capable of concurrently processing I/O requests, but initiating them as well. As such, there are two separate environments in an iAPX 432 system:

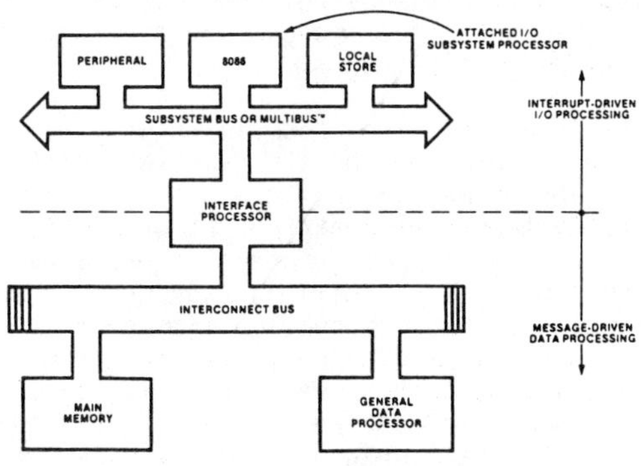

Figure 3
iAPX 432 SYSTEM PARTITIONING

a message driven data processing environment, and an interrupt driven I/O environment (Figure 3). Perhaps the most significant difference between the iAPX 432 and conventional machines is the object based architecture of the iAPX 432. Whereas the granularity of protection in a conventional machine is at the user/supervisor level, which basically prevents a malicious user from destroying the integrity of the system, the iAPX 432 provides very finely grained, per data structure protection. This allows for the highly protected sharing of data by multiple users, each of who may have different access rights, such as, read only, read/write, etc.

Incremental Performance Capacity

As discussed previously, it is likely that a large system will evolve over time, with more and more features being added, until the system's ability to interact properly with the physical world is impaired. An example of this situation would be the inability to sample a sense point every 10 ms, because all of the intervening calculations can no longer be completed before the next sample is required. With a traditional machine, this would be a situation that would require a significant analysis of system throughput to be undertaken, with the probable result that extensive hardware and/or software changes would be required. With the iAPX 432, one would simply add an additional processor, and without changing a single binary bit of software, an increment of processing power will be added to, and utilized by, the system.

This capability of the iAPX 432 is made possible by two unique attributes of the system, a high efficiency, low bus occupancy, multiprocessor interconnect, and a silicon operating system, which coupled with the object based architecture of the machine, provides self-dispatching processors that find their own work. (The silicon operating system will be discussed later.)

The multiprocessor interconnect, or Packet Interconnect Protocol, solves the problems of multiple processors sharing a common memory bus. It provides for separate packetized requests and replies which are of varying lengths, to help maximize bus efficiency (Figure 4).

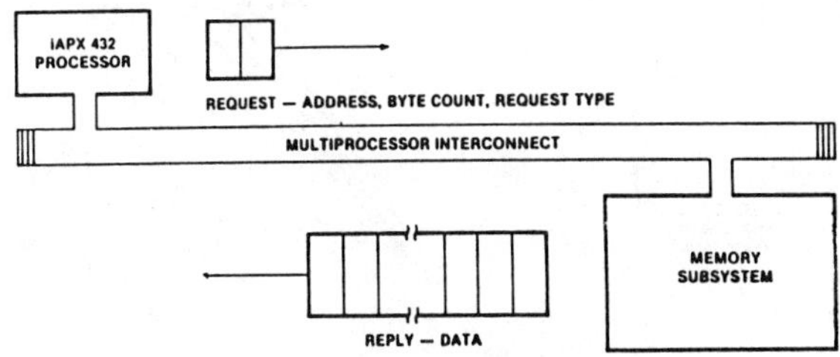

Figure 4
INTEL 432 PACKET PROTOCOL

The packet protocol specifies the logical implementation of the bus only; the physical implementation of the bus is definable by the user. This makes possible the tailoring of the physical bus structure to the requirements of the application. Sixteen, thirty-two, or sixty-four bit wide data busses can be implemented, and these can be either fully demultiplexed, or multiplexed with address and control information. The peak instantaneous bandwidth of the packet protocol, as emitted by the processor chip as a local bus, is sixteen megabytes per second.

With multiple processors utilizing a common bus, regardless of the level of bus structure sophistication, eventual saturation of the bus is inevitable. In fact, a single iAPX 432 memory bus will typically saturate with from three to four processors. To allow for a range of performance of from one to ten effective processors, using fifteen to seventeen physical processors, multiple memory busses are required. This capability will be provided by two interconnect components that will be available in 1982. That system configuration (Figure 5) and its performance range graph (Figure 6) are shown below:

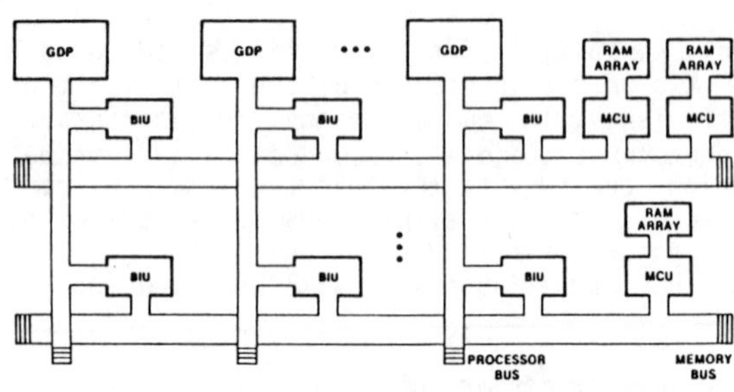

Figure 5
iAPX 432 SYSTEM WITH INTERCONNECT COMPONENTS

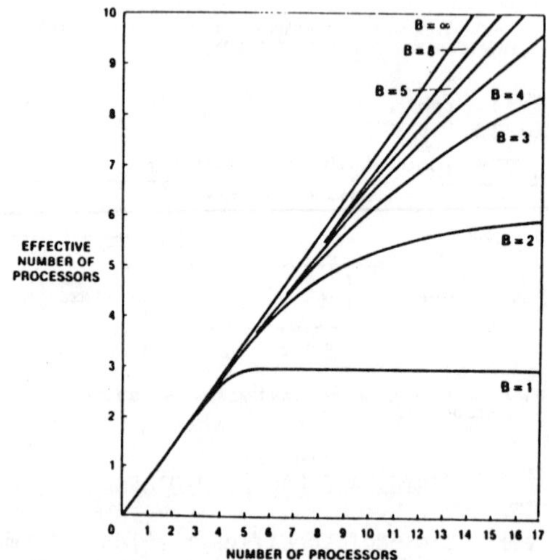

Figure 6
MULTIPLE BUS PERFORMANCE RANGE
(Assumes 200 ns Dynamic RAM)

Highly Dependable Hardware and Software

As an ever-increasing amount of responsibility is placed on computing systems, the need for highly reliable hardware and software becomes increasingly important. Patient monitoring, nuclear power plant instrumentation and control, and the "factory and office of the future", are just a few of the examples of applications where unreliable systems can play havoc with tremendous amounts of human and material resources, and can even be life threatening.

The iAPX 432 provides a unique set of capabilities to address these reliability issues. The finely grained protection that is intrinsic to an object based architecture provides a large measure of reliability, with regard to the confinement of software errors. In addition, all of the components in the iAPX 432 system have the capability of operating in a Functional Redundancy Checking mode, in which each component operates as either a master or checker. This allows two components, one master and one checker, to operate in lock step, with the master accepting inputs and driving outputs, and the checker using the same inputs to derive outputs, against which the master's outputs are checked, cycle by cycle, on chip, with no additional hardware. If an error occurs during any cycle, an error signal is raised, which software can detect and use to configure out a bad node. Note that there can be no determination of fault made between the master and checker; in fact, the two components are viewed as a single logical unit.

Finally, the ability to develop highly reliable software is provided by the selection of Ada, the new Department of Defense standard language, as the Systems Implementation Language of the iAPX 432. Ada is a language that provides object orientation, significant support for modularization, extensive compile time error checking, and configurable run time error checking. Ada is, in fact, the lowest level language that will be supported on the iAPX 432. This is not to say that the machine directly executes Ada source; it does have a symbolic machine instruction set. However, in keeping with the primary objective of the system, which is to significantly reduce the cost and time to market of large software intensive applications, it was not felt that an assembler would be an effective tool to deal with the scope of problems that the iAPX 432 is intended to solve.

Increased Programmer Productivity

A high productivity software environment for the development of iAPX 432 applications is assured in two ways. First, through the use of Ada, as discussed above, which was specifically designed to reduce software development and maintenance costs. Second, the incorporation of operating system functionality in the silicon, which provides a higher level interface to the machine than heretofore possible.

The silicon operating system deserves further discussion, in that it not only makes possible software transparent multiprocessing, but also contributes significantly to the overall level of productivity in the development of system software for the iAPX 432. There are, of course, potential problems when such high level functions become part of the silicon; users may have special operating system requirements, due to the nature of their application, that cannot be satisfied by a "general" approach. It is for this very reason that a significant amount of work was done to provide an effective partitioning of functions between the silicon and the software operating system. The primary goal of this work was to impose no limitations on the types of operating systems that could be implemented on the iAPX 432.

The partitioning was implemented in a manner that achieves this goal. The portions of the operating system that are implemented in silicon are the low level functions that are required by all operating systems, regardless of the high level functions and their manner of implementation, that are provided. Operations such as sending a message to a communications port, receiving a message, in a process blocking or non-blocking manner, and dispatching a ready to run process to run on an idle processor, are termed operating system <u>mechanisms</u>. These are low level functions that perform basic operations that all operating systems need, and these are implemented in the silicon. Scheduling algorithms, which define the manner in which an operating system allows the sharing of the processor resource(s) by multiple users, is termed an operating system <u>policy</u>. The selection of priority, round robin, first-in-first-out, or a combination of these scheduling algorithms, are <u>policy</u> decisions, which can only be made by the user, as dictated by the needs of the application. Therefore, these functions are left to the operating system software. So in order to execute a ready to run process, the user defines and implements the required <u>policy</u> for the scheduling algorithm (priority, round robin, etc.), and the iAPX 432 hardware will then utilize the silicon operating system's <u>mechanisms</u> of scheduling in the order indicated by the user's <u>policy</u>, and dispatching, according to the order in which they were scheduled, the ready to run process. This careful separation of <u>mechanisms</u> and <u>policies</u> provides a five to ten fold improvement in the performance of operating system functions, while in no way reducing the ability of the systems programmer to tailor the characteristics of the operating system to the needs of the application.

SYSTEMS IMPLEMENTATION

The implementation of the iAPX 432 can be divided into two portions; the silicon implementation, and the system level implementation, each of which will be briefly examined.

iAPX 432 Silicon Implementation

The silicon is implemented in three, sixty-four pin, quad in-line packages. These include the two chip General Data Processor, consisting of the iAPX 43201 Instruction Decode Unit, with one hundred and ten thousand devices; and the iAPX 43202 Execution Unit, with forty-nine thousand devices. The single chip iAPX 43203 Interface Processor, with sixty thousand devices, completes the set of three chips.

The three chip set is implemented on Intel's HMOS process, a mature, high volume manufacturing process. The current family of devices is offered at a clock frequency of five or eight megahertz.

The development of the iAPX 432 components required the use of sophisticated computer aided design (CAD) tools, many of which were developed specifically to support this program. This "suite" of CAD tools will allow Intel to easily move the iAPX 432 components to more advanced processes, such as our current HMOS II and beyond, in order to produce higher performance and lower cost devices.

iAPX 432 System Implementation

The first commercially available iAPX 432 system is the System 432/600 family. This is a single memory bus system, which is highly modular and extensible.

The system allows for a maximum of six processors, representing any mixture of General Data Processors and Interface Processors, with a minimum of one of each (Figure 7).

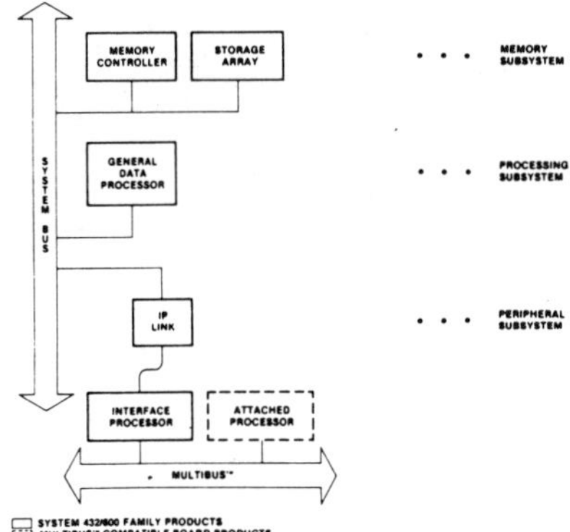

Figure 7
SYSTEM 432/600 BLOCK DIAGRAM
MINIMUM CONFIGURATION

The system utilizes a thirty-two bit multiplexed address and data bus, with a parity bit for each of the four bytes. There is also a set of dedicated control and status lines that coordinate system activity, perform parallel arbitration, and support memory interleaving. The structure of the system bus is such that it will saturate with three to four General Data Processors on the bus, so a typical extended configuration for the System 432/600 would include that number of General Data Processors, and two Interface Processors (Figure 8).

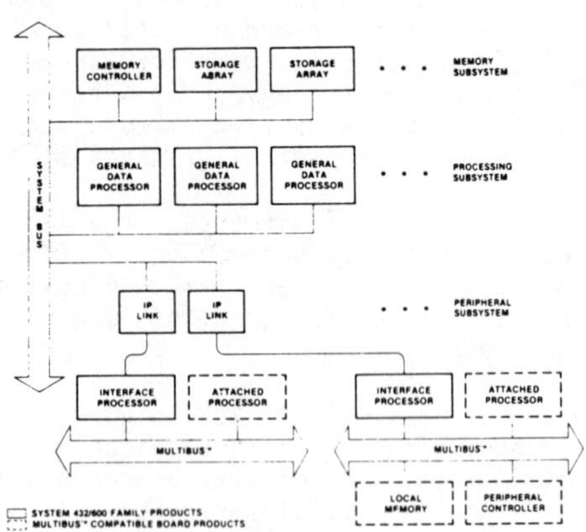

Figure 8
SYSTEM 432/600 BLOCK DIAGRAM
EXTENDED CONFIGURATION

System memory, which is expandable up to four megabytes, is implemented using modular, self-refreshing storage boards. The memory array includes 32 bits of data and seven bits of error correcting code (ECC) per word. The ECC facility allows for single bit error correction and double bit error detection on each module. Two types of storage array boards are available, with capacities of 128K and 256K bytes.

Storage array board types may be mixed within a system providing flexibility in memory size, incremental granularity, and upgradability. The only limitation exists when memory is interleaved, in which case paired boards must be of the same capacity.

The System 432/600 utilizes a single memory controller board. This board services processor memory requests, maps instruction addresses to the proper storage array board(s), supports memory interleaving, and centralizes hardware error logging.

The System 432/600 implementation will support a range of performance of from one to three "plus" effective processors, using from one to four physical processors.

SUMMARY

The iAPX 432 system provides a unique set of capabilities to specifically address the problems associated with the development of large, software intensive applications. By providing a tenfold range of data processing performance extensibility, via software transparent multiprocessing; I/O bandwidth extensibility, through multiple attached processors; Functional Redundancy Checking for hardware reliability, and the Ada programming language on an object based architecture, for software reliability; the iAPX 432 truly provides mainframe performance in a microcomputer form factor.

The Execution Unit for the VLSI 432 General Data Processor

DAVID L. BUDDE, STEVEN R. COLLEY, MEMBER, IEEE, STEPHEN L. DOMENIK, MEMBER, IEEE, ALLAN L. GOODMAN, MEMBER, IEEE, JAMES D. HOWARD, AND MICHAEL T. IMEL

Abstract—The microinstruction execution unit (MEU), which is one of two chips that implement a 32-bit VLSI object-oriented general data processor, is described. A companion paper describes the instruction decoding unit (IDU) that provides the microinstruction inputs to be executed by the MEU. A functional overview of the MEU is given and important design tradeoffs are described, including some of the motivations for the particular partitioning of the functions between the two chips. Finally, details of circuit implementation are described for some of the more interesting and important circuits on the chip.

Manuscript received May 3, 1981.

D. L. Budde, J. D. Howard, and M. T. Imel are with the Intel Corporation, Aloha, OR 97007.

S. R. Colley is with Falco Data Products, Sunnyvale, CA 94086.

S. L. Domenik is with the Intel Corporation, Santa Clara, CA 95051.

A. L. Goodman is with Tektronix, Inc., Beaverton, OR 97007.

INTRODUCTION

THE microinstruction execution and instruction decoding units (MEU and IDU [1]) form a generalized data processor (GDP) that efficiently executes the operator set of the GDP's architecture. Salient attributes of the GDP's architecture include software-transparent multiprocessing, virtual memory, self-dispatching processors, hardware-implemented interprocess and interprocessor communication, dynamic storage allocation, object-oriented addressing and protection, and operations defined for nine different data types, including three types of IEEE-compatible floating point [2].

The basic function of the MEU is to accept, decode, and execute any of 88 unique vertically encoded microinstructions

Reprinted from *IEEE J. Solid-State Circuits*, vol. SC-16, pp. 514–521, Oct. 1981.

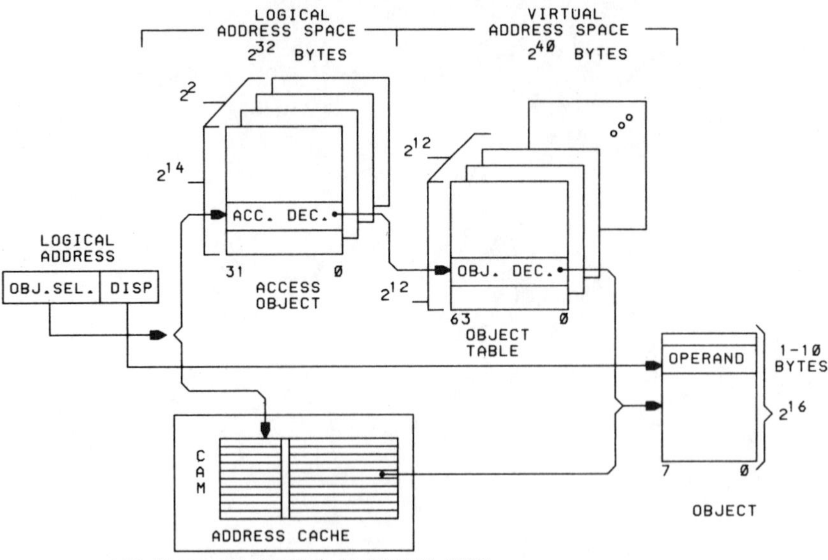

Fig. 1. Object addressing mechanism.

supplied by the IDU. These microinstructions control the registers and the arithmetic capabilities of the MEU to perform the GDP macroinstructions. The MEU is also responsible for interfacing with main memory; thus, it supports the required virtual-to-physical address translation mechanism and initiates all memory accesses on behalf of the processor.

The implementation of the GDP departs from conventional processor implementations in several ways. 1) No processor interrupts or service requests are recognized by the GDP. It does not support the concept of input/output address space. Instead, all input/output is accomplished using a hardware-supported message-based communication mechanism which is refered to as an interprocess communication. Thus, messages are sent through an interface processor, using objects (data structures) in main memory as the message buffering medium, to an attached I/O processor that performs the actual I/O operations with its associated I/O subsystem. More details about I/O are given elsewhere [3]. 2) There are no programmer-visible registers defined by the architecture. There are, however, nine different data types as well as complex hardware-recognized data types that are supported which can only be reasonably represented in main memory. This implies the need for a general and efficient addressing mechanism that is described in the following paragraph. The instruction formats and reference types are described in more detail elsewhere [1].

The object (virtual) addressing mechanism is depicted in Fig. 1. A logical address is comprised of two components, an object selector and a displacement. Each of these components has 16 bits, giving a total logical address space of 2**32 bytes. The physical address is computed in the following way. First, the object selector selects one of 16 536 entries in one of four access objects. The contents of this entry, called an access descriptor, contain access rights information about the operand being referenced, as well as two indices that select one of 4096 entries in one of 4096 object tables. This is the object descriptor which contains the 24-bit physical base address and the length for the object that contains the operand being referenced. The two indices together with the displacement give a total virtual address space of 2**40 bytes. Finally, the physical base address is added to the displacement component of the logical address, completing the reference mapping. Note that a reference may specify from 1 to 10 bytes, depending on the data type of the operand being referenced. The figure also shows the cache mechanism implemented on the MEU that bypasses the mapping once an object has been qualified. The cache is described below.

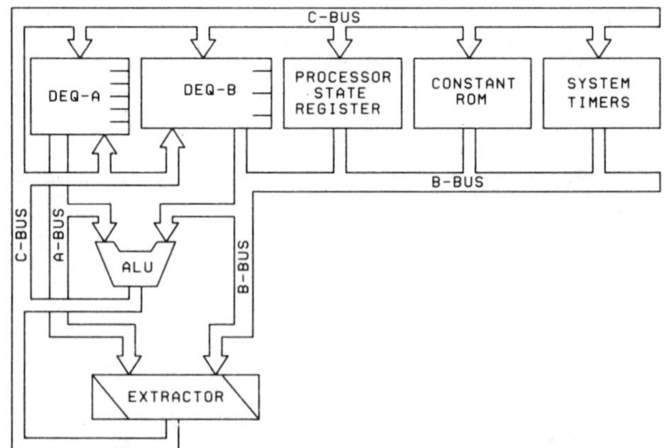

Fig. 2. Data manipulation unit block diagram.

Functional Description of the MEU

The MEU is comprised of two semi-autonomous subprocessors, a data manipulation unit (DMU) and a reference generation unit (RGU). The DMU block diagram is shown in Fig. 2. It contains the operand registers and functional units necessary to efficiently implement the macroinstruction set. The RGU (Fig. 3) contains the registers and the functional units that support logical-to-physical address translation and access rights verification. Both the DMU and the RGU contain state machines to control both fixed and variable cycle microinstructions.

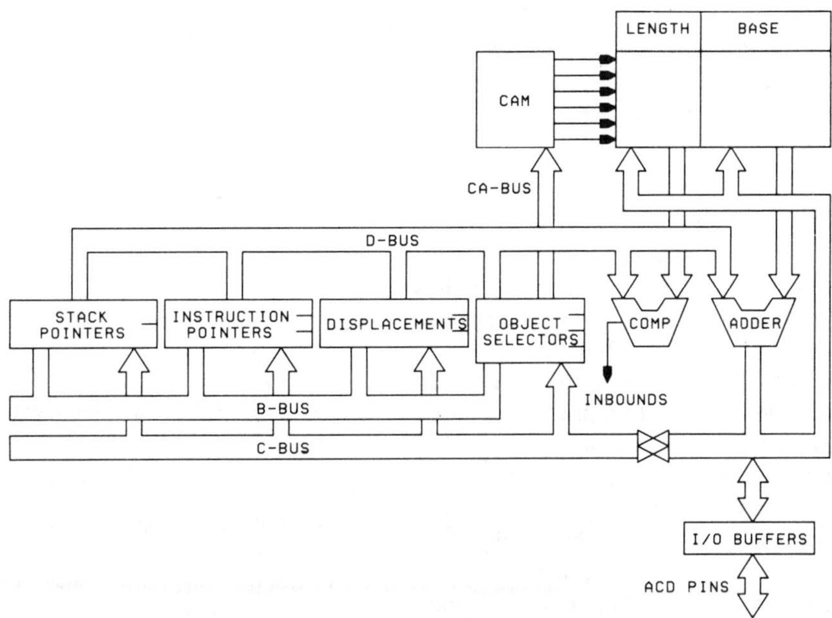

Fig. 3. Reference generation unit block diagram.

Data Manipulation Unit

The DMU is comprised of a variable length ALU, a variable length bit field extractor (a barrel shifter), two double-ended queues (DEQ-*A* and DEQ-*B*), processor state registers, a constant ROM, and two system timers. Three major buses are used to communicate information between the various blocks: the *A*-bus, the *B*-bus, and the *C*-bus. The *A*-bus and *B*-bus are operand buses and convey information from registers to function blocks. The *C*-bus is a result bus and is used to convey information from a function block such as the ALU or extractor back to the registers.

The ALU is a variable length arithmetic logic unit which supports all possible (16) logical operators of two variables, the unary arithmetic operators for increment, decrement, negate, absolute value, and square root, and the arithmetic operators of two variables for add, subtract, multiply, divide, and remainder. An arithmetic sequencer in the DMU allows the MEU to perform a large portion of the multiply, divide, remainder, and square root algorithms in response to a single microinstruction. The other portion of the algorithms are such as checking for pre- and postexceptional conditions, normalization, denormalization, and rounding is handled in microcode.

The extractor takes two inputs from the *A*-bus *and B*-bus and extracts a field from the combined value. A multiplexer at the input to the extractor allows each input to be sourced from one of four places: the *A*-bus, the *B*-bus, the value zero, or a temporary register. The temporary register can be loaded during an extract operation from the *A*-bus or the *B*-bus to be used in subsequent extract operations, thus creating the ability to perform multiprecision shifts.

The operand registers, implemented as double-ended queues, provide a performance optimized solution to the problem of handling arithmetic calculations on variable length operands with a fixed length (16-bit) bus. The DEQ's operate as a combination FIFO and STACK. As a FIFO, data can be inserted into the back of the DEQ and removed from the front. As a STACK, the DEQ can be pushed and popped from the front of the DEQ. With this structure, data can be stored least significant to most significant or vice versa. The combination of the two DEQ's, the ALU, and the extractor make a very efficient variable precision arithmetic unit. The basic computational data types and their formats that are supported by the MEU are shown in Fig. 4.

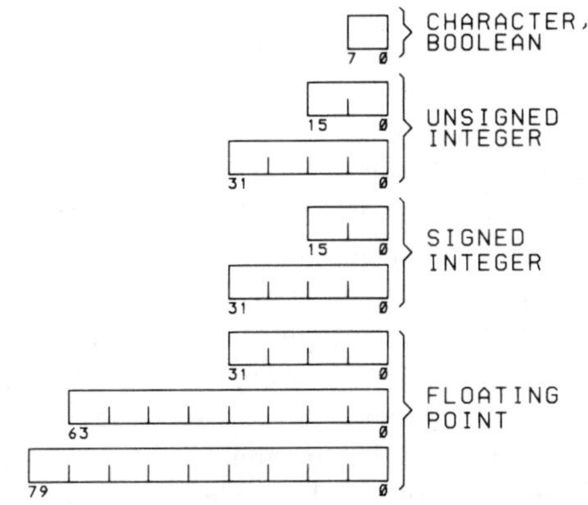

Fig. 4. Basic computational data types and formats.

Two timers are employed, a system timer that keeps track of systemwide time from processor reset and a process time quanta timer which is a 16-bit down counter that can be loaded, started, and stopped under microcode control. The process timer returns a fault when it is decremented to zero. This timer is used to allocate some time quanta to a specific process, and it initiates a process switch upon the exhaustion of the process's allocated time quanta. Both timers are clocked by an external clock, which is typically a multiple of the basic clock period.

The constant ROM is a 32-entry by 16-bit ROM that contains certain immediate values such as floating-point exponent biases and other important values. The processor state registers contain status information about the current process and the current context in which a process is running. For example, the rounding and precision control information for the various floating-point operations is contained here.

Reference Generation Unit

The RGU contains the registers and the functional units necessary to support the virtual addressing mechanism of the GDP architecture. The RGU internally stores the descriptors for hardware-recognized objects as well as user-defined objects. When the MIS requests the MEU to access an object, it is the RGU that translates the logical address to a physical address to be supplied to the external memory subsystem. The RGU may recognize an exceptional condition (e.g., access privilege violation or out-of-bounds memory access) during this translation process, and as a result, notifies the IDU that an object is not being appropriately accessed so that it can invoke a fault-handling microinstruction sequence that recovers from and records the exception. Finally, the RGU is responsible for tracking the state of a software-transparent on-chip extension to the operand stack object.

The major circuitry and busing that forms the RGU includes four independent stacks, four 16-bit buses, a 43-bit by 20-entry register array, an adder, an unsigned magnitude comparator, and a content addressable memory (CAM; see Fig. 3). The object selector stack contains 16-bit object selectors that point to user-defined objects. The stack pointer, instruction pointer, and displacement stacks store the displacement portion of a logical address into the operand stack object, the instruction object, and user-defined objects, respectively. This offset information is placed onto the *D*-bus and added to the appropriate object base address register to form a physical address that is sourced externally via the *M*-bus. Simultaneously, the appropriate object length register is being compared against the offset that is on the *D*-bus. If the offset into the object is larger than the object's created offset boundary (length), then an addressing exception is signaled to the IDU.

Access to user-defined objects is facilitated by the use of two independent and fully associative CAM's implemented in the RGU. Logical addresses of user-defined objects, represented internally by an object selector and a displacement, are compared against the entries in the CAM's, and if a match occurs, sufficient information is stored in the base/length register array and the displacement stack to immediately finish the logical-to-physical address translation.

Typical Data and Control Flow in the MEU

Execution of a particular microinstruction proceeds in a pipelined fashion. To illustrate the pipeline technique as it is applied to the MEU and to illustrate the operation of the DMU, an example microinstruction execution is described below. The microinstruction takes two source operands from the ADEQ and BDEQ register structures, performs a bit-wise logical AND function, and places the result back into the ADEQ (see Fig. 5).

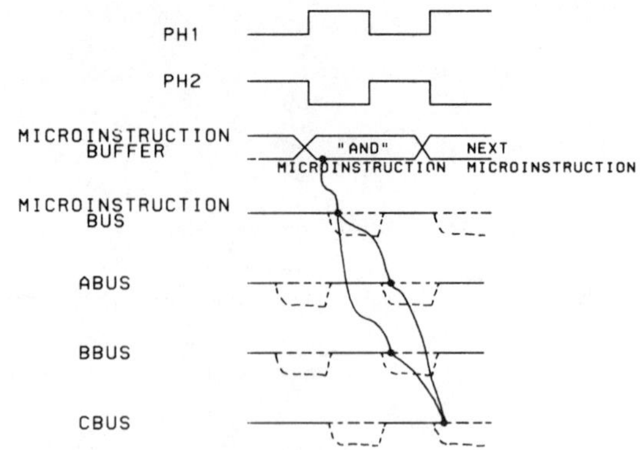

Fig. 5. Internal bus timing diagram.

The microinstruction is first loaded into the MEU's microinstruction buffer during the clock period phase 2 (PH2). Then the value in the microinstruction buffer is sourced to the microinstruction bus during phase 1 (PH1). The various fields of the microinstruction are decoded by the distributed control PLA's. Control signals from these PLA's during PH2 cause the ADEQ and BDEQ registers to source the operands to the source operand buses, *A*-bus and *B*-bus. These operands are then presented to the ALU logic, where a logical AND is performed during the latter part of the PH2 clock period. Meanwhile, a new microinstruction is being loaded into the microinstruction buffer. However, before this new microinstruction is decoded, the latched PLA control signals from the first microinstruction load the ALU result using the *C*-bus into the ADEQ during PH1. Now the new microinstruction can use the result just generated as one of its source operands. Thus, the ALU can generate one 16-bit result every clock cycle. The flow of data and control can be summarized in the following manner: buffer the microinstruction, decode the microinstruction, source the required operands, perform the desired function while buffering the next microinstruction, and store the result.

Microarchitectural Tradeoffs

The microarchitecture is the result of an effort to match the function to the implementation medium. System performance was optimized given the constraints imposed by silicon economics and packaging. Microarchitectural issues were resolved by ensuring that the resolution was consistent with optimum system performance and the following constraints.

1) Chip size for both the MEU and the IDU must be within manufacturable limits.

2) Silicon economics dictate that the chips be of roughly equal area.

3) The pin and power requirements must be within the capability of the 64-pin quad-in-line package (QUIP) developed for the chip set.

Deciding whether or not these constraints had been met required the ability to evaluate any additions or deletions of special hardware down to the topology level. For this purpose, it was necessary to arrive at a general layout scheme in the incipient stages of the design. This section reviews some of the major microarchitectural tradeoffs.

Microinstructions

A fundamental design decision resulted in the MEU being the final stage in a decoding-execution pipeline. First-order partitioning resulted in the MEU being realized as a distinct chip. This had strong implications for the microcode. Pin count minimization weighs in favor of reducing the microcode word width, while performance seemed to indicate the need for a wider word. Ultimately, a compromise was struck that called for a relatively vertical microcode word width that maintained performance by using numerous small local PLA's to decode control where it was required. This scheme has the further advantage of tending to balance the chip size by moving some of the control function burden from the IDU to the MEU. The numerous small PLA's exhibit better performance than the larger PLA's and help ease the chip internal wiring burden. The local decoding power they provide makes it possible to distribute a minimum number of microinstruction lines (16), thereby saving area.

Sequencers

Most microinstructions operate in a single clock cycle. However, having decided to employ the power of local PLA's for decoding microinstructions, it was obvious that further chip size balancing and efficiency could be achieved by sequencing appropriate operations locally as well. As microcode design proceeded, it became clear that the arithmetic operations and external bus control were obvious choices. In the end, three sequencers were created for the MEU.

The access sequencer is used to control the external bus and initiates all memory accesses on behalf of the GDP. It is necessary to respond to a wide variety of internal and external stimuli without tying up the external bus unnecessarily. Doing this via local control eliminates the need to pass condition information between the MEU and IDU chips, and thus reduces the MEU's response time to conditions that occur on the bus. This is a very important consideration since a memory-based architecture is expected to be accessing memory frequently.

The arithmetic sequencer is a PLA state machine and is responsible for controlling the sequence of multiple cycle arithmetic operations. Here again the sequencer serves not only the need to balance chip areas, but also minimizes the amount of status information that must be communicated between the two chips of the GDP.

The third sequencer (another PLA state machine) is responsible for controlling the sequence of a variety of short multiple cycle microinstruction flows. When exceptional conditions arise, it is also responsible for supervising the storage of fault-type information. Therefore, this sequencer provides the minimum sequencing ability required for supervising all other single, double, or triple cycle microinstructions supported by the MEU.

Data Buses

There are seven major data buses in the MEU. Three are primarily associated with the RGU, three are primarily associated with the DMU, and one is used as the microinstruction control bus. A regular structure layout discipline [4] that uses the DMU and RGU constituent cells as the channels for the buses makes liberal use of buses to optimize performance an appropriate design tradeoff.

FUNCTION	MICROCODE ALLOCATION	
	BITS	PERCENTAGE
BASIC INSTRUCTION SET	3680	6%
FLOATING POINT ARITHMETIC	11680	18%
RUN-TIME ENVIRONMENT	6400	10%
VIRTUAL ADDRESSING	4800	7%
FAULT HANDLING	2640	4%
SILICON OS	26400	40%
MULTIPROCESSOR CONTROL	8640	13%
DEBUG SERVICES	1280	2%
	64K BITS	100%

Fig. 6. Distribution of microcode.

Microcode Allocation Tradeoffs

Fig. 6 is a table that shows the amount and percentage of microcode allocation for several of the generic functions implemented in the GDP. The DMU is optimized to execute the operators for the basic instruction set and the floating-point operators. In other words, the partitioning tradeoffs and hardware versus microcode tradeoffs in the DMU are made to implement these two functions. Notice that only 24 percent of the total 64K bits of microcode is used to implement these functions. That leaves the remaining 76 percent of the microcode to implement some of the more interesting and algorithmically complex operators of the GDP architecture. These high level operators address some of the long-standing system and software problems that have plagued computers for many years. These include the programming language run-time environment support which consumes about 10 percent of the microcode and virtual addressing which takes only 7 percent. The RGU is optimized for this function. Fault handling and debug services combined only use 6 percent of the microcode. The silicon OS (i.e., the part of the operating system that is implemented in microcode) requires the most microcode, about 40 percent. And finally, multiprocessor control (the part of the microprogram which supports the notion of software transparent multiprocessing) requires 13 percent.

Implications of a Large Die Size

As a result of conservative design rules (HMOS 1) and integrating many functions into the MEU, the die is a relatively large 313 × 367 mils (Fig. 7). This presents several interesting but difficult circuit and interconnect problems. In particular, clock distribution and power busing are especially challenging.

Special attention has been given to the distribution of V_{CC} and V_{SS} throughout the chip. There are no fewer than five V_{SS} and four V_{CC} pins that evenly distribute the current load and reduce the current densities on individual internal power busing lines. Large output transistors are grouped together and placed on separate V_{SS} and V_{CC} pins. This allows the internal logic circuitry to function correctly in the presence of large current and voltage transients that may be generated by the large output transistors. In addition, no two V_{SS} or V_{CC} pins are internally connected together. Therefore, ground loop

Fig. 7. MEU photomicrograph.

problems or voltage differentials between any two power pins cannot destroy the internal power busing.

Internal distribution of the clock signals was also a challenge. The MEU employs a four-phase clocking scheme (Fig. 8) and thus requires four separate clocks to be internally buffered and distributed throughout the chip. The internal clock buffers must be capable of driving a large capacitive load (in excess of 100 pF) with small buffer delay and clock skew between any of the four phases, even though the capacitive loading on the different phases varies greatly. A sophisticated model of the clock interconnect was made to identify potential *RC* time delay problems due to poor routing of the interconnect or heavy loading of the clock lines. Several design changes (mostly rerouting of signals) were made as a result of this analysis.

Generation of timing signals for controlling access to wide internal data buses also received special attention. Fig. 9 shows a technique for reducing the delay of distributing control signal across a wide logic block through the use of multiple dynamic (clocked) AND gates. The clock lines are distributed at various intervals in parallel with the metal busing, and the actual AND gate is repeated at each instance of a clock line. This scheme shifts the high resistance line from the high capacitance node to a lower capacitance node, thus reducing the time constant of the output node by an order of magnitude (versus using a single dynamic AND gate).

Power dissipation also must be given careful consideration when designing a component that requires large amounts of silicon real estate. Several design tradeoffs were made on the MEU to minimize power and yet maintain good performance. Four-phase clocks are used internally, instead of the more

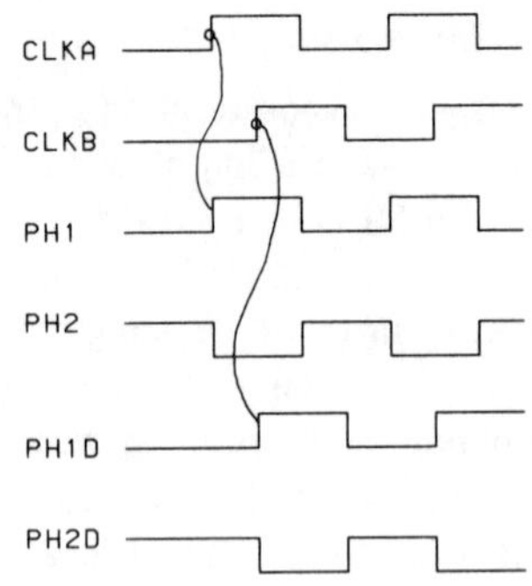

Fig. 8. Clocking scheme.

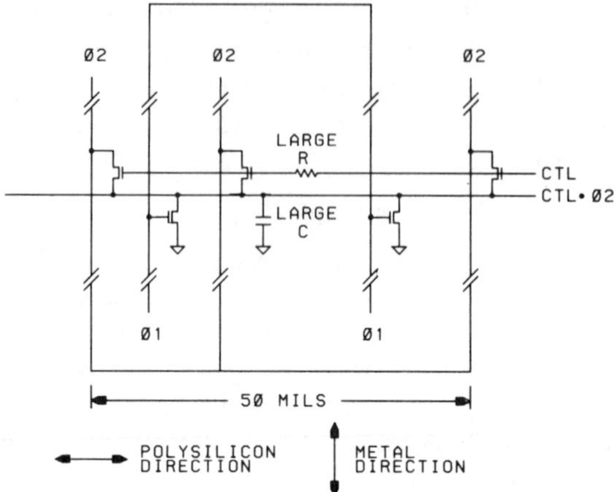

Fig. 9. High performance dynamic AND gate across 50 mils of metal.

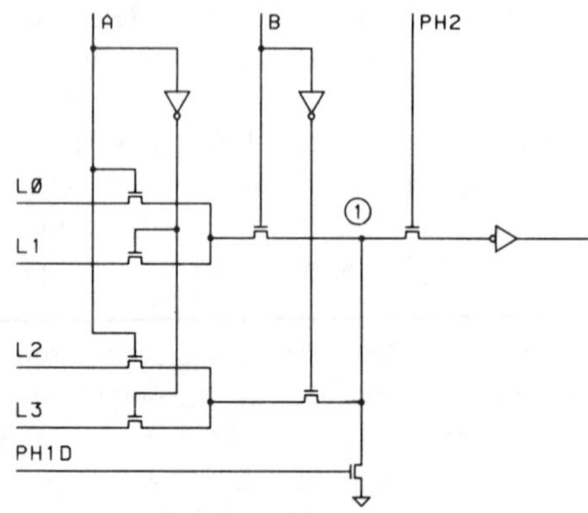

Fig. 10. Boolean function generator.

L3	L2	L1	LØ	FUNCTION
Ø	Ø	Ø	Ø	1
Ø	Ø	Ø	1	-A+-B
Ø	Ø	1	Ø	A+-B
Ø	Ø	1	1	-B
Ø	1	Ø	Ø	-A+B
Ø	1	Ø	1	-A
Ø	1	1	Ø	A• B+-A•-B
Ø	1	1	1	-A•-B
1	Ø	Ø	Ø	A+B
1	Ø	Ø	1	-A•B+A•-B
1	Ø	1	Ø	A
1	Ø	1	1	A•-B
1	1	Ø	Ø	B
1	1	Ø	1	-A•B
1	1	1	Ø	A•B
1	1	1	1	Ø

Fig. 11. Least recently used replacement circuit.

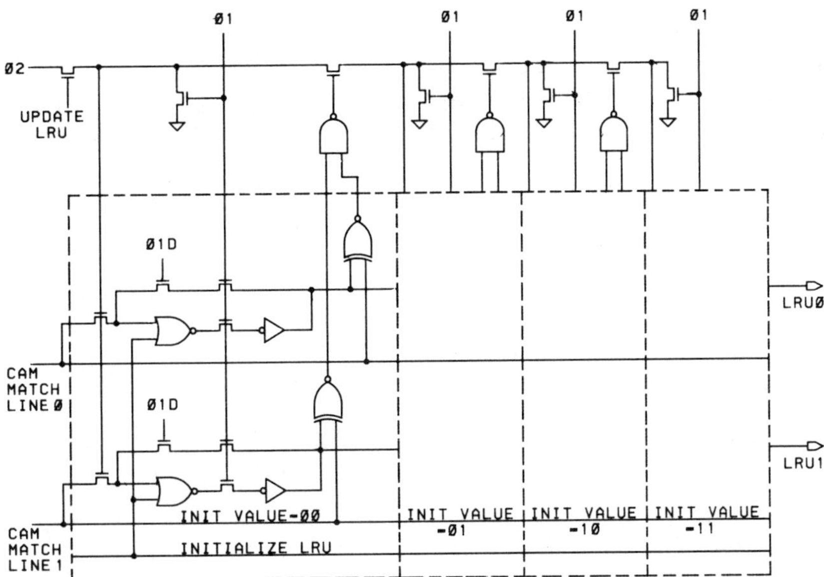

Fig. 12. LRU replacement circuit.

straightforward and traditional MOS two-phase clocking scheme, to allow much of the internal circuitry to be clocked-dynamic logic without sacrificing the speed at which the logic produces a result. In particular, almost all of the control signals on the chip that are sampled or used during the phase 1 clock period are generated from many small dynamic PLA's. Portions of the ALU and the extractor circuit are also dynamic to improve performance and decrease power dissipation.

Novel Circuit Implementations

Although most of the focus must of necessity be given to the design of a VLSI chip at the block or microarchitectural level (for reasons of decomposition of complexity), much energy is focused at the circuits level of design. In the case of the MEU, a Boolean function generator and a circuit associated with address caching logic are described in what follows.

A very compact fast circuit is used to implement the Boolean function generator portion of the ALU (see Fig. 10). This circuit is capable of generating all 16 Boolean functions of two variables. The node labeled 1 in Fig. 10 is first discharged, while the signals $L0 \cdots L3$ are held low. Then $L0 \cdots L3$ are driven, at the same time as PH2 is high, to the appropriate levels to generate the desired Boolean function. Fig. 11 is a table that shows the Boolean functions generated for the various $L0 \cdots L3$ encodings.

The circuitry depicted in Fig. 12 is used to implement a least recently used (LRU) cache replacement algorithm. That is, when a user accesses a previously unaccessed object, the object's base and length information is automatically cached on the MEU by replacing the address information that is associated with the least recently used cache entry. The LRU is a direct circuit realization of the true LRU algorithm. It exemplifies a unique aspect of VLSI design, which is a direct (i.e., nonlogic gate) implementation of a combinatorially complex problem. The LRU circuitry is implemented essentially as a four-entry by 2-bit variable length shift register. Each time a user-defined object is accessed, the UPDATE LRU signal is asserted. As a result, the 2-bit encoding of the address of the cache register that matches the current segment selector is placed into the most recently used slot (the leftmost cell in Fig. 12) of the shift register during PH2. The previous most recently used encoding is not overwritten until PH1; thus, it is used to determine whether or not the next most recently used slot of the shift register should be updated. If the previous most recently used cache is the same as the current most recently used cache, then the LRU shift register does not need to be shifted any more as there has been no change in the time ordering of accesses to the currently valid object address registers; however, if the previous most recently used encoding is not the same as the current match encoding (CAM MATCH LINE 1 and 0), the previous most recently used cache's encoding is shifted into the next slot of the shift register, indicating that this encoding points to the second most recently used data segment register. The third and fourth entries in the LRU shift register work in an identical fashion.

Conclusion

In the past, the design of chips was limited by semiconductor processing and fabrication technology; today the design of VLSI chips is increasingly being driven by the ability of designers to conceive and structure large numbers of transistors into a useful, testable, and very complex set of functions. The design of the MEU highlights some of these design problems that are beginning to be addressed by current chip implementers. These problems include circuit considerations like chip power dissipation and internal wiring RC delays, but also include the problem of being able to decompose an immensely complex design problem into smaller more tractable pieces. We believe that the application of a hierarchical design methodology has become necessary to fully exploit the potential of the rapidly evolving semiconductor technology.

Acknowledgment

Our thanks to the following for their valued contributions: G. W. Cox, D. K. Jackson, K. K. Lai, S. R. Page, J. F. Palmer, J. R. Rattner, C. D. Royce, R. C. Swanson, and J. L. Wipfli.

References

[1] J. A. Bayliss, S. R. Colley, R. H. Kravitz, G. A. McCormick, W. S. Richardson, D. K. Wilde, and L. L. Wittmer, "The instruction decoding unit for the VLSI 432 general data processor," *IEEE J. Solid-State Circuits*, vol. SC-16, pp. 531–537, Oct. 1981.

[2] Intel Corp., *iAPX 432 GDP Architectural Reference Manual*, 1981.

[3] J. A. Bayliss, J. A. Deetz, S. A. Ogilvie, C. B. Peterson, and D. K. Wilde, "The interface processor for the VLSI 432 32b computer," *IEEE J. Solid-State Circuits*, vol. SC-16, pp. 522–530, Oct. 1981.

[4] W. W. Lattin, "VLSI design methodology: The problem of the 80's for microprocessor designs," presented at the 1st Caltech Conf. VLSI, Jan. 1979.

[5] J. A. Bayliss, D. L. Budde, W. W. Lattin, J. R. Rattner, and W. S. Richardson, "A methodology for VLSI chip design," *Lambda*, 1981.

[6] W. W. Lattin and J. R. Rattner, "Ada determines architecture of 32-bit microprocessor," *Electronics*, Feb. 24, 1981.

The Interface Processor for the Intel VLSI 432 32-Bit Computer

JOHN A. BAYLISS, JOHN A. DEETZ, CHUN-KIT NG, SCOTT A. OGILVIE, MEMBER, IEEE, CRAIG B. PETERSON, AND DORAN K. WILDE, MEMBER, IEEE

***Abstract*—The Intel 43203 interface processor is designed to link conventional I/O subsystems and Intel's new 32-bit computer system, the iAPX432. The interface processor is an excellent example of how high density VLSI technology can be combined with innovative circuits to create highly functional systems on a single chip. This paper describes the function of the interface processor and some of the details of its implementation.**

INTRODUCTION

THE 43203 interface processor (IP) serves as a data and control interface between the protected 432 central system and an I/O subsystem. A subsystem processor called the attached processor (AP) provides the intelligence to control all I/O activity in the subsystem and transfers data through the IP between the subsystem and the 432 memory space. The IP acts as a slave to the AP and maps a portion of the AP's address space, called a window, into a segment of the 432 system memory known as an object. The IP operates in conjunction with the AP to logically form a 432 I/O processor. The AP can control the position of a window in its own address space, but the actual location of the object that it maps to in the 432 address space and the access rights to the object are controlled by a process in the 432 operating system. This organization prevents the AP from corrupting the environment of the central 432 computing system.

Internally, the IP is partitioned into two separate and independent functional units, the data acquisition unit (DAU) and the microexecution unit (MEU).

The DAU is responsible for such functions as address mapping from the subsystem to an object in main system memory, data transfer, and access control such as rights checking. It provides up to five windows which access different objects in the 432 main memory, including one that is dedicated as a control window. Datum written to a particular displacement in the control window is interpreted as the deposition of an IP macro-operator opcode. This causes an interrupt to be sent to the second IP functional unit, the MEU.

The MEU is a microprogrammed machine that is used to perform IP initialization, faults and interrupt handling, and execute 432 operators as may be requested by the AP. A few examples of AP requested operations are MOVE WINDOW (to another location in the AP address space), OPEN WINDOW, CLOSE WINDOW, and SEND or RECEIVE MESSAGE. During execution of an operator, the MEU retrieves the operand(s) and opcode from the control object in 432 central system memory, performs the function, and places results and status back into the control object.

Manuscript received May 19, 1981.
The authors are with the Intel Corporation, Aloha, OR 97007.

A TYPICAL FUNCTIONAL SCENARIO

To better understand the relationship of the MEU and the AP, consider the following typical scenario for their interaction. The AP writes through the DAU's control window into the control object requesting the MEU to execute a 432 macro-operator. The request is made by several accesses to the control object whereby the operands and the opcode of the request are deposited. Access to the opcode displacement location in the control object is recognized by logic inside the DAU which causes an interrupt to the MEU.

At this point, the MEU branches to a service routine, reads the opcode and operands from the control object, and services the request. After performing the requested function, the MEU will post status in the control object and interrupt the AP. At this time, the AP may make additional read accesses to the control object to determine the results of the request. Satisfied that the desired function was performed successfully, the AP software may proceed to issue further requests for service.

43203 GENERAL INTERNAL PHYSICAL DESCRIPTION

Four unique circuits in the 43203 will be described here. Two are located in the DAU, a static address mapping content addressable memory (CAM) and a byte packing buffer. The last two are located in the MEU, an interrupt handling structure, and a 2K by 16-bit 2-bit-per-cell ROM. First we will look at the general structure of the chip.

The 43203 chip block diagram in Fig. 1 shows all of the major data structures and buses on the 43203 and their relationships to each other. It is drawn in the approximate arrangement of the actual chip layout.

The chip photograph in Fig. 2 points out the major blocks on the chip. The most notable blocks are briefly described in the figure.

DAU OPERATION

The purpose of the DAU is to provide the ability for an AP to access a number of objects inside the 432 main memory. In addition, in the case of transferring large files or blocks of data, the DAU needs some provision for accommodating high-speed block transfers.

Reprinted from *IEEE J. Solid-State Circuits*, vol. SC-16, pp. 522–529, Oct. 1981.

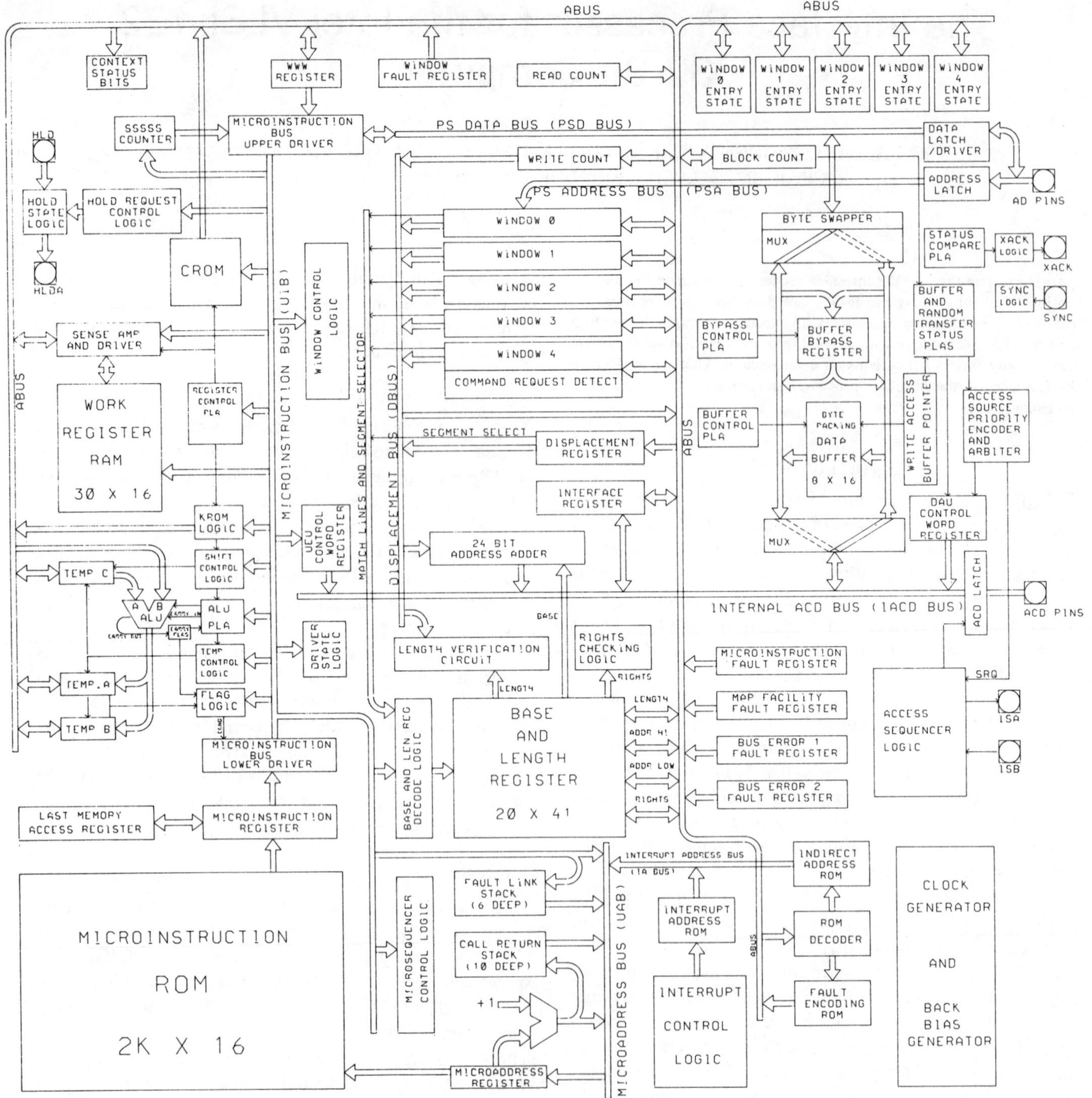

Fig. 1. 43203 block diagram.

Preliminary evaluations of the DAU requirements proved that the major design goals of the DAU should be to maximize data transfer rate while minimizing chip area. The compromise of these two normally conflicting goals was determined after architectural simulations showed that four windows would provide an AP with access to enough objects in 432 main memory to avoid excessive reallocation of windows by the AP. A fifth window was added for control and status purposes. Limiting the quantity of windows also helped contain the die size problem.

Additional performance study helped define the microarchitecture of the two functional units which compose the DAU. These are the address mapping section and the data transfer section.

Address Mapper

To perform its function, the address mapping section takes the AP address displacement into the subsystem window and adds it to the base address of the associated object in the 432 system. This produces the system physical address. Functionally, the address mapping section uses a CAM to detect if a subsystem address falls within one of the five windows. The

Fig. 2. Intel 43203 chip photograph. The work register RAM is used by the MEU as working registers for storage of temporary results and values while executing microcode. The microcode ROM contains the microprogram executed by the MEU. It is 2K by 16-bits and is implemented with analog 2-bit-per-cell structures. The interrupt control structure organizes interrupts which are sent to the MEU. The mapping CAM is used by the DAU to recognized AP accesses to windows and determine the offset from the base of the window. The base and length register block contains the base address of all the objects in 432 memory that are accessed by the windows and other special objects used by the MEU such as objects that contain the current processor object or process object. The byte packing data buffer is a special mechanism which can be associated with one window to provide high-speed block transfer operation.

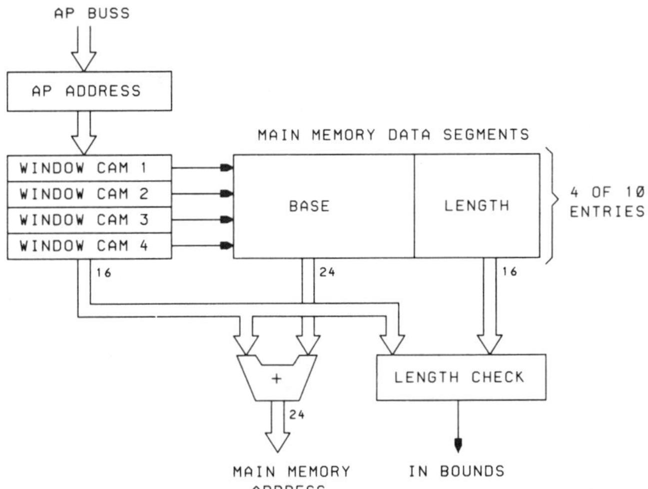

Fig. 3. Window address mapping.

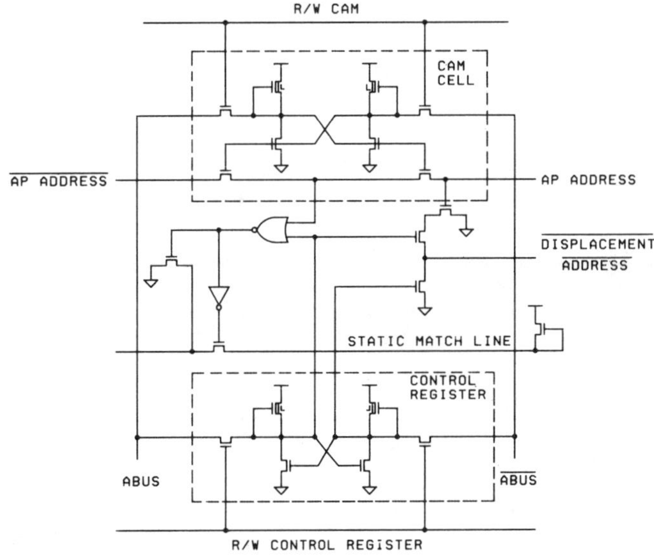

Fig. 4. Circuit diagram of the address mappers CAM cell and control registers.

subsystem address gets split into an upper and lower portion as defined by a mask register in the CAM. The upper portion of the subsystem address is used for a match compare to a base register in the CAM, while the lower portion is used, if a match occurs, as a displacement to be added to the base address of the corresponding 432 object. The particular object base address is selected by a match line which is derived from the CAM. This is illustrated in Fig. 3.

The CAM was the biggest challenge in the design of the address mapping section of the DAU. Analysis showed the AP address comparison function to be the performance-limiting function in the address mapping section. The CAM itself has to perform an address match comparison across a maximum of 16 bits in less than 35 ns and cause the return of an acknowledge back to the AP (if a match occurred and if other buffer full/empty status information is valid). In order to minimize this delay, a special CAM design was created. It allows the AP address to propagate through the CAM and status logic and return an acknowledge to the subsystem totally unclocked. The acknowledge is therefore purely a result of the propagation delay through the nonclocked CAM and some static circuits.

Fig. 4 shows the CAM cell, its static match line, and the accompanying mask and base control registers. There is one 16-bit word of these cells for each of the five windows in the 43203. After detection of an AP address match, the CAM is brought into synchronization with the rest of the chip by the external SYNC signal, the main system address calculation is performed, and the data access is completed.

Byte Packing Data Buffer

The data transfer section of the DAU is a sophisticated interface between the AP and the 432 system. Its most significant functional element is a byte packing data buffer that can be called into action in connection with the first window. It satisfies the design goal of accommodating high-speed block transfers.

The primary requirement of the data buffer was high data transfer speed. This resulted in the data buffers' designed-in property to prefetch data from 432 memory when in read mode, and to postwrite data to 432 memory when in write mode. When it prefetches or postwrites, it does so by normally

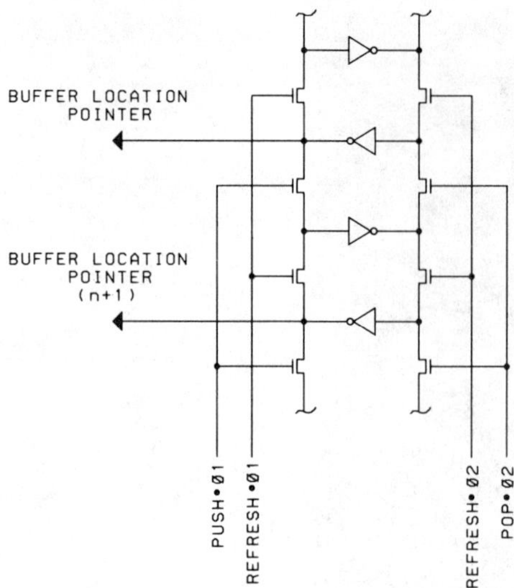

Fig. 5. Two stack pointer cells.

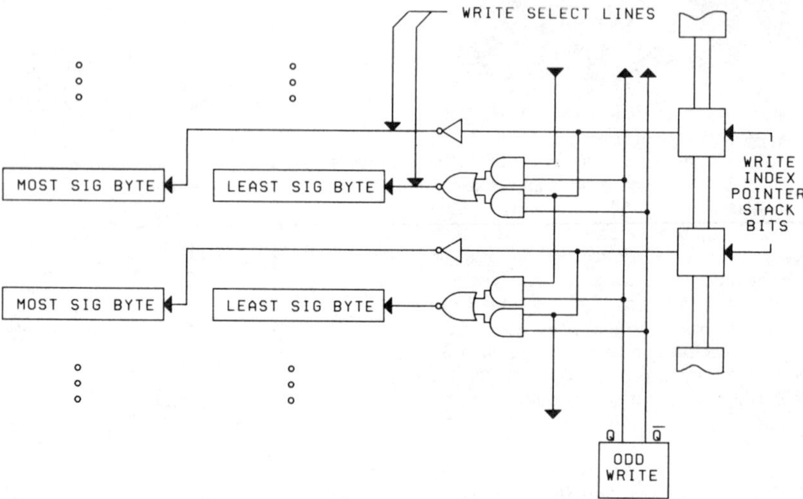

Fig. 6. General data buffer structure.

requesting or transferring 8 byte data packets. This implementation allows the AP access time to be greatly reduced since the AP only waits for the access time from the IP's internal data buffer instead of waiting for the IP to access memory.

Secondary requirements were for the data buffer to handle accesses from a wide variety of different type of AP's, such as 8- and 16-bit microcomputers. Such AP's may issue access requests of 8 or 16 bits of data at a time. Requests for 8 bits may be issued on the upper or lower data byte of a 16-bit bus. In addition, access types may even be mixed, with 8- and 16-bit requests during a single block transfer.

The data buffer has to accept these requests and be able to pack the data into fully filled right-justified packets of data when in the write mode. In the read mode, the buffer has to unpack right-justified packets that it received from the 432 memory and pass the data to the AP in the right order and requested format.

These requirements resulted in designing the buffer to be 8 words of 16 bits each. The buffer is read from one end like a 16-bit-wide shift register. Write data are selectively written into the buffer at a location specified by a 9-bit-deep by 1-bit-wide stack. The 1-bit-wide stack was used to implement the write index pointer since its physical size was small and it provided direct status on the fullness of the buffer. An additional status flip-flop, called oddwrite, indicates if the last written location is half full since the AP may write only one byte at a time. Figs. 5 and 6 show the general structure of the pointer stack and the oddwrite flip-flop relative to the buffer. Fig. 7 shows the structure of a data buffer bit cell.

The data path in nonbuffered windows uses the buffer bypass register for temporary storage. This register's inputs and outputs are connected to both the input bus and the output bus since the nonbuffered windows can make either read or write accesses independent of the direction of the buffered window. Fig. 8 shows how the bypass register and data buffer were nested together between an input and output bus. The byte swapper shown in the figure aids in packing and unpacking the data.

The buffer write index pointer stack (1-bit-wide stack) contains a "1" in a field of "0's" which points to the first 16-bit-word in the data buffer with an empty byte. The pointer stack

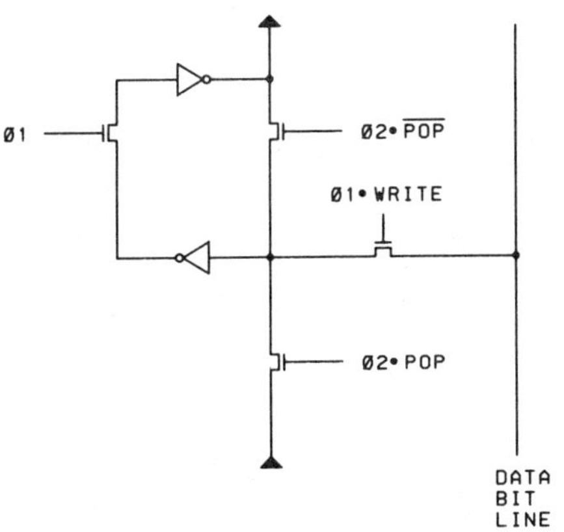

Fig. 7. Data buffer bit cell.

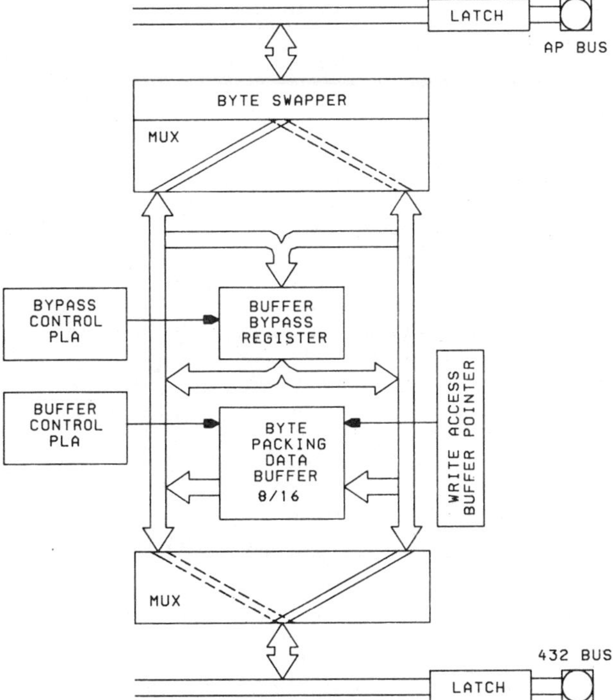

Fig. 8. Data path structure.

has zero fill on top and bottom so push and pop operations on the stack serve to move the pointer up and down. The oddwrite status flip-flop denotes whether the 16-bit word is completely empty (oddwrite = 0) or if only the MS byte (most significant byte) is empty (oddwrite = 1). Whenever a register is completely filled, the stack is pushed, and whenever both bytes in a register are read, the FIFO and the stack are popped.

When writing, the input data are packed in a right-justified format automatically by the data buffers. For example, if the input-byte-quantity input indicates one byte transfers, the first byte will be placed in the LS byte (least significant byte) of the first register and the next byte will be placed in the MS byte of the first register. The second location to be filled would be the LS byte of the next register, etc. When reading, the first byte accessed will be the LS byte, then the MS byte, then the LS byte of the next register, etc.

As noted before, data are read out of the buffer from one end. There is, however, a special condition which is monitored by a second status flip-flop called oddread. If a single byte read is performed to the buffer, a "hole" develops in the LS byte of the first word. This is because the buffer cannot be popped while there is still a second byte contained in that location. This condition sets the oddread flip-flop to a "1." Now, if a second read access is performed to the buffer requesting one byte, the buffer is popped and the oddread flip-flop is reset. If the second read access is a double byte, the MS byte of the first register is output and the LS byte of the second register is output. The bytes are then swapped by the byte swapper to restore the order of the data. The buffer is then popped and the oddread flip-flop remains set.

The stack, oddwrite, and oddread flip-flops provide all of the status information for determining the fullness of the buffer.

MEU Operation

The MEU is a microprogrammed machine that is used to perform IP initialization, faults and interrupt handling, and execute 432 operators as may be requested by the AP. The MEU includes an interrupt controller, an address sequencer, a 2K by 16-bit microcode ROM, a microinstruction bus and decoder, a 16-bit ALU, and all of the internal working registers. All microinstruction routines are initiated by the interrupt controller. The MEU idles in an infinite microinstruction wait loop while waiting for prompts from the interrupt controller. When the interrupt controller receives an interrupt request, it prioritizes it and initiates a microinstruction service routine. A microaddress sequencer provides for sequential execution, absolute branches, subroutine calls, and returns up to ten levels of nesting. The microinstruction ROM receives its address from this sequencer and outputs microinstructions onto the microinstruction bus. This bus runs vertically through most of the length of the chip. In order to minimize the amount of interconnect, control signals are decoded locally in the areas where they are used. This distributed control methodology proved to be very worthwhile. There are 32 16-bit registers which are available to the microcode for storing internal status and for using as a scratch pad. Register to register 16-bit operations such as ADD, SUBTRACT, INCREMENT, DECREMENT, ROTATE, AND, OR, INVERT, and XOR are all provided for in the ALU.

The MEU was pipelined to a high degree to make it possible to execute a new microinstruction each machine cycle. Up to five microinstructions can be in various stages of completion at one time. These five stages make up the basic internal pipeline of the MEU as listed below.

- Interrupt request and interrupt grant. Microaddress computed.
- Microcode ROM accessed.
- Microinstruction decoded. Operands accessed. 432 interface signals are sampled.
- Data movements and ALU operations performed.
- 432 interface signals are driven.

The Interrupt Controller

The parallelism of the IP makes it possible for many separate activities to make demands on the microinstruction unit. Often the MEU must resolve contention in order to provide services

CLEAR PROCESSOR
(CLRPU PIN)
BUS ERROR DETECTED
(ON THE ACD BUS)
PROCESS CLOCK TIC
(PCLK PIN)
432 ADDRESS DEVELOPMENT FAULT

FLAG TEST FAULT
(MICROCODE INTERNAL FLAG TEST)
OBJECT ALTERED FAULT
(OCCURS FIRST TIME AN OBJECT IS WRITTEN INTO)
MAPPING FAULT
(AN ERROR DETECTED DURING AP ADDRESS MAPPING OPERATION)
ALARM INTERRUPT
(ALARM PIN)
COMMAND INTERRUPT
(WHEN THE AP REQUESTS THAT A 432 OPERATOR BE PREFORMED)
INITIALIZATION INTERRUPT
(INIT PIN)
INTERPROCESSOR COMMUNICATION INTERRUPT
(WHEN AN IPC IS SIGNALED ON THE ACD BUS)

Fig. 9. MEU interrupts.

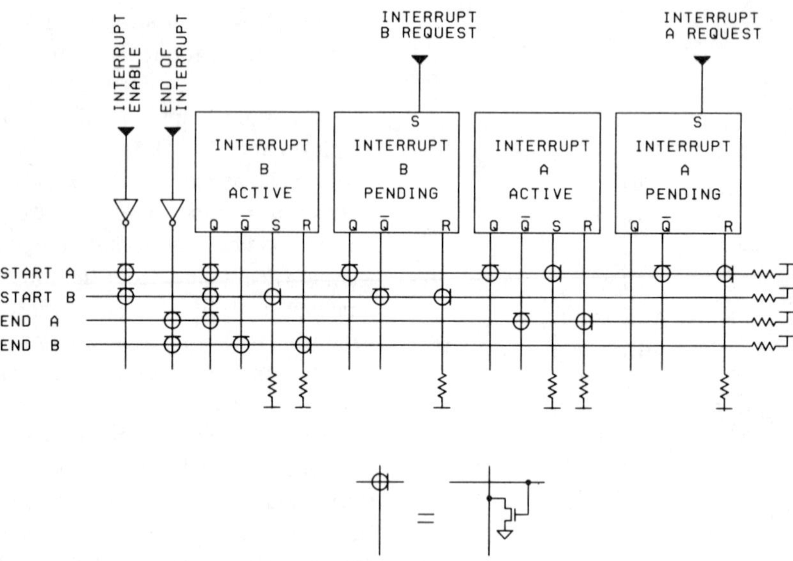

Fig. 10. The MEU interrupt control structure.

to all of these different sources. Requests for microinstruction flows are made by having the circuit that needs the service make an interrupt request. The MEU is totally interrupt driven and only executes a microcode flow in response to an interrupt made by some other circuit on the chip. Eleven such interrupts are handled (see Fig. 9).

To resolve contention for use of the MEU, it was necessary to design a controller to service requests for microcode flows in a priority type of arrangement and to design it so that it would implement well into silicon. A similar problem had been experienced on the 43201. The solution for the 43201 required a large amount of random logic and was difficult to lay out. On the 43203, a goal was to simplify the layout by making the design more regular than on previous chips.

After considering other alternatives, it was decided to implement the interrupt control logic in a regular structure called a storage logic array (SLA [4]). The SLA had the advantage that it was able to implement the interrupt controller design easily and there was no need for any external interconnect or additional random logic. Refer to Fig. 10 for a diagram of a sample circuit illustrating an interrupt controller for two interrupts and how the SLA was used to solve the interrupt controller problem.

There were two major objectives in the logic design of the controller. First, in case there was contention for use of the MEU, the interrupts had to be started in the correct order according to the their assigned priority. Second, once an interrupt had been started and was in execution, that service routine could not be interrupted by other interrupts of lesser priority. To acheive these requirements, two flags are associated with each interrupt: the pending and active flags. The pending flag indicates that an interrupt has been requested, but not serviced, and the active flag indicates that the interrupt has been serviced, but that the microcode service routine is not yet completed. Requests for interrupts come from all over the chip and are latched by the interrupt controller in the respective interrupt pending flags. A pending interrupt is started if it is of higher priority than the presently executing active interrupt. When an interrupt is started, the pending flag for that interrupt is reset and its active flag is set. Microcode then branches to the appropriate starting address in the microinstruction ROM and the interrupt service routine starts execution.

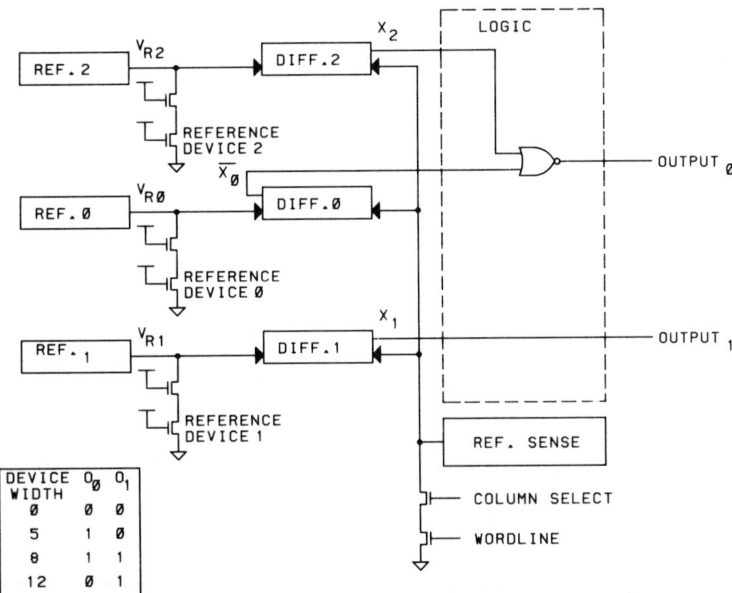

Fig. 11. ROM output section.

The MEU Microinstruction ROM

The microinstruction ROM on the IP is a 32-kbit ROM organized as 2K words by 16 bits. The important design goals were small area and a 100 ns cycle time. For the area goal, storing two bits per cell, using circuits similar to the ROM design of the i8087(1), requires the use of a static sense amplifier circuit. However, only approximately half of the area of a conventional ROM array was required. To meet the speed goal without using excessive power, the decoder circuits use dynamic design techniques.

The basic principle of the 2-bit-per-cell ROM is the use of multiple sized gates in the array to represent more than two states of information. For this design, four array device sizes were used to represent the data for two bits, but occupying only one physical location. The same principle can be used for even higher storage densities. The block diagram of the sense circuit shown in Fig. 11 contains three comparators and the logic necessary to determine the states encoded in the array device. The selected array device is part of a voltage divider circuit that creates a voltage that is proportionate to the array device size. Three reference voltage values are created using divider circuits similar to the circuit used on the column output. These voltage values divide the voltage range into four regions. Each region represents one of the states of the 2 bits of information encoded in the array device size. To determine the value of the array device, the column output is used as a common input into the three comparators. Each of these comparators uses one of the reference voltages as the other input. The output of these comparators is then decoded into the two output bits. Shown in Fig. 11 is the assignment of the device sizes to the output states. This assignment could be arbitrary, but this particular encoding was used to minimize the logic needed to determine the output state.

The voltage differences at the inputs to the comparator can be as little as 200 mV. This small difference is converted into normal logic levels by using a two-stage amplifier (Fig. 12). The first stage is a differential amplifier, and the second stage is a latch. The differential amplifier is a good high gain comparator, but the output from this stage is not a normal logic level. The second stage of the comparator adds gain and corrects the logic levels from the differential amplifier.

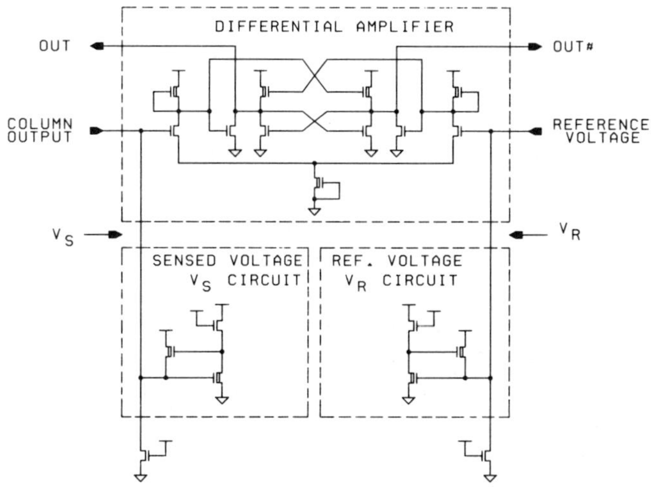

Fig. 12. Output circuits.

The circuit used for the X-decoder had to be small enough to fit in the pitch of the array cell and should use the least amount of time possible to select the word line. The two-stage dynamic decoder circuit shown in Fig. 13 is used to meet these requirements. The first stage uses a single clock (PHX) that is decoded into two subclocks by using the least significant bit of the X-address. This allows the second stage to share the common portion of the address so that it can be drawn in the pitch of two cells. To minimize the RC delay, the second stage is located in the center of the array. The Y-decoder is a conventional dynamic decoder and drives a 1-of-16 multiplexer which selects the columns.

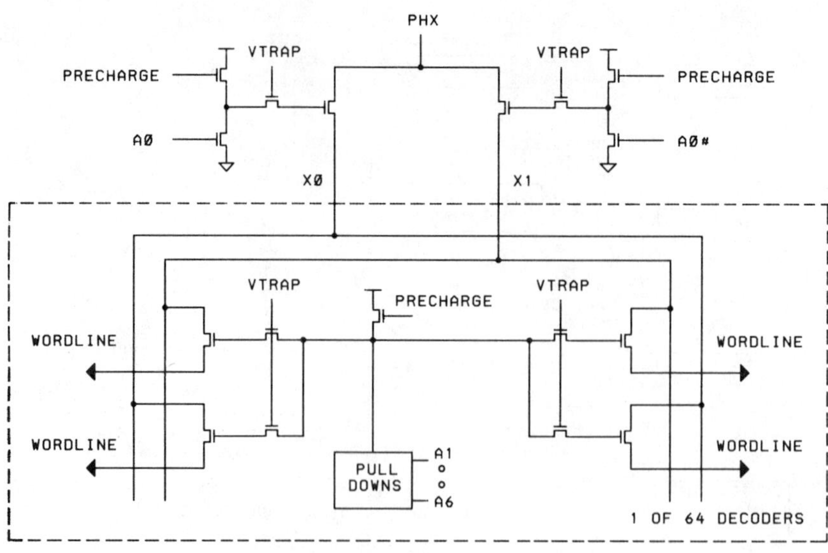

Fig. 13. *X*-decoder.

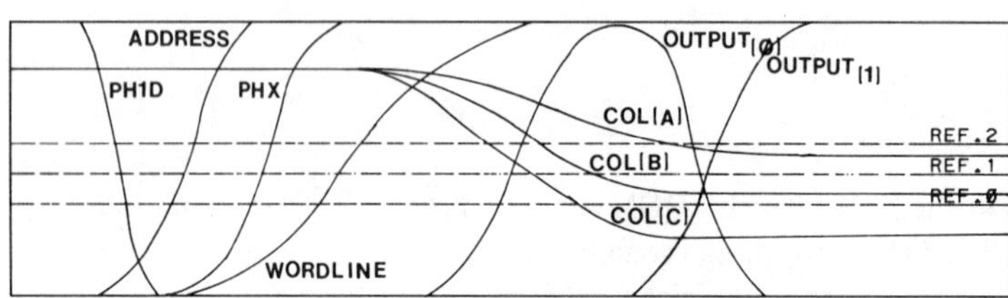

Fig. 14. ROM waveform.

Fig. 14 shows the voltage waveforms for a typical access cycle. The access cycle begins as the decoders are precharged and the address is sent from the microaddress register. On the falling edge of PH1D, the address is driven and the decoders are discharged. PHX is then used to drive the word and column lines selected. The clock signal PHX is designed so that the delay from PH1D to PHX precisely matches the discharge of the *X*-decoder. Special care was taken to ensure that this signal delay tracked the decoder discharge over a wide range of conditions. After the word and columns have been selected for the second half of the cycle, the sensing of 2 bits from each selected column begins. The columns are not precharged, and must move from their past state to the level determined by the array device size. Once this level is reached, the comparators will settle and the output is latched in the microinstruction bus driver circuit before the beginning of the next cycle.

Conclusion

During the design of the IP, much consideration was given to implementing logical functions in regular structures. This is becoming a necessity as chips are becoming more complex. Eventually, as chip complexity increases, nearly all of a chip's design time will be spent in defining the functions of the chip. As more is learned about implementation in regular structures, much of the lower level design could be automated. This will free the engineer to concentrate on higher level definition and evaluation. Below are some interesting numbers for the 43203.

Total possible device placements:	62 000
Total actual devices:	51 000
Estimated number of devices drawn/entered:	6300
Regularization factor (actual/drawn):	8.1
Programmable devices	
Microinstruction ROM	
Number possible device placements:	16 384
All other programmable arrays	
Number possible device placements:	8270
Total die area (mils):	326 X 358

Acknowledgment

Our thanks to the following for their technical contributions: G. W. Cox, D. L. Davis, B. Forbes, D. K. Jackson, K. K. Lai, J. R. Rattner, and D. N. Smith. And thanks, also, to M. A. McQueen for providing the illustrations.

References

[1] J. A. Bayliss, S. R. Colley, R. H. Kravitz, G. A. McCormick, W. S. Richardson, D. K. Wilde, and L. L. Wittmer, "The instruction decoding unit for the VLSI 432 general data processor," this issue, pp. 531-537.

[2] D. L. Budde, S. R. Colley, S. L. Domenik, A. L. Goodman, J. D. Howard, and M. T. Imel, "The execution unit for the 432 general data processor," this issue, pp. 514-521.

[3] R. Nave and J. F. Palmer, "A numeric processor," in *ISSCC Dig. Tech. Papers*, Feb. 1980, pp. 108-109.

[4] S. S. Patil and T. A. Welch, "A programmable logic approach for VLSI," *IEEE Trans. Comput.*, vol. C-28, pp. 594-617, Sept. 1979.

[5] W. W. Lattin, "VLSI design methodology: The problem of the 80's for microprocessor design," in *Proc. 1st Caltech Conf. VLSI*, vol. 1, 1980, pp. 247-252.

A 32-Bit Microprocessor with Virtual Memory Support

ASHER KAMINKER, LESLIE KOHN, YOAV LAVI, AVRAHAM MENACHEM, AND ZVI SOHA

Abstract—**A 32-bit microprocessor which supports demand paged virtual memory is described. The processor is implemented on a 290 mil^2 chip containing approximately 60K transistors with a 3.5 μm gate NMOS technology. The effect of software architecture and performance requirements on chip design is discussed, with particular emphasis on the special problems of supporting virtual memory. The methodology used to develop and verify the design is also discussed.**

I. Introduction

THE CPU[1] is the first of a family of 16/32-bit microprocessor components. To support large software systems, the CPU provides a 16 Mbyte uniform address space, virtual memory capability, and a 32-bit instruction set which is designed to be efficient for programs compiled from high level languages. The instruction set implemented by the CPU contains 82 instructions supporting operations on 8-, 16-, and 32-bit integers, strings, packed decimal, bits, bitfields, arrays, and high-level program control constructs. The instruction set may be extended in a software-transparent fashion through the use of slave processor chips. One such slave processor is a memory management unit (MMU)[2] which implements a demand-paged virtual memory system. Another slave processor chip implements 32- and 64-bit floating point arithmetic compatible with the proposed IEEE binary floating point standard. This three-chip set implements a software architecture comparable in sophistication to a high-end 32-bit minicomputer[3] with about half the performance and about two orders of magnitude lower in price.

II. Software Architecture

The CPU contains eight 32-bit general registers and seven 32-bit special purpose registers that are visible to the programmer (Fig. 1). To eliminate register allocation bottlenecks, the instruction set is symmetric with respect to memory and general register references. Every basic instruction allows any addressing mode to be used for any operand, so that memory locations may be used as accumulators or pointers. Instructions are also symmetric with respect to operand length. Any operation which works on 8-bit integers works on 16- or 32-bit integers and vice versa.

Manuscript received April 1, 1981; revised May 23, 1981.

The authors are with National Semiconductor Corporation, Santa Clara, CA 95051.

[1]NS16032

[2]NS16082.

[3]VAX 11/780.

General Registers

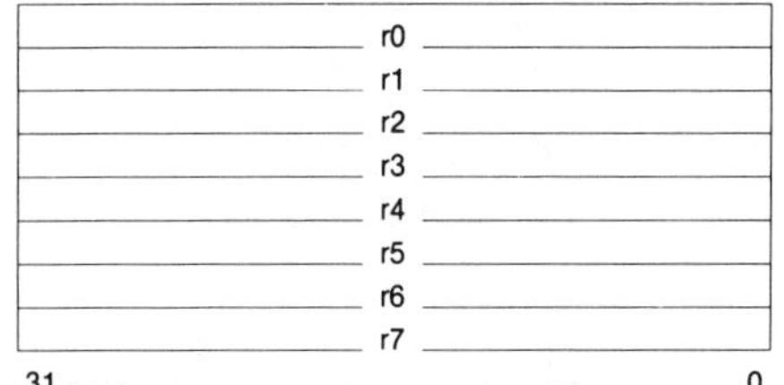

Floating Point Registers

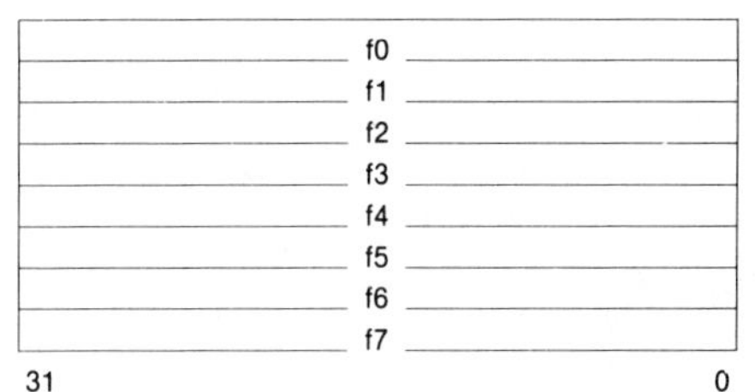

Special Purpose Registers

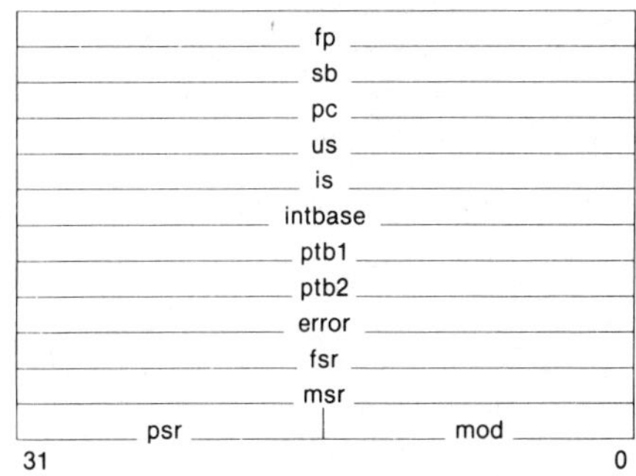

Fig. 1. Register set.

The CPU provides nine types of address modes (Fig. 2), which are chosen to directly support typical variable references of high-level language programs. Autoindexing address modes, which are not easily generated by compilers and cause virtual memory implementation problems, are not included. Address mode offset constants are frequency encoded so that small values (−64 to 63) take only one byte in the instruction stream, medium values (−8192 to 8191) take two bytes, and large values take 4 bytes (Fig. 3). By encoding the length in the upper two bits of the offset, any offset length may be used by any address mode without unduly increasing the size of the basic address mode field (five bits).

Instructions are aligned on 8-bit rather than 16- or 32-bit

Reprinted from *IEEE J. Solid-State Circuits*, vol. SC-16, pp. 548–557, Oct. 1981.

Number	Syntax	Name
0–7	r0 or f0	register
8–15	disp(r0)	register relative
16	disp(disp(fp))	frame memory relative
17	disp(disp(sp))	stack memory relative
18	disp(disp(sb))	static memory relative
19		reserved for future
20	value	immediate
21	disp	absolute
22	ext(disp)	external
23	tos	top of stack
24	disp(fp)	frame memory
25	disp(sp)	stack memory
26	disp(sb)	static memory
27	disp(pc)	program memory
28	mode[r0:b]	index byte
29	mode[r0:w]	index word
30	mode[r0:d]	index double
31	mode[r0:q]	index quad

Fig. 2. Addressing modes.

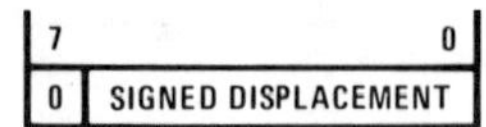

Byte Displacement: Range −64 to +63

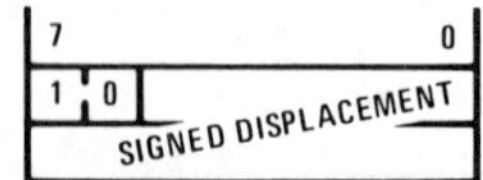

Word Displacement: Range −8192 to +8191

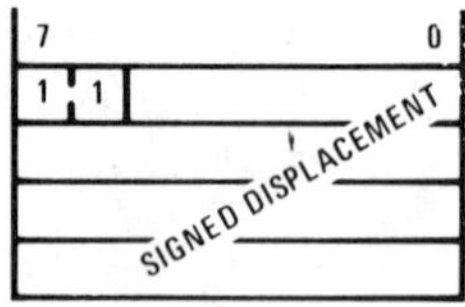

Double Word Displacement: Range (entire addressing space)

Fig. 3. Displacement constant encodings.

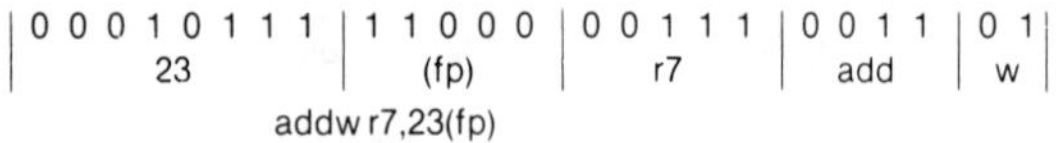

Fig. 4. Sample instruction encoding.

boundaries for code compactness, and they too are frequency encoded. Common zero-operand instructions (such as branches) have a one-byte opcode. Uncommon zero and common one- and two-operand instructions use a two-byte basic instruction. This provides for a large instruction set and a wide range of data types without sacrificing address mode or operand length symmetry. A sample of instruction encoding is shown in Fig. 4.

III. System Considerations

The CPU is packaged in a 48-pin package for cost and circuit board area considerations. This requires a multiplexed external bus of 24-bit address and 16-bit data, although internally all data paths and address calculations are 32 bits wide. As shown in Fig. 5(a), the CPU completes a memory cycle in four clock periods, which is 400 ns with a 10 MHz clock.

During definition of the architecture it became apparent that it was not practical to incorporate all the desired facilities on a single chip with available technology. Rather than compromise the architecture, a slave processor concept was developed. This concept allows advanced optional functions to be implemented in auxiliary chips in a manner which is transparent to software. As the technology improves, these functions can at some point be integrated onto a single chip with the software investment protected. When a program attempts to execute a slave instruction for a slave which is not present in the system, the CPU will trap to a software routine. The software routine can emulate the slave functions in a compatible lower cost, lower performance system.

When the CPU decodes an instruction for a slave that is present in the system, it broadcasts the instruction to all slaves using the slave processor control (SPC) pin and a special two-clock bus cycle shown in Fig. 6. The appropriate slave will recognize the instruction and enable itself for further bus transfers. The CPU then transfers any data operands not resident in the slave with the same two-clock bus cycle and waits for the slave to finish the instruction. When the slave finishes, it signals the CPU on the bidirectional SPC pin. The CPU then reads the slave's completion status and any results using the slave bus cycle. Because the CPU performs all address calculations and memory accesses, the slave chip can be fully devoted to the specialized functions it implements. The CPU provides instructions for user-defined slaves, so that specialized user functions can be implemented with the high-speed slave protocol.

When the CPU is used with the memory management unit, the addresses outputted by the CPU are translated by the MMU into physical addresses used by the rest of the system (Fig. 7). The CPU provides four system features to support the MMU. First, an extra clock cycle is added to the memory cycle to allow the MMU to place the translated address on the bus [Fig. 5(b)]. This allows the bus timing for the rest of the system to be the same as for a system without the MMU. Second, the CPU provides a "float" input pin which suspends the current bus cycle and floats the CPU off the bus. This allows the MMU to access memory tables when an address translation cache miss occurs. Third, a memory cycle abort pin on the CPU will cancel the current memory cycle and instruction and force a trap to a software routine. The instruction is cancelled in a way that allows it to be reexecuted at a later time. The abort pin is used by the MMU to signal that the virtual address does not currently map to physical memory in the system. Fourth, MMU slave instructions allow the operating system software to control the MMU using the slave mechanism described above.

IV. Internal Architecture

The CPU internal architecture is shown in Fig. 8. The order of the following subsections roughly parallels the chronological evolution of the design.

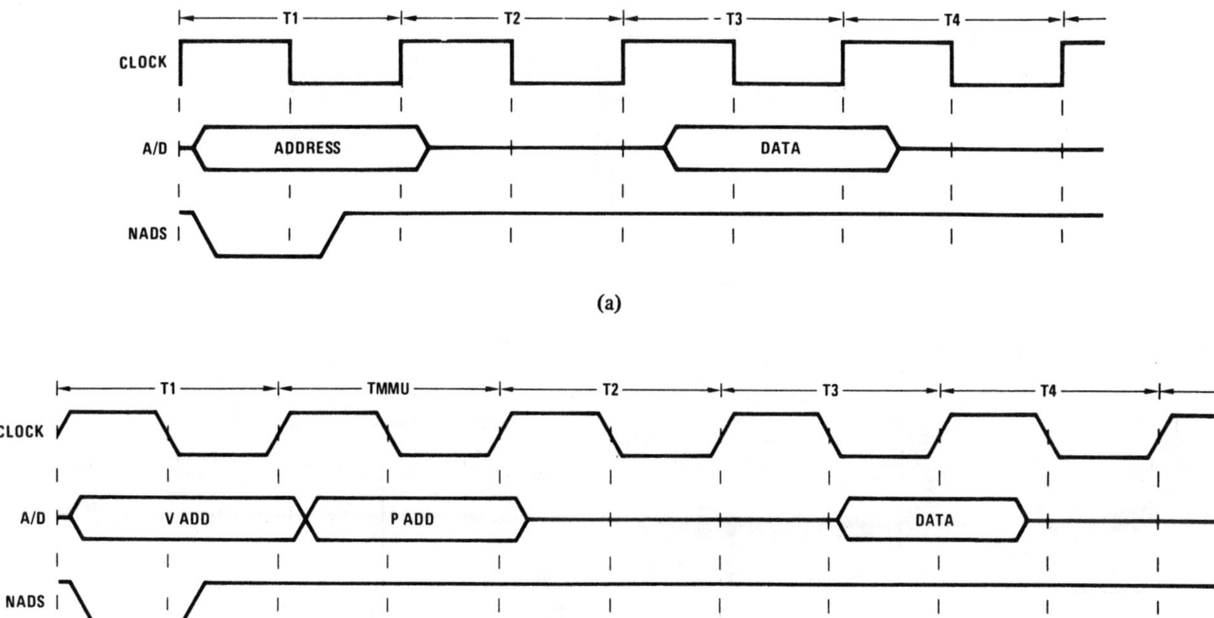

Fig. 5. (a) Memory cycle without address translation. (b) Memory cycle with address translation. (c) PHI1, A/D 9, NADS, and NWR with a "1" being written out to data bit 9.

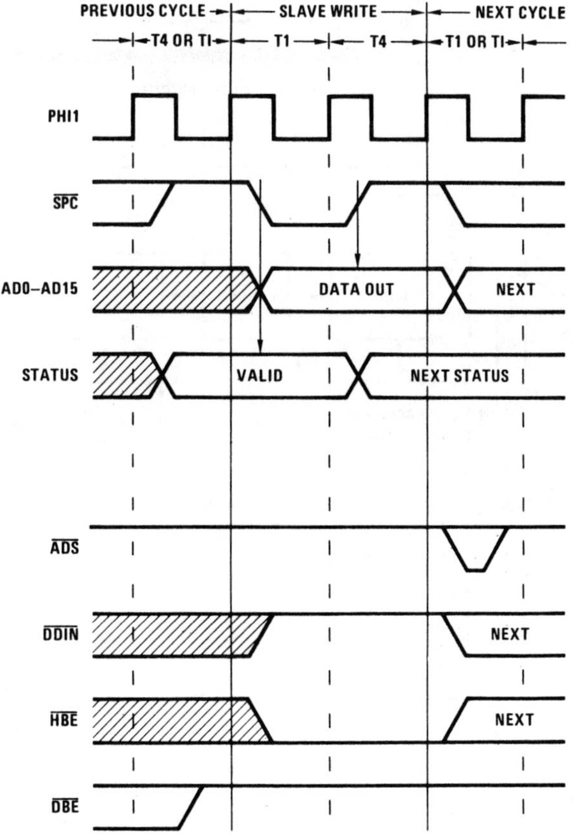

Fig. 6. Write slave processor timing.

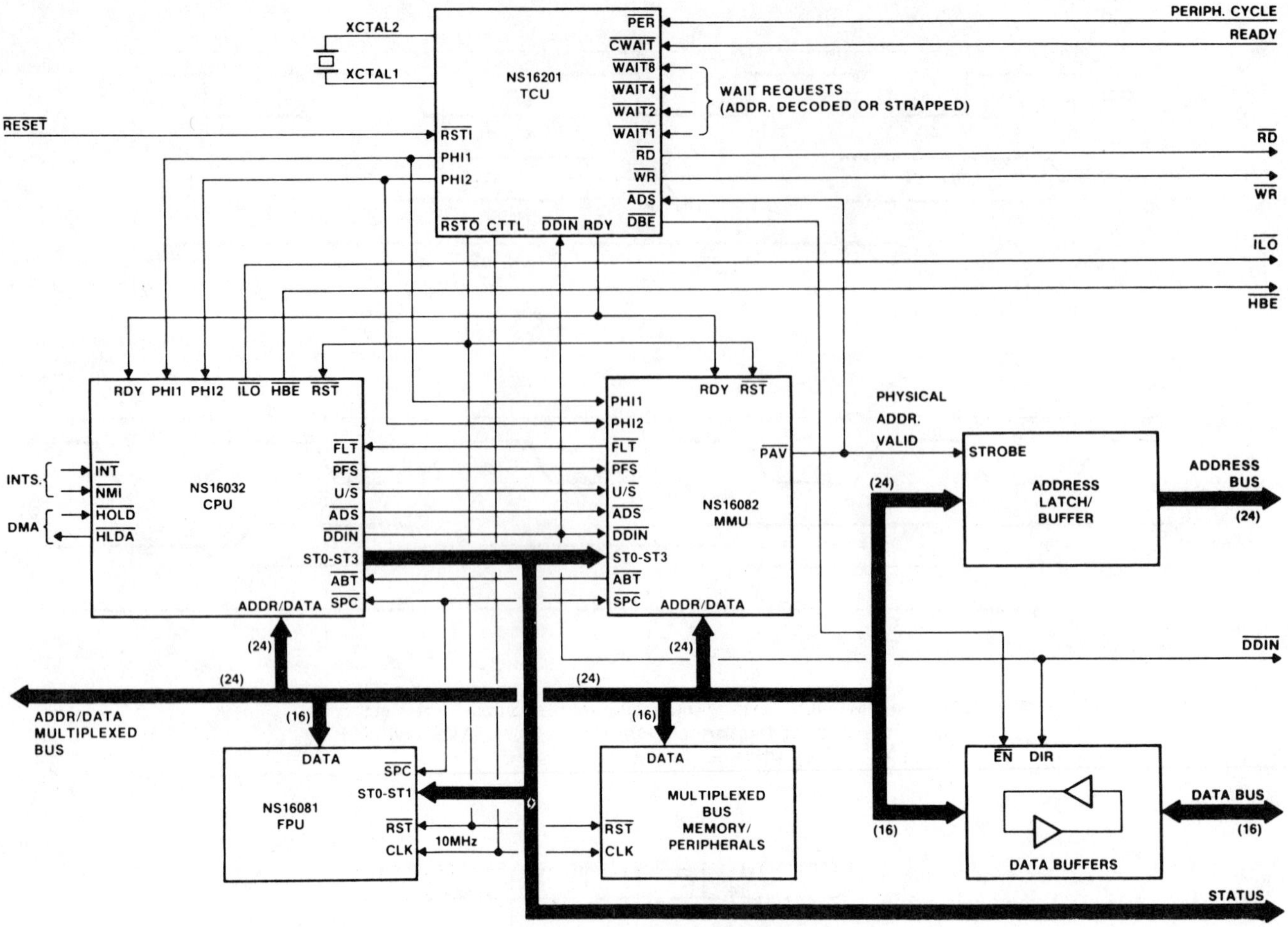

Fig. 7. System connection diagram.

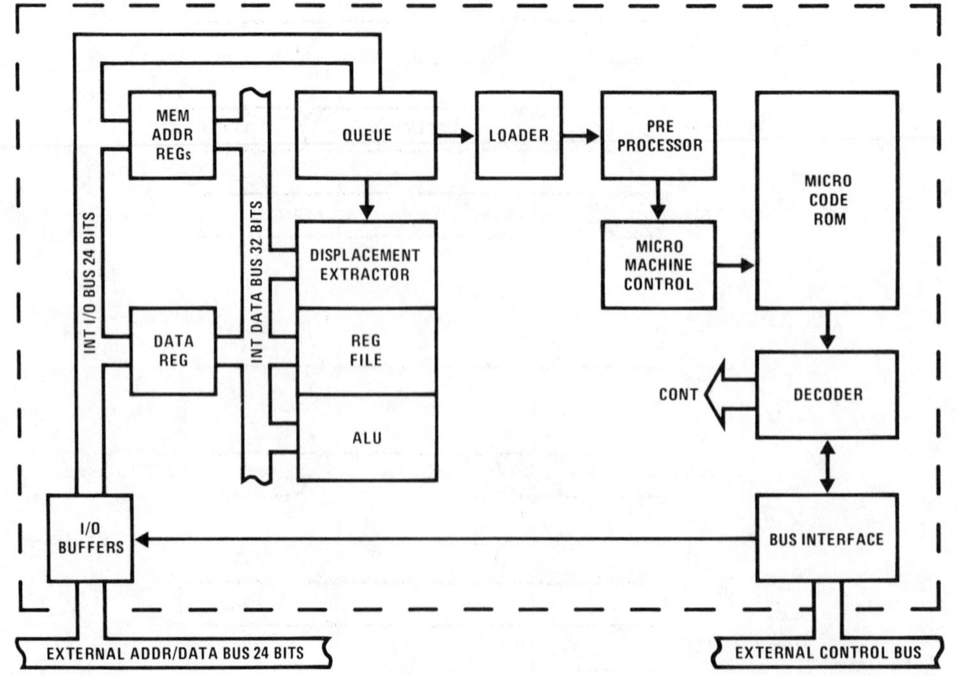

Fig. 8. CPU block diagram.

Selecting Machine Cycle Time

Selection of the machine cycle time is a functional design decision which determines to a large extent the internal architecture and performance of the CPU. To determine the cycle time, the basic internal functions were simulated to estimate their expected timing in the available technology. The main design criteria are: the fastest and most common functions should be performed in one machine cycle with more complicated functions taking more cycles; internal pipelining should be implemented to achieve throughput of one microinstruction per cycle; and the internal processing rate should be balanced with the external bus bandwidth.

Chip area constraints dictate the use of a single internal data path through the register file. In this case, the most common operation is data transfer over the internal data bus. This bus is used in about 90 percent of the machine's internal cycles. Simulations indicated that a 100 ns cycle time could be used for one data transfer over the bus. To complement this data transfer time, considerable effort was devoted to developing special ROM sensing circuitry to achieve microcode ROM access that is compatible with the 100 ns cycle time. This eliminates the space-consuming design complications involved with slow ROM access. A slow ROM would require reading several successive microwords at a time and multiplexing them into the microinstruction register at the basic clock rate.

The ALU design is tailored to fit this basic machine cycle. Circuit simulations showed that a 32-bit carry propagation could not be accomplished in a worst-case time of less than 150 ns. At first, it seemed that an ALU operation such as "destination register = accumulator + source register" should last four cycles:

1) transfer source to ALU temporary
2) and 3) carry propagation
4) transfer result to destination.

However, the final design succeeds in performing this operation in three cycles:

1) transfer source to ALU
2) start carry propagation
3) complete carry propagation, transfer result to destination.

Although carry propagation still takes 150 ns, the last 50 ns overlap the first half of the result transfer cycle (which is the internal data bus precharge phase). Moreover, during cycle 2 the internal data bus may be used by the microcode for other data transfer operations. Therefore, the internal data bus may be used during all cycles.

Register File and ALU

The architecture defines all internal registers as 32-bit elements. Although the most natural approach is to implement a 32-bit internal bus and 32-bit data storage and processing elements (ALU, temporary registers, memory data register), a 16-bit bus was considered during the design as a space-saving measure. However, selecting a 32-bit bus allows uniform processing that is independent of the operand length. The reduced microcode complexity and the elimination of multiplexing circuitry, together with the significant performance advantages, outweigh the space penalty of a full 32-bit bus.

The chip design is oriented towards efficiently handling the 8-, 16-, and 32-bit operand length variations of each instruction. The operand length is usually transparent to the microcode. A special two-bit length bus controls the register files and other data processing elements. In the case of a byte or word operation, only the 8 or 16 least significant bus bits are used. The length bus is driven by the length register containing the length field from the instruction. The microcode is capable of overriding the length bus, for handling operand lengths other than that specified by the instruction.

All the data processing elements are connected to the bus. The microcode specifies the source and destination for bus transfer operations by two five bit fields. Thus 32 bus elements are available. In addition to the general purpose and dedicated machine registers, additional 32-bit data processing elements were included such as three temporary registers, data shifter, bit decoder, displacement extractor, microloop repetition counter, condition code logic, memory address register, memory data register, etc. An interesting feature is the inclusion of the memory data register as a normal internal bus element. This enables fetching an operand from memory and using it in the following machine cycle as the source for the ALU operation.

The arithmetic and logic operations, including address-mode effective address calculations, are carried out by the 32-bit ALU. The ALU is a general purpose element that may be configured into one of 12 operating modes by the microcode or directly by the ALU control fields of the machine instruction. In addition to standard operations (ADD, SUBTRACT, AND, XOR, etc.), dedicated hardware enhancements suppory multiply and divide algorithms and BCD addition and subtraction.

Special Purpose Hardware

The tradeoffs between silicon area and performance were the main consideration in defining dedicated hardware elements. Special hardware is implemented when it contributes to the execution speed of critical instructions, when it is shared by many instructions, or when implementation without special purpose hardware would be impractical.

Some special purpose elements are tailored to the specific requirements of the instruction set. For instance, a bit decoder is implemented to support the bit and bit-field instructions. The bit decoder is a 1-out-of-32 decoder, decoding a 5-bit input, specifying the bit to be set, into a 32-bit output. The decoder input and output may be specified as data transfer destination or source, respectively.

Memory Accesses

The bus interface unit manages transfers between the CPU and slave processors, memory and I/O devices attached to the external bus. It operates asynchronously with respect to the microcode so that internal operations may be overlapped with bus transactions. The data transfer that the BIU handles as the result of a microcode request are

1) read or write of 8-bit/16-bit/32-bit data at odd or even byte addresses
2) read or write to slave processors, with an automatic check of slave processor completion status
3) read from interrupt controllers.

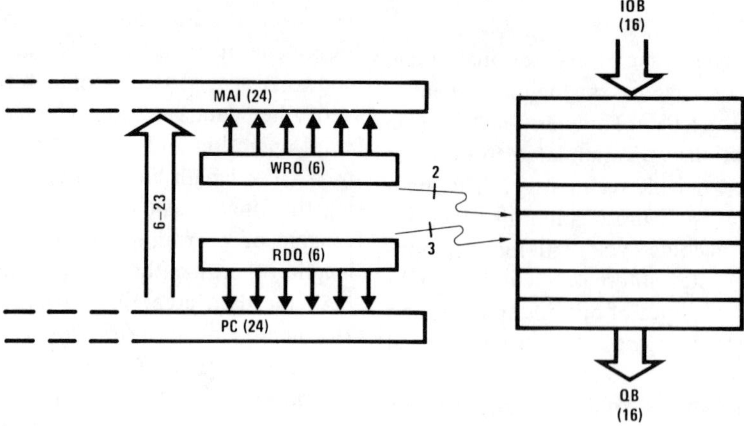

Fig. 9. Queue control.

Microcode semaphores are used for synchronizing the execution machine to the bus interface machine, and microcode algorithms are designed to maximize the parallelism available. A typical execution sequence is: request first operand fetch, perform operand independent operations, request second operand fetch, wait for completion of first operand fetch, process operand one, wait for completion of second operand fetch, process operand two. Note that the BIU is notified about the second operand fetch before the first operand memory cycle is completed so that no time is lost between memory cycles.

Instruction Queue

An instruction fetch-ahead queue is used to provide overlap of instruction fetch and execution and to align incoming instructions to 16-bit boundaries (Fig. 9). Fetch ahead cycles are initiated by the bus interface unit when there is space in the queue and no pending data requests from the microcode. The queue is organized as a double-ended 8-byte FIFO with 16-bit input and output buses. The RDQ and WRQ registers control data entry and removal from the queue, respectively. The PC register contains the address of the currently executing instruction. The WRQ in conjunction with the PC register is used to generate instruction fetch ahead addresses. The RDQ register is used to derive the next instruction PC from the current PC.

A displacement extractor unit is used to extract and process the frequency encoded address offset constants described in Section II. When specified by the microcode, as the source for a data transfer operation, it extracts a constant from the queue, decodes its length, sign extends it to 32 bits, transfer it to the internal data bus, and increments the RDQ register by the displacement length. The displacement extractor can extract and process two bytes of displacement data in 100 ns.

Instruction Execution

Instruction execution uses a three-stage pipeline as shown in Fig. 10. The instruction is extracted from the queue by the loader stage. The loader decodes the instruction into a basic opcode, an operand length, address modes, and ALU control fields. The loader can decode two bytes every 100 ns. Loader operation for the next instruction is initiated by the microcode when all instruction bytes have been extracted from the queue for the current instruction. The execution of the loaded instruction starts upon termination of the current instruction's execution. Thus, three successive instructions may be processed simultaneously by the CPU: the instruction being executed, the instruction being loaded into the instruction register, and the instruction being shifted through the queue.

Microcode and Preprocessor

The complexity of the instructions, some involving dozens of processing steps, leads to the use of microprogramming. Vertical microcode encoding is used to save microcode ROM space. However, careful construction of the microword allows almost all microsequences to fully utilize the internal data path and ALU. Thus, almost no performance degradation results from the limited parallelism of a vertical microcode structure because most of the available parallelism is extracted automatically by the BIU, loader, and preprocessor.

A two-operand instruction proceeds through three execution phases.

Phase 1: Fetch the first operand or calculate the effective address of the first operand.

Phase 2: Fetch the second operand or calculate the effective address of the second operand.

Phase 3: Execute (write result if necessary).

Phase 1 or 2 or both are omitted in one-operand and zero-operand instructions. Obviously, some kind of mechanism should be provided to allow efficient processing of the three phases. The main design problems were the following.

1) Each instruction may use any of the 15 addressing modes.

2) Each addressing mode calculation microcode may be shared by any instruction at phase 1 or phase 2.

3) At each phase, two variants are possible: calculate effective address of operand or actual operand fetch from memory.

The solution adopted is a two-level microcode technique which allows sharing of common effective address calculation routines by all the instructions and avoids time-consuming subroutine calls or space-consuming repeated microcode flows.

The outer level is the preprocessor which controls the sequence of instruction execution phases, while the inner level controls the individual execution steps. The preprocessor specifies which phase is to be executed and if it should involve actual operand fetch. The addressing mode fields of the in-

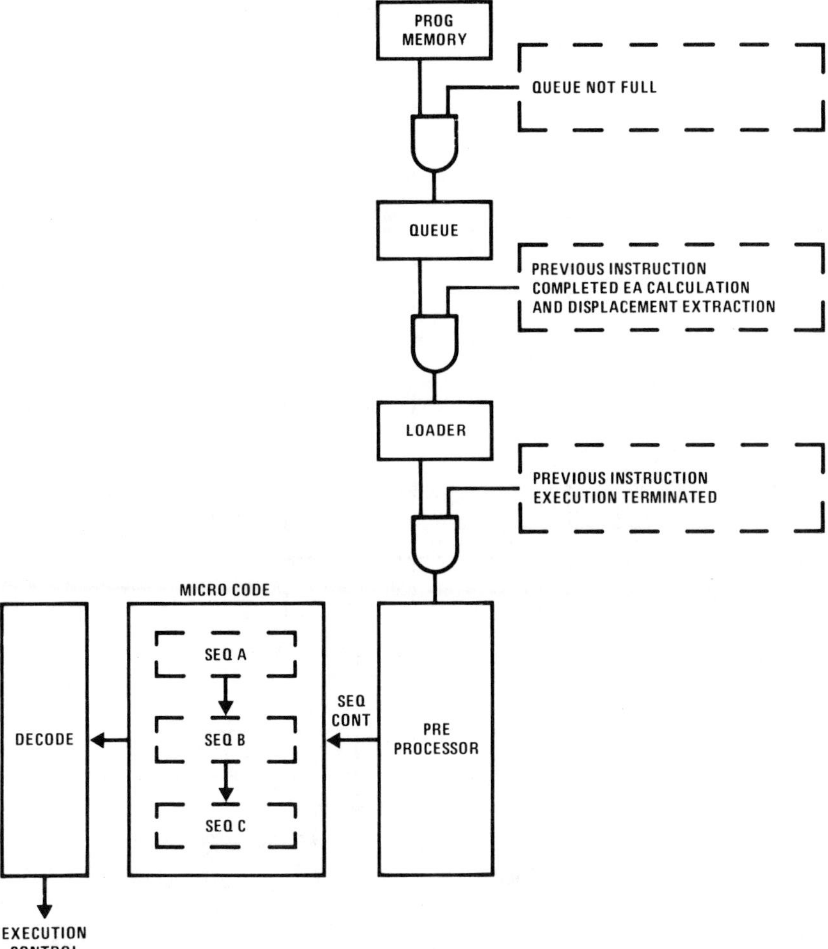

Fig. 10. Instruction processing pipeline of the CPU.

struction define the microcode ROM entry point in phase 1 and 2 and the basic opcode field defines the entry point used in phase 3. The preprocessor overlaps selection of the next phase (which may be the first phase of the next instruction) with execution of the current phase. A dedicated control flag in the microword signals the preprocessor of the end of a phase in time to allow it to initiate the next phase without any idle cycles between phases. The preprocessor can also select special microsequences for fast instructions to eliminate an operand fetch phase when the operand is in a general register.

Microinstructions within a sequence are normally executed sequentially, although microcode control instructions are implemented. These instructions are used for less speed-critical control transfers or conditional execution control. They allow a tradeoff between microcode size and preprocessor complexity. Control instructions include conditional jumps, microroutine calls, and repeat and loop mechanisms. A three-stage microlevel pipeline is used to achieve a 100 ns microinstruction execution rate. While microinstruction n is executed, microinstruction $n+1$ is decoded and microinstruction $n+2$ is selected by the microcode ROM address decoder.

Virtual Memory Support

Instructions that are cancelled by the abort pin must be reexecutable. This means that whenever the CPU changes one of its registers or a memory location, one of the following conditions is satisfied.

1) The old contents of the register are saved, so that they can be recovered in case of abort.

2) Writing into this specific destination does not inhibit instruction reexecution, if aborted.

3) No abort can possibly occur at this phase of the instruction execution (i.e., no more memory accesses in the current instruction).

A hardware backup mechanism saves the value of the processor status register, the stack pointer, and the program counter, so that they are automatically restored to their original values in case of abort. An abort on an instruction prefetch cycle requires special treatment. Prefetching an instruction preceded by a flow control instruction (e.g., CALL, RETURN, JUMP) may generate an abort, even though the instruction is not executed. The problem is solved by suspending the abort on instruction fetch until the abort-causing instruction is to be executed.

V. Circuit Considerations

Microcode ROM Design

Because entry points to microcode sequences are aligned on 16-word boundaries, it is desirable to have as few words as possible in each row of the ROM in order to reduce wasted space

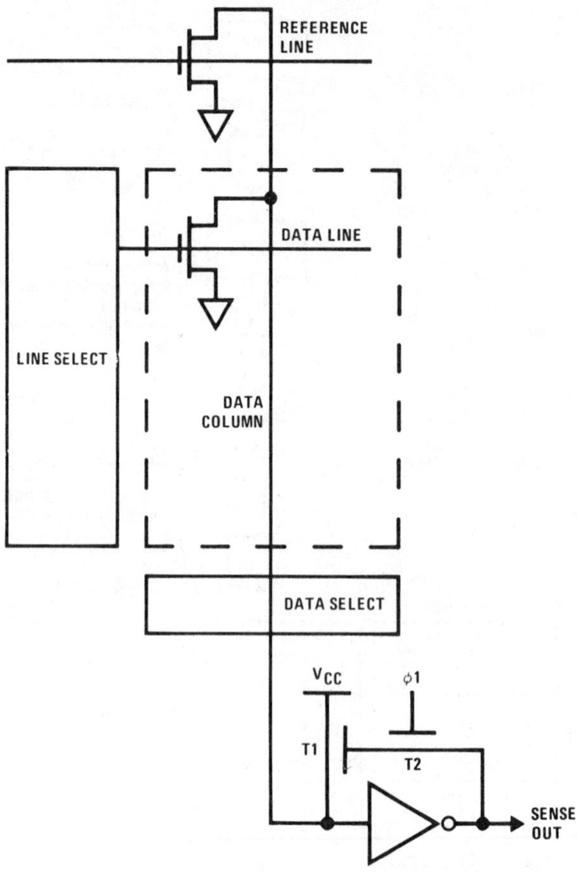

Fig. 11. Sense amp; ROM array organization is shown in simplified form.

caused by short sequences. Another reason for limiting the number of words in a row is to avoid the large *RC* delay introduced by long polysilicon select lines. The result of using such a narrow ROM architecture is that the long columns produce a very large capacitance on the sense amplifier inputs. To achieve the desired 100 ns microcycle time, a sense amplifier capable of detecting 40-100 mV voltage swings was developed.

Fig. 11 shows the basic sense amplifier circuit. Sensing is performed in two clock phases. In phase 1, all select lines except for a reference line are inactive and the line decoder is precharged. The transistors in the reference line are sized so that they conduct about half the current of a normal array transistor. During this phase, the negative feedback path on the sense amplifier is closed to bring the amplifier to its trip point. A reference current of half the normal array current now flows through *T*1. During phase 2, *T*2 opens the feedback path of the amplifier, but *T*1 continues to conduct the same reference current since the control voltage has been latched by the gate capacitance. If the selected cell in the array is empty (no transistor) the data line will charge. If there is a transistor in the selected cell, the data line will discharge since the array transistor conducts twice the current *T*1 supplies. Because the sense amplifier has been set to its trip point during the first phase, a very small change in the input voltage is required to make a transition. The sense amplifier output stabilizes in about 20 ns from the beginning of phase 2.

Several approaches were examined for the ROM array organization, including two-bit per cell and one and a half-bit per cell techniques. A shared ground/data line ROM is used, however, because it is faster and sensing is simpler than in the multiple bit per cell techniques. The space saving of the two-bit per cell technique is only 25 percent because the two-bit cell is 15 × 15 μm, whereas the one-bit cell is only 12.5 × 12.5 μm in the technology used.

Bootstrap Circuit

Another circuit widely used in the design is the bootstrap circuit shown in Fig. 12. The main idea is to increase the bootstrapping efficiency over conventional techniques by almost eliminating the charge sharing between nodes *A* and *B*. In this circuit, most of the current which charges node *B* will come through *T*2 from V_{cc} instead of node *A*. The result is that the initial voltage level on node *B* before the bootstrap starts is higher than the voltage produced using conventional techniques and this produces larger output swings and shorter rise times.

VI. Design Methodology

With a device as complicated as this CPU, and with the work being performed by a large team of designers, careful design procedures must be established to minimize design errors. The CPU design was divided into twelve functional blocks, so that a given block could be implemented by a single engineer. The design of each block was composed of the following steps.

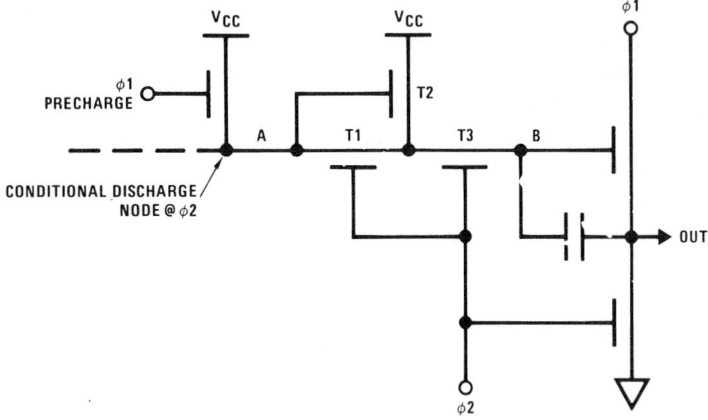

Fig. 12. Improved "boot" circuit.

1) Definition of the function, timing, and interface signals of the block.

2) A formal block definition review meeting with all engineers on the project, in which all interface signals and their corresponding timing were discussed and agreed upon.

3) Design of block, including register transfer level simulations, gate level simulations, and, finally, circuit simulations.

4) A formal design report documenting the design work of step 3.

5) A formal design review meeting with all the project engineers, in which the design report is presented and reviewed.

6) Mask design artwork is prepared and layout-based circuit simulations are performed.

This top-down approach did not prevent changes and modifications to the block functions if, during the course of the design, more efficient approaches were discovered. In particular, it was sometimes desirable to transfer functions from one block to another.

A software interactive register-transfer level (RTL) simulator was developed which can accept both high-level and gate-level block definitions. It was used to integrate all the block definitions for testing the entire chip design and for microcode debugging. The simulations were later extended to include the CPU in combination with the slave processors under development so that slave protocols and complex system interactions could be checked. Finally, the simulator is now being used to generate chip test patterns for debugging and production testing of the CPU. The RTL simulator has proven to be an extremely valuable tool, and enabled us to isolate problems at an early stage while they were still easy to fix.

VII. Conclusions

A chip photomicrograph is shown in Fig. 13. The register file and ALU occupy the left third of the chip with the ALU on the bottom. The queue, loader, preprocessor, and micromachine occupy the middle third of the chip. The microcode ROM, microinstruction decoder, and bus interface unit occupy the right third of the chip. Random logic is used in the loader, preprocessor, and bus interface unit instead of PLA's to save chip area. It is clear that with increasing chip complexity, more sophisticated design tools and methodologies must be devel-

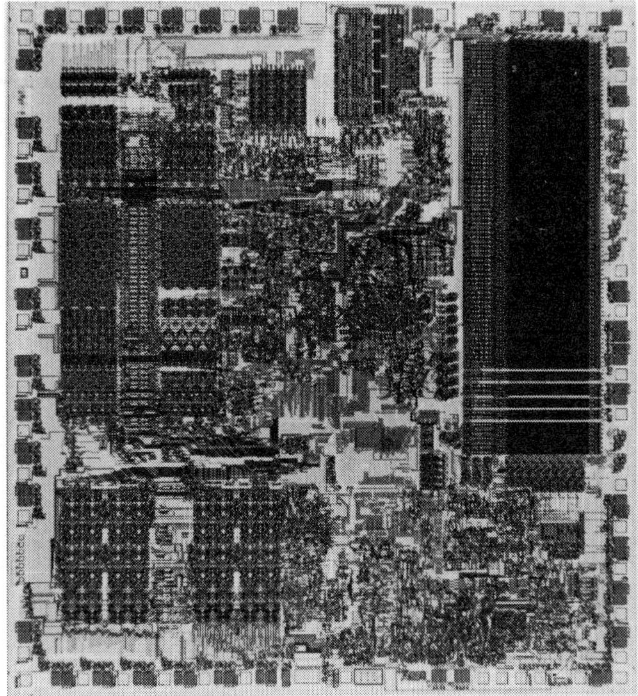

Fig. 13. 16032 silicon.

Operation	Data Type*	Exec Time (μs)
MOV R,R (Register to Register)	8b, 16b 32b	0.30 0.30
MOV M,R (Memory to Register)	8b, 16b 32b	1.10 1.50
MOV M,M (Memory to Memory)	8b, 16b 32b	1.70 2.50
ADD M,R (Memory to Register)	8b, 16b 32b	1.20 1.60
CMP M,M (Memory to Memory)	8b, 16b 32b	1.70 2.50
MULT R,R (Register to Register)	8b × 8b 16b × 16b 32b × 32b	3.50 5.10 8.30
BCC (Conditional Branch)	(Branch Taken) (Branch Not Taken)	1.60 0.80
ADDP R,R (BCD ADD, Register to Register)	8 Nibbles	2.00

Fig. 14. Typical instruction execution times.

oped. The need to minimize die size and to optimize performance of general purpose products which are intended for large volume production compounds this problem.

Typical instruction execution times are shown in Fig. 14. The CPU demonstrates that it is possible to integrate the full functionality of a high-end 32-bit minicomputer or mainframe computer onto a small number of chips in a conservative NMOS process and achieve a performance-to-price ratio which compares quite favorably with such systems. We believe there will be a major impact on the structure and applications of computer systems from highly integrated, high-functionality processors such as the one described in this paper.

Acknowledgment

The design efforts of the following people made this chip possible: A. Brish, A. Fisher, Y. Hollander, I. Kashat, A. Morgenstern, D. O'Dowd, A. Shani, R. Talmudi, A. Wilnai, and S. Yomtov.

The Operating System and Language Support Features of the BELLMAC™-32 Microprocessor.

Alan D. Berenbaum
Michael W. Condry
Priscilla M. Lu

Bell Laboratories
Holmdel, New Jersey

1. Acknowledgements

Many designers contributed to the design and development of the BELLMAC-32 microprocessor and we would like to acknowledge their work on this project. In particular, Anand Jagannathan provided much of the original design of the operating system interface. J. J. Molinelli and D. E. Blahut provided overall architectural specification. Other key contributors were Steve Pekarich and Lakshmi Goyal. L. C. Thomas and J. J. Molinelli, who are project managers for this development, contributed to the directions and the success of the BELLMAC-32 microprocessor.

2. Introduction

The BELLMAC-32 microprocessor is a 32-bit microprocessor, implemented with CMOS technology, designed to support operating system functions and high level languages efficiently. The architecture was designed with the following objectives in mind:

- High performance.
- Enhanced operating system support capabilities.
- High level language support.
- High reliability, availability and maintainability.

BELLMAC is a trademark of Western Electric.

The microprocessor has a 32-bit bidirectional bus with status decoding, bus arbitration for external access, DMA control, interrupt handling, and test/debug access to the system.

3. BELLMAC-32 Microprocessor Architecture

The BELLMAC-32 processor supports four data types: bytes, halfwords, words and bit fields (1 to 32 bits in length). Bytes, halfwords and words can be interpreted as either signed or unsigned in arithmetic or logical operations. Strings are supported by special block instructions (STRING COPY, STRING LENGTH). The string format conforms to the C language and is terminated by a "null" or zero byte.

Instructions are byte addressable, and defined by a one or two byte opcode followed by zero or more operand descriptors. All byte or halfword operands are sign or zero extended to 32 bits when they are fetched.

The operand descriptor identifies the location of the operand. There are several addressing modes: literal, byte/halfword/word immediate, register, register deferred, short offset (for frame and argument pointers), byte/halfword/word displacement, byte/halfword/word displacement deferred, and expanded operand type. These are covered in more detail in the following sections.

There is a special program counter register and fifteen other registers in the processor that can be referenced in any of the addressing modes. Three of the fifteen registers are privileged, ie, they can be written only when the processor is in kernel execution level. These three registers are used to support operations in the operating system. They are used as interrupt stack pointer, process control block pointer and processor status word. Another three registers are used by special instructions as a stack pointer, a frame pointer and an argument pointer.

Reprinted with permission from *Proc. Symp. Architectural Support for Programming Languages & Operating Syst.*, vol. 10, Mar. 1–3, 1982, pp. 30–38.

4. Programming Language Support

In designing the BELLMAC-32 microprocessor a major goal was to provide support for the programming language C [1]. The resulting architecture, however, supports the needs of high-level programming languages in general, as well as C. Language support features include useful instructions for implementing arithmetic and logical operations, special instructions for manipulating strings and bit fields, and both simple and high-level subroutine linkage operations. Several features of the BELLMAC-32 microprocessor simplify the interface to an operating system including the machine's "process oriented" design as needed for tasking and a special "controlled transfer" mechanism which implements both user defined and system exception control. This special transfer mechanism can be employed to implement packages, such as in Ada[2], and common libraries.

In discussing the relationship between machine design and compliers Wulf[3] suggested some principles of machine architecture to simplify compiler implementation and improve object code, for high-level languages in general. Specifically, Wulf suggests that instructions be consistent across functions, that operations, addressing, and data types be independent and composible concepts, and that the architecture should provide features for environment support. The BELLMAC-32 microprocessor follows these principles closely.

4.1 Arithmetic and Logical Instructions.

All machines provide some means for a compiler to implement arithmetic and logical operations; however, irregularity of operations (e.g., arithmetic operations are dyadic and triadic while logical operations are only dyadic) and inconsistency of operands (e.g., some must be registers) make generating efficient code complex. The BELLMAC-32 microprocessor's design eases this task similar to Wulf's ideas.

Instructions, addressing, and to some extent, data types are orthogonal concepts on the BELLMAC-32 microprocessor. The operation code defines the function to be performed, operand descriptor (or *addressing mode*) specifies how to determine the operand and these concepts function independently of one another. The operand descriptor can be any one of the possible addressing modes, including one that specifies the data type of the operand that provides conversion between data types as a component of operand data fetch. There are no register or data type restrictions on operands with any operation. Machine instructions associate a "default" data type with the operands if their data type is not otherwise specified.

The BELLMAC-32 microprocessor offers a complete set of the "usual" arithmetic and logical operations. These instructions are regular, where all functions are available in the same forms. Briefly the functions provided are:

logical:	clear (i.e., zero data), ones complement, inclusive or, and exclusive or
arithmetic:	negate, add, subtract, multiply, divide, modulus, increment and decrement (by one).

The unary operators negate and complement are formulated as a move instruction; consequently, the result can either replace the existing datum or be placed in a new destination[1]. All binary operators have both dyadic and triadic forms of instructions[2]. All operations are internally performed as 32 bit functions; however, an overflow occurs if the computation result size exceeds that of the output operand's size.

Having all operations occur in all the same forms is convenient for compilers. For example, using dyadic and triadic forms for evaluating an expression is sometimes ignored in compiler optimization because of operand restrictions. Coding the C expression

$$a = b + c * (d + e)$$

can be done easily with three instructions (assume all variables were integer words):

addw3	*d*,*e*,%r0	$R0 = d + e$
mulw2	*c*,%r0	$R0 = c^*(d+e)$
addw3	*b*,%r0,*a*	$a = b + c^*(d+e)$

where the variable names represent some operand descriptor to access the variable data. The same sequence could be used with different (binary) operators in the C expression with the corresponding opcode replacements, also, the variables need not be integer words.

One addressing mode of particular interest is the *short literal* mode that can represent a small integer (between −16 and 63) using only a single byte for data and descriptor. Using this mode provided an average space reduction of 5% and, as a consequence of this reduction, improved execution time by about 1.8%[3].

1. Under the present implementation, both the source and target operand addresses in a unary operation addresses are calculated, even though they may be identical.
2. The dyadic form stores the result in the second operand and the triadic form places the result in the third operand, with the first two unaltered.
3. These and other performance figures were determined by comparing a collection of benchmark programs with and without the feature.

The BELLMAC-32 microprocessor also has *immediate* modes for the different data types, where the data follows the mode descriptor. As with many machines, short literals and immediates need not be the same data type as the other instruction operands and these modes cannot be used as an operation destination[4].

An instruction associates a pre-defined data type with its operands, such as "add word" and "add byte." However, this default data type is essentially a convenience that provides abbreviated addressing descriptions. The BELLMAC-32 microprocessor has an *expanded type* operand mode that explicitly specifies the data type of the operand along with its addressing form[5]. Using this mode, operations are generic (e.g., all forms of add are just **add**) as each operand's mode defines its data type. As noted earlier, the BELLMAC-32 microprocessor executes arithmetic and logical operations internally in words; the machine performs any data type conversion while fetching and storing operands.

As an example of *expanded type* operands consider adding a byte integer (a) to a word integer (b) and storing the result in a halfword integer (c). Typically, this computation requires instruction several steps. The sequence of operations for most machines would look like[6]:

movbw	*a*, *temp*	convert *a* to word.
addw2	*b*, *temp*	compute the sum in a temporary
movwh	*temp*, *c*	convert result to a halfword.

Using the *expanded type* operands on the BELLMAC-32 microprocessor this operation needs only one instruction:

addb3 *a*,{word}*b*,{halfword}*c*

Where the desired operand data type is specified in brackets. In this example "add byte" was used as the instruction to specify the data type of the first operand; if the first operand also used an *expanded type* mode then any of the add instructions would produce identical computations.

As seen in above example, the *expanded type* mode is convenient when the operand data types happen to be inconsistent since its use eliminates temporaries that can compete for registers. *Expanded type* also provides some operations that are not directly available with the instructions; for example, these is no unsigned multiplication operation but this operation can be achieved with a multiplication instruction using unsigned *expanded type*'d operands. A final motivation for *expanded type* is to permit future type extensions. Three main points motivated the BELLMAC-32 microprocessor not to only offer generic instructions, always using *expanded type* addressing:

1. most computations involve data having identical types,
2. the *expanded type* address descriptor requires an extra byte and thus takes more space,
3. in most languages, compilers know the types of the operands and, unless conversion is necessary, generating the code for, say, "add word" as opposed to just "add" involves little additional complexity.

4.2 Other Data Type Operations.

Other data operations in the BELLMAC-32 microprocessor include functions to manipulate strings and bit fields. The string operations are designed specifically for a C string representation, where a *string* is a sequence of bytes ending in a null character (zero).

There are two string primitives:

string copy:	copy one string into another
string end:	locate the terminating (null) character in a string.

The addresses of the operands for these operations are specified in predefined registers. The *string end* operation can be used to compute the string length or in combination with *string copy* to produce a string append function. No length specification is given in either of these operations (string copy assumes target space is adequate and string end assumes the string is properly represented). These instructions are suitable for C but not necessarily for other languages. The BELLMAC-32 microprocessor also provides an instruction for moving a block of storage similar to the string copy except the length is specified.

A *field* on the BELLMAC-32 microprocessor is a variable length sequence of bits occurring entirely within a word. Instructions are provided to extract a field from storage and to insert a field, with the operations specifying the number of bits and bit offset of the bit field as well as the target and source addresses. Fields can be manipulated in terms of bytes, halfwords or words. Using these operations, most of the necessary bit manipulation functions for high level languages can

4. Such a semantically inconsistent operand construct generates an *invalid descriptor* exception.
5. The address can be specified with any addressing mode except *expanded type*.
6. The movXY instruction moves the data and converts from type X to type Y (b=byte, h=halfword, w=word).

be easily implemented.

The BELLMAC-32 microprocessor chip does not support floating point or decimal arithmetic; however, "extension" instructions are provided where the appropriate operations can be included. An auxiliary processor to perform decimal and floating point operations is under investigation.

4.3 Procedure Linkage

The BELLMAC-32 microprocessor offers high-level procedure linkage operations as well as a set of primitive instructions for subroutine jump and return. The high-level operations are useful for many programming languages, including C.

The high-level procedure linkage operations manipulate the stack frame, save registers, and transfer control between procedures. They are implemented to be efficient and include procedure call/return, and register save/restore. The push operation can be used to push arguments. The procedure linkage process manipulates the stack and execution. Four registers are modified:

pc: the program counter is changed to start executing in the subroutine and to return to the calling program.

sp: the stack pointer is adjusted properly to point to the top of the stack.

fp: the frame pointer points to the point in the stack just above the register save area (usually the start of local variable space for a procedure).

ap: the argument pointer points to a list of arguments used by the procedure. This list precedes the other linkage data on the stack.

In addition to these registers, other registers have a presumed semantics. Specifically, registers r0 through r2 are viewed as "temporaries" whose values are not saved between procedure calls. Registers r3 through r8 can be saved across procedure calls.

A typical stack frame, such as used in C, contains the arguments, return information, saved registers, and local variables. This stack frame is displayed in Figure 1 below.

Stack frames using the BELLMAC-32 microprocessor's high level linkage operations can differ from the above in the number of registers saved.

There are four instructions used in procedure linkage. The calling procedure uses the *call* instruction to save the **ap** and return address on the stack. The first instruction of each procedure is the *save* instruction that saves the old **fp** and a specified sequence of

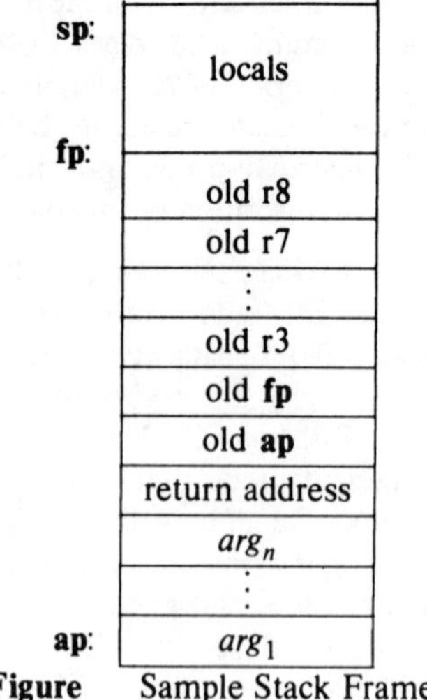

Figure Sample Stack Frame

registers from r8 to r3. Conceptually, only the registers to be used are saved. As noted earlier registers r0-r2 are not saved and consequently can be used to store the result. When the procedure completes it executes a *restore* instruction to restore any needed values in r3 through r8, and then a *return* instruction that resets the stack frame to that of the calling procedure and resume its execution. Arguments are typically placed on the stack with the push or push-address instructions; the return instruction automatically pops them off. Using these instructions proved to give a 20% speedup in execution time over direct coding of these four functions.

Coupled with the above procedure linkage scheme are two addressing modes called **ap**-offset and **fp**-offset. These modes provide a one-byte descriptor that can reference an datum whose address is an offset to the **ap** or **fp** registers in a range of 0 to 14. Since procedures typically have few arguments and often only a few local variables, most arguments and locals can be referenced with a one-byte descriptor. For example of where these modes can be used consider the variables in the C program:

```
foo(a,b,c)
int a,b,c;
{    int d,e,f;
        . . .
}
```

All the given variables (a-f) could be addressed with a one-byte descriptor. Our analysis showed that each of these addressing modes gave an average space reduction of 5% and an average execution speed improvement of 1.8% over not using these modes.

If it is inconvenient to use the above procedure linkage scheme, "jump to subroutine" and "return from subroutine" instructions are also provided. The "jump to subroutine" instructions act as in many machines by pushing the return address on the stack and changing control to the subroutine. This operation comes in both a jump (that gives the address) and branch (which gives an **pc** offset) formats. The "return from subroutine" unwinds this operation but is interesting in that in comes in a conditional form. That is, the execution of the return can depend on the condition codes, where all available codes can be tested.

4.4 Environmental Control: Tasks and Exceptions.

Providing "operating system" functions in a programming language, such as tasking and exception control, have typically been difficult to implement. Many articles on compilers have cried for assistance in machine architecture[3,4]. The BELLMAC-32 microprocessor provides some assistance to these problems, particularly with exceptions.

Traditionally, to implement tasking compilers have been forced to with the process design established by a specific operating system. The process-oriented architecture of the BELLMAC-32 microprocessor eases this requirement by establishing the process design with the machine architecture. A compiler can represent a task as a BELLMAC-32 microprocessor process with the appropriate memory mappings that can be constructed by either the language run time system or operating system. Using this approach, a task's design depends on the machine and not a specific operating system. Also, this approach simplifies the mutual exclusion aspect of task rendezvous [2], since it is provided by the hardware[7]. The other rendezvous issues, synchronization and data exchange, are not directly assisted by the hardware and need some assistance by the system scheduler. Section 5 on operating system design discusses this process structure for the BELLMAC-32 microprocessor.

The BELLMAC-32 microprocessor has a table-driven *controlled transfer* mechanism that is used to manage system exceptions (and other system calls) and can be employed to implement user exceptions as well. When a system-level exception occurs the BELLMAC-32 microprocessor effectively executes an *controlled transfer* call instruction using a predefined set of operand values. This transfer operation is best viewed as form of jump-to-subroutine where tables select the appropriate subroutine address. If the operating system provides an interface for modifying the *controlled transfer* tables, a user-written exception handler can be called automatically by inserting its address into the appropriate table entry. The user defined exceptions can be managed with this operation, by adding exception handler addresses for each user exception and having the user execute a *controlled transfer* call instruction when the exception occurs. The *controlled transfer* can transfer to a normal user routine. To resume processing at the point of the exception (user or system) the code for the handler simply executes an *controlled transfer* return instruction.

7. On a multi-processor, multiple activations of a task are assumed to be separate processes.

4.5 Common Libraries and Packages

One approach to implementing common libraries and packages (abstract data types) is to use the *controlled transfer* mechanism discussed above. Conceptually, the call to a package entry can be viewed as a user exception.

One (or more) of the transfer tables could be allocated to package control. Each entry in this table would correspond to a function entry in some package. To invoke a package procedure a *controlled transfer* call instruction would be used and each package procedure would return via a *controlled transfer* return. A major advantage of this approach is that code for package procedures could be shared across processes and generating code for package calls would be simplified.

5. BELLMAC-32 microprocessor Operating System Support

The BELLMAC-32 microprocessor was designed to provide an efficient environment for a sophisticated operating system. An operating system is not built into the processor, nor is the processor optimized for any particular operating system. Instead, the processor provides two mechanisms that can be used to manipulate processes, control transfers to the operating system, respond to interrupts and handle exceptions.

5.1 Processes

The BELLMAC-32 microprocessor supports a "process oriented" operating system; a particular model of a process is implicit in the machine architecture. This model has several characteristics:

- There are four levels of privileged execution to allow flexibility in constructing multi-level operating systems. The hierarchy among the four levels is enforced only by the controlled transfer mechanism.
- There is only one execution stack per process. This stack is used by the procedure call mechanism as well as the controlled transfer mechanism, and it is used independent of execution level.
- A process is defined to the processor by a Processor Control Block (PCB), which stores copies of the

processor's resources used by the process (e.g., the on-chip registers).

— It is intended that at least the kernel of the operating system reside in the address space of every process.

With four execution levels, a system that required a separate stack for each execution level would have to maintain at least four growable segments for stacks. With a single stack, the operating system need maintain only one, and a single stack overflow mechanism is sufficient to grow the stack. The stack fault mechanism, which handles overflow conditions as well other violations, is described below in the section *Stack Exception*. In addition, at least four registers would be required to point to these four stacks, and the management of such special registers is expensive in a VLSI design. The execution stack can also be used to pass arguments from user code to system functions; the regular parameter passing mechanism can be used without elaborate copying operations.

If the kernel of the operating system is in the address space of every process, copying of data from user buffers to system buffers is not required, since the system can access user buffers, and *vice versa*. A common address space for user and operating system code is necessary if the single execution stack mechanism is to work: changing the address space would lose the stack and the procedure chain it contains. The exception mechanism of the BELLMAC-32 microprocessor expects the kernel to be in the address space of every process, so the processor does not change memory management to access an exception handler.

Two data structures are associated with processes on the BELLMAC-32 microprocessor, the PCB and the Interrupt Stack. The PCB (see Figure 2) has space for the 14 registers used by a process. These are the 11 user registers plus three control registers, the Stack Pointer (SP), the Program Counter (PC) and the Processor Status Word (PSW). Two words in the PCB are used to store the upper address limit and the lower address limit of the execution stack; these bounds are checked in the controlled transfer mechanism. The rest of the PCB is unbounded in length and is intended to be used by (but is not restricted to) memory management. The Interrupt Stack is not associated with any one process, and contains pointers to PCB's. One of the two on-chip registers not associated with any one process, the PCB Pointer (PCBP), points to the PCB of the process running on the processor. The second of these registers, the Interrupt Stack Pointer (ISP), points to the top of the Interrupt Stack. Both the PCBP and the ISP are privileged in that they can only be written when the processor is in the kernel execution level.

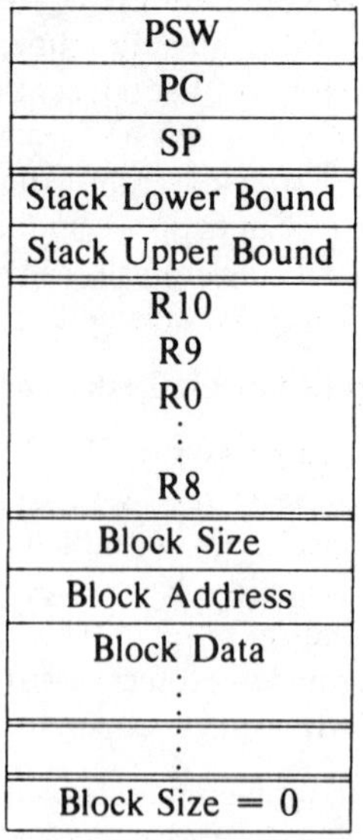

PSW
PC
SP
Stack Lower Bound
Stack Upper Bound
R10 R9 R0 ⋮ R8
Block Size
Block Address
Block Data ⋮
⋮
Block Size = 0

Figure 2. Process Control Block Layout

5.2 Process Switch

The first of the two mechanisms used to support operating systems on the BELLMAC-32 microprocessor is the Process Switch mechanism, which is used in process switching, interrupt handling and exception handling. The Process Switch mechanism has four parts that are used by the microsequences in various combinations:

I. Store the control registers in the PCB pointed to by the PCBP (the "old" PCB).
Store the user registers in the "old" PCB. (optional)

II. Update the PCBP to point to the "new" PCB.
Load the control registers from the "new" PCB.
Move PCBP past the initial context of the "new" PCB. (optional)

III. Perform a series of block moves. (optional)

IV. Load user registers from "new" PCB. (optional)

The data in the block move section of the PCB is intended to be a memory map specification. Since all I/O on the BELLMAC-32 microprocessor is memory mapped, the starting address in the block move section would be the base of translation registers in a memory management unit. With this mechanism, the process switch would automatically establish the virtual address domain of the new process without any further intervention by the operating system. Of course, if the BELLMAC-32 microprocessor's mechanism is undesirable for some application, it can be disabled by setting the block move count to zero in all PCB's.

5.2.1 Call Process/Return to Process. Explicit instructions are provided in the BELLMAC-32 microprocessor for switching processes by the operating system. They are not used for scheduling processes, which in the BELLMAC-32 microprocessor is still the responsibility of operating system software. Instead, they provide a means of dispatching processes, and coordinating process switches determined by the operating system with those that arise unexpectedly from interrupts. The two instructions, Call Process and Return To Process, are analogous to the pair Jump to Subroutine and Return From Subroutine. In the subroutine transfer instructions, the starting address defines the subroutine. The jump pushes a return address on the execution stack and the return pops the return address off that stack. In the process transfer instructions, the address of the PCB defines the process. The call pushes the address of the current PCB on the Interrupt Stack and the return pops the address of a PCB off the Interrupt Stack. Like the subroutine transfer instructions, the process transfer instructions only transfer flow of control and do not explicitly pass arguments.

The Call Process instruction has the address of a PCB as its argument. It saves the context of the old process in the old PCB, with the saved PC pointing to the next instruction to be executed, and gets a new context from the new PCB. The Return To Process instruction just loads a new context from the new PCB.

5.3 Interrupts

The interrupt mechanism of the BELLMAC-32 microprocessor is intended to be efficient, reliable and consistent with the process model of the processor. Since interrupts are asynchronous, they are not likely to be associated with the process running on the processor. Ideally, an interrupt should be handled by a new process, which is exactly what the BELLMAC-32 microprocessor does. This concept has a number of advantages. An interrupt process has an entirely new context and is unlikely to interfere with any other process. If the interrupting device is not a critical resource, the interrupt handler need not run in kernel mode, but can be dispatched directly in user mode. A special execution stack used by interrupts is not necessary, since each interrupt process gets a new execution stack that does not need any special treatment.

5.3.1 Interrupt mechanism. An interrupt in the BELLMAC-32 microprocessor is handled as an unexpected Call Process instruction. An interrupting device presents the processor with an 8-bit interrupt id. This id selects one of 256 PCB pointers in a table starting at a fixed virtual address. Each PCB pointer corresponds to an interrupt handler process. The microsequence is then exactly the same as in the Call Process instruction. The interrupt process will then run unless it is interrupted in turn by a higher priority interrupt. When the interrupt handler process is completed, a Return To Process instruction should be issued, which will restart the process that was suspended when the interrupt occurred.[8]

The Interrupt Stack keeps track of the nesting of interrupts. Unless the Interrupt Stack is explicitly manipulated by the operating system, the PCBP at the bottom of the stack points to the PCB of the first interrupted process. The entries above it point to the PCB's of interrupt handler processes of increasing priority, with the PCBP pointing the PCB of the highest priority interrupt currently in a state of execution.

5.4 Controlled Transfer

The controlled transfer mechanism in the BELLMAC-32 microprocessor provides a means for controlled entry into a procedure or handler along with a new PSW. It can be used as the system call mechanism. The controlled transfer consists of a "controlled call" and a "controlled return". The controlled call operates like the jump-to-subroutine instruction except that the PC/PSW pair is stacked and replaced. This instruction has two operands that operates as a double table index to determine the new PSW and the appropriate address to branch to. The PC/PSW pair is popped off the stack on a "controlled return".

At a predefined location in memory there is a "first level" table of pointers each of which can point to a "second level" table of PC/PSW pairs. The first index operand selects the appropriate "second level" table. The second index operand determines the appropriate address to branch to (see Figure 3). The "first level" allows for 32 entries and each "second level" table can have up to 4095 entries. The "second level" table can be located anywhere in memory. In particular, they may be shared by some (or all) of the users or be uniqued to a process.

5.4.1 Use of Controlled Transfer In more conventional architectures, a single Supervisor Call instruction exists, which loads a new PC and PSW from a predetermined location. It is up to the operating system software to determine which procedure to invoke.

In the BELLMAC-32 microprocessor, this software procedure is assisted by the processor internal architecture. The controlled transfer mechanism is the only way a processor can change its execution level.

8. unless the Interrupt Stack was modified.

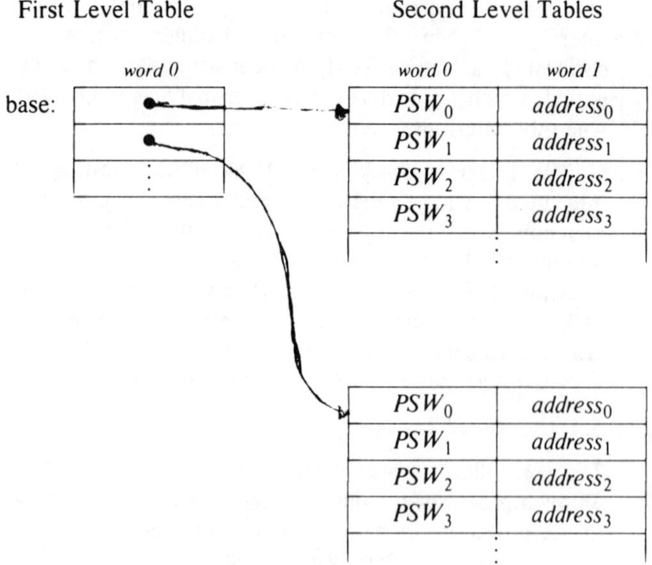

Figure 3. Controlled Transfer Tables

There is no notion of execution level in the microsequence implementating the call, because the new PSW will determine the execution level of the process. The controlled return instruction is the only place in the BELLMAC-32 microprocessor that explicitly identifies privilege: it will not allow a procedure to return to a more privileged one.

Since there is only one execution stack per process, it is especially important to maintain integrity of this stack. The controlled transfer mechanism is where the sanity of the stack is preserved. There are two entries in the PCB. These corresponds to the upper and lower bounds of the execution stack. The controlled call instruction checks to make sure that the stack pointer lies between these boundaries before executing the transfer. The operating system on the processor has to properly maintain the stack bounds in the PCB.

5.5 Exceptions

Exceptions are events that indicate something is wrong with the current execution. They can be detected internally by the processor or generated externally. The BELLMAC-32 microprocessor can handle all exceptional conditions without halting and it uses the two basic mechanisms provided for the operating system, the controlled transfer mechanism and the process switch mechanism. Four levels of exceptions are invoked by the BELLMAC-32 microprocessor, depending on the severity of the error and the resources available at the time. These levels are: normal exception, stack exception, process exception and reset exception.

5.5.1 Normal Exception. Most exceptions are normal exceptions. These include such internal exceptions as illegal instruction, integer overflow and privileged register access as well as externally generated memory faults. The processor records an index of the exceptions in a 4-bit field of the PSW called the Internal State Code (ISC). The action the processor takes is exactly the same as the controlled transfer call. The first level index is always zero, and the second level index is the ISC. Therefore, when any normal exception occurs, the controlled transfer mechanism automatically transfers control to a routine that can handle the exception. The exception handler need not be privileged or even part of the operating system. If the user provides an handler for an exception, it is sufficient to change the table entry of that exception to point to that code.

5.5.2 Stack Exception. The execution stack on the BELLMAC-32 microprocessor is a critical resource and hence must be maintained carefully. If the execution stack is bad, a normal exception sequence cannot be invoked, since the first thing a normal exception sequence does is push a PC/PSW pair onto the stack. Therefore, a special type of process switch is provided to handle stack exceptions. Stack exceptions are detected in the controlled transfer mechanism, either when the stack bounds check fails, or when a read from the stack or write to the stack fails. When a stack exception is detected, the processor fetches a pointer to a new PCB from a fixed virtual location. It then pushes the current PCBP onto the Interrupt Stack, saves the old control registers and loads a new set, obtaining a new stack. It does not execute the block moves, so the memory management is not forced to change. The new process can repair the stack, adjust the stack bounds, kill the process or whatever else it likes.

5.5.3 Process Exception. A process exception occurs when a read from or a write to the PCB during a microsequence causes a memory fault. Since the PCB is bad, the process is effectively dead; there is no way registers can be saved or the process restarted. All that the processor can do is to start a new process. When a process exception occurs, the processor fetches a pointer to a new PCB from a fixed virtual location, pushes the current PCBP onto the Interrupt Stack and loads a new set of control registers. Because the process exception handler should do its job quickly, it is more efficient to include one in the domain of every process and avoid executing the block moves of the process switch.

5.5.4 Reset Exception. A reset exception is invoked when all else fails or when the processor is reset externally. It occurs during a microsequence, when a memory fault occurs when reading from or writing to the Interrupt Stack, when a memory fault occurs in reading an address vector or it occurs when there is a memory fault in processing a process exception. When a reset exception occurs, the processor disables virtual addressing, fetches a pointer to a new PCB from a fixed physical location and loads a new set of control registers. If a memory fault occurs in processing a reset exception, another reset exception is generated and the processor tries again. The BELLMAC-32 microprocessor will not halt. The only way to halt the BELLMAC-32 is to turn it off — there is not even a HALT instruction.

6. Conclusion

The BELLMAC-32 microprocessor has provided a strong foundation for evolving towards more sophisticated features for supporting complex multiprocessor architectures. The BELLMAC-32 microprocessor is operational and is being used in BELL system applications. The next generation BELLMAC-32 microprocessor is underway and it aims at providing system level functions and control in a family of custom VLSI chips.

References

[1] Kernighan, B.W., and Ritchie, D.M., **The C Programming Language**, Prentice-Hall, 1978.

[2] **Ada Programming Language**, Department of Defense Military Standard MIL-STD-1815, December 10, 1980.

[3] Wulf, W.A., *Compilers and Computer Architecture*, Computer (July 81), pp 41-47.

[4] Denning, P.J., *A Question of Semantics*, Computer Architecture News Vol 6,8 (April 78), pp16-18.

[5] Johnson, S.C., *The Portable C Compiler*, Bell Labs technical report.

[6] Johnson, S.C., and Fraser, A.G., *The C Machine*, Bell Labs technical report.

A 32-Bit VLSI CPU Chip

JOSEPH W. BEYERS, MEMBER, IEEE, LOUIS J. DOHSE, JOSEPH P. FUCETOLA, RICHARD L. KOCHIS, CLIFFORD G. LOB, GARY L. TAYLOR, MEMBER, IEEE, AND EUGENE R. ZELLER

***Abstract*—A fully integrated 32-bit VLSI CPU chip utilizing 1 μm features is described. It is fabricated in an n-channel, silicon gate, self-aligned technology which is overviewed in a companion paper. The chip contains about 450 000 transistors and executes microinstructions at approximately one per 55 ns clock cycle. It can execute a 32-bit binary integer add in 55 ns, a 32-bit binary integer multiply in 1.8 μs, and a 64-bit floating point multiply in 10.4 μs. The instruction set provides the functions of an advanced mainframe CPU. Because the implementation of such a complex device poses an organizational as well as a technical challenge, the design philosophy that was adopted is summarized briefly. Careful attention was paid to designer productivity, and design flexibility and testability.**

I. INTRODUCTION

SINCE the advent of MOS microprocessors in the late 1960's, MOS technology has appeared attractive for low cost computer systems. Recent technological innovations have made higher integration density possible and have removed many of the performance limitations of MOS systems. The inherent simplicity of MOS process technology and its projected performance as a function of anticipated technology scaling make it worthy of consideration for functions traditionally reserved for TTL and even ECL implementations.

Over the last few years the price-performance ratio of MOS technology has been improving approximately 25 percent per year [1], limited in part by the weakly coupled communications between systems developers, systems users, IC technology researchers, and IC fabrication equipment vendors. A more cohesive approach to VLSI implementation that is described here has allowed us to achieve a significant acceleration in the rate of technology development. This paper and a companion paper [2] on technology development summarize the efforts of technology, circuit, and system groups working together to achieve a high performance device. The groups involved chose a challenging objective, then streamlined their tactical approach to address primarily the key limiting variables. This strategy can be characterized as "conservative application of aggressive design rules to systems design." Because of the limited resources involved, the approach was to minimize complexity wherever possible in our system, rather than to try to manage complexity. High on our list of concerns were issues of producibility, timeliness, and system performance/cost tradeoffs. These concerns led to carefully considered but simple strategies to improve design productivity, testability, and system performance. This

Manuscript received May 25, 1981; revised June 24, 1981.

The authors are with the Hewlett-Packard Company, Fort Collins, CO 80525.

Reprinted from *IEEE J. Solid-State Circuits*, vol. SC-16, pp. 537–541, Oct. 1981.

paper provides an overview of the 32-bit CPU chip, a summary of the operation of the chip, some performance benchmarks, and, finally, the design strategy and the ensuing methodology.

II. 32-Bit VLSI CPU Description

The chip described here is a 32-bit CPU containing about 450 000 transistors fabricated in an advanced 1 μm silicon gate technology with $3\frac{1}{2}$ layers of interconnect. The CPU itself is approximately 5.7 mm on a side (the chip is 6.3 mm on a side and includes some process parameter test devices). The chip has 83 pads, including a 32-bit address/data path, 25 control lines, and 26 power, ground, and clock pads. It dissipates approximately 7 W of power, and operates at a worst case clock frequency of 18 MHz. A map of the chip is presented in Fig. 1. It consists of seven major sections, including 1) a microcode control store ROM which is organized as 9216 38-bit words, 2) a PLA for decoding microinstructions, 3) a sequencing machine for controlling the flow of instructions from the ROM to the PLA, 4) a test condition multiplexer for decoding various test and branch conditions, 5) an extensive set of 32-bit registers for storage and manipulation of data, 6) a general purpose ALU, and 7) a memory processor bus (MPB) interface for communication with the external data paths.

The microcode ROM provides a major element of the chip functionality. Its 9216 38-bit words are arranged in 38 individual "bit slices," which are essentially separate ROM's. Each "bit slice" of the ROM is implemented as 32 × 16 18-bit "series FET" strings. The upper 9 bits of the ROM control store address select 1 of 288 sets of 32 bits of the "bit slice." An individual bit is then selected by the bottom 5 address bits. Each bit cell occupies an area of approximately 10 μm^2. This high performance implementation is made possible both by the ability to contact first layer metal to gate poly directly over active transistor area, and by the lack of significant substrate bias effect on series FET transistor strings.

Microinstructions which are accessed from the ROM are transmitted to the PLA, where they are decoded by the nearly 600 terms and ultimately drive control lines which determine the operations of the 32-bit register stack and the ALU.

The sequencing machine for controlling the flow of instructions from the ROM to the PLA contains nine 14-bit registers. The sequencer contains a microprogram counter, a set of incrementers, three registers for microcode subroutine return addresses, and a machine instruction opcode decoder. The opcode decoder generates the starting address in control store for the microcode routine that implements each machine instruction.

The test condition multiplexer uses a 6-bit microcode field to select one of 55 qualifiers that originate in various portions of the chip. These qualifiers are used in conditional jumps and skips in the microcode.

The register stack typifies one major segment of the chip design. It consists of a set of 28 identical 32-bit registers and the two data buses. In addition, it contains some special instruction-set-related logic such as top of stack registers, instruction registers, etc. Fig. 2 provides a block diagram of a typical register,

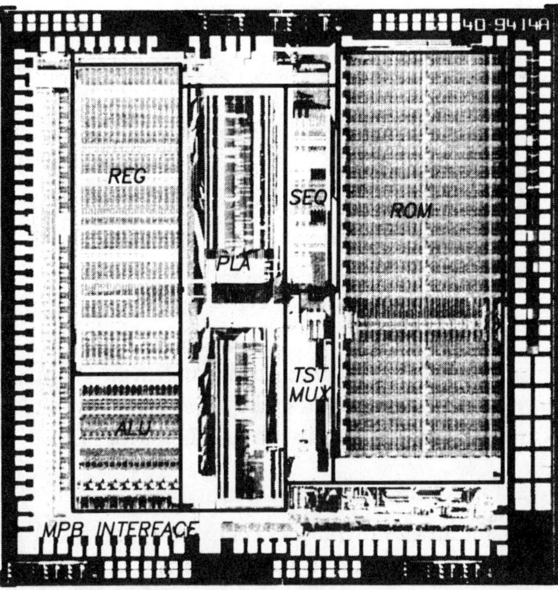

Fig. 1. 32-bit VLSI CPU chip showing the seven major subsections. The patterns on the right edge are parametric test devices; the patterns on the top and bottom of the chip include special resolution patterns, alignment marks, and alignment measurement patterns.

STRUCTURED CHIP DESIGN

CHIP
REGISTER
SECTION
CELL
A B
SET A
DUMP A
SET B
DUMP B

Fig. 2. Simplified diagram showing the composition of the register stack. The registers in the stack are comprised of identical bit cells driven by four control lines from the PLA.

which consists of 32 identical bit cells. Each bit cell has the ability to receive data from or dump data to either of the two data buses, as controlled by the PLA outputs. The typical register bit cell occupies an area of 33 × 35 μm and implements the schematic shown in Fig. 3. This cell has been optimized for size, speed, and power, utilizing the packing density offered by the minimum feature size and $3\frac{1}{2}$ levels of interconnect provided by the fabrication technology. Register cells utilize two phase nonoverlapping clocks with ratioed inverters and depletion loads. The 32-bit data buses are precharged dynamic buses.

The ALU contains an n-bit shifter, a 32-bit logical selecter, and a 32-bit full look-ahead adder. The selecter can perform logical operations on 32-bit quantities in one processor state (55 ns). The adder also completes its operation in 55 ns and is used in conjunction with some special hardware for performing integer multiplication and division. The ALU results can be stored in four result registers contained within the ALU.

The memory processor bus interface is the communication channel between the internal chip data buses and the external

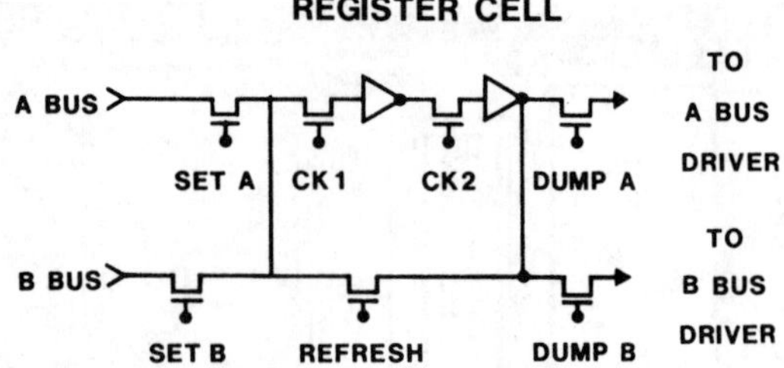

Fig. 3. Schematic of the register cell in Fig. 2. The inverters shown are ratioed circuits using depletion loads.

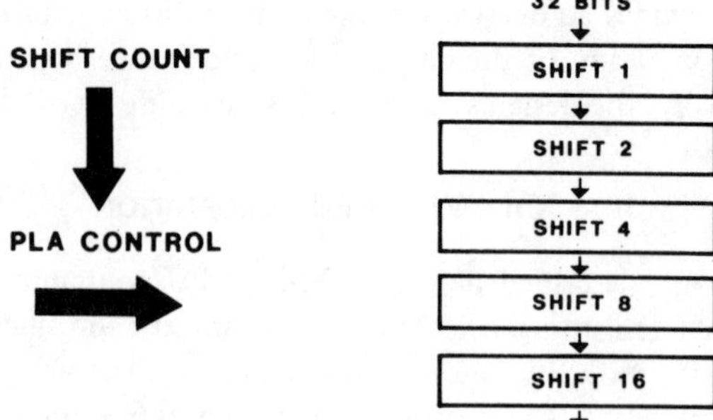

Fig. 4. Schematic representation of the *n*-bit shifter showing the shift count which is decoded in the PLA and fed through five sequential stages of combinational logic.

data bus. The interface protocol is implemented with seven 32-bit registers for addresses and data coming into and going out of the chip, and a special set of local control logic.

III. Design Methodology

Because the design of the CPU chip was undertaken with a relatively small group and in parallel with an emerging process technology, a structured design approach using limited but carefully specified objectives was fundamental. Special care was taken to minimize the design task, and to adopt a design approach that would produce a fast, flexible and testable chip.

In the early stages of this program, limited design tools were available. Consequently, a substantial effort was invested in reducing the overall design task by reusing many cell building blocks in the various registers and control sections, by extensive use of PLA concepts, and through the use of microcode to provide chip personalization. The entire CPU chip was fabricated with 100 unique cells whose performance was simulated on desktop computer systems. The computer simulation models employed were simplified and could simulate a maximum of 25 transistors. Nevertheless, the design productivity achieved by this technique was well in excess of the industry standard rate of 5–10 transistors per day [3], demonstrating the importance of conceptual simplicity and appropriate design methodology versus more generalized computer aided design approaches. To optimize the performance of the CPU chip given the engineering resource available, careful thought was given to operations which occur frequently in typical programs. Specific examples of critical performance limiters included 32-bit addition, qualifier testing, bit extraction, and address computation. These elements were optimized either by careful analysis of the critical timing paths or by development of special purpose hardware for specific functions. The "*n*-bit shifter" is an example of this special purpose hardware for supporting bit extraction operations. This shifter has the ability to shift a 32-bit quantity left or right 0 to 31 places in a single 55 ns clock cycle. The *n*-bit shifter consists of five stages of combinational logic, each stage capable of shifting left, right, or not at all as shown in Fig. 4. The shifter is controlled by PLA lines decoded from the microcode.

In a further effort to optimize the speed limiting functions, the CPU makes extensive use of pipeline techniques for microcode, for machine instructions, for ALU operations, and for memory accesses. For example, machine instructions are fetched and executed in a three-stage overlapping sequence. While a machine instruction is being executed, the following

CPU BENCHMARKS*

64-BIT	FLOATING POINT DIVIDE	16 μ SEC
64-BIT	FLOATING POINT MULTIPLY	10.4 μ SEC
64-BIT	FLOATING POINT ADD	6 μ SEC
32-BIT	LOAD FROM MEMORY	0.56 μ SEC
32-BIT	INTEGER DIVIDE	9.4 μ SEC
32-BIT	INTEGER MULTIPLY	2.9 μ SEC
32-BIT	INTEGER ADD	0.39 μ SEC
PROCEDURE CALL		3.3 μ SEC

* INCLUDES ALL OVERHEAD TIME FOR ERROR AND BOUNDS CHECKING

Fig. 5. Representative CPU performance measures.

instruction is being decoded and a microcode routine starting address is being generated from the opcode. Simultaneously, a third machine instruction is being prefetched from memory. Similarly, in the case of data accesses from memory, the CPU chip can issue several memory addresses before receiving the corresponding data words from memory. The microcode execution pipeline is another example where the machine function was optimized. Microcode execution as shown in Fig. 5 requires three phases: fetch, decode, and execute. If these steps were performed sequentially, one microinstruction would be executed every three cycles. However, the microcode sequencer, the ROM, and the PLA are designed so that these operations can occur simultaneously (except in a limited set of multistate microinstructions), leading to an average microcode execution rate of approximately one per clock cycle.

The selective optimization which we did undertake resulted in a CPU chip which is designed to operate with a 55 ns microcycle, worst case. It executes a broad spectrum of instructions at rates comparable to many mainframe computers, including a 32 X 32 bit integer multiply in 1.8 μs and a 64-bit floating point multiply in 10.4 μs. Additional performance data are provided in Fig. 6.

Flexibility was another major design objective. We chose to achieve flexibility by using microprogramming to utilize a technology strength in the ability to fabricate a high-density, high-speed ROM. The microcode words are arranged in seven fields which specify the sources and destinations for data on the buses, the operation for the ALU, the destination of the ALU result, and, finally, a qualifier for conditional microcode oper-

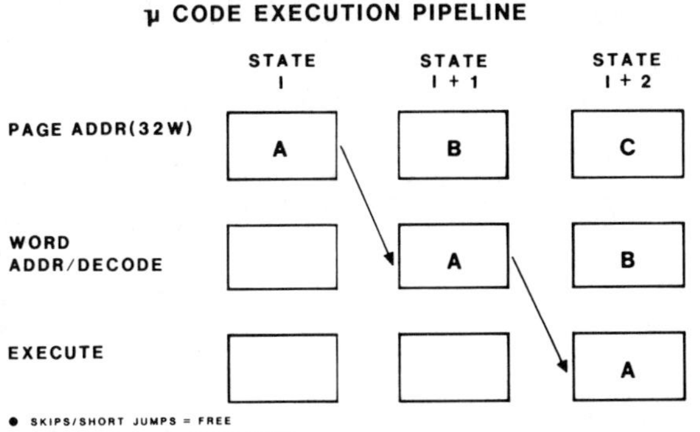

Fig. 6. Microcode pipeline showing accessing the data from the ROM and executing it.

ALU EXAMPLE

ABUS	ASTOR	BBUS	BSTOR	FUNC	STOR	TEST
SPO		SPI		SUBA		
TOSA		TOSB		ADD	C	
OPC	SP3	TOSC		ADD	A C	AOVF

SPI - SPO ⟶ SP3, SKIP IF OVERFLOW

TOSA + TOSB + TOSC ⟶ OPC

Fig. 7. Sequential states of executing ROM microcode.

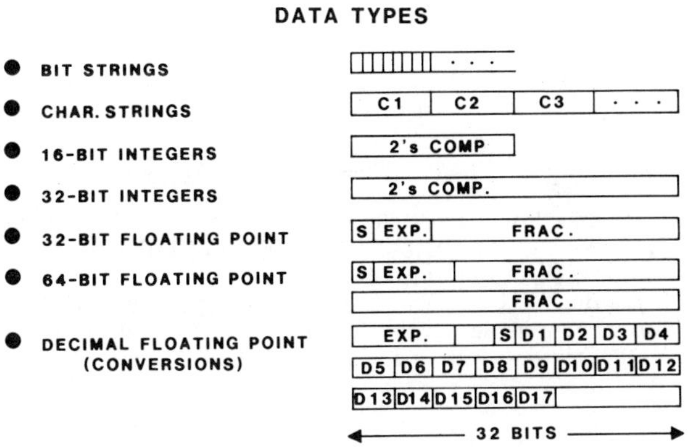

DATA TYPES

- BIT STRINGS
- CHAR. STRINGS — C1 | C2 | C3 | . . .
- 16-BIT INTEGERS — 2's COMP
- 32-BIT INTEGERS — 2's COMP.
- 32-BIT FLOATING POINT — S | EXP. | FRAC.
- 64-BIT FLOATING POINT — S | EXP. | FRAC. / FRAC.
- DECIMAL FLOATING POINT (CONVERSIONS) — EXP. | S | D1 | D2 | D3 | D4 / D5 | D6 | D7 | D8 | D9 | D10 | D11 | D12 / D13 | D14 | D15 | D16 | D17

⟵ 32 BITS ⟶

Fig. 8. Data format supported by on-board CPU microcode.

ations. This microcoding scheme provides general, flexible, and high-speed microcode operations at the expense of optimal microcode packing. Fig. 7 shows an example of microcode operations illustrating the utilization of the microcode fields, with both data buses and the ALU 100 percent utilized.

This CPU chip has been used to implement a very powerful machine instruction set which is stack based and contains support for virtual memory, multiprocessing, and multiprocessors, and supports IEEE standard floating point math. It has an address range of 500M bytes and supports a wide variety of data formats (see Fig. 8).

The instruction set is centered around a segmentation scheme which is shown in Fig. 9. Memory space is divided into four kinds of segments (code, stack, global data, and external data). Pointers to these segments are maintained in 32-bit on-chip registers and include, for example, in the case of code segments, the program base address, the program limit address, and the current instruction address. External data segments are accessed

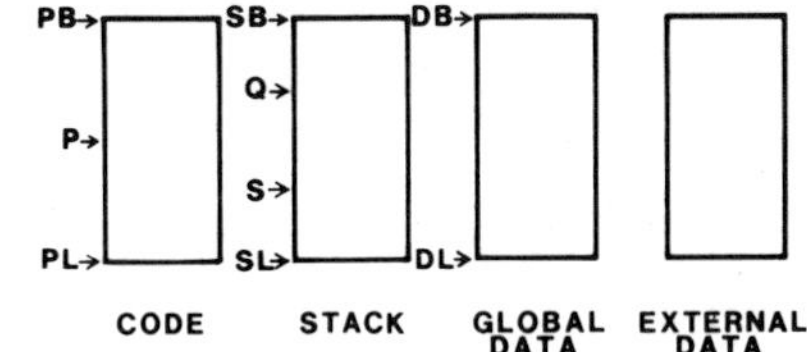

Fig. 9. Segmentation scheme supported by the CPU instruction set.

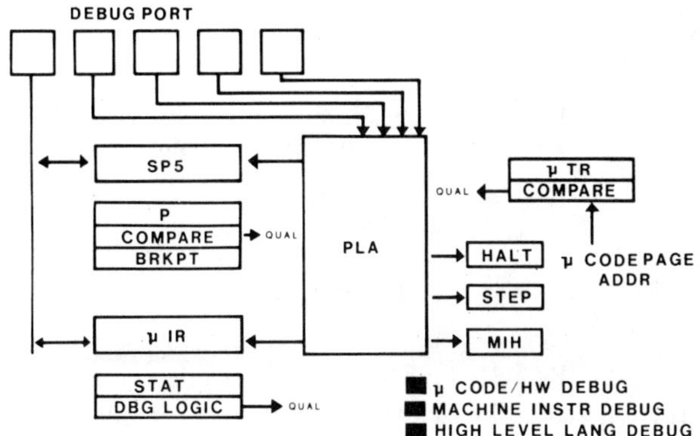

Fig. 10. Schematic representation of the debug hardware. Four pads drive the PLA, which provides control to two special registers, a scratch pad (SP5) and the microinstruction register (μIR). The debug data is loaded serially into these two registers, which can then be used to set or dump any other registers within the chip. Other registers shown provide support for higher level debugging.

via a set of memory resident tables. This scheme provides fully protected and relocatable segments.

Providing adequate testability for this chip was another major design challenge. The CPU has several levels of testability, including testability at the circuit verification, microinstruction, and high-level language levels. Explicit effort was made to provide testability at little silicon area cost and essentially no performance penalty.

Specific design features were built into the chip to verify chip function at the lowest level. Low level testability included 600 10×10 μm second-layer metal probe pads on key signal lines and a more sophisticated set of debug hardware (see Fig. 10). The debug hardware provides a mechanism for altering the normal sequencing of the machine. It provides for microcode breakpoints, single stepping microcode, single stepping machine instructions, executing externally supplied microcode, and altering the contents of any of the internal chip registers. This debug port uses only five pads, four for control and one for serial data input. The input data can be loaded either into the microinstruction register (and PLA) or into a scratch pad register.

At a higher level, special microcode routines have been included to provide the ability to implement high-level language breakpoints, single stepping, histograms of individual program line execution frequencies, and tracing both program variables and program procedures (see Fig. 11). Fig. 12 shows the chip area specifically devoted to all levels of chip debugging and testing aids. The small amount of real estate required is a consequence of the design approach and the simplicity of the overall chip design concept.

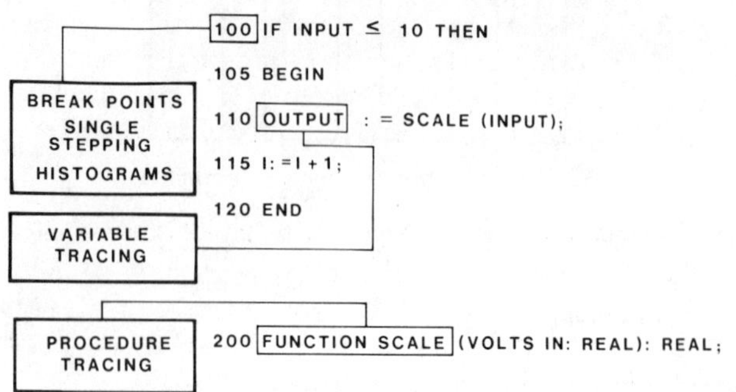
HIGH LEVEL LANGUAGE DEBUGGING
100 IF INPUT ≤ 10 THEN
105 BEGIN
BREAK POINTS
SINGLE STEPPING
HISTOGRAMS
110 OUTPUT : = SCALE (INPUT);
115 I: = I + 1;
120 END
VARIABLE TRACING
PROCEDURE TRACING
200 FUNCTION SCALE (VOLTS IN: REAL): REAL;

Fig. 11. The CPU supports special features which provide high level debugging aids such as are illustrated in the pseudolanguage example shown above.

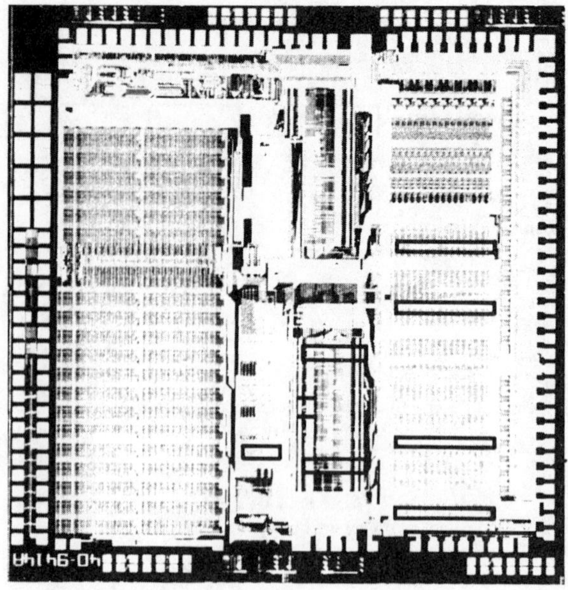

Fig. 12. The areas outlined in white delineate those circuits added specifically for testing and debugging, less than 1 percent of the total chip surface area.

IV. Conclusion

The 32-bit CPU chip described in this paper has been fabricated and fully tested. These chips execute the entire 220 instruction repertoire at or above the design frequency of 18 MHz and have met all the initial design goals. The design represents one approach to the VLSI fabrication problem and realizes a significant advance in the performance available on a single chip. It also represents an example of a successful design approach utilizing systematic design, close coupling between the circuit and system design teams, and advancements in process technology.

Acknowledgment

The results reported in this paper are the product of the efforts of engineers, managers, and fabrication teams of the Systems Technology Operation of Hewlett-Packard Company, too numerous to mention explicitly here, to whom we are deeply grateful. Our special appreciation goes to F. Wenninger, C. Christopher, M. Kolesar, and D. Maitland, who provided much of the technical insight and motivation in the early phases of this program, and D. Schulz and J. Anderson for their continued support of our efforts.

References

[1] R. N. Noyce, "Microelectronics," *Sci. Amer.*, vol. 237, pp. 63-69, Sept. 1977.

[2] J. M. Mikkelson, L. A. Hall, A. K. Malhotra, S. D. Seccombe, and M. S. Wilson, "An NMOS VLSI process for fabrication of a 32 bit CPU chip," this issue, pp. 542-547.

[3] B. Lattin, "VLSI design methodology–The problem of the 80's for microprocessor design," presented at the Cal. Tech. Conf. VLSI, California Inst. of Technology, Pasadena, Jan. 1979.

Gate array embodies System/370 processor

by C. Davis, G. Maley, R. Simmons, H. Stoller, R. Warren, and T. Wohr, *IBM Corp., Data Systems Division, East Fishkill, N. Y.*

The central processing unit of a System/370 mainframe computer now sits on a single chip (see Fig. 1). The goal was to see if the computer-aided design of gate arrays could meet the challenge of very large-scale integration, and it can—only nine months were required to encode the processor's logic design, automatically place and wire the logic gates, and generate and verify the test patterns. No commercial production of the device itself is planned, however.

On the chip . . .

Figure 2 shows how the chip connects to other system components, and Figs. 3 and 4 explain the chip architecture. A circuit count of nearly 5,000 and a 2.2-nanosecond NAND circuit—conservatively clocked at 4 ns—gives the machine a cycle time of 100 ns. The rich instruction set of the IBM System/370 requires a weighted average of 50 machine cycles for each instruction, resulting in a system performance rating of 200,000 instructions per second.

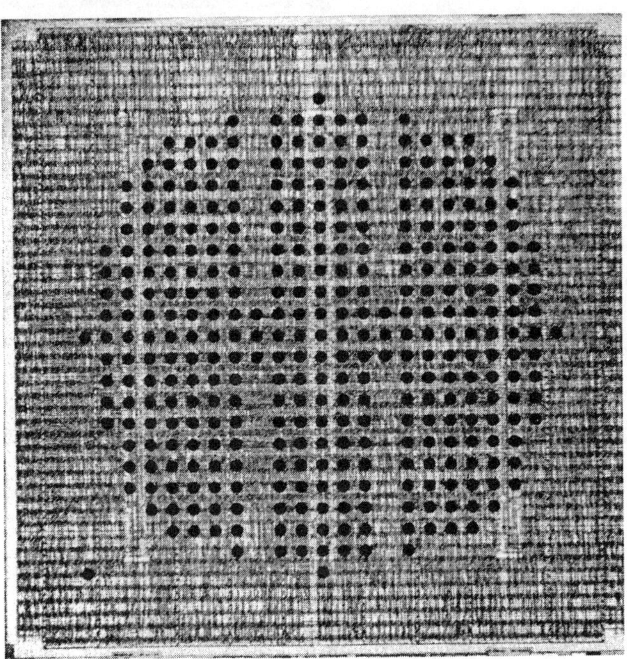

1. Master mainframe. Along 1,405 wiring channels and through 33,516 vias, 4,923 Schottky bipolar gates out of a possible 7,640 were automatically interconnected. The third and final metal level on the 7-by-7-millimeter (75,950-mil^2) die ties to 200 I/O solder dots.

An 8-bit arithmetic and logic unit is all that can be permitted if hardware assists such as program relocation are to be included. A shared incrementer/decrementer (I/D) is used rather than counters, because sequential circuits can be difficult to test.

. . . and off the chip

An off-chip control store, assumed to be read-only memory, provides overall control of the processor (see Fig. 2). The ROM word is 54 bits wide, including 3 parity bits. On the assumption that up to a quarter of a million bits of ROM would be required, a full 2 bytes of ROM addressing, gated off the CPU chip, is provided.

Enough pads (200) were supplied on the master slice to allow horizontal microprogramming. This means that system resources are controlled by microcode bits directly, without the need for vertical microprogramming. The directness of such an approach should reduce timing and logic errors, while its horizontal nature should lessen the testing problem and in general add to the flexibility of the chip.

The System/370 architecture requires many active registers that could not fit on the chip, so an off-chip high-speed local store is instead used for this purpose. Given the performance of the bipolar processor chip, this local store complies nicely with the requirement for a 100-ns machine cycle time. (The access time of the register bank is 60 ns.)

Data flow

The 8-bit ALU, incrementer/decrementer, and both off-chip memories are controlled by the 54-bit microcode word, as shown in Figs. 3 and 4. The microcode is also responsible for its own sequencing.

The ALU performs its arithmetic and logic operations on two 8-bit binary numbers, producing one 8-bit binary result with carry and overflow signals. It can also perform the same operations on two packed 4-bit binary-coded decimal numbers or on 8-bit binary numbers that represent alphabetic characters. It produces negative numbers in the 2's complement form.

Its three 8-bit logical operations are OR, AND, and exclusive-OR. Its arithmetic operations may be controlled directly from a microcode ROM field or indirectly through a bit located in the status register, S. This indirect control allows microprogramming routines to be shared for adding and subtracting operations.

The output of the ALU is connected to a bus that is used to pass the data to a series of machine registers. As for the input, two registers, A and B, each hold a byte for the ALU. Fields in the ROM word decide how the contents of the A and B registers are presented to the ALU. This gating is important to decimal operations because it gives easy access to each of the two 4-bit hexadecimal digits in each byte. The two hexadecimal digits in the A register can also be swapped—a feature that is very useful for the packing and unpacking instructions required by the System/370 architecture.

The incrementer/decrementer is really a 24-bit binary

Reprinted with permission from *Electronics*, vol. 53, pp. 140-143, Oct. 9, 1980.

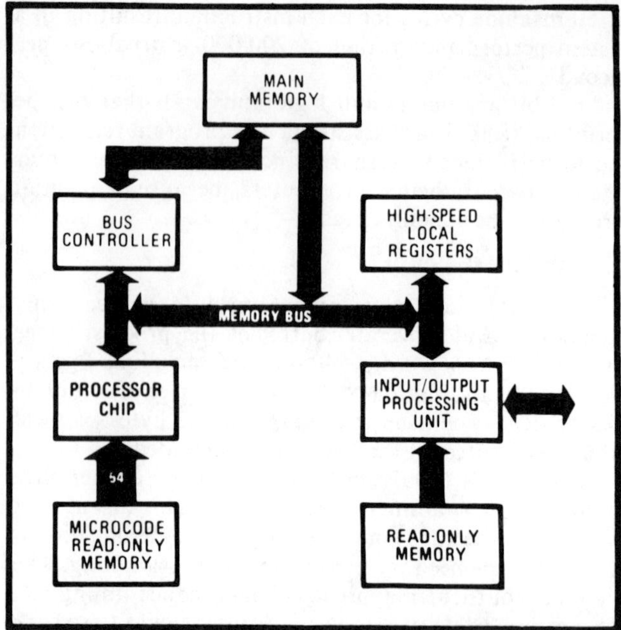

2. In its place. To complete the System/370 architecture, the processor chip talks to main memory, a high-speed local store, and a separate I/O channel processor over a multiplexed memory bus. Microcode is brought in directly over a separate 54-bit bus.

arithmetic unit having limited capabilities. It can perform only eight arithmetic operations: add or subtract the values 0, 1, 2, and 3. The primary input to the I/D comes from the 24-bit memory-address register. A ROM field selects which of the eight arithmetic operations is to be performed, as well as which set of registers is to feed the memory-address register (MAR) and thus the I/D. The output of the I/D is always returned to the same set of registers that feed the MAR.

A 24-bit shifter with a very limited number of complex instructions is connected in parallel with the I/D. The shifter primarily handles the 12-bit address field used for page addressing in a virtual storage system.

Memory control

Twenty-four address lines from the processor chip address 16 million bytes of main storage—another requirement of the System/370 architecture. The chip can accept or transmit memory data in either 1- or 2-byte increments. For reasons of performance, however, a 2-byte interface is preferred and is assumed here.

The parity of each data byte from the main store is checked by the chip. Parity generators affix a parity bit to each memory data byte leaving the chip, and these bits are tested when the bytes return.

The two main memories with which the chip works can have different speeds. Since they share the same address and data buses, they cannot be referenced on the same cycle. Two independent signals, generated by a ROM field, leave the chip and select either memory or neither memory. This arrangement allows I/O devices to be affixed to the same set of address and data lines as the main memories.

The CPU will operate at almost any memory speed, since the memories are asynchronous with it. Any mem-

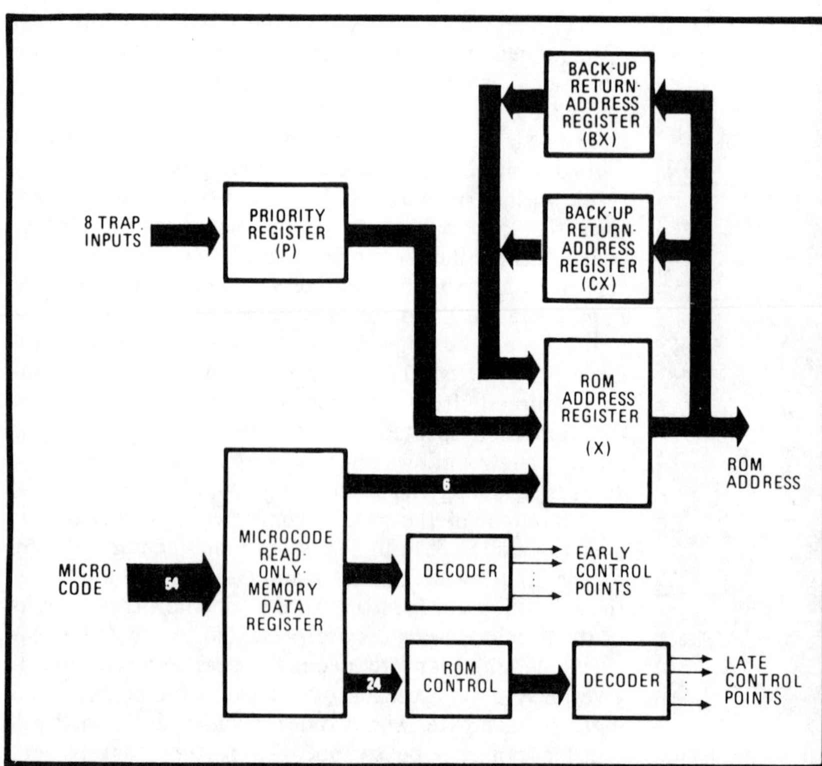

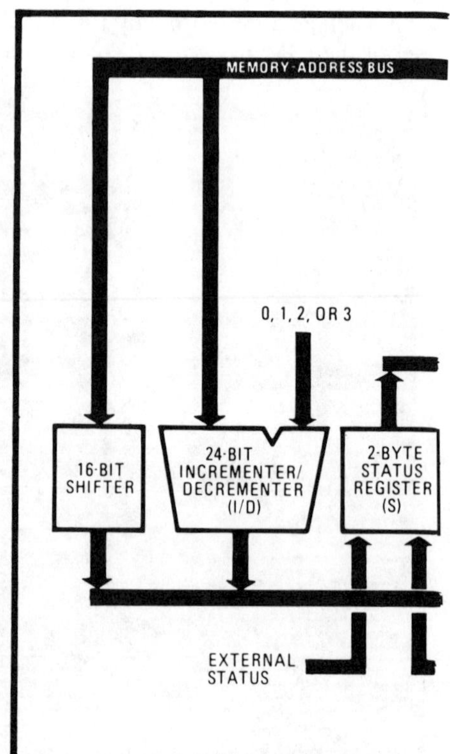

3. Decoding. The 54-bit microcode gets divided up for control and sequencing of the microcode ROM itself. The next address is based upon bits from the ROM, from trap inputs, and from backup registers holding return addresses if a trap was taken.

ory reference causes the processor to enter a wait state that lasts until a data-valid signal is received from the referenced memory. A separate control line from the chip requests a read or write operation.

A 16-bit ROM address is generated very early in each machine cycle to ready the next 54-bit microcode word (see Fig. 3). Thus, while one word controls the chip, the next word is being fetched. As the generation of the next ROM address requires 25 ns, the access time of the microcode ROM must be 75 ns for the 100-ns machine cycle time.

ROM addressing

The CPU generates 2 low-order bits of ROM address by examining conditions internal to the chip. Two fields in the ROM data word, one field for each bit, dictate which internal conditions the CPU is to consider. This technique provides a four-way conditional branch that appears to be adequate for a 1-byte CPU.

The next-higher 6 bits of the address are taken directly from a 6-bit field in the ROM data word, thereby enabling the ROM programmer to read any one of 64 words without consideration of the 2 branch bits. By setting each of the 2 branch bits to 0 or 1, a programmer can read any of 256 words without branching.

The memory address register is 3 bytes wide (refer to Fig. 4). Any bit pattern in this register will appear on the 24 address lines from the chip. The immediate source of the data to be placed in either the high-speed local store or the main memory is derived from one of four pairs of registers. Any of the 2-byte R, G, L, or H register pairs may be used as a memory-data register (MDR), significantly reducing the need for data transfer among registers. The G register pair has special ROM branching capabilities that dictate its use as an operation-code register.

A 3-byte instruction counter (the I register) is updated by having its contents passed through the I/D. Another 3-byte register, U, serves as an operand-address register for main store; it, too, can be updated by the I/D. The 2-byte T register is used for addressing local store, limiting the size of the local store to 65,536, or 64-K, words. Although this feature is not shown in Fig. 4, the I, U, T, and R registers can pass 2 bytes of data — with or without displacement information — among themselves to aid in implementing the virtual storage requirements of the System/370 architecture.

More registers

As mentioned, the S register is a CPU status register. The microprogram uses it for branching by altering the 2 low-order bits of the ROM address generated by the chip. The higher-order byte of the S register can be set and reset by external inputs.

The 1-byte F register is for interrupts, and all 8 of its bits may be set in accordance with external conditions. The response to the setting of these bits is under control of the microprogram, and action is usually delayed until the end of a System/370 instruction. This delay time can therefore vary from a few to hundreds of machine cycles.

The execution of some System/370 instructions may require hundreds of microinstructions. It is therefore

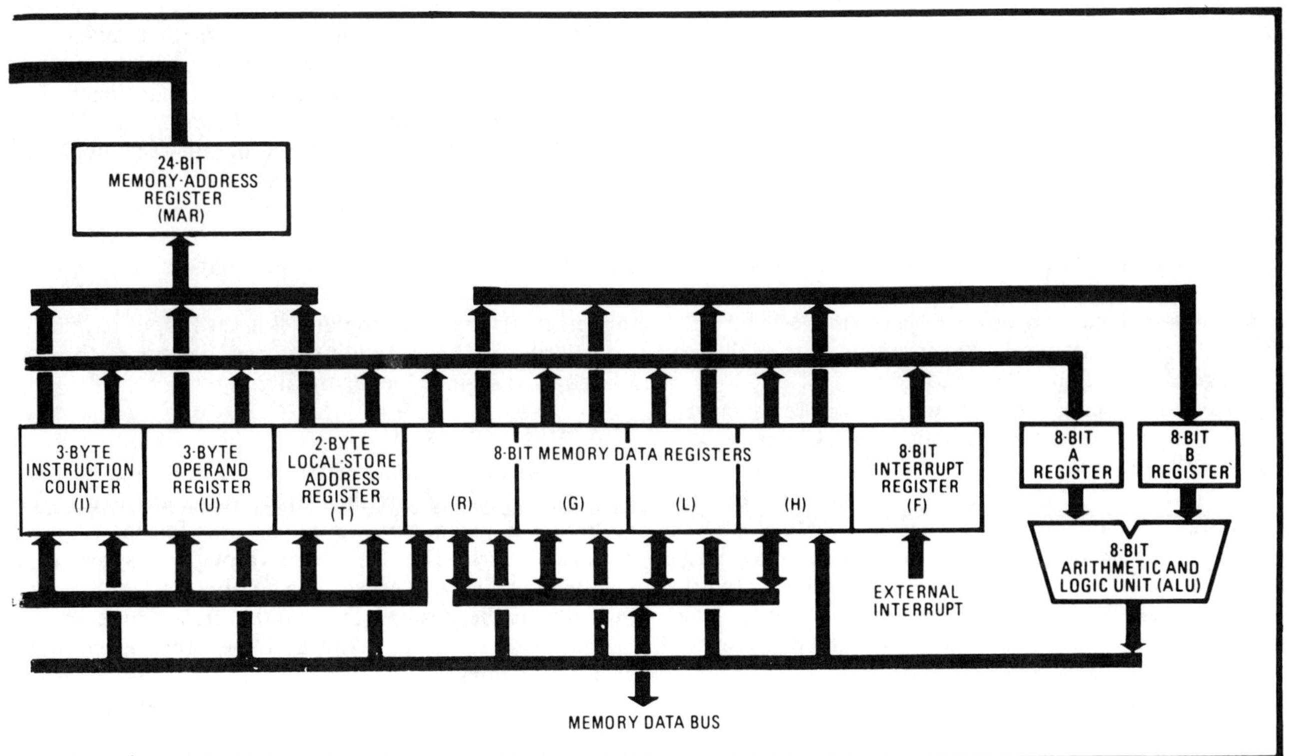

4. Architectural details. An 8-bit arithmetic and logic unit adds and subtracts, ORs, ANDs, and exclusive-ORs. The 24-bit memory address register feeds a 16-bit shifter and a 24-bit incrementer/decrementer that is actually an ALU with limited functions.

advantageous to provide a hardware-forced microprogram-entry, or trap, system to transfer control between microprograms on a microinstruction boundary rather than on a macroinstruction boundary. Once included, this hardware can be expanded to solve other difficult control problems such as the handling of parity errors, push-button interrupts like those generated through a front panel, and memory wraparound.

Eight trap levels

The processor chip incorporates eight trap levels, each of which forces a different address onto the ROM address lines. The eight levels are executed in the following order:

- Parity errors.
- Initial program load (IPL) request.
- Page overflow (virtual storage operation).
- Memory wraparound.
- Memory-protect violation.
- Stop request.
- I/O control.
- I/O control.

The last two levels are intended to handle high-speed I/O devices that cannot wait until the end of a System/370 instruction.

Once a trap has been taken, a latch is set and all future trapping is suspended until a microinstruction is executed to reset the latch. In addition, each of the seven low levels (all below parity error) can be individually masked off. As shown in Fig. 3, the ROM address register has two backup registers to save return addresses when a trap instruction is in progress.

No macrocircuits are used in the physical design of the logic. Every logic function on the chip—whether a register, latch, or one-shot—is created exclusively out of NAND gates.

Furthermore, every function was designed so that the placement program could locate the component NAND blocks anywhere on the chip. For example, the latches were designed to operate even if the four NAND blocks comprising the network were located at each of the corners of the chip. This approach was adopted because it gave maximum flexibility to the automatic placement and wiring programs.

Redundant logic can improve performance and reliability. Unfortunately, it cannot be used if high test coverage of stuck faults is desired.

Performance enhancement was therefore achieved without redundancies. For instance, clock timing was used to eliminate logic glitches (noise). In addition, for easier testing, all clock lines can be activated by test input signals, allowing data to be flushed through the registers. As a result, the entire chip becomes one large combinatorial—rather than a sequential—network. Moreover, all registers may be loaded directly from input pads and read directly from output pads, which further enhances testability.

Testing details

Manually generated test patterns were used to test the microprocessor chip. The initial objective was to select reasonably good chips from the first fabrication run through flush testing. Chips that passed this preliminary screening would then be mounted on modules and functionally exercised. The exerciser would clock the chips at full speed while executing test microcode.

A limited number of flush tests caught 40% of the stuck faults. Close to 100% may be caught by exercising the registers and propagating the stuck faults through the sequential circuits. Some test patterns could cause the chip to oscillate or lock up. These were spotted by means of a simulator and avoided.

The fault simulator produces an updated listing of the untested fault conditions. In working with this list, new test patterns are generated to cover the untested faults. Thus any degree of test coverage may be obtained.

The physical design

In the case of this gate array, 4,923 circuits had to be placed within 7,739 cells and 10,605 interconnections had to be wired on a 800-by-600-channel grid.

Two placement methods were pursued: fully automated placement and iterative structured placement. The automatic method ignored the functionality of the logic and instead grouped and placed the logic blocks on the basis of the interconnection matrix. This was possible because the basic logic gate had been designed to operate independently of the position of its constituent NAND blocks. Since not all the cells of the chip had to be used, rows of horizontal cells were kept clear of NAND blocks in order to provide avenues for additional horizontal wiring channels.

Three different automatic placement passes were made, and the most promising was chosen for automatic wiring. Each placement pass required approximately three hours of IBM System/370 model 168 data-processing time, as well as several hundred cylinders of disk space.

The structured, iterative placement method was pursued as an alternative in case the fully automatic method was unsuccessful. In addition, this method gives the designer greater control during failure analysis and greater freedom to correlate the physical placement of a set of NAND blocks and their logical function.

The same automatic wiring program was used on placements resulting from both methods. The best fully automatic placement was wired with only 68 overflows. Wiring for the best structured method produced over 200 overflows. The detailed printout of the wiring required a plot measuring about 4 by 5 meters. Using this printout, and with the aid of a card input language to describe the wire additions and deletions, the 68 overflows were imbedded manually.

Few errors

After wiring, a sophisticated pattern-recognition program for checking circuit shapes was used to test for ground-rule (geometry) violations and for logical and physical errors. The first pass through this program ferreted out just five errors in a total of 750,000 shapes involved in the design. Two of the errors were in the definition of the gate array and the other three were wiring violations.

The second pass was error-free. The shape-checking procedure required about four hours of processing time on the IBM System/370 model 168 and several hundred cylinders of disk space.

The physical design took about three months to complete. Allowance should be made for the fact that this was the first time that this array and automatic placement and wiring programs were used. A second-pass design would take much less time. □

Part IV
Performance Evaluation

UNTIL the advent of the third generation chips, microprocessors were simple in design. The instruction set was comprised of only about 50 instructions, and features to enhance throughput by pipelining and parallel operations were rare. Timings provided by manufacturers for common instructions (such as ADD and MULTIPLY) could be used to compare performance of chips from different manufacturers. This comparison was facilitated by the similarity of architectures and instruction sets of different microprocessors. For example, the Zilog Z-80 used a superset of the Intel 8080 instruction repertoire, enabling equitable comparison of chips of two different vendors. The selection of a chip was a fairly straightforward exercise.

Contemporary microprocessors are characterized by complex design differing enormously from one vendor to another, and even from one chip family to another of the same make (e.g., the Intel 80286 and the Intel 432). As seen in previous Parts of this book, the system architectures, the instruction sets, the addressing modes, the data-handling capabilities, and the multitude of auxiliary chips all contribute to making it infeasible to compare chips on the basis of raw instruction timings. Further, since modern microprocessors are consciously designed to support and process multiple jobs concurrently, comparison of chips requires a comprehensive identification of the computing environment and the jobs that can or will run in parallel.

This, in turn, brings us to the complicated domain of workload characterization. For the subset of chips that will be used in dedicated systems (e.g., on-line monitoring of processes), it may be feasible to accurately define input data rates and characteristics. But the greater usage of chips is in general-purpose systems—personal computers, word processors, desktop computers—environments in which it is virtually impossible to define "average" or "typical" usage, especially since the usage itself is heavily impacted by the speed and flexibility of the system.

The situation is akin to the task of evaluating computer mainframes. As computers became increasingly complex and the definition of the computing environment nebulous, it became essential to devise new performance evaluation techniques. Fortunately, many of those techniques can be easily transplanted into the realm of microprocessors.

Depending on the application scenario, one or more of the following evaluation criteria may be relevant.

1) Instruction Time

This reflects the time taken to execute a particular instruction or, more commonly, a set of instructions. The elapsed time is dependent on the kind of instruction, the location and size of operands, the exact instruction sequence, clock frequency, and other factors. When a particular chip is claimed to offer a processing power of 1 MIP (million instructions per second), this figure must be used cautiously if the exact instruction mix has not been defined.

2) Throughput

In the case of chips that can operate on several processes in parallel, it is useful to estimate the total "throughput" capabilities of the different chips. The total throughput will depend significantly on a programmer's ability to make maximum use of system resources.

3) Application-Related Measures

In the case of an electronic exchange application, for example, it is most pertinent to know the number of switchings the chip can handle. Similarly, for primarily data processing and text processing applications, it is appropriate to estimate the overall number-crunching and record-crunching abilities, respectively. However, most real-life applications constitute a mix of several different scenarios.

4) Overall System Productivity

Computer performance evaluation is the measurement of how well software is using hardware for a given job mix. With software functions now being gradually implemented in hardware, the essential criterion becomes how well the user programmer can benefit from the system. Thus, if the same user takes five minutes to solve a problem using System A, and an hour to solve the same problem using System B, then System A is 12 times as powerful as System B, provided the particular problem represents a close approximation of the totality of the user's work function. Such overall system productivity comparisons have yet to become widely available.

The evaluation criteria above, although by no means exhaustive, represent a spectrum of levels; the instruction level criterion at 1) represents the hardware end of the spectrum, and the overall productivity at 4) represents the user end of the spectrum. Microprocessors can be evaluated at different points along this spectrum.

In the first reprint in this Part, the above concept is emphasized by the identification of several distinct evaluation levels. Various hierarchical levels attempt to focus on hardware architecture, instruction sets, routines, support tasks, operating system functions, and user jobs. A set of evaluation kernels has been developed. These kernels have been used to identify the strengths and weaknesses of the Intel 8086, Zilog Z-8000, and the Motorola MC-68000 16-bit processors. The significance of the path length is outlined. Finally, the need for constructing an appropriate mix factor (AMF) based on the application scenario is emphasized.

In the next paper, R. K. Bell *et al*. also concentrate on the same set of three microprocessors. Their results are based on the timings for word processing applications—enter character, insert line, cursor to home, etc. They conclude that although all chips were equally usable from a hardware viewpoint, one particular chip was slightly superior in terms of lower timings and memory space, for the particular application.

Paul M. Hansen *et al.* provide insight into the overall speed and the size of code provided by the Intel iAPX 432, as compared to several different 16-bit microprocessors. Four programs (string search, sieve, puzzle, and Ackermann's function) were used. The results show that if the iAPX 432 is tested as a high-level language uniprocessor for integer and character programs, its potential benefits of transparent multiprocessing, data security, and increased programmer productivity are not reflected, and if one looks at timings alone, one may come to the erroneous conclusion that 32-bit microprocessors are slower than 16-bit microprocessors. The article reaffirms the extreme care needed to program meaningful benchmarks.

The survey articles on architectural comparisons of 16-bit and 32-bit microprocessors (Parts II and III of this book) contain comparisons of performance of several popular chips. The concluding sections of these articles also contain useful tips on selecting a microprocessor and on noncommercial issues, such as second-sourcing.

Several vendors of 16-bit microprocessors are now offering superior versions of their original chips. It is interesting to evaluate the performance of these chips in comparison to the 32-bit microprocessors. Based on information from [1] and from the vendors, comparative information on execution timings is summarized in Table I.

Table I shows that the Intel 80286 operates at 10 MHz and is significantly faster than the Intel iAPX 432. Even the HP-32 biter, operating at a much higher clock frequency, can barely compete with the Intel 80286. However, it is essential to remember that what is being compared represents the full power of the Intel 80286, but not all the advantages and the full power of the other 32-bit microprocessors. The choice of processor ultimately depends on the nature of the application and on the preferences of the designer.

References

[1] D. A. Patterson, "A performance evaluation of the Intel 80286," *Comput. Architecture News*, vol. 10, p. 17, Sept. 1982.

TABLE I
EXECUTION TIMES

Machine	Language	Word Size	Time (milliseconds) Search	Sieve	Puzzle	Acker
VAX-11/780	C	32	1.4	250	9400	4600
	Pascal (UNIX)	32	1.6	220	11 900	7800
	Pascal (VMS)	32	1.4	259	11 530	9850
68000 (8 MHz)	C	32	4.7	740	37 100	7800
	Pascal	16	5.3	810	32 470	11 480
	Pascal	32	5.8	960	32 520	12 320
68000 (16 MHz)	Pascal	16	1.3	196	9180	2750
	Pascal	32	1.5	246	9200	3080
8086 (5 MHz)	Pascal	16	7.3	764	44 000	11 100
432/rel. 2 (4 MHz)	Ada	16	35	3200	350 000	260 000
432/rel. 3 (8 MHz)	Ada	16	4.4	978	45 700	47 800
80286 (8 MHz)	Pascal	16	1.4	168	9138	2218
80286 (10 MHz)	Pascal	16	1.1	135	7311	1774
HP 32 biter (18 MHz)	Pascal	32	NA	NA	7450	2590
NS16032 (7 MHz)	Pascal	32	NA	NA	24 000	9900

Bibliography

[1] D.A. Patterson, "A performance evaluation of the Intel 80286," *Mini-Micro Syst.*, pp. 152–162, Dec. 1980.

[2] ——, "A tale of four μPs: Benchmarks quantify performance," *EDN*, pp. 179–185, Apr. 1, 1981.

[3] A. Gupta and H. D. Toong, "An architectural comparison of 32-bit microprocessors," *IEEE Micro*, vol. 3, Feb. 1983 (included in Part III of this book).

[4] J. Heering, "The Intel 8086, the Zilog Z8000 and the Motorola MC68000 microprocessors," *EUROMICRO J.*, vol. 6, pp. 135–143, 1980.

[5] H. D. Toong and A. Gupta, "An architectural comparison of contemporary 16-bit microprocessors," *IEEE Micro*, vol. 1, May 1981 (included in Part II of this book).

Evaluation Kernels for Microprocessor Performance Analyses

Hoo-min D. Toong and Amar Gupta
Massachusetts Institute of Technology, Cambridge, MA 02139, U.S.A.

Received 17 October 1981

Contemporary microprocessors offer several sophisticated technical features that were once the exclusive domain of large mainframes. The implementation of these capabilities in VLSI motivates the evaluation of these microprocessors at various hierarchical levels. This paper compares the basic architectures, the instruction sets and finally the overall performance of the three leading 16-bit microprocessors.

Keywords: Microprocessors, Performance Evaluation, Architecture, Instruction Set, Benchmark, Machine Independent Algorithm, Selection Methodology.

Introduction

The complexity of the new generation microprocessors requires greater effort in the evaluation and design of their software/hardware architectures. Previously, microprocessors were characterized by 8-bit and 16-bit structures that were relatively straightforward in design. However, the newer 16-bit devices incorporate features such as memory management, complex data manipulation and data movement instructions, and multiprocessor synchronization mechanisms [1]. The advent of more powerful 32-bit architectures will further complicate the task of performance measurement.

Microprocessors represent a unique combination of software and hardware. Traditional nonprocessor functions such as interrupt structures, bus arbitration, and memory management are now being incorporated directly into the hardware of the microprocessor. This tends to accentuate the coupling between software and hardware at the processor level. Consequently, to effectively evaluate a current generation device, it is necessary to employ both hardware and software measures. Functionally, a microprocessor can be tested at various hierarchical levels as depicted in Fig. 1 [2].

Reprinted with permission from *Performance Evaluation*, vol. 2, pp. 1–8, May 1982.

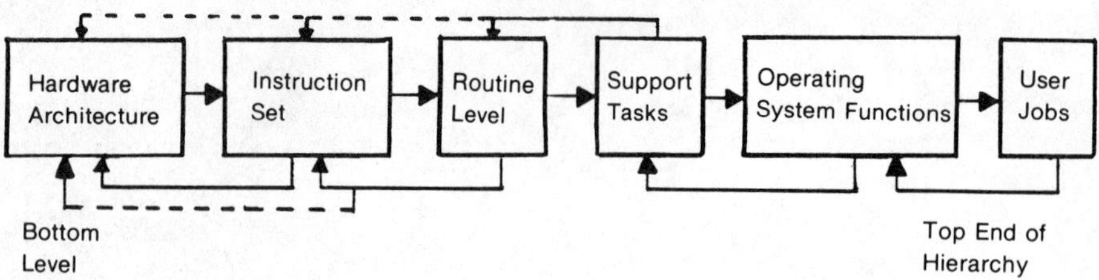

Fig. 1. Microprocessor measurement hierarchy.

Table 1
Comparison at hardware architecture level

Characteristic	8086	Z 8000	MC 68000
General:			
Basic clock frequency	5 MHz (4–8 MHz)	2.5–3.9 MHz	5–8 MHz
Number of transistors	21000 (MHz version)	17500	68000
Number of general purpose registers	14	16	16
Pin count	40	48/40	64
Addressing:			
Direct address range (in bytes)	1 M	6×8 M	16 M/64 M
Addressing modes	Immediate	Immediate	Immediate
	Register direct	Register direct	Register direct
	Register indirect	Register indirect	Register indirect
	Register indirect indexed	Register indirect indexed	Register indirect indexed
	Register indirect with offset	Register indirect with offset	Register indirect with offset
	Register indirect indexed with offset		Register indirect indexed with offset
		Register indirect with predecrement	Register indirect with predecrement
		Register indirect with post decrement	Register indirect with postincrement
	Absolute	Absolute	Absolute
		Absolute indexed	
		Relative	Relative
			Relative indexed with offset
Primitive data types:			
Bits	No	Yes	Yes
Integer byte/word	Yes	Yes	Yes
Integer double word	No	Yes	Yes
Logical byte/word	Yes	Yes	Yes
Logical double word	No	No	Yes
Character strings	Yes	Yes	No
BCD byte	Yes	Yes	Yes
Floating point	No	No	No
Timings:			
Bus cycle time	800 nsec (500 nsec for 8 MHz version)	750 nsec	500 nsec read 750 nsec write

At each level in this hierarchy, one must construct a set of benchmarks such that all higher levels can perform their measures using the appropriate combination of measures from previous stages. This ascending inclusion property depends heavily on identifying the Appropriate Mix Factor (AMF). The scope of each level is as follows:

Hardware architecture: from the hardware engineer's viewpoint, valid benchmarks compare architectural features such as registers, data paths, word widths, ALU sizes and other hardware features. All deficiencies identified by succeeding benchmarks at the next higher level will reflect themselves as architectural inadequacies at this level.

Instruction level: one compares on an instruction-by-instruction basis, especially when considering newly released processors.

Routine level: sample user tasks coded in assembly language are often represented as competitive analyses between processors by manufacturers. The application programs frequently reflect advantages unique to the 'winning' microprocessor.

Support task: support tasks for the operating system and user jobs are encoded to evaluate the level of sophistication of operating systems support. An example of a support task would be a multi-level queue management used by the process scheduling function of the operating system.

System functions: at this level, specific operating system and user tasks are encoded, e.g. memory management algorithms for segmentation.

User jobs: this benchmark spawns many processes, thereby exercising the operating system and all lower level benchmarks.

In this paper, the 16-bit microprocessors are evaluated at four different levels.

Hardware architecture

The current single-chip, 16-bit microprocessor market has three contenders:

(1) the 8086 (iAPX 86): designed by Intel; second-sourced by Mostek in the US and by Siemens in Europe [3];

(2) the Z 8000: designed by Zilog; second-sourced by AMD in the US by SGS/ATES in Europe, and by Sharp in Asia;

(3) the MC 6800: designed by Motorola [4]; second-sourced by AMD and Rockwell in the US by EFCIS in Europe, and by Hitachi in Asia [5]. In addition, National Semiconductor has announced the NS 16000 microprocessor chip family scheduled to be introduced during 1982 [6]. In the absence of availability of the National 16000 family chips, we shall concentrate on the 8086, the Z 8000 and the MC 68000.

Comparative information, at the hardware architectural level, pertaining to the three chips is summarized in Table 1.

Instruction level

All of these microprocessors offer a very powerful instruction set, as compared to earlier chips. The 8086 was introduced in 1978, Z 8000 in 1979 and the MC 68000 in 1980; as such, there is a general trend of increasing sophistication amongst the three chips. A notable exception is that the MC 68000 does not support string manipulation instructions, and that makes its use in text-processing applications quite difficult. At the same time, one must emphasize that the MC 68000 instruction set can be extended easily as it is microprogrammed.

The benchmark comparisons at the instruction level are summarized in Table 2a and 2b.

Routine level

At the routine level, the analysis is much more difficult and subjective than at the lower levels. The identification of representative routines, and

Table 2a
Instruction level comparisons

Instruction	8086	Z 8000	MC 68000
Primitive			
Move	Yes	Yes	Yes
Jump	Yes	Yes	Yes
Conditional branch	Yes	Yes	Yes
Multiway branch	No	No	No
Subroutine call	Yes	Yes	Yes
Condition code primitives	No	Yes	Yes
Bit instructions	No	Yes	Yes
Privileged instructions	No	Yes	Yes
String operations	Yes	Yes	No
Floating point	No	No	No

Table 2b
Instruction level comparisons (in microseconds)

Operation	Data type	8086	Z 8000	MC 68000
Register-to register move	Byte/word	0.40	0.75	0.50
	Double-word	0.80	1.25	0.50
Memory-to register move	Byte/word	3.40	3.50	1.50
	Double-word	6.80	4.25	2.00
Memory-to-memory move	Byte/word	7.00	7.00	2.50
	Double-word	14.00	8.50	3.75
Add memory to register	Byte/word	3.60	3.75	1.50
	Double-word	7.20	5.25	2.25
Compare memory to memory	Byte/word	7.00	7.25	3.00
	Double-word	14.00	9.50	4.00
Multiply memory to memory	Byte	13.00	20.25	N/A
	Word	23.00	16.00	8.75
	Double-word	115.20	85.75	43.00
Conditional branch	Branch taken	1.60	1.50	1.25
	Branch not taken	0.80	1.50	1.00
Modify index branch if zero	Branch taken	2.20	2.75	1.25
Branch to subroutine		3.80	3.75	2.25

their coding at identical levels of efficiency are major constraints in any benchmark creation exercise. In the present case, the following guidelines were used [7]:

(1) The benchmarks should be as machine independent as possible.

(2) They represent well-known and complete algorithms for the particular routine function.

(3) The algorithms must exhibit the following features:

(a) finiteness – the algorithm must always terminate after a finite number of steps;

(b) definiteness – each step of the algorithm must be precisely defined;

(c) input/output – the algorithm has zero or more predefined inputs and one or more outputs;

(d) effective – all operations to be performed in the algorithm must be sufficiently basic such that they can, in principle, be done exactly and within a finite length of time by a person using pencil and paper.

On the basis of the above considerations, two routines were identified and encoded. These are described in succeeding paragraphs.

The first routine, based on Booth's multiplication algorithm, evaluates register oriented instructions, such as shifts, rotates, and arithmetic operations. Also, the routine provides the multiplication capability required in some higher-level benchmarks. The flowchart of this algorithm is shown in Fig. 2. The assembly language programs were 24 instructions, 22 instructions and 21 instructions

Table 3
Results – Booth's algorithms

Case	8086		Z 8000		68000	
	Path length	Time (clocks)	Path length	Time (clocks)	Path length	Time (clocks)
0×0	225	2112	182	1635	182	1869
−3×−5	534	2186	470	1673	470	1913
Worst case	214	2944	182	1827	182	1985
Total (1)+(2)+(3)		7242		5135		5767
Performance relative to 8086		1.00		1.41		1.26

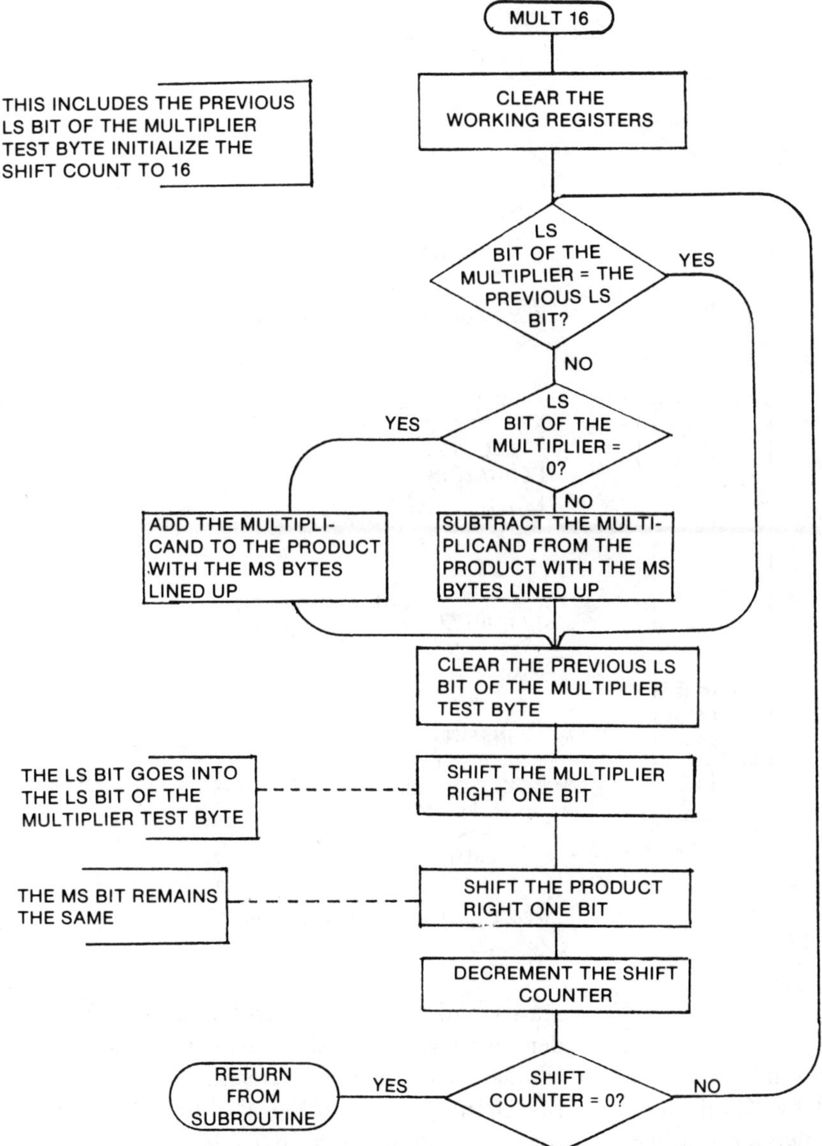

Fig. 2. Flowchart – Booth's algorithm.

long on the 8086, the Z 8000 and the MC 68000 respectively. Three different scenarios were considered, namely: multiplication of 0 by 0; multiplication of −3 by −5; and a worst case requiring alternative additions and subtractions. The total number of instructions executed (called the path length) and the corresponding time in 'clocks' are shown in Table 3.

Polynomial

The algorithm is a register test benchmark; since it is called by the hash table management task, it serves as a useful routine level module. The flowchart is shown in Fig. 3 and the performance figures are summarized in Table 4.

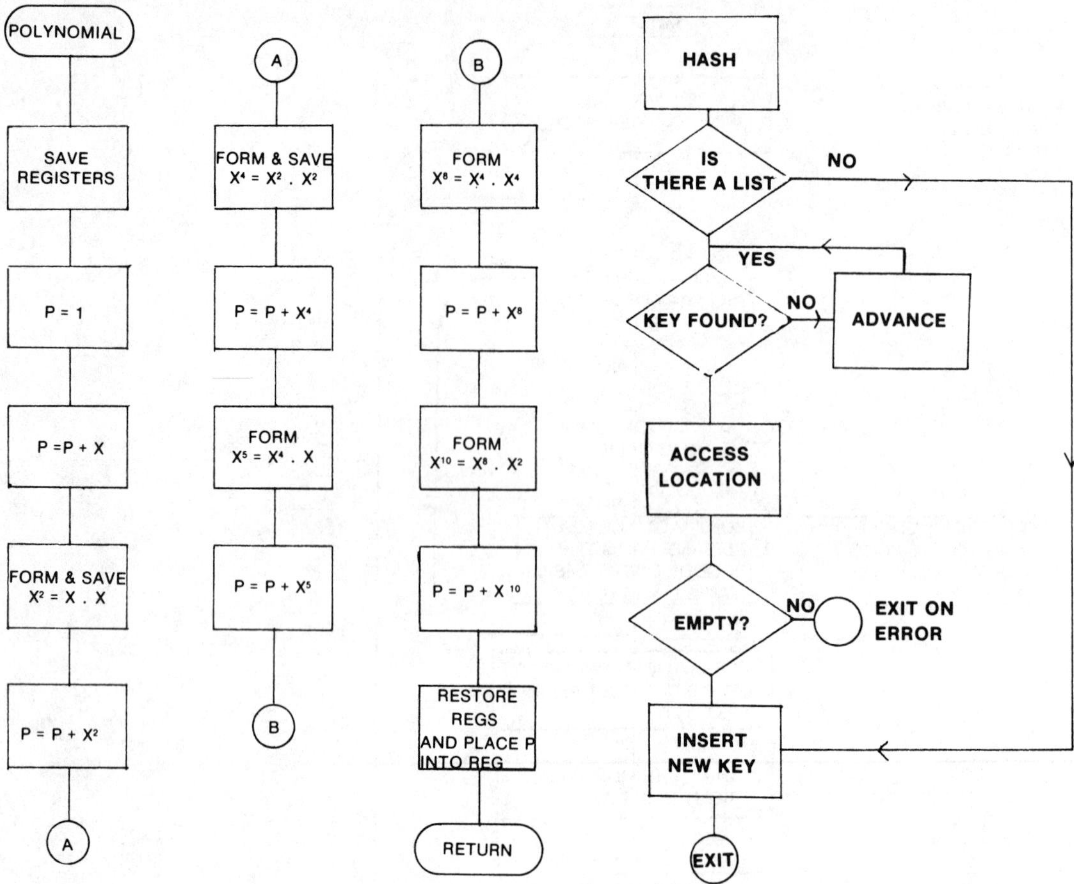

Fig. 3. Flowchart – polynomial evaluation.

Fig. 4. Flowchart – Hash algorithm.

Support task level

The algorithm used in this benchmark is the polynomial Hash algorithm used by Knuth, and builds upon the polynomial evaluation routine outlined in the previous section. Hashing is a common operation in tasks involving manipulation of data tables. This benchmark uses a table search and insertion algorithm as a vehicle for demonstrating the facility with which processors can handle common table manipulation tasks. The flowchart is shown in Fig. 4 and the performance figures are summarized in Table 5.

Another support task level benchmark encoded was designed to test the processor's ability to deal with stack operation. Since the manipulation of

Table 4
Results – polynomial evaluation

Characteristic	8086	Z 8000	68000
Program size	33	27	17
Path length (instructions)	33	27	17
Time in 'clocks'	870	484	441
Performance relative to 8086	1.00	1.80	1.97

Table 5
Results – Hash algorithm

Characteristic	86	Z 8000	68000
Program size (instructions)	24	26	18
Time in clocks	$144 + n * 48$	$188 + 66 * n$	$141 + 54 * n$

(where n is the number of searches before an open slot is found)

Table 6
Stack exerciser

S. No.	Table size	No. of tables	8086 Path length	8086 Time (clocks)	Z 8000 Path length	Z 8000 Time (clocks)	68000 Path length	68000 Time (clocks)
1	100	2	1838	18399	44	2220	436	5326
2	100	3	2751	27621	60	3332	648	7938
3	200	2	3638	36407	44	4236	836	10328
	Times $(n)+(2)+(3)$			82427		9788		23592
	Performance relative to 8086			1.00		8.42		3.49

tables often reflects a common use of stack, two table operation algorithms were chosen as a stack exerciser. The flowchart is shown in Fig. 5 and the program size was 32, 26 and 23 instructions on the 8086, Z 8000 and 68000 respectively. Three 100 entry by 16 bit tables are used as test data. The length and the width of the tables were selected to reduce the bias of the benchmark to a given task. To test the full width of a machine's data path, 16 bits was chosen. A medium size table was considered to be 100 entries. The results are summarized in Table 6.

Conclusion

Benchmark exercises have generally been either at the instruction level [8,9] or at the macro user job level [10,11]. In this paper, several intermediate evaluation levels have been identified. These intermediate levels are essential for any effective analysis of the increasingly complex microprocessor architectures. Besides fulfilling the essential criteria for constituting benchmark programs, namely – finiteness, definiteness, finite input/output, and effectiveness, the routines outlined in this paper represent very general mechanisms and as such have a very wide applicability. This is in sharp contrast to benchmarks based directly on user application, e.g. inventory control, automobile parts sorting, which serve only a very limited purpose. It is hoped that the hierarchical benchmark methodology [12] will provide a useful framework for comparative microprocessor performance analysis.

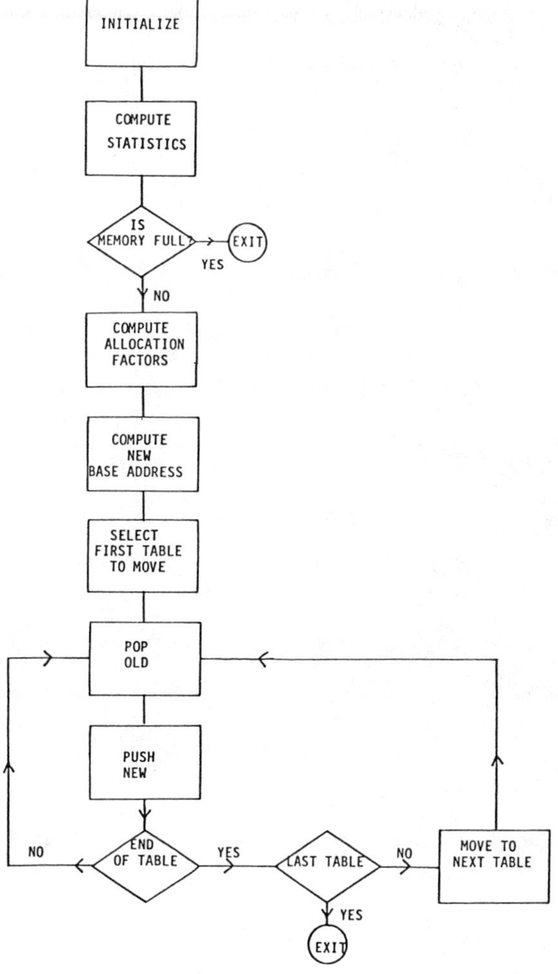

Fig. 5. Flowchart – Stack exerciser.

Acknowledgement

The authors thank John-Francis Mergen and Charles J. Smith for programming the benchmark routines.

References

[1] H.D. Toong and A. Gupta, An architectural comparison of contemporary 16-bit microprocessors, IEEE Micro (1981) pp. 26–37.

[2] H.D. Toong, Advanced microprocessor performance measurement, MRG Tech. Rept. #1, Center for Information Systems Research, M.I.T., Cambridge (1978).

[3] Intel Corp., 8086 User's guide, and other 8086 technical publications, 3065 Bowers Avenue, Santa Clara, CA 95051.

[4] Zilog. Corp., Z 8000 User's guide, and other Z 8000 technical publications, 10460 Bubb Road, Cupertino, CA 95014.

[5] Motorola Semiconductor, MC 68000 microprocessor user's manual, and other MC 68000 technical publications, Motorola IC Division, 3501 Ed Bluestein Boulevard, Austin, TX 78721.

[6] National Semiconductor Corp. The NS 16000 family of 16-bit microprocessors and other NS 16000 technical publications, 2900 Semiconductor Drive, Santa Clara, CA 95051.

[7] J.F. Mergen, C.J. Smith and H.D. Toong, Methodology for software measurement: routine level measures, MRG Tech. Rept. #2, Center for Information Systems Research, M.I.T. (1979).

[8] P.H. Callaway, Performance measurement tools for VM/370, IBM Systems J. 2 (1975).

[9] Zilog Corp., The Zilog Z 8000, an architectural overview, 10460 Bubb Road, Cupertino, CA 95014.

[10] S. Lapham and H. Kop, 8086 competitive analysis, Intel Corp., 3065 Bowers Avenue, Santa Clara, CA 95051.

[11] D. Ferrari and M. Spadoni, eds., Experimental Computer Performance Evaluation (North-Holland, Amsterdam, 1981).

[12] B. Kumar and E.S. Davidson, Computer system design using a hierarchical approach to performance evaluation, Comm. ACM 23 (9) (1980) 511.

THE BIG THREE - TODAY'S 16-BIT MICROPROCESSOR

R. K. Bell, W. D. Bell, T. C. Cooper, T. K. McFarland

Sperry Univac, Advanced Technology
General Systems Division, Salt Lake City, Utah

Abstract

This paper reports on the functional evaluation of the three 16-bit microprocessors, namely the Intel 8086, the Zilog Z8000, and the Motorola MC68000. These microprocessors were employed in several CRT applications, both monochrome and color. Execution time benchmark tests were made, mechanization problems compared and instruction/architectural characteristics highlighted. Conclusions and recommendations are made applicable to terminals and similar Sperry Univac products.

Introduction

The authors of this paper are members of the Advanced Technology Group of the Salt Lake City Development Center. Other members of the group were involved in the work supporting this paper. We recognize and give thanks to them for their contributions.

The purpose of the Advanced Technology Group is to study any and all new products and ideas which have use in communications and terminals products. The group's previous efforts in the 8-bit microprocessors lead directly to the development of the highly successful UTS 400 product. Among the many projects undertaken in the group is the effort directed towards the 16-bit microprocessors.

The 8-bit microprocessor opened the door to the intelligent terminals and we as a company stepped through that door. The 16-bit microprocessors, with their increased speeds, larger address spaces, and expanded support chips are making possible another major step in the capabilities of our communications and terminals products.

As the semiconductor industry has made new microprocessors available, we have obtained and evaluated the major 16-bit entries, namely the Intel 8086, Zilog Z8001, and Motorola 68000. These evaluations are geared toward giving us knowledge in using these devices and their support chips as they apply to Univac applications in the communications and terminals world. This paper is a statement of that knowledge obtained to date.

The paper is divided into hardware and software related sections, a section covering our benchmarks, followed by a summary.

Hardware Architecture

A discussion of hardware architecture can encompass a large variety of different concepts. It can span a wide variety of fields including definition of individual transistor functions or total system definition. This section will discuss microprocessor hardware architecture as it applies to the new 16-bit microprocessors but will limit the discussion to the input and output pins which are available to the hardware designer.

The input and output pin functions of a 16-bit microprocessor are limited because of the package limitations involved in providing over 64 I/O pins. This limitation results in multiple definitions for a single pin or the multiplexing of functions. If one looks at general architecture, the I/O functions can be divided into several categories. These are shown in Table 1 and are discussed separately in the sections which follow.

Address/Data Bus

Each microprocessor provides a means of transferring data, a means of identifying the location where the transfer will take place, and its direction. The transfer takes place on the address and data bus of the processor. The 8086 and the Z8000 microprocessors use a multiplexed data and address bus where an address is placed on the bus and a strobe is issued to indicate to the user when the address is stable. Data is transferred on the same bus and is also strobed by control signals. The 68000 demultiplexes these two buses by providing separate pins for each. The address is available continuously on an address bus and data can be transferred either in or out on a separate data bus. The multiplexed address bus requires that the user provide hardware to separate address and data. This requirement does not exist on a system where they are already separated. Large systems require that both data and address must be buffered by external components to provide the proper drive to the outside world. So, extra functions are required for either approach.

Reprinted from *Proc. 13th Annual Microprogramming Workshop*, 1980, pp. 126-138.

Table 1. I/O Functions

	8086 MIN	8086 MAX	Z8001	Z8002	68000
ADDRESS/DATA BUS	$AD_0 - AD_{15}$	$AD_0 - AD_{15}$	$AD_0 - AD_{15}$	$AD_0 - AD_{15}$	$D_0 - D_{15}$
ADDRESS BUS	$A_{16} - A_{19}$ BHE	$A_{16} - A_{19}$ BHE	-	$SN_0 - SN_6$	-
BUS CONTROL	ALE DT/R DEN RD WR M/IO	S0 S1 S2	AS DS MREQ READ/WRITE	AS DS MREQ READ/WRITE	AS E R/W VMA UDS VPA LDS DTACK
STATUS	S3 S4 S5 S6 S7	S3 S4 S5 S6 S7 QS0 QS1	ST0 ST1 ST2 ST3 Normal/System Byte/Word	ST0 ST1 ST2 ST3 Normal/System Byte/Word	FC0 FC1 FC2
BUS ARBITRATION CONTROL	HOLD HLDA	LOCK RQ/GTO RQ/GT1	BUSRQ BUSAK	BUSRQ BUSAK	BR BG BGACK
INTERRUPT	NMI INTR TEST INTRA	NMI INTR S_1, S_2, S_0 TEST	NMI VI NVI	NMI VI NVI Segment Trap	IPL0 IPL1 IPL2
CPU CONTROL	READY	READY	WAIT STOP	WAIT STOP	DTACK HALT
SYSTEM CONTROL	RESET	RESET	RESET	RESET	RESET
SYSTEM SIGNALS	Vcc GND CLK	Vcc GND CLK	Vcc GND CLK	Vcc GND CLK	Vcc GND CLK

The processor must be evaluated to determine whether the proper control signals are available to strobe the data and address at the correct time into the latches or transceivers. In all three of these microprocessor systems, the control signals are available to allow the user proper control.

Extended Address Bus

The data bus on the 16-bit microprocessors is, of course, 16 bits wide but these devices provide for wider than 64K bytes of addressing space. All of the processors provide expansion with additional address lines. The 8086 defines this address space as address bit 16 through 19. The Z8000 defines the address space as segment pins 0 through 6. The 68000 because of the separate data and address bus defines the address bus from address 0 to 23. This expands the address capability to one megabyte for the 8086, eight megabytes for the the Z8000, and 16 megabytes for the 68000. These lines are also controlled by address strobe lines.

Bus Control. Bus control signals are the functions which are provided to the user to indicate data direction and validity. They are either provided as output pins directly or decoded externally in a separate function from status pins.

The 8086 provides two modes of operation: in its minimum configuration, the signals are available to control address latching, data enable for tristate drivers, data direction for either read or write operations, and an indication of either memory or I/O device definition. The 8086 in max mode provides three encoded status lines: S0, S1, and S2. These lines are externally decoded in a bipolar circuit and provide the same information as indicated in the min-mode. A decode table is shown in Table 2.

Table 2. Decode Table

S2	S1	S0	
0	0	0	Interrupt Acknowledge
0	0	1	Read I/O
0	1	0	Write I/O
0	1	1	Halt
1	0	0	Instruction Fetch
1	0	1	Read Data from Memory
1	1	0	Write Data to Memory
1	1	1	Passive

The Z8000 provides an address strobe for latching address information, a data strobe to indicate tristate bus drive requirements, and a read/write signal which indicates data direction. Another signal available is a memory request which differentiates between memory and I/O operations. These signals must be logically combined externally to provide the necessary control for tristate drivers and receivers.

The 68000 provides an address strobe to indicate when address data is good, a read/write signal to indicate data direction and two data strobes to indicate either upper byte or lower byte selection. The 68000 data bus is asynchronous and the memory or I/O devices connected to the system must respond with a data acknowledge signal indicating that the data transfer is complete. A secondary bus control system in the 68000 provides for the control of 6800 microprocessor peripheral circuits.

Status

All microprocessors evaluated provide microprocessor status on output pins. These status functions require decoding in order to determine the various processor states. The 8086 provides internal microprocessor status, as well as queue status to the user. The Z8000 provides microprocessor status and information regarding system use of either normal mode or protected system mode. It also indicates whether bytes or words are being accessed. The 68000 provides internal status on three pins to indicate the state of the microprocessor. All of these functions can be decoded by the user to provide the necessary information regarding which state the microprocessor is operating in at any particular time.

Bus Arbitration Control

All of the microprocessors investigated provide some type of control which can be used to allow external peripherals or other microprocessors to gain control of the system bus. These signals all take the form of bus request and bus acknowledge or grant. The 8086 has two Req/Grant channels, each channel using a single bidirectional input/output pin which is time shared between the Request and Grant signals. The Z8000 implements this function using two pins. A request signal and a grant signal are used to pass bus control between two devices. The 68000 uses a three pin system consisting of a bus request, bus grant, and a bus grant acknowledge. Each system allows the user to move multiple microprocessors or peripherals on and off the system bus using the pins described above.

Interrupt Control. All three microprocessors evaluated provide for user interrupt functions. The 8086 has a non-maskable interrupt, a maskable interrupt, and a test pin to provide software interrupting capability. An acknowledge signal is used to indicate when an interrupt has been received. This acknowledge is passed to the 8259A interrupt controller which provides vectors and priority encoding. The Z8000 provides three interrupt functions. It has a non-maskable interrupt, one which cannot be disabled, a vectored interrupt, and a non-vectored interrupt. In the segmented version, a fourth function is added, called a segment trap. This is used to indicate that an error has taken place in segmentation. The 68000 provides three pins for interrupt control. This allows seven priority levels of interrupts with the 0 level being non-maskable.

CPU Control

All three microprocessors provide signals to allow the user to stop or delay the microprocessor system. These may be used to interface a slow memory system where the processor must wait until access time has been completed or it may be used as a debug technique to provide single step or breakpoint features. The 8086 has a single signal called READY which indicates to the processor that an external device is now able to continue an operation. The Z8000 provides a wait and a stop signal. The wait signal is used for slow memory or I/O devices and the stop signal used to provide a single step feature. The 68000 uses a data acknowledge signal to indicate memory and I/O speed and a halt signal to single step the processor.

System Control

Each microprocessor evaluated has a reset line to allow the processor to be driven to a known state. The 68000 also provides a bus error signal to allow the user to trap on an error condition. The reset signal on the 68000 can also be used as an output to control peripheral functions. The microprocessor can execute a reset instruction and drive this line to a reset condition.

System Signals

All of the microprocessors evaluated required a clock signal for the internal logic, as well as power and ground signals. The Vcc line on each microprocessor requires 5 volts and the Vss lines are tied to ground. Input and output signals are TTL compatible except for clocking signals which normally required higher voltages.

Implementation

Each of the microprocessors evaluated required approximately the same number of circuits to implement a buffered microprocessor system. Each was implemented on a single UTS 400 PC card and required approximately 30 to 35 additional integrated circuits to provide clocking, buffering, and decoding. Intel provides the external buffering and decode control circuits required for use with the 8086. They have a clock circuit, a bus control circuit, and the bus latches and tristate devices. The other two firms, Motorola and Zilog, did not provide special functions but these can be easily implemented using standard off-the-shelf TTL components. The same technique can be used in an 8086 design and the circuit count will not change dramatically. The clocks required for the three systems were higher than TTL levels and required special circuits to drive them. Of the three evaluated, the clock in the Z8000 was the most difficult to generate. It required a four transistor circuit to provide the necessary rise and fall times, and the clocking levels.

Overall, hardware implementation of the microprocessors is really rather simple and requires no special design expertise. Many of the problems which were present in early microprocessor designs have been eliminated and the necessary control signals are now provided on chip. The 8086 and the Z8000 are packaged in a standard .6 inch 40 pin DIP and the 68000 package is a .9 inch 64 pin DIP.

Program Architecture

The various microprocessor worlds, as seen by the programmer, are described in the following sections. Within the framework of program architecture are discussed the topics of address spaces, register models, addressing modes, and instruction sets. Some fairly extreme differences exist from a software point of view between the big three. These differences are contrasted and occasionally relative preferences are given.

Address Spaces

The addressing range of the three microprocessors has been expanded significantly from the days of the 8080, Z80, and 6800. The 8086 is capable of directly addressing one megabyte of memory, the Z8001 eight megabytes, and the 68000 sixteen megabytes. For those programmers working with the past limitations of 64K bytes, this new generation should keep them busy for at least a fortnight or two.

Register Models

Significant differences begin to occur when one contrasts the register models of the various microprocessors.

The 8086 is comprised of eight 16-bit general registers, four 16-bit segment registers, a 16-bit instruction pointer register, and a 16-bit flags register (Figure 1). Four of the 16-bit general registers can be considered as being made up of two 8-bit registers (high and low halves). Each 8-bit register component is uniquely addressable. The Intel model also uses a compact yet powerful encoding scheme which assumes some implicit register usage (Table 3).

```
15                      0
:------------------------:
:  (AH)    AX      (AL)  :
:------------------------:
:  (BH)    BX      (BL)  :
:------------------------:
:  (CH)    CX      (CL)  :
:------------------------:
:  (DH)    DX      (DL)  :
:------------------------:

:------------------------:
: SP - Stack Pointer     :
:------------------------:
: BP - Base Pointer      :
:------------------------:
: SI - Source Index      :
:------------------------:
: DI - Destination Index :
:------------------------:

15                         0
:--------------------------:
:   CS - Code Segment      :
:--------------------------:
:   DS - Data Segment      :
:--------------------------:
:   SS - Stack Segment     :
:--------------------------:
:   ES - Extra Segment     :
:--------------------------:

:--------------------------:
: IP - Instruction Pointer :
:--------------------------:
           Flags
:--------------------------:
:   O D I T S Z  A  P  C   :
:   F F F F F F  F  F  F   :
:--------------------------:
```

Figure 1. 8086 Register Model

The segment registers are designed to provide logical segmentation of the one megabyte address space. Segment sizes range from 16 to 64K bytes with four segments (reference types) being active at any one time. Instruction pointer references are made relative to the CS or Code Segment register. Stack references are relative to the SS or Stack Segment register. Data references are relative to the DS or Data Segment register. The ES or Extra Segment register is used to point to an extra memory segment which in practice usually contains data. A mechanism is provided by which the segment registers can be changed or temporarily overridden (Table 4).

Table 3. Implicit 8086 Register Usage

Register	Implicit Usage
AX	Word Multiple and Divide, Word I/O
AL	Byte Multiple and Divide, Byte I/O Translate, Decimal Arithmetic
AH	Byte Multiple and Divide
BX	Translate
CX	Loops, Repeat Operations
CL	Variable Shift and Rotates
DX	Word Multiply and Divide
SP	Stack References
SI	String Operations - Source Pointer
DI	String Operations - Destination Pointer
CS	Code References
DS	Data References
SS	Stack and BP Indexed References

Table 4. 8086 Segment Register Usage

Memory Reference Type	Assumed Segment Register	Alternate Segment Register	Offset
Instruction Fetch	CS	None	IP
Stack Operation	SS	None	SP
Data (Except Below)	DS	CS/ES/SS	Effective Address
String Source	DS	CS/ES/SS	SI
String Destination	ES	None	DI
BP Used as Base Pointer	SS	CS/DS/ES	Effective Address

```
15                                 0
:----------------------------------:
:        RH0      :      RL0       :R0    RR0
:        RH1      :      RL1       :R1          RQ0
:        RH2      :      RL2       :R2    RR2
:        RH3      :      RL3       :R3
:        RH4      :      RL4       :R4    RR4
:        RH5      :      RL5       :R5          RQ4
:        RH6      :      RL6       :R6    RR6
:        RH7      :      RL7       :R7
:                                  :R8    RR8
:                                  :R9          RQ8
:                                  :R10   RR10
:                                  :R11
:                                  :R12   RR12
:                                  :R13         RQ12
: Normal Stack Pointer (Seg No)    :R14   RR14
: Normal Stack Pointer (Offset)    :R15
:----------------------------------:

:----------------------------------:
: System Stack Pointer (Seg No)    :R14'
: System Stack Pointer (Offset)    :R15'
:----------------------------------:
```

Figure 2. Z8001 Register Model

The Z8000 is designed with sixteen 16-bit general purpose registers, R0 thru R15. The first eight 16-bit registers can be addressed as sixteen 8-bit registers RL0, RH0, RL1 .... RH7. In addition, the registers can be paired to form eight 32-bit registers or combined to form four 64-bit registers (Figure 2). RR14 is designated as the stack pointer for the Z8001. When the microprocessor is in systems mode a duplicate stack pointer register, RR14', is used.

In addition to the general registers, the Z8000 has a set of control registers. The control registers are the Flags and Control Word (32-bit) register - FCW, Program Counter (32-bit) register - PC, Program Status Area Pointer (32-bit) register - PSAP, and a memory refresh control (16-bit) register - REFRESH.

A 23-bit memory address is contained in a register pair with the 16 least significant bits being held in the odd numbered register and the seven most significant bits (segment number) being held in bits 8 to 14 of the even numbered register.

```
              Data Registers
31             16        8         0
:----------------------------------:
:               :        :         :  D0
:               :        :         :  D1
:               :        :         :  D2
:               :        :         :  D3
:               :        :         :  D4
:               :        :         :  D5
:               :        :         :  D6
:               :        :         :  D7
:----------------------------------:

            Address Registers

31             16                  0
:----------------------------------:
:               :                  :  A0
:               :                  :  A1
:               :                  :  A2
:               :                  :  A3
:               :                  :  A4
:               :                  :  A5
:               :                  :  A6
:  User Stack   :     Pointer      :  A7
:----------------------------------:

:----------------------------------:
:  Supervisor Stack Pointer        :  A7'
:----------------------------------:

      24
:----------------------------------:
:       :     Program Counter      :  PC
:----------------------------------:

15              8                  0
:----------------------------------:
: T  S   I I I  :    X N Z V C     :  Flags
:----------------------------------:
```

Figure 3. 68000 Register Model

The register model (Figure 3) for the 68000 contains eight 32-bit data registers (D0-D7), eight 32-bit address registers (A0-A7), a copy of A7 namely A7' that is used as a supervisor stack pointer, a 24-bit program counter register, and a

16-bit status register. The eight data registers can be loaded with 8-, 16-, and 32-bit values. The address registers can be loaded with either 16- or 32-bit values. In all cases, the values loaded are right justified in the register, i.e., loaded with the least significant bit of the value being the least significant bit in the register.

In our applications, the greatest potential for optimum register usage of the three machines is held by the Z8000 with its very regular structure and register pairing to form 8-, 16-, 32-, and 64-bit registers. The 8086 has 8-bit pairings which is very useful in character manipulation as well as general data handling. But the Z8000 has more. The 68000 is beset with the problem of not being able to easily access bits 8 thru 31 of the data registers. This makes byte and character handling unnecessarily difficult. Our vote here is for the Z8000 with the 8086 and the 68000 tieing for last place.

Addressing Modes

The addressing modes implemented within the architecture of the big three provide much of the individual personalities with which the programmer interfaces. Addressing modes are the windows the instruction set uses to interface to memory. Basically, each one of the three microprocessors under consideration is a register to memory machine. Stacks are used for return addresses interrupts and subroutines. Easy access is provided to the stack(s) so that registers and data, both system and user, can be pushed or popped.

The 8086 boasts of forty different operands which are usable over the entire applicable instruction set - less string primatives (Table 5). They call it orthoganality. It is somewhat restrictive and difficult to remember. Complex in one word. All string operations require the data addresses to be in SI/DS and DI/ES.

Table 5. 8086 Addressing Modes

R/M	MOD 00	01	10	11 w=0	w=1
000	(BX)+(SI)	(BX)+(SI)+d8	(BX)+(SI)+d16	AL	AX
001	(BX)+(DI)	(BX)+(DI)+d8	(BX)+(DI)+d16	CL	CX
010	(BP)+(SI)	(BP)+(SI)+d8	(BP)+(SI)+d16	DL	DX
011	(BP)+(DI)	(BP)+(DI)+d8	(BP)+(DI)+d16	BL	BX
100	(SI)	(SI)+d8	(SI)+d16	AH	SP
101	(DI)	(DI)+d8	(DI)+d16	CH	BP
110	d16	(BP)+d8	(BP)+d16	DH	SI
111	(BX)	(BX)+d8	(BX)+d16	BH	DI

Within the forty addressing operand formats are four variations of base indexing (two registers) which can be expanded by adding either an eight or sixteen bit displacement if required. In addition, there are four indexing modes - three with zero displacement and four with eight or sixteen bit offsets. All of the 16-bit, as well as the 8-bit registers are addressable.

Table 6. Z8001 Addressing Modes

Mode	Symbol	
Immediate Data	Im	
Register	R	Rm or RRn or RQp
Indirect Register	IR	(RRn)
Direct Address	DA	address
Indexed Address	X	(Rm) + address
Relative Address	RA	offset
Based Address	BA	(RRn) + displacement
Based Indexed Address	BX	(RRn) + (Rm)

Architecturally, the Z8000 has eight addressing modes, five of which are generally applicable to the general instruction set (Table 6). The last three entries in Table 6, RA, BA, and BX, are limited to specific instructions for their usage. The addressing modes do not limit register usage, i.e., any register pair can be used in the indirect register, based address, or based indexed addressing modes. The displacement field for the based indexed address mode is 16 bits.

Twelve effective addressing mode categories are used by the Motorola 68000 (Table 7). Unique addressing modes for the 68000 are the postincrement, predecrement, and PC indexed forms.

Table 7. 68000 Addressing Modes

Mode	
Data Register Direct	Dn
Address Register Direct	An
Address Register Indirect	(An)
Address Register Indirect w/Postincrement	(An)+
Address Register Indirect w/Predecrement	-(An)
Address Register Indirect w/Displacement	(An)+d
Address Register Indirect w/Index	(An)+(Ri)+d
Absolute Short	16-bit address
Absolute Long	32-bit address
Program Counter w/Displacement	(PC)+d
Program Counter w/Index	(PC)+(Ri)+d
Immediate Data	8-,16-,32-bit Value

In the postincrement mode, the specified address register is incremented by either one, two, or four depending on the instruction's operation length following the formation of the effective address. The predecrement form decrements the specified address register by the appropriate value prior to the formation of the operand address. With these two address modes, the move instruction can do both push and pop operations using any of the address registers as stack pointers.

Displacement values are 16 bits in length except for the address register indirect with index and program counter with index formats where the displacements are only 8 bits.

The 68000 has the richest set of addressing modes on the surface. The separation of address and data registers in their usage is a major limitation.

The postincrement/predecrement feature is very nice. The eight bit displacement field in the "indexed" formats, while workable, is also a minor limitation.

The Z8000 is missing the based indexed with displacement operand type. Both the 8086 and the 68000 have this feature in one form or another. The plus for the Z8000 is its regular register structure. Zilog's Z8000 does not distinguish between address and data registers, alla 68000, or limit the operands to a few specific registers used in a couple of predetermined combinations - 8086.

In this category, the 68000 is just a hair ahead of the Z8000. The 8086, while usable, just does not compare on the assembly language level to the competition.

Instruction Sets

Contrasting the instruction sets for the big three is a fairly complex task. This comparison will look at some general characteristics of the instructions as a whole and then break the comparison down into the various types or classes of operations.

8086 instructions consist of from one to five bytes. This very compact instruction map contains many one byte instructions and expands one byte at a time as required by the individual operations. The limited register set and general formats of the 8086 are efficiently encoded and intertwined with the instruction set organization.

The Z8001, on the other hand, uses an instruction set made up of instructions that range from two to eight bytes. 68000 instructions range from two to ten bytes. Both the Z8000 and the 68000 require their instructions to be aligned on even byte (word) boundaries and contain an even number of bytes.

On the surface, the Z8000 and 68000 instructions appear to be larger than those of the 8086. They are. But the flexibility of the instructions, register models, and addressing operands when taken as a whole, allow the assembler language programmer to code Z8000 or 68000 tasks in an equivalent memory or space requirement as that required for the 8086. Sometimes even a little less. This is due principally to the fact that with a large number of registers, one does not have to continually have to restore intermediate values or move items to specific registers for certain operations.

Move Type Instructions. The Z8000 and 68000 move 8-, 16-, and 32-bit quantities. The 8086 only moves 8- and 16-bit items.

A load/store multiple register feature has been implemented by both the Zilog and the Motorola devices, not Intel's. The Z8000 load register immediate as well as the 68000 move quick - MOVEQ - instructions are faster and shorter than the equivalent 8086 move immediate operation (one byte move). The 68000 is extremely fast with this operation using only two clock cycles.

Both Zilog and Motorola implemented clear - CLR - instructions. A move immediate or exclusive OR instruction is required by the 8086. It should be noted at this point that it is almost twice as fast for the Z8000 to clear a register by subtracting or exclusive oring a register with itself than by using the clear instruction. On the other hand, the 68000 clear operation is twice as fast as its equivalent logic or arithmetic operation.

The 8086 push and pop instructions assume the use of the stack pointer - SP - register. The Z8001 push and pop instructions allow any register pair to be used except RR0, while the 68000 move operation with the postincrement/predecrement addressing modes allow any of the address registers to be used with similar functionality. The 8086 supports one and only one stack. The Zilog and Motorola microprocessors support multiple stacks. For "controller type" sytems, this feature might not be as significant as systems intended to execute a variety of functions, both system and user, in a variety of environments.

The Z8000 and 68000 tie for first.

Arithmetic Instruction. All of the big three contain an almost complete set of arithmetic operations. Each one will perform 8- and 16-bit add, subtract, and compare operations. The Z8000 and the 68000 also do the equivalent 32-bit operations. Multiply and divide operations are described in Table 8. The Zilog machine does only signed arithmetic.

Table 8. Multiply/Divide Comparisons

	8-bit	16-bit	32-bit
Multiply			
8086	Yes	Yes	-
Z8000	-	Yes	Yes
68000	-	Yes	-
	16-bit	32-bit	64-bit
Divide			
8086	Yes	Yes	-
Z8000	-	Yes	Yes
68000	-	Yes	-

The increment and decrement instructions of the Z8000 and 68000, being 16 bits in length, contain space to specify an increment (decrement) constant. The equivalent - Increment/Decrement by more than one - task is performed within the Intel machine by doing an add or subtract immediate.

All three of the microprocessors provide for limited decimal arithmetic. Only the Intel 8086 appears to support limited operations with ASCII encoded numbers.

Logic Instructions. Each of the three machines contains a full set of common logic operations, i.e., AND, OR, EXCLUSIVE OR, COMPARE, and TEST (compare with zero). The 8086 performs these functions with 8- and 16-bit operands while the other two microprocessors add the 32-bit operations to the picture.

For our applications and environment, it is our opinion that a significant 68000 problem exists in this area. Logic operations within the 68000 are allowed on data addressing modes only. Address registers are not allowed here! Some very efficient queuing techniques use a logical operational to determine queue wraparound instead of the compare, jump, reset top of queue address sequence. To implement a similar function on the 68000 requires the programmer to do the following:

```
MOVE      D0,A0        .
ANDI      D0,#00FF     . Assume queue on 256
MOVE      A0,D0        . byte boundary
```

This requires two additional move instructions - four bytes and four cycles. While this does not seem like much, it is very annoying to the aesthetically based purist programmer.

Two additional architectural features should be noted here. First, the 8086 TEST instruction actually performs a logical AND between two source operands, without altering either one of them. This allows one to test for multiple bits or flags being set in only one operation.

The second feature is one where both arithmetic and logical operations can be performed between memory and a register with the final result being placed in memory. This feature is not supported by the Z8000, another minor annoyance.

Rotate and Shift Instructions. Each of the three machines contains a full complement of rotate and shift operators. All of the instructions are two bytes in length except for the Zilog shift instructions. They are four bytes long. This was done to allow static shifts of from zero to thirty two bit positions. The 8086 architecture allows static shifts of only one bit position while one to eight bit position shifts are supported by the 68000.

Dynamic shifts depend on a shift count being in CL, Rn, or Dn, respectively, for the 8086, Z8000, or 68000.

The rotate operations supported by the 68000 have the identical parameters as their shift counterparts. In a like manner, the 8086 shift and rotate operations have like parameters. The Z8000, on the other hand, allows for static rotates of one or two bit positions only. It has no dynamic rotate operations.

The Z8000 does feature a special rotate digit (4-bit nibble) left or right instruction. This allows one to rotate a four bit nibble through one byte register and into or out of another register.

The 68000 seems to be the winner here with a very flexible and consistent set of operations.

Program Control (Jump) Instructions. Table 9 describes the different types of jump and subroutine call instructions of the respective architectures.

The 68000's weakness appears to be that it does not have a call subroutine direct instruction. The flaw in the Z8000 is its limited relative addressing range. While the competition allows +/-32K bytes of relative displacement, Zilog gives us only +/-256 bytes in the jump case and +/-4K for subroutines. The weakness in the 8086 architecture is that the conditional jump displacement is only 128 bytes. A suggestion to Intel and Zilog: the flexibility of the Motorola relative conditional jump is very nice, and please do not rebut that good programming practices academically preclude jumps of over 128 bytes.

Table 9. Program Control Comparisons

	8086	Z8000	68000
Jump Direct	intersegment	Yes	Yes
Jump Relative	+/-32K, 128	+/-256	+/-32K, 128
Jump Condition Relative	+/-128	+/-256	+/-32K, 128
Call Direct	intersegment	Yes	No
Call Relative	+/-32K	+/-4096	+/-32K, 128

Intel's architecture supports true jump and call indirect instructions, not just indirection through a register as Zilog's, but indirection through memory (actually an effective address).

An additional subroutine return type is provided by Intel; capability to adjust the stack pointer after the return address is popped from the stack is provided-a help in parameter passing.

The 8086 and 68000 come in vying for next to last. The Z8000 is a clear second. In our opinion, all three of the architectures could be improved in this area.

Bit Instructions. Bit operations are elaborately supported by the 68000. Bit test, bit set, bit clear, bit test and either clear, set, or change functions have all been implemented. Zilog's bit instruction repertoire is comprised of bit test, bit set, and bit clear functions. Both manufacturers appear to have gotten into some minor trouble in implementing these functions. Motorola allows only byte memory references while Zilog has some strange register restrictions. Intel's 8086 came out smelling like a rose (?) - they did not implement bit operations.

String Instructions. Comparison of the string operations is simple for the 68000. They do not have any. 68000 string type operations necessitate the use of several instructions that, when taken together, run potentially slower than the competition.

The full set of string operations is featured within the Z8000 architecture. Move, compare, and translate functions are combined with increment and decrement with or without repeat.

The 8086 contains five string primatives which, when combined with Intel's repeat prefix and direct bit in the flags register, can be used to build string move and compare type operations. The only drawback is that the source address MUST ALWAYS be in the SI register (based on DS) and the destination address MUST ALWAYS be in the DI register (based on ES), an almost intolerable restriction.

I/O Instructions. Input and output transfers are done in the 8086 using much of the older 8080 philosophy. Single byte or word (16-bit) I/O is supported using the AL or AX register only.

The Z8000 extends the Z80 philosophy by supporting byte or word I/O using any register or memory address in a single or block transfer mode. Both the 8086 and the Z8000 support 256 static I/O ports or by use of the DX or any Rn register up to 64K I/O ports.

The 68000 is a memory mapped I/O system.

Processor Control Instructions. As larger and more complex systems are developed around microprocessors, the area of process control becomes more and more important. Multitasking and multiprocessing concepts are now being implemented in the microprocessor arena.

With the big three, support of these concepts is becoming a reality. Of course, the flags register is accessable and alterable by all the microprocessors. In addition, test and set type operations are also supported. The Intel method is not as elegant; requiring a suggested five instruction sequence. Intel uses an explicit lock command to control the system bus during the lock sequence. Both Zilog and Motorola have implemented their test and set lock instructions with an implied bus lock. In other words, it is done in hardware.

System mode or exec mode versus user mode is another feature of the Z8000 and the 68000. This mode setting is indicated by a bit in the flags register. It signifies whether the special set of privileged instructions can be executed and which stack pointer register to use.

Each of the three systems has a method (escape, system call, or trap) for allowing user programs to enter the operation system. The Zilog part also has a set of five instructions intended to be used in coordinating a multiprocessor configuration.

Interrupt Spaces

Interrupt vectors are used by each of the architectures. 256 vectors are supported by the 8086, Z8000, and 68000. The reason this topic has been introduced is to discuss specifically the location of the restart vector.

The restart vectors for the 8086 and Z8000 are logically separated from the other interrupt vectors. On restart the 8086 begins execution at the fixed address 0FFFF0. The 8086 vector space is fixed in lower memory at address 00000. This allows the 8086 system designer to place the interrupt vectors in RAM and initialize, or reinitialize them, appropriately.

The Z8000 uses an assumed restart vector which starts execution at the address specified in location 0000. Z8000 system initialization code is then required to point the special register - PSAP - at the program status area which contains the interrupt table. A very flexible design allowing for easy modification of the interrupt environment.

The 68000 implementation has all of the interrupt vectors fixed at location zero like the 8086. But unlike the Intel part, the 68000 restart vector is in locations 0000 through 0008. This is the most limiting design of the three since either all of the vectors need to be fixed in loader ROM or special hardware tricks must be employed to separate the zero vector from a RAM based, loadable interrupt vector space.

Environment

When looking at the environment of an executing activity, one must consider the following aspects:

Registers/Stacks
Memory Access - Code, data, etc.
Priviledge level - Exec, user, etc.

Any given activity will execute within the environment defined by these items. Each of the three microprocessors handle these items in a little different manner. Some do a good job and others....

The Z8000 and 68000 both have load multiple instructions. A nice extra which does save a little bit of memory and a few extra memory fetches at interrupt time. In addition, multiple stacks, i.e., system stack and user stack, are a must if any type of user programming is to be implemented with hopes of maintaining even a little bit of system stability. For our applications, this is a major limitation in the 8086 architecture.

System Architecture

The system designed to test and evaluate the 16-bit microprocessors was defined around a general purpose bus architecture into which each of the proposed test processors could fit. There are two possible approaches which can be used in defining a microprocessor system. The first approach is to design the processor system around the microprocessor architecture as it exists. This would mean that a multiplexed address and data bus structure would have to be developed for processors in the 8086 and the Z8000 class and a non-multiplexed processor function would be required to develop 68000 architecture. This approach allows the peripherals designed for use with the specific microprocessor to fit into the design bus structure. The evaluation of the 16-bit microprocessor functions took place before peripherals were available and consequently a different approach was used. The second approach defines a general purpose bus architecture and each microprocessor is modified to fit into that architecture. This approach does not allow the user to take advantage of special purpose peripherals which have been developed specifically for an individual microprocessor family. But since none exists, the approach worked well in our evaluation.

System Bus Structure

Address Bus:	A_0 - A_{31}
Data Bus:	D_0 - D_{15}
Byte Control:	Lower Sel., Upper Sel.
Read/Write Control:	Mem Read/Write, I/O Read/Write
Interrupt Control:	IR0 - IR7
Processor Control:	Reset, Wait, Bus Req, Bus Grant
Extra:	Clk, EMemRd, EMemWrite,
Status	

Figure 4. System Bus Structure

A general purpose system bus structure was defined for the processor evaluation system. This bus structure is shown in Figure 4. As can be seen, the address bus and the data bus were separated. The address bus was defined 32 bits wide to allow for future expansion into new microprocessor systems. The data bus was defined to be 16-bits wide. In order to fit into this structure, it was required that the 8086 and the Z8000 microprocessor buses be demultiplexed on the processor board. The 68000 having separate address and data bus structures, does not require demultiplexing. Byte control was provided in the bus structure through the means of a lower byte select and an upper byte select. When both selects are active, word operations are allowed. Read/write control was provided by using memory read, memory write, I/O read, and I/O write signals. This separation of memory and I/O functions allows the use of either specific I/O instructions such as those in the Z8000 and the 8086 or memory instructions in memory mapped I/O systems such as the 68000. A general purpose interrupt structure was developed allowing seven interrupt inputs into the microprocessor board. The I/O devices can use vectored interrupts if that option existed or can use non-vectored interrupts if that is necessary. If priority control is provided on chip that can be used, or external priority control can be used if it is available. Processor control signals were provided on the bus including reset, wait, bus request, and bus grant. The reset line provides power-on reset and a user reset. The wait signal is used to delay memory or I/O functions where extended times are required. The bus request and bus grant signals are used to implement multiprocessor systems or DMA functions where the processor is removed from the bus and the DMA or the second processor takes over. In functions where multiple request/grant is required such as in the 68000, the system is reduced to a single request and a single grant signal on board. Extra control functions were also provided in this bus structure to allow the passing of special control signals such as early memory read, early memory write, or system clocks. The system has been developed on an 81-pin backplane and bus signals, as well as power and ground, are passed across the entire backplane to each individual card.

System Definition

A CRT based system was designed to allow user interface into the microprocessor system under test. A block diagram of this test system is shown in Figure 5. The microprocessor system is surrounded by ROM and RAM resources and has various input and output capabilities.

The processor board contains the 16-bit microprocessor with its associated driving circuitry, as well as a bootstrap ROM, a scratch RAM, and the interrupt control necessary to interface the 7 external interrupt lines. The bootstrap ROM was programmed to perform simple keyboard input functions and to interface the display. It allows the user to display memory and to load software programs into RAM from which they can be executed.

A memory card consisting of 64K bytes of RAM was designed using 16K dynamic memory parts. This board contains the necessary decode and control to complete refresh, memory read, or memory write. This card was used to store user programs for execution and debug within the sytem.

Programs were assembled for each of the processors and then brought to the system via floppy disk. A floppy disk interface is used to load user programs into the system RAM card. This floppy disk interface is microprocessor controlled and consequently eliminates much of the overhead required. The user accesses the disk by placing data in a shared memory and then executing read or write commands accompanied by track and sector locations. Programs can be developed external to the system and then loaded into RAM for test and debug.

The display used in this test bed is a CRT monitor. An alpha-numeric CRT system was developed to allow data characters placed in the alpha-numeric CRT memory by the microprocessor to be displayed on the CRT system. A graphics interface was also developed using raster dot graphics capability. The processor interface into the raster dot graphics was through graphics memory.

Figure 5. Test System Block Diagram

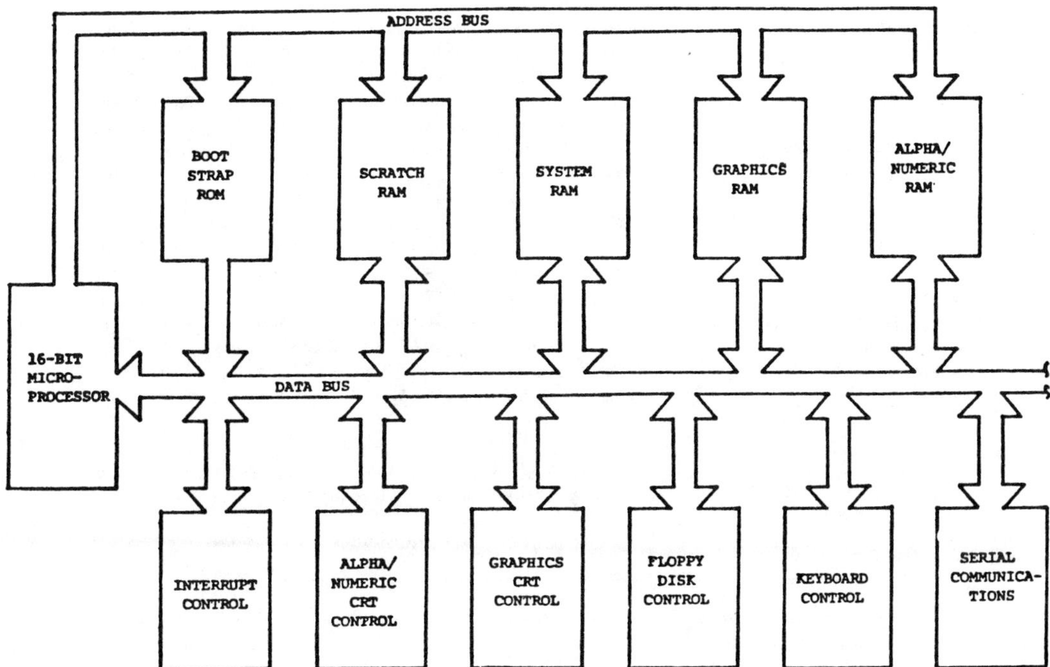

Data placed in that memory was displayed on the CRT. These two interfaces were ORed together allowing both alpha and graphic information to be displayed at the same time. Information transferred from the memories to the CRT controllers is transparent to the microprocessor which is being used and the processor wait line is used to remove contention.

User data is presented into the system via a keyboard interface. This keyboard interface is a parallel port into the microprocessor system and generates an interrupt whenever keyboard data is available for access. The 16-bit microprocessor accesses the data which is represented as ASCII characters and the microprogram discerns which function should be executed. The keyboard used is a UTS 400 keyboard providing both alpha, numeric, and multiple function keys. The multiple function keys can be defined for use in the graphics or other special purpose applications.

A serial communications interface which operates as an RS-232, UTS 400 protocol channel was developed for use with the system. A serial communications circuit was interfaced into the general system bus and the 16-bit microprocessor provides or receives data upon interrupt. This function is a multi-function serial interface allowing for either synchronous or asynchronous operation; however, program control usually provides a synchronous UTS 400 protocol channel.

The system as defined allows for multiple microprocessors to be interfaced without having to change the other cards within the sytem. Evaluation of the microprocessor then took place by programming the various interfaces to interact together as a terminal. Debug features and user aid codes were developed in the bootstrap ROM which existed on each microprocessor board while general interfaces could be programmed via the system RAM which could be loaded from floppy disk once the floppy disk loader was implemented in bootstrap.

Benchmark

This section is included to present the quantitative data collected to date on the three microprocessors under study.

Instruction comparisons give an idea of the times of the individual processors. However, those times do not tell the whole story. What is needed are timings for various functions using these instructions. This then gives timing comparisons which reflect how effectively the instructions go together to perform a given task.

These functions may be defined in many ways. Each will tend to favor one processor over the other. We have chosen to use the functions which normally occur in the products we build. There are other functions which could be used to compare the processors and some of those are being pursued.

Our timings, for this paper, are taken from the editing functions of Sperry Univac terminals. The functions were not defined to include the Field Control Character concept and thus, can not be directly compared to timings of any current product. They are, however, defined the same for

Table 10. Edit Function Timings (Raw Data)

Function	8080	6800	Z8000 (4 MHZ)	MC68000 (4 MHZ)	8086 (4.91 MHZ)
Enter Character	330.0us	280.0us	142-156us	168-176us	160-180us
Insert In Line	3.4ms	3.2ms	350-500us	720us	500-650us
Delete In Line	4.0ms	3.0ms	350-500us	700us	500-650us
Insert Line	51.0ms	51.0ms	5.5-6.0ms	8.8ms	8.8-9.2ms
Delete Line	53.0ms	49.0ms	5.5-6.0ms	11.5ms	8.8-9.2ms
Insert In Display	70.0ms	70.0ms	6ms	12.5ms	8.8-9.2ms
Delete In Display	87.0ms	65.0ms	6ms	11.5ms	8.8-9.2ms
Erase Line	3.2ms	3.0ms	400-500us	600us	350-500us
Erase Display	68.0ms	65.0ms	5.5-6.0ms	9.0ms	5.0-5.5ms
Line Duplicate	-	-	400-550us	660us	550-700us
Cursor Up	4.0ms	2.8ms	180-190us	235us	210-230us
Cursor Down	4.3ms	4.2ms	174us	210us	210-230us
Cursor Left	-	-	180-190us	230us	210-230us
Cursor Right	-	-	174-184us	210-220us	210-230us
Cursor to Home	320.0us	255.0us	170-180us	220us	190-210us
Return	4.5ms	4.5ms	210-230us	380us	270us

Table 11. Edit Function Timings (Extrapolated)

Function	Z8000 (6 MHZ)	MC68000 (8 MHZ)	8086 (8 MHZ)
Enter Character	98.0us	86.0us	104.0us
Insert In Line	280.0us	360.0us	353.0us
Delete In Line	280.0us	350.0us	353.0us
Insert Line	3.8ms	4.4ms	5.52ms
Delete Line	3.8ms	5.8ms	5.52ms
Insert In Display	4.0ms	6.2ms	5.52ms
Delete In Display	4.0ms	5.8ms	5.52ms
Erase Line	300.0ms	300.0us	261.0us
Erase Display	3.8ms	4.5ms	3.22ms
Line Duplicate	323.0us	330.0us	384.0us
Cursor Up	123.0us	118.0us	135.0us
Cursor Down	116.0us	105.0us	135.0us
Cursor Left	123.0us	115.0us	135.0us
Cursor Right	119.0us	108.0us	135.0us
Cursor to Home	117.0us	110.0us	123.0us
Return	147.0us	190.0us	166.0us

NOTES ON TABLES 10, 11:

A range is given on some of the functions. These variances appear to come from the randomness of memory wait states.

The 68000 Insert Line function was programmed using its 32 bit move instruction. The other Delete and Insert functions were not.

---

all three of our breadboard terminals giving a comparison of the three processors.

The functions work on a 24 X 80 screen, with each character position a sixteen bit value. This gives an 8-bit displayable character and eight bits of attributes making up each screen position.

The timings were taken using an oscilloscope which was triggered by the interrupt as a key was hit. A signal was then captured on the storage scope which changed levels when the code returned to the idle loop of the system, indicating the completion of the function. Nothing else was going on in the system, namely timer interrupts. These timings were taken several times for each case and a value arrived at for each function.

Table 10 shows the raw data for the specified functions with similar data taken years ago for the 8080 and 6800. This gives a feel for the improvements in speed of the 16-bit microprocessors over the 8-bit microprocessors. Unfortunately, we do not have numbers for the Z80.

The differences between the 8- and 16-bit microprocessors are even greater than it might appear on first glance. The 8-bit systems were only working with 8 bits/character screen positions so less data was being moved and worked with. If the 16-bit systems were defined the same, many of the functions' times would be even faster.

Since each processor has, or is, going to have faster versions of their parts, we have performed a linear extrapolation of the data in Table 10 to produce Table 11. Table 11 shows what numbers might be expected with the faster parts.

Summary

From our evaluation of these three microprocessors, we have concluded that, from a hardware point of view, all three are equally usable. However, from a software view point, we find many differences in the architectures. From the benchmark results, the size of code required for a given task and the ease of programming, the Z8000 is preferred for our communications and terminal applications. The amount of memory needed for the routines in the three systems was almost identical with the Z8000 needing slightly fewer bytes. The Z8000 addressing modes and instruction set make it easier to program. This results in fewer programming mistakes, faster generation of code, and a finished package which is produced sooner and is more easily maintained.

Aside from the technical aspects, discussed in this paper, other issues must be considered as one selects a microprocessor for a given product. Some of them are: second sourcing, availability, useable support circuits (not necessarily from the same manufacturer), costs, and follow-on upward compatibility migration paths.

The evaluation of any new generation of microprocessors brings with it the ability to do more with less. The challenge is to develop the ideas which spring from these additional capabilities.

References

MCS-86 User's Manual, February 1979

The 8086 Family User's Manual, October 1979

Z8000 PLZ/ASM Assembly Language Programming Manual, April 1975

Z8001 CPU Z8002 CPU Product Specification Preliminary, March 1979

MC68000 16-Bit Microprocessor User's Manual, September 1979

Trademarks

The following are trademarks of the respective businesses:

Sperry Univac	Sperry Corporation
Intel	Intel Corporation
Zilog	Zilog, Incorporated
Motorola	Motorola, Incorporated

A Performance Evaluation of The Intel iAPX 432

Paul M. Hansen, Mark A. Linton, Robert N. Mayo, Marguerite Murphy, and David A. Patterson

Computer Science Division
Department of Electrical Engineering and Computer Sciences
University of California, Berkeley
Berkeley, California 94720
May 17, 1982

ABSTRACT

We describe an experiment to test the 432 as a high-level language uniprocessor by comparing it with the 8086, 68000, and VAX-11/780 for four integer and character programs written in Ada, C, and Pascal.

Introduction

In 1981 Intel announced a 32-bit VLSI microprocessor incorporating several innovations [Intel 81]:

> "The Intel iAPX 432 represents a dramatic advance in computer architecture: it is the first computer whose architecture supports true software-transparent, multiprocessor operation; it is the first commercial system to support an object-oriented programming methodology; it is designed to be programmed entirely in high-level languages; it supports a virtual address space of over a trillion bytes; and it supports on the chip itself the proposed IEEE-standard for floating point arithmetic."

This microcomputer system was the result of a very extensive project that started in 1975 whose goals were [Mazor 81]:

- large scale computational power
- incremental performance capacity
- highly dependable hardware and software
- increased programmer productivity

An interesting question is how much performance is degraded because of the object-oriented architecture with software-transparent multiprocessing and fault tolerance. This report presents the results of a 432 performance study conducted by members of a graduate class at the University of California, Berkeley during the Fall quarter of 1981. We limited ourselves to studying uniprocessor performance and did not consider the following goals for the 432: object-oriented programming, floating point, multiple processes, and multiple processors. The 432 is intended to support Ada [Rattner and Lattin 81], so we used benchmark programs written in high-level languages to determine execution time and code size. Note that a high-level language system consists of the compiler and the machine, so we are not measuring just the architecture and hardware implementation. For purposes of comparison, these programs were run in Pascal on an Intel 8086, a Motorola 68000, and a VAX-11/780, and in C on a 68000 and VAX, as well as in Ada on the 432.

Reprinted with permission from *Comput. Architecture News*, vol. 10, pp. 17-26, June 1982.
Published by Association for Computing Machinery, Inc.

Description of Benchmarks

We measured the code size and execution time of four programs. The time allotted to our visit at Intel prevented us from running more. We did measure the size of other programs and found the results consistent with the measurements presented here. The programs are:

string search
: This program searches a 120 character string for a 15 character substring. It is taken from the performance study sponsored by *Electronic Design News* last year [Grappel and Hemmenway 81].

sieve
: This program computes prime numbers and has also been run on several machines [Gilbreath 81].

puzzle
: This program, created by Forest Baskett, is a bin packing program that solves a simple puzzle and has been run on a wide variety of machines.

acker
: This program computes Ackermann's function with arguments 3 and 6. Ackermann's function is a recursive computation requiring more than 170,000 procedure calls. This benchmark is useful in measuring the cost of a procedure call on a particular machine [Wichmann 76].

All the programs were initially written in C, then translated to Pascal and then into Ada. The C programs do **not** use register variables, pointers, or any other of the unusual features of C.

Accessing parameters and global variables is very expensive inside a procedure in release 2 of the 432 and will be much less expensive in release 3. This overhead can be avoided by either changing the compiler or modifying the program source to make local copies of parameters and globals. We ran Ada programs both translated directly from Pascal and modified to avoid expensive accesses. Table entries marked with a "*" refer to modified programs.

These programs have characteristics found in many high-level language programs except for the frequency of procedure calls and returns. Recent studies on several architectures show that 1 out of every 20 instructions executed is a procedure call or return [Clark and Levy 82] [Ditzel and McLellan 82] [McDaniel 82]. "Acker" is certainly on the high side with 1/7 being call or return, but the dynamic mix for the others is on the low side: 1/235 in "puzzle", 1/245 in "string search", and 1/125000 in "sieve".

Description of Machines

Microprocessor data sheets refer to two terms, *clock rate* and *wait states*, that are sometimes misunderstood. Each microinstruction generally corresponds to one or two clock ticks. Wait states refer to the the time, measured in clock ticks, that a processor is idle while waiting for memory. While we can predict the relative performance of models of the same architecture given the clock rate and wait states, we can not predict relative performance of different architectures given the same information.

The 432 timings were done on a release 2 system running with a 4 MHz clock and 12 wait states. This system is a half-speed prototype of an 8 MHz system. In December Intel plans to ship release 3 of the 432, the first version in which they have attacked the problem of performance. Timings of release 3 were obtained from a simulator. Size was measured from the output of the release 3 Ada compiler. The 432 systems support virtual memory and provide error correcting memory.

The 8086, announced in 1978, was measured on an Intellec MDS III development system using a 5 MHz part with no wait states. The Pascal compiler was version X125, the first Intel Pascal compiler for the 8086.

The 68000, announced in 1979, was measured on three systems.

- Dual Systems Corporation of Berkeley has a single user UNIX† based 68000 system that uses a variant of the MIT C compiler. The Dual 8312 uses an 8 MHz 68000 built on S-100 cards that needs 2 wait states.

- Motorola's first development system, the EXORMACS, uses an 8 MHz 68000 with 4 wait states: 2 for the memory management unit and 2 for the memory system. The Motorola Pascal compiler is version 2.0, distributed April 10, 1982.

- Finally, Motorola has a 16 MHz 68000 on a board with high-speed memory that runs without wait states.

The VAX-11/780, announced in 1978, supports virtual memory and provides error correcting memory. It was measured with three compilers: the VMS Pascal compiler, the UNIX C compiler, and the Berkeley UNIX Pascal compiler. Berkeley Pascal has an option to get greater performance at the expense of code size by expanding some procedures in line. We ran the programs both ways, with the average change being 4% larger to gain 7% in performance. We selected the time and size of the higher performance choice.

These programs assume a standard word size. The 8086 uses 16 bits, the VAX uses 32 bits, and the 68000 and 432 programs were run with both sizes.

Experimenters

Some of us (Linton, Mayo, and Murphy) ran the 16-bit 432/670 experiments at Intel in Aloha, Oregon. Subsequently, Konrad Lai of Intel ran the programs using 32-bit variables for release 2 and then all the programs for release 3 on a simulator. Ackermann's function was calculated for (1,2) and then multipled by the ratio of acker(3,6) to acker(1,2) on the VAX. Dave Trissel of Motorola ran the 68000 Pascal benchmarks. Members of our department ran the rest of the experiments in Berkeley: Robert Henry measured Pascal programs on the Intel 8086 and the VAX-11/780 under VMS, Keith Sklower ran the C 68000 programs, Peter Kessler did UNIX Pascal on the VAX-11/780, and we ran the UNIX C programs on the VAX-11/780 ourselves.

---

†UNIX is a registered trademark of Bell Laboratories.

Measurements

Table 1(a) shows the execution times of the programs as measured on real hardware. Table 1(b) shows the relative performance of each of the machines with respect to VMS Pascal; entries greater than 1 indicate a faster time than on the VAX.

TABLE 1(a): EXECUTION TIME

Machine	Language	word	Time (milliseconds)			
		size	search	sieve	puzzle	acker
VAX-11/780	C	32	1.4	250	9400	4600
	Pascal (UNIX)	32	1.6	220	11900	7800
	Pascal (VMS)	32	1.4	259	11530	9850
68000 (8 MHz)	C	32	4.7	740	37100	7800
	Pascal	16	5.3	810	32470	11480
	Pascal	32	5.8	960	32520	12320
68000 (16 MHz)	Pascal	16	1.3	196	9180	2750
	Pascal	32	1.5	246	9200	3080
8086 (5 MHz)	Pascal	16	7.3	764	44000	11100
432 (4 MHz)	Ada	16	35	3200	350,000	260,000
	Ada	16	14.2*	3200	165,000*	260,000
	Ada	32	16.1*	3200	180,000*	260,000

TABLE 1(b): RELATIVE PERFORMANCE

Machine	Language	word	Ratio to VMS Pascal (>1 => **faster**)				
		size	search	sieve	puzzle	acker	avg±sd
VAX-11/780	C	32	1.0	1.0	1.2	2.1	1.3±.4
	Pascal (UNIX)	32	.9	1.2	1.0	1.3	1.1±.2
	Pascal (VMS)	32	1.0	1.0	1.0	1.0	1.0±.0
68000 (8 MHz)	C	32	.3	.4	.3	1.3	.6±.4
	Pascal	16	.27	.32	.36	.86	.5±.2
	Pascal	32	.24	.27	.35	.80	.4±.2
68000 (16 MHz)	Pascal	16	1.1	1.3	1.3	3.6	1.8±1.0
	Pascal	32	.95	1.0	1.3	3.2	1.6±.9
8086 (5 MHz)	Pascal	16	.2	.3	.3	.9	.4±.3
432 (4 MHz)	Ada	16	.04	.08	.03	.04	.05±.02
	Ada	16	.10*	.08	.07*	.04	.07±.02
	Ada	32	.09*	.08	.06*	.04	.07±.02

Table 2(a) shows the number of bytes of object code and constants for each of the programs. Space necessary for libraries and the operating system was **not** counted. Table 2(b) shows the code sizes relative to VMS Pascal; entries less than 1 indicate code that is smaller than on the VAX.

Although the 432 has bit-variable length instructions, it requires more space than either the 68000 in Pascal or the VAX in C. Reasons include the lack of immediates and the inability to refer to a local variable or constant using fewer than 16 bits of address. On the other hand, the 432 programs are 60% of the size of Pascal on the VAX. Nothing simple explains this seeming contradiction; perhaps a VAX Pascal system requires more sophisticated compiler technology than is currently available.

TABLE 2(a): CODE SIZE

Machine	Language	word size	Size (bytes)			
			484	sieve	puzzle	acker
VAX-11	C	32	764	156	2220	152
	Pascal (UNIX)	32	802	512	4336	244
	Pascal (VMS)	32	636	411	2904	340
68000	C	32	578	228	2940	172
	Pascal	16	578	120	1742	124
	Pascal	32	592	126	1862	130
8086	Pascal	16	756	348	2301	311
432 (rel. 3)	Ada	16	612	180	2443	144

TABLE 2(b): RELATIVE CODE SIZE

Machine	Language	word size	Ratio to VMS Pascal (< 1 => **smaller**)				
			search	sieve	puzzle	acker	avg±sd
VAX-11	C	32	.60	.38	.77	.45	.5±.2
	Pascal (UNIX)	32	.95	1.24	1.49	.72	1.1±.3
	Pascal (VMS)	32	1.0	1.0	1.0	1.0	1.0±.0
68000	C	32	.79	.55	1.01	.50	.7±.2
	Pascal	16	.72	.29	.60	.36	.5±.2
	Pascal	32	.74	.31	.64	.38	.5±.2
8086	Pascal	16	.94	.85	.79	.91	.9±.1
432 (rel. 3)	Ada	16	.76	.44	.84	.42	.6±.2

Normalized Performance

Table 3 shows the normalized execution times of 8 MHz versions of the 432 in Ada and the 68000 and 8086 in Pascal. The 8086 performance is predicted from the 5 MHz measurements assuming 0 wait states, the 432 programs were run with 4 wait states for both versions of the Ada programs for release 2 and also for release 3. The 4 wait state 68000 was measured on the EXORMACS and the 0 wait state times were computed by doubling the times for the 16 MHz 68000. Times for a 0 wait state 432, while not available as we go to press, are expected to be about 25% faster. The average performance relative to the 68000 is show in figure 1.

TABLE 3: NORMALIZED 8 MHz, 16-bit PERFORMANCE

Wait States	Machine	Language	Time (milliseconds)			
			search	sieve	puzzle	acker
4	68000	Pascal	5.3	810	32470	11480
	432 (rel. 2)	Ada	17.5	1600	175,000	130,000
	432 (rel. 2)	Ada	7.1*	1600	82500*	130,000
	432 (rel. 3)	Ada	4.4	978	45700	47800
0	8086	Pascal	4.6	448	27500	6938
	68000	Pascal	2.6	392	18360	5500

1983 Performance

In the first quarter of 1983, Intel plans to deliver 432/800 systems (release 3, 4 wait states). They also plan to deliver 10 MHz 432 chips. To be fair, we will forecast the 1983 performance of the VAX, 68000, and 8086 as well.

DEC is working on a new Pascal compiler that we expect will result in programs 1.2 to 1.4 times faster than the current version. Since next year marks the fifth anniversary of the VAX-11/780, a faster VAX must be on the horizon.

Motorola has announced two new products for the next year. The 68010 handles page faults, is slightly faster (less than 25%), and is scheduled for this summer. The 68020, scheduled for the end of 1983, has 32-bit internal and external busses plus an on-board instruction cache; however, only one of the three measured 68000 systems has memory management. It seems you must add wait states to add memory management to a 68000, but Sun Microsystems Incorporated has an 8 MHz 68000 with memory management and no wait states. Nevertheless, we believe that faster 68000's will require wait states for memory management. Thus next year we expect systems 1.5 to 3 times faster than the EXORMACS development system with 4 wait states.

Intel has also moved ahead with successors the the 5 MHz 8086. 8 MHz parts are commonly available and Intel has announced 10 MHz versions. The 80286, announced this year, includes an 8086 compatibility mode that runs the same programs many times faster. We thus expect the 1983 version of an 8086 system to be at least 3 times faster than the 5 MHz MDS system.

Conclusion

Our experiment was to test the 432 as a high-level language uniprocessor for integer and character programs. Figure 2 summarizes our findings. The bar graph shows both measured performance on real hardware (solid box) and predicted performance (dotted box). A single 4 MHz, release 2 432 is currently about 1/20th of a VAX-11/780, and we expect Ada programs on the 1983 version to run about 1/5th the speed of Pascal programs on the 1983 VAX. For some applications a 432 system consisting of 5 processors may perform as well as a VAX-11/780. We need multiprocessing benchmarks that could assess such systems.

If performance were the only measure of system cost, then software development would always be done in assembly language. Obviously there are other important aspects, thus we should not disregard the potential 432 benefits of programmer productivity, transparent multiprocessing, and data security. One could attempt to build these 432 functions into software around a 8086, 68000, or VAX, but until then we can not compare completely equal systems. Rather than speculate on the performance of such a system, we have instead tried to evaluate the time and space cost of the 432 approach.

Acknowledgments

Intel has been helpful to us in our study, particularly in allowing us to visit Aloha and run the benchmarks on their release 2 system and release 3 simulator. Konrad Lai and Justin Rattner of Intel were especially helpful in explaining the subtleties of the 432 design. We would also like to thank Tony Anderson and Bill Lattin for arranging the visit. Dave Trissel of Motorola deserves special credit for getting the programs to run on the Motorola Pascal systems, and thanks go to Les Crudele for making the arrangements. We would like to thank several people at Berkeley who helped with the measurements: Wayne Graves, Robert Henry, Paul Israel, Peter Kessler, and Keith Sklower. We are also grateful to Doug Clark, Robert Henry, William Kahan, Carlo Sequin, and John Wakerly for suggesting improvements to this paper.

References

[Clark and Levy 82]
Clark, D., and Levy, H., "Measurement and Analysis of Instruction Use in the VAX-11/780," *Ninth Annual Symposium on Computer Architecture*, Austin, Texas, April 26-29, 1982, pp. 9-17.

[Ditzel and McLellan 82]
Ditzel, D., and McLellan, R., "Register Allocation for Free: The C machine Stack Cache," *Symposium on Architectural Support for Programming Languages and Operating Systems*, Palo Alto, California, March 1-3, 1982, pp. 48-56.

[Gilbreath 81]
Gilbreath, J., "A High-Level Language Benchmark," *Byte*, vol. 6, no. 9, September 1981, pp. 180-198.

[Grappel and Hemmenway 81]
Grappel, R. G., and Hemmenway, J. E., "A Tale of Four Microprocessors: Benchmarks Quantify Performance," *Electronic Design News*, April 1, 1981, pp. 179-265.

[Intel 81]
Introduction to the iAPX 432 Architecture, Intel Corporation, Santa Clara, CA, 1981.

[Mazor 81]
Mazor, S., *432 Architecture Workshop Version 2*, Intel Corporation, July 1981.

[McDaniel 82]
McDaniel, G., "An Analysis of a Mesa Instruction Set Using Dynamic Instruction Frequencies," *Symposium on Architectural Support for Programming Languages and Operating Systems*, Palo Alto, California, March 1-3, 1982, pp. 167-176.

[Rattner and Lattin 81]
Rattner, J., and Lattin, W., "Ada Determines Architecture of 32-bit Microprocessor," *Electronics*, vol. 54, no. 4., February 24, 1981, pp. 119-126.

[Wichmann 76]
Wichmann, B. A., "Ackermann's Function: A Study in the Efficiency of Calling Procedures," *BIT*, vol. 16, 1976, pp. 103-110.

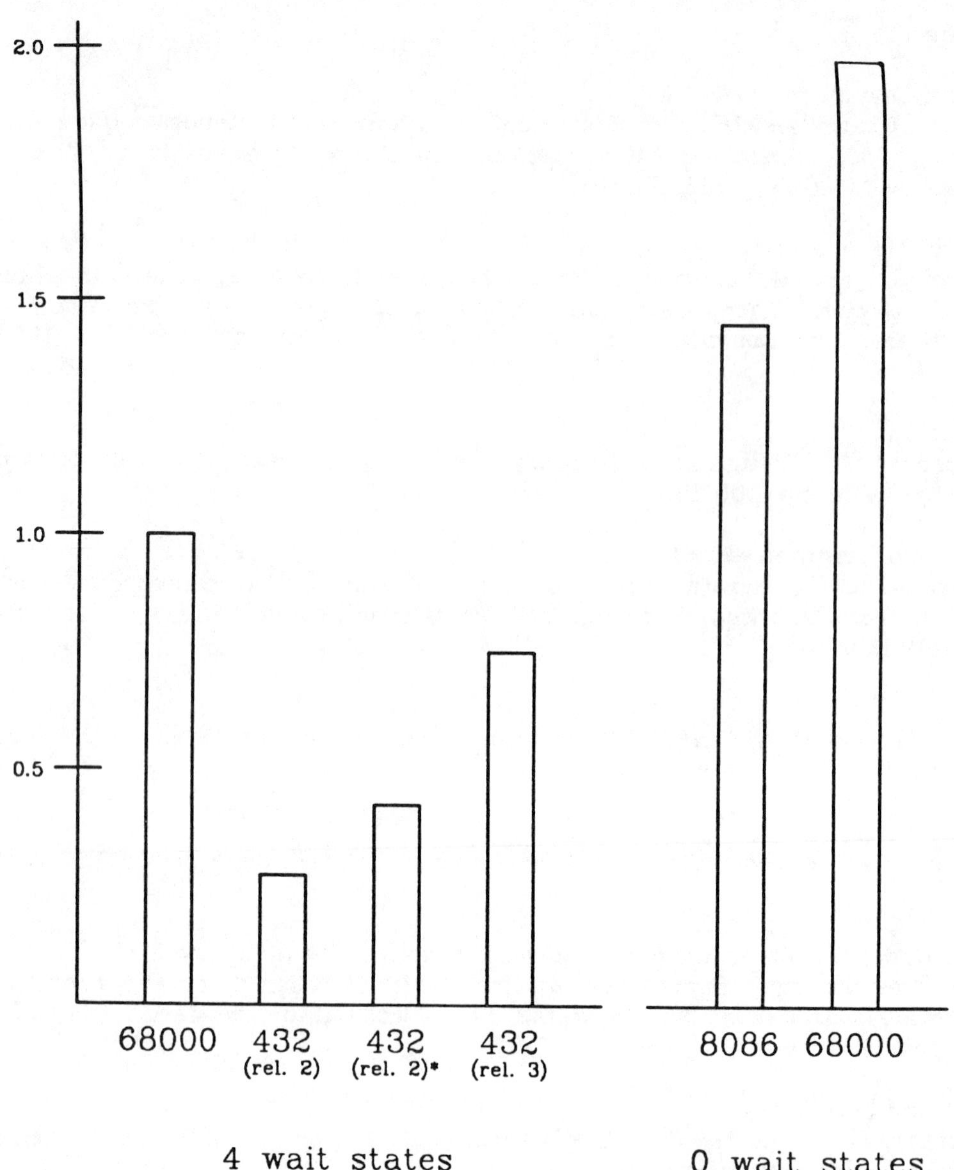

Figure 1: Predicted 8 MHz performance

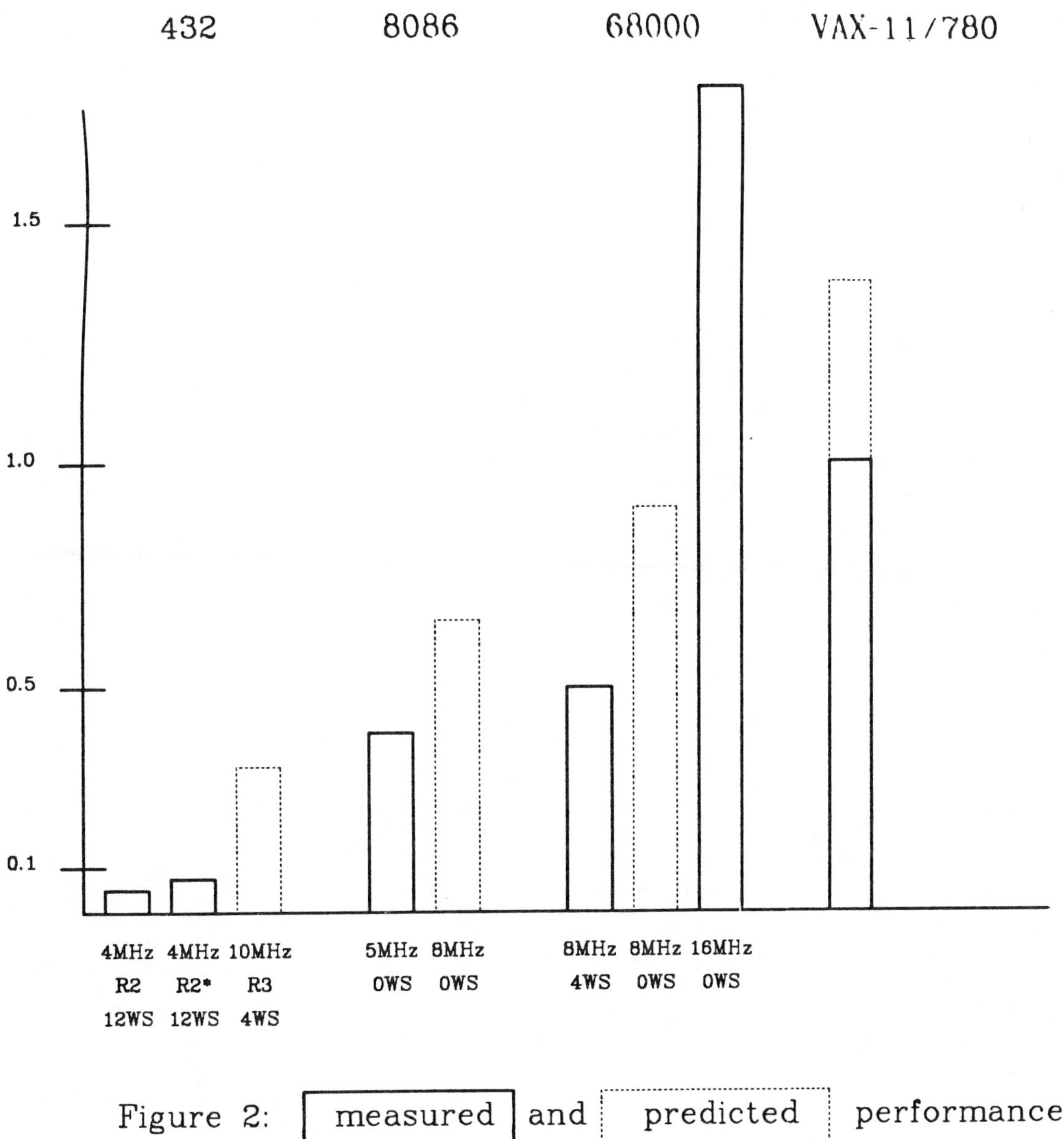

Figure 2: measured and predicted performance

Part V
Related Technologies

THE microprocessor revolution represents a trend towards implementing all the components of a computer on a small number of chips. Any computer system, irrespective of size, power, and capabilities, combines three classes of subsystems: CPU's (for arithmetic, logic, and control functions), memories [Read/Write (RAM) and/or Read-Only (ROM)], and input/output interfaces for peripheral control. Early microprocessors performed the basic CPU functions only. Additional chips were required to generate timing signals, to provide primary memory for program and data storage, and to interface with peripheral units. As better technology became available to enable integration of a larger number of devices on the same chip, it became feasible to implement an increasing number of auxiliary functions on the microprocessor chip itself. *Single-chip microcomputers* constitute an important subset of microprocessors in which all functions, including program and data memory, are implemented on the same chip. In view of the chip area devoted to auxiliary functions, there is always a time lag between the introduction of a microprocessor chip of a given word size and the introduction of a microcomputer chip of an equivalent word size. For example, the first 8-bit single-chip microcomputer, the Intel 8048, was introduced in 1976, four years after the introduction of the first 8-bit microprocessor, the Intel 8008 [1].

At the other extreme of the spectrum, there are applications that require higher computing power or better accuracy than that provided by single-chip microprocessors. For such applications, *bit-sliced organization* enables linking several identical modular chips in parallel to achieve higher throughput and accuracy. Thus, by using multiple 4-bit chips of this kind, one can easily integrate systems offering an effective word size of 8, 12, 16 bits, or even more. Note, however, that although the Intel iAPX 432 uses a three-chip set, it does *not* represent an example of bit-sliced architecture, as the three chips are neither capable of operating individually, nor are they identical to each other.

Since single-chip microcomputers and bit-sliced architecture chips cater to more specialized markets, their popularity of usage has been significantly lower than that of single-chip microprocessors. Also, with the advent of wider word-size general-purpose microprocessors, the primary merit of using bit-sliced microprocessors for higher accuracy has been gradually eroded over the years. For these reasons, instead of presenting brief articles on individual chips, the emphasis in this part of the book is on survey articles that offer a comprehensive treatment of the principles involved in designing systems using these building blocks.

In the first article, Cragon describes the elements of single-chip microcomputer architecture, and emphasizes the characteristics that distinguish single-chip microcomputers from conventional architectures. Because of the large volumes in which single-chip microcomputers are purchased, real estate per chip must be minimized. For instance, a 20 percent savings on a $2 microcomputer can result in savings of $400 000 for a million units. Using examples of several systems, it is shown that no single section can be optimized at the expense of another. This article examines architectural tradeoffs, memory design factors, instruction sizes, memory addressing techniques, and other issues of concern in the domain of single-chip microcomputers. Various techniques are discussed for extending the address space such as: implied indirect addressing, page addressing, indexing, and the use of base registers. All of these addressing modes are considered in light of the single-chip microcomputer architect's design constraints with respect to area, performance, and run-time parameters. Major differences in the architectural approach of a "Harvard machine" versus a "von-Neumann" architecture are shown. For the latter approach, the use of a single memory for both instructions and data is presented. Common architectural elements between the two are demonstrated in their use of asynchronous inputs, status registers, context switch, operating registers, instruction sets, and data I/O. Cragon has identified architectural characteristics of single-chip microcomputers which distinguish them from more traditional architectures.

In the second paper, Patterson and Sequin predict the design specifications of a hypothetical single-chip microcomputer of the mid-eighties. A typical chip of this time will contain about a million transistors, offering a tremendous potential for implementing many sophisticated features in hardware. The processor section of the chip could include on-chip memory hierarchy, multiple homogeneous caches for enhanced execution parallelism, support for complex data structures and high-level languages, a flexible instruction set, and communication hardware. More than four-fifths of the transistors on the chip are expected to be allocated for memory functions. Although architecturally this computer-on-a-chip will compare favorably with modern computers in terms of throughput, implementation of processors such as the CDC 7600 or the CRAY-1 on a single chip is not likely to happen until the end of the eighties.

In the third article, Hayes surveys the domain of bit-sliced computer design. This article introduces the basic concepts, traces historical origins, and considers and compares in detail three representative familes of bit-slice components, from Advanced Micro Devices, Intel, and Texas Instruments. Finally, the design of bit-sliced central processing units to emulate a popular general-purpose microprocessor is described. This technique can be used to emulate instruction sets of popular mainframes. It is useful to note an example of a recurring phenomenon in the semiconductor industry. In 1972, just a year after the commencement of the microprocessor era, American Micro-Systems Inc. announced the AMI 7200, the first 8-bit processor slice, or "byte-slice"; such slices became more of a commercial reality with the introduction of the Fairchild F100200 in 1979. The need for caution in depending on chips which use the leading edge of technology cannot be overemphasized.

Almost all leading semiconductor vendors offer single-chip microcomputers. New chips are announced in conferences like Wescon, Midcon, and Electro. In addition, trade journals such as *Electronics*, *EDN*, and *Electronic Design* usually publish an annual survey of microcomputers. A list of recent articles is provided in the Bibliography.

References

[1] R. N. Noyce and M. E. Hoff, Jr., "A history of microprocessor development at Intel," *IEEE Micro*, vol. 1, pp. 8–21, Feb. 1981.

Bibliography

[1] "Single-chip microcomputers: Performance and features," *Electron. Des.*, pp. 130–139, Oct. 14, 1982.

[2] P. R. Brown, "Advanced hardware features of the Z8 microcomputer family," in *Proc. Midcon 1981*, Session 21, Paper 5, pp. 1–10.

[3] J. Chiang, "Microprocessor-resident tiny basic interpreter speeds program development," in *Proc. Electro*, Session 25, Paper 3, pp. 1–4.

[4] R. Dumse, "Applications using multiple single chip computers," in *Proc. Electro 1982*, Session 29, Paper 2, p. 7.

[5] —, "New programming philosophy for dedicated applications," in *Proc. Electro 1982*, Session 25, Paper 5, pp. 1–5.

[6] —, "High level language in single chip microcomputers," in *Proc. Midcon 1981*, Session 24, Paper 2, pp. 1–7.

[7] —, "Expanded applications of one chip microcomputers," in *Proc. Midcon 1981*, Session 21, Paper 3, pp. 1–7.

[8] D. Folkes, "An instruction set architecture for a high performance single-chip microcomputer," in *Proc. Electro 1982*, Session 29, Paper 4, 7 pp.

[9] —, "Single chip microcomputers in distributed control applications," in *Proc. Midcon 1981*, Session 21, Paper 1, pp. 1–9.

[10] V. Goler and M. W. Cruess, "Programming single-chip microcomputers without pain," in *Proc. Midcon 1981*, Session 24, Paper 1, pp. 1–5.

[11] B. Huston, "Self-programmed single-chips—The MC68705s," in *Proc. Electro 1982*, Session 29, Paper 1, 13 pp.

[12] W. D. Huston, "Microcomputers—Heritages and the future," *IEEE Trans. Consum. Electron.*, vol. CE-26, pp. 129–141, Feb. 1980.

[13] L. V. Kaplan, "The TMS 7000: Programming and microprogramming," in *Proc. Electro 1982*, Session 25, Paper 2, pp. 1–11.

[14] T. Knowlton, "μPD7500 family of 4-bit microcomputers—Big jobs with small programs," in *Proc. Midcon 1981*, Session 24, Paper 5, pp. 1–5.

[15] J. A. Langan, "The programming ease of the M6805 family," in *Proc. Electro 1982*, Session 25, Paper 1, pp. 1–9.

[16] K. McDonough *et al.*, "Microcomputer with 32-bit arithmetic does high-precision number crunching," *Electronics*, pp. 105–110, Feb. 24, 1982.

[17] J. Millar, "Versatile microcomputers for the 1980s," in *Proc. Electro 1982*, Session 29, Paper 3, 11 pp.

[18] —, "Single-chip microcomputer programming made easy with the TMS 7000," in *Proc. Midcon 1981*, Session 24, Paper 3, pp. 1–11.

[19] P. E. Nyman, "A common sense approach to choosing CMOS microprocessors," in *Proc. Electro 1982*, Session 33, Paper 1, 4 pp.

[20] J. Paradise, "CDP1800 series multiprocessing for maximum performance," in *Proc. Electro 1982*, Session 33, Paper 4, 11 pp.

[21] M. Patrick and J. Millar, "An innovative microcomputer for the 1980's," in *Proc. Midcon 1981*, Session 21, Paper 4, pp. 1–13.

[22] E. Peatrowsky, "New peripherals for CMOS microprocessors," in *Proc. Electro 1982*, Session 33, Paper 3, 6 pp.

[23] —, "EPROM MCU's reduce hardware liability," in *Proc. Midcon 1981*, Session 21, Paper 2, pp. 1–3.

[24] S. Sanghavi, "NSC 800 family provides high performance/low power solutions," in *Proc. Electro 1982*, Session 33, Paper 2, 5 pp.

[25] D. E. Smith, "New high performance one chip microcomputer," *Electron. Eng.*, pp. 56–65, Feb. 1982.

[26] M. Stevens, "Software techniques for single-chip microcontrollers," in *Proc. Midcon 1981*, Session 24, Paper 4, pp. 1–5.

[27] J. T. Twardy, "Fourth generation architecture allows performance of larger jobs with smaller programs," in *Proc. Electro 1982*, Session 25, Paper 4, pp. 1–8.

Unique—and sometimes obscure—characteristics distinguish single-chip microcomputers from conventional architectures. Current examples show that no one section can be optimized at the expense of another.

The Elements of Single-Chip Microcomputer Architecture

Harvey G. Cragon
Texas Instruments Incorporated

The advent of the single-chip microcomputer in the mid-1970's has brought a new philosophy to computer architecture. Because processor, memory, and input/output logic are contained on a single chip of silicon, the design trade-offs differ from those well proven in the design of computers and minicomputers. Not intended to present a detailed analysis of any one single-chip microcomputer—this article uses various products to illustrate a particular architectural feature which may be common to a number of products.

The cost trade-offs discussed in this article should be considered in the context of the markets served by these devices. These markets are quite cost-sensitive. After a fixed level of performance is established by the intended application, cost becomes the dominant consideration. For example, a microcomputer performing the control function for a radio must provide only this function and at the lowest possible cost.

This design requirement places heavy responsibility on the designer to create an architecture which uses a minimum of chip area. The financial consequence of excessive chip area is severe. For a typical NMOS process used in the manufacturing of microcomputers, the manufacturing cost[1] is

$$\text{manufacturing cost} = K\,(10^{.0243\,A})$$

where A = area of chip in square mils ÷ 1000
K = constant, for a given process

The exponential increase in cost with area drives the design to minimum chip area. Small decreases in chip area can yield large decreases in manufacturing cost; conversely, increases in area increase manufacturing cost exponentially.

The area of a single-chip microcomputer is sensitive to the area occupied by the processor and memory. The complete device, as shown in Figure 1, has three regions: processor, memory, and buffers and bonding pads. The geometry of the buffers and pads is a "picture frame," usually 15-20 mils wide, around the CPU and memory. Thus, the approximate area of a square chip is

$$\text{area} = (\sqrt{\text{CPU} + \text{memory}} + 40)^2$$

Where the memory area is fixed due to the selected technology and the quantity of memory, the CPU area has a significant influence on area and cost. For example, assume two designs. Design A has a memory area of 15,000 square mils and a CPU of 5000 square mils. Design B has the same memory area and a CPU of 7500 square mils—a 50 percent increase in area. Design A results in a

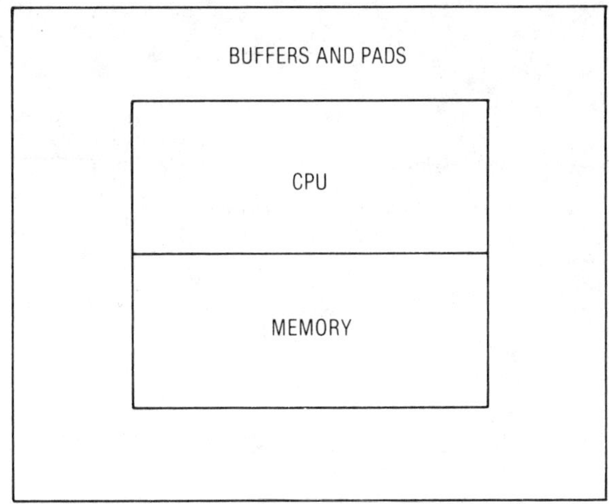

Figure 1. Single-chip microcomputer chip partition.

Reprinted from *IEEE Computer*, vol. 13, pp. 27-30, 32-41, Oct. 1980.

chip area of 32,900 square mil at a relative manufacturing cost of 1, while Design B provides a chip area of 36,100 square mil at a relative cost of 1.20. Therefore, the 2500 square mil increase in CPU area increased the chip area by 3200 square mils and the manufacturing cost by 20 percent.

The necessity of reducing manufacturing cost becomes clear when the production volumes associated with these devices are considered. A 20 percent savings in the cost of a $100,000 computer system is easy to understand—it is $20,000. On the other hand, a 20 percent savings on a $2 microcomputer is only 40¢. However, these devices are purchased in large quantitites, and $400,000 can be saved with the purchase of a million units.

Architecture trade-offs. Since no one section of a microcomputer can be optimized at the expense of another section, we will examine all sections of the microcomputer and discuss their interdependence. Comparisons to computer features will be made to clarify the differences.

Program efficiency. There are two characteristics of a program which are of interest to the microcomputer architect.[2] The *static* characteristic of a program is the frequency of occurrence or use of the instructions. The *dynamic* characteristic is the frequency of execution of the instructions. In the discussion that follows, the word "used" refers to static and the word "executed" refers to dynamic characteristics.

A microcomputer designer is primarily interested in the static characteristic of his product. Memory is a fixed, limited quantity. Each byte saved is of real value. In terms of space occupied in the program memory, there is no difference between instructions that execute only once in every pass through the program and those that execute hundreds or thousands of times. All instructions occupy a portion of the limited memory space.

CPU efficiency. The microcomputer's CPU capabilities must be determined by the dynamic characteristics of the program to be executed. The number of times a feature is executed will help determine if the use of CPU area is worthwhile. A feature should be included in the design if it is needed to achieve a performance level. Low frequency of execution suggests that the feature should not be included but should be programmed.

An example would be the inclusion of decimal arithmetic instructions. Since they generally have low static but high dynamic characteristics, decimal arithmetic instructions are included in the architecture of most microcomputers. This example is noteworthy, since an architect who was only familiar with minicomputer design and use statistics would probably not include decimal instructions due to their high cost.

Memory design factors. The computer or minicomputer designer is always aware of the limited memory bandwidth at his disposal. Providing high memory bandwidth can result in a costly design. Techniques for interleaving memory modules and having the memory provide multiple computer words each cycle all add to the cost of a memory system. Nevertheless, these techniques must always be used when the necessary bandwidth exceeds the bandwidth of a single memory module.[3,4]

On the other hand, a microcomputer designer is never forced to restrict the number of bits in the word to save memory bandwidth. In most cases, an increase in the number of bits per word can be obtained at reduced cost—the opposite of the situation faced by the computer designer.

As illustrated in Figure 2, a standard semiconductor memory device is designed as a square matrix to minimize chip area, because minimum chip area is obtained when the X and Y decodes are of the same size. The X decode selects one of the words, and the Y decode selects one of the bits in that word. For a 64K-bit memory device, X = Y = 256. Notice that to obtain a "by one" organization, which is needed to minimize the number of package pins, 255/256 or 99.6 percent of the available memory bandwidth is not used!

For the microcomputer designer, this bandwidth is there for the asking. Because the memory is on the chip with the processor, no external pins are needed, as with standard memory devices; thus, there is no need to select only one bit with the Y decoder. In fact, if the word length is made 4, 8, 16, or 32 bits, Y decoder circuits are saved and the chip area is reduced.

This discussion of unlimited memory word length should not be taken to mean that memory cycles are not important. The number of memory cycles to random locations needed to execute an instruction will determine the speed of the microcomputer. Nevertheless, the number of bits per instruction or data word does not pose a bandwidth constraint for the designer.

The trade-off that must be made by the designer is complicated by the bus which provides the communications between the memory section and the other sections of the microcomputer. The wider the bus, the more difficult to route, and more chip area is used. Therefore, to save bus area, the number of bits per word is minimized. Memory and bus widths of 8 and 16 bits seem to provide the best compromise. However, some new products, such as the Intel 8089,[5] have a 20-bit register length and internal bus.

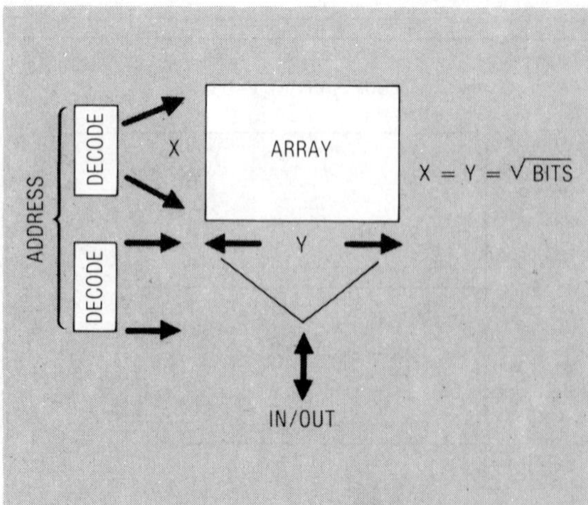

Figure 2. Standard memory device architecture.

Harvard architecture

The Mark I calculator,[6] developed by Howard Aiken of Harvard University in the 1940's, provided the architectural concepts for what are known today as "Harvard machines." It accepted a program on punched paper tape, which controlled the electromechanical calculator. Four decades later, Aiken's work, which started in 1939, still provides the basic architecture for many microcomputers.

Instruction and data word length. In the "Harvard machine" architecture, the program memory and the data memory are disjoint. This separation of the two memory functions of instruction storage and data storage gives the microcomputer designer great flexibility in word size selection. A major advantage of this architecture, derived from its use of two memories, is that the increased bandwidth permits an overlapping of instruction and data accesses which will increase the performance, for a given technology, over that possible with a single-memory von Neumann architecture.

In a von Neumann architecture,[7] both data and instruction must reside in the same memory. Therefore, when a computer designer selects an operand or data word size, he has specified the instruction word length as well. For example, if he selects a data word size of 16 bits, the instruction word length will be 16 bits or factors of 16 bits.

A "Harvard" microcomputer is not restricted in this way. If the microcomputer is to operate on four-bit quantities, the instruction word length can be of any length—eight bits, nine bits, etc.—since there is no need to have these instructions reside in the same memory.

Furthermore, the various registers of the microcomputer need not be of lengths which are multiples of the data word. Microcomputers have a program counter, for example, which is of a length sufficient to address only the memory on the chip. The saving of return addresses is usually handled by a small stack dedicated to this task—not by a stack in the data memory. Thus, the designer is not constrained to have the addressability of the program storage equal to a data word length.

Instruction and data memory size. The number of words of storage for instructions and for data must be considered as separate, unique problems by the microcomputer designer. The instructions will be stored in a ROM and the data in a RAM.

Experience has shown that a microcomputer needs 16 to 32 times more instruction memory words than data memory words[8-12] (see Table 1). While many computer systems are characterized by "small programs processing a large data set," the microcomputer system is a "large program processing a small data set." There is some indication that the ratio of ROM to RAM will grow even greater in the future. This is a consequence of having several programs, not one large program, in the ROM. Each of these programs needs the same relatively small data storage. Since only one of these programs is active at any time, the data storage provided is only large enough to satisfy the most demanding program, not all the resident programs.

Table 1.
Instruction and data memory size.

MICROCOMPUTER	INSTRUCTION WORDS (BITS/WORD)	DATA WORDS (BITS/WORD)	RATIO
TMS1000	1024 (8)	64 (4)	16:1
TMS1100	2048 (8)	128 (4)	16:1
S2000	1024 (8)	64 (4)	16:1
M3870*	2048 (8)	64 (8)	32:1
18021*	1024 (8)	64 (8)	16:1

*Multiple byte instructions are required for some instructions.

The relative cost of RAM to ROM—4:1 to 8:1—provides an incentive to minimize RAM. Instruction-intensive programming techniques are employed to save data memory.

Data memory addressing. The microcomputer designer must create an architecture which addresses a relatively small memory and does not burden the instruction with unnecessary bits. Binary addressing schemes are very wasteful of bits when small memories are implemented. A fifth bit added to a four-bit address adds only 16 words to the memory. However, a sixteenth bit added to a 15-bit address adds 32,768 words to the memory. The designer is working in a wasteful memory size, where even short addresses can add a significant burden to an instruction set. Six address bits added to a six-bit opcode is a 50 percent burden for data addressing. Thus, due to this overhead burden, direct addressing is not commonly used.

Two techniques commonly used to cope with the data memory addressing problem are indirect addressing and zero page addressing.

Implied indirect addressing. Some early supercomputers, such as the CDC 7600,[13] were designed with short instructions because large memory bandwidth was costly. By reducing the length of the instructions, the available bandwidth was used most effectively. The technique employed was to have two fields of three bits each which pointed to two groups (A&B) of eight registers which contained the addresses of the operands. This gave the effect of a three-bit address capable of pointing to a memory whose size was determined by the length of the pointed-to address register. Instructions were provided to load, index, and test these address registers. This type of indirect addressing should not be confused with the more conventional type, where a direct address to memory finds the address of the operand.[14]

The microcomputer architect has taken this indirect addressing scheme one step further. If there is but one data memory address register, there is no need for bits in the instruction to select an address register. Those instructions which need to address the data memory use the one available address register; the use is implied in the instruction.

The TMS1000 illustrates implied indirect addressing. As shown in Figure 3, the 64 words (four bits per word) data memory is addressed by a six-bit register. This

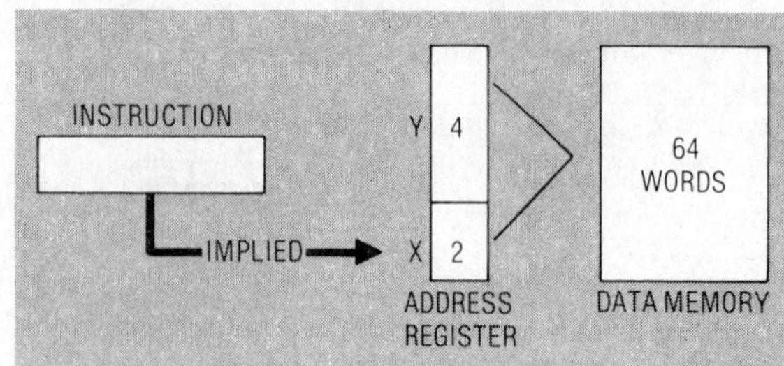

Figure 3. TMS1000 implied direct addressing.

register is divided into two sections, the two-bit X register and the four-bit Y register. Any instruction which references the memory uses the address pre-established in the X and Y registers. Other uses for the TMS1000 X and Y registers will be discussed later.

As with the CDC 7600, there are instructions which load, increment, and test the address register. In some products, such as the AMI S2000 and TMS1000, the incrementing of the address register occurs automatically and concurrently with some instructions. The probability of the next location containing the desired data is so high that this compound instruction saves code space and execution time.

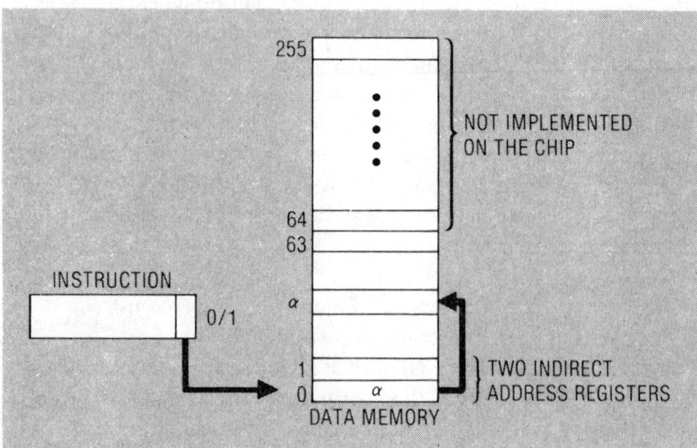

Figure 4. I8021 indirect addressing.

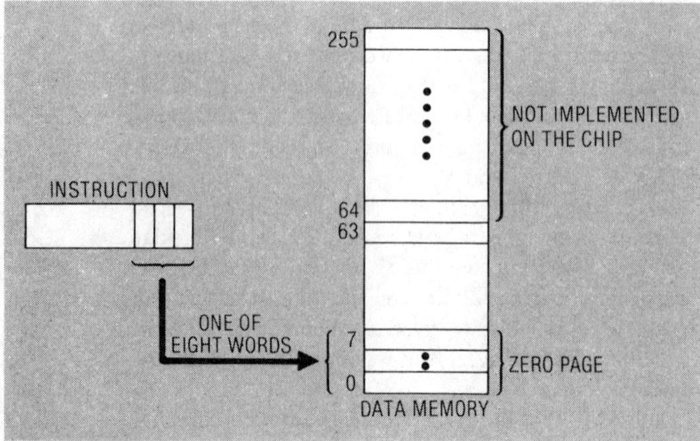

Figure 5. I8021 zero page addressing.

Indirect addressing. A more conventional form of indirect addressing is found on devices such as the Intel 8021.[12] Here, address registers are located in the data memory and are pointed to by a field in the relevant instructions. In the case of the I8021, locations 0 and 1 of a 64-word memory are the address registers, and one bit in the instruction is needed to select between them.

With the indirect address registers located within the data memory, the address length is constrained to be the length of the data word or a multiple of the data word. The I8021 has an eight-bit operand and data word memory, resulting in a data addressability of 2^8 or 256 words (see Figure 4).

A benefit of having the indirect address registers in data memory is that the usual instructions for operating on data are useful for manipulation of the indirect addresses. The major disadvantage of this approach is that the already limited data memory capacity is reduced by the use of data memory words for dedicated functions.

Zero page addressing. This technique is based on two considerations. First, since the data memory will be small, only a small address is needed. Second, a short address can be used in a base + displacement addressing scheme, such as the IBM 370 architecture.[15]

Combining these ideas, a single implied base register is assumed to contain the value "zero." The short address is then a displacement off this implied "zero base" which addresses "zero page." The number of bits carried in the instruction for addressing within the zero page can be small. For example, I8021 uses three bits which gives a zero page of eight data words (see Figure 5). The Rockwell R6500/1[16] uses an eight-bit address for a zero page of 256 words.

As a provision for growth in the data memory above the zero page size, an additional mode of addressing may be provided which takes the address out of the "zero page." The R6500/1 uses a conventional two-byte direct address to address out of the "zero page." The I8021 uses indirect addressing for data outside of the zero page.

Indexing. The invention of indexing[6]—or the "B Box" as it was called at the University of Manchester—was stimulated by the need to compress code. A program loop could address an array of data by having a value added to the address in the instruction. This value would be incremented or decremented (indexed) after each use, thereby accessing the data array.

The motivation of saving code space is still dominant for the microcomputer architect. The microcomputer does not need the generality of a true index register. If the indirect or implied indirect address registers can be incremented, decremented, and tested for zero or a value, array addressing can be performed. The hardware features necessary to support relocation of code are not necessary in a microcomputer. Thus, no address in the instruction is needed—only the index value in the indirect address register.

As described earlier, the TMS1000 addresses data memory with two registers, the X of two bits and the Y of four bits. This six-bit address can be manipulated with the following instructions. (Underlined instructions indicate operations on portions of the implied addressed register.)

Transfer accumulator to memory and increment Y
Transfer constant to memory and increment Y
Increment Y, if carry, 1 → status
Decrement Y, if no borrow, 1 → status
$Y \neq A$, 1 → status
$Y \neq C$, 1 → status
Complement X

With these instructions, a loop can be established which not only generates the addresses to the data memory but also controls the length of the loop itself.

The F8/3870[17] illustrates another architecture using implied indirect addressing. The indirect scratchpad register addresses the data memory. This register of six bits can have the low order three bits automatically incremented or decremented during instruction execution which reference the data memory. Moving from one group of eight registers to another requires that the higher order three bits are modified by a load ISAR upper instruction. The lower three bits of ISAR can be tested for all ones and a branch taken for loop control. Note that the two segments of the register are manipulated separately, similar to the TMS1000's X and Y registers.

The I8021 also combines the indirect address register concept with indexing. The instruction "Decrement register and jump on R not zero" provides for using R_0 and R_1 both as an indirect address register and as the index register. The three indexing systems described above are summarized in Table 2.

Base registers. Computer architects have relied on the base register to solve two problems which do not exist for the microcomputer architect. The computer architect is usually faced with the task of extending a limited address—say 8 to 12 bits—to a larger address. A base register is used to point to a region of memory where the displacement is effective.[15] The microcomputer architecture usually has only a small data memory space—in many cases, smaller than the available zero page address span. Thus, no need exists to expand the data addressability.

Table 2.
Indexed instruction sequences.

MICRO-COMPUTER	SEQUENCES	INSTRUCTIONS	BYTES
TMS1000	OPERATION	AMAAC	1
	INCREMENT	IYC	1
	TEST AND BRANCH	BR	1
F8/3870	OPERATION AND INCREMENT OR DECREMENT	ASD	1
	TEST AND BRANCH	BR7	2
I8021	OPERATION	ADD	1
	DECREMENT, TEST, AND BRANCH	DJNZ	2

The I8048 has, in effect, two zero pages. The data memory is divided in half, and an instruction is provided which will select bank 0 or bank 1. This in effect provides two base registers with implied selection. What is increased is not the memory space but rather the flexibility to invoke another set of indirect address registers and another zero page. The use of this feature in context switching will be discussed later.

The second reason for using base registers in a computer is to provide a convenient technique for program segment relocation. This also is not a problem with microcomputers. As the programs are stored in ROM, the binding of the program segments into an absolute address system must be accomplished so that the part can be manufactured. Run-time relocation cannot occur; thus, base registers for instructions are not needed.

Instruction memory addressing. As with data memory addressing techniques, the microcomputer designer is concerned with addressing the instruction or program memory with as small an address as possible. This memory will be referred to as ROM in the following sections.

The minimum increment of ROM is usually 1024 (1K) bytes. The size of the ROM in new products is increasing; 4K products are in production. There are two basic addressing needs for ROM. The first is the program counter which points to the location of the current program step. Simple incrementing of the program counter is needed to change its value. The second need is a random address system which will change the value of the program counter for branching, subroutine calls, and subroutine returns.

The design of this portion of the microcomputer architecture can have a profound influence on the static program storage efficiency. Branch and subroutine calls constitute 25-50 percent of all functional instructions used.[18] These are the instructions which need to have the longest address in the architecture. The problem is trading off high frequency of use and long addresses.

Segmented instruction addressing. For many microcomputers, the ROM is subdivided into pages and chapters. A page size is determined by the number of bits which can be contained within an eight-bit instruction word. For the TMS1000 and S2000, for example, six bits are reserved for the address within the page of 64 words. The technique for using six of eight bits for an address will be discussed later in regard to instruction format. Branches and calls within a page are quite efficient in their use of instruction bits.

The addressability of the ROM is extended beyond the page limit by another register which addresses the pages. The TMS1000 and S2000 have four-bit page address registers for addressing 16 pages. Extensions beyond the 10-bit limit are accomplished by adding additional bits to the ROM address. Instructions must be dedicated to the manipulation of these registers. A branch out of a page requires that two branch instructions are executed. The first prepares to branch into a new page by changing the value in a page address buffer—not the page address register. The branch instruction loads the six-bit immediate value into the six-bit program counter and swaps the contents of the page address register and the page buffer. Table 3 illustrates a branch from location 173 to 754—a long out-of-the-current-page branch. The S2000 employs a similar technique with the instruction "Prepare page or bank."

Similar procedures are employed for subroutine calls with provisions to save the return address in a stack. As mentioned earlier, these architectures employ a dedicated stack to save return addresses.

Nonsegmented instruction addressing. Several architectures avoid the ad hoc extension procedure of the segmented memory system by establishing a framework of easy expansion. The F8/3870 illustrates this technique.

A 16-bit logical address is created in the architecture. A shorter address register, 11 bits, is implemented in the hardware.

The F8/3870 has three forms of the branch or jump and two forms of the call instructions. For short branches and calls, an eight-bit displacement is added to the program counter. Using a short relative address conserves program storage. The five forms of these instructions are

Branch (2) conditional, 8-bit immediate, relative
(2) unconditional, 8-bit immediate, relative
(3) unconditional, 16-bit immediate, absolute

Call • (1) computed, 16-bits in R12 and R13, absolute
(3) unconditional, 16-bit immediate, absolute
[(X), number of bytes in the instruction]

The use of the relative addresses will reduce the average bytes per branch or call to approximately two, while giving the full flexibility of a large logical address space.

The F8/3870 also uses a dedicated stack for saving return addresses. The length and depth of this stack is a design option which, in the F8/3870, is limited to one level. Variations of the TMS1000 have extended the depth of the dedicated stack to three levels.

Table lookup. The requirement for table lookup poses unique problems to the architect of a Harvard-class microcomputer. The disjoint data and instruction memories must have some connective path so that a value in the data memory or accumulator can serve as an address to the ROM. The value in the addressed ROM location is returned to the processor as the desired table entry. The I8021 and F8/3870 solve the problem with specific hardware and instructions.

The I8021 has an instruction—MOVP A, @A* —which takes the eight-bit value in the accumulator as an address in the active or current ROM, page. The value in the ROM location is returned to the accumulator as the table entry. The major disadvantage of this technique is that the tables must be associated with the program which will reference the table. If common use tables are needed—degrees C to degrees F, for example—a call into the table page would be required before the table is accessed. A return to the main program is then required.

The F8/3870 provides two registers, which can be 16 bits in length, to address the ROM for table lookup. These registers are named "data counter" and "auxiliary data counter." Instructions are provided to load and store the DCs from RAM, load with a 16-bit immediate value, and exchange the contents of DC and DC1.

A set of arithmetic, logical, load, and store instructions operate with the accumulator and ROM as addressed by the data counter. This facility, therefore, provides not only table lookup but also ready access to constants and masks.

Memory expansion techniques. There will be cases where the architect will want to provide off-chip memory expansion capability for the microcomputer. The instruction memory and/or data memory, external to the microcomputer, must be addressed. This may seem like a strange requirement, for if the memory needs of a particular application exceed the capabilities of the microcomputer, a microprocessor with almost unlimited memory can be employed. For architectures which are not members of an expandable family, memory expansion is frequently provided.

Instruction memory expansion. The instruction memory expansion technique employed on the S2000 is typical. In addition to the six-bit word address and the four-bit page address, a three-bit bank address register is provided, which can obviously point to one of eight banks of 1024 words. Bank "0" is on the chip, banks 1 through 7 are off the chip. A three-bit value is loaded into the address buffer with the same instruction used to load the page buffer, prepare page, or bank. One occurrence of this instruction in a program will load the page buffer. A pair of these instructions, in sequence, will load the page buffer and then the bank buffer. As with the TMS1000, these new values are not transferred into the program counter until a branch or call instruction is executed. Thus, a branch or call to external instruction memory takes three instructions of one byte each.

Instruction memory expansion for the I8048 starts after the 1K bytes which are on the chip. The program counter is 11 bits in length, plus a bit called "MB" which is set and reset with special instructions. The effective 12-bit address enables 4K bytes of instruction storage. Addresses above 1023 are automatically routed to the external program memory.

Table 3.
TMS1000 long branch.

INSTRUCTION	PAGE ADDRESS BUFFER	PAGE ADDRESS REGISTER	PROGRAM COUNTER	LOCATION
INITIAL CONDITIONS	XXXX	0010	101101	173_{10}
LDP, 1011 →	1011	0010	101110	174_{10}
BR, 110010	1011	1011	110010	754_{10}

The 12-bit address is transmitted to the external memory via pins 20-23 for the four high order bits and pins 12-19 for the eight low order bits. Pin 9 carries a signal $\overline{PSEN}$ to activate the external instruction memory. The addressed external instruction returns to the I8048 via pins 12-19.

Data memory expansion. The I8048[19] also illustrates data memory expansion. Direct addressing to words 64-255 external to the chip is not provided. A pair of move instructions permit one word at a time to be moved between the accumulator and external data memory. To process a block of data in external memory, the block is moved to the accumulator and then to the internal RAM. This requires a three-instruction loop per word transferred.

Von Neumann architectures

The major difference of the von Neumann architecture[7] from the "Harvard machine" architecture is its single memory for both instructions and data. This architecture has one address space, and data and instructions can be intermixed within that space. Futhermore, instructions can be used as data (processed by other instructions), and data may be used as instructions. Microcomputers of von Neumann architecture are starting to emerge from the manufacturers; the TMS9940[20] and R6500/1 will serve as examples in the discussion that follows.

Word lengths. Due to the common data and instruction memory, instructions and operands must have lengths which are equal and/or are factors of each other, as shown in Table 4. That is, if the memory word length is 16 bits, instruction and operand lengths must be 16 bits or factor lengths, such as 8 or 24 bits. In practice, all lengths have become multiples of the eight-bit byte. In those cases where registers are not a natural multiple of eight, bits are wasted or left unused so the word can be stored in memory.

Instruction addressing. Instruction addressing is accomplished by a full 16-bit program counter. Even though the memory size in all of today's microcomputers is much less than 2^{16}, the full length program counter is used in the architecture. In some cases, only the number of bits required to address the on-chip memory are implemented. This technique was employed with the F8/3870.

Branch addresses are usually one of two forms—a short one-byte branch, relative to the program counter, and a long absolute two-byte branch address. The short branches conserve instruction space, since a high percentage of the branches are within ± 127 of the current program counter location.

The program counter contents are saved in the memory, either random or stack, during a subroutine call, interrupt service, or other context switch. This is convenient, because the lengths are equal or multiples—i.e., memory word length is equal to the program counter length or is equal to one-half the program counter, etc.

Unlike most of the "Harvard machines" discussed earlier, no special instructions to manipulate the various program counter segments are required in von Neumann architecture.

Table 4.
Register and word lengths in bits.

REGISTERS	TMS9940	R6500/1
PROGRAM COUNTER	16	16
OPERANDS	8,16	8
INDEX REGISTERS	16	8
ACCUMULATOR	16	8
STATUS WORD	16	8
INSTRUCTION	16,32,48	8,16,24

Data addressing. Data addressing has the same uniformity of instruction addressing. Two address lengths are usually provided—short register or zero page address and a long full memory address. The R6500/1 and the TMS9940 differ in the generation of these two address forms.

The R6500/1 has addressing modes similar to many minicomputers:

- Zero page addressing is accomplished by a second byte in the instruction. Only six of the bits are used to address up to 64 locations. Expansion capability up to 256 locations is provided in the architecture.
- Absolute addressing of 2^{16} locations is accomplished by two bytes in a three-byte instruction.
- Two eight-bit index registers (X or Y) are provided which can be selectively added to either the zero page address byte or the two-byte absolute address.
- Eight-bit immediate operands are contained in the second byte of the instruction.
- Two forms of indirect addressing are provided. In the first form, the second byte of a two-byte instruction is added to the X index register. The sum addresses a pair of zero page bytes (16-bits) which address the full address space for the operand. The second form provides that the second byte of a two-byte instruction addresses a zero page location. The contents of this location, and the next, are added to the Y index register (eight bits) to generate a 16-bit address.

The TMS9940—a register architecture—has four addressing modes. The architecture is designed to operate on 16-bit data and have a 16-bit-wide memory. For this reason, all data addresses, index registers, and immediate values are 16 bits. While this produces a static code space penalty for small memory applications, the penalty should decrease as more memory is added to the chip.

The TMS9940 data addressing forms are:

- *Immediate.* Bytes three and four of a four-byte instruction contain the value.
- *Direct.* Four-bit addresses are contained in the two-byte instruction. These addresses point to the 16 registers which contain the value.

- *Indirect.* The contents of the addressed register addresses memory.
- *Indexed.* Bytes three and four of a four-byte instruction contain index values which are added to an addressed register. The sum is the data address.

Common architectural elements

In most cases, architectural elements common to both the Harvard and von Neumann architectures are insensitive to the characteristic of a common or disjoint memory. In those cases where the memory architecture does influence how the capability is included in the architecture, the differences will be described.

Asynchronous inputs. A microcomputer is required to have facilities for detecting the occurrence of an external asynchronous event and to perform some processing task associated with the event. Two techniques commonly used to achieve this facility are polling and interrupt.

Polling. A polling architecture provides that asynchronous inputs will be detected by the action of an instruction which looks to see if the input has occurred. A sequence of instructions called a "polling loop" tests the various input lines at a rate which will provide the desired system response time. The poll of the inputs is an action at a time which permits the processing task associated with the input to be accomplished.

Two architectural requirements exist for polled inputs. First, there must be a flip-flop associated with each input which will recognize and retain the presence of an input. If the input flip-flop is not present, the polling must be fast enough to detect the input change. Secondly, there must be instructions which test the conditions of these flip-flops and, if set, branch to the service program.

The I8021 has an input, T1, which can be tested by two instructions. The JT1 jump to a new program if $T=1$ and the JNT1 will jump if $T=0$ ($T\neq1$). These two instructions require two bytes, the first byte containing the operation code and the second an eight-bit address. This is a direct address within the current or active 256-byte program page.

The TMS1000 polled input architecture represents another technique for detecting the presence of an asynchronous input. One input bus of four bits, called the K inputs, is tested by an instruction. This instruction, KNEZ, looks at all four input lines, and if any one of these lines is a logical "one," the status bit is set to a one. A second instruction, BR, branches if status = one. As discussed earlier, the branch address is six bits for a short branch. Two and sometimes three bytes are required to poll an input and branch into the service routine.

The major advantage of the polled input system is simplicity of hardware and software. For most applications, response time is satisfactory, and the possibility of programming error is reduced because the input is serviced when the processor can attend to the event.

Interrupts. Interrupts, as the name indicates, have the characteristic of interrupting the normal program execution at any time to demand service. Something must be done as a result of the interrupt—even if only to place the request for service in a queue. Interrupts were first used in the late 1950's on the Remington Rand 1103.[6]

The most significant difference between a polling architecture and an interrupt architecture is that an interrupt architecture must have facilities for saving the state of the processor and restoring the state to its original condition after the interrupt has been serviced or deferred. This demand can occur at any time, and sufficient state information must be saved to reestablish the processing.

Since there will be times when the interrupt must be ignored, a provision for disabling the interrupt is provided. This disabling is sometimes used when an interrupt is being serviced and no more interrupts are wanted. As will be discussed, some architectures provide that interrupts can be "stacked"—i.e., a new interrupt can be serviced by suspending the service of the current interrupt. In this case, the status of the interrupted interrupt service routine must also be saved. In addition to the enable/disable control, a flip-flop is also included in the interrupt line to "save" the interrupt when it occurs. This flip-flop performs the same function as the save flip-flop of a polled architecture.

Some architectures provide for accepting interrupts from more than one source. In this case, some means must be provided to resolve the conflict when more than one of these interrupts arrive simultaneously or a second interrupt arrives while the first is being processed. The facilities for resolving this problem are called priorities. The hardware may be configured to recognize the priority of one interrupt over another or a polling of the inputs.

The F8/3870 has two interrupts, an external and an internal timer. Two bits in an eight-bit I/O status word, called port 6, enable or disable these two interrupt sources. A third bit, the interrupt control bit, allows or disallows either interrupt to occur.

Upon receipt of an interrupt, one of two hard-wired addresses is transferred into the program counter which causes a jump to the proper interrupt service routine. The old value of program counter is pushed into the one-level stack for recall after the interrupt is serviced. With only one level of stack, only one interrupt can be serviced at a time.

Saving the status of the machine after the receipt of an interrupt will be discussed in the following sections.

Status registers. The development of the concept of status is contained in the development of subroutine calling and interrupt techniques. The architecture proposed by John von Neumann in 1946 had no convenient way of determining the return location from a subroutine which could be called from more than one place.

When a subroutine is called, if the contents of the program counter are stored in some known location, restoring the program counter to its value prior to the call is quite easy. The contents of the program counter are, thus, a basic portion of the machine's "status." The program counter must be incremented by one either before it is stored or after it is recalled.

The development of interrupts stimulated the need to add other factors of the machine's state to the "status."

While a subroutine call, as an input poll, occurs at a time of the programmer's choosing, an interrupt can occur at any time. Thus, more information needs to be saved so that the complete state of the machine can be restored after the interrupt is serviced.

There are two levels of status: that which is saved on a subroutine call or poll, and that which is saved on an interrupt. Status consists of two classes of information: results from the execution of the program, and conditions which are established by the program for use in the future. Examples of the first class—results from the program—are the program counter value, overflow bit, and carry bit. Examples of the second class—conditions set by the program—are interrupt enable, internal timer enable, internal counter enable, and internal flags.

The microcomputer architect must decide which items of status must be saved by the hardware under the conditions of subroutine call and interrupt. This trade-off becomes one of evaluating the area in the CPU for status-saving hardware versus the ROM bits required to save status by programming. If there is a heavy use of subroutines, polling, or interrupts, area can be saved by hardware-saving of status. Table 5 illustrates the type of information saved under various conditions. Performance is not the critical issue, and the time to execute the code is of little consequence, but the code space in ROM must be considered paramount.

Context switch. When the sequential flow of instructions is diverted due to a subroutine call or interrupt, the status of the microcomputer must be saved. After the task is completed, the prior status can be restored and the sequential flow reestablished. There are three architectural techniques for saving the microcomputer context: a dedicated stack, a stack in the data memory, and a form of linked list as used on the TMS9940.

Dedicated stack. The TMS1000, the F8/3870, and the S2000 use a dedicated stack to save the program counter, a technique which has already been discussed. These architectures have a minimum of status information, the program counter, and are limited as to the depth of calling subroutines or serving polled inputs and interrupts. One to three levels of stack depth have been considered satisfactory for this class of product.

Table 5.
Status information saved.

CONTEXT SWITCH	TMS1000	I8021	F8/3870
SUBROUTINE CALL	PROGRAM CTR	PROGRAM CTR*	PROGRAM CTR
INTERRUPT	NONE	NONE	PC, ICB, SIGN, CARRY, ZERO, OVERFLOW
POLLED	(1) Set C = 1 (2) JUMP ON C = 1 TO SUB-ROUTINE.	(1) TEST BIT AND BRANCH TO SUB-ROUTINE.	(1) SET Z = 1 (2) JUMP ON Z = 1 TO SUB-ROUTINE.

*Since the RETURN instruction does not restore four bits of the PSW, these bits cannot be preserved during a subroutine; only the program counter is preserved.

Stack in RAM. The I8021 has a simple stack in RAM for saving return addresses. Locations 8-23 of the data memory are assigned as the stack. These sixteen bytes provide eight two-byte locations which will permit stacking up to eight levels. A three-bit counter points initially to location eight. A CALL instruction increments this counter by one and a RETURN decrements it by one, with each count representing two bytes.

This architecture has a fixed depth, which is less than the data memory capacity. The stack registers can be used as conventional data memory.

The R6500/1 carries the generality of the stack in data memory one step further. A dedicated register of eight bits in length points to the stack in the zero page of RAM. An instruction is provided to load this stack pointer with a value which establishes the location of the stack in RAM. This context-switching instruction increments or decrements this pointer as required.

TMS9940 context switching. The TMS9940 has a unique context-switch mechanism designed to minimize overhead. The architecture has sixteen registers in which the various operations are performed. These registers are in memory and are pointed to by the contents of the workspace pointer. A context switch initiated by an interrupt fetches a new workspace pointer value and program counter value from the interrupt vector. The current workspace pointer, program counter, and status register value are stored in locations 13,14, and 15 of the new workspace region. This stacking of context into successive workspace regions can continue to any depth.

A shorter version of this instruction takes the new value for the program counter from an addressed memory location and stores the current value of the program counter into location 11 of the *current* workspace region. Return instructions are provided to return control and status to the original condition.

Register content storage. After the status information is stored, the poll or interrupt service routine must store away the contents of the accumulator and/or working registers so that these facilities will be available for the service routine.

To facilitate this action, some microcomputers—such as the I8048—have a dual bank of registers which can be selected by a single instruction in the service routine. On the surface, it would seem wasteful to have two banks of registers. However, in any case eight words (bytes) would be allocated out of the limited address space as a place to store the registers during a context switch. The unused bank of registers can be used as normal data storage, since this bank is within the indirect address space. Care must be exercised that a program does not cause an error by modifying the contents of a register in the currently unused bank.

Because the accumulator does not reside in either the status word or the register area on the 8048/21/22, the start of the service routine must, if required, store the accumulator in the RAM and restore its contents as the conclusion of the service routine.

Comparisons. The major characteristics which distinguish context switch systems are levels of stacking, a dedicated or RAM-located stack for storing the program counter and any status bits, and hardware and/or software techniques for storing register contents.

The architect must trade off CPU area versus ROM area in selecting a context-switch system. Heavy use implies a more complex CPU to save ROM bytes, while light use implies the opposite. The problems of programs writing into stacks and registers in the data memory must also be comprehended. Table 6 compares the various architectures mentioned.

Operation registers. The question of the operation register architecture for microcomputers has been decided in favor of the single accumulator by most designers. Register, memory-to-memory, and evaluation stack architectures are not used in any Harvard architecture. The TMS9940 and R6500/1 von Neumann architectures are register-file and accumulator architectures, respectively.

The reason for the almost universal use of accumulator architecture is that, with one address implied—the address of the accumulator—a minimum number of bits are required in an instruction. Take, for example, the I8021. Within a one-byte instruction, an operand in the eight-word zero page can be addressed along with the implied accumulator and the operation code. The entire 64 words of data memory, which could be expanded to 256 words, can also be addressed, along with the implied accumulator, by indirect addressing in a one-byte instruction. The necessity to address a second location or register for a register-to-register operation would add three or more bits to the instruction.

In some applications, the exclusive use of the accumulator can produce a computational bottleneck which slows down execution. While this is of little consequence in most microcomputers, some new architectures—the TMS9940 and Zilog Z-8,[21] for example—are employing architectures which are register-to-register in orientation. In general, some sacrifice in instruction density is made to achieve the higher performance obtainable with a register-to-register architecture.

The R6500/1 is an accumulator machine. Thus, like the Harvard machines, many instructions need only one data address since the other address is implied.

The TMS9940 and Z-8 are register-file machines of unusual design. Sixteen registers are provided in the architecture. These registers are not in the CPU; however, they are in memory. A 16-word (two bytes per word) block is pointed to by a workspace pointer. Until the contents of this pointer are changed, the registers are fixed. Normal register-to-register and register-to-memory operations are implemented.

Instructions. The architecture of an instruction set must meet two needs. First, what instructions will be included in the set? Second, how will these instructions be formatted into the instruction word?

The instruction set selection. The instructions to be included in the set are determined by the dynamic characteristics of the application environment. Frequently executed functions should be included, while infrequently executed functions should not be included. Of equal importance to the function selection is the selection of addressing modes consistent with the basic architecture.

Further considerations are that all registers—including I/O—must be loadable and storable, a useful set of branch and jump instructions must be provided, subroutine calls and returns must be provided for, and asynchronous inputs must be acceptable.

In addition, the set should be useful in building up more complex functions (don't make multiply an inefficient subroutine) and the operations should be symmetrical, if possible. That is, there should be a left shift as well as a right shift, a store register as well as a load register, etc.

The architect of a microcomputer instruction set must also keep in mind that he is designing a computer which will have its program in ROM. Computer features needed for relocation of programs have no value in a microcomputer, except when family compatibility must be preserved.

The I8021 instruction set. The I8021—a Harvard single-accumulator architecture—will be used to illustrate the selection of an instruction set. Its data addressing modes are:

- register or zero page (eight words),
- indirect reference to memory register, and
- immediate eight-bit value.

Five operations using these addressing modes were selected:

- add to accumulator,
- add with carry to accumulator,
- logical AND to accumulator,
- logical OR to accumulator, and
- logical XOR to accumulator.

Note that one address is always the accumulator. Symmetry would suggest that a subtract instruction be included; it was not included because a short instruction sequence will yield the same result for this infrequently used operation.

Table 6.
Comparison of architectures.

MICROCOMPUTER	TYPE OF STACK	DEPTH OF STACK	CONTENTS OF STATUS
TMS1000	DEDICATED	1	PROGRAM COUNTER
S2000	DEDICATED	1	PROGRAM COUNTER
F8/3870	DEDICATED	1	PROGRAM COUNTER
I8021	DEDICATED IN RAM	8	PROGRAM COUNTER
R6500/1	RAM	64	PROGRAM COUNTER STATUS REGISTER CONTROL REGISTER
TMS9940	LINKED LISTS IN WORKSPACE	(AN IMPLEMENTATION LIMIT)	PROGRAM CONTROL STATUS REGISTER WORKSPACE POINTER

Table 7.
I8021 register transfers.

MOVE FROM: TO:	ACCUMULATOR	DATA MEMORY	REGISTER OR ZERO PAGE	IMMEDIATE VALUE
ACCUMULATOR	R	✓	✓	X
DATA MEMORY	✓	R	B	X
REGISTER OR ZERO PAGE	✓	A	R	X
IMMEDIATE VALUE	✓	✓	✓	X,R

R = redundant move
X = an absurdity
✓ = an instruction in the set

Table 8.
I8021 I/O transfers.

MOVE FROM: TO:	ACCUMULATOR	PORT	EXPANDER	TIMER
ACCUMULATOR	R	✓	✓ MOVE AND OR	✓
PORT	✓	R	TWO INSTRUCTIONS	TWO INSTRUCTIONS
EXPANDER	✓	TWO INSTRUCTIONS	R	TWO INSTRUCTIONS
TIMER	✓	TWO INSTRUCTIONS	TWO INSTRUCTIONS	R

These 15 instruction variations—five types with three modes—are augmented by 10 instructions which operate on the contents of the accumulator only: increment, decrement, clear, complement, swap UH/LH, rotate left, rotate left through carry, rotate right, rotate right through carry, and decimal adjust. Note that—due to the heavy use of decimal arithmetic in this class of product—a decimal adjust of the accumulator is provided.

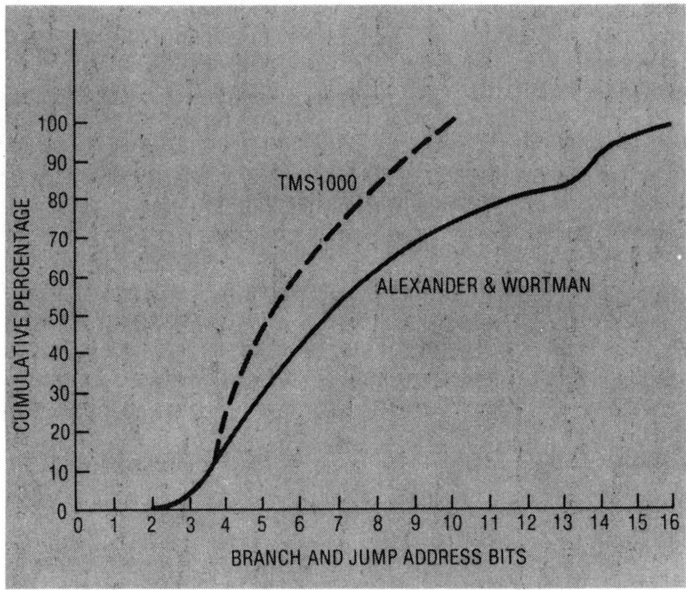

Figure 6. Distribution of branch distance.

The requirement to load and store registers is met in the I8021, as illustrated in Table 7. Several things can be noted from this table:

(1) Storing in the immediate field of an instruction is an absurdity when the program is in ROM, as signified by an X in Table 7.

(2) Two moves take two instructions:

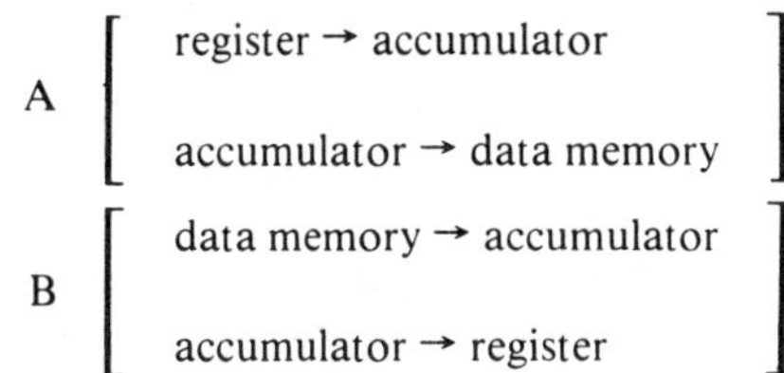

Four address bits would be required to perform these moves in one instruction.

(3) The redundant moves, each marked with an R in Table 7, are excluded from the instruction set.

Two additional instructions added to the set perform frequently needed exchanges:

accumulator ⇄ register or zero page
accumulator ⇄ data memory

A similar matrix will be used in Table 8 to illustrate the I/O paths of the I8021.

Note that this set of moves provides that any move can be accomplished in one or, at most, two instructions. For example, two instructions can move the contents of the timer to the port by way of the accumulator. In addition to simple moves, logical operations can be performed on the expander with a mask held in the accumulator. The balance of the instruction set—a total of 21 instructions—are used for loop control (4); jumps, branches (9); subroutine calls and returns (2); table lookup (1); and status changes (5).

Instruction formats. The assignment of formats to instructions is influenced by the static characteristics of the application environment. Those functions most frequently used should have the shortest, most compact instruction format.[22,23] This is counter to the philosophy of computer architecture, where short formats are used for most frequently executed operations to conserve memory bandwidth.

In addition, ease of decoding and control are of great importance since complicated, multi-field, multi-step formats complicate the control logic of the microcomputer. Experience has shown that it is much better to have a sequence of two or three simple instructions for a function than to implement a multi-step, single-function instruction. The number of instruction bits is not increased, and the control complexity is reduced. The multi-instruction function will usually have a longer execution time, and this must be evaluated in the light of the anticipated dynamic statistics and the available execution time for the application environment. The execution is longer because the cycle time of the ROM is much slower than the logic time needed to perform the complex operation. The TMS1000 illustrates the technique of instruction format assignment.

Static statistics from a larger number of TMS1000 programs indicate that the call and branch instructions represent 25 to 50 percent of all functions used. Sometimes it is difficult to determine whether statistical results are a consequence of an architecture or the application. While an absolute distinction cannot be made, one cannot ignore the overwhelming use of calls and branches in these applications.

To conserve bits in the jump address, the microcomputer architect must look at the distribution of branch address distances. Figure 6 plots data from Alexander and Wortman[2] and TMS1000[18] experience. In the case of the TMS1000, 60 percent of all branches are within a 2^6 or 64-word page. Because of a memory capacity of 1024 instructions, 100 percent of all branches are within 10 bits of address.

It is interesting to note that the TMS1000 family has a short jump address of six bits while many minicomputers and microprocessors with a 16-bit long jump address have short jump addresses of eight bits. Both six and eight bits are near optimum short address lengths.

All instructions of the TMS1000 are eight bits in length. The branch and call instructions are:

Branch	10	X X X X X X
Call	11	X X X X X X

These short branch/call instructions are augmented by the load page buffer instruction to give a long branch:

Load page buffer	0 0 0 1	X X X X

The next most frequently used instructions load various registers with four-bit or two-bit constants. Thus, these instructions take the following forms:

OP	X X X X

OP	X X

The final instruction format has no address or immediate fields. It is a pure eight-bit operation code. All addressing is implied:

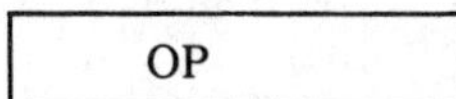

OP

These four instruction formats accommodate the following requirements:

- All are one length.
- Static frequency encoding is used.
- All are simple to decode in the control section of the microcomputer.

The TMS1000 and S2000 devices depart from the rule of instruction set selection which requires that the instruction set be useful in building up more complex functions. With these devices, the reverse is true. Simple functions—such as logical operations—must be programmed as routines of more complex operations. When these operations are required, major code space inefficiencies result.

Data input/output. The microcomputer's environment is unlike that of a computer. In general, the devices attached to the microcomputer are low-speed and bit-oriented. Examples are keyboards which must be scanned and read, lights and relays which are turned off and on, and phototransistors which must be sensed.

The heavy emphasis on bit I/O is a consequence of the problems solved by the microcomputer. In general, today's problems are dominated by performing BCD arithmetic and logical operations based on binary inputs and/or data comparisons. Thus, the major I/O format is the single-bit or four-bit characters. Only in rare and unusual applications do today's microcomputers need high bandwidth byte or word I/O.

There are two techniques[24] in use today for dealing with microcomputer I/O. These techniques—bus or port I/O and bit I/O—are discussed below.

Bus or port I/O. The first technique divides the available I/O pins into eight-bit groups called a bus and/or port. A small number of bits—say, two—in the instruction word can address four of these ports giving coarse addressability of 32 bits. Fine addressing within the eight bits is accomplished by a logical operation of a mask and the port.

For output:

port (operation) mask → port
(The result is latched into the port)

For input:

Port (operation) mask → accumulator
or
port → accumulator
accumulator (operation) → accumulator

The logical operations for output are:

Set a "one." The OR function

P +	M	P′
0	0	0
0	1	1
1	0	1
1	1	1

Reset to "zero." The AND function with $\overline{M}$

P •	$\overline{M}$	P′
0	0	0
0	1	0
1	0	0
1	1	1

Complement. The XOR function

P ⊕	M	P′
0	0	0
0	1	1
1	0	1
1	1	0

As discussed earlier, the I8021 can perform two of the most frequently used logical operations—AND and OR—with a single instruction. The mask must be in the accumulator. Thus, two instructions must be executed to set or reset an output bit line:

mask → accumulator (2 bytes)
AND or OR to port (1 byte)
(4 bytes total, including the mask)

To complement an output port requires three instructions:

Port → accumulator (1 byte)
accumulator ⊕ mask → accumulator (2 bytes)
accumulator → port (1 byte)
(5 bytes total, including the mask)

Input is treated in like manner. To test the value of an input bit requires that the byte containing the bit be read into the accumulator. The desired bit is extracted by the AND operator and the accumulator is tested for one or zero. In the I8021 instruction set, this is:

port → accumulator (1 byte)
accumulator • M → accumulator (2 bytes)
jump on accumulator = zero (2 bytes)
(6 bytes total, including the mask)

The R6500/1 employs a variation of the bus or port architecture. With this architecture, four memory locations are declared to be I/O ports. Bits in these ports are manipulated, similar to the I8021, with moves and logical instructions. The major difference is that no additional explicit I/O instructions are required in the instruction set. The normal instructions which address memory perform the I/O functions. The R6500/1 requires a total of six bytes, including the mask to set or reset a bit.

The R6500/1 I/O architecture is referred to as "memory-mapped I/O." This technique generally requires more bits in the instruction stream than the technique to be discussed below, but the CPU control is simpler and of smaller area. Thus, a good case can be made for this architecture where the use of bit I/O is low.

In those cases where higher-bandwidth, byte-wide I/O is required, microcomputers such as the I8021 can transfer data to or from the data memory and a port by a program loop which transfers the data through the accumulator.

Bit I/O. Several architectures specifically recognize the importance of bit I/O and provide architectural features and instructions for it.

The TMS1000 and TMS9940 are typical examples of this I/O architecture. The TMS1000 has 16 bit output pins. Each of these pins is addressed, with an implied address, with two instructions: "Set R bit" and "Reset R bit."

Due to the implied addressing used, one additional instruction is usually required to set up the address in the same Y register which addresses the data memory. Thus, in the worst case, two bytes are required to perform these instructions.

The TMS9940 extends this concept to 32 pins of addressable I/O. These pins can be used as input or output with the following two-byte instructions: "Set bit to a one," "Set bit to a zero," and "Test bit." An eight-bit address is used to select the I/O bits. Addresses between 32 and 255 are provided for external expansion.

High bandwidth multi-byte I/O is provided by two instructions which specify a transfer between the I/O pins and a memory location. The number of bits—1 to 16—transferred are specified in a four-bit field of the instruction.

Scanning a keyboard can be considered as either a bit I/O or a special case of the bus or port I/O. With some microcomputers, it is easier to turn on and off the bit lines which address the keyboard matrix. With others, the transfer of a word containing only one "one" is more effective.

This article has attempted to identify those architectural characteristics of single-chip microcomputers which distinguish them from more conventional architectures. These characteristics have been illustrated by examples from various microcomputers which are on the market today. A complete examination of all of today's products was neither desired nor attempted.

Hopefully, this article will serve as a guide for understanding the sometimes obscure architectures found in single-chip microcomputers. ■

Acknowledgment

I wish to acknowledge the unknown designers of single-chip microcomputers. They were not bound by dogma and were able to understand the unique architectural needs of their products. Without their work, this article would not have been written.

References

1. Turner Hasty, Texas Instruments Incorporated, private communications.
2. W. G. Alexander and D. B. Wortman, "Static and Dynamic Characteristics of XPL Programs," *Computer,* Vol. 8, No. 11, Nov. 1975, pp. 41-46.
3. Kenro Murata and Kisaburo Nakazawa, "Very High Speed Serial and Serial-Parallel Computers HITAC 5020 and 5020E," *AFIPS Conf. Proc.,* Vol. 26, 1964 FJCC, p. 187.
4. P. Fagg, J. L. Brown, J. A. Hipp, D. T. Doody, J. W. Fairclough, and J. Green, "IBM System/360 Engineering," *AFIPS Conf. Proc.,* Vol. 26, 1964 FJCC, p. 228.
5. K. A. El-Ayat, "The Intel 8089: An Integrated I/O Processor," *Computer,* Vol. 12, No. 6, June 1979, pp. 67-78.
6. Saul Rosen, "Electronic Computers: A Historical Survey," *Computing Surveys,* Vol. 1, No. 1, Mar. 1969, p. 7.
7. Arthur W. Burks, Herman H. Goldstine, and John von Neumann, "Preliminary Discussions of the Logical Design of an Electronic Computing Instrument," Institute for Advanced Studies, 1946.
8. "TMS1000 Series MOS/LSI One-Chip Microcomputers," Manual No. CM 122-1, Texas Instruments Incorporated, Nov. 15, 1975.
9. "AMI S2000 Microcomputer," Mar. 1977, preliminary.
10. "F8 Users Guide," No. 67095665, Fairchild Camera and Instrument Corp., 1976.
11. "Mostek F-8 Microprocessor Devices, Single-Chip Microcomputer, MK 3870," Apr. 1977, preliminary.

12. "8021 Single Component 8-Bit Microcomputer," Intel Corp., Oct. 1977.

13. P. Bonsiegneur, "Description of the 7600 Computer System," *Computer Group News,* Vol. 2, No. 9, May 1969, p. 11.

14. J. L. Greenstadt, "The IBM 709 Computer," *New Computers: A Report from the Manufacturers,* Western Joint Computer Conf., ACM, Los Angeles, Calif., Mar. 1957, p. 93.

15. IBM System/370, Principles of Operation, GA 22-7000-5.

16. "R6500/1 One-Chip Microcomputer," Document No. 29000 D51, Rockwell International Corp., May 1978.

17. Dave Caulkins, "Critique of the F8 Microprocessor," *Computer,* Vol. 10, No. 8, Aug. 1977, p. 83.

18. Charles Brixey, Texas Instruments Incorporated, private communications.

19. John F. Wakerly, "The Intel MCS-48 Microcomputer Family: A Critique," *Computer,* Vol. 12, No. 2, Feb. 1979, p. 22.

20. J. D. Bryant and Rick Longly, "TMS9940 Single Chip Microcomputer," *Proc. Electro 1977.*

21 "Z8 MCU Microcomputer, Product Specification," Zilog Corp., Mar. 1979.

22. D. R. Allison, "A Design Philosophy for Microcomputer Architectures," *Computer,* Vol. 10, No. 2, Feb. 1977, pp. 35-41.

23. Andrew S. Tanenbaum, "Implications of Structured Programming for Machine Architecture," *Comm. ACM,* Vol. 21, No. 3, Mar. 1978, p. 237.

24. John F. Wakerly, "Microcomputer Input/Output Architecture," *Computer,* Vol. 11, No. 2, Feb. 1977, pp. 26-33.

Design Considerations for Single-Chip Computers of the Future

DAVID A. PATTERSON AND CARLO H. SÉQUIN, MEMBER, IEEE

Abstract—In the mid 1980's it will be possible to put a million devices (transistors or active MOS gate electrodes) onto a single silicon chip. General trends in the evolution of silicon integrated circuits are reviewed and design constraints for emerging VLSI circuits are analyzed. Desirable architectural features in modern computers are then discussed and consequences for an implementation with large-scale integrated circuits are investigated. The resulting recommended processor design includes features such as an on-chip memory hierarchy, multiple homogeneous caches for enhanced execution parallelism, support for complex data structures and high-level languages, a flexible instruction set, and communication hardware. It is concluded that a viable modular building block for the next generation of computing systems will be a self-contained computer on a single chip. A tentative allocation of the one million transistors to the various functional blocks is given, and the result is a memory intensive design.

I. Introduction

THIS Joint Special Issue is devoted to the results of an interaction between computer architecture and very large-scale integration (VLSI). Rather than discussing existing designs or applications, this paper explores the design of a processor to be built with the VLSI technology of 1985. We start with a brief review of current trends and future expectations of that technology.

In the first 15 years since the inception of integrated circuits (IC's), the number of transistors that could be placed on a single chip (with tolerable yield) has doubled every year [1]. Over the past few years this growth has slowed to a rate of doubling every 18 to 24 months. The 1980 state of the art is about 70K devices per chip, e.g., the Motorola MC68000 or the 64K memory chip. Over the next four to eight years we can expect about 16-fold increase in the number of devices:

1) halving the present design rules will lead to a factor of four increase in density;

2) increased chip size should yield about another factor of three;

3) improved layout techniques, which minimize wasteful interconnections by proper structuring of the signal paths and placement of useful functions underneath bus-lines (see Section II-F), should also add a small factor.

Manuscript received July 9, 1979; revised October 25, 1979. This work was supported by the Defense Advanced Research Projects Agency (DoD), ARPA Order 3803, monitored by the Naval Electronic System Command under Contract N00039-78-G-0013-0004.

The authors are with the Computer Science Division, Department of Electrical Engineering and Computer Sciences, University of California, Berkeley, CA 94720.

Thus, somewhere between 1984 and 1988 the technology will be ready to put a million transistors on a single chip. Fig. 1 illustrates this trend with two curves, one for a sequence of memory chips and another for microprocessors. While the number of transistors on a microprocessor chip is traditionally smaller than that of memory parts, this gap is narrowing due to the increasing share of memory circuits within newer products.

On several occasions Gordon Moore has made the statement that the technology to make chips with a million transistors will be here shortly, but that systems designers have neither the imagination nor the tools to exploit the complexity of such a chip. While a dramatic improvement in available design tools is desperately needed, the following paper will show that a million transistors on a chip can indeed be put to good use. In Section II we will first review the constraints that the emerging VLSI technology places upon such a complex single-chip design. Section III explores desirable architectural features of future processors and the implications of these features for the circuit modules of such a chip. In Section IV we attempt to bring a subset of these desirable features in line with the capabilities of a single-chip processor with a million active devices. For easy reference this processor will tentatively be called "P1985."

II. P1985 in the Framework of VLSI

The evolution of hardware technology typically drives the development of computers, and silicon integrated circuit technology is no exception. The strongest current driving force is the emergence of a VLSI capability in most semiconductor houses, which will make VLSI building blocks readily available for the construction of the next generation of computers.

A. Functional Blocks of General Use

Due to high design costs, integrated circuits must be aimed at high volume applications. With VLSI, more than ever, the emerging products have to be carefully designed to be of general usefulness in order to guarantee large volume and thus a reasonable price. In the past, such a general-purpose building block was the NAND gate. Later the modular components became MSI chips such as registers, decoders, and multiplexers, and LSI chips for pure memory functions. Defining the proper modular components is an exercise in systems partitioning. High bandwidth paths should be confined to within

Reprinted from *IEEE Trans. Comput.*, vol. C-29, pp. 108-115, Feb. 1980.

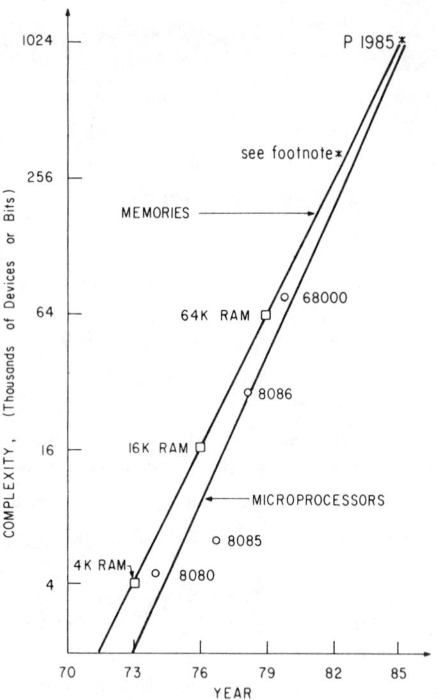

Fig. 1. Trend in the evolution of large-scale integrated circuits.

one and the same chip. This has led to bit-slice processor parts [2], [3]. Since P1985 can be substantially more complex than the bit-slice parts, the partitioning problem has to be rethought in the light of VLSI components.

Because of the different loading capacitances, the delay-power product of a connection residing entirely inside an IC chip is significantly smaller than that of a path interconnecting separate chips. At present there is a ratio of more than two orders of magnitude, which will become even larger as proper scaling of MOS circuits [4] leads to smaller and faster circuits operating at lower power levels. Since the delay-power product ideally decreases with the third power of the scale factor, the difference may grow another order of magnitude by 1985.

By building large and power-consuming driver circuits onto the chip, it would be possible to drive the signals going through the package pins as fast as minimum-size gates can drive internal signal paths. However, at present, practical tradeoffs typically lead to external signal speeds which are about an order of magnitude slower. It is estimated that five years hence such tradeoffs will lead to speed ratios of about 25:1. In any case, bringing a signal from one chip to another will result in a major performance penalty, either as increased power consumption or as an exorbitant delay.

In the bit-slice parts, the high bandwidth data paths are inside the chip, while the chip boundaries cut through the lower bandwidth signals such as carry lines and control signals. With a million transistors, the whole data path can be placed on a single chip. The path with the next highest bandwidth then becomes the connection to the memory. In P1985 as much local memory as possible should therefore be included on the same chip. As a result, one general-purpose component of the next generation will be a self-contained, single-chip computer [5].

B. *Multiprocessor Systems*

The inherent maximum speed which can be extracted from silicon integrated circuits is limited by material constants and by the smallest feasible dimensions in the active devices. For a system of a given complexity, a significant increase in compute power can only be obtained with a switch to an intrinsically faster technology, e.g., gallium arsenide circuits or Josephson junctions. To get more computational power out of a given technology, the complexity of the system has to be increased so that more computational steps are done simultaneously. One possible approach leads to pipelined computers such as the CDC 7600 or the CRAY-1 [6]. These are among the largest, fastest, and most expensive machines available today. Their complete data paths with the necessary associated local registers and memory elements are too complex to fit even on a million-transistor chip (see Section V). Thus the intrinsically high circuit speed available on paths completely internal to a chip could then not be exploited fully. In addition, difficulties inherent in the design of VLSI circuits (see next section) may make these architectures unsuitable for the next generation of highly integrated computers.

An alternative approach uses a multitude of similar processor components interconnected with a suitable communication network to achieve enhanced parallelism of computational tasks. This has the advantage that a smaller number of different building blocks has to be designed. With one of the general-purpose building blocks of the next generation being a self-contained computer, this will naturally lead to multiprocessor systems. Several research projects are investigating the problem of how powerful computer systems can be constructed from hundreds or thousands of microprocessors [7], [8]. We expect that by 1985 the construction and effective usage of such systems will be well understood.

C. *Feasible Designs*

The complexity of future VLSI chips, the lack of suitable design tools, and the difficulties in testing these chips (see next section) necessitate the use of the simplest and most regular designs possible. This is one reason why memory parts achieve a higher degree of integration than microprocessors. The most difficult part in a processor is the control circuitry. Control has traditionally been implemented with carefully minimized logic functions using gates that are placed irregularly in the available space between other circuit modules. Recently, the more structured, microprogrammed approach, which uses programmable logic arrays (PLA's) or read only memories (ROM's) or combinations [9], has become dominant. This leads to a more regular layout which is easier to design, debug, and modify. In addition, layout may proceed concurrently with microprogramming, which may decrease product development by several months. Product modifications can be achieved more easily by changing the bit pattern in one mask, whereas changing logic implies a new layout [10].

Microprogramming thus appears to be the appropriate technique for implementation of control in VLSI processors.

Among the latest generation of microprocessors, the Intel 8086 [11] and the Motorola MC68000 [12] are microprogrammed, and the only nonmicroprogrammed processor, the Zilog Z8000 [13], experienced serious design delays.

D. *Design for Testability*

The ratio of the number of internal nodes to the number of accessible points in integrated circuits is also experiencing an exponential growth. It will not be possible to test VLSI circuits by simply impressing test patterns from the outside, just as it is impossible to test an IBM 370/158 CPU with access to only the address, data, and I/O buses. VLSI single-chip computers will have to be tested "inside-out," i.e., a significant amount of self-testing has to be built into the devices. Testing at the microlevel, called "microdiagnostics," has been shown to be crucial because it is much closer to the hardware than machine level programming [14]. Microprogramming may thus become a necessity simply for the testing of future complex designs. To obtain full freedom to exercise internal parts of the computer in any desired manner, it will even be necessary to have a writable part in the microprogram memory [15].

E. *Power Limitations*

VLSI has changed the accounting of hardware complexity. The number of transistors or logic gates in a circuit is no longer an appropriate measure for the cost of a VLSI circuit. The relevant parameters are the amount of power dissipated and the area of silicon used, since these quantities have rather rigid upper limits for a given state of technology. The total number of gates that can be put onto a single chip of silicon may be limited by power dissipation rather than by the potential transistor density of the technology. Memory parts were recently developed which have a low-power standby mode. This capability should be implemented into individual functional blocks on VLSI chips, allowing the processor to keep all but the most recently used blocks in standby mode. It is conceivable to implement this power-down feature within rather small modules. The activation control for the various modules is contained in each microinstruction. The microprogrammer now has the additional responsibility to keep peak or average power load within specified limits. By carefully planning the distribution of power in time and space, it will be possible to extend the maximum functional complexity of a single chip.

F. *Layout Strategies*

As the data path of a processor gets wider, an ever larger fraction of the chip area may be wasted by mere interconnections. This space is rather poorly utilized. Typically, the silicon crystal plays no active part in the area underneath the buses, which logically do not add to the function of a particular chip. One of the challenges to IC designers will be to make better use of the silicon area by a suitably structured layout and by functionally integrating the buses with the circuits which they service [16]. Software tools which help the designer in this approach are currently being developed [17].

III. Desirable Features for P1985 Architecture

Without paying attention to the stated limitations and constraints in the previous section, we will discuss desirable architectural features for future processors and the hardware required for their implementation.

A. *Large Local Memory*

In the previous section we concluded that it was advantageous to place the memory that contains programs and data on the same chip as the processor. This memory and its connection to the processor should be as fast as possible, since they will determine the processing speed of P1985. Ideally, the memory should be large enough to contain the complete working set of program and data for a particular problem, since memory accesses off the chip will reduce performance. The growing need of memory for programs and data is made evident by the increasing address spaces provided by small computers. The previous generation of microprocessors used 64K bytes, but their successors have grown to 1024K (8086), 8192K (Z8000), and 16384K (MC68000) bytes.

A high-density on-chip memory, implemented with dynamic RAM or charge-coupled devices (CCD's), will thus be required. While CCD's offer more density than RAM, their serial organization is not suitable for primary memory. Furthermore, CCD's require more complicated clocking schemes, they have lower yield in fabrication, and potentially waste power since all information in a loop has to be moved in order to access a specific bit of information. These drawbacks render CCD's unattractive for integration with a general-purpose processor. Single-transistor RAM cells are almost as dense as CCD cells, and are easier to use from the systems designer's point of view.

Dynamic storage cells in a large memory array are not as fast as register cells, and are thus not suitable for all storage needs in P1985. Faster access times are obtained with static memory designs. For any given technology, memory blocks can be designed with a wide range in access times. The design typically involves complicated tradeoffs between the construction of the individual memory cell (dynamic-static), cell area, power consumption, and overall size of the memory block. Reasonable compromises for some of the latest memory parts, which were presented at the International Solid-State Circuits Conference in 1979, show the latter dependence quite clearly. Cycle times for static memories of 1K, 4K, and 16K storage, all built with the same scaled-down, 2-μm NMOS technology (minimum gate delay of 0.4 ns, speed-power product of 0.5 pJ) are 15, 22, and 40 ns, respectively [18], [19]. For a given size of memory, the access times have been reduced exponentially by about an order of magnitude every five years [19]. At the same time, dynamic RAM's with 16K and 64K bits have access times of 80 and 120 ns, respectively [20], [21] and cycle times which are about twice as long. Thus, as an overall rule of thumb, dynamic RAM's are about four times slower than static RAM's of comparable size. This variation in speed and density permits the construction of an effective memory hierarchy on the chip. Just as traditional memory hierarchies have exploited different technologies (disk, core, semiconductor), one can exploit different implementations of memory cells within the same technology to obtain the best overall results. A suitable combination of relatively small caches, built from the faster static memory, with a large backing memory, built from the denser dynamic RAM's, will result in a memory system with an effective density close to that of dynamic RAM and the desired access time of static cache cells. By proper design of these cells, the relative speed and storage capacity of the different components of this memory hierarchy can be tailored to achieve an optimum balance between overall performance, silicon area and total power consumption.

This cache based approach exploits locality of reference, i.e., the clustering of references within a few small areas of program memory and data memory. The cache automatically keeps copies of the most recently used information, thereby making accesses to the larger but slower backing store unnecessary most of the time. In a similar manner, all the on-chip memory can act as a buffer to the slower *external* semiconductor memory or mass storage devices.

B. Error Correction

The amount of memory on a chip can be increased by shrinking the memory cell, but the higher soft-error rates of these smaller cells may require on-chip error correction. The use of error correction codes (ECC's) in the main memory as a means to enhance reliability, which is common in present-day computers such as the DEC VAX 11/780, HP 300, IBM 370, or Tandem, will also invade the domain of single-chip computers. If ECC is provided on the smallest modifiable unit, then the space overhead is very high, e.g., with 8 bits of data, 4 ECC bits are needed for single-bit error correction (SEC), and one more bit for double error detection (DED). The space overhead is reduced if ECC is provided over larger blocks (e.g., 64 bits of data needs only 8 bits for SEC and DED), but it incurs two types of performance overhead. First, each *read* or *write* of any portion of a block will require reading of the rest of the block to be able to calculate the correct ECC. Thus, *reads* imply reading the whole block and *writes* take two memory accesses. Second, a practical approach to the calculation of parity and comparison for 71 bits (64 data + 7 ECC) may require eight levels of logic, increasing memory access time by eight gate delays. To avoid this delay, the data could be sent to the processor in parallel with the calculation of the ECC. This would require, however, a more complex design because the processor would have to be able to restart any operation with the corrected data.

In P1985, the logical place for error correction is between the cache and the memory (Fig. 2). The ECC size overhead is low because caches normally transfer large blocks, which are natural units for the calculation of ECC, and the processor can usually make memory references to the cache which are not slowed down by ECC. Error correction between the cache and the central processing unit (CPU) can be avoided. The larger and more powerful static cells are less likely to be subject to random switching errors. Secondly, with the proper update strategy (write-through), memory behind the error correction circuitry maintains a good copy of everything in the cache. Thus, by simply checking parity, a fault in the cache can readily be detected and subsequently be corrected by replacing the invalid block with the appropriate copy in memory.

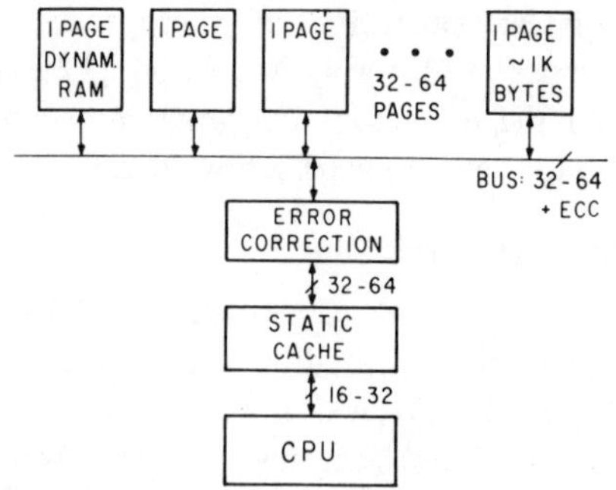

Fig. 2. Block diagram of on-chip memory hierarchy showing dynamic memory, static cache, and error correction circuitry.

C. Multiport Memory

Three logically distinct items must be accessed during execution: instructions, addresses, and data; they must then be transferred to different destinations: instruction decoder, address register, and data ALU, respectively. For best performance, all three items should be fetched in parallel from the local main memory of P1985, and the memory must thus be capable of delivering three words from different locations simultaneously. However, the limited drive capability of single-transistor dynamic memory cells and the topological difficulties in the overall layout make dynamic RAM's unsuitable for multiport memory designs.

Another possible approach is to partition the memory into three sections containing separately instructions, addresses, or data. The disadvantage of this approach lies in its inflexibility. Each section would have to contain sufficient storage space for extreme cases, which would result in rather poor memory utilization for the average case. A single contiguous block of memory with "flexible" boundaries is much more effective.

A better solution is to modify the memory hierarchy. Separate cache memories, devoted specifically to handling either programs or addresses or data, are connected to the output port of the main memory (Fig. 3). For example, an operand required in the ALU is requested from the data cache, and if it is not available, the corresponding block will be brought in from the local main memory. With this approach the common data path between the various caches and the main memory may now represent a bottleneck. However, cache designs that lead to successful cache hit ratios should also minimize contention for the memory bus. Determining the proper cache parameters will require extensive studies.[1]

The multicache approach not only leads to enhanced execution parallelism, but also facilitates layout of the VLSI chip. The cache designs can be based upon known memory struc-

[1] A study of the PDP-11, with total cache and main memories about the size of those considered in Table I, shows that a cache hit probability of 0.95 can be achieved [22]. The insertion of a well-designed cache should then reduce memory traffic by at least 80 percent.

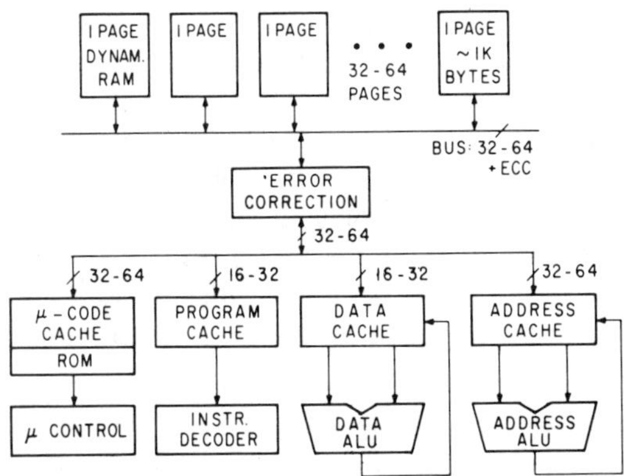

Fig. 3. Expanded view of the memory hierarchy showing the multiple caches dedicated to microcode, instructions, data, and addresses.

tures and form natural building blocks, which are used several times.

D. *Support for Complex Data Structures*

The only types of data that can be manipulated by the traditional 8-bit microprocessors are 8- and 16-bit integers. The newer 16-bit processors have expanded the data types to include 32-bit integers, 16- and 32-bit addresses, characters and word strings, and 4-bit packed decimal numbers (BCD's). Eventually these microprocessors will also support 32- and 64-bit floating-point numbers. This expanded architectural support leads to performance improvements in applications which rely on these more sophisticated data types. It also makes these processors safer and easier for machine or assembly language programming, or alternatively, makes compilation of programs simpler.

The next step is to include support for *arrays* and *structures* (*records*). Special hardware must be added to calculate the address of an element, and to check that it is within the bounds of the structure. Some bounds checking can be found in the CHK instruction of the MC68000, which checks to see if a register is between 0 and some specified limit, and traps to a special routine if it is not. While bounds checking can always be implemented in software or in microcode, special-purpose hardware avoids performance degradations. Fig. 4 shows the necessary circuitry to perform bounds checking in parallel with the address calculation for the case of arrays. An additional ALU and a pair of comparators have been added to calculate the address of an array element and to check if the index is within specified bounds. The address and bounds are obtained from a data structure descriptor via the descriptor cache memory whenever the array is accessed [15]. There are difficult tradeoffs between the "cost" of such circuitry and the improved performance and safety obtained through execution-time bounds checking in hardware.

E. *High-Level Language-Oriented Instruction Set*

At present, most programs developed for microprocessors are written in assembly language, but an ever-increasing percentage is being written in high-level languages (HLL's) such as Fortran or Pascal. HLL's typically reduce the costs of coding, debugging, and maintenance since the programmer can think at a higher level of abstraction, allowing the compiler to do more of the menial tasks associated with the details of data or program structures. Ease of programming will become a major selection criterion for computers as the cost of software continues to account for an ever larger fraction of total expenses.

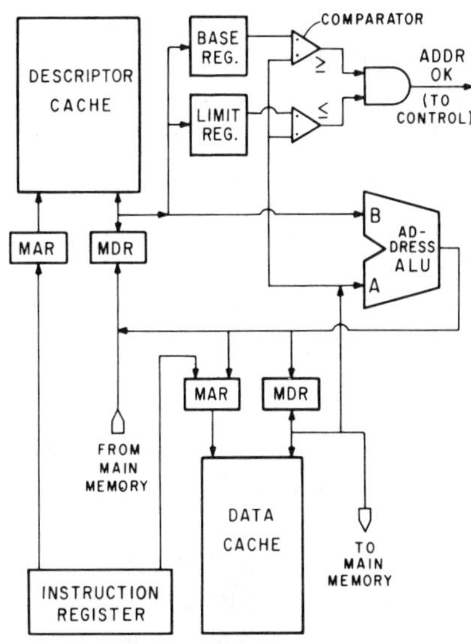

Fig. 4. Hardware support for array address calculation and bounds checking.

The choice of the proper HLL is strongly applications dependent. To be a general-purpose building block, P1985 should be able to support several different languages efficiently. The design of a corresponding instruction set is still an open research issue. The real goal is to build future architectures which lead to efficient implementations of high-level language computer *systems.* The term *system* purports a combination of software and hardware that looks to the user as if the high-level language program is executed directly [23]. While definitive solutions to these issues are still being sought, a microprogrammed control store provides the necessary flexibility and adaptability. For a general-purpose processor, a writable control store (WCS) has the additional advantage that its instruction set can readily be switched among different HLL's. Customers with changing types of applications can store the various sets of microcode in secondary memory and load the proper set for a particular application as required. In some cases this ability has provided an order of magnitude increase in performance [24], [25]. The most sophisticated users may even want to develop their own microcode.

F. *Flexible Instruction Sets*

P1985 should be provided with both fixed and alterable memory for microcode. The ROM will contain the basic instruction set and some of the operating system kernel. The WCS will be integrated with the main memory, which contains programs, addresses, data, and microcode. The execution of instructions implies simultaneous access to instructions as well as microcode; thus, the multiple cache scheme proposed above will need a separate cache for microcode (Fig. 3). Putting swappable microcode in the address space simplifies the task of loading control memory, which traditionally has been a difficult problem. In P1985, microcode gets swapped over the same path as data and programs, and thus requires no separate I/O pins. By sharing the main memory and using special caches, we can provide flexible instruction sets without special hardware to load the control memory.

G. Compact Code Representation

Careful, frequency-based encoding of the instructions, in which the most frequently used instructions have the shortest representation, can lead to a reduction of program size of 3 : 1 [26]. This compaction is equivalent to an increase in the effective size of the program memory and the program cache, and, for a given amount of memory on the chip, will result in improved compute power because of fewer cache misses and fewer memory references off the chip. The primary cost of effective encoding is the extra time needed to decode the more compact instructions. By including a small amount of logic between the program cache and the instruction processing unit, the compact, varying length instructions can be expanded into a regular, more easily decodable format. Such a two-stage decoding process will not degrade performance if this decoder is suitably incorporated into an instruction lookahead unit. Since a significant percentage of the circuitry will be dedicated to memory functions, even a small amount of code compaction justifies the necessary decoder.

An instruction set that is more difficult to expand may constitute a secondary cost of compact encoding. To avoid the problem, some opcodes could be reserved for future expansion; alternatively, the instruction set could be made independent of its internal representation [26].

H. Support for Process Switching

Structured programming encourages the use of several concurrent processes, each handling a particular aspect of the overall job. This approach is particularly suitable for operating systems [27]. The operating system is normally a significant part of most computing systems, and suitable hardware support in the processor is important.

The notion of a "process" can be understood as a "program piece in execution." In a computer with only a single instruction execution unit, these processes have to be multiplexed. A switch from one process to another involves saving the environment or context of the old process and restoring the context of the new process. For performance reasons, the processor should execute such a process switch as fast as possible.

In register architectures, a process switch includes saving registers for the current process and loading registers for the new process or flushing register banks. Memory-to-memory architectures, such as the Texas Instruments 990, eliminate the need for general register flushing, but pay the price in longer latency for "register" access, since these references must go to the common memory. For P1985, a memory-to-memory architecture is preferred where the "registers" are located in the caches. The caches should have sufficient capacity to hold the register contents associated with more than one process, so that very fast process switching can be achieved when the context for the new process is already in the cache.

To make the high-speed buffers or caches effective, hit probabilities should range from about 0.85 to 0.95. Most published data concern hit ratios for a single program. In this context, the question arises whether process switching will reduce cache hit probability to the point where the cache becomes ineffective. In a study of caches and main memory comparable to those considered for P1985 (see Table I), Strecker analyzed the effect on hit probabilities assuming the cache is cleared at regular intervals [22]. The results were as follows:

Cleared every 300 memory accesses:	hit ratio 0.70
Cleared every 3000 memory accesses:	hit ratio 0.87
Cleared every 30000 memory accesses:	hit ratio 0.94
Never cleared:	hit ratio 0.95.

These statistics support the above ideas. If the process switches occur infrequently, then it has very little impact on cache performance. Alternatively, if the processor switches frequently between a small set of processes, the hit ratio should be even better than in the case above where the cache was cleared completely because the data needed by a process may still be in the cache. Thus, acceptable cache performance for P1985 is expected.

I. Interprocessor Communication

The self-contained, single-chip computers which have appeared on the market in the last few years are mostly used in stand-alone control systems. A single-chip computer of the next generation should be designed with the idea of a modular multiprocessor system in mind [7]. Current single-chip computers (e.g., 8048) are unsuitable for multiprocessor systems since the communication issues have not been properly addressed. Eventually, all necessary communication hardware may become an integral part of the single-chip computer. For the near future, the necessary switching circuitry for message-based communication [28] may have to be implemented on a separate VLSI chip or may even have to be built from many small, standard building blocks. P1985 may thus contain only a minimum of communication hardware, capable of packaging all information into suitable messages which obey the communications protocols of the network. The necessary hardware may involve several small buffer memories, the necessary logic for multiplexing several messages over one and the same communications link, and a finite state machine to control the link allocation to the different message channels [29].

IV. Device Allocation in P1985

While a million transistors may still seem very large by today's standards, it is not an infinite number, and this resource has to be carefully allocated. Table I gives a range of desirable values for the various memory blocks within P1985, showing anticipated ranges for the number of bits per word, number of words per page or block, and number of blocks. These estimates are based in part on an examination of microprocessor chips (e.g., 8048 and MC68000) and in part on the examination of mainframe computers such as the PDP-11 or the VAX 11/780. The number of bits per word in the dynamic memory

TABLE I
TENTATIVE ALLOCATION OF THE AVAILABLE DEVICES ON A MILLION-TRANSISTOR CHIP TO THE VARIOUS FUNCTIONAL BLOCKS IN P1985

Memory	Bits/Word	Number of Words	Number of Blocks	kbytes	k-FET's
Dyn. RAM blocks	32-64	128-256	32-64	16-128	128-1024
Stat. RAM μ-code	32-64	256-1024	1	1-8	32-256
Instr. cache	16-32	256	1	0.5-1	16-32
Data cache	16-32	256	1-2	0.5-2	16-64
Adrs. cache	32-64	64	1	0.25-0.5	8-16
Descriptors	16-64	64	1	0.125-0.5	4-16
Process cache	32-64	16	1	0.063-0.125	2-4
Stack	16-64	64	1	0.125-0.5	4-16
ROM μ-code	32-64	1024-2048	1	4-16	32-128
All Memory					242-1556
ALU	16-32		2		20-40
Control					20-80
Comm. & I/O					10-10
All Circuitry					292-1686

and in the caches is determined as a compromise between an effective size for error correction and a reasonable bus width. The RAM and ROM microcode memories are expected to be 32-64 bits wide because most mainframe computers have microinstruction formats in this range [30]. Since the latest generation of microprocessors have 16-bit ALU's, and have only just started to enter the domain of 32-bit ALU's [12], it is reasonable to assume that P1985's ALU will be 16-32 bits wide. The number of words per block for each memory part is also an extrapolation of the corresponding components in mainframe computers. The choice of a number of blocks is governed by the wish for as many dynamic memory blocks as possible.

Given those values, Table I shows corresponding numbers for the amount of storage, expressed in kilobytes and also in kilo-FET's (thousands of transistors), for an estimate of complexity. For the latter estimate a dynamic RAM cell is equated with a single transistor, while the static cache cells are assumed to be four times larger. Also included in Table I are estimates of size for the ALU, the controller, and the input/output sections. These estimates are based upon the complexity of the corresponding circuits in current processors.

From these numbers, rough percentages of the chip circuitry devoted to all particular functions were derived. It is interesting to note that all memory functions combined will utilize about 80-90 percent of all transistors, even though the corresponding chip area will be a smaller fraction. The high-density main memory on the chip will account for 50-70 percent of all memory circuitry or 45-65 percent of all chip circuitry. ALU and control circuitry are both in the range of a few percent, and together are definitely less than 15 percent of the total chip. Communications and input/output functions, i.e., buffers, bonding pads, and associated drivers, will account for only 1-3 percent of all transistors and for less than 10 percent of the chip area. The reason for this departure from the traditional trend, where these I/O functions account for almost a quarter of the chip area of a present-day microprocessor, lies in the fact that memory and processor are on the same chip. This combination requires significantly fewer pins for communication and for addressing. In principle, the P1985 module could be placed in a package with only 24 pins. In reality, though, the desire for special control signals (interrupts) or for the possibility to extend local memory and the need to dissipate the power will lead to the use of a significantly larger package.

V. SUMMARY

This paper has considered the design of a hypothetical processor, P1985, built from a million transistors using the VLSI technology of the mid 1980's. P1985 includes the processor, memory, and some communication hardware on the same chip. The memory is hierarchically organized and constructed with a combination of static and dynamic circuitry in order to maximize storage capacity and to minimize access time and power consumption. The use of several special-purpose caches gives the chip the potential performance of a processor with register architecture, but retains all the advantages of a memory-to-memory architecture, and in particular, can provide fast process switching.

The state of the art in design tools and the need to minimize development time advocate regular layouts and a microprogrammed implementation of processor control. A writable control store (WCS) appears important for several reasons. The manufacturer needs the WCS in testing to provide full freedom in the selection and the size of microdiagnostic routines. WCS also provides the simplest scheme for correcting microcode errors. To the user the WCS is invaluable in order to provide a flexible instruction set. One important case is the support for various high-level languages; another is the possibility to tailor a general-purpose multiprocessor system to specific applications.

To be successful, future processor architectures must be much more responsive to the specific needs of operating systems and software in general. The corresponding hardware in P1985 includes a special cache approach to improve context switching, potential support for high-level languages through a microprogrammed implementation of the instruction sets, and special circuitry to aid in address calculation and in execution-time bounds checking for arrays or other high-level data structures.

The allocation of transistors in Table I shows that 80-90 percent of P1985 is dedicated to various memory functions. In the face of difficult design decisions, a memory-based solution is frequently found to be most suitable: microprogrammed control, fast instruction and data access via static caches, and enhanced execution parallelism via multiple homogeneous caches. Such a memory-intensive approach reduces design time, simplifies layout and debugging, and is thus the preferred choice for VLSI circuits.

Overall, the architecture of P1985 is an evolutionary extension of the processors appearing on the market today. The availability of even a million transistors is just barely sufficient to implement a modern processor with a useful amount of memory on a single chip. For many applications the available amount of local memory may be marginal, even when a large number of these building blocks are effectively combined into a closely coupled multiprocessor system. For this reason the implementation of processors such as the CDC 7600 or the CRAY-1 on a single chip will not be possible until several years after the realization of P1985.

With the inevitable evolution of multiprocessor systems, the question arises whether it pays to place more than one processor onto a single chip. Because of the different bandwidths of signals internal to the chip and signals leaving the package, the silicon chip must always be considered as a separate building block. Thus, the above question becomes whether the particular function that this block must perform is better implemented with a single, rather sophisticated processor or with several smaller processors. From the foregoing analysis we conclude that it will not be advantageous to perform the function of a building block for a general-purpose computer with an on-chip multiprocessor system, that is, not until the degree of integration has reached substantially higher levels than a mere million transistors.

Acknowledgment

Too many people to be mentioned individually have contributed their ideas and have thus influenced the thinking of the authors. We would therefore like to globally thank all individuals inside and outside the University who have contributed directly or indirectly to this study. Special thanks go to A. Despain and S. Fehr who have taken part in long discussions about the topics presented in this paper, and to J. Goodman for suggesting write-through to correct cache errors.

References

[1] G. E. Moore, in *Tech. Dig. Int. Electron Devices Meeting*, Dec. 1-3, 1975, pp. 11-13.

[2] Intel Corp., Santa Clara, CA, "Central processor design using Intel 3000 computing elements." Appl. Note AN-16, 1975.

[3] J. R. Mick, "AM 2900 bipolar microprocessor family," in *Proc. 8th Annu. Workshop on Microprogramming*, Sept. 21-23, 1975, pp. 56-63.

[4] R. H. Dennard *et al.*, "Design of ion-implemented MOSFET's with very small physical dimensions," *IEEE J. Solid-State Circuits*, vol. SC-9, pp. 256-268, Oct. 1974.

[5] C. H. Séquin, "Single-chip computers, The new VLSI building blocks," presented at the Caltech VLSI Conf., Jan. 22-24, 1979.

[6] R. M. Russell, "The CRAY-1 computer system," *Commun. Ass. Comput. Mach.*, vol. 21, pp. 63-72, Jan. 1978.

[7] A. M. Despain and D. A. Patterson, "X-TREE: A tree structured multi-processor computer architecture," in *Proc. 5th Annu. Symp. on Comput. Architecture*, Apr. 3-5, 1978, pp. 144-151.

[8] S. H. Fuller *et al.*, "Multi-microprocessors: An overview and working example," *Proc. IEEE*, vol. 66, pp. 216-228, Feb. 1978.

[9] B. Hashizume and W. N. Johnson, "The LSI-11/23 control store microarchitecture," in *Proc. Fall COMPCON*, Sept. 1979.

[10] E. Stritter and N. Tredennick, "Microprogrammed implementation of a single chip microprocessor," in *Proc. 11th Workshop on Microprogramming*, Nov. 19-22, 1978, pp. 8-16.

[11] S. P. Morse *et al.*, "The Intel 8086 microprocessor: A 16-bit evolution of the 8080," *Computer*, vol. 11, pp. 18-27, June 1978.

[12] E. Stritter and T. Gunter, "A microprocessor for a changing world: The Motorola 68000," *Computer*, vol. 12, pp. 43-52, Feb. 1979.

[13] B. L. Peuto, "Architecture of a new microprocessor," *Computer*, vol. 12, pp. 10-21, Feb. 1979.

[14] S. S. Husson, *Microprogramming: Principles and Practices.* Englewood Cliffs, NJ: Prentice-Hall, 1970, pp. 109-112.

[15] D. A. Patterson, E. S. Fehr, and C. H. Séquin, "Design considerations for the VLSI processor of X-TREE," in *Proc. 6th Annu. Symp. on Comput. Architecture*, Apr. 23-25, 1979, pp. 90-101.

[16] C. A. Mead and L. S. Conway, *Introduction to VLSI Systems.* Reading, MA: Addison-Wesley, 1979.

[17] D. Johannsen, "Bristle blocks: A silicon compiler," in *Proc. 16th Design Automation Conf.*, San Deigo, CA, June 25-26, 1979, pp. 310-313.

[18] R. M. Jecmen *et al.*, "A 25ns 4K static RAM," in *Dig. Tech. Papers, Int. Solid-State Circuits Conf.*, Feb. 14-16, 1979, pp. 100-101.

[19] R. D. Pashley *et al.*, "A 16K by 1b static RAM," in *Dig. Tech. Papers, Int. Solid-State Circuits Conf.*, Feb. 14-16, 1979, pp. 106-107.

[20] J. M. Lee *et al.*, "An 80ns 5v-only dynamic RAM," in *Dig. Tech. Papers, Int. Solid-State Circuits Conf.*, Feb. 14-16, 1979, pp. 142-143.

[21] I. Lee *et al.*, "A 64Kb MOS dynamic RAM," in *Dig. Tech. Papers, Int. Solid-State Circuits Conf.*, Feb. 14-16, 1979, pp. 146-147.

[22] W. D. Strecker, "Cache memories for PDP-11 family computers," in *Proc. 3rd Annu. Symp. on Comput. Architecture*, Jan. 19-21, 1976, pp. 155-158.

[23] D. R. Ditzel and D. A. Patterson, "Retrospective on high-level language computer architecture," in preparation.

[24] A. M. Abd-Alla and D. C. Karlgaard, "Heuristic synthesis of microprogrammed computer architecture," *IEEE Trans. Comput.*, vol. C-23, pp. 802-807, Aug. 1974.

[25] H. Weber, "A microprogrammed implementation of EULER on IBM System/360 Model 30," *Commun. Ass. Comput. Mach.*, vol. 10, pp. 549-558, Sept. 1967.

[26] W. T. Wilner, "Design of the Burroughs B1700," in *Proc. 1972 Fall Joint Comput. Conf.*, 1972, pp. 489-497.

[27] R. C. Holt *et al.*, *Structured Concurrent Programming.* Reading, MA: Addison-Wesley, 1978.

[28] C. H. Séquin, "Message switching circuits for multi-microprocessors," submitted to COMPCON, Feb. 25-28, 1980.

[29] C. H. Séquin, A. M. Despain, and D. A. Patterson, "Communication in X-TREE, A modular multiprocessor system," in *Proc. ACM Nat. Conf.*, Washington, DC, Dec. 1978.

[30] A. K. Agrawala and T. G. Rauscher, *Foundations of Microprogramming: Architecture, Software, and Applications.* New York: Academic, 1976.

A Survey of Bit-Sliced Computer Design*

JOHN P. HAYES†

Abstract—**This paper surveys a class of modular LSI components that implement a design concept called bit slicing. A bit-sliced system S_m^n is formed by cascading *n* copies of a basic component or slice S_m. If S_m performs a certain set of operations on *m*-bit words, then S_m^n can perform the same operations on *nm*-bit words. Bit slices are typically used for design of the execution unit (data processing part) and the control unit of a microprogrammable computer. Section I introduces the basic concepts of bit-sliced system design. The historical origins of bit slicing are traced, and a summary of commercially-available bit-sliced devices is presented. The design of microprogrammable control units and the major applications of bit-sliced systems are briefly considered. Three representative families of bit-slice components, the Advanced Micro Devices 2900, the Intel 3000, and the Texas Instruments 481 series, are discussed and compared in Section II. Section III presents a case study on the design of bit-sliced central processing units that emulate the 8080 microprocessor. In Section IV, two important issues in bit-sliced system design, microprogram specification and test generation, are discussed. An easily testable processor slice is presented, and its test requirements are examined.**

Index Terms—**Bit-sliced systems, emulation, microprocessors, microprogramming, testability.**

1. INTRODUCTION

The term *bit-sliced* is most often applied to microprocessors and similar complex integrated circuits (ICs) that have the following characteristics:

1. The basic module or *(bit) slice* S_m performs a specified set of operations F on operands or data words of length *m* bits where $m \geqslant 1$.
2. A set of *n* copies of S_m can be connected in the form of a 1-dimensional array or cascade as depicted in Fig. 1 so that the resulting *bit-sliced system* S_m^n performs the same set of operations F on *mn*-bit words.

A bit-sliced system that can act as the *execution unit* or E-unit of a computer's central processing unit (CPU) is called a *bit-sliced (micro-) processor*. An E-unit contains the registers and arithmetic-logic circuits necessary to execute a set of externally applied (micro-) instructions. It operates in conjunction with an *instruction unit* or I-unit which provides the E-unit with the instructions to be executed. To give added flexibility to the system designer, the I-unit of a bit-sliced processor is usually designed to be *microprogrammable*. This means that the E-unit is controlled by a set of user-defined microinstructions which can exercise greater control over its operation than is possible in non-microprogrammable or hardwired machines. The I-unit of a typical microprogrammable CPU has two main parts: a *control memory* (CM) which stores the microinstructions and a *microprogram sequencer* which generates the addresses of the microinstructions to be executed. As will be seen later, the microprogram sequencer may also be bit-sliced. However, the use of bit slicing in the E-unit alone suffices for a computer to be called bit-sliced.

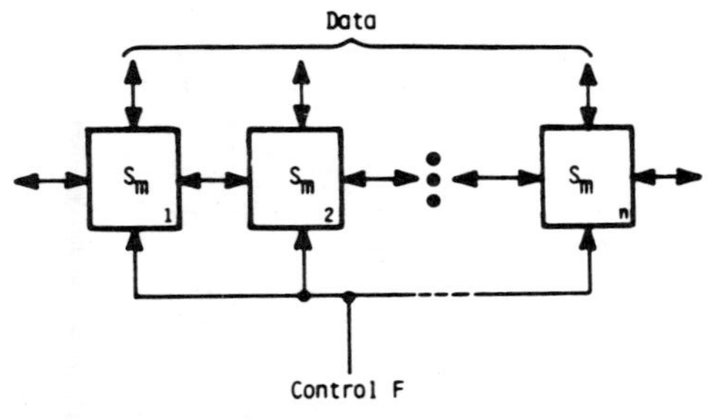

Fig. 1. General structure of a bit-sliced system S_m^n composed of *n* *m*-bit slices S_m

1.1 Rationale

An obvious advantage of bit-slicing is that it allows a designer to customize the word size of a system. Thus, using typical 4-bit processor slices, 8-, 16-, and 32-bit processors can easily be built. Since the processors perform the same set of operations F, they can be viewed as executing a common (micro-) instruction set I. Bit-slicing therefore makes it possible to design families of computers that employ different word sizes but use the same basic software. It should also be noted that many computers have instruction sets that process operands of several different sizes. A bit-sliced implementation allows such operands to be processed in a fairly uniform manner.

An important reason for the introduction of commercial bit-sliced microprocessors in the early 1970s was to overcome the manufactur-

* This work was supported by the Air Force Office of Scientific Research under Grant No. AFOSR-77-3352.

† Departments of Electrical Engineering and Computer Science, University of Southern California, Los Angeles, California 90007.

Reprinted with permission from *J. Digital Syst.*, vol. 5, pp. 203–250, Fall 1981.

ing problems associated with high-speed LSI processors using bipolar technologies such as ECL and Schottky TTL. High speed implies large power dissipation, which limits the number of components (gates) that can be placed on a single IC chip. Most non-bit-sliced processors employ MOS or unipolar technologies, which allow higher component densities, but are usually significantly slower than equivalent bipolar devices. By building bipolar processors with very short word sizes, manufacturers could obtain the lower component densities necessary for acceptable power dissipation and reasonable production yields. At the same time, by using the bit-slice concept, these components could be combined relatively easily to accommodate the larger word sizes required in many applications.

Bit-sliced systems are characterized by the use of uniform slices with simple and regular interconnections between the slices. While these properties are helpful in designing systems with many ICs, they are also extremely useful in the internal design and layout of complex IC chips. The cost of VLSI chip specification is greatly reduced by the use of uniform components (cells) with simple interconnections. For example, bit-slicing is used extensively in the design of the E-unit chip of the Caltech OM-2 computer [Mead and Conway 1980].

The uniformity of the slices and their interconnections also facilitates the testing and maintenance of bit-sliced systems. Although not a significant factor in the commercial introduction of bit-sliced components, it provided motivation for several early computer design projects [Forbes et al. 1965; Levitt et al. 1968], as well as some recent research [Ciompi and Simoncini 1977; Wakerly 1978; Sridhar and Hayes 1979].

In a survey conducted in 1976, Walker found that applications of commercial bit-slice components were approximately evenly divided among three areas: general-purpose processing, control-oriented processing, and arithmetic-oriented processing. Almost three-quarters of the 30 projects surveyed cited the higher processing speeds attainable with bit-sliced processors as the primary reason for choosing them over conventional non-bit-sliced microprocessors.

A number of factors contribute to the speed of bit-sliced computers: the fast IC technology used, the ability to design processors for long data formats, and the fact that complex operations can be microprogrammed. Thus in the missile guidance and control application described by Lowe [1977], bit-sliced modules (the 2900 family) were selected over conventional 1-chip microprocessors for the following reasons:

1. The required speed of about 700,000 instructions per second was then beyond the capabilities of most non-bit-sliced processors.
2. Designers needed the flexibility to modify and enlarge the instruction set with little change in the hardware, so microprogrammability was deemed necessary.
3. An instruction set with an unusually large proportion of multiply instructions was to be used, hence the desirability of fast (microprogrammed instead of programmed) multiplication.
4. Most arithmetic operations required relatively long 16-bit words, with occasional use of 32-bit (double-precision) words.

1.2 History

The term bit slicing was not widely used until the advent of microprocessors in the early 1970s. However, the underlying concept of processor design using cascades of uniform modular components can be traced to several computer projects a decade earlier. The IBM DX-1, a self-diagnosable computer designed in 1962, contained a CPU consisting of two identical cascaded "partitions," i.e., slices, each capable of testing the other [Forbes et al. 1965]. Referring to the DX-1 some ten years later, Ramamoorthy and Chang [1972] define "bit-slice or byte-slice design" as design in which "all logic associated with a particular bit (byte) position (input-output, logic, arithmetic and memory circuits) is packaged in the same integrated circuit." Also motivated by fault diagnosis and repair considerations, Levitt et al. [1968] defined a byte-sliced organization as one in which "each major system block is realized as a one-dimensional cascade of identical elements." The "macromodules" developed at Washington University in the mid-1960s were basically single-function 12-bit slices [Ornstein et al. 1967]. Macromodules consisted of devices such as adders and registers, all realized in modular form using discrete transistor technology. They were designed so that several macromodules of the same type could be plugged together to increase word size without affecting the operations being performed. The term bit slice also appears to have been used in the 1960s in the context of associative processors [Thurber and Wald 1975]. An associative array processor such as the Goodyear STARAN can process simultaneously all bits B_i in any fixed position i in a set of k words. The set B_i is called a bit slice through the k words. In the sequel we will only be concerned with bit-sliced modules designed for constructing conventional computers. Such modules first became available commercially in the early 1970s with the advent of microprocessors.

As LSI circuits became feasible in the late 1960s, several companies experimented with the design of multifunction processor slices. An early example is the AS-80 "LSI array" developed by Raytheon around 1969 [Langley 1970]. This is an 80-gate chip—80 gates/chip was then considered large-scale integration—capable of performing each of the following eight functions on 4-bit operands: clear, shift left, shift right, hold, load, complement, increment, decrement. Fig. 2a shows the external connections of these modules, while Fig. 2b shows how three of the modules are connected to form a 12-bit processor. Note that neighboring slices are directly connected via carry and shift lines. Ripple-carry propagation between adjacent slices is the primary mechanism by which arithmetic operations (increment and decrement in this case) can be extended to words of arbitrary length. Similarly the left/right shift lines allow shift operations to extend across the entire array. No direct communication between the cells is required for data transfer (clear and load) or logical (complement) operations. Note how the data input lines have been grouped into three 12-bit buses which correspond to the X, Y, and L data-in buses of a single module. Similarly, the Z lines form a 12-bit data-out bus. The interconnection structure of Fig. 2b is typical of all subsequent bit-sliced processors.

Bit-sliced processors became available commercially soon after the introduction of the first microprocessor, the Intel 4004, in 1971 [Lapidus 1972]. In 1972 American Micro-Systems Inc. announced a

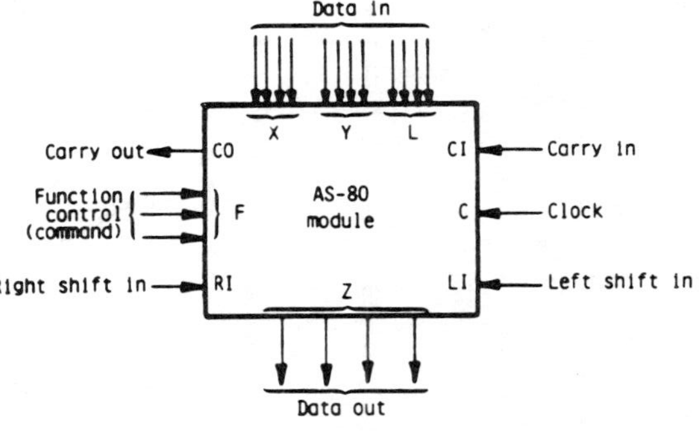

Fig. 2a. Main external connections of the Raytheon AS-80 4-bit processor slice

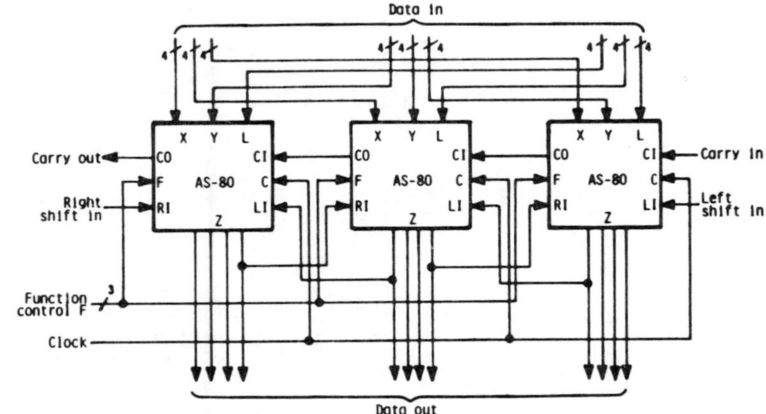

Fig. 2b. A 12-bit processor constructed from three AS-80 slices

"byte slice" or 8-bit processor slice, the AMI 7200 [Schultz and Holt 1972]. This was intended as a building block for the E-units of 8- or 16-bit minicomputers. Even though the 7200 employed MOS technology, it was found to require a chip that was too large for reasonable production yields at that time, and it was abandoned by AMI shortly after its announcement. Eight-bit processor slices did not appear again until the introduction of the Fairchild F100200 in 1979.

The first company to market microprocessors based on the bit-slice concept was National Semiconductor which, in 1973, introduced the GPC/P (General Purpose Controller/Processor) system design kit [National Semiconductor 1973; Reyling 1973]. The GPC/P is based on a 4-bit processor slice called a RALU (register and arithmetic logic unit) which uses PMOS technology and contains a simple arithmetic-logic processor, seven general-purpose registers, and a 16-word stack memory. The I-unit of GPC/P employs a single IC called a CROM (control read-only memory) which combines the functions of microprogram sequencer and control memory. National also supplied its own pre-microprogrammed versions of GPC/P in 4-, 8- and 16-word sizes, called the IMP (Integrated Micro Processor) series [National Semiconductor 1975]. In 1974 Intel introduced the 3000 bit-slice series [Rattner et al. 1974; Hoff 1975]. Like most subsequent bit-slice families, it employs bipolar instead of MOS technology, resulting in significantly higher operating speeds (clock rates of 10 MHz or more). A unique feature of the 3000 series is its use of a 2-bit slice for the 3002 CPE (central processing element). Also introduced in 1974 was Monolithic Memories 5701/6701 4-bit processor slice [Wyland 1975]. This was soon followed by (and eventually superseded by) the very similar Advanced Micro Devices 2901 [Advanced Micro Devices 1978; Mick and Brick 1980]. The 2900 series of bit-slice modules has since become one of the most popular.

In recent years, bit-slice components for computer design have been introduced by many semiconductor manufacturers [Adams 1978; Adams and Smith 1978; Myers 1980]. These components may be grouped into families that are hardware and software compatible. The E-unit or processor slice is usually called a microprocessor. In addition to a bit-sliced processor, each family normally includes a microprogram sequencer, memories, IO interface circuits, and other support devices. In some cases—for example, in the Motorola 10800 series—the microprogram sequencer may be bit-sliced with respect to control memory address words. This means that *n* copies of a microprogram sequencer that generates *m*-bit control memory addresses can be cascaded to produce *nm*-bit addresses. In families like the Texas Instruments 481, the I-unit and E-unit functions are partly merged in a single IC slice, allowing more complex operations such as multiplication and division to be implemented in a bit-sliced organization. Table I lists the main characteristics of the bit-slice families produced up to 1980.

1.3 Design Concepts

The bit-slice families listed in Table I constitute powerful building blocks for the digital system designer. They provide the high switching speeds of bipolar SSI and MSI circuits, but allow complex systems to be constructed from far fewer ICs. On the other hand, bit-sliced systems generally require more ICs than systems based on conventional non-bit-sliced microprocessors. As observed earlier, the latter lack the flexibility of bit-sliced processors, and generally use slower MOS technologies. Microprocessor families like the Intel MCS-80 series that do not use bit slicing have a CPU (the 8080 microprocessor in the MCS-80 case) whose organization and instruction set are fixed by the manufacturer. In the case of bit-slice families, however, no instruction set or CPU organization is defined a priori; this must be done by the system designer. Furthermore, the designer must also specify how the instructions are interpreted, a task normally implemented by microprogramming. Other considerations common to all microprocessor-based systems include specifying the system interconnection (bus) structure, and the mechanisms such as interrupts for communication between the CPU and the IO devices.

Table I

Commercial Bit-Slice Devices Introduced Before 1980

Primary Manufacturer	Series Name	Circuit Technology	Processor Slice					Microprogram Sequencer			
			Part No.	Slice Width	Clock Rate (MHz)	No. of Instr.	No. of Pins	Part No.	Address Width	Bit Sliced?	No. of Pins
Advanced Micro Devices	2900	Schottky TTL	2901 2903	4 4	10 10	16 25	40 48	2909 2910	4 12	yes no	28 40
Fairchild	Macrologic Macrologic 100200	Schottky TTL CMOS ECL	9405 34705 100200	4 4 8	10 2 25	64 64 27	24 24 68	9408	10	no	24
Intel	3000	Schottky TTL	3002	2	10	40	28	3001	9	no	40
Monolithic Memories	6700	Schottky TTL	6701	4	5	32	40	6710	9	no	40
Motorola	10800	ECL	10800	4	20	64	48	10801	4	yes	48
National Semiconductor	GPC/P (IMP)	PMOS	00A/520 (RALU)	4	5	8	24	4A/521 (CROM)	4	yes	24
Texas Instruments	SBP0400 481	I^2L Schottky TTL	SBP0400 74S481	4 4	5 10	512 24,780	40 48	74S482	4	yes	20

Figure 3 shows the structure of a typical microprogrammable bit-sliced computer. It can be regarded as having two levels of control, the instruction and microinstruction levels. At the instruction level the CPU repeatedly performs a sequence of operations which constitute the *instruction cycle*, the main steps of which are as follows:

1. The CPU fetches from main memory M the opcode of instruction I whose address is stored in the program counter PC.
2. The opcode is placed in the instruction register IR where it initiates execution of a microprogram MP(I) that carries out all the operations specified by I.
3. The contents of PC are altered to indicate the next instruction to be fetched on termination of MP(I).

The operations taking place at the microinstruction level are quite similar to those at the instruction level. The *microinstruction cycle* involves the following steps:

1. The microprogram sequencer fetches a microinstruction μI from the control memory CM. The address of this microinstruction is normally specified by the microprogram counter μPC.
2. The microinstruction μI is placed in a microinstruction register from which are derived all the control signals necessary to carry out the operations specified by μI.
3. The contents of μPC are altered to indicate the next microinstruction to be fetched.

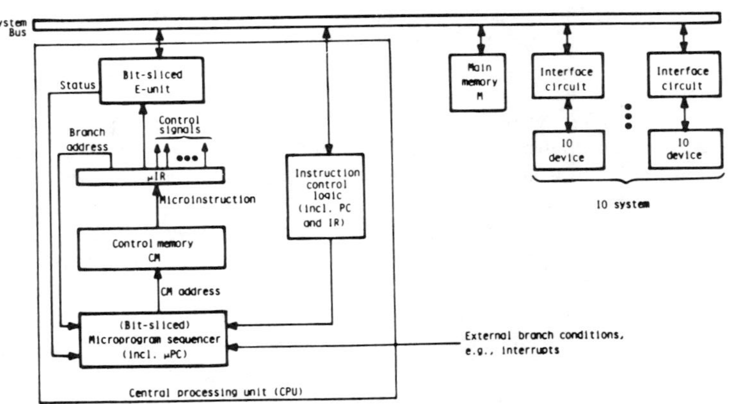

Fig. 3. Structure of a typical microprogrammable bit-sliced computer

Microinstructions are stored in CM in their normal execution sequence, hence by incrementing the microprogram counter μPC we obtain the address of the next microinstruction. As can be seen from Fig. 3, the microprogram sequencer can also obtain CM addresses in other ways. The current microinstruction may itself supply the next microinstruction address; in other words, it may include a branch or jump address. It is also desirable to be able to alter the microinstruction sequence based on status information from the ALU such as overflow/underflow signals, and interrupt signals from devices external to the CPU. The microprogram sequencer is designed to select one address from these various possible sources.

A microinstruction is divided into a number of fields which collectively specify the (micro-) operations to be performed. Figure 4 shows a typical example, the microinstruction format of the AMD 8080 Emulator [Shavit 1978] whose 56 bits are grouped into 24 fields. (This machine is examined in Section III.) Most of the fields are *control fields*, each of which controls a particular device such as a register, a functional unit, or a set of control lines. The control fields typically are used to select the functions to be performed by multifunction units such as the ALU, to set or reset control signals and associated registers, and to control the routing of information by activating data paths in the CPU and other parts of the computer. In the simplest case, each control field is one bit wide and defines a single microoperation. Often several nonconcurrent operations are associated with a control field, each of which is assigned a unique code. For example, a 3-bit field is required to specify the function F performed by the processor array of Fig. 2b.

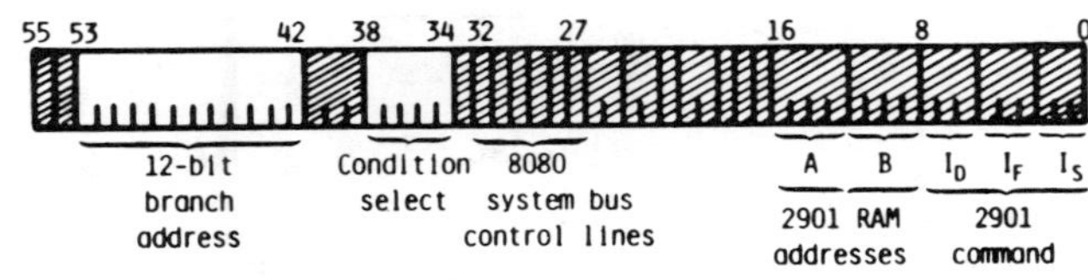

Fig. 4. 56-bit microinstruction format of the AMD 8080 Emulator (control fields are shaded)

In addition to the control fields, a microinstruction may contain one or more *branch address fields* used to implement conditional or unconditional branching. The conditions to be tested in the case of microinstructions with conditional branch capability are specified by *condition select fields.* An example of a conditional branch at the microinstruction level is: if the ALU overflow signal OVF is set to 1, jump to CM address 1000, otherwise execute the next sequential microinstruction. An enormous variety of microinstruction formats have been developed for microprogrammable computers; they range in length from a dozen or so bits to several hundred [Agrawala and Rauscher 1976; Salisbury 1976].

Microprogramming allows changes to be made to the system's instruction set by altering the contents of the control memory; in most cases no costly hardware changes are required. Moreover, complex operations such as floating-point arithmetic can be performed more rapidly by implementing them at the microinstruction or *firmware* level instead of at the instruction level. The advantages of microprogramming are not attained without some cost, however. System design is complicated by the need to specify and use a detailed and usually non-standard microprogramming language. More ICs are required than if a non-microprogrammed microprocessor family is used.

2. SURVEY OF BIT-SLICE FAMILIES

In this section three representative bit-slice families, the Advanced Micro Devices 2900, the Intel 3000 and the Texas Instruments 481 are examined (see Table I). These devices include 2-bit and 4-bit processor slices, and both bit-sliced and non-bit-sliced microprogram sequencers. All employ Schottky TTL bipolar IC technology.

2.1 AMD 2900 Series

The 2900 family which was introduced in 1976 appears to be the most widely used series of bit-sliced modules [Advanced Micro Devices 1978; Mick and Brick 1980]. Its popularity stems from its relatively straightforward design, and the availability of many support chips. In this section we describe in detail two key 2900-series members, the 2901 processor slice and the 2909 microprogram sequencer slice.

Figure 5 shows the internal organization of the 2901 4-bit processor slice. It contains a 16×4-bit RAM which is used as a set of general-purpose or scratchpad registers, an ALU capable of performing eight operations on 4-bit operands, and various support circuits. The ALU input operands may be obtained from five sources: the A and B data

outputs of the internal RAM, an external data bus D, an internal results register Q, or a logical zero. The output F of the ALU can be transferred to the RAM, to register Q, or to a set of data output lines Y.

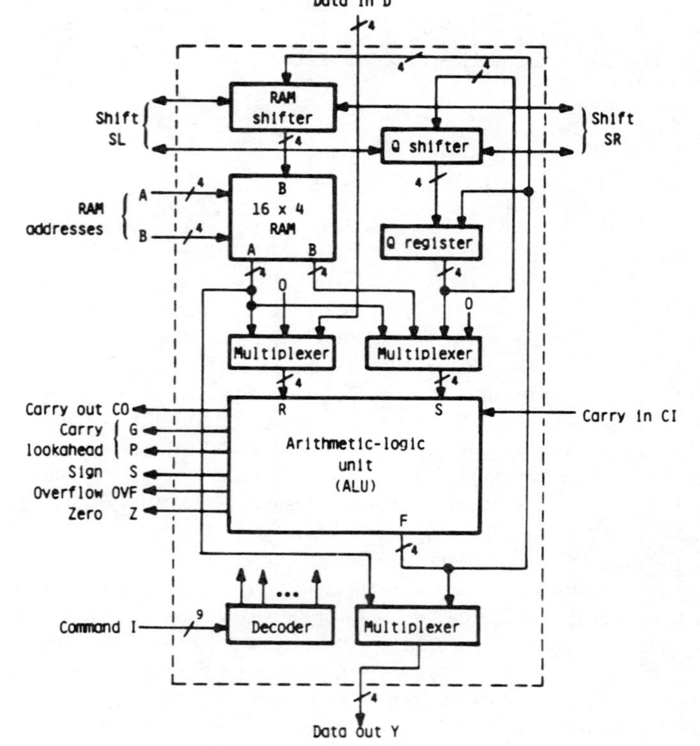

Fig. 5. The AMD 2901 processor slice

There are nine main control or command lines denoted here by I which define the operations to be performed by the 2901. These lines are grouped into three 3-bit fields I_F, I_S and I_D which define, respectively, the ALU operation to be selected, the source operands to be applied to the ALU input ports R and S, and the actions to be taken with the results. Table II lists the functions that can be specified by I. I_F defines one of three arithmetic and five logical operations. Twos complement numbers are used for all arithmetic operations. The result F produced by the ALU can be transferred to the data output lines Y, the Q register, or the B data input of the RAM, as specified by the I_D

or destination field. I_D may also be used to cause data to be shifted one bit position before it is transferred to Q or to the RAM. In Table II left and right shifts are denoted by multiplication and division by 2, respectively. In operations involving the internal RAM, the RAM registers to be connected to its two output data ports and its single input data port are identified by the signals applied to the A and B address buses.

Table II

Definition of the 2901 Command Lines I

I_S Code	ALU source operands R	S
000	A	Q
001	A	B
010	0	Q
011	0	B
100	0	A
101	D	A
110	D	Q
111	D	0

I_F Code	ALU Function
000	$R + S$ (add)
001	$S - R$ (subtract)
010	$R - S$ (subtract)
011	$R \vee S$ (or)
100	$R \wedge S$ (and)
101	$\bar{R} \wedge S$ (complement-and)
110	$R \bullet S$ (exclusive-or)
111	$\overline{R \bullet S}$ (exclusive-nor)

I_D Code	Destination(s) of ALU result F and related data		
	RAM port B	Q register	Y bus
000	not used	$Q \leftarrow F$	$Y \leftarrow F$
001	not used	not used	$Y \leftarrow F$
010	$B \leftarrow F$	not used	$Y \leftarrow A$
011	$B \leftarrow F$	not used	$Y \leftarrow F$
100	$B \leftarrow F/2$	$Q \leftarrow Q/2$	$Y \leftarrow F$
101	$B \leftarrow F/2$	not used	$Y \leftarrow F$
110	$B \leftarrow 2 \times F$	$Q \leftarrow 2 \times Q$	$Y \leftarrow F$
111	$B \leftarrow 2 \times F$	not used	$Y \leftarrow F$

The I_F, I_S, I_D, A and B lines typically correspond to five control fields in the user-defined microinstructions controlling a 2901-based processor; see Fig. 4. Many different operations can be specified by these fields. Suppose, for example, that it is desired to transfer the contents of RAM register 7 to register 11. This simple data transfer is specified by the following (partial) microinstruction in the format of Fig. 4:

$$A, B, I_D, I_F, I_S = 0111, 1011, 010, 011, 100 \quad (1)$$

Here registers 7 and 11 are designated the A and B registers, respectively. As can be deduced from Table II, (1) performs the "dummy" OR operations $0 \vee A$ which causes the A data to pass unchanged through the ALU.

A $4n$-bit processor can be formed by cascading n copies of the 2901. The ripple-carry scheme of Fig. 2b may be used, in which case the carry-out line CO of each slice is connected to the carry-in line CI of its left neighbor. Ripple-carry propagation suffers from the drawback that addition and subtraction time increases rapidly with the number of slices. Figure 6 depicts an alternative method for handling carry signals which is included in the 2901 and most other bit-sliced processors. Here the CI signals of each slice are obtained from an external carry-lookahead generator such as the 2902 IC. The inputs to the 2902 are obtained from the G and P outputs of each slice, which specify the slice's need to generate (G) or propagate (P) a carry signal. The advantage of this technique is that the carry-lookahead generator can produce the CI signal for every slice simultaneously, resulting in faster arithmetic operations.

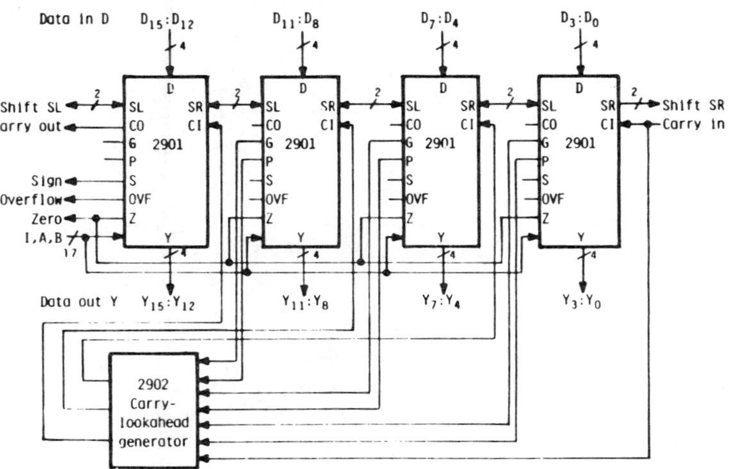

Fig. 6. Expansion of the 2901 to form a 16-bit processor with carry lookahead

Figure 6 also illustrates some other aspects of processor expansion. The RAM and Q shift circuits are cascaded directly via two sets of lines SL and SR, thereby extending the shift logic from 4 to 16 bits. The 2901 generates three status bits: S which is the most significant bit of the ALU result and may specify the sign of a number, OVF which is set to indicate overflow resulting from a signed arithmetic operation, and Z which is set to 1 when the ALU result is zero. These status signals are used to control microinstruction branching as illustrated in Fig. 3. Clearly, in the processor array of Fig. 6, only the S and OVF signals from the most significant (leftmost) slice are of interest; the corresponding signals from the other slices are not used. In the case of the zero result signal Z, however, the Z signals from each slice must be logically ANDed in order to obtain a valid Z signal for the entire array. The 2901 has been designed so that the Z lines can be directly connected as in Fig. 6 to form a wired-AND gate which yields the desired output signal.

The 2909 is a 4-bit microprogram sequencer slice whose organization appears in Fig. 7. The output data generated by the 2909 is a 4-bit address word Y which can be used to address a control memory containing up to 16 microinstructions. Y is selected from one of the four sources: a microprogram counter register μPC, a direct input bus D, a register R, and a 4-word LIFO stack ST. The external control lines S_0 and S_1 specify which address source is to be selected.

The register μPC may be viewed as the usual source of microinstruction addresses. After a microinstruction has been fetched, μPC can be incremented by one to point to the next sequential microinstruction. The R and D input buses are typically used to transfer branch addresses to the 2909 where they can be used to define Y or replace the contents of μPC. The 2909 has five input lines OR_0:OR_3 and $\overline{ZERO}$ which are also used to allow external conditions to modify the address being generated. For instance, if OR_0 is set to 1, and the output X of the main multiplexer is ddd0, then the final output Y becomes ddd1, causing the microinstruction whose address is ddd0 to be skipped. When $\overline{ZERO} = 0$, Y is forced to 0000. The stack ST is intended for implementing subroutines within microprograms. To initiate a call or jump to subroutine operation, a "push" signal is sent to the 2909 which transfers the current contents of μPC (the return address) to the stack ST, and replaces it by D or R. After execution of the subroutine, a return operation is implemented by causing ST to "pop" the previously stored return address. Four addresses may be stored in ST in this manner, allowing up to four nested subroutine calls.

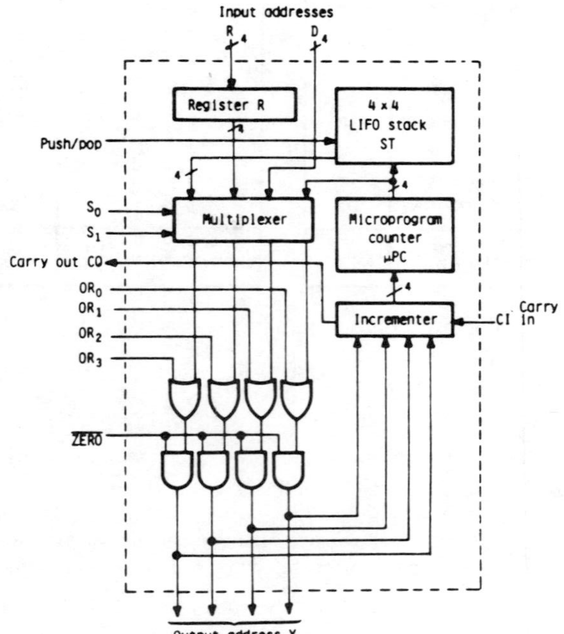

Fig. 7. The 2909 microprogram sequencer slice

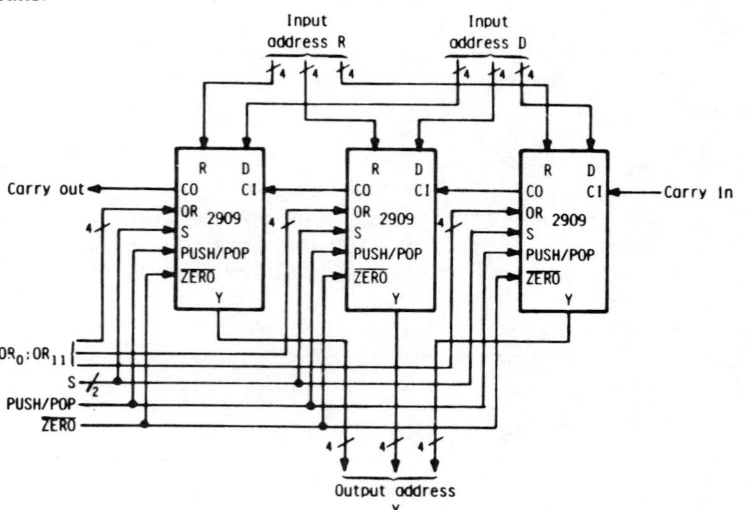

Fig. 8. Expansion of the 2909 to form a 12-bit microprogram sequencer

Expansion of the 2909 is quite simple as illustrated by Fig. 8; n slices are cascaded to generate $4n$-bit addresses. The various sets of address lines are juxtaposed, while corresponding control lines are directly connected. The only local link between adjacent slices is a carry line that allows ripple-carry propagation between the incrementers of the various slices.

2.2 Intel 3000 Series

The 3000 series is one of the earlier bit-sliced microprocessor component families [Rattner et al. 1974; Intel 1976]. It has been widely used, but has some features that now must be viewed as obsolete. The principal members of the series are the 3002 processor slice and the 3001 microprogram sequencer. The 3002 processes 2-bit words, thus requiring roughly twice as many ICs to build an n-bit processor as a 4-bit slice such as the 2901. The 3001 is not bit-sliced; it generates a fixed-length 9-bit address which limits control memory capacity to $2^9 = 512$ words.

The internal structure of the 3002 appears in Fig. 9. Like the 2901 it has an ALU capable of twos-complement addition and subtraction,

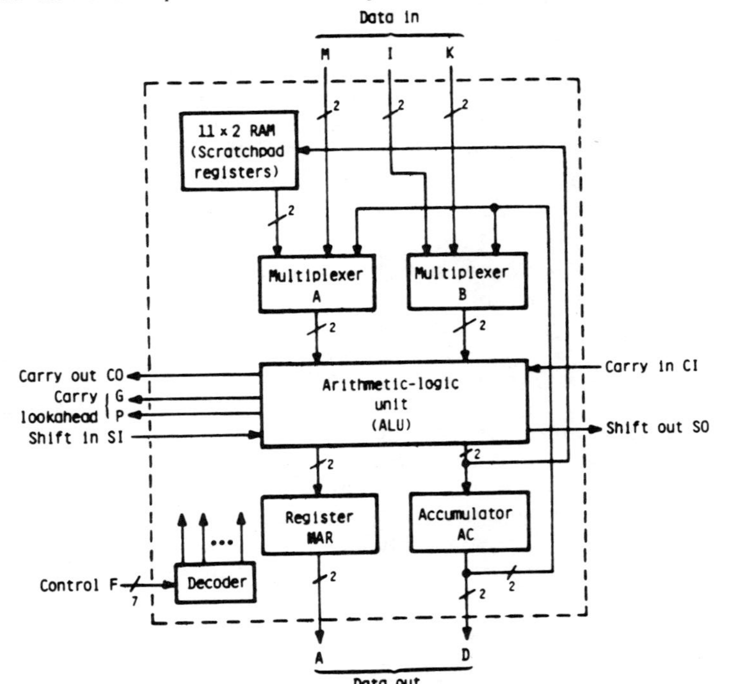

Fig. 9. The Intel 3002 processor slice

and the standard logical operations. The ALU generates the signals P, G and CO needed for both ripple-carry propagation and carry lookahead. The 3002 contains a conventional accumulator AC which is the principal ALU results register. A second ALU results register MAR is intended as an address register for external main memory. There are also 11 general-purpose scratchpad registers R_0:R_9 and T, all two bits wide. The 3002 has an unusually large number of input-output data buses, each of which is two bits wide. The M and I buses are general-purpose input data buses. M may, for example, be connected to main memory, while I can be connected to a peripheral device. D is a general-purpose data output bus connected to AC. The A bus is connected to MAR and is intended specifically for transferring addresses from the 3002 to main memory.

The function to be performed by a 3002 processor is specified by the 7-bit command bus F. In general, the three bits F_4:F_6 specify an operation to be performed, while F_0:F_3 specify one or more operands, usually registers or data buses. A rather complex format is used for F. The 2-line K bus, originally called the control memory data bus [Hoff 1975], allows the external I-unit's control memory to supply constants and masks to the 3002. Hence the K-bus increases the number of functions that can be specified. In a typical operation, the K-bus contents are ANDed with one of the main operands. For example, F = 1111001 specifies the EXCLUSIVE-NOR microoperation

$$R_9 \leftarrow R_9 \bar{\oplus} (\mathrm{AC} \wedge \mathrm{K}) \qquad (2)$$

The implicit operand AC is automatically ANDed with K. If K = 11, then (2) becomes

$$R_9 \leftarrow R_9 \bar{\oplus} \mathrm{AC}$$

while if K = 00, (2) reduces to the complement operation

$$R_9 \leftarrow \bar{R}_9$$

The values K = 11 and K = 00 are particularly useful; K = 11 effectively includes AC in the main operation, while K = 00 excludes AC. The other two values of K are useful for testing the individual bits of a word. Note that the 3002 lacks explicit status signals such as the zero, sign and overflow signals produced by the 2901. The absence of an arithmetic overflow indicator has been judged a major design deficiency of the 3002 [McWilliams et al. 1977].

The 3001 is a non-bit-sliced microprogram sequencer of fairly simple design. It contains a single 9-bit register which stores the current microinstruction address. The next address to be used is specified by means of 11 conditional and unconditional "jump commands" placed on seven address control lines J of the 3001. Since each 7-bit jump command can only specify part of a 9-bit microinstruction address, an unusual technique for defining branch addresses is used. The 512-word control memory address space is treated as a 32 × 16 matrix. A 9-bit address a_8:a_0 therefore consists of a 5-bit row address a_8:a_4 and a 4-bit column address a_3:a_0. Microinstruction branches are confined to a small group of rows and columns related to the current address. For example, the unconditional "jump in current column" command JCC is specified by $J = 00d_4d_3d_2d_1d_0$. The effect of JCC is to replace the current address $A = a_8a_7a_6a_5a_4a_3a_2a_1a_0$ by the new address $A = d_4d_3d_2d_1d_0a_3a_2a_1a_0$ in which the column address $a_3a_2a_1a_0$ is unchanged. This idiosyncratic approach to address control makes microinstruction sequencing rather complex in computers using the 3000 series.

2.3 Texas Instruments 481 Series

The main components in this series, which was introduced in 1976, are the 74S481 4-bit processor slice and the 74S482 4-bit microprogram sequencer [Horton et al. 1978; Texas Instruments 1979]. Unlike most slices, the 74S481 contains few general-purpose registers; main memory is used to provide most of the scratchpad or working registers normally included in the CPU. This is the *memory-to-memory architecture* found in the TI 990 series of mini- and microcomputers [Texas Instruments 1975]. Another feature of the 74S481 not found in earlier bit-sliced microprocessors is the inclusion of the relatively complex operations multiplication and division in the basic command set. The 74S482 microprogram sequencer is quite similar to the 2909 chip discussed earlier, and will not be considered further. The 74S481 and 74S482 are compatible with standard 74S00 series Schottky TTL devices, which are used as support chips when constructing a complete computer.

Figure 10 shows the organization of the 74S481 processor slice. It contains a fairly conventional 4-bit ALU capable of twos-complement addition and subtraction, left and right shifting, and the standard logical operations. Multiplication and division are implemented via sequential shift-and-add/subtract algorithms which are stored in a special memory within the 74S481. These wired-in algorithms, which are invoked by single commands applied to the F lines, add significantly to the computing power of the 74S481. In processors such as the 2901 and 3002, multiplication and division require user-written microprograms which must be stored in the I-unit.

The 74S481 contains only four 4-bit registers. Two of these, the program counter PC and the data counter DC, are designed as main memory address registers. The working register WR acts as the main accumulator. XWR, the extended working register, is intended as an

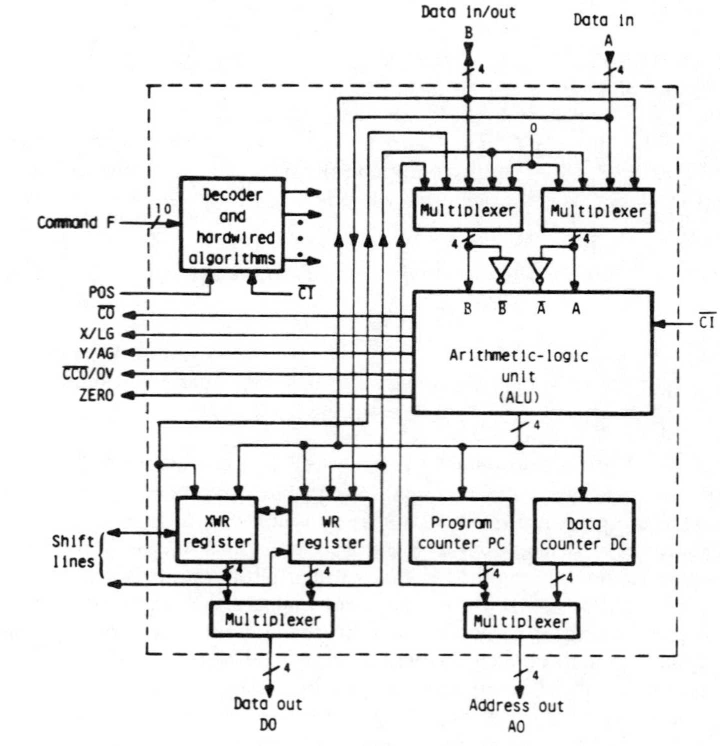

Fig. 10. The Texas Instruments 74S481 processor slice

extension of WR for operations such as multiplication and division that produce double-length results. It also facilitates the programming of double-precision operations. The data input/output buses A and B allow direct connection of the ALU to main memory. ALU operations may therefore use main memory locations in the same way that processors with the more usual general-register architecture use scratchpad registers in the CPU. This involves some speed penalty since it generally takes longer to access main memory than to access local registers. However, the memory-to-memory architecture of the 74S481 may allow faster transfer of control between programs required, for example, when processing interrupts, since there is no need to save the CPU's working registers in main memory. As Fig. 10 suggests, the 74S481 allows considerable flexibility in the routing of data among its registers, processing circuits and IO ports. For example, the contents of the WR can be transferred to either of the two

ALU input ports in either true or complemented form. Thus many different operand sets can be associated with the basic commands of the 74S481, resulting in an unusually large number of distinct command possibilities (24,780 by the manufacturer's count).

Extension of the 74S481 to a multislice processor is fairly conventional. Facilities are provided for both ripple-carry propagation and carry lookahead (see Figs. 2b and 6). A powerful feature of the 74S481 is its ability to carry out most arithmetic operations using either signed or unsigned numbers. In signed operations, the most significant (leftmost) bit MSB of a data word being processed by a 74S481 array must be distinguished. It is also useful to distinguish the least significant bit LSB, for example, in circular shift operations. To this end, the 74S481 contains a control line POS called the relative position control. POS is set individually in each slice to one of three voltage levels that indicate if the slice contains the MSB, the LSB or neither. POS also determines the use of the three multifunction ALU output lines X/LG, Y/AG and $\overline{CCO}$/OV. These lines provide the standard carry lookahead and overflow signals; they are also used to indicate the results of various arithmetic comparison operations [Texas Instruments 1979].

2.4 Evaluation

In evaluating bit slices as design components, the following criteria appear to be the most important: word size, processing speed, functional capabilities, register and bus organization, and ease of microprogramming.

The word size of current processor slices is restricted by technology factors, in particular, by the maximum chip component densities that allow reasonable manufacturing yields. Word size is also limited by power dissipation and, to a lesser extent, by pin count. Most microprocessor slices operate on 4-bit words; only the Intel 3002 uses 2-bit operands. Eight-bit slices like the Fairchild 100220 and, eventually, 16-bit processor slices can be expected to appear as technology improvements permit. Longer word sizes are desirable in processor slices for several reasons. The more ICs in a processor array, the higher its cost. The fact that most applications for bit-sliced microprocessors use word lengths of 16 bits or more [Walker 1976] suggests the desirability of larger slices. The speed of a processor array may be reduced by interchip propagation delays, particularly if ripple-carry propagation is used. Carry-lookahead circuits can reduce carry propagation delays, but at the expense of additional logic circuitry.

There is less need for bit-slicing in the case of microprogram sequencers, hence not all bit-slice families contain such devices. The 9-bit non-bit-sliced 3001 can address up to 512 microinstructions, which is adequate for many applications. The more recent non-bit-sliced 2910 microprogram sequencer can generate 12-bit addresses [Advanced Micro Devices 1978]. If much shorter or much longer addresses are needed, then bit-sliced devices such as the 2909 are most suitable.

Among devices with similar functional characteristics such as instruction set, word size, and register and IO port organization, the primary determinant of processing speed is the IC technology used. Bit-sliced microprocessors use bipolar technologies, which is the primary reason for their speed advantage over conventional MOS microprocessors. Low-power Schottky TTL is presently the preferred technology among bit-slice families as Table I indicates. An important design advantage of these devices is the vast range of compatible TTL devices that are widely available. ECL families such as the 10800 and 100220 are significantly faster. Their main disadvantages are more complex physical design rules resulting from their high operating speeds and high power dissipation.

The functional capabilities of a bit-sliced module are defined mainly by its command lines. The commands executed by most current processor slices are rather simple. All are limited to fixed-point arithmetic and most cannot perform multiplication or division. The functional capabilities of bit-sliced processors can be increased significantly by transferring some of the functions of the I-unit to each processor slice. This has been done to a limited extent in the 74S481 and the 2903, another 4-bit processor slice in the 2900 family [Coleman et al. 1977]. In both cases, complex functions such as multiplication are implemented largely via hardwired control algorithms within the processor slice. While this may result in the control algorithms being duplicated in every processor slice, it also reduces the complexity of the microprograms that must be stored in the external control memory CM, and hence reduces the size of CM and its associated circuitry.

The design of the microprogram sequencer also has an important impact on the overall capabilities of a bit-sliced system. The 3001 is the most primitive of the microprogram sequencers that have been discussed here: it has only one address input port, it has no subroutine capability, and it uses an unusually complex scheme for generating branch addresses. The 2901 provides several independent address sources and has a 4-register stack for implementing subroutines.

The bit-sliced series surveyed above take several different approaches to CPU register organization. The 2901 and 3002 have a general-register CPU organization in which each processor slice contains a dozen or so general-purpose working registers. The 2901 has the advantage of a dual-port internal RAM allowing two operands to be fetched from this RAM simultaneously. The 3002 has a single-port internal RAM which requires the use of more instructions than the 2901 for some operations. The 74S481 has only one or two internal registers, and so must use external register sets or main memory for its working registers. Internal working registers can generally be accessed more rapidly than external ones. On the other hand, their number is somewhat limited and they cannot be easily extended when necessary. (This problem is alleviated in the 2903 which has the same register organization as the 2901, but has extra logic to facilitate the expansion of its register set using external registers.) The memory-to-memory organization of the 74S481 allows large sets of working registers to be used. This is an advantage when frequent rapid transfer of program control is required—for example, when processing interrupts from many high-speed IO devices. Each program can be assigned its own set of working registers and, since most working registers are outside the CPU proper, little time is required to save the old program state. Thus the general register and memory-to-memory architectures involve tradeoffs affecting the number of working registers, the access time of the working registers, and the speed with which working registers can be reassigned.

There are also substantial differences in the register organizations associated with the various microprogram sequencers. The 3001 is clearly deficient in this regard. The stacks of the 2909 and 74S482 are very useful since they allow efficient implementation of subroutines within microprograms. Both of these stacks allow up to four subroutines to be nested, which is adequate for most microprogramming tasks. The inclusion in the microprogram sequencer of the loop counter of the type found in the 2910 also facilitates microprogramming.

Closely related to register organization is the structure of the IO bus system associated with both processors and microprogram sequencers. Generally speaking, it is desirable to have as many independent IO buses as possible to increase the number of devices that can be connected directly to the chip. Pin count is the obvious limiting factor on the number of IO lines available. Among the processor slices, the 2901 is most deficient in IO buses, having only one input and one output data bus. The 3002, taking advantage of its small word size and the resulting need for fewer pins, has five independent data buses, while the 74S481 has four.

Probably the most difficult aspect of design with bit-sliced modules is specifying the microinstruction format and writing the necessary microprograms. Each microinstruction may contain 50 bits or more, and microprograms often contain hundreds of microinstructions. Two factors which have a large impact on microprogrammability are the functional capabilities of the bit-sliced modules themselves, and the software tools available to aid in writing microprograms.

It is obviously advantageous to have powerful and well-organized command sets for both the processor and the microprogram sequencer. Thus the complex functions implemented in the 74S481 and 2903 simplify the writing of microprograms that use such functions. Also desirable is a processor that provides comprehensive status information; the 3002 is most lacking in this regard. The ability of the 74S481 and the 2903 to perform signed arithmetic operations automatically also aids in the microprogramming of arithmetic functions. Among the microprogram sequencers, a comprehensive and systematic set of jump commands is very desirable. The most widely available design aids for microprogramming bit-sliced computers are microassemblers [Powers and Hernandez 1978]. They allow microprograms to be written in a symbolic language similar to an assembly language. Microassemblers are commercially available for all the widely used bit-sliced families. A specific microassembler, AMDASM, is discussed in section 4.1

3. DESIGN EXAMPLE: 8080 EMULATION

The 8080 microprocessor introduced by Intel in 1973 is one of the best-known and most widely used "second generation" microprocessors [Shima and Faggin 1974; Intel 1975]. It is the first in a family of partly compatible microprocessors that includes the Intel 8085 and the Zilog Z80. The 8080 is of special interest here because several well-documented bit-sliced systems have been designed that execute its instruction set, i.e., emulate it. Two of these 8080 emulators will be described and compared in this section: an emulator designed by AMD which uses 2900 series components [Shavit 1978], and one designed by Signetics which uses the 3000 series [Lau 1978; Signetics 1977].

The main justification for building bit-sliced emulators of existing machines such as the 8080 is to obtain faster execution of the instruction set of the target machine. In addition, the basic instruction set may be enhanced with additional microprogrammed instructions. Among the contributing factors to the speed advantages of the emulator are—

1. its use of a faster IC technology than that of the target machine;
2. the inclusion of architectural improvements such as (micro-) instruction overlap to increase throughput;

3. the implementation in firmware of functions such as multiplication which must otherwise be implemented at the instruction level.

The bit-sliced systems considered here are intended as replacements for a CPU built around a standard 1-chip 8080 microprocessor. An 8080 emulator must present to the outside world a set of address, data and control lines with all the characteristics of the 8080 system bus. In addition it must contain the logic circuits and microprograms necessary to interpret and execute the 8080 instruction set.

3.1 8080 Microprocessor

In order to appreciate the design of the 8080 emulators, some understanding of the system to be emulated is required. We begin therefore by summarizing the organization and instruction set of the 8080 microprocessor [Intel 1975].

The 8080 has the general structure depicted in Fig. 11. It contains an 8-bit ALU, an accumulator A and a set of six 8-bit general-purpose scratchpad registers designated B, C, D, E, H and L. The 8080 is designed to address up to $2^{16} = 64K$ bytes of main memory, and so

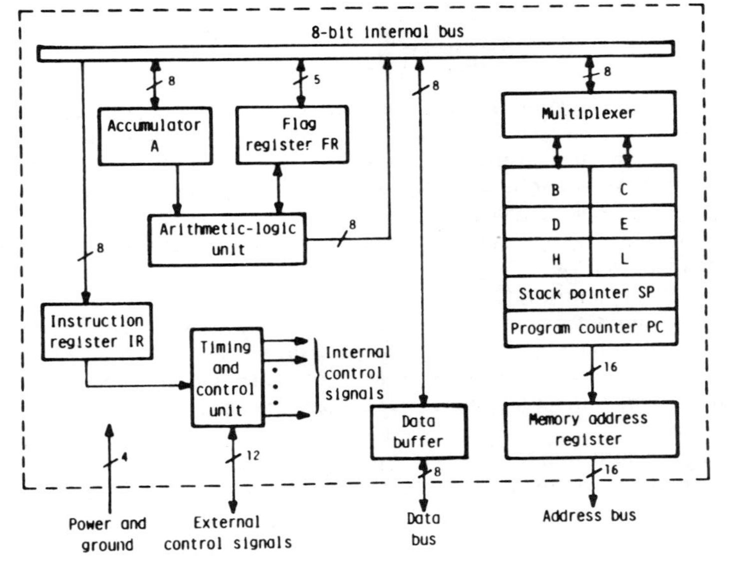

Fig. 11. Organization of the 8080 microprocessor chip

uses 16-bit memory addresses. There are two main 16-bit address registers in the 8080, the program counter PC and the stack pointer SP. SP is used to hold the topmost address of a user-defined LIFO stack in main memory. Additional address storage registers are provided by the six scratchpad registers which may be paired to form three 16-bit registers BC, DE and HL. The 5-bit flag register FR stores status information or condition codes concerning the results generated by 8080 instructions.

The 8080 has a fairly conventional repertoire of over 70 instructions including data transfer, arithmetic, logical, conditional and unconditional branching, and input-output instructions. Most 8080 instructions use 8-bit operands; there are, however, some 16-bit instructions, and most instructions involve processing 16-bit memory addresses. Instruction operands may be immediate, i.e., in the instruction itself, in 8080 registers, or in main memory. There are two memory addressing modes: direct in which the instruction contains a 16-bit memory address, and register indirect where the instruction specifies a register-pair containing the main memory address to be used. There are no indexed or relative addressing modes. Instructions may be one, two, or three bytes long. The 1-byte instructions are mainly register-to-register operations, or memory operations where indirect addressing is used. The first or opcode byte of all instructions defines the operations to be performed. The second and third bytes in multi-byte instructions contain immediate data or direct memory addresses.

3.2 2900-based Emulator

The AMD Emulator [Shavit 1978] is based on the 2901 4-bit processor slice and the 2909 4-bit microprogram sequencer slice, both of which were described in Sec. II. The 16-word RAM of the 2901 (see Fig. 5) can clearly accommodate the small number of registers used in the 8080. Although the 8080 is usually thought of as an 8-bit processor, it performs many operations on 16-bit addresses, suggesting the use of a 16-bit processor in the emulator. The AMD Emulator therefore uses an array of four 2901s as the heart of its ALU. The size of the 2909 array is determined by the number of microinstructions to be stored. In this case 352 microinstructions are used, so three 2909s supplying a 12-bit control memory address are required. The AMD Emulator uses about 60 ICs to implement an 8080-based CPU.

The 56-bit microinstruction format shown in Fig. 4 is used in this machine. The 12-bit branch address field provides the next control memory address when microinstruction branches are required. The 5-bit condition select field is used to specify conditions to be tested in the case of conditional branch microinstructions. The remaining 39 bits are divided into some 22 control fields which specify a variety of control functions, most of which are peculiar to the design of the AMD Emulator.

Figure 12 shows the organization of the microprogrammable I-unit. This unit replaces the instruction register IR and the hardwired timing and control unit of the 1-chip 8080 (see Fig. 11). The purpose of the mapping PROM is to translate 8-bit instruction opcodes into 12-bit control memory addresses. These addresses are sent to the D inputs of the 2909 microprogram sequencer array, and thence to the microprogram counter μPC inside the 2909s. The μPC is normally incremented to obtain the next address. The 12-bit branch address field in each microinstruction is transferred to the 2909 array via its R inputs. Address selection within the 2909 array is controlled by the address selection logic unit. This circuit monitors the microinstruction condition select field, the 8080 status flags, external interrupt lines, and

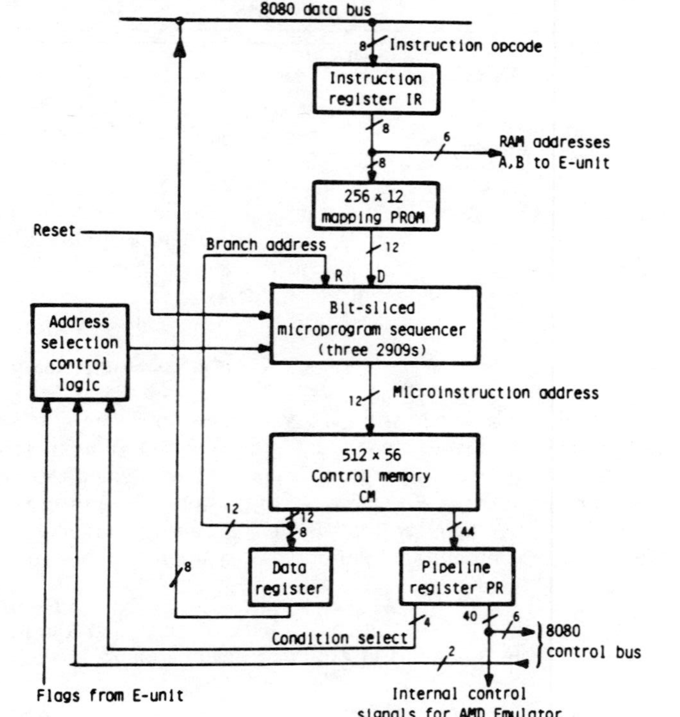

Fig. 12. Microprogram control unit (I-unit) for the AMD 8080 Emulator

Table III

Allocation of 2901 Registers in the AMD Emulator

2901 Scratchpad Register (RAM) Address	Left (high-order) 8-bit Processor	Right (low-order) 8-bit Processor
0000	B	C
0001	C	B
0010	D	E
0011	E	D
0100	H	L
0101	L	H
0110	not used	A
0111	A	not used
1000	not used	not used
1001	$SP_{15}:SP_8$	$SP_7:SP_0$
1010	scratchpad	scratchpad
1011	scratchpad	scratchpad
1100	00000000	00111000
1101	00111000	00000000
1110	not used	not used
1111	$PC_{15}:PC_8$	$PC_7:PC_0$

other conditions that affect microinstruction sequencing. When branching is not required, the microprogrammer may use the branch address field to store data such as numerical constants, masks, etc. The 8-bit register connected to the control memory is intended to hold such data. Finally, the I-unit contains a 44-bit pipeline register to store microinstruction control fields. The purpose of this register is to allow the fetching of the next microinstruction to be overlapped with the execution of the current microinstruction. It does so by providing buffer storage for the current microinstruction control information while the next microinstruction is being read from control memory.

As noted earlier, the E-unit or data processing part of the AMD Emulator contains four 2901 4-bit processor slices. The data and address registers are assigned to the 2901 scratchpad memory in the manner indicated in Table III. This apparently complex and redundant allocation is ingeniously designed to allow register names appearing in the 8080 instruction opcodes to be applied to the A and B address ports of the 2901 array with a minimum of decoding logic.

The 2901 processor array consists of four 2901s which are organized into two largely independent 8-bit processors: the left processor consisting of the high-order pair of 2901s, and right processor consisting of the low-order pair. The left and right processors can be coupled to form a single processor for 16-bit operations. Eight-bit operations are implemented by having the left and right processors operate simultaneously on separate but identical data. When a 16-bit operation alters the contents of a register pair, say BC, the complementary pair CB must also be updated. The overhead associated with this updating is considered small.

The organization of the E-unit for the AMD Emulator is given in Fig. 13. It has a general resemblance to the data processing part of the 8080 microprocessor, cf. Fig. 11. Note that the ALU and all the 8080 registers except the data, memory address, and flag registers are contained within the 2901s. A certain amount of special logic is needed to generate the 8080 flags. For example, a parity generation circuit is needed to obtain the parity flag P, since P is not included among the 2901 flags.

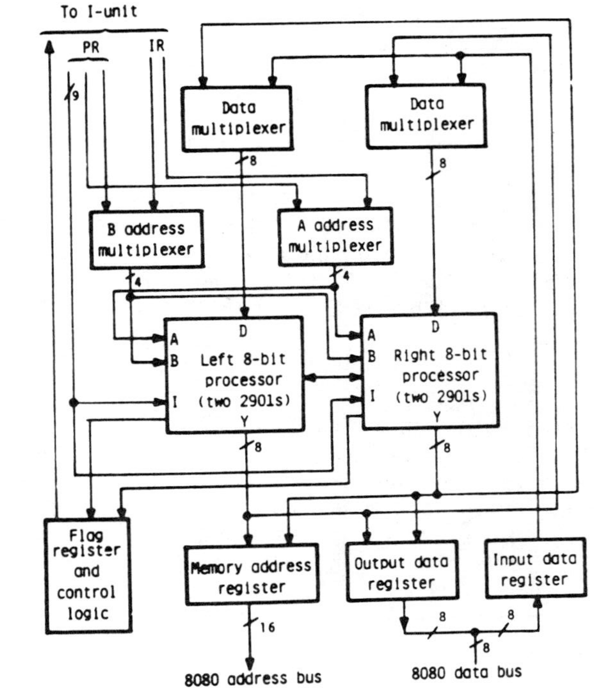

Fig. 13. E-unit of the AMD 8080 Emulator

We now briefly outline the organization of the microprograms used in the AMD Emulator to emulate the 8080 instruction set. A small set of microinstructions starting in control memory location 000_{16} constitute a RESET microprogram which serves to initialize the Emulator. Activation of the reset line of the 2909s (see Fig. 12) forces the contents of μPC to 000_{16} causing RESET to be executed. The RESET routine places in the 2909 stack the initial address of a microprogram FETCH, whose function is to fetch instructions from main memory. On termination, RESET transfers control to FETCH.

FETCH, which consists of two microinstructions, executes a main memory read operation using the PC as the address source. It transfers the opcode of the incoming instruction to the instruction register IR. The opcode is then used to produce a control memory address via the mapping PROM; this address is the start address of a microprogram which emulates the instruction that has just been fetched. After execution of this microprogram, control is normally transferred back to FETCH, so that the next instruction can be fetched and executed. The transfer to FETCH can be accomplished easily by restoring to μPC the starting address of FETCH which was saved in the stack of the microprogram control unit. The FETCH routine of the AMD Emulator is also designed to respond to interrupt requests.

The microprograms used to emulate 8080 instructions range in length from one to nine microinstructions. Consider, for instance, the design of the microprogram MOVRR which executes 8080 instructions of the form MOV R_1,R_2 specifying the 8-bit register-to-register data transfer $R_1 \leftarrow R_2$. The register addresses R_1 and R_2 are contained in 3-bit fields in the instruction opcode. The register allocation of Table III has been chosen so that the opcode address fields can be sent directly to the A and B address ports of the 2901 processor array. These register addresses are sent unchanged to the left 8-bit processor, whereas the least significant bit is complemented before sending the same address to the right 8-bit processor. The only available data transfer path from one processor register to another is through the ALU. We must therefore define the ALU command fields so that the ALU in each 8-bit processor passes data from the A output data port of the RAM back to the B input data port without altering it. This can be done in several ways, for example, by the 2901 command

$$I_D, I_F, I_S = 010, 011, 100$$

As can be verified from Table II, this command performs the dummy OR operation $B \leftarrow 0 \vee A$ which accomplishes the desired data transfer. Besides setting the I, A and B address fields as indicated above, MOVRR must also set the unused microinstruction fields to inactive values. Finally, MOVRR must check to see if there is an active DMA request from an external device; if there is, control must be transferred to a microprogram designed to handle such requests. If no unusual condition is pending, control is transferred back to FETCH. The design of the AMD Emulator allows all the operations of MOVRR to be included in a single microinstruction; thus three microinstructions are required to implement a MOV R_1,R_2 instruction cycle: two FETCH microinstructions and the MOVRR microinstruction.

3.3 3000-based Emulator

The Signetics Emulator [Lau 1978; Signetics 1977] is a commercial product based on the 3002 2-bit processor slice and 3001 microprogram sequencer. It has many similarities to the AMD Emulator, so discussion here will be confined to its distinctive features.

Figure 14 shows the organization of the E-unit of the Signetics Emulator. Like the AMD Emulator, the Signetics E-unit contains a pair of 8-bit bit-sliced processors which can operate independently, or

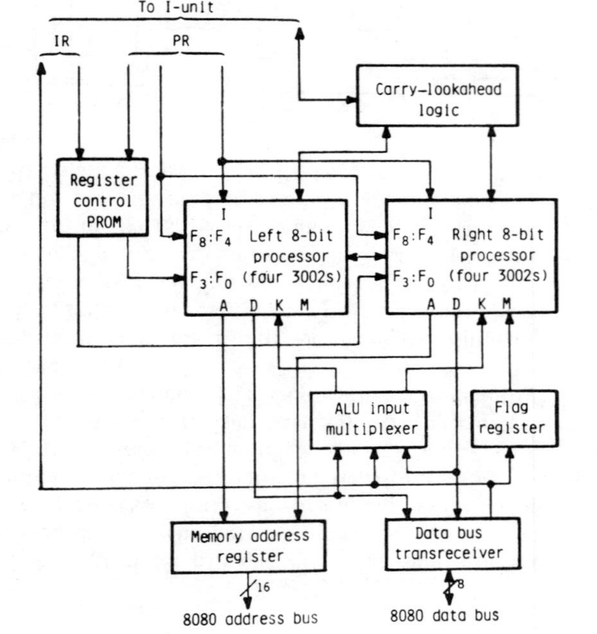

Fig. 14. E-unit of the Signetics 8080 Emulator

can be coupled to form a 16-bit processor. The 8080 registers are assigned to the 3002 registers in a manner that closely matches the register layout used in the 8080 chip; only the 8080 accumulator A is duplicated in the left and right 8-bit processor. Each 8-bit processor employs a separate carry-lookahead circuit. A third carry-lookahead generator is used to produce a carry output for 16-bit operations.

The Signetics Emulator takes advantage of the relatively large number of IO ports in the 3002 processor by using several independent data buses to connect the processor to the outside world. The A buses of all slices are combined to yield a 16-bit main memory address bus. The output D buses of each 8-bit processor are routed to the (bidirectional) 8080 data bus. Input data from the 8080 data bus is sent to the left and right processors via their K buses. This is an unconventional use of the K bus which allows data to be routed to any 3002 register. The M bus is used to connect the 8080 flag register to the right 8-bit processor as Fig. 14 indicates. The I-bus is used as a mask source, a role normally filled by the K bus.

As in the AMD Emulator, the processor commands, which here are applied to the 3002 F bus, are derived from microinstruction control fields stored in the microinstruction pipeline register PR and, in some cases, from the instruction opcode stored in the instruction register IR. A PROM called the register control PROM is used to map the relevant microinstruction and opcode information into the 3002 command formats. Note that the register allocation of the AMD Emulator eliminates the need for this PROM.

The I-unit of the Signetics Emulator is similar to the AMD I-unit appearing in Fig. 12. A single 3001 chip forms the microprogram sequencer in place of the three 2909s. A 48-bit microinstruction format is used, which results in a 512×48 control memory. The microinstruction format contains 25 fields. More complex coding is used within the control fields than in the AMD Emulator [for details see Signetics 1977]. Pipelining is used in the same way in both the AMD and the Signetics Emulators to allow the fetching and execution of microinstructions to be overlapped. In the Signetics machine the pipelining concept is extended to the instruction level, so that during the execution of one instruction, the next can be fetched from main memory.

To illustrate microprogramming in the Signetics Emulator, consider the 8080 instruction MOV R_1,R_2 which was used as an example earlier. Four microinstructions specify the complete instruction cycle. The first microinstruction transfers the address of the MOV R_1,R_2 instruction to the main memory address register shown in Fig. 14 and initiates a memory read. It then transfers the incoming instruction to the instruction register IR. The second microinstruction uses the opcode and the mapping PROM to determine the address of the first of two microinstructions which execute the move operation. It also increments the addresses in the memory address registers and the program counter PC. The third microinstruction transfers the contents of the source register R_2 to the 3002 accumulator AC in the appropriate (left or right) processor. The fourth microinstruction completes the instruction execution by transferring the contents of AC to the destination register R_1 via the external D bus. If R_1 is A, the 8080 accumulator, the final transfer is made to the A registers in both the left and right processors.

During the final microinstruction cycle of every instruction cycle, a main memory fetch operation can be carried out, thus overlapping instruction fetch and execution. Note that if the instruction being executed results in a branch to a new instruction address, the prefetched instruction cannot be used; and the instruction address pipeline comprising PC, the 3002 array's internal memory address register, and the external memory address register must all be reloaded.

3.4 Evaluation

The AMD and Signetics Emulators are broadly similar in overall design philosophy and complexity. Each uses about 60 ICs to model an 8080 CPU, and about 350 microinstructions to emulate the 8080 instruction set. A conventional microprogram control unit with overlapped microinstruction fetch and execute is used in both cases. Both E-units contain 16-bit bit-sliced processors which can also be used as parallel 8-bit processors. The ability to dynamically reconfigure the E-unit for 8-bit or 16-bit operations allows fast processing of both the 8-bit data and 16-bit address operations required by 8080 instructions. While adequate performance data is not available for either machine, it appears that the Signetics design uses, on the average, slightly fewer machine cycles per 8080 instruction than the AMD Emulator. This is not surprising in view of the fact that the AMD Emulator was designed for demonstration purposes only. It is likely that if it were designed to maximize processing speed, it would run at least as fast as the Signetics Emulator. The main architectural feature of the Signetics machine not found in the AMD design is the overlapping (pipelining) of instruction fetch and execute.

The two emulators demonstrate many of the strengths and weaknesses of the bit-slice families used in their design. The command formats of the 2901 are simpler and more flexible than those of the 3002. This enables the AMD Emulator to obtain control signals directly from the 8080 opcodes, whereas in the Signetics design, a (mapping) PROM is used. However, the AMD design uses a more complex scheme for allocating 8080 registers to the registers in its bit-sliced processor. The 3002 processor arrays contain twice as many slices as the corresponding 2901 arrays, which results in higher signal propagation delays through the 3002 arrays. This problem is partly overcome by the use of carry lookahead. Of course, carry-lookahead circuits would also speed up the 2901-based processors in the AMD Emulator. The 2901 has the advantage of a dual-ported RAM which allows instructions such as MOV R_1,R_2 to be executed by a single microinstruction in the AMD Emulator. The 3002 has a single-port RAM resulting in the need for two microinstructions to execute MOV R_1,R_2. Other 8080 instructions, however, benefit from the larger number of independent IO buses connected to the 3002.

4. DESIGN ISSUES

Bit-sliced computers share most of the design problems associated with computers that are built from LSI modules. These problems include (1) deciding which functions to implement in hardware and which to implement in software, (2) specifying the detailed hardware and software designs, (3) debugging the resulting system, and (4) devising appropriate testing and maintenance procedures. Bit-sliced systems also have some special design problems resulting primarily from their use of microprogrammed control. The specification of microinstruction formats and the writing of microprograms entails an enormous amount of detail, which requires efficient management of the design process. The most widely used specification media are microassembly languages which are analogous to the assembly languages used at the instruction level. The characteristics of microassembly languages for bit-sliced computers are discussed in this section.

As the level of integration of the design components increases, so does the difficulty of testing both the individual components and complete systems. This is due to the vast number of possible physical failure modes, as well as the difficulty of gaining access to the internal components of IC chips. Traditional fault models and test pattern generation methods, which treat elementary circuit components (gates) and interconnecting lines on an individual basis, are no longer applicable to such systems [Breuer and Friedman 1976]. Here we show that the structural regularity of bit-sliced systems has some special advantages which greatly simplify the LSI testing problem.

4.1 Microassembly Languages

The main advantages of assembly languages compared to machine languages lie in their use of symbolic names for operations and data. The assembly languages used at the microinstruction level, which are usually called *microassembly languages*, differ in several respects from those used at the instruction level. First, a much larger number of fields must be specified in each (micro-) instruction statement. Second, the format of the microinstruction and the symbolic names used in control fields must be specified by the user. The cost of writing microprograms is higher than that of writing most forms of software, hence it is important to have powerful, easily understood, and well-supported microprogramming languages.

A number of microassembly languages and supporting software have been developed specifically for the design of bit-sliced computers [Powers and Hernandez 1978]. Most are intended for use with specific bit-slice families. The translators (microassemblers) for the languages in question are usually written in high-level programming languages such as FORTRAN or PL/1, and so may be used with many host computers.

Most microassembly systems require that microprogram specifications be written in two major parts: a *definition part* which specifies the microinstruction formats and the symbolic names to be used, and an *assembly part* which specifies the microinstructions using the previously defined formats. The complete description is then translated by a microassembler which produces executable code in a form that can be loaded directly into the control memory of the target machine. We now outline some of the main features of a typical and widely used microassembly language AMDASM, intended primarily for use with 2900-based systems [Advanced Micro Devices 1978].

Input to the AMDASM microassembler consists of a definition part and an assembly part. In the definition part, the designer specifies the microinstruction length, and the positions and lengths of its internal fields. Symbolic names may be given to the microinstruction fields (field names), and also to the values (value names) that can be assigned to the fields. In general, a mnemonic name may be given to any desired field or group of fields. Different field names can also define the same fields, so that AMDASM allows field specifications to overlap.

An AMDASM definition statement partitions the microinstruction word into regions of several types:

1. Don't care regions denoted by X whose values are left undefined.
2. Fields with fixed numeric values which may be specified in the definition itself using the standard binary (B), octal (Q), decimal (D), and hexadecimal (H) codes.
3. Fields with variable values which are specified only when the item being defined is invoked during the assembly phase. Default values indicated by # may be included in the definition statement.

To illustrate AMDASM field definitions, consider the 56-bit microinstruction format appearing in Fig. 4. Suppose that it is desired to be able to specify the 2901 ALU function field I_F consisting of bits 5:3 using the field name FUNCT. Furthermore, suppose that we require that FUNCT always assign the constant value 1110 to bits 21:18. Let 001 be the desired default value for the 3-bit I_F field. This information is all included in the following definition (DEF) statement for FUNCT:

```
FUNCT: DEF 34X, B#1110, 12X, 3VQ#1, 3X.
```

Here 34X indicates that the leftmost 34 bits of the microinstruction are unspecified. The next four bits are assigned the fixed binary pattern 1110. The I_F field is declared to be a 3-bit variable field (3V) with the octal (Q) default value of 1. Whenever FUNCT is invoked, this default value is used unless an alternative value is supplied as a parameter of FUNCT. The possible values of the I_F variable field may be assigned mnemonic names in the definition phase using the EQU statement; for example:

```
 PLUS:   EQU  Q#0
MINUS:   EQU  Q#2
```

Careful choices of field groupings and field names greatly enhance the readability of the subsequent programs.

The assembly part of an AMDASM description consists of a sequence of microprograms, each containing one or more microinstructions. A microprogram is assigned a symbolic name which also serves as the (symbolic) start address of the microprogram. Each microinstruction consists of a list of field names, including any required variable field parameters, separated by the symbol &. During the assembly process, the individual fields are combined or "overlaid" to yield a complete specification of every bit in the microinstruction. Note that each bit position must be assigned either the same value or else a don't care value by every field name. (Conflicts occurring in bit specifications are automatically detected and reported by the AMDASM assembler.)

Returning to the previous example, suppose that we have the definition statement

XX: DEF 50D#0, 3X, 3Q#7

We can now define a microinstruction called ADD by overlaying FUNCT and XX thus

ADD: FUNCT PLUS & XX

Here the PLUS parameter is being substituted into the FUNCT variable field. The result is overlaid with XX yielding the following 56-bit pattern:

00000000000000000000000000000000011100000000000000010111

4.2 Testability Considerations

Conventional approaches to test pattern generation for LSI devices like microprocessors usually employ heuristic methods. These methods often lead to very large test sets, for example, over 12,000 test patterns in the case of the 2901 4-bit processor slice [McCaskill 1977]. The ability of heuristic tests of this kind to detect or locate faults, i.e., their fault coverage, is very hard to estimate. However, bit-sliced devices are also amenable to non-heuristic analytic testing approaches [Sridhar and Hayes 1979]. The short word sizes of most processor slices permit the use of powerful functional fault models. These in turn make it possible to generate test sets of near-minimal size whose fault coverage can be precisely determined. Furthermore, the regular array structure of bit-sliced systems can be exploited to obtain tests for the entire array directly from the tests for a single slice. This interconnection regularity can also be used to advantage in the design of self-testing systems [Forbes et al. 1965; Levitt et al. 1968; Ciompi and Simoncini 1977; Wakerly 1978; Sridhar and Hayes 1981].

Figure 15 shows a model C of a general-purpose processor slice developed for the study of fault diagnosis in bit-sliced systems [Sridhar and Hayes 1979]. It differs from current commercial processor slices primarily in the fact that its word size is just one bit. (Note, however, that 1-bit non-bit-sliced microprocessors such as the Motorola 14500 are commercially available [Motorola 1977].) As we will see later, test data for a one-bit slice of this kind can readily be extended to larger slices. The overall structure of C is very similar to that of the 2901 processor appearing in Fig. 5. Table IV lists the functions of the command lines of C, which are essentially the same as those of the 2901; cf. Table II. Two working registers A and T are used; in this respect C

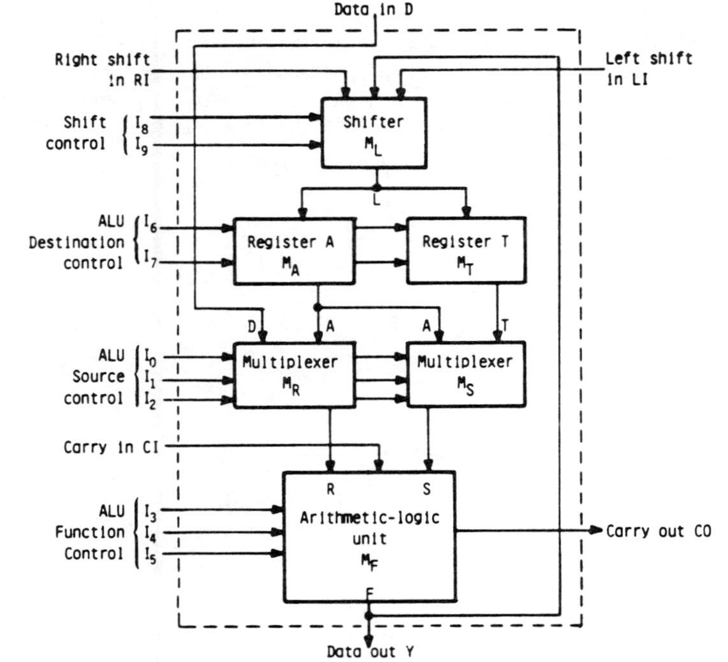

Fig. 15. An easily-testable 1-bit processor slice C

resembles the 74S481. Only ripple-carry propagation is allowed since external carry-lookahead circuits destroy the 1-dimensional array structure of bit-sliced systems, which plays an important role in their testing. It is interesting to note that in the bit-sliced VLSI chip that forms the E-unit of the OM-2, an experimental 16-bit microcomputer, ripple carry is also preferred to carry lookahead [Mead and Conway 1980]. The OM-2 designers observe that carry lookahead circuits would greatly increase circuit complexity without much gain in performance.

As illustrated by Fig. 15, C is viewed as a network of a small number of register-level modules such as multiplexers, registers and a combinational ALU. The internal structure of the modules is not of interest; indeed, such information is normally unavailable to the system designer. A fault model based on the functions performed by the modules is defined as follows. Let M be any combinational or synchronous sequential logic module in C. Let z denote the function realized by M, and let s be the number of internal states of M; $s = 1$

Table IV

Definition of the Command Lines I of C

I_2	I_1	I_0	R	S
0	0	0	0	A
0	0	1	0	T
0	1	0	D	A
0	1	1	D	T
1	0	0	A	A
1	0	1	A	T
1	1	0	D	0
1	1	1	A	0

ALU source control

Fcn.	I_5	I_4	I_3	F output
f_0	0	0	0	$R+S$
f_1	0	0	1	$S-R$
f_2	0	1	0	$R-S$
f_3	0	1	1	$R \vee S$
f_4	1	0	0	$R \wedge S$
f_5	1	0	1	$\bar{R} \wedge S$
f_6	1	1	0	$R \oplus S$
f_7	1	1	1	$\overline{R \oplus S}$

ALU function control

I_7	I_6	Function
0	0	$A \leftarrow L$
0	1	$T \leftarrow L$
1	0	$A,T \leftarrow L$
1	1	not used

ALU destination control

I_9	I_8	L output
0	0	F
0	1	RI
1	0	LI
1	1	not used

Shift control

if M is combinational. A malfunction F of M is called a *(functional) fault* of M if F permanently changes M to a module M^F realizing z^F, where $z \neq z^F$ and the number of states s^F of M^F is not greater than s. It is assumed that at most one module in C is faulty at any time.

Next we consider the task of generating a test sequence T_C for all functional faults in C. Let T_i be a test that detects all functional faults in an isolated module M_i. If M_i is combinational, then it is necessary and sufficient for T_i to be the set of all 2^n inputs to the module, where n is the number of distinct input lines of M_i. If M_i is a sequential circuit, then the checking sequence approach is used in constructing the test T_i [Breuer and Friedman 1976]. This approach has been shown to yield test sequences of minimal or near-minimal length in the case of the small sequential modules considered here. When M_i is a component of C, faults in M_i are detected by a test T_i^*, which when applied to the primary inputs of C causes T_i to be applied to M_i, and causes the responses of M_i to be propagated to the observable outputs of C. Since at most one module is allowed to be faulty, a composite test T_C for the entire circuit is obtained by combining all the T_i^*, many of which contain common test patterns.

C contains six modules M_L, M_R, M_S, M_F, M_A and M_T as shown in Fig. 15. The modules M_L, M_R, M_S and M_F are combinational, while M_A and M_T contain (synchronous) sequential logic. Each of these modules has one or two output lines. The output signal of every module must be observed at one of the output lines Y or CO of C. For example, to test the shifter module M_L, which has five input lines, the test set T_L consisting of all $2^5 = 32$ 5-bit binary patterns must be applied to M_L. The responses of M_L to T_L can be propagated to the observable output Y by applying appropriate constant values to those inputs of C which are not also inputs of M_L. Figure 16 shows a suitable configuration of C for testing M_L. The output signal L of M_L

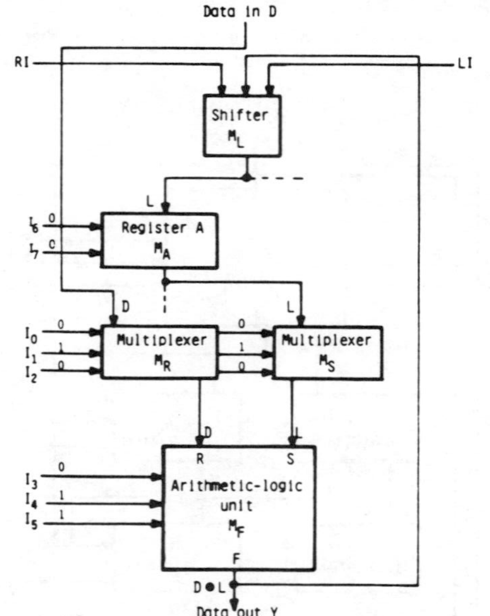

Fig. 16. Set-up of C for testing the shifter module M_L

is sent to the register M_A and thence to the right input port S of the ALU module M_F. The input data line D is applied to the left input port R of M_F. The control signals I_3, I_4 and I_5 of M_F are set to specify the EXCLUSIVE-OR function, resulting in the ALU output signal F $= D \oplus L$. Since F is connected to the primary output line Y of C, and D is a primary input of C, the output signal L of M_L has been made observable at Y. Furthermore, by means of D we can control the next value of F which is to be applied as an input signal to M_L. Thus T_L^* can easily be constructed to have the same number of test patterns as

T_L, namely 32. The ALU module M_F can be tested with 64 test patterns in much the same way as M_L. The multiplexers M_R and M_S require 32 tests, most of which can be combined with tests for the ALU. It is easily shown that at most 98 test patterns suffice for all four combinational modules of C.

The register modules M_A and M_T are assumed to be Moore-type sequential machines each with a state diagram of the type shown in Fig. 17. Clearly this diagram is Eulerian; i.e., there is a single path

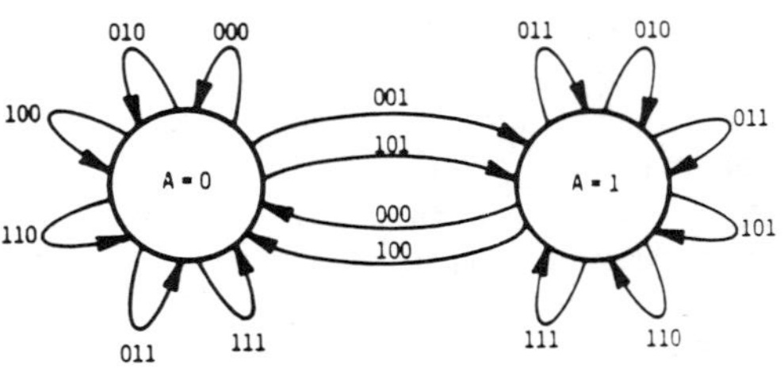

Fig. 17. State diagram for register module M_A with inputs I_7I_6L

passing through every transition of the state diagram exactly once. An Eulerian path that covers every transition exactly once corresponds to a minimum-length checking sequence that detects all functional faults in the register. This follows from the fact that the next state, which is also the register's output signal, can be made observable at the primary output Y of C by suitable selection of the ALU source and function control signals, as was done for M_L. The following easily-derived sequence of length 16 serves as an optimal test sequence T_A for register M_A.

Inputs of M_A	I_7:	0 0 1 1 1 0 1 1 1 0 0 0 0 1 0 1
	I_6:	0 1 1 1 0 1 0 1 1 0 0 1 0 0 1 0
	L:	0 0 0 1 1 1 1 0 1 0 1 0 1 0 1 0
Output (state)	A:	0 0 0 0 0 1 1 1 1 1 0 1 1 1 0 0 0

The corresponding optimal test sequence T_A^* is also readily constructed. The test sequences T_A^* and T_T^*, being essentially the same, can be merged into a single sequence T_{AT}^* of length 16 which tests the sequential part of C. Thus the entire processor C can be tested by a sequence T_C containing 98 + 16 = 114 test patterns. Note that this is less than twice the minimum number of test patterns (64) required to test M_F alone.

N copies of C can be cascaded as in Fig. 2b to form an *N*-bit processor array $C_0, C_1, \ldots, C_{N-1}$. Figure 18 shows the layout of an integrated circuit chip that implements a 4-bit version of this processor array using NMOS technology. The chip was designed by T. Sridhar and the author using the Caltech/Xerox VLSI design software [Mead and Conway 1980]. In order to test an array of this type, it is necessary to apply the test sequence T_C to each slice C_j in the array

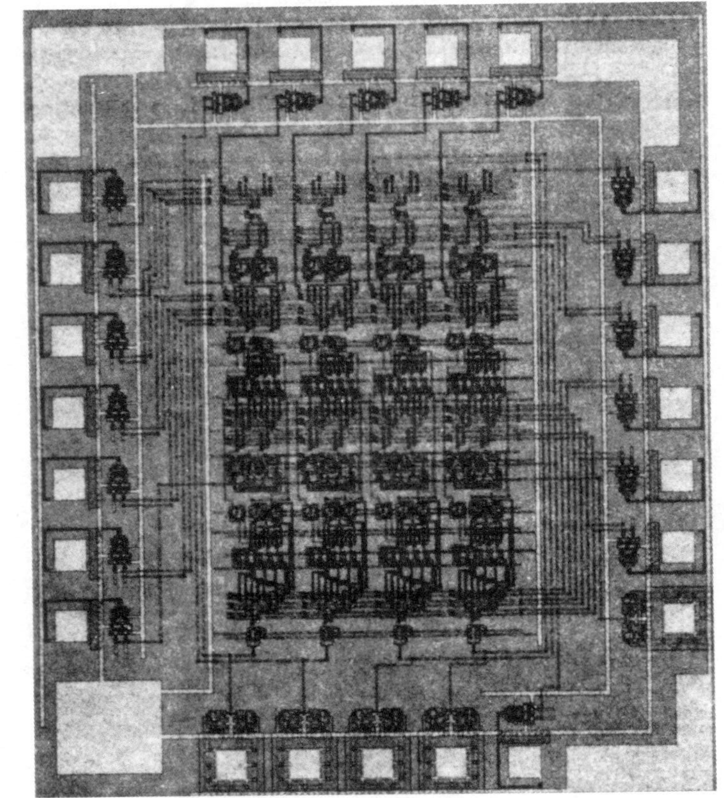

Fig. 18. Layout of an IC chip containing a 4-bit processor composed of four copies of C

irrespective of its position. In addition, the responses of C_j to T_C must be propagated to the observable outputs of the array, which comprise the lines $Y_0{:}Y_{N-1}$ and the array carry out line. Most of the tests of the form T_i^* for a module M_i in C can be applied simultaneously to every copy of C in the array since they do not affect the interslice shift and carry lines. Certain test patterns involving the shift and carry lines cannot be applied simultaneously to every slice; for instance, a test that results in CI≠CO. It can be shown [Sridhar and Hayes 1979] that such cases can be covered by applying one type of test pattern to even-numbered slices, and another to odd-numbered slices. These test patterns can be so ordered that the entire array is completely tested using the same number of tests as used for C alone. Moreoever, the tests for the array are easily computed from the tests T_C for C. Consequently, testing a bit-sliced array of arbitrary length constructed from C is only a little more difficult than testing C itself, and the testing time is constant.

The 1-bit slice C of Fig. 15 can be extended to more closely resemble commercial bit slices without destroying its desirable testing properties. For example, Fig. 19 shows a slice C^k which is a k-bit version of the original 1-bit slice C. In expanding the word size from one to k, a straightforward replication technique is used; in most cases a module M_i from C is replaced by k copies of M_i in C^k. For example, the multiplexer module M_R of C is replicated k times to form the k multiplexer modules $M_{R_0}, M_{R_1}, \ldots, M_{R_{k-1}} = M_{R_0}:M_{R_{k-1}}$ of C^k. The module M_{R_i} operates on the ith bit of the k-bit word obtained from the direct input bus $D_0:D_{k-1}$, and the corresponding ith bit obtained from the registers $M_{A_0}:M_{A_{k-1}}$. The same technique is used to expand the modules M_L, M_A, M_T and M_S. The ALU module M_F, however, has been retained as a single module operating on the k-bit operands $R_0:R_{k-1}$ and $S_0:S_{k-1}$. This permits the use of any fast carry propagation scheme such as carry lookahead within C^k. The analysis applied earlier to C can also be used to derive a complete test set T_{C^k} for C^k. The k-bit combinational ALU module requires 2^{2k+4} test patterns, but the other modules require roughly the same tests needed for the corresponding modules in C. It can be shown that C^k, and any array formed from C^k, can be completely tested with no more than 2^{2k+4} + 80 test patterns.

Bit-sliced systems of the foregoing type have the very desirable properties that (1) comprehensive test sets are easy to compute, and (2) test generation complexity is, at least to a first approximation, independent of word size. Thus the fundamental property of bit-sliced systems that their functional behavior is independent of word size can also be extended into the realm of test generation. It should be noted, of course, that commerical processor slices are often more complex than C or C^k and their test generation problems are correspondingly more difficult. The significance of the C and C^k models is that they demonstrate that bit slicing can be used to build realistic processors that are far easier to test than equivalent non-bit-sliced processors.

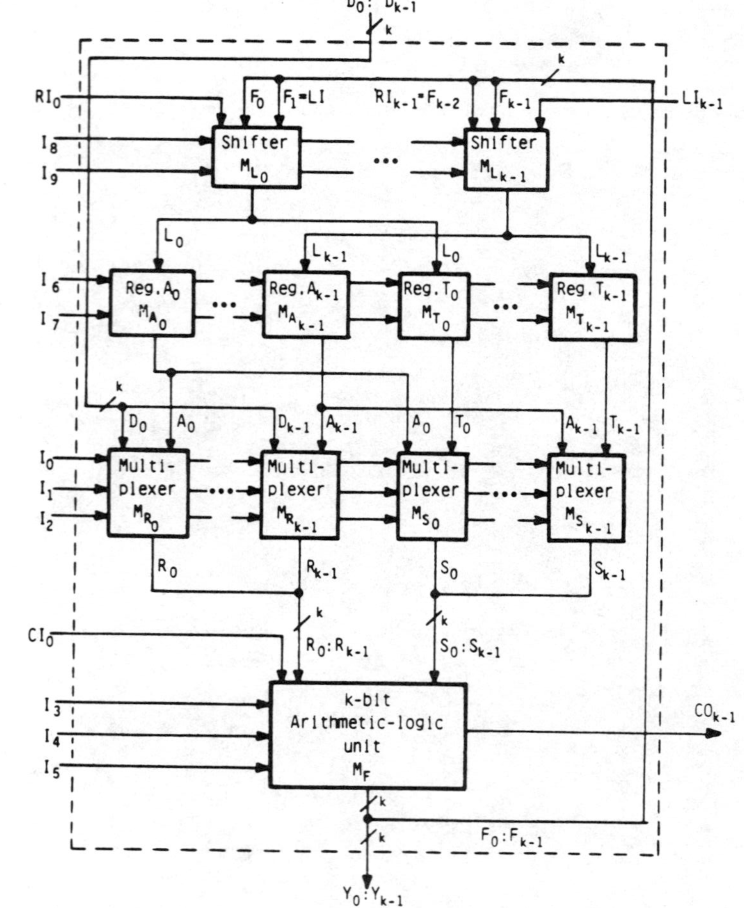

Fig. 19. A k-bit processor slice C^k derived from C

It is well-known that microprogrammable control greatly increases the ability of a computer to test itself. Several reasons may be adduced for this.

1. Microprogramming allows a great deal of flexibility in the construction and application of test patterns. Special diagnostic microprograms can be written which exercise the CPU in ways that cannot be reproduced using hardwired control.
2. Test routines can be stored in the control memory of the CPU

and can be executed periodically in ways that interfere very little with normal data processing.

3. Testing performed at the microinstruction level can access components that are not directly accessible at the instruction level. This allows faults to be identified more quickly and precisely.

The existence of many separate processor slices in a bit-sliced computer can also be exploited to increase testability. These possibilities have been investigated by Ciompi and Simoncini [1977]. They have proposed a scheme in which the test responses of each slice in a bit-sliced array are transmitted to, and evaluated by, the two neighboring slices. This permits many processor faults to be isolated very quickly to one or two adjacent slices. Most current microprocessors would require some modification to make this design approach feasible.

The number of test patterns required by a bit-sliced processor composed of well-structured slices, like C, is relatively small. It is therefore feasible to store these patterns and their associated responses in a ROM in the processor's control unit. Explicit storage of the test responses can be eliminated by using check circuits to compare the responses of the individual slices [Sridhar and Hayes 1981]. The processor can be tested on-line by periodically applying the stored test patterns and checking the observed responses. The small size of the test set means that all tests can be applied to the bit-sliced processor very quickly, so that the test process interferes very little with its normal operation.

4.3 Status and Prospects

Bit-slice design modules are currently produced by many IC manufacturers. They are grouped into families characterized by a common circuit technology, usually bipolar. Processor word sizes range from two to eight bits, with four bits being most common. All bit-slice families use microprogrammable control units organized around a microprogram sequencer which may also be bit-sliced.

As design components, bit-slice modules are intermediate in complexity between MSI circuits and conventional 1-chip microprocessors. They allow systems to be designed with far fewer ICs than an MSI-based system. On the other hand, they involve more ICs than a design based on non-bit-sliced microprocessors. The complexity of the design process using bit slices is intermediate between designs using MSI and those using conventional microprocessors. Bit-slice modules are clearly the most desirable components available for designing microprogrammable computers.

Most current applications that employ bit-sliced systems do so primarily because of speed considerations. The speed advantages of bit-sliced families have several sources.

1. The use of high-speed bipolar IC technologies; most non-bit-sliced processors use slower MOS technologies.
2. The ability to optimize word size for the particular application.
3. The fact that functions can be implemented more efficiently in microcode than they can be at the instruction level.

The speed advantages that depend on circuit technology can be expected to diminish considerably as faster non-bit-sliced microprocessors using similar techniques become available.

Perhaps the most fundamental attribute of bit-sliced computers is their ability to process operands of different lengths in a uniform manner. This can simplify software design, since programs can be written that are independent of data length. Examples of this approach were seen in the 8080 emulator designs covered in Section III where the CPU sometimes acts as an 8-bit processor and sometimes as a 16-bit processor. We may thus attribute to bit-sliced processors the ability to vary word size dynamically with minimal hardware and software changes.

Most computer systems constructed to date using bit-slices have fairly conventional architectures. There is considerable potential, as yet largely unexplored, to exploit the unique features of bit slicing in designing unconventional systems that provide higher performance or reliability than can be achieved by other systems of comparable cost. Among the more interesting possibilities are systems capable of parallel processing, and self-testing systems.

5. ACKNOWLEDGEMENT

The author wishes to thank T. Sridhar for his comments on this paper.

6. REFERENCES

Adams, P.M. Microprogrammable microprocessor survey, Part I. *SIGMICRO Newsletter*, vol. 9, no. 1, pp. 23-49, March 1978; Part II, *ibid.*, no. 2, pp. 7-38, June 1978.

Adams, W.T. and Smith, S.M. How bit-slice families compare, Part I. *Electronics*, vol. 51, no. 16, pp. 91-98, Aug. 3, 1978; Part II, *ibid.*, no. 17, pp. 96-102, Aug. 17, 1978; Postscript, *ibid.*, no. 18, pp. 138-139, Aug. 30, 1978.

Advanced Micro Devices. *The Am2900 Family Data Book*. Sunnyvale, Calif., 1978.

Agrawala, A.K. and Rauscher, T.G. *Foundations of Microprogramming: Architecture, Software and Applications*. New York: Academic Press, 1976.

Alexandridis, N.A. Bit-sliced microprocessor architecture. *Computer*, vol. 11, no. 6, pp. 56-80, June 1978.

Breuer, M.A. and Friedman, A.D. *Diagnosis and Reliable Design of Digital Systems*. Rockville, Md.: Computer Science Press, 1976.

Carlstead, R.H. and Huston, R.E. Test techniques for ECL microprocessors. *Digest 1977 Semiconductor Test Symp.*, Cherry Hill, N.J., pp. 32-35, 1977.

Chu, P. ECL accelerates to new system speeds with high-density byte-slice parts. *Electronics*, vol. 52, no. 16, pp. 120-125, Aug. 2, 1979.

Ciompi, P. and Simoncini, L. Design of self-diagnosable minicomputers using bit-sliced microprocessors. *J. Design Autom. and Fault-Tolerant Computing*, vol. 1, pp. 363-375, Oct. 1977.

Coleman, V.; Economidis, M.W.; and Harmon, Jr., W.J. The next generation four-bit bipolar microprocessor slice—the Am2903. *Wescon 77 Conf. Record*. San Francisco, paper no. 16/4, Sept. 1977.

Forbes, R.E. et al. A self-diagnosable computer. *Proc. 1965 Fall Joint Computer Conf.*, pp. 1073-1086.

Hoff, Jr., M.E. Designing central processors with bipolar microcomputer components. *AFIPS Conf. Proc.*, vol. 44, pp. 55-62, Fall 1975.

Horton, R.L.; Coppersmith, L.; and Bergler, R.M. Make the most of bit-slice flexibility and design high-performance processors. *Electronic Design*, vol. 26, no. 21, pp. 226-235, Oct. 11, 1978.

Intel. *Intel 8080 Microcomputer System User's Manual*. Santa Clara, Calif., Sept. 1975.

Intel. *Series 3000 Reference Manual*. Santa Clara, Calif., 1976.

Langley, F.J. Small computer design using microprogramming and multifunction LSI arrays. *Computer Design*, vol. 9, no. 4, pp. 151-157, April 1970.

Lapidus, G. MOS/LSI launches the low-cost microprocessor. *IEEE Spectrum*, vol. 9, no. 11, pp. 33-40, Nov. 1972.

Lau, S.Y. Emulate your MOS microprocessor. *Electronic Design*, vol. 26, no. 8, pp. 74-81, April 12, 1978.

Levitt, K.N., et al. A study of the data commutation problems of a self-repairable multiprocessor. *Proc. 1968 Spring Joint Computer Conf.*, pp. 515-527.

Lowe, E.H. A 16-bit minicomputer for missile guidance and control applications. *Proc. 1977 Joint Automatic Control Conf.*, San Francisco, pp. 17-21, June 1977.

McCaskill, R. Wring out 4-bit μP slices with algorithmic pattern generation. *Electronic Design*, vol. 25, no. 4, pp. 74-77, May 10, 1977.

McWilliams, T.M.; Fuller, S.H.; and Sherwood, W.H. Using LSI processor bit-slices to build a PDP-11—a case study in microcomputer design. *AFIPS Conf. Proc.*, vol. 46, pp. 243-253, 1977.

Mead, C. and Conway, L. *Introduction to VLSI Systems*. Reading, Mass.: Addison-Wesley, 1980.

Mick, J.R. and Brick, J. *Bit-slice Microprocessor Design*. New York: McGraw-Hill, 1980.

Motorola. *M10800 High Performance MECL LSI Processor Family*. Phoenix, 1976.

Motorola. *MC14500B Industrial Control Unit Handbook*. Phoenix, 1977.

Myers, G.J. *Digital System Design with LSI Bit-Slice Logic*. New York: Wiley-Interscience, 1980.

National Semiconductor. *GPC/P Product Description*. Pub. no. 4200005B. Santa Clara, Calif., Oct. 1973.

National Semiconductor. *IMP: The Modular Concept for Microprocessors from 4 Bits to 16 Bits*. Santa Clara, Calif., 1975.

Ornstein, S.M.; Stucki, M.J.; and Clark, W.A. A functional description of macromodules. *AFIPS Conf. Proc.*, vol. 30, pp. 337-355, 1967.

Powers, V.M., and Hernandez, J.H. Microprogram assemblers for bit-sliced microprocessors. *Computer*, vol. 11, no.7, pp. 108-120, July 1978.

Rallapalli, K., and Verhofstadt, P. MACROLOGIC—versatile functional blocks for high performance digital systems. *AFIPS Conf. Proc.*, vol. 44, pp. 67-73, 1975.

Ramamoorthy, C.V., and Chang, L.C. System modeling and testing procedures for microdiagnostics. *IEEE Trans. Computers*, vol. C-21, pp. 1169-1183, Nov. 1972.

Rattner, J.; Cornet, J-C.; and Hoff, Jr., M.E. Bipolar LSI computing elements usher in a new era of digital design. *Electronics*, vol. 47, no. 18, pp. 89-96, Sept. 5, 1974.

Rauscher, T.G., and Adams, P.M. Microprogramming: a tutorial survey of recent developments. *IEEE Trans. Computers*, vol. C-29, pp. 2-20, Jan. 1980.

Reyling, Jr., G. LSI building blocks for parallel digital processors. *1973 IEEE Intercon Tech. Papers*, vol. 6, Paper no. 21/3, New York, March 1973.

Salisbury, A.B. *Microprogrammable Computer Architectures*. New York: Elsevier, 1976.

Schultz, G.W.; and Holt, R.M. MOS LSI minicomputer comes of age. *AFIPS Conf. Proc.*, vol. 41, pp. 1069-1080, 1972.

Shavit, M. *An Emulation of the Am9080A*. Advanced Micro Devices, Sunnyvale, Calif., 1978.

Shima, M.; and Faggin, F. In switching to n-MOS microprocessor gets a 2-microsecond cycle time. *Electronics*, vol. 47, no. 8, pp. 95-100, April 18, 1974.

Signetics. *Signetics 8080 Emulator Manual*, Sunnyvale, Calif., March 1977.

Sridhar, T., and Hayes, J.P. Testing bit-sliced microprocessors. *Digest Ninth Symp. Fault-Tolerant Computing*, Madison, Wisc., pp. 211-218, June 1979.

Sridhar, T., and Hayes, J.P. Self-testing bit-sliced microcomputers. *Digest Spring COMPCON 81*, San Francisco, pp. 312-316, February 1981.

Texas Instruments. *990 Computer Family Systems Handbook*. Manual no. 945250-9701, Austin, Oct. 1975.

Texas Instruments. *The Bipolar Microcomputer Components Data Book*. 2nd Ed., 1979.

Thurber, K.J.; and Wald, L.D. Associative and parallel processing. *Computing Surveys*, vol. 7, pp. 215-255, Dec. 1975.

Wakerly, J. *Error-Detecting Codes, Self-Checking Circuits and Applications*. New York: North-Holland, 1978.

Walker, R. Applications of bit-slice MPUs. *1976 WESCON Professional Program*, Los Angeles, Paper no. 26/3, September 1976.

Wolfe, C.E. Bit-slice processors come to mainframe design. *Electronics*, vol. 53, no. 5, pp. 118-123, Feb. 28, 1980.

Wyland, D.C. Design your own computer by using bipolar/LSI processor slices. *Electronic Design*, vol. 23, no. 20, pp. 72-78, Sept. 27, 1975.

Part VI
System Issues

APART from the processor itself, the performance of a microprocessor-based system is dependent on the performance of the other system components (memory, peripherals, input–output devices), on the efficient interconnection and interfacing of various system resources, and especially on the software used to control the operations of the subsystems. In previous parts of this book, the emphasis was on the processor alone. Now, we look at other components of the system.

Concurrent with the development of basic processors, manufacturers have developed sophisticated chips for auxiliary functions—memory management, control of DMA operations, control of peripherals, bus management and arbitration, control of communications, and control of input and output functions. However, a particular chip of this kind is designed to support only a particular family of microprocessor chips of a particular vendor. Exhaustive lists of chips are published annually in several trade magazines. Usually there is a time lag between the introduction of the processor chip itself and the introduction of support chips. This results in extra effort in implementing systems based on recently introduced microprocessors.

In order to take over applications previously handled by minicomputers and mainframes, users demand that microprocessor-based systems offer high throughput, ease of use, and friendliness of system. To optimize utilization of resources and to minimize user effort, an *operating system* is used. It is used for some or all of the following functions:

1) Processor allocation management
2) Memory management
3) Peripheral management
4) File management
5) User-oriented facilities like command-line interpreter
6) Miscellaneous features to support networking, utilities, and high-level languages.

In order to fully comprehend the emerging trends in microcomputer software, it is relevant to know a little about the history of the popular operating systems.

The earliest uses of microprocessors were in embedded control applications. Programs were written on mainframe computers, cross-assembled for the micro, and loaded as object code into the micro's memory for execution. To aid in the writing of such control programs, in 1972 Intel Corporation hired MAA (Microcomputer Applications Associates, later to become Digital Research) to design and implement a systems programming language. This language, called PL/M (Programming Language for Microcomputers) used ideas from PL/I, Algol, and XPL, the computer-writing language. PL/M became quite popular and is still used.

Along with PL/M, MAA proposed a small operating system, called CP/M (Control Program for Microcomputers), to enable applications to be written and compiled on the Intel 8080-based microcomputer. As Intel was reluctant, MAA developed the product independently in 1974. CP/M subsequently became the most popular operating system for microcomputers; now there are 200 000 installations using 3000 different hardware configurations. It has become a de facto standard, judging by the fact that vendors in both the U.S. and abroad support it on their 8-bit and 16-bit microprocessors. CP/M dominates the single-user environment.

UNIX, developed during the seventies at Bell Laboratories, is the premier example of an operating system optimized for program development by professional programmers in a multiuser interactive environment. The popularity of UNIX can be judged by the vast number of look-alike operating systems, such as: Coherent and Xenix on the 8086; Zeus, Onix, and Xenix on the Z-8000; Uniflex, Idris, Coherent, and Xenix on the 68000; Cromix, UNIX, and Idris on the Z-80; and Idris, Xenix, and Coherent on LSI-11 and PDP-11 systems.

According to Kenneth Thompson, the principal architect of the UNIX operating system, "the UNIX kernel consists of about 10 000 lines of C code and about 1000 lines of assembly code. The assembly code can be further broken down into 200 lines included for the sake of efficiency (they could have been written in C) and 800 lines to perform hardware functions not possible in C. The code represents 5 to 10 percent of what has been lumped into the broad expression 'the UNIX operating system.' The kernel is the only UNIX code that cannot be substituted by the user to his own liking" [1]. Some companies like Microsoft have adapted this hardware-dependent code for several microprocessors. Others, like Mark Williams Company, have chosen to rewrite the entire code based on the UNIX design.

Inspired by UNIX, Digital Research, the originator of CP/M, has developed the MP/M operating system. Similar to UNIX, MP/M is a multitasking operating system. But unlike UNIX, MP/M has a real-time kernel that can be either interrupt-driven or dependent upon device polling. Also, MP/M uses multilevel directories rather than the tree structure provided by UNIX, thus enabling records to be automatically locked for greater safety and convenience. In the UNIX environment, a fast disk file is used as a buffer to communicate between two processes. Such "pipes" are opened and closed as standard files, but are limited to character I/O only. MP/M permits variably sized messages to be written to and to be read from an unlimited number of processes, through buffers maintained in the memory. Each such "queue" has a name and is treated like other disk files. Furthermore, queues can be optimized for message sizes. UNIX, on the other hand, offers a large array of excellent system development tools and the ability to link utilities through a single command.

The advent of personal computers has resulted in a growing popularity of the MS-DOS operating system developed by Microsoft. This operating system is supported on many leading computers of the U.S. and Japan. Unfortunately, in all of these cases, even though the same operating system is supported on several operating systems, the differences in hardware generally make it essential to modify application programs to execute under the same operating system on different systems.

New techniques are evolving that enable such differences to be transparent to end-users. For example, the UCSD p-system, originally developed by the University of California at San Diego, permits maximum level of software portability through use of intermediate code, called p-code, into which all its high-level languages are compiled. When a new processor is introduced, the p-system is implemented simply by writing an interpreter that translates p-code into the new processor's native code. The penalty is in terms of reduced execution speed of interpreted code. The advantage is in terms of ability to execute the same program under different environments like 8086, Z8000, 68000, TI 9900, and others. As microprocessors offer increased speeds, and as programming costs continue to escalate, it is likely that more users will accept the penalty of reduced execution speeds and opt for using techniques of intermediate code to aid conversion of programs at the software compatibility level.

In the domain of large computer systems, Fortran and Cobol became industry standards by virtue of their availability on a large number of systems. This does not, however, imply that all vendors offered identical languages. The traditional problem of incompatible higher level languages has been carried over to the microprocessor area. Although Basic is supported on almost all systems, the different vendors offer significantly different versions, depending on word size, memory addressing, and other factors. Frequently, multiple versions of Basic are available for the same machine (for example, on Apple and IBM Personal Computers). The current trend in new operating systems is to support Pascal and ADA. These two languages are likely to dominate the scene in coming years.

Unlike during the early years of microprocessors when standalone applications dominated the scene, the need to transmit and receive data and programs is an important characteristic of current generation systems. Communication between microprocessor-based systems can be analyzed at different levels. The International Organization for Standardization has developed a reference model of open systems interconnection (OSI), comprised of seven layers as follows [2], [3]:

1) physical layer
2) data link layer
3) network layer
4) transport layer
5) session layer
6) presentation layer
7) application layer.

The *physical layer* deals with transmission of raw bit streams, and the electrical protocols. For example, RS 232 is a physical link protocol that specifies the required voltages, number of wires, and transmission speeds over a serial communication link. The *data link* layer deals with issues of converting unreliable transmission links into reliable ones by using techniques like checksums to validate information received over the line. Although virtually every leading vendor is proposing a somewhat different protocol, two protocols (carrier sense multiple access (CMSA/CD) and tokenpassing) currently dominate the consideration for standards embodied in the IEEE 802 specification. The *network layer* deals with conventions that govern the transmission of data messages over the communication highway, for example, X.25. The *transport layer* is used to shield the customer's portion of the network from the carrier's portion; thus, change in carrier should be transparent to the computers at the two ends of the link. The *session layer* deals with setting up, managing, and splitting down process-to-process connections. The *presentation layer* deals with transformations (like data compression) on the data to be transmitted. The *application layer* is at the discretion of the users and refers to the ability of application programs involved in communication to freely exchange data and programs. Although the goal is to enable efficient communication at the application level, this goal involves efficient communication at the other levels as well. Efficient communication, especially between dissimilar systems, is critically dependent on the protocols and standards for interconnection.

The first three articles in this Part focus on operating systems, languages, and related software issues. Contemporary microprocessors offer very sophisticated architectures, which need to be matched by good software to yield systems that offer high throughput, ease of use, and user-friendliness.

Schindler describes the current trends in the domain of microcomputer software. While CP/M is the dominant operating system for microprocessors, UNIX constitutes a serious rival. Unlike early operating systems, new products are designed to support several users concurrently and to carry out multiple tasks in parallel. The trend is towards multiuser multitasking operating systems.

Cramer describes the concept of multitasking operating systems for microprocessors. By definition, a multitasking operating system permits multiple programs or tasks to be active simultaneously. Such an operating system requires a carefully designed scheduler and resource manager; furthermore, it must provide for interprocess communication and synchronization.

In the third article, James presents an insight into a proposed standard for extending high-level languages for microprocessors. The motivation is to develop a minimal common set of language extensions that will address the greatest number of needs of microprocessor users. This would enable enhanced portability of software from one system to another.

The three papers on communication issues describe three different bus standards that have evolved after careful consideration by IEEE standardization committees. Boberg describes the IEEE 796 bus, which was originally initiated by Intel as its Multibus. Wright describes the IEEE 696.1 bus, which is an extension of the S-100 bus originally used in the first personal computer, the Altair 8800; the IEEE 696.1 is designed to support both 8-bit and 16-bit processors. Allison describes the 896 bus protocol, evolved internationally on a manufacturer- and processor-independent basis to support fully distributed control of 32-bit multiplexed address/data paths by up to 32 masters, via a single 34-pin connector; a fully compatible 96-pin configuration has also been specified to provide across-the-bus error detection and additional control capabilities. In view of the different widths of data paths and the investments made by vendors on designing equipment that is compatible with a particular bus standard only, it is likely that all of these different standards will co-exist for the near future. It is also pertinent to point out that these standards are not static, but evolve with enhancements and refinements [4].

The microprocessor world is dynamic in all respects. This is what makes it a revolution!

REFERENCES

[1] K. Thompson, *Bell Syst. Tech. J.*, vol. 57, part 2, p. 1931, July–Aug. 1978.

[2] H. Zimmerman, "OSI reference model—the ISO model of architecture for open systems interconnection," *IEEE Trans. Commun.*, vol. COM-28, pp. 425–432, Apr. 1980.

[3] A. S. Tanenbaum, "Network protocols," *ACM Comput. Surveys*, vol. 13, pp. 454–489, Dec. 1981.

[4] R. G. Stewart, "Notes, comments, and asides . . . and news of the final IEEE-696 draft," *IEEE Micro*, vol. 2, pp. 76–79, Nov. 1982.

BIBLIOGRAPHY

[1] "The latest in microcomputer operating systems," *Electron. Des.*, pp. SS46–SS64, Mar. 18, 1982.

[2] L. D. Adams, "Functional architecture: Optimizing a powerful system bus solution," in *Proc. Wescon 1981*, Session 27, Paper 4, pp. 1–9.

[3] T. Balph and J. Black, "Multiprocessing could bring out a system's best," *Electron. Des.*, pp. 219–224, Mar. 18, 1982.

[4] J. Black and J. Kister, "VERSA bus: A powerful structure for multiprocessing applications," in *Proc. Midcon 1981*, Session 25, Paper 6, pp. 1–6.

[5] P. L. Borrill, "Microprocessor bus structures and standards," *IEEE Micro*, vol. 1, pp. 84–95, Feb. 1981.

[6] W. C. Cummings, "STD bus: A standard for the '80s," in *Proc. Midcon 1981*, Session 25, Paper 1, pp. 1–11.

[7] R. Dilbeck and J. Barthmailer, "The multibus/IEEE P796 bus standard and microcomputer system architecture for the 80's," in *Proc. Midcon 1981*, Session 25, Paper 2, pp. 1–8.

[8] H. A. Freeman and K. J. Thurber, Eds., *Micromputer Networks—A tutorial* (IEEE Computer Society). New York: IEEE Press, 1981.

[9] R. Gilbert, "The general-purpose interface bus," *IEEE Micro*, vol. 2, pp. 41–51, Feb. 1982.

[10] M. Graube, "Local area nets: A pair of standards," *IEEE Spectrum*, pp. 60–64, June 1982.

[11] T. J. Harrison, "IEEE Project 802: Local area network standard," in *Proc. Electro 1982*, Session 17, Paper 1, pp. 1–11.

[12] R. C. Johnson, "Operating systems hold a full house of features for 16-bit microprocessors," *Electronics*, pp. 113–120, Mar. 24, 1982.

[13] S. P. Joshi, "Ethernet controller chip interfaces with variety of 16-bit processors," *Electron. Des.*, pp. 193–200, Oct. 14, 1982.

[14] G. Kotelly, "EDN's third annual μC operating systems directory," *EDN*, pp. 80–157, Sept. 15, 1982.

[15] C. Myers and G. Munsey, "A multiprocessor minicomputer designed for Unix," *Comput. Des.*, pp. 87–96, Feb. 1982.

[16] T. A. Rolander, "Microcomputer software meshes with local nets," *Electron. Des.*, pp. 96–99, Jan. 27, 1982.

[17] R. Ryan *et al.*, "Intel local network architecure," *IEEE Micro*, vol. 1, pp. 26–41, Nov. 1981.

[18] R. M. Schell, "Multi-user systems from advanced processor chips," *Comput. Des.*, pp. 149–158, Nov. 1982.

[19] M. Schindler, "Operating systems help micros act like minis," *Electron. Des.*, pp. SS41–SS45, Mar. 18, 1982.

[20] A. S. Tanenbaum, "Network protocols," *ACM Comput. Surveys*, vol. 13, pp. 453–489, Dec. 1981.

Operating systems help micros act like minis

The number of new microcomputer operating systems may have decreased, but the capabilities have grown, and even a few *de facto* standards are emerging.

Microcomputer operating systems are coming of age. For microcomputers to penetrate markets that used to belong to minicomputers, they must act like minis. The hardware is shifting relentlessly toward 16 bits, often with a 32-bit address space, and the operating system must support all the utilities that such systems need, both for handling numerous peripherals and complex applications programs.

Hence, though fewer new systems have come out since last year's survey (ELECTRONIC DESIGN, March 19, 1981, p. 179), they typically are more powerful than last year's entries (see table). For example, of the 32 new systems listed in the table entitled "The Latest in Microcomputer Operating Systems" (p. ss47), all but seven handle multitasking, nearly half can work with multiple CPUs or users or both, and a sizable majority (over 60%) are equipped for networking.

Supported languages provide additional insights into the growth of microcomputer operating systems. Basic, long the ruler of the microcomputer world, is fighting a losing battle with Pascal, the preferred language of professionals. Of the new systems tabulated, two-thirds offer Pascal, while Basic shows up in barely more than one-third of the releases (Fig. 1). Fortran's 40% share indicates that many of the new systems are aimed at engineers, while Cobol's 26% points to the continuing penetration of the small-business market.

The growth of both Fortran and Cobol support seems to have slowed down since last year, but primarily because of Pascal's tremendous gains. Since only a few of the operating systems listed last year were taken off the market, the language support for all systems listed in the tables has changed much less than it did last year (Fig. 2).

As the figure illustrates, Basic support is still offered in nearly two-thirds of the listed microcomputer operating systems, but both Pascal and Fortran are not far behind. Cobol has held its own, while the "Other languages" category has lost even more support than Basic. However, many uncommon languages, like Forth or Lisp, are available on computers that support the CP/M system, whose number has greatly increased since last year.

Max Schindler, Software Editor

Standard systems are gaining

In fact, Digital Research, the originator of CP/M, claims 200,000 installations on no fewer than 3000 different hardware configurations. Although CP/M has not fully shed its hobbyist image, the new 16-bit version, as well as the forthcoming CP/M 3.0 release, will finally establish CP/M as a well-documented and maintained *de facto* standard. Often-heard complaints about lacking user friendliness (e.g., cryptic file names, lack of feedback) hopefully will be alleviated.

The single-task CP/M system consists of a module (BIOS) that provides basic I/O access and is tailored to the CPU; a disk handler (BDOS) that finds, creates, accesses, deletes, and renames files; a console command processor; and an area for transient programs like compilers or other routines. All told, the system takes up less than 70 kbytes, most of which is needed in the transient area. A multitasking version, MP/M, is organized essentially the same way, but needs about

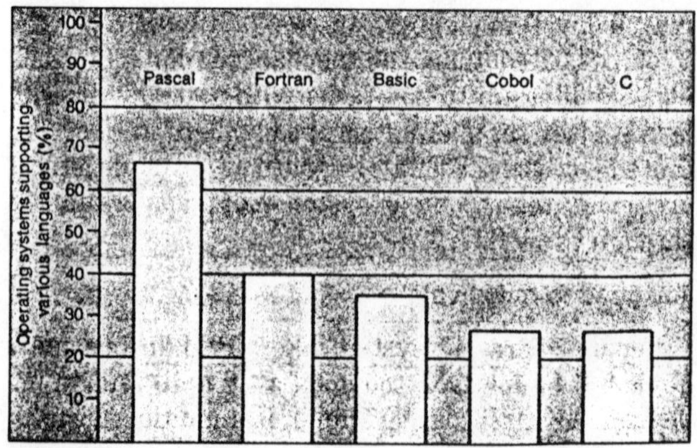

1. Among the languages supported by the new operating systems tabulated on p. ss 47, Pascal has a commanding lead. Riding the coattails of Unix popularity, C rivals Cobol, and lags Fortran and Basic by only a small margin.

Reprinted with permission from *Electron. Des.*, vol. 30, no. 6, pp. ss41–ss45, Mar. 18, 1982.

10 more kbytes of RAM (MP/M II will be discussed thoroughly in a future issue).

The evolution of a standard operating system, albeit an imperfect one, will have far-ranging consequences on the microprocessor industry. With IBM, Hewlett-Packard, and Xerox offering CP/M on their personal computers, writers of CP/M-compatible software are assured of a large market, and users of a huge selection of ready-to-run programs. Many of the 5000 programs in the *International Microcomputer Software Directory* will run under CP/M.[1] Digital Research's own catalog lists programs from over 300 sources.[2]

On the other hand, operating-system standards will encourage chip makers to tailor their products to fit the system, and—in the long run—to put at least some of the chip into firmware. The table of new operating systems provides some indications of the emerging firmware trend, notably Intel's 80130, which contains the kernel of the iRMX-86 operating system, and

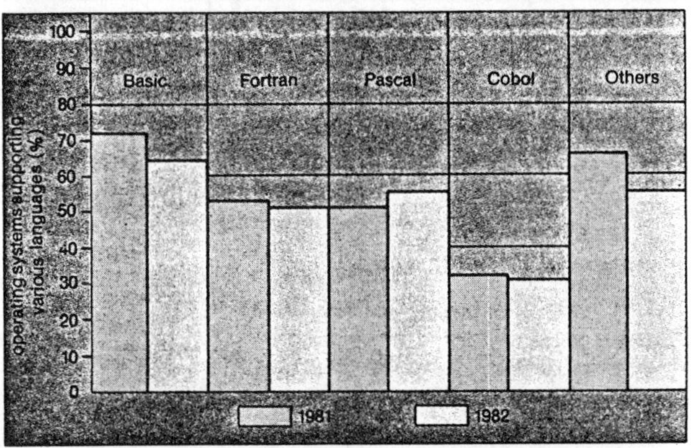

2. Compared with last year, today's operating systems support Basic less, Pascal more. The only other significant change is a drop in the "Other Languages" category, because more CP/M-supported languages were counted separately last year.

Hunter & Ready's VRTX real-time executives for the 8002, which competes with Zilog's own ZRTS/8000 plug-in system kernel. In two 2716 PROMs, the VRTX/8002 contains the mechanisms for multitasking, handling up to 256 tasks with as many priority levels. User-supplied interrupt handlers can be integrated via the Z8002's NPSA (new program status area) feature, as long as system-call traps are routed through the VRTX.

Too good to remain alone

For an operating system like CP/M to become a standard is, however, too good a thing to remain unchallenged. Oasis, for example, is a multiuser, multitasking operating system from Phase One Systems that can communicate with IBM mainframes and has already found many implementations; it will compete head-on with MP/M II. So will the USCD P-system from SofTech Microsystems, which has already blossomed into a complete software environment.

But the most formidable challenger comes not from the microcomputer world, but from the world that microcomputers are about to invade: industrial research laboratories and their powerful minis. Developed in the 1970s at Bell Laboratories (Murray Hill, N.J.) first for the GE 645 and then for the PDP-7, Unix is finally emerging as the prime contender for an operating-system standard that can satisfy the professional programmer.

Unix, for which the high-level implementation language C was developed, consists of a kernel and a shell. While the kernel is an excellent operating system in its own right, sporting features that are still superior after a decade in the field, it is the Unix shell that has made the system so popular. What in other systems would simply be a command interpreter has, in Unix, turned into a very-high-level language. At a time of huge projected programmer shortages, such a productivity tool appeals to most computer buyers.

The Unix shell lets the user string together whole sequences of programs, as if they were so many function calls. The output from one command can be directed into the input of another, as in

```
tr < name A-Z a-z | sort | uniq.
```

This command line translates all upper-case characters in a file to lower case, sorts them in alphabetical sequence, and then deletes multiple occurrences of the same lines. The vertical bars that separate commands are called pipes, and the shell programs (tr, sort, uniq) filters—typical of the often esoteric Unix nomenclature that has generated much criticism.

Since Western Electric Co. (Greensboro, N.C.), the distributor of Unix, gave the system freely to universities, but charged others a $20,000 license fee, Unix grew up in an academic environment, spawning an ever growing collection of software tools. Many of them have since been assembled in the Programmer's Workbench, and contribute in no small manner to Unix' popularity. In fact, many of them have moved into environments outside Unix—not an easy undertaking, since the Workbench, like Unix, is written in C. But Fortran and Pascal versions are in the making.

One of the first to seriously harness Unix for microcomputers was Microsoft, when it developed Xenix for the Z8000 (ELECTRONIC DESGN, Sept. 13, 1980, p. 19). But now, Unix-like operating systems are sprouting like mushrooms. Zilog's Zeus rules over that company's System 8000; TNIX is the heart of Tektronix' 8560 development system, whose Guide program helps coordinate software design by many users; Codata's Unisys powers the 68000-based CTW-300; the P/40 from Plexus (Santa Clara, Calif.) has been explicitly designed around Unix; and the list goes on.

Summary of existing operating systems

Company	Name	Applications: General-purpose	Development systems	Industrial control	Small-business	Comments or changes
Advanced Micro Computers (Santa Clara, Calif.)	CP/M	★	★			
Altos Computer Systems (San Jose, Calif.)	Amex				★	
American Microsystems Inc. (Santa Clara, Calif.)	Amix		★			No longer available
Apollo Computer Inc. (Billerica, Mass.)	Node OS	★				Addresses 3.5 Mbytes; disk capacity is 66 Mbytes, max.
Apple Computer Inc. (Cupertino, Calif.)	DOS 3.3	★			★	
	SOS 1.0		★	★		
Boston Systems Office (Waltham, Mass.)	UMDS-10,30	★	★			Universal cross assemblers
Central Data Corp. (Champaign, Ill.)	ZMOS	★			★	
CGRS Microtech Inc. (Langhorne, Pa.)	FDOS	★	★			
	PDOS	★			★	
Commercial Computer Inc. (Minneapolis, Minn.)	CP/M	★			★	Now R2E of America (see "The Latest in Microcomputer Operating Systems," p. 000)
Computer Automation Inc. (Irvine, Calif.)	Omega 4, 4 Plus	★	★	★	★	
	OS4	★	★	★	★	Also for lab automation and data processing
Control Systems Inc. (Kansas City, Kans.)	MT809, MT809-E			★		Also offers UCSD system, Unix
Convergent Technologies Inc. (Santa Clara, Calif.)	CTOS	★				
Cromemco Inc. (Mountain View, Calif.)	CDOS; Cromix	★				Cromix resembles Unix
Data General Corp. (Westboro, Mass.)	DOS	★	★		★	Peripherals: ASLM (4 disks deleted)
	RTOS	★		★		Now has Basic (ALM deleted)
	ICOS	★	★		★	For CS/10, 30, supports 4 users
Digital Equipment Corp. (Maynard, Mass.)	RT-11, RSX-11M	★	★			
	RSX-11S			★		
Digital Research Inc. (Pacific Grove, Calif.)	CP/NET 1.0	★	★	★	★	Works with CP/M and MP/M II
Digitek Inc. (Kenmore, Wash.)	DK/DOS	★		★		
Emulogic Inc. (Westwood, Mass.)	ECL-3211	★	★			
Heath Co. (Benton Harbor, Mich.)	HT-11	★	★		★	Now Zenith Data Systems, Glenview, Ill.
Hemenway Corp. (Boston, Mass.)	SP6800, SP/Z8000	★	★		★	Superseded by entries in "The Latest in Microcomputer Operating Systems"
Heurikon Corp. (Madison, Wis.)	CP/M 2.2 MP/M 1.1	★	★			
	M-DAQ	★	★			
	ZRAID-DAQ			★		Price changes, more disk support
Hewlett-Packard Co. (Palo Alto, Calif.)	64000 OS		★			Now $550, up to 960 Mbytes of disk, CRT editor
	RTEL, RTEXL	★		★		RTEXL also for development

Summary of existing operating systems

Company	Name	Applications: General-purpose	Development systems	Industrial control	Small-business	Comments or changes
Industrial Programming Inc. (Jericho, N.Y.)	MTOS series	★		★		4 systems for 8- and 16-bit microcomputers
InfoSoft Systems Inc. (Westport, Conn.)	I/OS, Multi-I/OS	★	★		★	Now 36 disk controllers, real-time applications, networking
Intel Corp. (Santa Clara, Calif.)	iRMX-80, iRMX-88	★		★		OEM license available
Ithaco Inc. (Ithaca, N.Y.)	TMS			★		Base price $4995. Has GPIB-3000
Language Resources Inc. (Boulder, Colo.)	RS-86		★			Uses IEEE-700 Pascal
Micromation (San Francisco, Calif.)	MP/M 2.0	★	★			Runs on Z80-based Mariner
Monolithic Systems Corp. (Englewood, Colo.)	MSOS	★				
Mostek Corp. (Carollton, Texas)	DT-ASMB-80		★			Discontinued
Motorola Inc., MOS Systems (Phoenix, Ariz.)	MDOS		★			
	RMS09	★				For Micromodules 17, 19, 19-A. Fast interrupts
National Semiconductor Corp. (Santa Clara, Calif.)	Starplex I DOS		★			Now supports Z80, line printer
Northern Telecom Inc. (Minneapolis, Minn.)	NT405 to 585	★			★	
North Star Computers Inc. (San Leandro, Calif.)	NS/HDOS	★				Now 59 to 72 Mbytes of mass storage
Ohio Scientific Inc. (Aurora, Ohio)	OS-65D, OS-Pascal	★		★	★	Also available for 1 to 8 small-business users, as OS-65U
Onyx Systems Inc. (San Jose, Calif.)	Onix	★	★	★	★	Unix-like. Also offers CP/M, UCSD operating systems
Percom Data Corp. (Garland, Texas)	OS-80	★			★	Size: 7 kbytes; mass storage: 0.8 Mbytes (4 floppies)
Phase One Systems Inc. (Oakland, Calif.)	Oasis	★	★			Z80-based systems, $500 (16-user system, $850)
Pro-Log Corp. (Monterey, Calif.)	MP4		★			
RCA Corp., Solid State Division (Somerville, N.J.)	CDOS	★	★			
Rockwell International Corp. (Anaheim, Calif.)	AIMOS	★	★	★		Both handle CRT terminals, parallel port
	OS3/65		★			
Smoke Signal Broadcasting (Westlake Village, Calif.)	DOS68, 69; BOS	★	★		★	BOS works with 6800 CPU
	OS-9, Flex-09	★		★	★	OS-09 comes in levels 1 and 2
Systems & Software Inc. (Downers Grove, Ill.)	REX80	★	★	★		$200. See "The Latest in Microcomputer Operating Systems" for new address
Whitesmiths Ltd. (New York, N.Y.)	Idris	★	★			Unix-like
Xycom Inc. (Saline, Mich.)	SPDS	★		★		
	Basic	★			★	

Of 16 recently introduced microcomputers costing $4000 or more (ELECTRONIC DESIGN, Jan. 21, 1982, p. 71), seven boast a Unix-like operating system.

The makings of another Pascal

Unix-like systems are proliferating wildly, spurred primarily by Western Electric's recent dramatic price cuts, which could reduce license fees to as little as $40, for a package that even includes the Programmers' Workbench. So, a question arises over whether a potential standard for high-end microcomputer operating systems is being nipped in the bud. Why, one might ask, are so many micro makers proudly hailing their Unix-like operating systems while few—if any—claim simply to run plain Unix?

As in the case of Pascal, a great tool has been discovered by the microcomputer industry, and—in true Pascal style—been found wanting. Having been developed by software designers for software designers and having grown uncontrolled in the fertile soil of academia, Unix suddenly finds itself in the limelight as a would-be product, which it was never meant to be.

Unix is powerful, versatile, and adaptable, but not user friendly: in the hands of a novice programmer, its power can turn destructive. Born in the days of sluggish printers, Unix was made to save time with capricious abbreviations and lack of user feedback. Without warning, a user can destroy a whole day's work, just by adding or omitting a blank space. No wonder Unix enhancements are beginning to rival those of Pascal in number.

The potential purchaser of a Unix-like operating system must weigh the benefits of specific enhancements against the loss of portability. Some systems are legitimate supersets of Western Electric's Version 7 or the more recent Unix System III; others are not. The would-be buyer may be well advised to join one of the many Unix user groups, for example Uni-Ops, which tries to serve as an umbrella organization (P.O. Box 5182, Walnut Creek, CA 94596, (415) 933-8564). Perhaps user organizations can persuade AT&T (which can no longer plead helplessness due to regulatory shackles) to design and enforce a standard before the task becomes unmanageable. □

References

1. *International Microcomputer Software Directory*, Imprint Editions Inc., Chadwell Heath, Romford, Essex, England, and Fort Collins, Colo., 1982.

2. *The CP/M Compatible Software Catalog*, Digital Research, Pacific Grove, Calif., 1982.

MULTITASKING OPERATING SYSTEMS FOR MICROPROCESSORS

Tom Cramer
Applications Engineer
Zilog, Components Division
10460 Bubb Road
Cupertino, California 95014

PREFACE

Microprocessors, because of their low cost, low power consumption, and small size, have caused an explosion in the number of innovative computer applications. Although there is a great deal of variation in microprocessor applications software, there is relatively little variation in the operating-system-level software from one application to the next. Nonetheless, operating system software, especially when multitasking is involved, can be very time consuming and expensive to develop.

The major microprocessor manufacturers have acknowledged the need for operating systems in microprocessor applications and are now supplying real-time multitasking operating system software that is adaptable to a wide variety of user systems. Use of this existing operating system software will decrease the number of redundant operating system development efforts, thus freeing programmers to work on more creative and productive problems.

INTRODUCTION

This paper discusses the basic terminology and concepts involved with multitasking operating systems. It is intended to provide a general understanding of the subject, so that the reader will be prepared to evaluate specific operating system software according to his or her needs.

OVERVIEW

An operating system is a collection of software that provides a convenient interface between applications software and computer hardware. The operating system and the application can be thought of as distinct **layers** of software. A well-structured operating system can also be broken down into layers as in Figure 1. At the heart or **kernel** of an operating system is software for scheduling and synchronizing programs. Most operating systems include resource management, device drivers, and a file system as the next layer above the kernel. Other programs that are often considered part of the operating system are editors, language translators, linkers, debuggers, diagnostics and security systems, but these programs are usually not part of the structure supporting the running applications software.

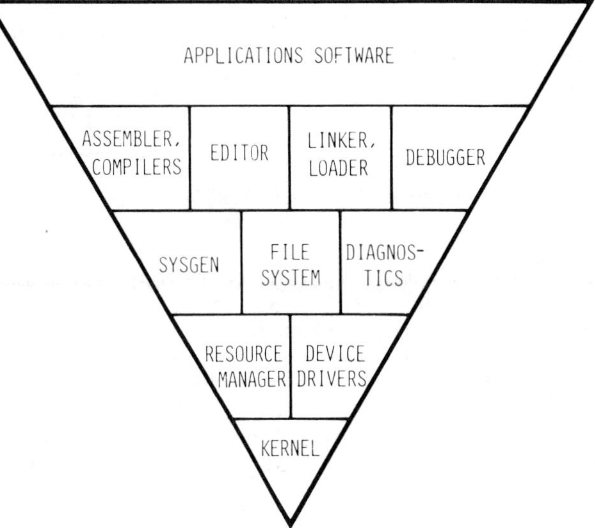

Figure 1. An Example of Layered Software

A multitasking operating system permits multiple programs or **tasks** to be active simultaneously. Although only one program can be running at a time, the system can switch back and forth between different programs, giving the illusion of executing them simultaneously. Programs often spend much time waiting for some asynchronous event, such as an I/O device action or operator input. A multitasking system can use this time to execute other programs. Multitasking is, therefore, a method for efficiently using CPU time.

Multitasking operating systems are used in multiterminal or multiuser systems, such as timeshare systems. Other uses include process control, where multiple devices are controlled in **real time** by a single processor. Communications controllers that handle multiple channels can also be implemented using multitasking techniques.

TASKS

A task, sometimes called a **process**, is a program that can have four states: **ready, running, suspended** and **undefined** (see Figure 2). Any number of tasks can be ready or suspended, but only one can be running on a given processor at a given time. A task is ready when it has all the information and resources it needs and is waiting on

Reprinted with permission from *Wescon Conf. Rec.*, 1981, pp. 26.0.1-26.0.4.

a **ready queue** to be run by the **scheduler.** A task is suspended when it **is waiting** for some event to take place. When the event occurs, the task is **activated** or **awakened** by being placed on the ready queue. A suspended task is sometimes referred to as being **deferred** or **asleep.**

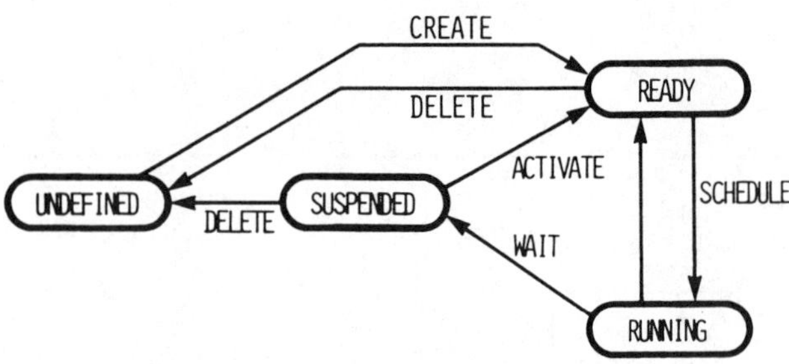

Figure 2. Task States

Each task in a multitasking operating system has a **context block** associated with it. The context block contains the status of the task, in other words, the instruction pointer, register values, and pointers to its allocated resources. When a task is suspended, all of the information necessary to resume execution (after the desired event takes place) is stored in its context block.

SCHEDULER

The scheduler is the program responsible for removing tasks from the ready queue and running them. The context block for each task supplies all the information needed to start the task running.

When more than one task is ready, it is up to the scheduler to decide which one will be run next. There are many different algorithms for determining which task to run. The ready queue, which is usually a first-in first-out (FIFO) linked list of context blocks, is a helpful mechanism in many schemes.

In a **nonpreemptive** scheduling algorithm, a running task is allowed to run uninterrupted until it suspends itself to wait for an event. In **preemptive** scheduling, a running task can be suspended by a higher priority task or by a system clock that limits the run time of a task. For example, in a time-sharing system, the scheduler allots a maximum run time (**a time slice**) to each task before it is suspended and sent to the back of the ready queue. This assures that no task can capture all the CPU processing time and that every process gets a chance to run.

When a running task is suspended, the scheduler looks to the front of the ready queue for the next task to run. If all tasks have the same priority, the task at the front of the queue has been ready the longest. In a prioritized system, tasks of higher priority might be placed in front of other tasks. In some situations, it may be advantagous to have more than one ready queue, where higher-priority queues are checked by the scheduler before lower-priority queues. The particular scheduling algorithm that most efficiently utilizes CPU time depends on the number, length, and relative priority of tasks as well as the the overhead involved in **context switching.**

INTERPROCESS COMMUNICATION AND SYNCHRONIZATION

In a multitasking system, software is often organized into functional units called **modules.** A module consists of a number of tasks working together to perform a particular function or several related functions. These tasks should be coordinated so that when one task is waiting for an event, another task can perform a part of the function that is independent of the event. For example, an assembler might need to perform disk I/O, output information to a CRT, and create a listing on a printer. If the disk, CRT, and printer handlers are independent tasks, the assembler can send a line of characters to the printer task and, while the printer task is waiting for the printer to do its work, the disk task can input another line of source to be translated. In order to accomplish this coordination, the tasks must have mechanisms through which to communicate and synchronize with each other.

Data can be transfered between tasks via shared memory, but some mechanism is needed to coordinate the writing and reading of data so that each task knows when it is all right to do so. One such mechanism is an **event flag.** The flag is initially off, indicating that the transmitting task may write into the shared area. When the transmitting task has finished writing, it turns the flag on. When the receiving task detects the flag on, it knows that the data is ready to be read. After the data is read, the receiving task turns the flag off to indicate that the shared memory is clear for future data. One problem with the event flag mechanism is that it must be polled by tasks to determine its state. Polling is a nonproductive activity, so it is undesirable in a multitasking system. Another problem with event flags is that they are limited to controlling one-way transfers with a single transmitting task.

A nonpolling mechanism for passing information between tasks consists of **messages** and **mailboxes.** A message is a structure containing a **header** and a **body.** The header contains a link that permits the message to be queued into various linked lists. The system may have a **free list** of message buffers from which tasks can draw. Each receiving task has a FIFO list, called a mailbox, for receiving messages. Two operations are associated with mailboxes:

- SEND: places a message in the appropriate mailbox and activates the receiving task if it was waiting on the mailbox.

- WAIT: is used for extracting a message from a mailbox. If the mailbox is empty, the task is suspended.

The SEND and WAIT operations must be **atomic** (in other words, execute uninterrupted from start to finish) or else problems could occur. For example, assume task A, while executing a WAIT, were to be suspended for some involuntary reason between the time it finds an empty mailbox and the time it suspends itself on the mailbox. Suppose that task B then tries to send a message to task A. The message would be placed in the mailbox, but task A would not be activated, because it has not yet been suspended on the mailbox. When task A is subsequently run by the scheduler, task A suspends itself on the mailbox. Unless some other message is sent to it, task A will never be activated. Operations can be made atomic by disabling interrupts during the operation's execution.

Resources such as memory, I/O devices, and programs can be shared by multiple tasks in a multitasking system. Software dealing with shared resources must sometimes be atomic in order to avoid confusion as to which data belongs to which task. This software is referred to as a **critical section.** Critical sections may be too time consuming to be made atomic by keeping interrupts disabled, so a software mechanism, called a **semaphore,** is often used. A semaphore allows only one task at a time to be in a critical section.

Semaphores consist of a flag and a queue. Like mailboxes, semaphores have two atomic operations associated with them:

- PASS: is executed by a task desiring to enter a critical section. If the flag is clear, the task sets the flag and continues into the critical section. Otherwise, the task is suspended and placed in the queue.

- SIGNAL: is executed by a task that has just finished with a critical section. The queue is examined to see if any tasks are waiting in it. If not, the flag is cleared. If there are tasks waiting in the queue, the flag stays set and the task at the front of the queue is activated. When the activated task is run by the scheduler, it resumes executing immediately after the PASS where it had been suspended.

Semaphore operations are so common that some microprocessors have an instruction, called TEST AND SET, that is designed to be used in the PASS operation.

RESOURCE MANAGEMENT

Memory space, disc files, and peripheral devices are examples of operating system resources. In a multitasking system, tasks must compete with one another for the use of these resources. The operating system function of allocating resources to tasks is known as **resource management.**

The need for formal management of a particular resource depends upon the number of tasks competing for the resource and the **divisibility** of the resource. For example, a printer is indivisible (ie. it cannot be divided into separate components), so it can be used by only one task at a time. Placing a semaphore PASS and SIGNAL at the beginning and end, respectively, of the printer driver is sufficient to manage this device. By contrast, memory space and disk storage are divisible resources, because they can be partitioned into sections to be used by many tasks. This partitioning must be **dynamic** (in other words, vary with time) in order to meet the changing needs of tasks. **Memory managers** and **file handlers** are examples of formal resource managers.

When a task requires memory for its stack or variables, it must obtain the memory from a **memory pool.** There are various strategies for managing the memory pool.

In some systems, the memory pool initially consists of one contiguous portion of RAM. When a task requests memory, the memory manager **allocates** a **segment** of contiguous RAM that is

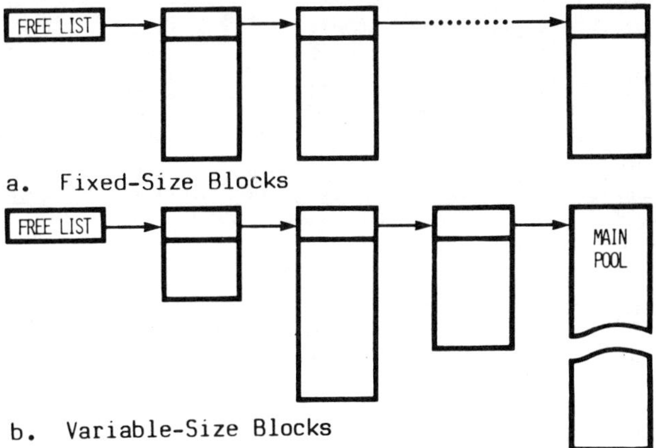

Figure 3. Memory Pools

exactly as long as is needed. When a task is finished with its segment, the segment must be returned to the pool. Since tasks may keep segments as long as they wish, the pool cannot remain contiguous, so the returned segments are linked into a **free list** (see Figure 3b). When further requests for memory are made, the memory manager must search the free list for segments large enough to fill the requests. The manager must occasionally go through the free list and merge contiguous segments together in order to avoid a total **fragmentation** of memory.

Another memory management scheme partitions memory into fixed-size memory blocks (see Figure 3a). When a task requires more memory than is contained in one block, blocks can be linked together to form a linked list of memory blocks. It is more difficult for tasks to access their data in this scheme than in the segmented memory scheme. However, with fixed-size blocks, there is no fragmentation problem, so the memory manager has less housekeeping to do.

Another aspect of memory management deals with program memory. In most microprocessor systems, programs are **fully resident** (in other words, they reside entirely in system memory). In some systems, however, there may be more programs than can fit into system memory at any one time. The programs not currently in use can be **swapped** out to secondary storage. The memory manager has the responsibility of deciding when to swap programs and where to locate them.

A problem universal to all resource management is the problem of **deadlocks**. A deadlock can occur when two or more tasks are competing for common resources. For example, suppose task A obtains resource X and then requests resource Y, but task A is suspended because task B currently owns resource Y. If task B then requests resource X, both tasks will be suspended indefinitely. Programmers must be careful to avoid deadlock situations, because the only way to recover from a deadlock is for the system to abort tasks until enough resources are available to resume operation.

CONCLUSION

Multitasking operating systems have two major benefits: they increase processing power by managing CPU time and system resources, and they provide a structured foundation on which multiuser and process control applications software can be built and maintained. Applications software that is logically separated from operating system functions is generally easier to maintain and upgrade than software that encompasses all levels.

Multitasking operating systems can be quite complex, and their development can be expensive and time consuming. Fortunately, multitasking operating systems are now readily available for many microprocessors. Some microprocessor manufacturers are offering multitasking software at nominal prices. Microprocessor users who take advantage of this software will enjoy reduced product development costs and more rapid product introductions.

REFERENCES

Zarella, John. Operating Systems Concepts and Principles, Microcomputer Applications, 1979.

Zilog, Inc. Zilog Real Time Software (ZRTS) User Manual, 1981.

A Proposed Standard for Extending High-Level Languages for Microprocessors

IEEE Task P755

Introductory remarks
by Richard E. James, III

Over the years language implementers have found it desirable to provide additional statements allowing users to get to some of the features of the hardware and operating system. Such new features partially eliminate the need for dropping into assembly language. With the wide use of microprocessors and microcomputers, and with the growing number of language implementations being made on them, it is time to ask, what is the minimal, common set of language extensions that will address the greatest number of needs of microprocessor users? The proposed standard published here tries to address this question with the following thoughts in mind:

- suitability for common languages (we chose Basic, Fortran, and Pascal for demonstration purposes);
- minimum number of syntax changes needed to implement the features.

Microprocessor applications interface to an arbitrary and inflexible environment characterized by such conditions as hardware-dictated memory layout, I/O via ports or memory mapping, interrupts, and prepackaged machine language subroutines with alien calling sequences. The extensions proposed here fall into several groups:

- Hardware requirements specify which addresses are read-only (ROM), which are read-write (RAM), which are inaccessible (so the compiler does not allocate code or data there), and which are hardware-specific (memory-mapped I/O). The proposed standard enables the user to tell the compiler where to put pieces of the object program, and also enables him to read and write specific locations. (We apologize for using PEEK and POKE, but they are the de facto standards.)

- Microcomputers are often used in low-level applications (e.g., as device drivers), where they need to get at the hardware I/O and where perhaps there is no operating system to provide I/O subroutines. Therefore, the proposed standard calls for access to the hardware input and output instructions (if any). Access to file systems is beyond the "minimal" scope of this standard.

- The high-level language must provide for an interface to those things that the user decides to do in assembly language. The proposed standard provides a general mechanism. The new routines GETREG and PUTREG may not actually touch the registers ("state elements") indicated; instead, CALLER may move values between temporary areas used by GETREG and PUTREG and the hardware registers.

- A minimal interrupt servicing mechanism is provided, but, in deference to other standardization efforts, concurrency is not.

- Masking functions are provided to deal with hardware bits, even though such functions may be deemed redundant with respect to other features of the language (e.g., Pascal SETs and PACKED RECORDs).

There are two main advantages to standardized extensions—they minimize the retraining process for programmers who move between machines and/or languages and, more important, they encourage language implementers to include necessary features that might otherwise be left out. These advantages will enhance the usefulness of high-level languages and will be a blessing to programmers who prefer to stay away from assembly language.

The proposed standard provides some portability—concepts and syntax are portable between programs and between processors but individual programs are not necessarily portable, because of differences in environments. We should note that the proposed standard is not as strong as it may seem—there are a number of

Reprinted from *IEEE Micro*, vol. 1, pp. 70–75, May 1981.

"should's" which specify recommendations as well as ways around truly implementing some of the "shall" (obligatory) features. For example, a Fortran manual could say: "PEEK is not provided, but can be implemented by the arithmetic statement function PEEK (J) = K (1 – LOCF(K(1)) + J), given that K is dimensioned." It then is up to the user who wishes to adhere to the standard to use PEEK and its definition as needed, instead of the nonstandard LOCF. Note, however, that for the implementation to conform to the standard, the reference manual must include any such auxiliary code.

Richard Karpinski is to be thanked for initially chairing the P755 working group. We also thank Robert Stewart, chairman of the IEEE Computer Society's Computer Standards Committee, for believing in standards enough to instigate this work, and Tom Pittman, for his expertise in grammar and word processing.

The IEEE Computer Society is publishing this proposed standard to allow comments prior to its submission to the IEEE Standards Board for adoption as an IEEE Standard. Your comments should be sent to

Richard E. James, III
3705 Eastwood Circle
Santa Clara, CA 95050
(408) 988-3048

Comments should be mailed to arrive no later than June 17, 1981.

If you would like to participate in this or other efforts of the Microprocessor Standards Committee, please contact either of its cochairmen, Steve Diamond or Michael Smolin at

Synertex Inc., MS 39
3001 Stender Way
Santa Clara, CA 95051

The Proposed Standard

IEEE Task P755

(Draft 3.0, December 5, 1980)

Abstract

This standard specifies extensions to high-level languages for the purpose of accommodating environmental restrictions common in microprocessor applications. The extensions include ways to access memory, I/O ports, and arbitrary subroutines; to service interrupts; and to bind entities to specific memory locations.

Foreword

(This Foreword is not a part of 755/D3.)

This standard represents the consensus of the High-Level Languages Working Group of the Microprocessor Standards Subcommittee of the IEEE Computer Society Computer Standards Committee.

While microprocessors are not qualitatively different from the more traditional computer systems (minicomputers and larger mainframes), their applications tend to be characterized by the need to interface to an arbitrary and inflexible environment. That environment may manifest itself in external hardware requirements or in pre-existing software. The failure of high-level languages (HLLs) to deal with this environment has historically precluded their use from such microprocessor applications.

Two reasons for the use of HLLs are

- to enable the application to be conceived and encoded in a language more oriented to the application than to the machine on which it is implemented, and
- to facilitate the transportation of encoded programs from one environment to another.

To the extent that microprocessor applications are entangled in the environment, this second purpose is defeated. This normally occurs, however, in only a small part of each well-coded application program; this part needs recoding for any transportation, regardless of the other constraints.

The purpose of this standard is to extend existing standard languages (which already afford a degree of portability and problem-orientation) in order to facilitate their interface to the inflexible environment of microprocessor applications. This extension should not do violence to the language. With most HLLs these extensions consist primarily of a set of predefined (library) subroutines and functions, which therefore require no language changes at all.

Suggestions for improvement of this standard are welcome. Readers are particularly encouraged to suggest implementations for items *a* through *e* of Section 1.3. All comments should be sent to the chairman of the High-Level Language Working Group, Richard E. James, III, at the address given in the introductory remarks.

The following working group members are responsible for this draft:

Richard E. James, III
Richard Karpinski
Dennis Paull
Tom Pittman
Robert G. Stewart

1.0 Scope

1.1 Languages

This standard specifies extensions to high-level languages for microprocessor applications. It covers computer languages for which there exist either ANSI or IEEE standards, or draft standards in preparation by existing ANSI or IEEE committees. Except as herein provided, the language extended by this standard shall conform to the existing standard for that language.

This standard explicitly extends three languages: Basic, Fortran, and Pascal. Other languages may be implicitly extended by the consistent application of the naming conventions and rules for extension specified in this standard.

1.2 Inclusions

This standard specifies

a) direct access to memory,
b) direct access to processor input and output instructions,
c) access to external subroutines not coded in the extended HLL,
d) facilities for servicing interrupts in the extended HLL, and
e) the ability to bind constant and variable parts of the program to specific regions of memory.

1.3 Exclusions

This standard does not, but some future revision of it may, specify

a) specific operating system capabilities,
b) facilities for concurrency,
c) access to internal processor functions not related to input/output or memory access (such as special instructions or functional modes),
d) access to file systems (other than by individual input/output operations), or
e) the effects of run-time errors (such as values too large for destination memory locations or registers, etc.).

This standard does not specify

f) machine architecture,
g) means of implementing specified extensions,
h) resource allocation in the extended HLLs (except in the case of memory), or
i) extensions to languages not compatible with microprocessors or not allowing for library subroutines (except Basic).

2.0 Definitions

HLL—High-level language to be extended by this standard. HLLs so extended are sometimes known as systems implementation languages.

Library routine—A function (which returns a value) or a procedure (wich does not return a value) supplied with the implementation of the HLL. For the purposes of this standard, a short routine coded entirely in the language supported by the implementation, but which the user is obliged to include with the application program, is said to be a library routine if its complete specification (i.e., source listing) is included in the user documentation.

State—The condition of the target microprocessor, given in terms of the contents of its registers, internal flags, local memory, etc. A **state element** is a microprocessor component containing a distinguishable part of the state information, such as a single register.

Shall and **should**—In this standard, the use of the word "shall" signifies that which is obligatory in any conforming implementation; the use of the word "should" signifies that which is strongly recommended—i.e., that which is in keeping with the intent of the standard, despite architectural or other constraints beyond the scope of this standard that, on occasion, may render the recommendations impractical.

3.0 Form of extensions

With two exceptions, extensions specified in this standard consist of intrinsic or library subroutines and functions supplied by the implementer of the language. Whether a language processor directly generates the corresponding machine-language instructions or simply invokes a call to the library routine is implementation-dependent.

The two exceptions are as follows:

- Standard Basic allows for library functions but has no facilities for calling named subroutines from a library. This standard follows the accepted practice of defining new statement types in the place of such subroutine calls.
- Memory allocation (e.g., to read-only memories) is intrinsically done prior to execution; it is meaningless to refer to subroutines or functions for this extension. The standard specifies the means to effect this extension in Section 8.0

Other than memory allocation, this standard identifies for each extension the subroutines or functions to effect the extension, and gives the names of the routines for each of the three languages, Basic, Fortran, and Pascal. To apply this standard to another language, the implementer should use the specified routine names in the normal calling sequence for the new language.

4.0 Memory access

All addressable memory shall be accessible to the program in the extended HLL for examination or modification, as appropriate. An addressable memory location is one which is uniquely identified by only one integer address value. For example, in a byte-addressable, 16-bit machine, the width of each memory location is eight bits. Memory access shall be provided by means of two routines, as specified in this section of the proposed standard. Memory may be examined by means of the integer function PEEK, with a single argument which evaluates to the integer address of the memory location to be examined. Memory may be modified (insofar as the hardware allows it) by means of a subroutine POKE, whose first argument is an integer address as in PEEK, and whose second argument evaluates to an integer appropriate to the width of a memory location. Both PEEK and POKE shall access the specified memory location, and not its neighbors, exactly once for each reference.*

In the following examples, the variable M is assigned the value of the memory datum at the location whose address is in variable L; that same memory location is then set to the value of the variable Q.

In Basic

```
400  M=PEEK(L)
410  POKE L,Q
```

In Fortran

```
M=PEEK (L)
CALL POKE (L,Q)
```

In Pascal

```
M: = PEEK (L);
POKE (L,Q)
```

If the microprocessor supports multiple-location memory access, or if the implementer desires such access, additional routines (PEEK2, POKE2, PEEK3, POKE3, etc.) may be supplied to access consecutive memory locations.

5.0 Input and output

All of the input and output capabilities of the microprocessor shall be supported in the HLL.

5.1 Memory mapped I/O

Some microprocessors have no hardware or instructions for input or output of data except by memory access. Section 4.0 specifies all that is necessary to meet the I/O requirement of this standard for these processors.

5.2 Port and discrete I/O

Many microprocessors have special instructions to permit access to particular external logic that is distinct from memory. Most of this external logic is configured into "ports," each having some numerical address. A few microprocessors also have discrete input or output lines not associated with the normal ports. The language implementer shall assign "port numbers" to the discrete I/O signals also; these should be distinguished in some way, such as by being outside the range of normal port numbers. Special-purpose hardware registers may also be accessed in this way.

Input from the external world to the microprocessor shall be specified by a function having a single integer argument corresponding to the port number. An implementation may restrict this argument to a constant. The value of the function is a value appropriate to the actual input datum. The name of the function shall be INP.

Output to a port shall be specified by a subroutine with two arguments. The first argument is a port number as above. The second argument evaluates to a value appropriate to the nature of the designated port; for discrete outputs, the value may be limited to 0 or 1. The name of this subroutine (or statement) shall be OUT.

In the following examples, the variable D is assigned the value of the input port number 3; that value is then sent to output port number 4.

In Basic

```
500  D=INP(3)
510  OUT 4,D
```

In Fortran

```
D=INP (3)
CALL OUT (4,D)
```

In Pascal

```
D: = INP (3);
OUT (4,D)
```

5.3 Simultaneous I/O

If a microprocessor has instructions which do simultaneous input and output, the function name IOP shall be used; its two arguments are the same as specified for OUT.*

6.0 Interrupts

The extended HLL should permit the application program to respond to some or all of the hardware interrupt capability of the processor. The number of interrupts thus supported and the amount of overhead processing imposed by the HLL (and possibly also by the operating system) are implementation-dependent.

An "interrupt number" shall be defined for each supported interrupt. The HLL application program may enable any such interrupt and attach an otherwise undistinguished routine to it by means of an interrupt enabling subroutine, as specified in this section. Thus, interrupt service routines may also be called in the ordinary way.

The name of the subroutine (or statement in Basic) shall be ARM. Its first argument is an integer interrupt number; its second argument is the name (or line number in Basic) of the routine that is to be attached to the interrupt.** An implementation may require the first argument to be a constant.

The interrupt service routine shall be detached by calling the subroutine DISARM with a single argument identifying the interrupt number, as above. This may also disable the interrupt. In block-structured languages like Pascal, the effect of exiting a scope in which the service routine is declared shall be implementation-defined.

An implementation may specify that service routines for certain interrupts have arguments and/or return a value. This is particularly useful for operating-system-generated interrupts or traps.

*This is intended to accommodate memory-mapped I/O, where the act of access may be significant. Note that PEEK may thus have side effects which may interact with the order of evaluation of expressions.

*For example, the Z80 input instruction "IN A,n" sends out the previous contents of the accumulator during an input.

**Both Fortran and Pascal permit subroutine names to be passed to another subroutine as arguments.

In the following examples, the routine INTS (Basic line number 1000) is to be attached to interrupt number 3, and interrupt number 5 is to be disabled:

In Basic

```
600  ARM 3, 1000
610  DISARM 5
```

In Fortran

```
EXTERNAL INTS
CALL ARM (3, INTS)
CALL DISARM (5)
```

In Pascal

```
ARM (3, INTS);
DISARM (5)
```

7.0 Machine language subroutines

The extended HLL shall allow the application program to call externally supplied machine language routines.

7.1 Compatible linkage

If the subroutines can be identified by name, and if the implementation-dependent linkage provided by the HLL is compatible with that required by the external routine, then the calling sequence in the HLL program shall be the same as for normal named subroutine calls. Special directives (such as EXTERNAL) to identify such named subroutines may be required.

The subroutine linkage supported in this way shall be implementation-defined.

7.2 Incompatible linkage

In order to allow the application program to call an externally supplied subroutine that can only be identified by its address in memory, or that requires a machine state at entry or exit incompatible with the HLL calling conventions, the subroutine CALLER shall be provided as specified in this section.

CALLER takes a single argument that evaluates to the integer address of the machine language subroutine to be called. CALLER saves whatever state information the HLL needs to have preserved across the call; the specified machine language subroutine is entered in such a way that the normal return instruction of that subroutine will cause the saved state to be restored and the HLL program to resume execution. Furthermore, CALLER shall initialize all programmable state elements (i.e., registers, flags, etc., of the microprocessor) on entry to the specified routine and unload them on exit.

Three support routines shall be supplied to enable the user to adequately specify the initial state and to recover any results from the exit state. The implementer shall specify an integer or some other identification for each distinct state element (register, etc.); this may, at the implementer's option, be restricted to a constant. A subroutine with the name PUTREG shall be used to assign to the state element identified in its first argument the value of its second argument. When the machine language routine requires an address rather than a value, the integer function MEMLOC shall be provided, which returns the memory address of its argument. The implementer shall specify the conditions under which the address value returned by MEMLOC may become invalid. The function GETREG shall return the value of the state element identified by its argument, as set by either PUTREG or CALLER.

In the following examples, the variable V is assigned the value of the memory address of the variable W, which is subsequently assigned to state element (register) number 4. Similarly, state element A is assigned the value in variable J. Then the machine language routine whose address is in variable M is called. Finally, variable X receives the value returned in state element number 2:

In Basic

```
700  V = MEMLOC (W)
710  PUTREG 4, V
720  PUTREG A, J
730  CALLER M
740  X = GETREG (2)
```

In Fortran

```
V = MEMLOC (W)
CALL PUTREG (4, V)
CALL PUTREG (A, J)
CALL CALLER (M)
X = GETREG (2)
```

In Pascal

```
V: = MEMLOC (W);
PUTREG (4, V);
PUTREG (A, J);
CALLER (M);
X: = GETREG (2)
```

8.0 Bit manipulation

In order to facilitate direct control of individual bits and subfields in peripheral registers, the following bit manipulation functions shall be provided:

```
IAND (A,B)
IOR (A,B)
IXOR (A,B)
INOT (A)
GETFLD (A,N,M)
PUTFLD (A,N,M,B)
```

8.1 Logical functions

The four logical functions, IAND, IOR, IXOR, and INOT, operate on the binary representations of integers of an implementation-defined length, are considered as bit vectors, and return an integer whose binary representation is the logical *and, inclusive or, exclusive or,* and *one's-complement,* respectively, of the arguments. The logical operations are performed bitwise-parallel on the binary integer representations of the arguments, irrespective of the actual internal representation of the numbers.

The implementer shall define the treatment of negative numbers. Thus,

IAND (5,6) = 4
IOR (5,6) = 7
IXOR (5,6) = 3
IAND (INOT (5), 15) = 10

8.2 Subfield functions

The other two functions provide field extraction/insertion and shifting. In each case, the second and third arguments are integers denoting the bit positions (counting the least significant bit as position 0) of the ends of a bit string considered as a substring of the binary integer representation of the first argument. GETFLD extracts, right-justifies, and returns the designated subfield as an integer. PUTFLD positions its fourth argument to replace the designated subfield and returns the composite as an integer. The bit position arguments shall be acceptable in either left-to-right or right-to-left order. Thus,

GETFLD(13, 2,1) = GETFLD(13,1, 2) = 2
PUTFLD (255, 4, 4, 0) = 239

9.0 Address binding

The extended HLL shall permit the application program to specify separately the memory address locations to be used for the constant (including code) and variable parts of the program.

9.1 Global bindings

Directives shall be accepted to establish collections of memory. Each such collection shall be identified as either a constant part (called "ROM") or a variable part (called "RAM"). Both constant and variable parts of an application program that specifies only a variable-part directive shall be located in that collection of (RAM) memory. The implementation may designate further distinctions as appropriate.* These directives should be accepted at the beginning of programs or, if appropriate, in the input to linkers or loaders.

9.2 Local bindings

The implementation should accept a directive (called "ADDRESS") that specifies the memory location to be used for the immediately following declaration of one variable or procedure. Where the declaration of variables is not permitted, the variable name itself should be included in the directive. Note that such local bindings may constitute aliasing with another program part residing at the same memory location, whatever the manner in which that part has been placed in that location. Such aliasing should be reported to the user.

*For example, if instructions reside in an address space separate from that for data, then instructions and data may each have constant and variable parts.

9.3 Syntax

Both the form of the directives and the form of the memory location specifications within the directives shall be implementation-defined. The implementation should accept memory location specifications in decimal, hexadecimal, and octal; the default should be decimal, but suitable notation should permit specification in any of these number systems.**

When there is no conflict with other HLL requirements, directives within the program text should be specified by a comment which begins with the currency symbol "$".

In the following examples, memory locations 4096 through 6143 are to be allocated to the constant part of the program (i.e., the instruction code), and locations 6144 through 8191 to the variable part, except for the variable X, which is to be assigned to location 92 (or as many locations as necessary, beginning with 92):

In Basic

```
900 REM$ROM 4096-6143
910 REM$RAM 6144-8191
950 REM$ADDRESS 92, X
```

In Fortran

```
C$ROM 4096-6143
C$RAM 6144-8191
C$ADDRESS 92
            REAL X
```

In Pascal

```
(*$ROM 4096-6143*)
(*$RAM 6144-8191*)
(*$ADDRESS 92*)
VAR   X: REAL;
```

(End of text of proposed standard)

**For example, the *Microprocessor Assembly Language Draft Standard* (IEEE P694) uses Q '117 for octal, D '79 for decimal, and H '4F for hexadecimal.

Offered here for public comment before submission to the IEEE Standards Board, this proposed standard allows manufacturers to produce varied but compatible microcomputer modules.

Proposed Microcomputer System 796 Bus Standard

IEEE Task P796/D2

Introductory comments by
Richard W. Boberg, Chairman
IEEE 796 Bus Working Group

The proposed IEEE 796 bus is a commercial-quality bus for use in a microcomputer-based system. The board modules that connect to the bus may be slaves (memory and/or input/output), masters (CPU and/or controllers), or both.

The 796 bus provides an electrical and mechanical specification to allow many different manufacturers to produce varied but compatible microcomputer modules. This offers the user the flexibility to choose the modules that solve his microcomputer system problem in the most complete and cost-effective manner.

The proposed bus is a departure from the minicomputer market, where each major manufacturer defines its bus without regard for its potential use by other systems or manufacturers. The 796 bus, though initiated by Intel as their Multibus, is a cooperative industry effort toward establishing a standard for a large number of manufacturers and users of microcomputer modules.

The original development of the Multibus was done at Intel by their initial systems engineering group—Bob Garrow, Rich Boberg, Hap Walker, and Mike Yen—with significant input by Fred Coury, a consultant. The bus was designated the Multibus, an Intel trademark, and was used as the basis for Intel's Intellec Microcomputer Development System introduced in 1975. Intel decided to use the same bus for its subsequent iSBC product line. The success of these reliable OEM board products produced hundreds of competitive and complementary products, all made to be compatible with this commercial-quality bus. This diverse offering of modules compatible at the board level has provided customers with a comprehensive and cost-effective product selection—even with second-sourcing at the board level. The customers of these boards are companies whose value-added consists of their own special-purpose hardware and software; they use the standard CPU, memory, I/O, and peripheral controller modules as the basis for their systems. The version of the bus standardized by the Task 796 Working Group of the IEEE Computer Society's Microprocessor Standards Committee will help assure the user community that the compatibility and high commercial quality of the bus will be maintained from one manufacturer to another.

The currently available draft of the standard, of which this is a subset, is complete and accurate. However, as expected, the 796 bus will continue to evolve with enhancements and refinements. The general philosophy being followed for these changes is to maintain upward and downward compatibility, where possible, while creating a clean, professional standard. In some cases, the Task 796 Working Group has elected to specify the bus in a way that will cause technical incompatibility with existing products. The removal of the −5 volt power supply from the bus pins is an example. In these cases, it is felt that there is minimal impact since the products can still be used (by making exceptions to the standard) until the products are changed or their lifetimes expire. This temporary inconvenience permits the deliberate focusing of all new or redesigned products onto the preferred standard.

Two of the issues being considered by the Task 796 Working Group for future revisions are

- Four more address lines to bring the total to 24 (for a 16M-byte addressability).
- Edge connector and board size(s) additions and details.

It should be noted that Intel has patents pending on the byte-swap aspects of the bus, first introduced in 1978, as partially described in Sections 2.1.3.2.2 and 2.2.2.4. If patents are granted, Intel has expressed a readiness to offer a one-time licensing fee for use of this aspect of the bus. While we know of no other patents covering this bus, they may exist.

The IEEE Computer Society is publishing this standard in draft form to allow comments on it prior to submission

Reprinted from *IEEE Computer*, vol. 13, pp. 89-105, Oct. 1980.

to the IEEE Standards Board for adoption as an IEEE standard. Since space limitations prohibited the inclusion of the full specification, only Section 1 (General), Section 2 (Functional description), and Section 5 (Levels of compliance) are presented in full below. Excerpts are presented from Section 3 (Electrical specifications) and Section 4 (Mechanical specifications). Complete copies of the full specification are available upon request. Your comments on the proposed standard should be sent prior to November 1, 1980, to:

Richard W. Boberg
Microbar Systems, Inc.
1120 San Antonio Road
Palo Alto, CA 94303
(415) 964-2862

Although the original work in creating the 796 bus was done at Intel Corporation, the current specification represents the work of individuals from many different companies. These individuals include the members of the Task 796 Working Group of the IEEE Computer Society's Microprocessor Standards Committee:

Rod H. Allen, Microbar Systems, Inc.;
Mark Bagula, Data General;
Richard W. Boberg, Microbar Systems, Inc.;
Robert Garrow (original chairman of the working group), Convergent Technologies;
Bill Holloway, Signetics;
Jim Johnson, Intel Corporation;
Jim Kelley, Relational Memory Systems, Inc.;
Craig Kinnie, Intel Corporation;
Jim Konsevich, consultant;
Martin A. Newman, Microbar Systems, Inc.; and
Tung-sun Tung, National Semiconductor.

In addition, other individuals made contributions verbally, by mail, or in surveys. Intel has currently established Gary Fielland at the Aloha, Oregon, facility as their 796 bus specialist. ■

The proposed standard

1. General

1.1 Scope

One of the most important elements in a computer system is the bus structure that supplies the interface for all the hardware components. This bus structure contains the necessary signals to allow the various system components to interact with each other. It allows memory and I/O data transfers, direct memory accesses, generation of interrupts, etc. This document provides a detailed description of all the elements and features that make up the 796 bus.

The bus supports two independent address spaces: memory and I/O. During memory cycles, the bus allows direct addressability of up to one megabyte using 20-bit addressing. During I/O bus cycles, the bus allows addressing of up to 64K I/O ports using 16-bit addressing. Both memory and I/O cycles can support 8-bit or 16-bit data transfers.

The bus structure is built upon the master-slave concept where the master device in the system takes control of the bus and the slave device, upon decoding its address, acts upon the command provided by the master. This handshake (master-slave relationship) between the master and slave devices allows modules of different speeds to be interfaced via the bus. It also allows data rates up to five million transfers per second (bytes or words) to take place across the bus.

Another important feature of the bus is the ability to connect multiple master modules for multiprocessing configurations. The bus provides control signals for connecting multiple masters in either a serial or parallel priority fashion. With either of these two arrangements, more than one master may share bus resources.

This document has been prepared for those users who intend to evaluate or design products that will be compatible with the 796 system bus structure. To this end, the necessary signal definitions and timing and electrical specifications have been covered in detail.

This standard deals only with the interface characteristics of microcomputer devices: not with design specifications, performance requirements, and safety requirements of modules.

1.2 Object

This standard is intended:

(1) To define a general-purpose microcomputer system bus.
(2) To specify the device-independent electrical and functionai interface requirements that a module shall meet in order to interconnect and communicate unambiguously via the system.
(3) To specify the terminology and definitions related to the system.
(4) To enable the interconnection of independently manufactured devices into a single functional system.
(5) To permit products with a wide range of capabilities to be interconnected to the system simultaneously.
(6) To define a system with a minimum of restrictions on the performance characteristics of devices connected to the system.

1.3 Definitions

The following general definitions apply throughout this standard. More detailed definitions can be found in the appropriate section.

Throughout this standard, the term "system" denotes the byte or word interface system that, in general, includes all the circuits, connectors, and control protocol to effect unambiguous data transfer between devices. The term "device" or "module" denotes any product connected to the interface system that communicates information via the bus and that conforms to the interface system definition.

1.3.1 General system terms

Compatibility. The degree to which devices may be interconnected and used, without modification, when designed as defined in Sections 2 and 3 of this standard.

Bus cycle. The process whereby digital signals effect the transfer of data bytes or words across the interface by means of an interlocked sequence of control signals. "Interlocked" denotes a fixed sequence of events in which one event must occur before the next event can occur.

Interface. A shared boundary between two systems, or between parts of systems, through which information is conveyed.

Interface system. The device-dependent electrical and functional interface elements necessary for communication between devices. Typical elements are: driver and receiver circuits, signal line description, timing and control conventions, and functional logic circuits.

Override. A bus master overrides the bus control logic when it is necessary to guarantee itself back-to-back bus cycles. This is called "overriding" or "locking" the bus, temporarily preventing other masters from using the bus.

System. A set of interconnected elements which achieve a given objective through the performance of a specified function.

Timeout. Any data transfer cycle terminated by the master before the transfer acknowledge (XACK*) signal is received.

1.3.2 Signals and paths

Bus. A signal line or a set of lines used by an interface system to connect a number of devices and to transfer information.

Byte. A group of eight adjacent bits operated on as a unit.

Word. Two bytes or sixteen bits operated on as a unit.

High state. The more positive voltage level used to represent one of two logical binary states.

Low state. The more negative voltage level used to represent one of two logical binary states.

Signal. The physical representation of data.

Signal level. The relative magnitude of a signal when compared to an arbitrary reference. Signal levels in this standard are specified in volts.

Signal line. One of a set of signal conductors in an interface system used to transfer messages among interconnected devices.

Signal parameter. That element of an electrical quantity whose values or sequence of values convey information.

2. Functional description

This section provides an overall understanding of how the 796 bus functions, and describes the elements that connect to the bus, the signals that provide the interface to the bus, and the different types of operations performed on the bus.

2.0 Notation

In this section, as well as throughout the specification, a clear and consistent notation for signals has been used. The memory write command, MWTC, will be used to explain this notation. The terms "one:zero" and "true: false" can be ambiguous, so their use will be avoided. In their place, we will use the terms electrical high and low, H and L. A nathan (asterisk) following the signal name (MWTC*) indicates that the signal is active low as shown:

MWTC* = asserted at 0 volts

The nathan or asterisk is not a negation operator or a footnote. It is an indicator of an electrically low condition for the active state. This asterisk is verbalized by the word "star," in consequence of the prior use of "overbar" or "bar." The following is used to further explain the notation used in this specification:

		Definition	
Function	*Electrical*	*logic*	*State*
MWTC	H	1 true	active, asserted
	L	0 false	inactive, not asserted
MWTC*	L	1 true	active, asserted
	H	0 false	inactive, not asserted

An active low signal, such as MWTC*, driven by a three-state driver will always be pulled up to Vcc when not asserted. The only exceptions to this rule are BPRO* and BPRN*, which are normal TTL lines.

The historical notation used for the address and data busses has employed a hexadecimal radix. The notation used in this proposed IEEE standard will use a decimal radix in order to be consistent with other IEEE bus standards. The historical notation will be considered in full compliance until January 1984 for existing stocks of boards and documentation. Artwork for new boards and documentation should move to the new nomenclature.

2.1 IEEE 796 bus elements

This subsection describes the elements, masters and slaves, that interface to the bus and the 796 bus signal lines that comprise this interface.

2.1.1 Masters

A master is any module having the ability to control the bus. The master exercises this control by acquiring the bus through bus exchange logic and then generating command signals, address signals, and memory or I/O addresses. To perform these tasks, the master is equipped with either a central processing unit or logic dedicated to transferring data over the bus to and from other destinations. Figure 1 depicts a system that includes a master and two slave models.

The 796 bus architecture can support more than one master in the same system, but in order to do this, there must be a means for each master to gain control of the bus. This is accomplished through the bus exchange logic (see 2.4).

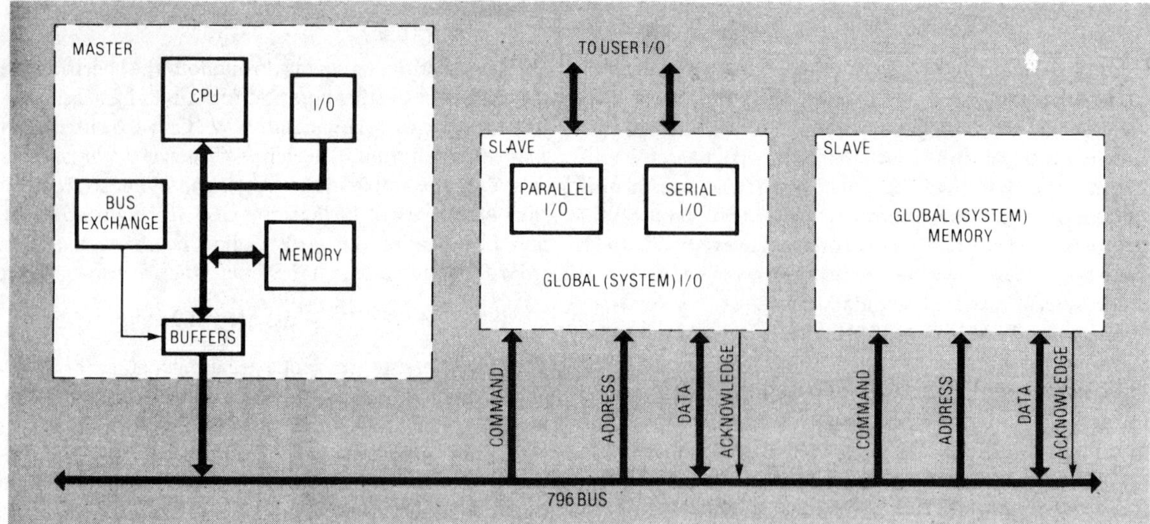

Figure 1. 796 bus master and slave example.

Masters may operate in one of two modes of operation. However, a particular configuration should have either all mode 1 masters or all mode 2 masters. Modes 1 and 2 are defined as follows:

Mode 1: Masters are limited to single bus transfers per bus connect. System timing is rendered deterministic by compliance with a maximum bus busy period. That period is limited by the maximum value of the parameter t_{BYSO} (see 3.2.5 in full specification).

Mode 2: Masters are unlimited in the bus control. They may invoke bus override. Bus timeouts are allowed. Compliance with the maximum busy period is not required.

The last classification is included to allow for a very broad class of operations, giving users maximum flexibility in meeting these applications' needs. The first mode of operation is defined to allow systems designers to predict the overall performance of their systems without concern for uncontrolled timing parameters such as bus timeout.

2.1.2 Slaves

Another type of module that can interface to the bus is the slave. Slave modules decode the address lines and act upon the command signals from the masters. The slaves are not capable of controlling the bus. Some examples of bus slaves are shown in Figure 1.

2.1.3 IEEE 796 bus signals

Signals transferred over the bus can be grouped into several classes based on the functions they perform. The classes are:

(1) Control lines
(2) Address and inhibit lines
(3) Data lines
(4) Interrupt lines
(5) Bus exchange lines

The following subsections explain the different classes of 796 bus signals.

2.1.3.1 Control lines

The following signals are classified as control lines:

Class	*Function*	*Signal*
Clocks	Constant clock	CCLK*
	Bus clock	BCLK*
Commands	Memory write	MWTC*
	Memory read	MRDC*
	I/O write	IOWC*
	I/O read	IORC*
Acknowledge	Transfer acknowledge	XACK*
Initialize		INIT*

2.1.3.1.1 Clock lines

(1) *Bus clock (BCLK*).* A periodic signal used to synchronize the bus contention logic; it may be slowed, stopped, or single stepped. The bus clock shall be generated by one and only one source within the system. This means that each bus master must have the capability of generating an acceptable clock that can optionally be connected to, or disconnected from, the bus. In a multi-master system, only one of the masters shall have its clock connected to the bus.

(2) *Constant clock (CCLK*).* A periodic signal of constant frequency, which may be used by masters or slaves as a master clock. The constant clock shall be generated by one and only one source within the system. This means that each bus master must have the capability of generating an acceptable clock that can optionally be connected to, or disconnected from, the bus. In a multi-master system, only one of the masters shall have its clock connected to the bus. The constant clock signal has a period of 100 nanoseconds minimum, 110 nanoseconds maximum.

2.1.3.1.2 Command lines (MWTC, MRDC*, IOWC*, IORC*)*

The command lines are elements of a communication link between the masters and slaves. There are two command lines for memory and two command lines for I/O. An active command line indicates to the slave that the address lines are carrying a valid address and that the slave is to perform the specified operation. In a data write cycle, the active command line (MWTC* or IOWC*) additionally indicates that the data is valid on the bus. In a data read cycle, the transition of the command (MRDC* or IORC*) from active to inactive indicates that the master has received the data from the slave.

2.1.3.1.3 Transfer acknowledge line (XACK)*

This line is used by the slaves to acknowledge commands from the master. XACK* indicates to the master that the requested action is complete and that data has been placed on, or accepted from, the data lines.

2.1.3.1.4 Initialize (INIT)*

The INIT* signal is generated to reset the entire system to a known internal state. This signal is usually generated prior to starting any operations on the system. INIT* may be generated by any or all of the bus masters or by an external source such as a front panel switch.

2.1.3.2 Address and inhibit lines

The address and inhibit lines are used for the following signals:

Function	*Signal*
Address lines	A0* - A19*
Byte high enable	BHEN*
Inhibit lines	INH1* and INH2*

2.1.3.2.1 Address lines (20 lines)

These lines, which specify the address of the referenced memory location or I/O device, allow a maximum of one megabyte (1,048,576 bytes) of memory to be accessed. When addressing an I/O device, a maximum of 16 address lines (A0* - A15*) are used, thus allowing the addressing of a maximum of 64K devices. An I/O module must also be able to be configured to decode only eight address lines (A0* - A7*) and ignore the upper eight lines (see 2.2.2.3).

2.1.3.2.2 Byte high enable line (BHEN)*

This byte control is used to enable the upper byte (bits 8-15) of a 16-word bit word to drive the data bus lines. The signal is used only on systems that incorporate 16-bit memory modules.

2.1.3.2.3 Inhibit lines (INH1 and INH2*)*

The inhibit lines can be invoked for any memory read or memory write operation (MRDC* or MWTC*). An inhibit line is asserted by a slave to inhibit another slave's bus activity during a memory read or write operation. The inhibit signal generated by the inhibiting slave is derived from decoding the memory address lines. The inhibiting slave can decode a single address, a block of addresses, or any combination of single and block addresses.

When it detects the specific address during an actual command (MRDC* or MWTC*), the inhibiting slave generates an inhibit signal, which is sensed by the inhibited slave. When so inhibited, this slave module disables its drivers from all data, address, and acknowledge bus lines, although it may actually perform internal operations. (All modules that may be inhibited must have completed internal operations within 1.5 microseconds from the start of the command line. This interval [1.5 microseconds] is also the minimum acknowledge timing for modules issuing inhibits. This guarantees that inhibited modules have enough time to return to their normal state before the current bus command is completed.)

2.1.3.3 Data lines (D0 - D15*)*

These 16 bidirectional data lines transmit and receive information to and from a memory location or an I/O port. (D15* is the most significant bit and D0* is the least significant bit). In 8-bit systems, only lines D0* - D7* are valid.

2.1.3.4 Interrupt lines

The interrupt lines consist of the following signals:

Function	*Signal*
Interrupt requests	INT0* - INT7*
Interrupt acknowledge	INTA*

2.1.3.4.1 Interrupt request lines (INT0 - INT7*)*

Interrupts are requested by activating one of the eight interrupt request lines. INT0* has the highest priority and INT7* has the lowest priority.

2.1.3.4.2 Interrupt acknowledge (INTA)*

In response to an interrupt request signal, an interrupt acknowledge signal can be generated by a bus master with bus vectored interrupt capability. The interrupt acknowledge signal is used to freeze the interrupt status and request the placement of the interrupt vector address on the bus data lines.

2.1.3.5 Bus exchange lines

The bus exchange lines are the following signals:

Function	*Signal*
Bus clock	BCLK*
Bus request	BREQ*
Bus priority	BPRN*, BPRO*
Bus busy	BUSY*
Common bus request	CBRQ*

A master gains control of the bus through the manipulation of these signals.

2.1.3.5.1 Bus request (BREQ)*

A signal used by the bus masters in a priority resolution circuit to indicate a request for control of the bus.

2.1.3.5.2 Bus priority (BPRN and BPRO*)*

The priority functions allow masters to break deadlocks that occur when more than one master concurrently requests the bus. The bus priority in (BPRN*) signal indicates to a particular master that no higher priority master is requesting use of the bus. The bus priority out (BPRO*) signal is used in serial (daisy chain) bus priority resolution schemes. In such a scheme, BPRO* is passed by one master to the BPRN* input of the master with the next lower bus priority; when active, the BPRO* signal indicates that the higher priority master does not require control of the bus.

2.1.3.5.3 Bus busy (BUSY)*

A signal activated by the master in control of the bus to indicate that the bus is in use. This prevents other masters from gaining control of the bus.

2.1.3.5.4 Common bus request (CBRQ)*

A signal that maximizes a master's data transfer rate to the bus by sensing the absence of other bus requests. The CBRQ* signal does this by serving two functions. It indicates to the master controlling the bus whether or not another master needs to gain control of the bus. To the other masters, it is a means of notifying the controlling bus master that it must relinquish control of the bus if it is not using the bus.

2.2 Data transfer operation

The primary function of the 796 bus architecture is to provide a path for the transfer of data between modules on the bus. The following subsections describe the different types of data transfers and the means by which they are implemented using the signals previously described. Figure 2 can be referenced during the following discussion.

The discussion of the data transfer operation of the bus is covered in three parts:

(1) an overview of the operation,
(2) a detailed description of the signals used in the transfer, and
(3) a discussion of the specifics pertaining to the different transfers.

It is assumed in this discussion that there is only one master on the bus, and therefore no bus contention exists. The bus exchange logic is discussed in 2.4.

2.2.1 Data transfer overview

A data transfer is accomplished as follows. First, the bus master places the memory address or I/O port address on the address lines. If the operation is a write, the data would also be placed on the data lines at this time. The bus master then generates a command (I/O read or write, or memory read or write), which activates the appropriate bus slave. The slave accepts the data if it is a write operation, or places the data on the data lines if it is a read operation. A transfer acknowledge signal is then sent to the bus master by the bus slave, allowing the bus master to complete its cycle by removing the command from the command line and then clearing the address and data lines. Figure 3 and Figure 4 show the basic timing for a read and write data transfer operation.

2.2.2 Signal descriptions

This subsection provides a detailed description of the 796 bus signals. Included are timing, signal origination, and other information pertaining to the specific function that each signal performs in the data transfer operation.

2.2.2.1 Initialize (INIT)*

Prior to any operation of the bus, all system modules should be reset to a known internal state. This can be accomplished by an INIT* signal initiated by one of three sources:

(1) a power-on clear circuit (RC network), which holds INIT* low until the power supplies reach their specific voltage outputs;
(2) a reset button, which is sometimes provided on the system front panel for operator use (note that this button must be debounced); or
(3) a software command that can be implemented to pull down the INIT* line.

The INIT* line is driven by open-collector gates and requires signal conditioning to meet the electrical specifications of the bus.

2.2.2.2 Constant clock (CCLK)*

The constant clock signal, which is driven by only one source, provides a timing source for any or all modules on the bus. CCLK* is a periodic signal with a specified frequency and is driven by a clock driver circuit. Section 3 contains the required frequency and tolerance specifications.

2.2.2.3 Address lines (A0 - A19*)*

The address lines are used to specify the address of the memory location or the I/O device that is being referenced by the command. There are 20 address lines, binary coded, to allow up to 1,048,576 bytes of memory to be referenced. These lines are driven by three-state drivers and are always controlled by the master using the bus.

For I/O bus cycles, master modules have the option of generating 8-bit or 16-bit addresses. Because of this, all

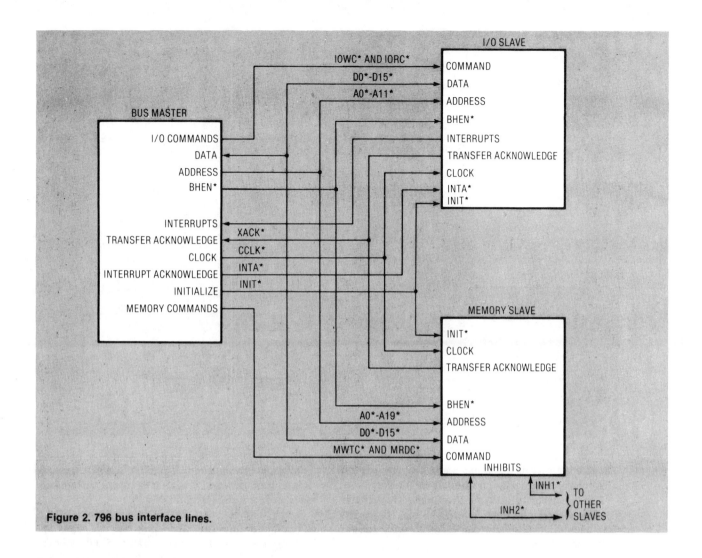

Figure 2. 796 bus interface lines.

I/O slaves must be capable of being configured to decode address bits (A0* - A7*) and ignore the upper address bits or to decode all 16 bits of address (A0*-A15*). Note that in a system using 8-bit I/O addresses, the value of the upper 12 bits of address is unknown. A master generating only 8-bit address may set the upper 12 address bits to any arbitrary value.

Refer to Figure 5 for an example of address line usage.

2.2.2.4 Data lines (D0 - D15*)*

These are 16 bidirectional data lines used to transmit and receive information to and from a memory location or I/O port. The 16 lines are driven by the master on write operations and by the addressed slave (memory or I/O) on read operations. Both 16-bit and 8-bit transfers can be accomplished by using only lines D0* - D7* (with D0* being the least significant bit).

There are three types of transfers that take place across the bus:

(1) transfer of low (even) byte on D0* - D7*,
(2) transfer of high (odd) byte on D0* - D7* (using swap byte function), and
(3) transfer of a 16-bit word.

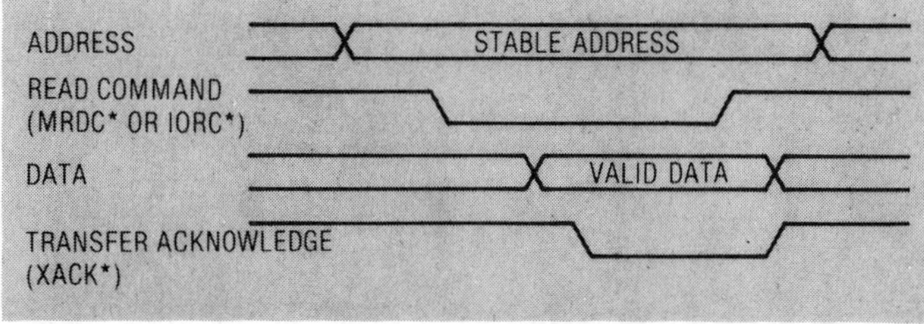

Figure 3. 796 bus read operation. (Note: Since bus cycles are asynchronous, the time scale is not necessarily linear.)

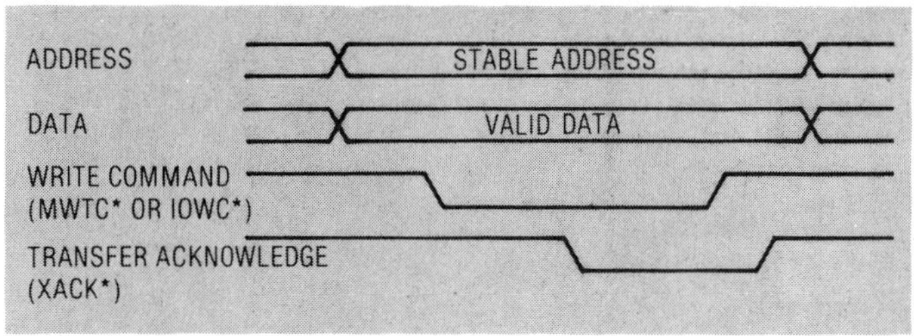

Figure 4. 796 bus write operation. (Note: Since bus cycles are asynchronous, the time scale is not necessarily linear.)

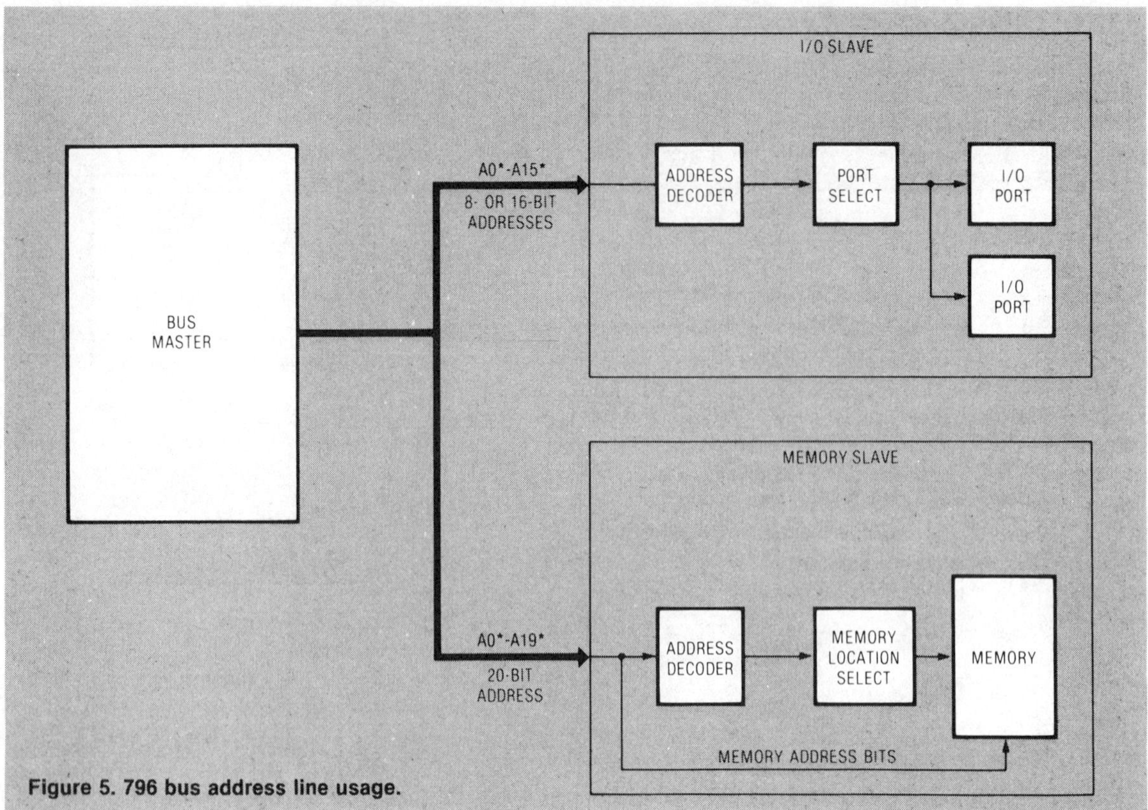

Figure 5. 796 bus address line usage.

Figure 6 shows the data lines and the contents of these lines for the three types of transfers mentioned.

Two signals control the data transfers. Byte high enable (BHEN*) active indicates that the bus is operating in the 16-bit mode, and the address bit 0 (A0*) defines an even-byte or odd-byte transfer.

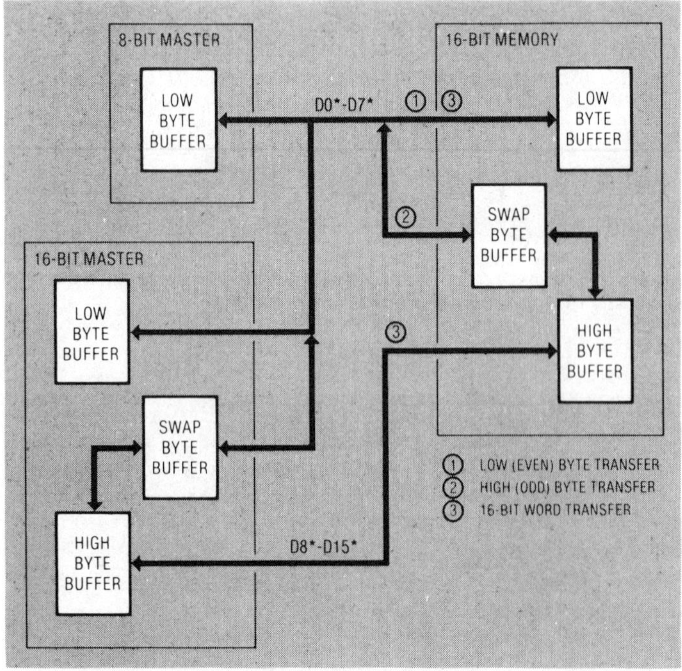

Figure 6. 796 bus data line usage.

For an even byte transfer, BHEN* and A0* are inactive, indicating the transfer of an even byte. The transfer takes place across data lines D0* - D7*.

For an odd-byte transfer, BHEN* is inactive and A0* is active, indicating the transfer of an odd byte. On this type of transfer, the odd (high) byte is transferred through the swap byte buffer to D0* - D7*. The high (odd) byte is transferred across on D0* - D7* to make 8-bit and 16-bit systems compatible.

For a 16-bit transfer, BHEN* is active and A0* is inactive. On this type of transfer, the low (even) byte is transferred on D0* - D7* and the high (odd) byte is transferred across the bus on D8* - D15*.

The 796 bus data lines are always driven by three-state drivers.

2.2.2.5 796 Bus commands

In this subsection, we will discuss the command lines and how they work in conjunction with other lines to accomplish a read or a write operation. There are four command lines:

Function	*Line*
Memory read command	MRDC*
I/O read command	IORC*
Memory write command	MWTC*
I/O write command	IOWC*

The command lines, which are driven by three-state drivers on the bus master, indicate to the slave the action that is being requested.

2.2.2.5.1 *Read operation*

The two read commands (MRDC* and IORC*) initiate the same basic type of operation. The only difference is that MRDC* indicates that the memory address is valid on the address lines, whereas IORC* indicates that the I/O port address is valid on the address lines. This address (memory or I/O port) must be valid on the bus 50 nanoseconds prior to the read command being generated. When the read command is generated, the slave module (memory or I/O port) places that data on the data lines and returns a transfer acknowledge (XACK*) signal, indicating that the data is on the bus. When the bus master receives the acknowledge, it strobes in the data and removes the command (MRDC* or IORC*) from the bus. The slave address (memory or I/O port) remains valid on the bus a minimum of 50 nanoseconds after the read command is removed. XACK* must be removed from the bus within 65 nanoseconds after the command is removed to allow for the next bus cycle. Figure 7 shows the timing for the memory read or I/O read command.

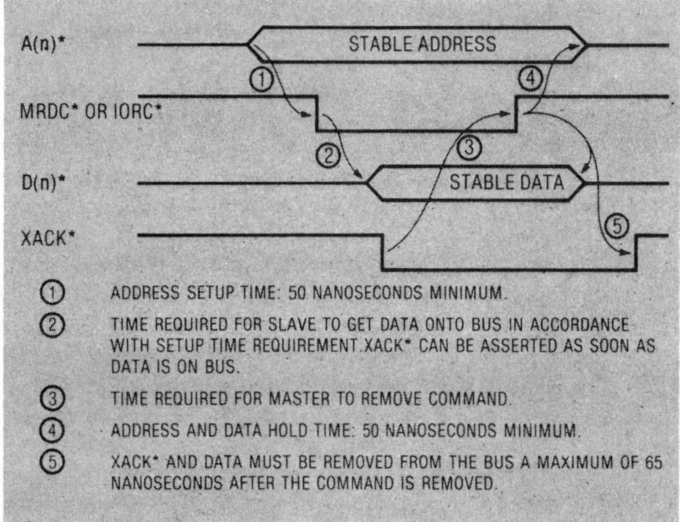

Figure 7. Memory or I/O read timing.

2.2.2.5.2 *Write operation*

The write commands (MWTC* and IOWC*) initiate the same basic type of operation. MWTC* indicates that the memory address is valid on the address lines, whereas IOWC* indicates that the I/O port address is valid on the address lines. The address (memory or I/O) and data must be valid on the bus 50 nanoseconds prior to the write command being generated. This requirement allows data to be latched on either the leading or trailing edge of the command. When the write command (MWTC* or IOWC*) is asserted, that data on the data lines is stable and can be accepted by the slave. The slave indicates acceptance of the data by returning a transfer acknowledge (XACK*), allowing the bus master to remove the command, address, and data from the bus. XACK* must be removed from the bus within 65 nanoseconds to allow for the next bus cycle. Figure 8 shows the timing for the memory write or I/O write command.

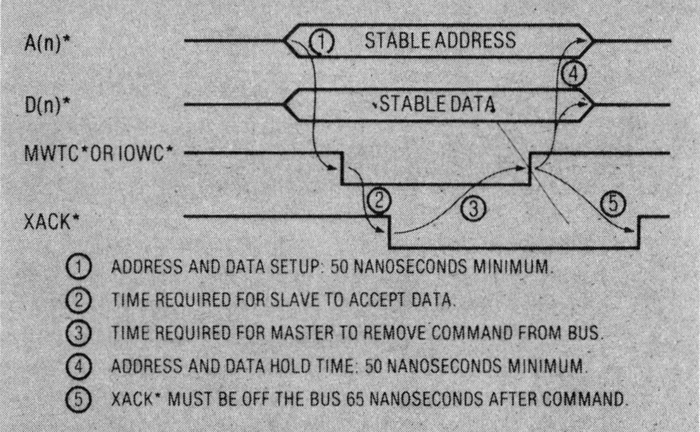

Figure 8. Memory or I/O write timing.

2.2.2.6 *Transfer acknowledge (XACK*)*

The transfer acknowledge (XACK*) signal is the response from the bus slave (memory or I/O) indicating that the commanded read or write operation is complete and that the data has been placed on, or accepted from, the data lines. In effect, this signal (XACK*) allows the bus master to complete the current bus cycle.

If a bus master addresses a nonexistent or malfunctioning memory or I/O module, an acknowledge will not be returned to the master. If this should occur, the bus master would normally wait indefinitely for an acknowledge and would therefore never relinquish control of the 796 bus. To avoid this possibility, a bus timeout function can optionally be implemented on a bus master to terminate a bus cycle after a preset interval, even if no acknowledge has been received. A bus timeout can therefore be defined as any data transfer cycle terminated by the master before the transfer acknowledge (XACK*) signal is received. The minimum allowable bus timeout interval is 1.0 millisecond.

2.2.2.7 *Inhibit (INH1* and INH2*)*

The inhibit lines can be invoked for any memory read or memory write operation (MRDC* or MWTC*). An inhibit line is asserted by a slave to inhibit another slave's bus activity during a memory read or write operation. The inhibit signal generated by the inhibiting slave is derived from decoding the memory address lines (t_{ID} = 100 nanoseconds maximum). The inhibiting slave can decode a single address, a block of addresses, or any combination of single and block addresses.

When it detects the specific address during the actual command (MRDC* or MWTC*), the inhibiting slave generates an inhibit signal, which is sensed by the inhibited slave. When so inhibited, this slave module disables its drivers from all data, address, and acknowledge bus lines, although it may actually perform internal operations. (All modules that may be inhibited must have completed internal operations within 1.5 microseconds from the start of the command line. This 1.5-microsecond interval is also the minimum acknowledge [t_{ACC}] timing for modules issuing inhibits. This time interval guarantees inhibited modules enough time to return to their normal state before the current bus command is completed.)

The slaves involved in the inhibit operation fall into three inhibit classes: top (inhibit) priority, middle priority, and bottom priority. In reference to the above paragraphs, a higher priority slave module would be the inhibiting slave and a lower priority slave would be the inhibited slave. INH1* is asserted during the appropriate address by a middle priority slave, such as a read-only memory module or memory-mapped I/O module, to inhibit the bus activity of a bottom priority slave, such as a read/write RAM module. INH2* is asserted at the appropriate address by a top priority slave, such as an auxiliary or a bootstrap ROM module, to inhibit the bus activity of a middle priority slave. The top priority slave shall also assert INH1* so that a bottom priority slave will also be inhibited. The inhibit lines shall be asserted low by open collector or equivalent drivers. When both a middle and a top priority inhibiting slave are activated, INH1* will be asserted by drivers on both modules.

The use of the inhibit signals during memory reads (MRDC*) shall not cause any adverse effects within the inhibited slave module. That is, data in the inhibited slave shall not be altered and its status register, if any, shall not be affected.

The use of the inhibit signals during memory writes (MWTC*) shall be allowed and might or might not affect the data within the inhibited slave. If the data is affected, it shall be only within the one byte (or word) that is being addressed. (No other data within the inhibited slave shall be altered.)

The inhibit signals, when issued, shall be generated within 100 nanoseconds (t_{ID}) after the address is stable. (See Figure 9.) A command may be generated as early as 50 nanoseconds (t_{AS}) after the address is stable. This timing can cause the inhibit to occur after the command has been received by the inhibited module. To prevent false acknowledges, modules that can be inhibited must not generate an acknowledge until the inhibit signals have had time to become valid (50 nanoseconds after the command).

Figure 9 shows the timing for an inhibit operation. In this example, both PROM and RAM have the same memory addresses; therefore, the PROM inhibits the RAM.

Although inhibit signals may be generated during IORC*, IOWC*, or INTA* operations, these signals are ignored by other slaves, including the slave that should respond to the INTA*, IORC*, or IOWC*.

2.3 Interrupt operations

The following subsections explain the 796 bus signal lines used in the interrupt operation, and the two different types of interrupt implementation.

2.3.1 Interrupt signal lines

2.3.1.1 Interrupt request lines (INT0 - INT7*)*

A set of interrupt request lines (INT0* - INT7*) is provided on the bus. An interrupt is generated by activating one of the eight interrupt request lines with an open-collector driver. All interrupts are level-triggered, rather than edge-triggered. Requiring no edge to trigger an interrupt allows several sources to be attached to each line. The interrupt request lines are prioritized, with INT0* having the highest priority and INT7* having the lowest priority.

2.3.1.2 Interrupt acknowledge (INTA)*

An interrupt acknowledge line (INTA*), driven by the bus master, requests the transfer of interrupt information on the bus. The specific information applied to the bus depends on the implementation of the interrupt scheme. In general, the leading edge of INTA* indicates that the address bus is active; the trailing edge indicates that data is present on the data lines.

2.3.2 Classes of interrupt implementation

There are two types of interrupt implementation schemes: non-bus vectored (NBV) and bus vectored (BV). The two schemes are explained in the following subsections.

2.3.2.1 Non-bus vectored interrupts

Non-bus vectored (NBV) interrupts are those interrupts handled on the bus master that do not require the 796 bus for transfer of the interrupt vector address. The interrupt vector address is generated by the interrupt controller on the master and transferred to the processor over the local bus. The slave modules generating the interrupts can reside on the master module or on other bus modules, in which case they use the 796 bus interrupt request lines (INT0* - INT7*) to generate their interrupt requests to the bus master. When an interrupt request line is activated, the bus master performs its own interrupt operation and processes the interrupt. Figure 10 shows an example of NBV interrupt implementation.

2.3.2.2 Bus vectored interrupts

Bus vectored (BV) interrupts are those interrupts that transfer the interrupt vector address over the 796 bus from the slave to the bus master using the INTA* command signal.

When an interrupt request occurs, the interrupt control logic on the bus master interrupts its processor. The processor on the bus master generates the INTA* command, freezing the state of the interrupt logic for priority resolution. The bus master also locks (retains the bus between bus cycles) the 796 bus to guarantee itself back-to-back bus cycles. After the first INTA* command, the bus master's interrupt control logic puts an interrupt code on the 796 bus address lines. The interrupt code is the address of the highest priority active interrupt request line. At this point in the BV interrupt procedure, two different sequences can occur because the 796 bus can support masters that generate either two or three INTA* commands.

If the bus master generates two INTA* commands, one more INTA* command will be generated. This second

INTA* causes the bus slave interrupt control logic to transmit its interrupt vector address on the 796 bus data lines. The address is used by the bus master to service the interrupt.

If the bus master generates three INTA* commands, two more INTA* commands will be generated. These two INTA* commands allow the bus slave to put its two-byte interrupt vector address on the 796 bus data lines (one byte for each INTA*). The interrupt vector address is used by the bus master to service the interrupt.

NOTE: The 796 bus can support only one type of bus vectored interrupt in a given system. However, the 796 bus can support both bus vectored (BV) and non-bus vectored (NBV) interrupts within the same system.

Figure 11 depicts an example of BV interrupt implementation.

2.4 796 Bus exchange

The 796 bus can accommodate several bus masters on the same system, each taking control of the bus as it needs to effect data transfers. The bus masters request bus control through a bus exchange sequence.

The discussion of the 796 bus exchange will be separated into three parts. The first part explains the signals involved, the second part discusses the bus exchange priority techniques (serial and parallel), and the

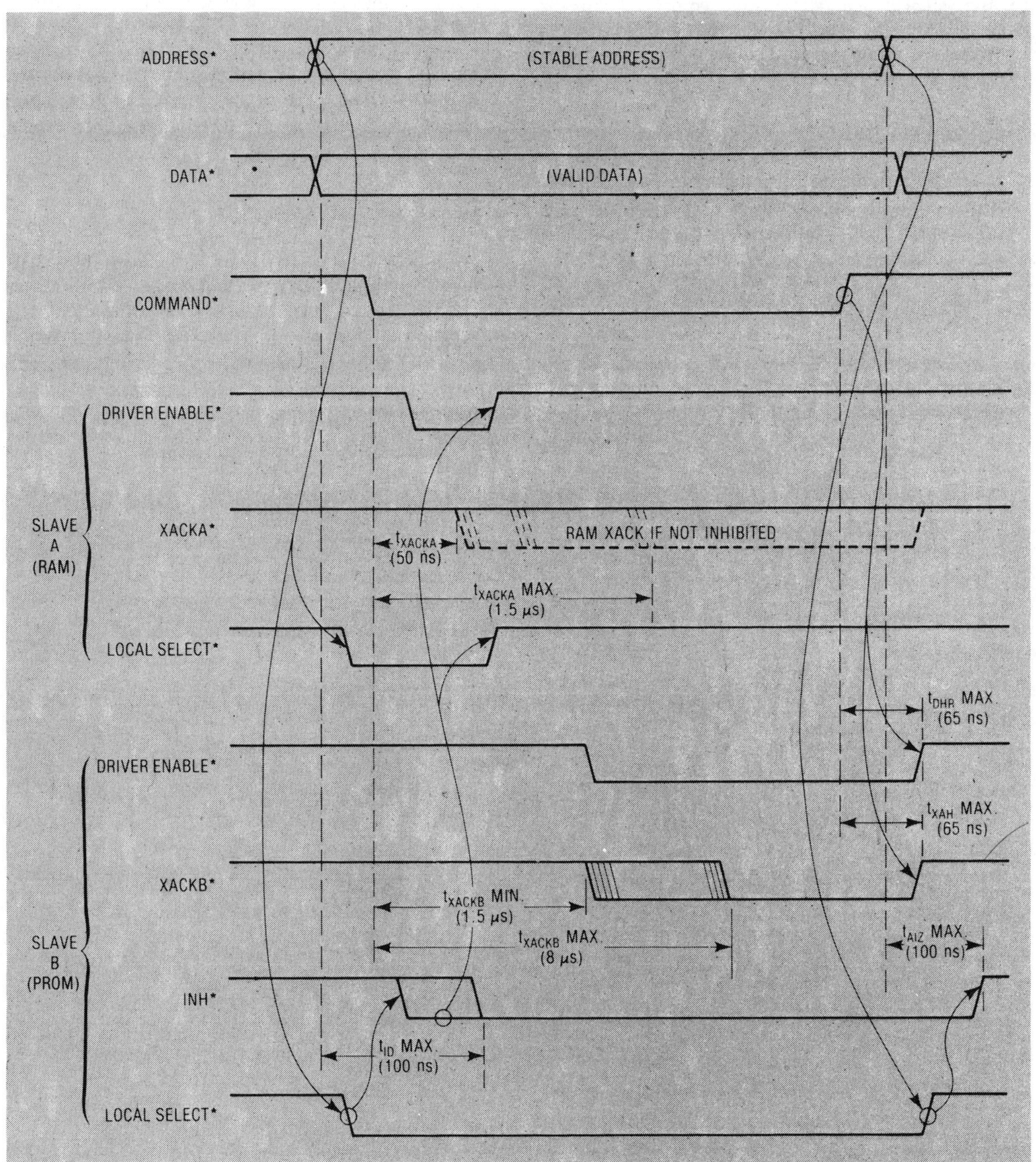

Figure 9. Inhibit timing for write operation. (Note: Since bus cycles are asynchronous, the time scale is not linear.)

third part explains the implementation of the exchange logic.

2.4.1 796 Bus exchange signals

A set of six signals is used to implement the bus exchange operation. All bus exchange signals are synchronized by BCLK*.

2.4.1.1 Bus clock (BCLK)*

This periodic clock signal is used to synchronize the exchange logic, with synchronization occurring on the trailing (high-to-low) edge of the pulse. BCLK* has a duty cycle of approximately 50 percent, a maximum frequency of 10 MHz, and can be slowed, stepped, or stopped as called for by system design. There is no requirement for synchronization between BCLK* and CCLK*, but they may be derived from the same source. The BCLK* line is driven by a TTL clock driver.

2.4.1.2 Bus busy (BUSY)*

This signal is driven by the master in control of the bus. All other masters monitor BUSY* to determine the state of the bus. This bidirectional signal, which is driven by an open-collector gate, is synchronized by BCLK*.

2.4.1.3 Bus priority in (BPRN)*

A non-bused signal that indicates to a master that no master of higher priority is requesting control of the bus. BPRN* is synchronized by BCLK* and driven by TTL gates. In a serial resolution scheme, this is the master's input from the priority chain. In a parallel resolution scheme, this is the master's input from the parallel priority circuit.

2.4.1.4 Bus priority out (BPRO)*

This non-bused signal, when activated by a bus master, indicates to the bus master of the next lower priority that it may gain control of the bus (i.e., no higher priority requests are pending for control of the bus). This signal is used only in a daisy-chained serial priority resolution scheme and should be connected to the bus priority in (BPRN*) input of the next lower priority bus master. BPRO* is driven by TTL gates and is synchronized by BCLK*.

Each bus master must allow its BPRO* signal to be disconnected from the BPRO* line on the 796 bus so that, if desired, a parallel priority resolution scheme can be used. This capability is to allow some bus masters to have their BPRN* inputs driven by a central parallel resolution circuit instead of by the BPRO* of the next higher priority master.

2.4.1.5 Bus request (BREQ)*

The bus request (BREQ*) line is used with the parallel priority resolution scheme, and is a request of the master for 796 bus control. The priorities of the BREQ* from each master are resolved in a parallel priority resolution circuit. The highest priority request enables the BPRN* input of that master, allowing it to gain control of the bus. BREQ* is synchronized by BCLK* and is a TTL output.

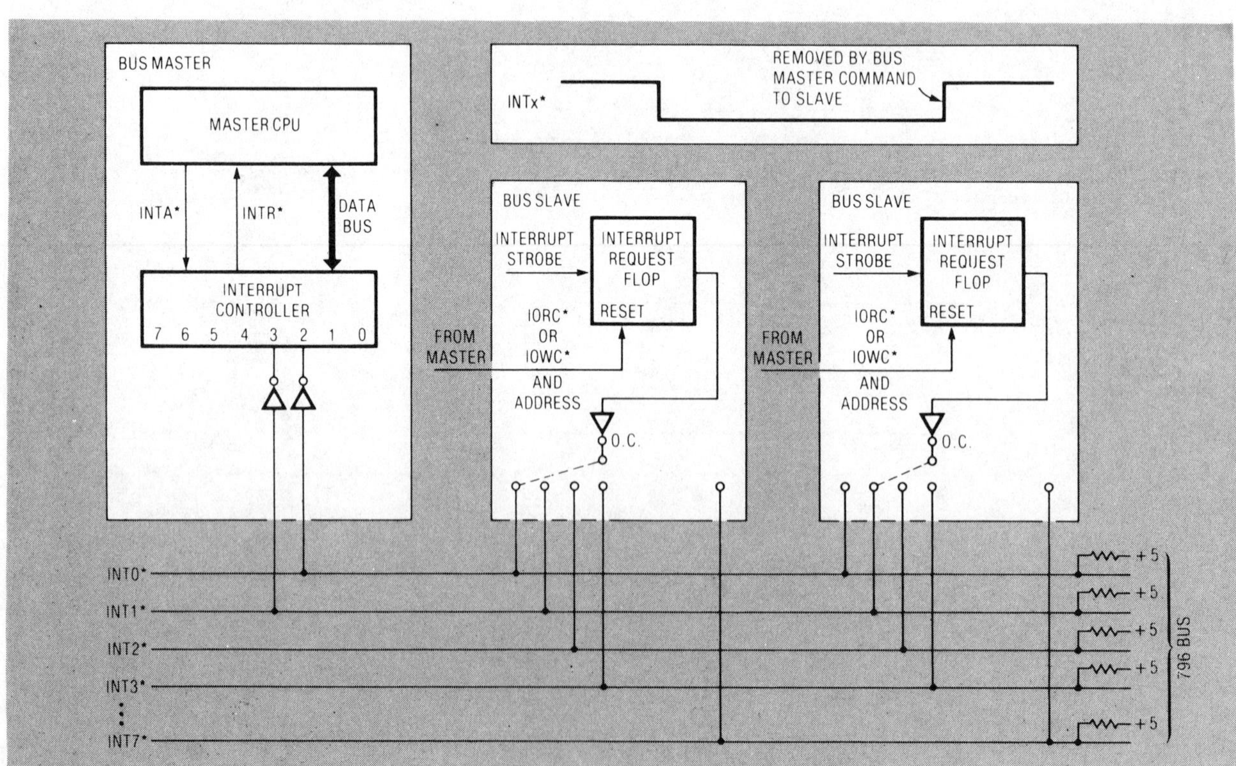

Figure 10. Non-bus vectored (NBV) interrupt logic.

2.4.1.6 Common bus request (CBRQ) (optional)*

Any master that wants control of the 796 bus, but does not control it, can activate CBRQ* with an open-collector gate. If CBRQ* is high, it indicates to the bus master that no other master is requesting the bus and therefore the present bus master can retain the bus. There are times when this can save the bus exchange overhead for the current master. This is because quite often when a master is controlling the bus, there are no other masters that are requesting the bus. Without CBRQ*, only BPRN* indicates whether or not another master is requesting the bus and, for BPRN*, only if the other master is of higher priority. Between the master's bus transfer cycles, in order to allow lower priority masters to take the bus if they need it, the master must give up the bus. At the start of the master's next transfer cycle, the bus must be regained. If no other master has the bus, this can take approximately three BCLK* periods. To avoid this overhead of unnecessarily giving up and regaining the bus when no other masters need it, CBRQ* may be used. Any master that wants but does not have the bus must drive this line low (true). The master that has the bus can, at the end of a transfer cycle, sense CBRQ*. If it is not low, then the bus does not have to be released, thereby eliminating the delay of regaining the bus at the start of the next cycle. (At any time before the master's next cycle, any other master desiring the bus will drive CBRQ* and cause the master to relinquish the bus at that time.)

Masters that use CBRQ* must be able to disable that function such that they can be used with masters that do not generate the CBRQ* signal.

2.4.2 Bus exchange priority techniques

Two bus exchange priority techniques are discussed: a serial technique and a parallel technique. Figure 12 and Figure 13 illustrate these two techniques. Note that the parallel and serial schemes are compatible and therefore can be combined and used together on the same bus. The

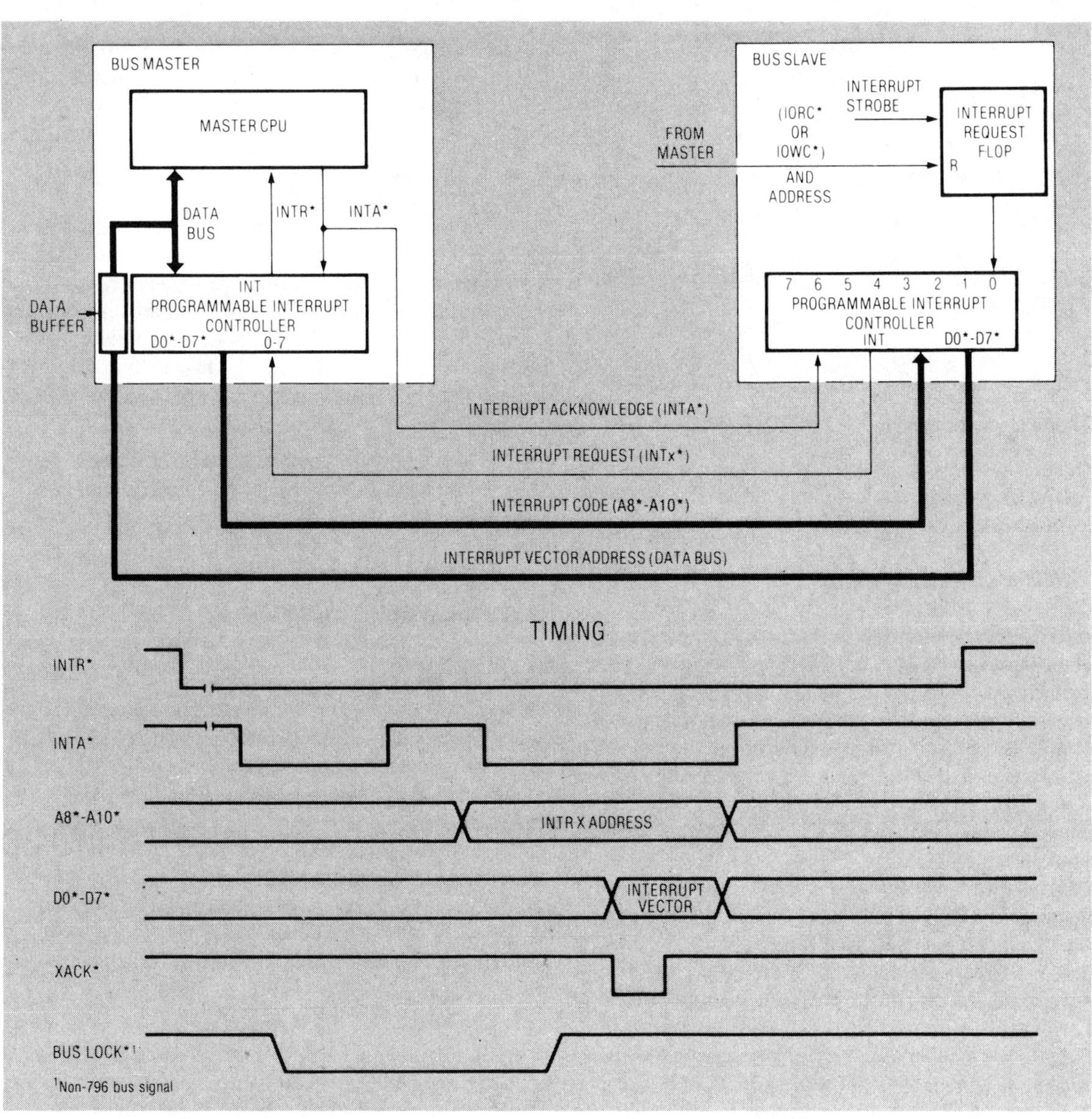

Figure 11. Bus vectored (BV) interrupt logic.

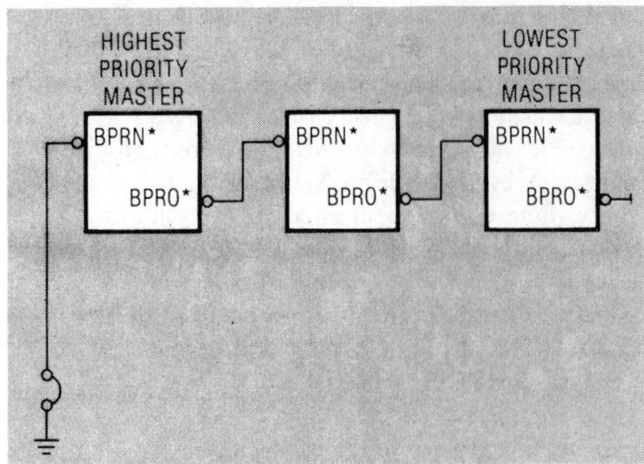

Figure 12. Serial priority technique.

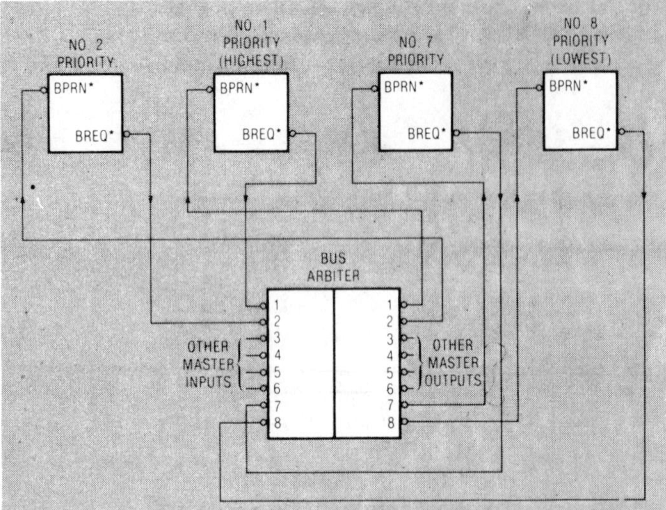

Figure 13. Parallel priority technique.

bus exchange implementation discussed in 2.4.3 is the same for both techniques.

2.4.2.1 Serial priority technique

Serial priority resolution is accomplished with a daisy-chain technique (see Figure 12). With such a scheme, the bus priority output (BPRO*) of each master is connected to the bus priority input (BPRN*) of the next lower priority master. The BPRN* of the highest priority master in the serial chain shall either be always active or connected to a central bus arbiter as described in 2.4.2.2. The latter connection would be used if a parallel-serial priority structure were used.

Serial priority resolution is accomplished in the following manner. The BPRO* output for a particular master is asserted if and only if its BPRN* input is active and that master is not requesting control of the bus. Thus, if a master requests control of the bus, it shall set its BPRO* high, which in turn disables the BPRN* of all lower priority masters. The number of masters that can be linked in a serial chain is limited by the fact that the BPRN* signal must propagate through the entire chain within one BCLK* cycle. If the maximum BCLK* of 10 MHz is used, then the number of masters in a serial chain is limited to three.

2.4.2.2 Parallel arbitration technique

In the parallel technique, the bus allocation is determined by a bus arbiter (see Figure 13). This may be a priority scheme, which determines the next master by a fixed priority structure, or some other mechanism for allocation (e.g., sequential). The BREQ* lines are used by the arbiter to signal the next master on the appropriate BPRN* line. The BPRO* lines are not used in the parallel allocation BPRN* scheme.

3. Electrical specifications

This section presents the electrical specifications for the 796 bus as follows:

(1) general bus considerations of the state relationships, signal line characteristics, and power supplies;
(2) timing specifications for the bus signals; and
(3) specifications for the signal line drivers and receivers, as well as the electrical termination requirements.

When electrical specifications indicate minimum or maximum values for the bus, they must be measurable at any point on the bus.

Note that a particular implemented bus could have any amount of bus propagation delay and ringing (before setup times), as long as all bus parameters (e.g., setup, hold, and other times) are met at all points on the bus. However, to facilitate the design of a compatible set of modules (masters and slaves) that use the bus, the standard maximum bus propagation delay will be specified as t_{PD} (max).

NOTE: The rest of this chapter is omitted because of space limitations. Full specification copies can be obtained by writing to the address given in the introduction.

4. Mechanical specifications

4.0 Introduction

This section describes all the physical and mechanical specifications that a designer must be concerned with when designing a 796 bus backplane or when designing printed circuit boards that will plug into the 796 bus interface.

The P2 connector does not have any specific pin assignments. P2 is not to be defined (NDEF) by this specification, and there are not necessarily any bussed lines for P2 on the motherboard.

Only the basic board's standard vertical height is currently specified.

NOTE: Due to space limitations, only the following three figures and one table [Figures 14-16 and Table 1] are presented here from this chapter. Full specification copies can be obtained by writing to the address given in the introduction.

5. Levels of compliance

This section presents the concept and notation of levels of compliance with the 796 bus standard as follows:

(1) variable elements of capability composing the essence of 796 bus standard compliance,
(2) general discussion of compliance relationship for masters and for slaves, and
(3) notation for describing level of compliance with the 796 bus standard.

The notion of levels of compliance is introduced to facilitate the use of 796 bus products of varying capability manufactured by diverse vendors. It bounds the variability allowed within the 796 bus specification and provides a succinct and convenient notation for these variables.

5.1 Variable elements of capability

The 796 bus is very versatile, allowing systems to be constructed with boards of varying capability. The 796 bus allows for variations in data path width, I/O address path width, and interrupt attributes. In addition, it is recognized that some vendors' products have differing memory address path widths.

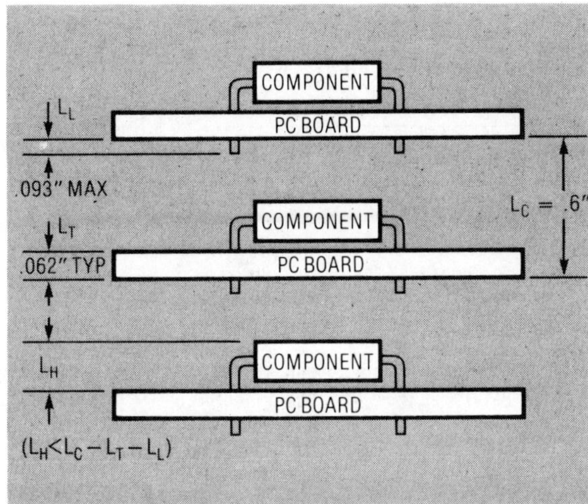

Figure 14 [Figure 31 in full specification]. IEEE 796 Bus backplane card-to-card separation.

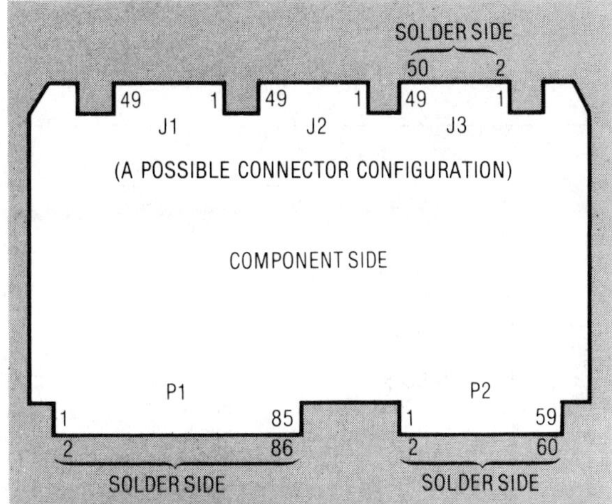

Figure 15 [Figure 33 in full specification]. Connector and pin numbering.

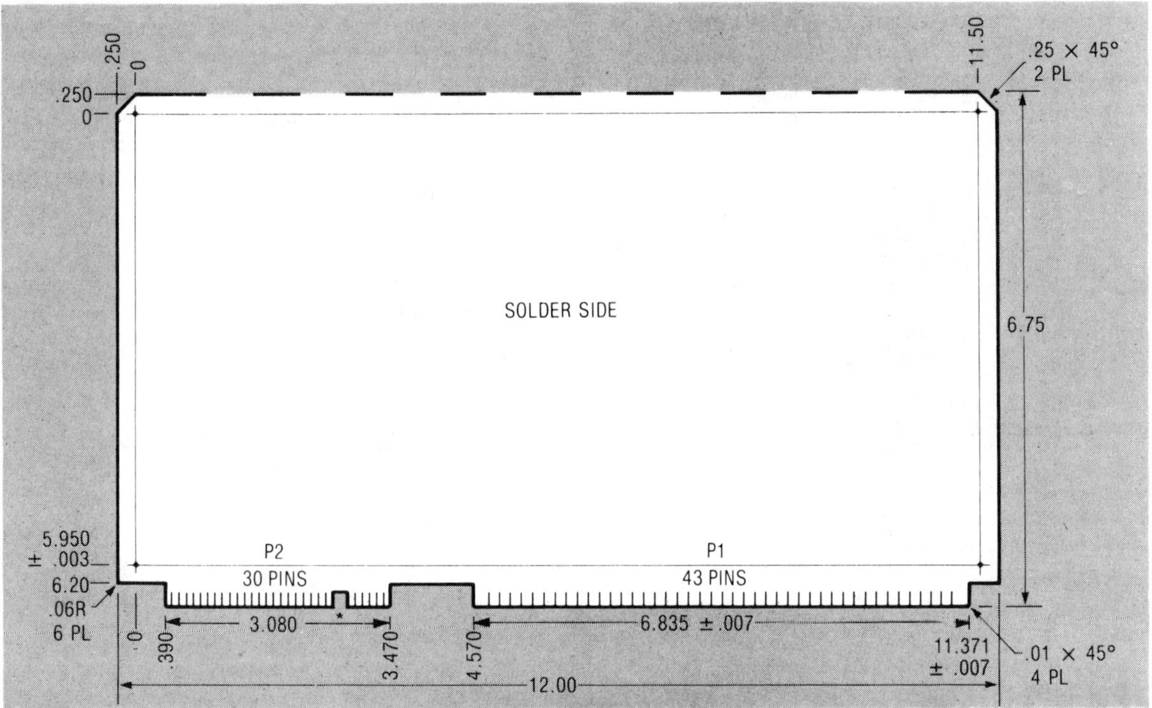

Figure 16 [Figure 34 in full specification]. Standard PWB and PCB outline. (Note: A more complete mechanical drawing is included in the full specification.)

5.1.1 Data path

The 796 bus allows for both 8- and 16-bit data path products. The 16-bit data path products use the byte swapping technique described in paragraph 2.2.2.4, thus allowing the 8- and 16-bit products to work together.

5.1.2 Memory address path

The 796 bus standard designates a 20-bit address path. In many systems a 16-bit address path may be sufficient, though not fully 796 bus compatible.

5.1.3 I/O address path

The 796 bus allows for both 8- and 16-bit I/O address paths. The 16-bit path products must also be configurable to act as 8-bit path products.

5.1.4 Interrupt attributes

The 796 bus (Section 2.3) allows for considerable variety in interrupt attributes. A product may support no interrupts, non-bus vectored (NBV) interrupts, two-cycle bus vectored interrupts, and three-cycle bus vectored in-

Table 1.
[Table 4 in full specification]
Pin assignment of bus signals on IEEE 796 bus board connector (P1).

	(COMPONENT SIDE)			|(CIRCUIT SIDE)		
	PIN	MNEMONIC	DESCRIPTION	PIN	MNEMONIC	DESCRIPTION
POWER	1	GND	Signal GND	2	GND	Signal GND
SUPPLIES	3	+5V	+5Vdc	4	+5V	+5Vdc
	5	+5V	+5Vdc	6	+5V	+5Vdc
	7	+12V	+12Vdc	8	+12V	+12Vdc
	9	RFU	Reserved†	10	RFU	Reserved†
	11	GND	Signal GND	12	GND	Signal GND
BUS	13	BCLK*	Bus clock	14	INIT*	Initialize
CONTROLS	15	BPRN*	Bus pri.in	16	BPRO*	Bus pri. out
	17	BUSY*	Bus busy	18	BREQ*	Bus request
	19	MRDC*	Mem read cmd	20	MWTC*	Mem write cmd
	21	IORC*	I/O read cmd	22	IOWC*	I/O write cmd
	23	XACK*	XFER acknowledge	24	INH1*	Inhibit 1 (disable RAM)
BUS	25	RFU	Reserve†	26	INH2*	Inhibit 2 (disable PROM or ROM)
CONTROLS	27	BHEN*	Byte high enable	28	A16* (ADR10*)	
AND	29	CBRQ*	Common bus request	30	A17* (ADR11*)	Address
ADDRESS	31	CCLK*	Constant clk	32	A18* (ADR12*)	Bus††
	33	INTA*	Intr acknowledge	34	A19* (ADR13*)	
INTERRUPTS	35	INT6*	Parallel	36	INT7*	Parallel
	37	INT4*	Interrupt	38	INT5*	Interrupt
	39	INT2*	Requests	40	INT3*	Requests
	41	INT0*		42	INT1*	
ADDRESS††	43	A14* (ADRE*)		44	A15* (ADRF*)	
	45	A12* (ADRC*)		46	A13* (ADRD*)	
	47	A10* (ADRA*)	Address	48	A11* (ADRB*)	Address
	49	A8* (ADR8*)	Bus††	50	A9* (ADR9*)	Bus††
	51	A6* (ADR6*)		52	A7* (ADR7*)	
	53	A4* (ADR4*)		54	A5* (ADR5*)	
	55	A2* (ADR2*)		56	A3* (ADR3*)	
	57	A0* (ADR0*)		58	A1* (ADR1*)	
DATA††	59	D14* (DATE*)		60	D15* (DATF*)	
	61	D12* (DATC*)		62	D13* (DATD*)	
	63	D10* (DATA*)	Data	64	D11* (DATB*)	Data
	65	D8* (DAT8*)	Bus††	66	D9* (DAT9*)	Bus††
	67	D6* (DAT6*)		68	D7* (DAT7*)	
	69	D4* (DAT4*)		70	D5* (DAT5*)	
	71	D2* (DAT2*)		72	D3* (DAT3*)	
	73	D0* (DAT0*)		74	D1* (DAT1*)	
POWER	75	GND	Signal GND	76	GND	Signal GND
SUPPLIES	77	RFU	Reserved†	78	RFU	Reserved†
	79	−12V	−12Vdc	80	−12V	−12Vdc
	81	+5V	+5Vdc	82	+5V	+5Vdc
	83	+5V	+5Vdc	84	+5V	+5Vdc
	85	GND	Signal GND	86	GND	Signal GND

†All reserved pins are reserved for future use and should not be used if upwards compatibility is desired.
††Signal mnemonics within parentheses are for historical reference.

Preliminary—Subject to Revision

terrupts. There are two methods of interrupt sensing: the preferred level-triggered, and for historical compatibility only, edge-level-triggered.

Level-triggered. The active level of the request line indicates an active request. Requiring no edge to trigger an interrupt allows several sources to be attached to a single request line. Sources for level-triggered sense inputs should provide a programmatic means to clear the interrupt request.

Edge-level-triggered. The transition from the inactive to the active level indicates an active request if and only if the active level is maintained, at least until it is recognized by the master. The requirement for a transition precludes multiple sources on a request line. But edge-level triggering removes the requirement that the source have a programmatic means to clear the interrupt request.

NOTE: Edge-level triggering is described only to allow for historical compatibility. New designs shall use level triggering.

A master may support either or both of the above interrupt sensing methods. It is necessary to configure the system such that the sources of the interrupt requests correspond to the interrupt sensing method of the master. Note that a source which is compatible with level triggering is also compatible with edge-level triggering.

5.2 Masters and slaves

When constructing 796 bus systems, it is not necessary that all modules have identical capabilities. One may, for instance, have a master with an 8/16-bit data path and a slave with an 8-bit data path. The system is completely functional, though the application must restrict itself to 8-bit access to the slave.

The key concept when constructing a 796 bus system is that of required capability versus supplied capability. Each product will provide some set of capability. A transaction between two such products will be restricted to use that capability which is the intersection of the sets of capability of the two products. In some cases the intersection may be null, implying fundamental incompatibility. It is the responsibility of the system designer to assure the viability of this intersection.

5.3 Compliance level notation

A notation is introduced which allows a vendor to succinctly and accurately specify a product's level of compliance with the 796 bus standard. For boards which may act as either masters or slaves, the compliance levels must be specified for both cases. Increasing levels of compliance subsume lesser levels for data path width, memory address path width, and I/O address path width. Interrupt attributes are listed discretely, since they are independent of one another. The lack of an element (i.e., no I/O address path) specification normally implies no capability for this element. An exception is that level-triggered interrupt sensing is to be assumed unless edge-level sensing is specified.

5.3.1 Data path

D8 represents an 8-bit data path.
D16 represents an 8/16-bit data path.

5.3.2 Memory address path

M16 represents a 16-bit memory address path.
M20 represents a 20-bit memory address path.

5.3.3 I/O address path

I8 represents an 8-bit I/O address path.
I16 represents an 8- or 16-bit I/O address path.

5.3.4 Interrupt attributes

V0 represents non-bus vectored interrupt requests.
V2 represents two-cycle bus vectored interrupt requests.
V3 represents three-cycle bus vectored interrupt requests.
E represents edge-level triggering only.
L represents level triggering only.
EL represents level or edge-level triggering.

The interrupt attribute notation can be concatenated to indicate multiple capabilities.

5.3.5 An example

A versatile combination I/O and memory slave board which supports an 8/16-bit data path, a 20-bit memory address, and 8- or 16-bit I/O address, NBV interrupt requests, and two- and three-cycle bus vectored interrupt requests would be specified as follows:

796 bus compliance: slave D16, M20, I16, VO23

5.3.6 Compliance marking

The compliance levels of a card shall be clearly marked on the printed circuit board as well as in the printed specifications. ■

THE BUS WHOSE TIME HAS COME
(IEEE 696.1)

Malcolm T. Wright
Electronic Enginneering
SSM Microcomputer Products, Inc.
2190 Paragon Drive
San Jose, Calif. 95131

INTRODUCTION

The IEEE 696.1 standard defines a very flexible microcomputer bus structure supporting both 8 and 16 Bit processors. For over 2-1/2 years the IEEE subcommittee reviewed microcomputer development and future hardware needs to maximize the 696.1's flexibility in an ever-changing computer market. Many requirements, like multiple DMA devices, direct addressing of 16 megabytes, 16-bit processors, etc., can be easily supported on the 696.1 bus. Presently this bus is being used in industrial control applications, business applications such as bookkeeping and word processing, and R&D work.

HISTORY

The birth of the IEEE 696.1 bus dates back to January, 1975, with the announcement of one of the first personal 8-bit computers for under $400. The Altair 8800 computer, as it was called, based its interconnection on a 100-trace bus with up to 16 PC card connectors. The Altair, as designed by its principal inventor Ed Roberts of MITS Inc., used an Intel 8080 microprocessor. Only 81 of the bus traces were committed, so that future enhancements in architecture could be supported by adding signals. Due to the simple bus structure, a low-cost power supply requirement, and low-cost LSI technology, the Altair bus structure became very popular.

The microcomputer market place exploded over the next two years with the creation of many new businesses to support the Altair and other personal computers. Companies like Cromemco Inc., NorthStar Computers Inc. and Vector Graphics were formed at this time supporting the Altair bus. The Altair bus (evenually renamed the S-100 bus) was the most supported computer system during the first personal computer show in April 1977. Over 160 exhibitors displayed their products at the show with over half of these S-100 related.

As the variety of hardware and the number of 8-bit processors increased, a committee was formed to document the S-100 bus requirements formally. In late 1978, Dr. Robert Stewart chaired IEEE committee meetings to standardize the interface requirements for the S-100 bus 696.1, MULTIBUS (R) 796, and Microbus (TM) 696.3. The S-100 bus as defined by the subcommittee for the IEEE 696.1 standard was enhanced to 93 signals to meet future 16-bit processor applications. The S-100 bus presently supports the 8080, 8085, 6502, 6809, 8088, 8086, Z80, Z8000, WD16 and TMS9900 processors.

FEATURES

The IEEE 696.1 bus offers signal traces to support the following:

1. 8- or 16-bit microprocessors
   *The bus has 16 data lines for passing data between a master and a slave device.
   *Handshaking lines are provided for mixing 8- and 16-bit slaves (memory & I/O) on the bus.

2. DMA control
   *Address lines to allow up to 16 DMA masters.
   *A detailed arbitration circuit set forth by the 696.1 standard.

3. 24 Address lines
   *Direct addressing possible up to 16 megabytes.

4. Interrupts
   *Eight interrupt lines set aside for vectored interrupts.

5. Error detection
   *One line for power fail.
   *One line for general systemerror (hardware or memory).

Reprinted with permission from *Midcon Conf. Rec.*, 1981, pp. 25.3.1–25.3.10.

6. Simple power supply
   *+8 volts unregulated but filtered.
   *+16 volts unregulated but filtered.
   *-16 volts unregulated but filtered.

INTERCONNECTION

The motherboard (696.1 interconnection PC board) for the computer system can be purchased in four- to 22-connector lengths. Per the 696.1 standard, the motherboard is specified for operations up to 6 MHz, but many manufactures have already tested their motherboards up to 10 MHz to better support the 8086, Z8000 and 68000 processors. [Seattle Computer Products and CompuPro are already running processors up to 8 MHz.] Each bus trace is normally terminated by approximately 250 ohms at 2.6 volts to reduce pulse reflections and cross-talk at speeds above 4 MHz.

POWER

The power traces on the motherboard are only on the end pins of the 100-pin PC board connector to each card. To guarantee low resistance for the main logic power, two pins are provided for the +8 volts and five pins for the ground. Two additional power sources of +16 and -16 volts are provided for I/O, CPU, memory, analog, or other special applications.

Since each 696.1 PC board has its own on-board regulator, the main power source can be simply a power transformer, diode bridge, and a filter capacitor.

TIMING

The main CPU timing is available to all 696.1 boards through two signal lines.

PSYNC [Pin 76]
: A positive going pulse to indicate the start of a read/write data cycle.

PHASE 2 [Pin 24]
: System clock generated by the permanent bus master.

For additional peripheral board timing, a 2 MHz (0.5%) clock is available from the bus called CLOCK.

DATA LINES

The 696.1 uses eight lines to write data (DO) and eight lines to read data (DI) into the bus master to maintain compatibility to its 8-bit CPU heritage. To support 16-bit processors, two handshaking lines (SXTRQ & SIXTN) are present to control data transfers. A 16-bit bus master can request 16 communications with a slave device by driving the SXTRQ line low. If the slave device can operate in the 16-bit mode, then the SIXTN line is driven low to acknowledge 16-bits, and the data bus goes bidirectional.

ADDRESS LINES

The original S-100 bus had only 16 address lines to support up to 64K bytes of memory. The 696.1 subcommittee added eight additional address lines (commonly known as "Extended Addressing") to support the 68000 microprocessor that was announced by Motorola. The full 24 address lines gives this bus direct access to 16 megabytes of memory. The address lines are labeled A0 thru A23.

READ/WRITE LINES

Two strobe signals are present on the bus to perform read/write operations.

PDBIN [Pin 78]
: A positive-going pulse to read data into the bus master.

PWR* [Pin 77]
: A negative-going pulse to write data out to the slave.

[NOTE: There is a second write signal on the bus called MWRT that is used for memory write operations only. This signal is not recommended for present or future 696.1 use; it had been used by the front control panel of the old Altair and IMSAI computers to allow manual memory deposits.]

CONTROL LINES

The 696.1 bus has four main status lines to control memory versus I/O operations. The signals on these lines occur in advance of the read/write signals to allow for setup time in the slave device.

SMEMR [Pin 47]
A logic high level during memory Read cycles.

SWO* [Pin 97]
A logic low level during I/O or memory write cycles.

SINP [Pin 45]
A logic high level during I/O read cycles.

SOUT [Pin 46]
A logic high level during I/O write cycles.

Additional control signals from the CPU acknowledge interrupt, DMA, halt mode, 16-bit mode or valid status periods.

SINTA [Pin 96]
Acknowledges that the interrupt was accepted by the master.

PHLDA [Pin 26]
Acknowledges that the processor has given up normal bus control for another master. [DMA protocall is defined in detail in the IEEE 696.1 Proposed Standard.]

SHLTA [Pin 48]
Acknowledges that the processor is in a halt state.

SIXTN [Pin 60]
Acknowledges that the slave will operate in 16-bit data mode.

PSTVAL [Pin 25]
Acknowledges by a low logic level that the status signals (bus names that begin with an "S") are stable.

To flag the beginning of an instruction fetch cycle, one status signal is available.

SM1[Pin 44]
A logic high level during an opcode fetch.

CLEAR LINES

To clear hardware on power-up of the system or to restart the system, the 696.1 has 3 reset lines.

POC* [Pin 99]
Power-on-clear is a low-going pulse during system power-up.

RESET* [Pin 75]
Driven low to reinitialize the hardware. RESET is low during power-on-clear also.

SLAVE CLR* [Pin 54]
Driven low to reset bus slaves. Pin 54 is low during power-on-clear also.

INTERRUPT LINES

To support vectored interrupts the following signal lines are available:

VIO* [Pin 4] thru VI7* [Pin 11]
Highest priority interrupt level (request line) is VIO*.

INT* [Pin 73]
Master interrupt line from the interrupt controller to the bus master.

NMI* [Pin 12]
Non-maskable interrupt line.

DMA LINES

To allow for multiple DMA masters on the 696.1 bus, four address lines and two handshaking lines are used to prioritize up to 16 masters.

DMA0* [Pin 55] thru DMA3* [Pin 14]
The LSB of DMA device selection is the line DMA0*.

HOLD* [Pin 74]
DMA request line.

PHLDA* [Pin 26]
DMA acknowledge line.

ACCESS SPEED CONTROL

To synchronize the bus master to the response speed of a slave device, two lines are provided.

RDY [Pin 72]
General ready line to the bus master. High logic state from the slave equals "Ready".

XRDY [Pin 3]
Special ready line to the bus master. Normally this line is used by front control panels.

READ/WRITE SEQUENCE

All read/write operations are preceded with a PSYNC pulse from the bus master. The order of events on the 696.1 bus could be listed as follows:

Sequence

1st PSYNC
;Start of operation

2nd ADDRESS
;Address set-up

3rd STATUS ("S" signals)
;Type of operation indicated

4th PSTVAL
;Status-valid indicated

5th Send READY(RDY)
;Slave indicates Ready or Not Ready.

6th PDBIN or PWR*
;Start of read or write strobe.

7th Test for READY (RDY)
;Delay, if slave not ready.

The address, status, and the read-/write strobe must all be valid for a slave/master data transfer. The RDY signal must be true also for the CPU to complete the read/write operation. The following signal combinations must be true for memory or I/O communications:

Memory Read
= SMEMR . PDBIN . ADDRESS

Memory Write
= -SOUT . -PWR* . ADDRESS

I/O Read
= SINP . PDBIN . ADDRESS

I/O Write
= SOUT . -PWR* . ADDRESS

Note: + = OR, . = AND, * = Inverted signal, - = NOT

CONCLUSION

As we have seen, then, the S-100 bus is now well-defined. Moreover, the proposed IEEE document on the bus also specifies timing requirements, which will guarantee interchangeability of boards. Thus, in the changing world of microcomputers, 696.1 is truly The Bus Whose Time Has Come.

And the variety of products available for the S-100/696.1 bus continues to grow daily. For example:

* Up to eight serial I/O channels on one board
* IEEE 488 interfaces
* Up to 64 kbytes of RAM
* Up to 32 kbytes of EPROM
* High-density graphics
* High-speed, floating-point processors
* Sound synthesizers
* 8- and 16-bit CPUs
* Relay control boards
* A/D and D/A boards
* Video interface boards
* Floppy disk interfaces
* Hard-disk interfaces
* Real-time clock boards
* Printer interface boards

The number and variety of applications for the 696.1 bus are also increasing. Among others, we can already list

* Numerical-control equipment
* Banking systems
* Automatic layout of PC boards
* Multiprocessor systems
* Word processing
* Accounting
* Environmental controls
* R & D projects

This level of maturity and acceptance of the 696.1 bus means that the systems designer can now be confident that an extensive infrastructure exists--an infrastructure that supports and complements the technically sound reasons for using the 696.1 bus, and which includes

* an existing base of knowledgeable hardware and software engineers, which decreases training costs and increases the availability of personnel;

* a diverse list of plug-compatible manufacturers, yielding a constantly improving system "workability" through competitive cost reductions and new-technology introductions;

* a dropping price/performance ratio--because the 696.1 standard encourages

additional hardware and software investments, which in turn provide increased performance.

In summary, the S-100/696.1 bus has evolved into a very capable design alternative...one that definitely justifies the business decision to "go" with the bus, the related investment in development, and the on-going product support.

(R) MULTIBUS is a trademark of Intel Corporation.
(TM) Microbus is a trademark of National Semiconductor Corp.

PROPOSED 696.1 BUS LAYOUT

pin 1	+8 Volts	pin 51	+8 Volts
pin 2	+16 Volts	pin 52	-16 Volts
pin 3	XRDY	pin 53	GROUND
pin 4	VI0*	pin 54	SLAVE CLR*
pin 5	VI1*	pin 55	DMA0*
pin 6	VI2*	pin 56	DMA1*
pin 7	VI3*	pin 57	DMA2*
pin 8	VI4*	pin 58	SXTRQ*
pin 9	VI5*	pin 59	A19
pin 10	VI6*	pin 60	SIXTN*
pin 11	VI7*	pin 61	A20
pin 12	NMI*	pin 62	A21
pin 13	PWRFAIL*	pin 63	A22
pin 14	DMA3*	pin 64	A23
pin 15	A18	pin 65	NDEF
pin 16	A16	pin 66	NDEF
pin 17	A17	pin 67	PHANTOM
pin 18	SDSB*	pin 68	MWRT
pin 19	CDSB*	pin 69	RFU
pin 20	GROUND	pin 70	GROUND
pin 21	RFU	pin 71	RFU
pin 22	ADSB*	pin 72	RDY
pin 23	DODSB*	pin 73	INT*
pin 24	PHASE 2	pin 74	HOLD*
pin 25	PSTVAL*	pin 75	RESET*
pin 26	PHLDA	pin 76	PSYNC
pin 27	RFU	pin 77	PWR*
pin 28	RFU	pin 78	PDBIN
pin 29	A5	pin 79	A0
pin 30	A4	pin 80	A1
pin 31	A3	pin 81	A2
pin 32	A15	pin 82	A6
pin 33	A12	pin 83	A7
pin 34	A9	pin 84	A8
pin 35	DO1(8),DATA1(16)	pin 85	A13
pin 36	DO0(8),DATA0(16)	pin 86	A14
pin 37	A10	pin 87	A11
pin 38	DO4(8),DATA4(16)	pin 88	DO2(8),DATA2(16)
pin 39	DO5(8),DATA5(16)	pin 89	DO3(8),DATA3(16)
pin 40	DO6(8),DATA6(16)	pin 90	DO7(8),DATA7(16)
pin 41	DI2(8),DATA10(16)	pin 91	DI4(8),DATA12(16)
pin 42	DI3(8),DATA11(16)	pin 92	DI5(8),DATA13(16)
pin 43	DI7(8),DATA15(16)	pin 93	DI6(8),DATA14(16)
pin 44	SM1	pin 94	DI1(8),DATA9(16)
pin 45	SOUT	pin 95	DI0(8),DATA8(16)
pin 46	SINP	pin 96	SINTA
pin 47	SMEMR	pin 97	SWO*
pin 48	SHLTA	pin 98	ERROR*
pin 49	CLOCK	pin 99	POC*
pin 50	GROUND	pin 100	GROUND

* = Inverted signal
RFU =Reservedfor future use
NDEF = Not defined

(8) = 8-bit mode
(16) = 16-bit mode

Cromemco, Inc. 280 Bernardo ave Mountain View, CA 94043 (415) 964-7400	Z80 systems Multi-User Software Boards and Boxes
Scion 8455-D Tyco Road Vienna, VA 22180 (703) 827-0888	High-Res. Graphics B&W and Color
Intersystems, Inc. Dept. B 1650 Hanshaw Road P.O. Box 91 Ithaca, NY 14850 (607) 257-0190	Z80 & Z8000 Systems Software Boards and Box
SSM Microcomputer Products, Inc. 2190 Paragon Drive San Jose, CA. 95131 (408) 946-7400	8080 & Z80 CPU Boards
CompuPro (Div. of Godbout Elec.) Box 2355 Oakland Airport, CA. 94614 (415) 562-0636	8085, Z80 & 8088 CPU Boards
California Computer Systems 250 Caribbean Drive Sunnyvale, CA 94086 (408) 734-5811	Z80 System 6502 CPU Boards and Box
Systems Group(Div. of Meas. Sys. & Controls, Inc.) 1601 Orangewood Ave. Orange, CA 92668 (714) 633-4460	Z80 System
Measurement Systems & Controls, Inc. 867 N. Main Street Orange, CA 92668 (714) 633-4460	Boards
Vector Graphic, Inc. 31364 Via Colinas Westlake Village, CA 91362 (800) 423-5857 or (800) 382-3367	Z80 System
Corvus Systems 2029 O'Toole Ave. San Jose, CA 95131 (408) 946-7700	Hard Disks & Interface Back-End & Local-Area Networks
Konan Corporation 1448 N. 27th Ave. Phoenix, AZ 85009 (800) 528-4563	Hard Disks & Interfaces Boards

Zobex P.O. Box 1847 San Diego, CA 92112 (714) 571-6971	Z80 System
Electronic Design Associates P.O. Box 94055 Houston, TX 77018 (713) 999-2255	Color Video & Sound Generator
Seattle Computer Products, Inc. 1114 Industry Drive Seattle, WA 98188 (206) 575-1830	8086 CPU Boards
Adaptive Data & Energy Systems 2627 Pomona Blvd Pomona, CA 91768 (714) 594-5858	31-MB Hard Disk & Interface
Executive Systems, Inc. 15300 Ventura Blvd. Sherman Oaks, CA 91403 (213) 990-3457	30-MB Hard Disk with Tape Backup & Interface
Dual Systems Control Corporation 1825 Eastshore Highway Berkeley, CA 94710 (415) 549-3854	32K CMOS Memory Boards
SD Systems P.O. Box 28810 Dallas, TX 75228 Telex 6829016	Z80 CPU Boards
Netronics R&D Ltd. 333 Litchfield Road New Milford, CT 06776 (203) 354-9375	Memory Board
Action Computer Enterprise, Inc. 55 W. Del Mar Blvd. Pasadena, CA 91105 (213) 793-2440	Multiprocessor Sys.,Z80 Single-Brd computer,Z80
Sierra National Corporation 5037 Ruffner Street San Diego, CA 92111 (714) 277-4810	Z80 Systems
Tarbell Electronics 950 Dovlen Place Suite B Carson, CA 90746 (213) 538-4251	Z80 Systems Floppy Disk Interfaces Boards
Vista Computer Company 1317 E. Edinger Ave. Santa Ana, CA 92705 (714) 953-0523	Floppy Disks & Interface

Pickles & Trout P.O. Box 1206 Goleta, CA 93116 (805) 685-4641	488 Interface
Microbyte 1198 E. Willow Street Signal Hill, CA 90806 (213) 595-8571	Z80 CPU Boards
Electronic Control Technology 763 Ramsey Ave. Hillside, NJ 07205 (201) 686-8080	Board and Box
OSM 2364 Walsh Ave.,#4 Santa Clara, CA 95051 (408) 496-6910 ext 40	Multiprocessor Sys.,Z80
Microbyte Computer Systems 2626 Union Ave. San Jose, CA 95124 (408) 377-4691	Single-Brd Computer,Z80
Delta Products 15392 Assembly Lane Huntington Beach, CA 92649 (714) 898-1492	Z80 System
TEI 5075 S. Loop East Houston, TX 77033 (713) 738-2300	Z80 System Boards and Boxes
Central Data Corporation 713 Edgebrook Drive P.O. Box 2530 Station A Champaign, IL 61820 (217) 359-8010	64K Dynamic Memory
Mullen Computer Products Box 6214 Hayward, CA 94544 (415) 783-2866	Extender/Logic Test Bd Boards
Innovative Products 7131 Owensmouth Ave.,#21D Canoga Park, CA 91303 (213) 883-3244	Memory(by Computer Sys. Resources)
Digital Graphic Systems 441 California Ave. Palo Alto, CA 94306 (415) 494-6088	Color Graphics with frame digitizer.
Integrand 8474 Ave. 296 Visalia, CA 93277 (209) 733-9288	Boxes

S.C. Digital P.O. Box 906 Aurora, IL 60507 (312) 897-7749	Z80 CPU Boards
North Star Computers 1440 Fourth Street Berkeley, CA 94710 (415) 527-6950	Z80 System Boards
Acom Electronics 4151 Middlefield Road Palo Alto, CA 94303 (415) 494-7499	8088 CPU
Digicomp Research Terrace Hill Ithaca, NY 14850 (607) 273-5900	Serial Interface
Sunny International 22129 1/2 S. Vermont Ave. Torrance, CA 90502 (213) 328-2425	Power Supplies
Lobo Drives International 354 South Fairview Ave. Goleta, CA 93117 (805) 683-1576	Floppy Disk Drives
Morrow Designs 5221 Central Ave. Richmond, CA 94804 (415) 524-2101	Floppy & Hard Disk Dr.
Vector Electronic Co., Inc. 12460 Gladstone Ave. Sylmar, CA 91342 (910) 496-1539	Box and Protoboards
Sci Tronics Inc. 523 S. Clewell Street P.O. Box 5344 Bethlehem, PA 18015 (215) 868-7220	Real-Time clock Board
Alpha Microsystems 17881 Sky Park North Irvine, CA 92714 (714) 957-1404	WD-16 System
Dynabyte Inc. 115 Independence Dr. Menlo Park, CA 94025 (415) 329-8021	Z80 System
Industrial Micro Systems 628 N. Eckhoff Street Orange, CA 92688 (714) 978-6966	Z80 System

Micropolis 21329 Nordhoff Street Chatsworth, CA 91311 (213) 709-3300	Floppy & Hard disk drives
Marinchip Systems Computer Power and Human Reason 16 St. Jude Road Mill Valley, CA 94941 (415) 383-1545	TMS9900 System
Quest Electronics 2322WalshAve Santa Clara, CA 95051 (408) 988-1640	4-Slot Motherboard Boards
Ackerman Digital Systems, Inc. 110 N. York Rd. Suite 208 Elmhurst, IL 60126 (312) 530-8992	6809 CPU Boards

---

This paper was originally prepared for, and presented at,

Wescon/81

ADVANCED MICROCOMPUTER SYSTEM BUS

(IEEE P896)

Andrew A. Allison
Chairman, P896 Subcommittee
IEEE Computer Society Microprocessor Standards Committee
27360 Natoma Road
Los Altos Hills, CA 94022

The Advanced Microcomputer System Bus is designed to be processor, technology and manufacturer independent. Level 1 of the proposed standard provides fully distributed control of the 32-bit multiplexed address/data path by up to 32 masters, via a single 64-pin connector. A fully compatible 96-pin configuration of the same connector (Level 2) will be specified to provide across-the-bus error detection and additional control capabilities.

This report on the activities of the P896 (Advanced Microcomputer System Bus) Subcommittee of the IEEE Computer Society's Microprocessor Standards Committee describes the origins of the subcommittee and the status of the proposed specifications as of its May 14, 1981 meeting. It must be emphasized that, while representing the fruits of many months of effort on the part of a joint US/European working group, the specification is incomplete and subject to change, at the time of writing.

A subcommittee on microprocessor standards was set up by the IEEE Computer Society in August, 1977. By the middle of 1978, the committee's efforts toward developing standard specifications for the S-100 (P696) and Multibus* (P796) buses had made clear the need to consider future system bus requirements before the emergence of yet another generation of de facto but incompletely specified and incompatible buses.

The working group set up to consider this need concluded that the buses then being specified by the Microprocessor Standards Committee could not be extended to satisfy the requirements anticipated for future microprocessor-based systems. Three major categories of bus - backplane, local network, and residential - were identified. A backplane bus subcommittee was set up in June, 1979, and Project Authorization Request Number P896 was approved by the IEEE Standards Board in September of the same year. EDISG - the European Distributed Intelligence Study Group - set up a subgroup in May, 1980 to interact with the IEEE work. (EDISG is one of the working groups supported by the Commission of European Communities for promoting standardization in the field of data processing.)

P-896 is intended to be a manufacturer-and processor-independent bus offering 32-bit multiplexed address and data paths, while also supporting 16-and 8-bit data paths. Very completely handshake bus transfers are supported, and distributed bus arbitration provides for at least 32 bus masters. Multitask operation is facilitated by the provision of a serial interprocessor link that also incorporates interrupt arbitration. Recommendations will be given for operating system compatibility. IEC standard mechanical specifications are proposed for modules, backplanes, and racks. In recognition of the high overall system cost associated with each signal path, every effort is being made to minimize pin count.

Bus timing and control are specified in such a way as to facilitate increased performance as interface technology permits, with an initial maximum clock rate in excess of 10MHz. If electrical and mechanical interface constraints are ignored, the upper limit on clock frequency is anticipated to be governed by four end-to-end bus propagation delays plus a limited number of gate delays.

Information on the status of the P896 activity may be obtained from:

Andrew Allison, Chairman
P896 Working Group
27360 Natoma Road
Los Altos Hills, CA 94022

or

Prof. J.-D. Nicoud, Vice-Chairman
LAMI-DE-EPFL
Bellerive 16
CH-1007 Lausanne (Switzerland)

STATUS - MAY 1981

Scope

P896 defines a family of upwardly compatible, technology- and processor-independent bus structures that includes two configurations:

Level 1. Supports 32-bit multiplexed address and data operation on a 64-pin connector.

Level 2. Supports additional control capability and error detection and correction on a 96-pin, fully compatible extension. Upward compatibility is guaranteed; i.e., any Level 1

*Multibus is a registered trademark of Intel Corporation.

Reprinted with permission from *Midcon Conf. Rec.*, 1981, pp. 25.5.1-25.5.6.

module shall operate in a Level 2 system.

The backplane bus is specified as having a maximum length of 500 mm and as capable of supporting up to 32 modules. An active extension cable may be used for increasing the number of modules at the expense of transfer speed.

Object

P896 is intended to satisfy, for at least 10 years, a full range of interconnection requirements for 8-, 16- and 32-bit microcomputers, from simple systems to multiprocessing, multitasking ones.

Definitions

The backplane is a set of lines on which connectors for receiving physical modules are installed. Three functional entities may be implemented on these modules: masters, slaves, and supervisors. Two kinds of transaction can take place: data transfer and resource management.

A slave can be selected by a master and perform the requested data transfer. Arbitration between masters is required before one of them can use the single data transfer path.

A master can receive, from another master or from a slave, task management information.

A supervisor can act as a master or slave and shall have, in addition, the ability to monitor and/or modify bus transactions.

Backplane Bus Overview

Four sets of lines make up the P896 backplane:

Power bus. Provides multiple ground and +5V lines.

Data bus. Consists of 32 multiplexed address and data lines, plus mode/status and timing lines.

Arbitration bus. Consists of priority arbitration lines and control lines. Bus arbitration occurs in parallel with data transfer.

Resource management. Carried out via a synchronous serial line. A management protocol, handled by a smart interface, allows task notification. May also be performed over the A/D bus.

Simple task management (i.e., interrupts) has other possible implementations. The parallel data transfer bus can be used with reserved addresses (i.e., can be operated in user-dependent fashion).

Standard Configurations

A typical P896 system includes several masters with their own memories and with I/O interfaces. Common memory is accessible on the bus. Simple I/O with high performance requirements (fast A/D) might occasionally be put on the bus, but most I/O interfaces are expected to be smart, with their own microprocessor and local memory.

Functional specifications

Notation. Byte - Group of eight adjacent bits operated as a unit.

Doublet - Two bytes, or 16 adjacent bits.

Quadlet - Four bytes, or 32 adjacent bits.

Octlet - Eight bytes, or 64 adjacent bits.

Funct. signal - Representation of a boolean value having two possible states - active (or asserted) or inactive (not asserted).

Bus signal - Physical signal on the bus, active high or active low.

Partitioning. The backplane bus connects a set of modules to allow exchange information, i.e., data transfer and resource management. All modules connected to P896 must belong to one of the following categories:

Master. A master can activate an information transfer. Only one master at a time is granted control of the bus, according to its priority. A master that obtains the bus keeps it until another master requests it. A master can have four states:

USING:	It will not release the bus.
GRANTED:	It has the bus and keeps it for the next transfer.
ARBITRATING:	It is participating in arbitration for the next use of the data bus, according to its priority code.
LOCAL:	It has no interest in bus resources.

Slaves. Devices acting as bus slaves monitor all bus cycles and, if addressed during a particular bus cycle, accept or send the requested device-dependent message on a set of lines. A slave can be either:

SELECTED:	It has been addressed by a master and is participating in the current transfer(s).
UNSELECTED:	It is not participating in

the current transfer.

Supervisor. A supervisor monitors all bus transactions and can modify them by changing the timing, changing the content of the information lines (address and data), or changing the type of operation.

The supervisor can act as a master or as a slave. It has two states:

ACTIVE:	It is intervening in current bus cycles.
NOT ACTIVE:	It is monitoring but not intervening.

A system can have no supervisor, or more than one, of which any one may be active at any given instant in time.

There are two categories of information exchange in a multiple-processor system:

Data transfer. Between CPU and memory, as in single-processor systems. These transfers involve a master/slave pair. In master-slave communication, the transfer can be READ (from slave to master), WRITE (from master to slave), BROADCAST (multiple slaves), or CHANNEL (channel address).

Resource management. This is similar to the usual interrupt technique but is more sophisticated so that it can perform efficiently in multiple-processor environments. It involves two or more masters. Master-to-master communication may be supported by two different mechanisms - a serial interprocessor link or parallel information lines. P896 may support either or both of them with appropriate operating system definitions.

<u>Bus Arbitration.</u> P896 resolves contentions among up to 32 masters by means of a high-speed distributed logic arbitration system. Arbitration occurs in parallel with, and is independent of, other bus operations. In order to reduce possibility of a high-priority master monopolizing the bus, an optional fairness scheme is provided in the priority mechanism.

Parallel arbitration using five priority lines and two control lines has been adopted.

A processor that has been granted the bus keeps BUS BUSY active until that processor loses an arbitration and concedes control of the bus.

<u>Parallel Information Transfers.</u> A set of parallel lines allows fast information transfers between a master having access to the bus and a slave, for 8-, 16-, and 32-bit or up to 128-bit words.

Several kinds of transaction can take place on this bus. In usual transfers, address and data are multiplexed. Indivisible and block transfers are supported.

Four lines are used for the timing control of parallel transfers.

Data is byte-justified on the bus. Specific hardware must be built on the processor board to match the 32-bit bus words.

<u>Transfer Control.</u> When a master has access to the bus and wants to transfer information (with other devices considered as slaves), it uses the following handshake lines:

AS	Address strobe (inverted, active low on the bus). Activated by the master. Falling edge on bus indicates address or event, plus transfer mode, valid.
DS	Data strobe (inverted, active low on the bus). Activated by the master. Falling edge indicates data valid.
AK1	Supervisor acknowledge. Indicates that no supervisor intervention will occur in the present bus cycle.
AK2	Responder acknowledge. Acknowledges completion of the address and data cycles of each bus transaction.

Timing requirements specify only positive set-up times on the bus. Full handshaking takes care of additional propagation delays on boards.

<u>Transfer Modes.</u> Simultaneously with address transfer, the four Ci lines plus the two low-order address lines encode the transfer mode as shown in Figure 1.

<u>Feedback Status.</u> The Ci lines are used by the slave to provide a detailed acknowledge of the transfer, as indicated below:

C3	C2	C1	C0	
0	0	0	0	Normal Cycle
0	0	0	1*	Error Corrected in Address
0	0	1	0	Error Corrected in Data
0	1	0	0	Write Protected Memory
0	1	0	1	Temporarily Busy
0	1	1	0	Nonexistent Memory or I/O
1	0	0	0	Permanent Bus Error
1	0	0	1	Unrecoverable Error on Address
1	0	1	0	Unrecoverable Error on Data
.	.	.	.	Other States Reserved

* "1" Means Active Low on the Bus

Serial Link. P896 provides a serial link which uses a dedicated backplane line and which is synchronized by the clock available on the backplane. This link allows short messages to be interchanged between modules in a clock-synchronous mode.

A proposed implementation of resource management functions:

The messages can be sent by any source to any destination on the bus. They have a fixed format, as illustrated below:

BESYNC SOURCE DESTINATION FUNCTION
ARGUMENTS ACK ENSYNC

Beginning-of-message and end-of-message synchronization delimit the message frame. As the link is bused, an arbitration over the source identifier is used to determine the current bus master. The destination may specify a single receiver, a pool of receivers, or a broadcast mode. The function field defines a set of services provided by the link. The arguments are used to transmit information or to execute arbitration for some of the functions.

The acknowledge field consists of two slots - NOK (not acknowledge), and ACK (acknowledge), which contain the receiver's reply.

Services provided. The serial link provides an easily expandable variety of functions:

User functions. Most of the functions are left open to the user, who may use the link in a particular application, e.g., transmission of I/O data to several destinations at the same time. Part of the function field and the argument field are then free for user data.

Immediate functions. The serial link may be used for directly activating signal lines on the processor board. This allows the implementation of HALT or RUN functions to remotely start a processor or to initialize the system, for example. A particular application of this function is error detection and recovery, which provides for the disconnecting of faulty modules and for system reconfiguration.

A set of function codes are reserved for these functions. It is the responsibility of the system designer to implement the required functions or a subset of them.

System Interrupt. The serial link may be used to transmit an interrupt from one processor to any other processor. This feature is important for a multiprocessor system, since it implements the basic redispatch tool needed for a multiprocessor operating system. Although the previous functions can also result in the generation of an interrupt, the system interrupt is more sophisticated in the sense that the interrupt priority and the interrupt vector are part of the message.

The first byte of the message is the interrupt priority and the second byte is the identifier of the task that should be started. It is up to the system designer to implement the arbitration and to generate the processor-specific interrupt vector, possibly by using a mapping scheme.

In this mode, the NOK and ACK fields of the message may be asserted simultaneously, indicating that the message has been accepted but that the interrupt itself has too low a priority to be accepted.

Notify-to-redispatch. The serial link has a special mode of operation which performs the notify-to-redispatch function. The NRP is a message that is addressed to a pool of processors and that indicates that a task with a given priority should be executed on one (and only one) processor of the pool. The priority of this task is the first argument of the message.

All processors of the pool will participate in an arbitration over the argument field in order to compare the respective priorities of all tasks running on the pool.

If there is a task running that has a priority lower than that of the waiting task, the processor in the pool running the lowest priority task will be selected to execute the waiting task.

Other high-level functions. Other functions are reserved to notify-to-deactivate (notify-to-remanage) and notify-to-ready. These functions use the message-passing service of the serial link and do not require any special arbitration. However, there must be a system-wide agreement on the meaning of these functions.

Error Checking and Correction. Eight error-checking lines will be defined in Level 2.

System Initialization. A reset line may be required at power-up; such a line would facilitate debugging.

Reserved Lines. Reserved lines may exist. They will be inactive for all present implementations and cannot be used in any other systems complying with the standard.

Mechanical Specifications. See IEC-297 Pub. -48D.

Pinout. A possible pinout for P896 is given in Figure 2; the connector is DIN 41612.

C3	C2	C1	C0	AD1	AD0	
0	0	0	0	x	x	Read/Block Read byte xx
0	0	0	1	y	0	Read/Block Read doublet y
0	0	0	1	0	1	Read/Block Read quadlet
0	0	0	1	1	1	Reserved
0	0	1	0	x	x	Write/Block Write byte xx
0	0	1	1	y	0	Write/Block Write doublet y
0	0	1	1	0	1	Write/Block Write quadlet
0	0	1	1	1	1	Reserved
0	1	0	0	x	x	Read/RMW byte xx
0	1	0	1	y	0	Read/RMW doublet y
0	1	0	1	0	1	Read/RMW quadlet
0	1	0	1	1	1	Reserved
0	1	1	z	z	z	Level 2 codes (reserved)
1	z	z	z	z	z	CSR operations

Note: Block transfer and Read/Modify/Write are detected by successive data strobes without an intervening address strobe and differentiated by C2.

Figure 1. Control Codes

	1	2	3	4	5	6	7	8	9	10	11	12	13	14	-	30	31	32
a	GND	+5	CK	GND	BP4	BP2	BP0	RES	AK1	AS	C2	C0	GND	AD1	-	AD31	+5	GND
b	GND	+5	IL	GND	BB	BP3	BP1	RES	AK2	DS	C3	C1	GND	AD0	-	AD30	+5	GND

Figure 2. Proposed pin-out as of May 14, 1981

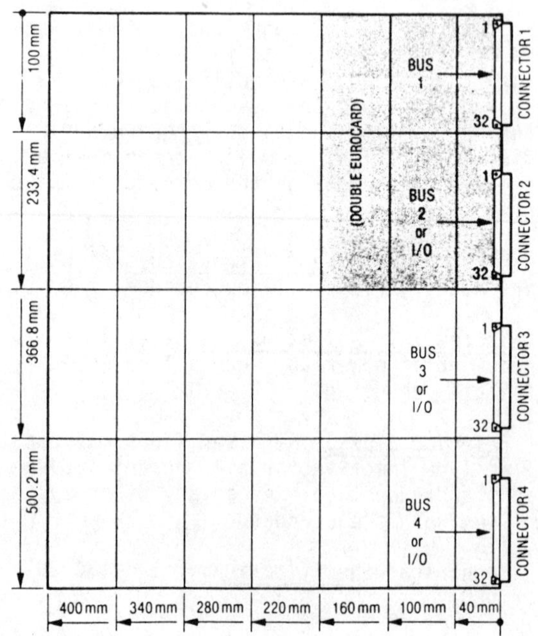

Figure 3. Standard Card Sizes

See Table 1 for a signal summary.

Card Layout. Card size will follow IEC standards (IEC-297 and DIN 41494), as shown in Figure 3. Bus drivers shall be placed as close as possible to their connectors, and control logic shall be placed at the "top" of the board (Figure 3).

System Philosophy

P896 may be logically separated into two different transmission media: the parallel bus (P-Bus) carries information between the processor and memory at high speed, using most of the 64/96 lines available and the serial bus (S-Bus) carries interprocessor information, which has a lower throughput but often a higher urgency than memory data. The main function of the S-bus is to support task redispatching for the operating system.

The P896 bus is intended for multiprocessor applications. Therefore, we assume that all stations on the bus are processors, in the sense that they all can access a common memory, send messages, and take some logical system decisions (Figure 4).

Furthermore, P896 is aimed at true multiprocessor systems, i.e., ones in which there is no explicit master/slave relationship between the processors (but in which the use of coprocessors is allowed). This reflects the trend toward each peripheral having a dedicated processor controlling it. Smaller peripherals like ADC's or TTY's are assumed to be directly connected to the local bus of a processor.

As a matter of definition, a group of processors which share the same memory, and which are capable of an atomic operation (semaphore) on a memory location, is termed a NODE.

Processors of a node which are interchangeable with respect to the tasks that they can run form a POOL. Each processor in a pool is identified by a processor identifier (PROC ID) and a pool identifier (POOL ID). A message can be sent to an individual processor, to a whole pool or to the whole node.

Since P896 is a system bus, some classical notions are altered. DMA is not relevant to the P896 concept, for example, since every memory transfer on P896 is a DMA. There is no centralized bus controller. Some other notions, like interrupt, have to be extended.

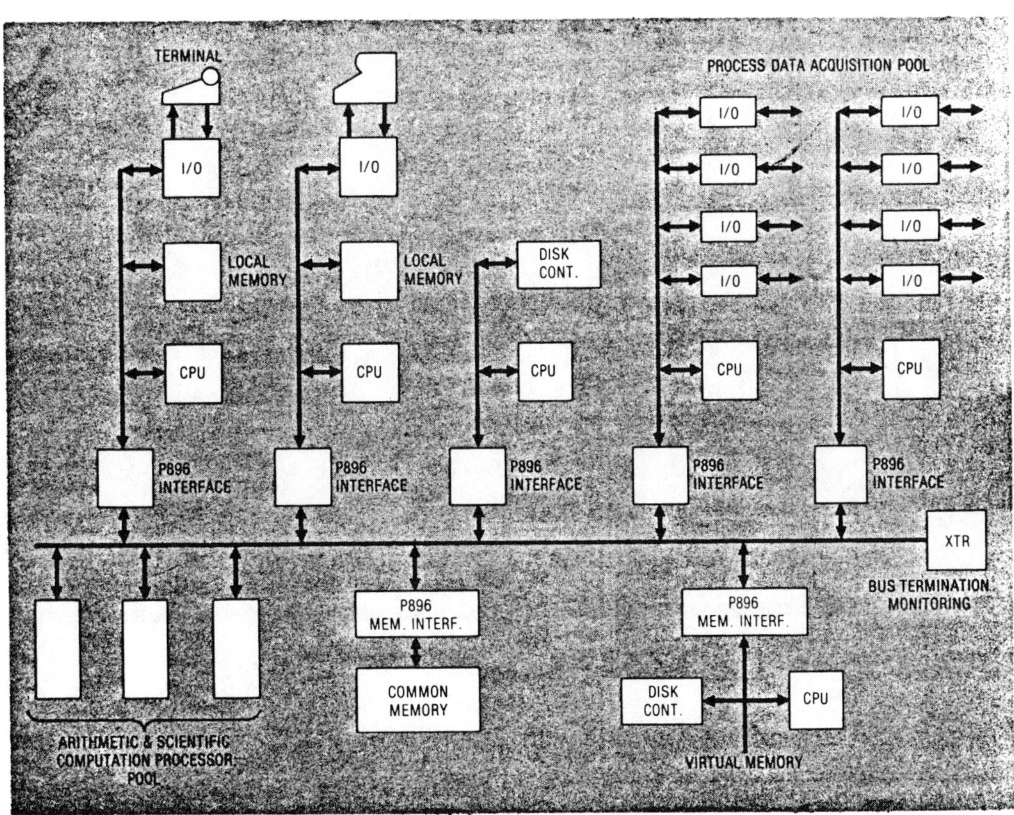

Figure 4, P896 System Philosophy

(This paper was originally presented at Wescon/81)

Author Index

Subject Index

Editors' Biographies

Amar Gupta received the B.Tech. degree in electrical engineering from the Indian Institute of Technology, Kanpur, in 1974, the M.S. degree in management from the Massachusetts Institute of Technology, Sloan School of Management, Cambridge, in 1980, and the Ph.D. degree in computer technology from the Indian Institute of Technology, Delhi, in 1980.

He is a postdoctoral associate in the Sloan School of Management. His interests include multiprocessor architectures, performance measurement, decision support systems, analytic modeling, office automation, and international technology transfer. He has been involved in research on tightly-coupled SIMD and MIMD machines.

Dr. Gupta was awarded the Rotary Fellowship for International Understanding in 1979, and in the 1980-1981 academic year, he received the Brooks' Prize, honorable mention, for his M.S. thesis at M.I.T.

Hoo-min D. Toong (S'71-M'76) received the B.S. degree in 1967, the M.S. and E.E. degrees in 1969, and the Ph.D. degree in electrical engineering and computer science in 1974, all from the Massachusetts Institute of Technology, Cambridge.

He is on the faculty of the Sloan School of Management, M.I.T., which he joined in 1978. His research interests include very large database architectures, multiprocessors, distributed operating systems, and the organizational impact of such systems. He is active in teaching microcomputer systems, personal computers, and business applications of the microprocessor technology. He has won several awards for excellence in teaching. Before joining the Sloan School, he was on the faculty of the Department of Electrical Engineering and Computer Science, M.I.T.

Dr. Toong is a member of Tau Beta Pi, Eta Kappa Nu, Sigma Xi, and the ACM.